SHANGHAI '37

Ja✧

1996.

Shanghai '37

Vicki Baum

With an Introduction by
H. J. Lethbridge

HONG KONG OXFORD NEW YORK
OXFORD UNIVERSITY PRESS

Oxford University Press

Oxford   New York
Athens   Auckland   Bangkok   Bombay
Calcutta   Cape Town   Dar es Salaam   Delhi
Florence   Hong Kong   Istanbul   Karachi
Kuala Lumpur   Madras   Madrid   Melbourne
Mexico City   Nairobi   Paris   Singapore
Taipei   Tokyo   Toronto

and associated companies in
Berlin   Ibadan

Oxford is a trade mark of Oxford University Press

First published by Doubleday, Doran & Company, Inc., 1939
First issued, with permission and with the addition of an Introduction,
in Oxford Paperbacks 1986
Fourth impression 1995

Published in the United States
by Oxford University Press, New York

ISBN 0 19 583876 9

Printed in Hong Kong
Published by Oxford University Press (China) Ltd
18/F Warwick House, Taikoo Place, 979 King's Road, Quarry Bay, Hong Kong

Introduction

VICKI Baum's name is inescapably linked with her best-selling novel, *Grand Hotel*. She once acknowledged, 'you can live down any amount of failure, but you can't live down a great success'. *Grand Hotel*, first published as *Menschen im Hotel* in a popular German weekly, the *Berliner Illustrierte*, in 1928, and in book form the following year, went on to achieve international success when it appeared in an excellent English translation. The play-adapter, Edward Knoblock, at once sensed its theatrical possibilities — the novel is constructed in film-like tableaux — and swiftly produced a stage version. In 1931 it played to full houses in London and in New York, where it became the Play of the Year in a lavish production by Max Reinhardt at the Guild Theatre.

The popularity of the novel was further attested by the 1932 Hollywood film of the same name produced by Irving Thalberg, with a cast of now legendary actors and actresses, including Garbo, the two Barrymores, Joan Crawford, and Wallace Beery.

The spectacular success of *Grand Hotel* in each of its avatars rocketed Vicki Baum to fame and transformed a 44-year-old Viennese popular novelist (hardly known outside Austria and Germany) into a cosmopolitan author and international celebrity. The book's success inspired her move to Hollywood — a migration that was to have a decisive influence on her life and fortunes — and conditioned, as we shall see, the writing of her Far Eastern novels, including *Shanghai '37*. (It is worth noting here that her book on Shanghai first appeared in German in 1939 under the title *Hotel Shanghai*. The American edition, reproduced here, was entitled *Shanghai '37*, the British edition, *Nanking Road*. For the sake of convenience, the book will be referred to here as *Shanghai '37*.)

Vicki Baum, an only child, was born in 1888, in Vienna, then the capital of the polyglot Austro-Hungarian Empire, and educated at the Vienna High School of Music. There she studied the harp. Later, she became a professional musician with various Austrian and German orchestras. She grew up in a period when Modernism in the arts had come to the fore and when Vienna was host to a remarkable galaxy of savants and artists. She was no modernist or innovator as a novelist; she was a straightforward storyteller. But her books are neither mawkish nor sentimental, and some, such as *Stud. Chem. Helene Willfuer* (1929), are brutally frank and starkly realistic. There is not much *gemütlichkeit* in her writing, the quality for which Austrians are notorious.

Her father was a bookkeeper/accountant; her mother, born into an established bourgeois family, went mad early on in her marriage and died comparatively young. Vicki Baum's first marriage to a shady Bohemian journalist, Max Prels, did not last long. He was too complaisant a husband — if it suited his interests. In 1915 she married the opera intendant, Ernst Lert, brother of the conductor, Richard Lert. Ernst, a rather prickly and difficult fellow, as she candidly admitted, experienced several ups and downs in his career. To succeed as an opera intendant in Germany one had to move up a scale of prestigious posts, to arrive finally at Berlin, the German musician's Mecca. Lert never achieved this supreme height. He remained restive in provincial cities.

By now they had three children; and money was often lacking. It was easy to write when the children were abed, and so Vicki Baum started to pen small pieces for newspapers, then short stories and novelettes. She began to supplement the family income. After the First World War, she at last obtained a permanent post, with Ullstein und Co. (the famous House of Ullstein) in Berlin, the largest and most successful publishers of books, journals, and newspapers in all Germany. The House of Ullstein, owned by four German-Jewish brothers, became her publishers, encouraging and promoting her books. For them she wrote romances and novels. By the late 1920s, she had emerged as a popular novelist, widely known in the German-speaking world.

She did not attempt to emulate such writers as Thomas Mann. 'I'm a first-rate second-rate author', she wrote in her autobiography. This is too modest an assessment since she was always a good professional writer and a gifted story-teller. Although she did not invent the 'hotel' novel, both *Grand Hotel* and, to some degree, *Shanghai '37* are good examples of this 'genre'. The essence of such a novel is that the hotel provides the framework for the resolution of the plot, the framework for the fortuitous coming together of a varied and unrelated cast of characters, who find themselves, for one reason or another, all lodging under the same roof. Propinquity then encourages social relations; love-affairs bloom; and destinies become intertwined. It is the hotel that acts as a catalyst, particularly so in *Shanghai '37* where death in the hotel precincts unites nine people.

This device had been utilized before, notably by Zola in *Pot-Bouille* (1882), in which the lives of a cross-section of people living in a large Paris apartment-block become enmeshed; and repeated by him in *Au bonheur des dames* (1883), though in this latter the locale is a department store. Arnold Bennett, a writer always enthralled by the spectacle of luxury and high living, despite his early absorption in the grim life of the Five Towns, wrote *The Grand Babylon Hotel* in 1902. In the same year that *Grand Hotel* appeared in its English translation, Bennett's *Imperial Palace* was published, another hotel saga, and he was greatly chagrined that Vicki Baum's popularity and sales outdid his own. One should also mention Eugène Dabit's *Hôtel du Nord* (1930), set in a small hotel in a poor district of Paris. It too was turned into a film, with Louis Jouvet in the starring role. All these later novels, in fact, were cinematic in technique, and their authors, one surmises, had been influenced by the new art form — the film.

In 1931 Vicki Baum went to the United States to see the dramatized version of *Grand Hotel*, which had become such a smash hit with New Yorkers. She intended to stay only for a fortnight, but at once fell in love with the country and decided to make it her home. That year she brought her family from Germany and settled in California. In time they all became American citizens. Resident in Hollywood, she worked for the film industry as an adviser on screenplays and as a script-writer; but her principal activity, as always, was the writing of a book a year, and much travelling.

She did not, in those early days, write in English but was fortunate in having Basil Creighton, an Englishman, as her main translator. She found him reclusive; he avoided meeting her; they corresponded from afar. The mystery behind his secretiveness was solved when she discovered finally that he could *read*, but not *speak*, German. 'Only years later', she wrote,' when I had learned English, did I succeed in meeting and thanking him in person for what he had done for me'. Basil Creighton had done much for her: his fluent, readable translations had helped to popularize her books and extend her fame throughout the English-speaking world.

The Baums were Jewish: moving to America in 1931 possibly saved their lives. The Ullsteins, her publishers, likewise were Jewish. When racial legislation was introduced by the Nazis, the House of Ullstein, founded in 1877, was forced in 1934 to go out of business, and the brothers left Germany. No one in Germany could now publish her books. Other popular Austrian novelists, like Franz Werfel and Stefan Zweig, suffered the same fate. Hence the German edition of *Shanghai '37* was published in Amsterdam. Her old father, however, was reluctant to emigrate, as she urged, and was murdered in Yugoslavia by Hungarian Nazis in 1943. Vicki Baum and her family then were far away in California, and secure.

America was important for other reasons. The New World widened her horizons and provided new vistas. The settings of her novels were now no longer purely German. Affluent at last, she could travel at will, by ocean liner across the Pacific from Los Angeles to Japan, China, Malaya, and the East Indies (then Dutch). These regions provided her with plots and new locations — the material for her two Balinese books, *Das Ende der Geburt* (*A Tale from Bali*) and *Liebe und Tod auf Bali*, and notably for *Shanghai '37*, a novel which reveals much first-hand knowledge of China. She visited Shanghai in 1937 and found it extraordinarily interesting, a congenial, vibrant, yet brutal city. The International Settlement, where she stayed, a self-governing foreign enclave, was one of the few territories where stateless persons (those without valid passports) could find sanctuary and reside; hence, many Jewish refugees moved to it after 1933, the year Hitler became German Chancellor. It is estimated that over 20,000 Jews were domiciled there in 1941. Former Austrian and German friends were living in Shanghai and they provided her with much gossip about personalities, the convoluted politics of China, and the secret life of the great city. When she came to write *Shanghai '37* she was well prepared. The English edition of the book appeared in 1939, again nicely translated by Basil Creighton.

When Vicki Baum sat down to write *Shanghai '37* she was hoping to repeat the success of *Grand Hotel*, the novel on which her international reputation was based. There had indeed been a flood of her books after that epochal date — 1930 — not only of new novels but also reissues by Ullstein of those she had previously published in cheap or popular editions; these, in turn, were to be translated by the indefatigable Basil Creighton and by others. Vicki Baum's bibliography is confusing.

None of her books achieved such spectacular sales or acclaim as had *Grand Hotel*. The hotel described in that novel was the Adlon, the Claridges of Berlin; the hotel depicted in *Shanghai '37* was the Cathay (also known as Sassoon House and now renamed the Peace Hotel), located at the junction of Nanking Road, a main thoroughfare, and the Bund, Shanghai's celebrated waterfront. The Palace Hotel, equally famed, was on the other side of Nanking Road from the Cathay.

The Cathay, built by Sir Victor Sassoon, philanthropist and magnate, was a landmark in the International Settlement and was famous for its comfort, cuisine, and cabaret, and for its tea and dinner dances. Noel Coward, prostrated by a bout of influenza in 1929, wrote *Private Lives* in one of its bedrooms. It was a focus of entertainment for opulent Shanghailanders (as they liked to be called), of whom there were plenty, since at that time Shanghai was the wealthiest city in the Far East, the most modern and the most Americanized, and was commonly regarded as the most sinful city east of Suez (in the world some would say).

Shanghai '37 is not, in the precise meaning of the term, a 'hotel' novel, but the destinies of the nine people, whose life stories are detailed in a sequence of almost independent novellas, reach their conclusion within its confines. Nine people from different backgrounds and starting-points meet finally in the Shanghai Hotel: it is the bourne to which each has been ineluctably moving. The year is 1937, the year when the Sino-Japanese War started with a minor skirmish (if it can be so termed) at the Marco Polo Bridge. Soon the conflict spread to the environs of Shanghai and fighting broke out between Chinese and Japanese troops in the Chinese-administered areas of Shanghai, which surrounded the International Settlement and the French Concession. The climax of the novel is based on a true incident, 'Bloody Saturday'.

As Dick Wilson writes: 'On Saturday afternoon — 14 August 1937 — foreign residents sipping cocktails in the Palace Hotel bar saw two Chinese aeroplanes coming towards them high over the river … The two planes circled under the clouds and then dropped four bombs, two on a crowded crossroads, one on the roof of the Palace Hotel and another on the neighbouring Cathay Hotel. Over a thousand people were killed'. This sombre event — a massacre of innocents — was a sign of things to come, the end of sanctuary. Vicki Baum, by highlighting this incident, showed percipience, for both Nationalists and Japanese showed scant regard for the neutrality of European-controlled Shanghai. In 1943, at the Cairo Conference, the Allies agreed that *all* Shanghai should come under Chinese jurisdiction. It was the end of the special status that foreigners had enjoyed for almost a century.

The British edition of *Shanghai '37* states, on the verso of the title-page, that its characters are fictitious — a conventional disclaimer, oddly omitted in the American edition. However, the portrait of B.G. Chang in the novel is obviously based on Tu Yueh-sheng (1888–1951), the great Shanghai crook and head of the feared 'Green Dragon Society', who colluded in 1927 with the right wing of the Kuomintang to slaughter Shanghai's Communists. Known as the unofficial Mayor of Shanghai, as legendary a personage in that city as Al Capone was in Chicago, Tu was so dominant a figure in the 1930s, so conspicuous in his bullet-proof limousine with armed bodyguards on it running-boards, that Vicki Baum felt compelled to put him in her book. Jelena Trubova, an amoralist straight out of a Michael Arlen novel, is sketched from an adventuress she met in Shanghai, for the city abounded with White Russians who had been migrating to Shanghai from soon after the Russian Revolution; by 1939 the count was around 30,000. As in Paris between the wars, they were notorious for adopting bogus identities and masquerading as former Tsarist officials or generals, members of the nobility and aristocracy or landed gentry. Many were great charmers, a lot were charming liars. In *Shanghai '37* Vicki Baum's characters were mostly drawn from life, her practice as a novelist.

Hergé (the Belgian author-artist, Georges Remi) presents a picture of Shanghai in the late 1930s in *Le Lotus bleu*, one of his series of Tintin books. Secret agents and conspirators, crooks and adventurers, dope fiends and assassins, all figure in his marvellous comic strip. Hergé, like Vicki Baum, had viewed Shanghai in the 1930s when, it seemed, Japan was on the road to hegemony in China. He depicts in bright colours not only the scenery and architecture of the city but also the social types found there: British officials, taipans, Sikh policemen, oriental flunkeys, Japanese spies, Chinese crooks and Chinese patriots, the Insulted and the Injured — the variegated strata of a vast seaport city teetering on its dangerous edge. This is the scene that Vicki Baum surveyed in 1937, and wrote about. Like Atlantis, it is now all legend.

After the war, she continued writing, though not at her 1930s' pace. In 1964 her autobiography appeared, a frank, gossipy, meandering account of her life, written in English. Her character is revealed: insouciant, curious, tolerant, a lover of life and its best things — conversation, music, books, and travel. She was a most likeable woman, as Sinclair Lewis discovered when they first met in New York in 1931. She died in Los Angeles in 1960.

When Arthur Hailey embarked on *Hotel* — his world best-seller — he diligently consulted the books of Arnold Bennett and Vicki Baum on his chosen theme. Both *Grand Hotel* and *Shanghai '37* are now regarded as her finest achievements; they have both remained popular with readers. *Shanghai '37* is more than good documentary, clever reportage disguised as fiction; it is a very readable and absorbing novel of a city where, for foreigners, the clocks stopped in 1941, and never chimed again.

H. J. LETHBRIDGE

Select Bibliography

Baum, Vicki, *Feme* (Berlin, Ullstein, 1927).

———*Stud. Chem. Helene Willfuer* (Berlin, Ullstein, 1929).

———*Menschen im Hotel* (Berlin, Ullstein, 1929).

———*Grand Hotel,* translated by Basil Creighton (London, Geoffrey Bles, 1930).

———*Die andern Tage* (Berlin, Ullstein, 1931).

———*A Tale from Bali,* translated by Basil Creighton (London, Geoffrey Bles, 1937).

———*Hotel Shanghai* (Amsterdam, 1939).

———*Shanghai '37*, translated by Basil Creighton (New York, Doubleday, Doran, 1939).

———*Nanking Road*, translated by Basil Creighton (London, Geoffrey Bles, 1939).

———*Vor Rehen wird gewarnt* (Cologne, Kiepenhauer & Witsch, 1951).

———*I Know What I'm Worth* (autobiography) (London, Michael Joseph, 1964).

———'Obituary', *The Times*, 31 August 1960.

Baum, Vicki, and Golden, John, *Divine Judge: A Play in Three Acts* (New York, Samuel French, 1934).

Bennett, Arnold, *The Grand Babylon Hotel* (London, Chatto & Windus, 1902).

———*Imperial Palace* (London, Cassell & Co, 1930).

Dabit, Eugène, *Hôtel du Nord* (Paris, 1930).

Drabble, Margaret, *Arnold Bennett* (London, Weidenfeld and Nicolson, 1974).

Hailey, Arthur, *Hotel* (London, Michael Joseph, 1965).

Hergé, *Le Lotus bleu* (Paris, Casterman, 1946).

Ullstein, Hermann, *The Rise and Fall of the House of Ullstein* (London, Nicholson & Watkins, 1944).

Ullstein und Co., *50 Jahr Ullstein 1877–1927* (Berlin, Ullstein, 1927).

Wilson, Dick, *When Tigers Fight: The Story of the Sino-Japanese War, 1937–1945* (New York, The Viking Press, 1982).

Zola, Émile, *Pot-Bouille* (Paris, Charpentier, 1882).

____*Au bonheur des dames* (Paris, Charpentier, 1883).

Contents

v

Introduction

THE TOWN which is the scene of the events here reported exists no longer; its face has been altered, as so often before. There has been fighting in its streets on innumerable occasions but never fighting so desperate as in the late summer and early autumn of 1937. For eighty-eight days this town was besieged, shelled and bombed. Hundreds of thousands died, and the smell of charred human flesh for long hung in thick clouds above it.

One of the first bombs to be dropped from the air hit the Shanghai Hotel, the large, new building erected four years before, soon after the fighting of 1932. A colonnaded building of eighteen stories, surmounted by its celebrated roof garden, it stood in Nanking Road halfway between the Bund and the English racecourse.

The bomb did considerable damage. All the windows were shattered, and a gaping hole in the façade tore open several rooms, exposing their interior to view. The Japanese maintained that the bomb was dropped by Chinese fliers, whereas the Chinese insisted that the bomb was Japanese. The foreign correspondents inclined to the view that this bomb was meant for the Japanese warships on the Whangpoo River but had been badly aimed by a Chinese airman. Protests were made and apologies were published, for although the Chinese quarters had been shelled to bits from time to time, it was always taken for granted that the International Settlement in the heart of the city was inviolable. Those who had lived long in the East and were well acquainted with its subtle methods of waging war appeared to be convinced that with this bombing the Chinese intended to indicate to the Japanese that they would not tolerate a repetition of what occurred in 1932. On that occasion a detachment of Japanese marines, on the pretext that the Japanese had a share in the International Settlement, occupied the center of it and abused the neutrality of the International concessions by making them a basis for warlike operations.

Whichever side dropped the bomb, the Shanghai Hotel was damaged, many people wounded and nine killed—nine of the thousands who were destined to die on that first day of hostilities.

In the following pages an account is given of the roads that led those nine people to Shanghai, of the course of their lives and of the hour of their death.

PART I

The People

Better a dog in peace than a man in war.
                                    Chinese Proverb.

I

B. G. Chang

CHANG WAS BORN in a boat. At night he came into the world, the river lapped against the planks, his mother loosed him from her with a rusty knife. In the morning she was dead. He had no father, the boat was house and home for many people, for his family and their children. It found its way with the eyes painted on its bow. A mat laid over a rounded bamboo framework was its roof. His sister, who was seven years older than he, went into the prosperous village where they anchored and begged beans for the orphan; she squeezed a thin milk from them, he sucked it hungrily from her fingertips. Thus he took hold of life.

He lay wrapped in rags on the bottom of the boat, with only the planks between him and the living water. He watched his sister bending and leaning her weight on the oar and urging the boat forward. The veins stood out on her small arms. When he cried she took him up and tied him on her back and labored on at the heavy oar. Back and forth, back and forth. The regular motion sent him to sleep. As there were no parents to choose a good name for him, he was simply called Ah Tai, a big one. To his sister he stayed devoted all his life, although she was only a girl. The river was his father and his teacher. He grew tall and strong and pushed his elder cousins aside or threw them into the water. They made merry over him.

He was always hungry, all his thoughts had mostly to do with food. Sometimes the boat lay idle and motionless in a bend of the river below a village. Then food became scarce and finally disappeared altogether. Chang dreamt of noodles, of bread and hot cabbage. He stole garlic from a little acre and chewed a piece of wood

3

as if it were bread. If they had a cargo to take downstream there were good times. Sometimes there was poultry in a cage or a young pig. The men laughed and ate, played Kaipu for little pierced coins, quarreled, made it up, and their merriment knew no end. The women and children got what was left over. The joy of a full belly came seldom to Ah Tai. Nevertheless he flourished.

The river rose after the summer rains and flooded the fields. It was gray and covered with white mist in the morning and yellow after the rains. Down through the tree roots at its banks it was clear and dark green. Chang grabbed for fish among the roots and took his booty to the fishmongers at the nearest market. His uncle snatched the money out of his hand. Ah Tai stood over the gigantic pots of the itinerant cooks; his round black nostrils distended as he swallowed down the good smell together with his hungry spittle.

Nobody took any care of him. His head and his jacket were full of lice. His sister undressed him and, kneeling at the river's edge, spread his clothes on a stone and beat them with a stick to wash them. Chang sat on the edge of the boat in the sun, dangling his legs, and felt the warmth tingling on his skin and saw the light reflected from the river making patterns on the boat's side; it looked like lizards made of light. He was hungry. He put on his clothes again as soon as they were dry, folding his trousers round his waist and tying the string tight that served him as a belt. The next moment he was scratching again.

As soon as he had his wits about him he begged in the towns near which they were anchored, and it was not long before he learned how to steal. A handful of chestnuts from a stall or a pumpkin from the open field; great, full, glorious, secret meals.

His sister grew heavy with child, nobody knew who the father was. The river people were not particular, they had little virtue and a lot of fun. The boats plied upstream and downstream, at night they anchored and by morning they were gone. Children were born and there were always more hungry bellies to be filled. The man whom Chang called Uncle beat Elder Sister. Chang watched laughingly, for it was funny. That night he saw Elder Sister bending over the boat's side and throwing something into the water. In the morning her belly was flat again. A month later she began to cough, but she worked on at the oar.

By this time Chang was helping to load and unload the sacks of meal. He hoisted sail, steered, pushed with the pole when they stuck in the mud, piloted the boat past others with shouts and cries. He did not know how old he was, for no one counted his years, but he was now the strongest man on the boat, a young giant with large powerful shoulders. He had a quarrel with his uncle, and the elder man struck him between the eyes with a leather thong. That night Chang jumped ashore from the boat and hid among the graves on a hillside. He was afraid of the spirits, for that reason he shouted rude threats into the darkness. He stayed there until the boat went on and the search for him had been given up. As he was strong, the spirits seemed to fear him and did him no harm. He ate raw cabbage and little red onions which he pulled out of the ground. He was famished with hunger. As the boat was being rowed downstream he set off upstream.

He came to a neighborhood he had never seen before, for the boat had always plied only between Sekuang and Gantsing. A temple with a beautiful roof stood on a hill, rich people were being carried up the steep road in litters and chairs. Chang followed, filled with curiosity, for he had never been in a temple. He gazed at the great gilded Buddha in the first courtyard of the temple with open-mouthed astonishment. A bald priest beat a gigantic gong hanging from the pillars. The air was clouded with incense. Priests and pilgrims knelt below the table on which were the incense vessels and the bronze vases full of golden lotus flowers. A god with innumerable arms and hands leaped to view from the darkness of a side altar. In the first courtyard outside the temple the pious were burning money made out of silver and gold paper and dealers sat in rows selling incense and food.

Chang's eyes devoured and devoured all these new and wonderful sights. He stood laughing stupidly from sheer astonishment. The chair bearers were sitting in front of the outer gate eating noodles. A seller of tea was standing behind them pouring tea into blue-and-white cups.

Chang's mouth watered. He went up to them. One of the bearers called out a greeting to him in jest: "Have you eaten?"

Politeness required the answer: "I have eaten." But Chang was entirely uneducated. "No, my belly is empty," he shouted out.

The bearers burst with laughter. One of them held out his bowl in which a little of the meal was left, noodles and vegetables. It was only lukewarm but marvelous all the same. Chang grabbed for the bowl, but the man slapped his hand and the others laughed louder than ever. One of them, an old and toothless one, rolled about with laughter and slapped his thighs in his mirth at the joke. Chang let out and brought his two fists down on the shoulders of the joker like two sledge hammers. The man went small. Chang took the bowl with noodles from him and began to eat. The bearers were still for a moment, then they complimented him on his strength. He laughed good-naturedly and stuffed himself. The man whose noodles he had taken looked surprised. Chang Ah Tai held the bowl to his mouth and crammed in the food with his chopsticks as fast as he could.

After he had eaten he felt fine and great and full of courage. He hung around the bearers and waited for further events. When they carried their patrons down the hill again late in the afternoon Chang kept pace with them, singing the songs that were sung on the river. There were three bearers to each chair, two who carried it and one as spare man. Chang watched with interest how the spare man put his shoulders under the poles and took over from the other man without breaking step. The man who had been relieved went to the edge of the path, coughed and spat, wiped the sweat from his face with his arm, and then followed the chair until it was time for him to relieve one of the others again. "I could carry without being relieved," Chang thought, and he said so too. The bearers laughed about him pantingly. One of them, after being relieved, dropped behind, he doubled up and vomited at the wayside. He was an elderly man and he had a piece of red plaster stuck to his ailing body with a holy saying on it.

Chang stood beside him and watched him being sick. "How much if I carry for you?" he asked.

The man, more exhausted now that he had emptied his stomach, waved him aside.

But Chang insisted. In the end he took the bearer's place and got no money but a second helping of noodles.

He slept with the bearers in the village at the foot of the hill and stayed with them for a while. Now he had enough to eat every day, and he saw many people who came by boat on pilgrimage to the temple on the hill. Strict old ladies with their slave girls, fat, wealthy men, with swollen livers and short of breath, scholars with faces like ivory. Once a mandarin came to visit the temple with his son in order to pray for success in the imperial examination which the young man was going to take in Peking. He had his own bearers, runners, outriders, and his litters had their blue curtains drawn. As Chang was well nourished he sang and talked a lot, even when he was going uphill, and so he learned a great deal about the comings and goings of the gentry he carried. After his meal at night he fell asleep at once on the ground, wrapped in a tattered mat. Just before he fell asleep he was always in the boat on the river, hearing the waves lap against its sides, smelling the moist air that smelt of reeds and rushes and many fish, listening to the subdued coughing of his sister. But he did not know that he was homesick for all this.

It was only that after a time he grew restless, although he was prospering and his belly was contented as never before. So one day he left the hill and the temple and went off, this time downstream. He did not know what drove him, for no one had beaten him. The bearers were witty fellows, he had learned some funny stories from them and also a little politeness through his relations with the great.

For a time he helped to pull a heavy boat upstream, and the rope chafed his shoulders raw until his skin got used to it and grew calluses. This time he received money, one piece of silver and seventeen coppers. He bought himself straw sandals and a worn blue jacket, for his was gone and he had worked naked from the waist.

It got cold, he took shelter in a peasant's hut where there were only women and children. The men had all died, black in the face of a plague. "I can do the work of five men," Chang boasted, and the women surveyed his gigantic frame with respect and pleasure. There was not much work for him to do, but bandits often descended on the village from the hills and pillaged the peasants. Chang knocked three of them down, and one of them did not get up again. Since then the house had been left in peace. There was little to eat, although the women kept almost nothing for themselves and tried only to content their protector. The silkworms ate dwarf-oak leaves on the frames, it sounded like the steady, steady patter of rain. Chang slept with all the women who were not too old and left his seed behind him when he went on his way in the spring.

Once he saw the boat on which he had been born gliding past, and he called to Elder Sister, who was standing at the oar. But she looked in front of her as though asleep as was her habit, and Chang lay down again in the grass on the bank, for he had no desire to meet his uncle.

Early in the summer of that year the dragon bestirred himself and the river went far beyond its banks and flooded the villages and towns. It carried houses and cattle and corpses on its back to the sea, and great misery overwhelmed the Province-East-of-the-Mountains. When the floods subsided and the people set about rebuilding their houses, Chang helped to carry the beams for the house of a teacher and assisted the carpenters.

Lo Si, the teacher, was one of the many scholars whose lives ran to waste while they tried to pass the three imperial examinations: the first in the district capital, the second in the provincial capital, the third in the northern capital itself, in Peking, in the temple of Confucius. In his youth the teacher had passed the first examination with great distinction. Then he was prevented for two periods of three years from taking the next examination, as he had to go into mourning first for his grandfather, then for his mother. When after nine years he went up for the second examination, his head had grown stiff and forgetful, his excitement made the brush tremble in his hand. He failed, went back to his village, resolved to wait until the prescribed three years were over and then to venture a second time. When he flunked this time too, his ambition withered. Now he had settled down in his native village, giving lessons to the small boys for slender payment which often consisted only of eggs and flour.

Yet the teacher had handed down his ambition to his son, a lively boy with red cheeks and a pleasing voice. Chang quickly made friends with him and learned from him the first eight characters: Heaven, Earth, Sun, Moon, Mountain, Water, Ground and Tree. The old teacher also explained to him one day the meaning of the symbol carved in the door of the house where Chang had often seen it: a circle divided into two parts, one black and one white, whose curved edges fitted completely one within the other. This was the sign Yin and Yang, the male and the female elements, Heaven and Earth, Cold and Heat, Light and Darkness, Day and Night—all things that are opposed and together make the whole: the meeting of the poles, the balance in the sum of all things. To Chang it meant Hunger and Satiety, Poor and Rich. He never forgot the time he spent with the teacher, for from that time on he was free of lice.

Working now at this, now at that, and always following the river's course until it became flatter and broader, and slower like an aging man, at last he reached the sea. There by the sea was the great city Chang Ah Tai had already heard of. He could not help learning a great deal on his wanderings, and now he had left the river people far behind in understanding. He did not hide his learning under a bushel; on the contrary he was proud of it, showed it off on all occasions. "This is the sign Tien," he would say. "It represents the sky." His companions would look with awe at the sign which could be seen in many shops: the sign of the sky, immense and mighty, with a little man sitting beneath it and eating from his bowl. This picture expressed complete contentment, and Chang himself knew this contentment well. Yes indeed, a little man leaning against the great sky, but sitting on the earth and his rice bowl full.

Chang had never seen a town so large as this. For three days he merely stood about and gaped. The streets of the silk dealers, the open-air kitchens, the bakers, the basket weavers, the coffin makers, the candle makers, the incense sellers, and then the markets, the stalls of beef, pork, poultry; then the smoked ducks hanging in rows by their long necks; the sacks of rice from the South; the quiet stores of the tea merchants, who sat in the elegance of their silken robes among their ten thousand tin boxes; the stags' antlers, dried snakes and tigers' hearts exhibited by the medicine men. Ten thousand banners and flags hung above the streets, and lanterns and signs of every sort; all covered with written characters inviting customers to enter, praising the goods or perhaps merely offering a prayer for happiness and contentment. Since Chang had learned to understand a few of the signs he was troubled by the many others which were incomprehensible to him. He pushed his way through the crowd, and his shoulders were always above the others. The children ran after him and cried out: "Big one, big one, was your father a dragon?"

Following the advice of a friend, Chang asked his way to the house in which the Porters' Guild had its headquarters. It was a little house near the harbor, and two old men who were sitting there sipping tea, clothed in long black robes which though not of silk were of great elegance, asked him certain questions. "It is known that the men of Shantung are the tallest men in the Middle Kingdom, but you are as a seven-storied pagoda compared with them," the elder of the two said. Chang bowed in acknowledgment. He became a member of the guild, work was found for him and he paid his contributions.

A thousand ships of every sort and size lay in the harbor. Although Chang Ah Tai had sometimes heard on his wanderings about ships of such a size as this, he had taken it all for fairy tales and tall talk. But there they lay in the water, larger than the temple on the hill. They could roar like beasts and exhale black smoke like gigantic dragons. They were the ships of the foreign devils, and Chang might have feared them if he had known what fear was. He carried coals on his back up long narrow swaying plankways; a procession of men carried coal into the bellies of the great ships, going and returning, a chain of coal heavers that never ceased from sunrise until the yellow dusk. They sang the coolie song that sounds like a groan and helps to regulate the breath. But Chang's breath was big and inexhaustible. In the harbor he saw, for the first time, the foreign devils of whom lately there had been so much talk. They were hideous and impertinent, and it was said that they cooked and ate small children. Chang, who was very fond of children, could not think of it without feeling a hot tremor in his huge fists. Most of the dock porters were afraid of the foreigners, but he went right up to them, measured his height and strength against theirs; he was sure that he was stronger than their Number One man.

As Chang now had regular work he nearly always earned enough to feed himself well. There were teahouses for the porters and seamen in the narrow streets along the harbor, and at night a dense crowd moved to and fro under the lanterns. Women's voices could be heard singing from many of the houses; that's where the girls were. Chang began to do without his second bowl of noodles and saved the money in his girdle in order to buy himself his pleasure with a whore. When he had saved up enough copper coins to exchange for two small silver pieces he went to the teahouse from where the singing came. Men sat below eating and drinking as in every drinking shop, but a narrow stair led up and an old woman drew him into a small room.

"How much money has the gentleman?" she asked.

Chang Ah Tai showed his two silver pieces; they looked lost and small in his immense palm.

The woman pulled a face and spat. "Do you come here with those two dwarfs?" she asked contemptuously.

A girl came in, and Chang was so excited that he did not see what she looked like, his eyes were riveted on her tiny, embroidered, red silk shoes. When he went up to the girl she pushed him back and laughed. "Go away. You stink," she cried out. "I have nothing to do with stinking porters." The old woman joined in at once in a shrill voice and called him a crazy egg. Chang's face flushed at the insult. He had just enough presence of mind to call the girl a lean, lazy whore and the old woman a daughter of a bitch. He put the two silver pieces back in his belt, kicked over a wooden bucket, spilling the water over the mats, and tramped down the stairs and out the door.

Although he tried to put the gnawing and smarting humiliation out of his mind it must have remained hidden somewhere in his memory, for Chang the porter, who up to then had been contented and happy as long as he had food and sleep, began to be tortured by ambition. Now he would stare into vacancy for hours, indulging in a beautiful dream. In this dream it always happened that he arrived at the house of the singsong girls borne in a litter. He got out, he was clothed in fine silk raiment, wearing over it a jacket of heavy black silk such as he had seen the wealthy merchants wear. He held his hands in his sleeves as he entered the house, and his servant flung down a handful of large, heavy silver pieces. The girls threw themselves down and scuffled for the coins. Chang saw the girls distinctly, heard the ring of the silver pieces. He was never quite clear whether he then would leave the house again, observing that the girls were too old and ugly for a man of his rank, or whether he would graciously permit them to entertain him with their arts. Nor did he know whence the money and his prosperity were to come, for rich was rich and poor was poor and there was no bridge leading from one to the other.

At that very time, however, there was a great rising against the foreign devils and many were killed, for so it was ordered by the Empress, the Old Tiger who lived in the Northern Capital, and these orders were proclaimed throughout the country. Chang armed himself with an old razor which he bought in the market—for he had now got beyond stealing—and he and a large band broke into a house and killed two of the men and one woman. While the rest were plundering and finally setting fire to the house he quietly searched the clothing of the dead. Sewn into the lining of the foreign-looking coat of the elder of the two men he found some paper notes printed with foreign characters. He did not know whether this was the money of the foreigners, but he knew that the paper must be of value, for otherwise the dead devil would not have hidden it on his person. He cut the shining buttons from the woman's jacket with his razor, for they too looked precious, and left the house just before the blazing roof fell in.

When order was restored again in the town, Chang confided his loot to a money-changer and received forty taels for the foreign paper, enough money for a mandarin. Now that he could realize his dream, he was reluctant to throw away the good solid money on whores. Instead of that he went to a pawnbroker, whom he had got to know in a teahouse, and offered him the money at interest, for money begets money as everyone knows. "I must make money, for it is time I took a wife and had sons," he explained to the pawnbroker who listened with a polite smile. "That is so, that is so," he agreed. He drew up a document, which Chang unfortunately could not read, and kept the money, promising to pay him a piece of silver every month as interest. He himself got six silver pieces a month on the capital, but Chang did not know that yet, although he was too clever to be a porter forever.

Foreign warships put in at the harbor, guns thundered and regiments of foreign soldiers came out of the ships' bellies. They all looked exactly alike and marched as stiffly as if they were not living people but figures of wood to frighten the people. Some great war lords were with them and took over the command of the town. The soldiers soon began to dig fortifications, and there was no more talk of killing all the foreign devils, for there were too many of them and they carried fire sticks over their shoulders.

One night when Chang was sitting in the harbor peacefully humming to himself and looking up into the sky where the moon was sailing like a boat, he happened to get into a dispute with some of the foreign soldiers. For once he was not in the mood for a scrap; the night was beautiful, he felt as happy and contented as the little man on the sign who leans against the heavens, but the soldiers, three young fellows with vacant eyes, were drunk and above themselves and they wanted to show the world what great face they had. They kicked Chang, who lost his balance and fell from the paved edge of the quay into the water. It tasted of mud and the refuse of the new town drains, and he got out dripping, breathless, very angry. The soldiers were still standing there laughing, shouting down to him in their barbarous speech.

Chang Ah Tai wiped the water from his eyes and looked at the soldiers. They wore small swords at their sides, but they did not have their fire sticks with them. He remembered the thunder of the ships' guns and was about to go on his way, dripping and insulted as he was. They shouted something after him, he heard their noisy, hard-soled feet following him. Dirty barbarians, he thought; for that was how they were described in many edicts. They overtook him, one of them barred his way. Chang pushed him aside. The soldier swore, he swore in Chang's own language. "A whore bore you, fatherless one," he shouted loudly and distinctly.

Chang had never known his mother, and it did not occur to him that the soldier was shouting out the only Chinese words he knew. He raised his fist, and it came down on the soldier with the force of a sledge hammer. The other two threw him to the ground. He defended himself, for now rage roused all his strength. He knelt on the chest of the one he had felled, and pressing his thumbs into his eye sockets he beat his skull with all his strength again and again against the stone pavement of the quay. He felt the man beneath him go limp and die.

A cold sweat ran down into his mouth, but he stood up and, thrusting the two others aside, ran away. His wind was good and he knew the harbor. He concealed himself in a little boat under the bows of a large ship. Next morning the harbor was searched for him. His friends of the Porters' Guild hid him for a few days, then they got frightened. His closest friend advised him to flee, for the foreigners had now put a reward on his head and it was certain that someone would betray him.

It was autumn and there were gray mists over the red-and-yellow foliage as Chang once more set out on his travels. The pawnbroker had refused to deliver up to Chang's friends the forty taels, and Chang had not ventured to put himself in his hands by going in person. The loss tasted bitter, but instead of repining he gained new impetus from it, as he had from the disastrous visit to the brothel.

At the beginning of the winter Chang joined a gang of bandits and robbers who lived in huts in the mountains. They were a wretched, famished lot, and it was little they could extort from the peasants in the district. They had given their leader the name Hung Tsi, the Red, because he had a large burn on his left cheek. He was a slow-witted man, and he had to eat a great deal to keep up his strength. He was now lean and wasted and was fond of telling boastful stories of the courage and strength he had shown in past adventures. Chang laughed him to scorn, for he himself was aware of hunger only in his belly and not in the muscles of his arms or in the adventurous courage of his heart. As the peasants of the district had made a complaint to the imperial prefect of the district, a body of soldiers was sent against the bandits, and the peasants were sorry that they had added this new peril to the old one.

The Red was killed in a fight with the soldiers; Chang led the survivors to safety and became their leader. In the new spring he moved off downstream with them to the mountain and the temple he knew already. But they did not haunt the populous, paved roads by the river's bank. They kept to the hidden trails in the hills. Chang had bigger and more enterprising ideas, he was tired of extorting bread or a handful of flour from impoverished peasants. The whole district was in distress, for the silkworms had got a sickness and died and the mulberry trees were unprofitably occupying ground which ought to have been sown with grain.

In his years of restless wandering and hard labor ambition must have been mounting in Chang's heart like a deep water whose depth could not be plumbed. He could not endure staying where he was; he had to go on to something else. Perhaps this uncommon and peculiar discontentedness was due to his having been begotten and born on a moving boat and on flowing water. In any case Chang Ah Tai, as leader of a band of robbers, was not content with petty theft; he went all out for a big scoop.

In the village at the foot of the hill on which the temple stood, and also among the bearers, he had spies who let him know when unusually wealthy and important pilgrims were coming. By this means he got news of the pilgrimage of Wu Tsing the banker, who had arrived by boat with his own retainers but without his own bearers. Chang held his people down until the banker was leaving again and being carried down from the temple in the dusk; then he fell on the train and the bearers ran away, for they were in the game. The banker's retainers put up just enough fight to preserve their face, and then took refuge in a junk. They then bargained from a distant village about the ransom and sent food and warm coverings for the prisoner, who was in poor health. Chang Ah Tai did all he could to treat the banker as a guest while his agents negotiated with the agents of Wu Tsing's family at the foot of the temple hill. He waited on him, told him the stories and jokes he had picked up in the course of his travels, and it was only a pity that the banker, who came from the South, could hardly understand his northern speech. He played Kaipu and Mahjong with him, games he had learned in the tea-houses of Kiaochow, and he sat by with his mouth watering while Wu Tsing ate the food sent for him and which Chang scrupulously handed over. His thoughtful family sent opium too, and under its soothing influence the banker came at last to take great pleasure in the stalwart young bandit.

Wu Tsing's affairs were not in a flourishing condition. His health and energy were undermined by opium. His doctors had advised him to give up smoking it, and this had caused him acute physical pains and restlessness of mind. For this reason he had gone on pilgrimage to the famous temple in order to pray for peace of mind and the fortitude to give up the vice. He had taken to the opium pipe when his three sons died and his sorrow was not to be borne.

Chang thought over all the banker told him; he thought it over so intently that he could not sleep. When he had thought it out to the end he made his proposal. He forfeited a part of the ransom and asked in return to be taken into Wu Tsing's bank, which was far away in the South in the town of Hangchow on the Western Lake. Fantastic as this demand appeared at first, the banker finally had no choice but to fall in with it. Possibly, too, his weary heart had become so deeply attached to the robust young man that he did not wish to part from him. The ransom was divided among Chang Ah Tai's band and Wu Tsing took Chang away with him. And thus began the career that made of Chang Ah Tai the banker Chang, one of the richest and most influential men of China.

"A coolie, yet he has no monkey's heart but the heart of a lion," Wu Tsing said when Chang made his first ten thousand taels for the bank. Wu Tsing was a tired man, inclined to caution, and he had conducted his business on the lines of making small loans to merchants of good standing who were certain to pay back. But where there is no risk there is little gain, as Chang knew, although he could not count beyond his fingers. He knew how to gamble, and as he had no fear he was always successful. He won wealth as he had his first dish of noodles—by force and brutality and fearlessness. He financed the great landowning families. He seized their land if they did not pay punctually at New Year, and he grew opium on all the land he got possession of in this way. A case of opium fetched over six thousand taels, more than a case of silver. He bribed officials and made them his puppets. The bank's money was at the service of great men, magistrates and prefects, if they needed it to retain their face, and in return they were his friends and did all they could for him. Wu Tsing went back to his opium pipe and left his young partner a free hand.

At first Chang, who came from the North, felt himself a foreigner in this southern land. The people were different to look at, they spoke another language. They were yellow, small, and their skin had an oily sheen. Among them he looked like the big figure of the red-faced guard in the temple of Lin Ying, and they laughed at the way he spoke. He did not mind and laughed louder than they did. In time he realized that he was not a foreigner but after all a Son of Han, just like the people of Hangchow. The banker, Wu Tsing, his boss, undertook his education, and soon Chang shone like a freshly minted silver tael with his new learning and polite manners. As soon as he began to enrich both himself and the bank, Wu Tsing gave him a new and better name. Thenceforward Chang was known no longer as Ah Tai, which was a worthless appellation, but as Bo Gum, precious gold.

"I am rich enough to buy myself eyes, ears and understanding," Bogum Chang boasted. He sent for the poor village schoolmaster in whose house he had learned to read the first eight characters. The teacher was thankful to come, and Chang settled him and his whole family in an outer court of his house, for by this time he had even a house of his own. It was the old rambling house of a great family which had fallen on bad times and let it go to ruins. On its outer walls there were still traces of red paint to be seen, the token of imperial favor in earlier days. It was situated on the slope of a hill near the lake; there were courtyards and gardens, bamboos and pine

trees, ponds and tiny bridges, artificially constructed cliffs and winding paths and galleries connecting the various buildings and pavil-
ions.

The schoolmaster was but ill acquainted with the southern dialect,
but he made great parade of the mandarin speech of the educated,
and the glamour of his culture was reflected on Chang just as
Chang's wealth gilded the existence of the needy teacher. Bogum
Chang took him about with him whenever there was any occasion
for reading documents. He made use of him as old men with weak
eyes make use of spectacles. But at night Chang sat down with paper
and paintbrush and learned the difficult art of reading and writing.
There was no need for him to know the ten thousand characters
required by a student; in a month he could distinguish most of the
two hundred and fourteen chief characters, and in a year he knew
about six hundred letters—enough to read the edicts, trade signs and
contracts that came his way.

Once more he sent out messengers to the province of Shantung to
inquire for the boat of the Chang family that plied with cargo between Sekuang and Gantsing. The schoolmaster wrote an elaborate
letter in which Chang informed his family that there was room for
them all in his house and that he, Chang, the banker, invited them
to do him the honor of eating his rice. As the river people could not
read, Chang gave the messengers the same message in briefer words,
and about three months later, on the fourteenth day of the seventh
month, two of his messengers returned with the news that his honorable family had just entered the north gateway of the town. Chang
ordered his chair-bearers, put on his most gorgeous dress and went
to meet his family borne on the shoulders of his own coolies in his
own palanquin. He had taken care to send plenty of fine clothes
with the messengers and had impressed on them that they were to
escort his relations into the town in a befitting manner. And now
there they were, seven mouths to feed, including the children—his
old uncle, lean and bent, his younger uncle with wife and sons, his
ancient grandmother, who was blind and had always lain in the
bottom of the boat looking like a dirty little bundle of old clothes,
and his sister, bent with labor, gnarled as a root, in an embroidered

robe with a fan in her hand, coughing and spitting. "Even the Emperor has relations in straw sandals," the schoolmaster said, quoting the old saying.

They were all struck dumb as they were carried through the black, metal-plated doorway into the first court of Chang's house and as the doorkeeper bowed before them and exclaimed: "The great and honorable family of the great lord Chang has come!" The men were as brown as old wood, their hands were twisted with labor, and the women and girls had large feet that had never been bound up; but Chang was a man of too strong a character to be ashamed of his own people. "I was born on a boat and I have been a coolie," he often said without shame, and it sounded almost like a boast. "But the strength of my forefathers in me has raised me to the position of a rich man." He had tablets of his ancestors made, and set them up so that he could bow before them daily, as was the practice in great families. As he had suffered much from hunger, there were always plentiful offerings of rice and fruit before the altar. But on special feast days he offered his forefathers pigs roasted whole. He bought a fine coffin for his old grandmother and had it placed beside her bed to rejoice her heart. Though she was blind she could feel it with her gnarled hands and was so flattered that she giggled like a young girl. Only his old uncle could not refrain from saying: "And so you have gone over to the rice eaters and made your fortune among the dwarfs." And he said that because, if Chang had towered above the men of the Province-East-of-the-Mountains, here in the South he was a giant among dwarfs. He had two good cooks in his household and soon he grew as heavy and stout as he was tall, for now he ate all the food of which before he had only dreamed. As for Wu Tsing, the old banker, he called Chang son and praised him for all he did.

Owing to the restless and unsettled way in which he had spent his youth, Chang had long passed the age when his parents would have had him married if they had been alive. He had long since blotted out his disastrous adventure with the whores in Kiaochow, and there were plenty of pretty young slave girls in his house who were sold to him for a handful of coppers. But now he became impatient to beget sons, and Wu Tsing sent out his own wife to find the right bride for Chang.

Lilien, the lotus flower, was the daughter of a magistrate who was entitled to the imperial distinction of the coral button on his cap. It was said that Lilien was sixteen years old and had had the best of educations. Although no man had ever seen her, since she always resided in the inner court of her father's house, the fame of her beauty was spread through the markets and streets by slaves and slave girls. As a child she had been betrothed to a cousin of the third degree, but the young man was robbed and murdered in an inn when he was on his way to the northern capital to sit for the third examination. Thus she was free for other suitors.

Chang Bogum had made up his mind to marry into the family of an official belonging to the literati. Lilien's father, one of the greatest and most distinguished persons in the province, had got deeply into debt owing to various circumstances. He had had to come to the assistance of the family of the murdered young man when they had to equip soldiers to catch and execute the murderers. Also he was one of the few who obeyed the old and strict imperial edict against opium and had given up the cultivation of it on his lands. As he drew no salary he was supposed, as all other officials were, to extort money from the people by abusing his office. But the magistrate had a gentle hand and could not clench his fist. His income had become smaller year by year while he could not, without losing face, restrict the size of his household, the pomp of his funeral celebrations, the number of his servants, slaves and coolies, or diminish the expenses of hospitality and the number of presents he gave. So he had borrowed large sums in one quarter and another, which were gladly advanced to him. Many of the lenders may have had no thought of repayment; they would have been content with the interest and with the advantages that came of serving a magistrate. Chang bought all these debts off the people, and this lent considerable force to his suit. His ruthlessness in calling in debts was notorious, and the magistrate knew that New Year's Day would not go by without costing him dignity and face if he were not able to pay the bank; so he submitted to the undesired proposal with a polite and inscrutable smile. When he handed over his daughter to the one-time coolie he may have felt as a poor man does who sells his child as a concubine. But the subtle and enlightened mandarin gave no outward sign; the documents were drawn up and the wedding took place with all pomp. The red silk curtains of the palanquin in which Lilien was carried to the house of her husband were so richly embroidered with gold that the people in the street stood still exclaiming their admiration. There was also a long train of porters following with clothing and household goods which were partly hired for this pageant and partly belonged to the bride's dowry. For some days before the wedding all the gifts were displayed in the magistrate's house, and visitors came and went and marveled at the hairpins and the jewelry of precious jade which the bridegroom had sent to the bride. But Lilien sat with her youthful friends and wept, as convention demanded, and besides she was in great fear of the man who, it was said, looked like a gigantic demon.

When Chang Bogum knelt with his bride on the mat before the ancestral altar and shared wine and rice with her in token of their union, he was as excited as he had once been in the house of the singsong girls, and again he saw nothing but the tiny feet in the embroidered shoes. Lilien too cast down her eyes and wafted intoxicating breaths of perfume; and a little later Chang saw her hands as well—fingers of carved ivory. His chest expanded with great laughter. He made her his wife in the intimacy of the night within the drawn curtains of the marriage bed, and it made him laugh again and again to feel how small and finely turned she was. And her skin was like finest silk which has lain in the sun, and her limbs were warm and supple and young, and his property. He could feel her fine ribs beneath his hands; and he was careful not to break something so fragile. For the first time a woman inspired the feeling which he had only known before when he lifted up a child. But he did not know that this was tenderness.

Lilien served him thenceforward with great politeness, and he sometimes caught himself in the act of wondering about her. He would have given a lot to know whether she was happy or sad, whether she cared for him or whether she was afraid of him. But her eyes were always downcast, her voice gentle and her gestures expressive of a refinement and politeness that betrayed nothing. Now that Chang had his wife in his bed he paid no attention for weeks to the slave girls in his courtyards, and every one of his limbs seemed to have its own joy and contentment. During this time, too, he saw for the first time that his house was not only expensive and smart but beautiful: the floors polished as smooth as mirrors with Ningpo polish, the pillars which supported the narrow galleries lacquered red, fan-tailed fish in the little ponds, flowers and trees, shadow and scent in all the courts.

The house stood on a hill, and from the gallery in the third court-yard you could look down on the lake. In the distance on the other side of the lake a slender, tall, needle pagoda rose into the sky, the hills lay peacefully in the dusk, the water was still and smooth, and from the pavilion in the middle of the lake people like dots, with lanterns in their hands, moved through the evening over the Bridge-of-the-Nine-Windings. Wild geese, emblem of marriage, flighted high above with the soft beat of their wings. Music and far-away laughter came floating up from the boats on the lake. Chang had the symbol Yin and Yang carved in the outer gates of his house and painted in gold and red, and this time it meant for him: man and woman. His life felt round and unified within him as the two signs that com-pleted one another.

In the third month of his marriage his sister announced that his wife bore a child within her, for Lilien confided in the elder woman as though she were her mother. Chang had sucked his earliest nour-ishment from her fingertips, now she served his young wife with devoted affection. There was great joy in the Chang household, and the women had themselves carried in their curtained litters to the Temple-of-the-Purple-Cloud, to pray for the birth of a son. In the first flush of his pride Chang invited friends in, and there was much eating and still more drinking and a great tumult and disorder in the hall. But Chang was too strong to be affected by wine, next morning he went about his business with a head as hard and clear as before. Yet the soft light and peace that lay over the first weeks had fled, and soon he was once more an honored guest at the teahouses and brought light girls into his house, for one night or ten nights.

When the time drew near, Chang went secretly and alone the fifteen li to the rock temple which was called In-the-Shadow-of-the-Spirits, feeling rather ashamed, for prayers were the business of women. He turned to the god of happiness, Mi Lei Fo, in whom he had most confidence because he was fat and laughed. But instead of praying, burning paper money and putting sticks of incense in the holders on the altar, he menaced the god with evil imprecations in case a girl should be born and promised him a hundred taels in spirit money and candles in return for the birth of a man child. Chang was a good man of business and did not pay for goods until they were delivered. The god seemed to take these curses and promises to heart, for on the seventh day of the eighth month Lilien bore a son with a golden skin, and when he opened his tiny mouth to cry the women saw that the new-born baby already had a tooth, which was a great miracle and gave promise of boundless might in the days to come. The astrologer who cast the horoscope of the hour of his birth foretold that the first-born son of the house of Chang would be a leader of thousands, mightier than a war lord. But he concealed the fact that the stars prophesied an early death.

The son was given the name of Yutsing, which means a star, because the little shining tooth in his mouth looked like a star and because the man in the fairy story with a mole like a star became the leader of thousands. On his first birthday all the relatives and friends came to wish him joy. They showed the child all kinds of objects, money and jade, paintbrush and books, a flute and a sword. His future could be told from the object he grasped. But Yutsing took hold of nothing he was offered; instead he flourished his tiny fists and knocked everything over. Chang, the father, laughed out loud. "He is going to be a coolie as his father was," he shouted in his mirth.

Two years after the birth of Chang's son, a new edict against the cultivation and use of opium was issued, and this edict, which gave three years' grace for the common people but imposed the severest penalties on officials and mandarins who could not break themselves of the vice within half a year, was taken very seriously by those in authority over towns, districts and provinces. Chang's father-in-law exerted all his power and influence to carry out the edict in his district and advised the peasants to cultivate more tea, the celebrated tea of Chekiang. But Chang Bogum, who could smell a spring of water when it was three li away, had a good nose for money also. If less opium was grown, then its price would go up: this was his very simple calculation. He had a discussion with his old partner, who spent most of his time in drowsy contentment, and one day, not long after, he had himself carried to the house of the fire wagons which had been built a short while ago outside the town. He got without fear into one of the little houses which were attached behind the head of the dragonlike monster, and traveled in it to the City-by-the-Sea, Shanghai.

Chang Bogum had often already done business with foreigners in his bank, when they wanted to rent land in the bank's possession. He liked doing business with them, for they were too stupid to bargain over the price and there was no need to lose time over politeness, as they were entirely ignorant of good manners and, further, they kept their promises. It made him laugh to hear his friends call the foreigners devils, for devils are crafty and sly and these red-haired people were exactly the opposite. They did inexplicable things such as collecting new-born girls and feeding them instead of destroying or selling them; they opened schools for coolie children whose fathers could pay nothing in return; they encouraged all the sick of the town to come to their white house and put them in good clean beds and gave them medicine and occasionally even made them well —all without payment and for no apparent reason. Since the publication of the opium edict they did a new thing. They endeavored to help those who were afraid of the punishment and could not break themselves of the habit of smoking, when their pains became unendurable and the craving for the Great Smoke made them go mad and writhe like worms. They took them into that house of theirs, locked them in and gave them soothing medicines and watched over them until they were cured of the vicious habit. Chang laughed as he tried to explain the folly of the foreigners to his old partner: "First they smuggle the dirt into the country. With the money they make on it they build their senseless schools and sick-houses. Then they go and cure the people of the opium they have sold them. If nobody smoked opium any more in the Middle Kingdom, where would they get the money for themselves and their servants?" Wu Tsing shook his head and could say nothing but: "They are devils and they ought to be driven out."

Chang had sent one of his nephews to the foreigners' school to learn their language. Now he had taken the young man into his bank to assist him as interpreter in his dealings with the foreigners. But he did not entirely trust him and felt sure he would make higher profits if he understood the language himself. So he had his nephew explain to him the characters and the words of those stupid devils, and he soon found out that they were in truth barbarians, as his honored father-in-law always said. A three-year-old child could take in their bellyful of letters in a day, their language was poor and had only one pitch of voice and one word where his own language had five tones of voice and fifty words. In order to help out their poverty they twisted and contorted their words to give them a fine appearance; but Chang lost no time over these tortuosities.

In the wagon, which bore him along more swiftly than a storm, were seated two foreigners whom he had never seen before. Chang tried his linguistic abilities on them, and they not only understood him but seemed to be overcome with joy that he could speak to them. He drank tea with them, in which jasmine flowers floated, and a servant went round and poured on boiling water as often as he had drunk up his tea. Chang did not believe the official at the station when he said how short the journey would be to the distant town. Therefore he had taken a servant with him, who sat trembling in a corner holding a large bundle with food for his master on his lap. Chang invited the foreigners to join him at his meal, and finally it became a feast in which all his fellow travelers took part. The foreigners brought out bottles, in which they had their strong and burning sort of wine, and if Chang had not been a giant at drinking, as he was in all else, it would have gone to his head. His servant in any case was ill merely from the speed, although he had drunk nothing, and vomited in a corner. Two of the other passengers sank to the floor and fell asleep there, while Chang chewed melon seeds and adroitly spat out the husks upon them.

Although there were many marvels in Shanghai, Chang lost no time in marveling at them. He was pleased to see that there were buildings as much taller than other buildings and ships as much bigger than other ships as he himself was taller and bigger than other men. He visited Wu Tsing's business friends, and they in turn introduced him to their business friends. He found that where he made ten thousand taels and thought himself a big man, the banks here made a hundred thousand. Shanghai was the open door through which opium poured into the country. The foreigners paid no attention to the edict, and the laws that had their origin in the northern capital did not bind them. Also a subterranean murmur of discontent ran through the Chinese quarters of Shanghai, and Chang learned for the first time that some provinces were resolved to shake off the dominion of the Manchus. A young man got up in a teahouse after he had drunk too much yellow rice wine and made a speech: "How long are we going to run around with long pigtails like slaves or like buffaloes whose master has burnt his brand on them? The foreign oppressors have laid this upon us as a sign of subjection, and we obey like sheep. A pigtail hanging from the head of a Chinese is a sign that he is a slave of the Manchus. Who rules the Middle Kingdom? The Old Tiger? The palace eunuchs in Peking? The mandarins who squeeze the marrow from our bones so that they can grow fat and lazy? When will you wake, China, and throw off your chains?"

Chang put his hand in dismay to his long, smooth pigtail, of which he had always been proud. You learn some new things in this town, he thought in amazement. An elderly man with the bent shoulders of a scholar said in a loud tone—and his voice had the ring of common sense after the mouthing of the young man: "Confucius teaches: A good man in the service of the sovereign always strives to show the utmost loyalty in his master's presence and in his leisure hours considers how to make good the mistakes his master may have committed." The young man sprang to his feet again. "Confucius did not know our rulers," he shouted. "He never taught that we had to obey thieves and blackmailers who break our rice bowls. He taught: Set yourself against wrong commands." His voice broke in his excitement; someone crowed in a corner as unpracticed cockerels crow, and another shouted: "Without pigtails we shall be laughed at as tailless dogs," and the dispute was drowned in laughter.

Next morning Chang bought newspapers, Chinese as well as English, and after three days he understood something of stocks and shares and the money market. He also observed that the smarter men of the town did not tie their trousers round their ankles and that jackets were worn without sleeves. He paid a visit to a barber's shop, the like of which he had never seen before, and he paid with silver instead of coppers and for days after he smelled as lovely as a whore. He found plenty to amuse him in this town, with friends and feasting, eating and drinking, singsong girls and driving in open gigs drawn by two ponies. He saw so many novelties in those days that he was not surprised when the foreigners told him that there were carriages that pulled themselves and that men had flown through the sky in newfangled rickshas and come down again alive.

As he had so much to do with opium, he wanted to know what this earthy-smoke was that was dearer to so many men than eating or sleeping with women. He visited an opium den with one of his new friends and sniffed the sickly odor that hovered with its faint fragrance over all the houses and streets of the country as though the walls were saturated with it; but in this den it was so thick that you could almost touch it. He lay down on a bench, rested his head on the hard neck rest and looked at the handsome boy who prepared the opium for him. He gave two pulls at the pipe, had it filled again, sucked at it and again had it filled; it tasted neither good nor bad, and he waited for the magic results that were supposed to follow. But nothing happened, after the fifth pipe Chang was every bit as sober as he had been at first. He did not become brilliant and excited as some did, nor drowsy as others. Opium made him neither philosophic nor drunk: it left him just as it found him—a jolly giant of a man. He got up, pushed the table and opium lamp aside, gave the boy a few coins and went out with a laugh. When he got home he smote his mighty chest and thought: I am stronger than the Great

Smoke. Before returning to the town by the Western Lake he affiliated his bank to the banks which were combining to monopolize the opium trade, and he bought a case of twelve bottles of whisky, that hot drink of the foreigners in which he found particular pleasure.

He had enjoyed his visit to Shanghai so much that after the death of his partner Wu Tsing he transferred his bank to Shanghai and invested much money in real estate. As he had foreseen, the price of opium soared, he made a lot of money on his own account and also for his clients. He saw how the town sprawled in all directions like a young growing animal, and he could smell money in land that was not yet built up.

Very soon Chang could touch nothing that did not turn to money. The revolution found him on the right side, for he had seen it coming. The foreign shares he bought went up. He had a finger in everything that went on in Shanghai, and his capital was at work in many places at once. He owned hotels in the center of the foreign town and sheds on the outskirts where the coolies lived. He owned cotton shares and railway shares, he was the first man to buy himself a motorcar such as the foreigners had. He had shares in a company that hired rickshas and in the earliest cinemas and in a Chinese theater in the Rue Edouard VII and in many brothels, Chinese, Korean, Japanese and International. But more profitable than all else to B.G., as he was soon called in Shanghai, were the civil wars, the exploits of generals and war lords and the warring of provinces against provinces. Some of the war lords were friends of his; he drank with them and gave them banquets at which they were waited on and entertained by girls. He sold them arms and munitions at a profit, lent them money at high interest to pay for what they bought, and in return they mortgaged the taxes they extorted from their districts. Chang helped them to invent new taxes. He thought only of the simplest things that arise in the lives of everybody—birth, marriage, death. With the money he made on the coffin tax he bought the government its first airplane.

He was a good friend to his friends and a relentless enemy to his enemies. He could sleep for forty-eight hours and do without sleep for forty-eight hours; he could drink any man under the table and then go and put through an intricate deal. On his forty-fifth birthday he made a bet that he would sleep with ten whores that night, and he won the bet. A bevy of concubines, servants, hangers-on and parasites accompanied him wherever he went. He loved to look on at executions and ran over people, dogs and pigs when he raced along the frightful roads of China in his motorcar; he attended all races and was passionately fond of flying. He spoke English and French well and understood enough Russian to hold his own with White Russian night-club girls and Soviet emissaries. He gave and received many presents, huge, heavy, silver salvers with long-winded inscriptions and the price ticket still attached. When a newspaper attacked him he bought it up and broke the rice bowls of the journalists who were responsible. From then onwards the papers described him as the benefactor of China. His were the money, the strength and the might.

There was only one vacant and aching spot in his life of violence and success: his son, Chang Yutsing. He was his only son, for the giant was unable to beget another son either with his wife or any of his concubines. While Chang attended to his many interests in Shanghai, traveled the country, now to Canton, where the revolutionaries were in power, now to Peking, where one war lord after another was in the saddle and where now and again even an emperor was set up; while his life spread out in ever-widening circles, his house by the Western Lake remained almost unaffected and unaltered. Behind the black double gateway the courts and buildings extended where the family lived, the servants and slave girls worked, where incense smoldered before the tablets of his ancestors and where Lilien flowered and faded. But Yutsing, who had come into the world with a tooth in his mouth, was not the man his father wished. He had not been born on the river but in a silken bed, and the older he grew the more he resembled his mandarin grandfather. He had trouble over teething, had many childish ailments. Every time news reached Chang that his son was sick he let all his affairs drop and journeyed home. He tried to subdue his heavy step and his loud voice and sat at the bedside of his feverish son trying to breathe his own strength into him. But the child gazed solemnly at him and did not smile when he saw his father. He had the narrow chest, the rounded shoulders and the ivory face of an old learned family. Soon after his third birthday he began to ask what the characters meant that were written on the rolls hanging on the wall. Although he was always polite and respectful to his father, his manner showed that he was afraid of him. Chang took great pains over his son, greater pains than he had ever taken with any person or thing in his life. But they remained on opposite banks of a wide river and drew no nearer to one another.

The old schoolmaster still lived in one of the outer courtyards, and his son, who had likewise become a teacher, with him. Yutsing soon learned from these two the first characters, the two hundred and fourteen which his father too had learned in his day, and the first teachings of Confucius. Chang was opposed to this. Since the revolution Confucius was superseded; there was better learning than the parrotlike gabble of the scholars. There were too many women in the household, there were no men for Yutsing to measure himself against or conflict with. His mother became ever more polite, but it looked as though a steady flame of obstinate hostility burned in her. She and her son stuck closely together; they had secrets of their own, their suppressed laughter died away the moment Chang joined them. There were soft clouds over the lake; Yutsing chewed candied lotus kernels as the concubines did; he was the precious and only offspring, the jewel, spoiled and petted. Chang consulted his friends in Shanghai, and one day he took the child back with him to the great town and put him to school with the foreigners. True, they made a Christian of him there, but as Chang had little opinion of religions he did not care to what gods his son prayed.

The one thing Yutsing seemed to have inherited from his father was the stubborn mind and discontent which had sent Chang on his travels in his youth. But this discontent drove the boy in the opposite direction—away from the riches and the highhanded achievements that fell to his father's lot. Chang discovered too late that he had sent his son to the wrong school, where he learned nothing of the submission and reverence proper to a child. Chang's rebelliousness had driven him from the bottom to the top: Yutsing's led him in the opposite direction. It took him out of the upper classes to which he belonged down to the poor, to the millions of little men who made up China.

He took part in every rising and always on the wrong side, on the side his father opposed. It is only his youth, Chang thought; youth talks big, and reflection is far from it. He thought of all the people he had killed by the time he was Yutsing's age. He himself had grown tame; he no longer killed anybody, at best he now and then looked on at a mass execution. Yutsing too would calm down.

Of course, he married the girl his parents had betrothed to him in his childhood. But immediately after the wedding he forsook the great house in Hangchow and took his wife with him in defiance of all convention. He became a student in Canton. After three years he turned up in a tattered uniform as a partisan of the Reds. At this Chang's patience gave out. He shouted at his son who was so sunk in folly, and Yutsing committed the unheard-of crime of shouting back. Chang raised both his fists and struck the boy. He ordered him to drop his callow notions and to enter the bank and lead a sensible life. His son, green in the face and trembling like a willow leaf, replied that the bank was a stinking quagmire, stained with the blood of the poor. This tactless and bombastic speech threw Chang into a fury. He felt capable of murdering the son he had begotten. He put his hands in his sleeves, kept them there to ward off a disaster. Yutsing, the weakling, had an attack of nosebleeding. He had been born with a tooth in his mouth, now he stood there in his tattered uniform, pale and trembling and sniffing back the blood into his nose.

Every coolie has a son to obey and respect him, Chang thought. But I, the most powerful man in Shanghai, am insulted by my son.

He had built up a kingdom for his successor, who threw it in his teeth. He told the boy to go. He was afraid he might kill him if he remained any longer in his sight. Yutsing went out of the door without a word of parting. There were some drops of blood on the floor, and Chang trod on them with the felt sole of his shoe. He will come back and beg for forgiveness, he thought with an impulse of relenting weakness.

But it was four years before he saw his son again.

II

Dr Emanuel Hain

EMANUEL'S FATHER was called Rosenhain and was the owner of the well-known Rosenhain bookstore near the Hauptwache which Emanuel's grandfather, Sigmund Rosenhain, had built up out of trading in wastepaper and secondhand books. It was said that his great-grandfather had gone from door to door with a sack on his back; on the other hand, this old, South German family had in every generation produced a scribe or even a rabbi and thus handed on to all its descendants an inborn familiarity with intellectual matters together with a tendency to short sight.

At the instance of his wife, Emanuel's father applied for permission to alter his name and by dropping its first two syllables it lost its Jewish sound and became German. Emanuel's mother was a beautiful and charming woman with light brown hair and a white skin, who was fond of traveling. "Is there any reason why we should be known for Frankfort Jews every time we sign a hotel register?" she asked, and her husband, who was indolent in such matters, did as she wished. His brother, Dr Paul Rosenhain, often twitted him about it, with an undercurrent of malice in his mockery. He was not particularly eminent in medicine, but he was a good, reliable family doctor and a contented bachelor, of whom children were particularly fond. His clients were mostly Christians, as Jewish doctors were reputed to be the best.

One of the old chestnuts in the repertoire of Emanuel's mother was the story of his behavior at his christening. According to her, he had first looked earnestly at old Pastor Meiners, blinking tensely, and had then suddenly and quite unexpectedly uttered a loud crow, laughed with toothless gums and tried to pull the pastor's hand from his head—an astonishing exhibition of strength and understanding in an infant only three weeks old. Emanuel heard this little tale so often in later years that in time he came to believe that he could remember his own christening, the candles, Pastor Meiners' clean-shaven face, the cold dry smell of the cathedral.

Emanuel's grandparents lived with his parents until he was born, but a month after his christening they moved into lodgings with large lofty rooms and gas. They gave no particular reason for this change of abode, for they were too civilized in the Rosenhain family to quarrel and too clever to say openly what they meant. It was not until old Sigmund Rosenhain got into bed for the first time in their new dwelling, with two hot bottles, which had previously held Kümmel, placed at his cold feet by his wife, that he said, sighing half in resignation and half in relief: "Why then should Frau Geheimrat Schönchen run into two old Jews every time she calls?"—expressing his meaning in a question, after the manner of the Jews. Frau Geheimrat Schönchen, Emanuel's godmother, and his mother's closest friend ever since their schooldays, was responsible for the Christian leanings of the Hain family.

It was the age of the liberal bourgeois class in Germany, ten years after the victory of Sedan. Everywhere there was prosperity and progress. Banks flourished and housed themselves in sumptuous buildings in the style of the Palazzo Pitti. The Hains' house was in the Paulsgasse in the new quarter which arose on the right of the old fortifications of Frankfort. It was built in old German style, which was the latest fashion, with an unsuccessful attempt to imitate the gables of the German Renaissance. Although there were the finest examples of old timbered buildings in the old town, the modern architects could only produce an ostentatious mixture of styles. But the townsfolk, lulled by their security and their wealth, felt perfectly happy amidst sham marble and wallpapers stamped in imitation of old Spanish leather, and heavy carved furniture, the dusting of which was exalted to a rite.

There Emanuel grew up behind thick dark curtains, in the care of a nurse from the Hessian hills. On Sundays the house smelt of roast goose and cucumber salad, of coffee and fresh yeast cakes and his father's cigars. At night a delicate perfume was wafted into his room—Mama, dressed for the opera or a party. He loved Mama, he stroked the fine suède of her long gloves, and when the door closed behind her again he would have liked to cry a little. But he did not cry, for he was a man, so at least Uncle Paul said, who also saw to it that he was rubbed down in cold water and went for regular walks.

Emanuel was wrapped in peace and security—a security so profound and certain that it seemed to him incredible in later years. It was as though all mankind slept enclosed in a cradle or a shell, the child Emanuel part of this repose.

Behind the house was a garden, at first very large but growing ever smaller as Emanuel grew up. In autumn the walnuts were beaten down from the walnut tree; they fell with a thump into the grass in their green rinds and had a bitter smell of autumn. The rinds made dark stains on his fingers, then Mama was cross. Papa only laughed behind his newspaper in a cloud of cigar smoke. When vintage time came round there were jolly family expeditions to the vineyards of the Pfalz.

Emanuel's first sorrow was having to wear skirts like a girl. But on his third birthday he was put into trousers and shiny boots, which he loved so dearly that he took them to bed with him. When he went to school he wore a little sailor suit, as all the better-class children of the town did, with a sailor knot emerging from under the wide collar. He parted with tears from his nurse and unwillingly made friends with Mademoiselle, who took her place. A little sister, Pauline, had made her appearance, a helpless dribbling creature; and properly brought up people had to know French. With a sigh Emanuel resigned himself to the two disagreeables.

Every Friday evening he was taken to the grandparents', and it is to be presumed that Grandfather purposely selected Friday evenings for the visits of his grandson; for on that evening the Sabbath began and there was white damask on the table and a plaited loaf and two lighted candles in old silver candlesticks over which Grandfather murmured a blessing. Moreover, he wore a little black cap on his head and a fine white, fringed silk shawl with gold thread woven in it over his shoulders.

You could easily tell in Frankfort when it was a Jewish holyday, for there were many gentlemen to be seen in the street wearing shining top hats and virtuously carrying prayerbooks under their arms. They were going to the temple to pray, Emanuel was told. He too was taken to the temple once, but only once. Hand in hand with his grandfather he walked through the old town with its squares and gables and fountains to a small and very ancient, hunchbacked house. There were many lighted candles inside, and a funny smell, and people sang in nasal voices. Emanuel began to feel afraid and started to cry. Uncle Paul often teased him about it afterwards. Mama said to Father, "I can't help it, it's quite unnecessary, why must Grandfather agitate the child?" And although the Hains too had been baptized in the meanwhile, Frau Hain still made use of a question instead of a statement. From the date of this visit to the temple Emanuel's evening with the grandparents was changed to Wednesday, and he soon forgot the Friday-evening Sabbath atmosphere. It was not until he had passed his fiftieth year that Dr Hain remembered his grandfather with increasing distinctness, and the candles, the plaited bread, the warm feeling of security as he put his hand in Grandfather's hand on that one and only walk to the temple.

He cried when Grandfather died, but he was not taken to the funeral; instead he had to spend a few days with Frau Geheimrat Schönchen, and he broke a coffee cup which had belonged to Goethe; and then he inherited Grandfather's violin.

Grandfather was very fond of music; he loved Mozart and Beethoven, Mendelssohn and Chopin, and Rossini and Meyerbeer too. On the other hand, Grandfather, with an embittered and fanatical hostility, warned his grandson against a swindler and devil called Richard Wagner. When Emanuel in later years was taken for the first time to a performance of a Wagner opera he listened at first with dread and horror, and the exciting surge of sound made a weird impression on him. Afterwards his dislike turned to a passionate and rather intoxicated love. But it had not got to that yet. Emanuel was still going to the elementary school; he got up at a chill and early hour, was ruthlessly submitted to the cold tub ordained by Uncle

Paul, trotted off to school holding Mademoiselle's hand, learned reading, writing and arithmetic, and also geography and history, from which he received an extremely one-sided picture of Germany as the central point and navel of the world, the greatest empire on earth, peopled by heroes and valiant kaisers and never conquered. When he was ten years old he was removed to the grammar school, had Latin drilled into him and later, with much sweat and agony, Greek as well. This classical education filled every crevice of his brain to bursting, and in the third year he missed his promotion. A new spurt got him through, then things were easier, as he was a year ahead of his classmates in age and experience. Mama was almost pleased over his failure, for the classes in the grammar school of Frankfort were composed of Catholics, Protestants and Jews, and the Jewish boys were always the best scholars. The better a boy's family, the worse his performance in class. Count Moltke, an elongated youth, was almost at the bottom, and it took the united efforts of all concerned to push him along until he was old enough to enter the army. In Mama's eyes it gave Emanuel a certain claim to nobility that he too had failed once. Father was annoyed and talked about the seriousness of life.

Confirmation, his first watch (a present from Frau Geheimrat Schönchen), dancing lessons, a blue suit with long trousers, his first pimples, the first trace of a mustache, his first attack of puppy love—an oppressive time of growing pains and suppressed fears. The examinations were a torture which haunted Dr Hain's dreams at intervals for the rest of his life. One of the boys (his name was Karl Blei) went out of his mind while they were doing the mathematics paper; he was led out struggling madly and vanished into an asylum. But Emanuel got through.

"What are you going to be?" Father, Mama, Uncle Paul and Frau Geheimrat Schönchen all asked him. For a time it seemed that music had taken complete possession of him. Ever since, as a fourth-year schoolboy, he had picked out his first tunes on Grandfather's violin, he was regarded in the family as a prodigy. "A second Sarasate!" exclaimed all their acquaintances, to whom he now sometimes had to play a violin sonata. But Emanuel surprised his parents with the decision that he was too fond of music to make it his career. And so music was to remain friendly to him throughout his life, a gentle relief in difficult moments. Uncle Paul had given him a microscope for his confirmation day, and this turned the scales. "Why should the boy not be a doctor and take over my practice later on?" Uncle Paul asked. And "Why should he not?" was Emanuel's father's answer. There was no question of his taking on the bookstore. "The business cannot support two families," his father said. He had taken to complaining frequently about the state of his business round about the turn of the century. "People do not read as much as they used to," he said.

What did people do then, now that they had electric light and could very well spend the evenings over a book? Well, they did this and that, they played lawn tennis, for example, the new game imported from England, and they went for bicycle rides into the country. People altered, gradually, almost unnoticeably. Emanuel's sister played tennis and fell in love, although she was only sixteen, and there were secret meetings and Mademoiselle got fired and there were scenes. Then came the crash of the stock market, and it seemed that everyone in Frankfort had lost money. All of a sudden Emanuel's father looked gray in the face and his shoulder blades stuck out. The end of it was that he decided to take Paula's young man into the business. Emanuel could be a doctor. Emanuel agreed. First of all he had to do his one year's military service as a volunteer with the 12th Artillery Regiment at Wiesbaden.

Emanuel remembered that year as the happiest and jolliest of his whole life. He loved the service, the uniform, the comrades, the discipline. It was freedom from his home, which in the last two years had become oppressive. Mama suffering from nephritis, Father from worries; the furniture too heavy, the curtains too thick, the rooms too dark. Vacations from too much thinking. Emanuel's brain took a rest, his body stretched, he got broader in the shoulders. Wiesbaden was at its zenith, the Kaiser and many of his generals took the cure, beautiful women walked on the esplanades, and a new theater, which belonged to the Kaiser, provided cheap seats for officers and volunteers. By day Emanuel did his drill, in the evening he soaked himself

in music and opera and at night he sometimes visited a girl of bad
reputation but pleasing manners.

When he came home on leave at Christmas he surprised his parents by the announcement that he would like best to become an
officer. His father laughed at him. His mother shut her lips tightly.
"How can you be an officer?" she asked. "Don't you know that old
Rosenhain was your grandfather? For those people you'll always be
a Jew." It was the first and only time his mother spoke to him about
his origin.

"Your great-grandfather was still going round with a sack on his
back buying up wastepaper," his father put in.

Something crashed down in Emanuel. He had a bad week of it
and from now onward he searched the faces of his comrades. Did
they accept him as one of themselves? Or did they say of him as they
did of some others: "A Jew—but not a bad fellow in spite of it"? Up
to now he had heard such remarks without any personal feeling, but
now a small, almost unnoticeable sore spot began to form. After all,
he was the son of Jewish parents, in spite of Pastor Meiners' bap-
tismal water. But I don't feel Jewish, he told himself.

A photograph was taken of him at this period of his life: a lean
slender boy in uniform with a frank and pleasing face, with a half-
shy and half-energetic look in his heavy-lidded but clear eyes. A Jew
disguised as a soldier. In the autumn, when he had served his year,
he took to spectacles and went to Heidelberg University.

As a changed person he came home for his first vacation. New
thoughts and new spirits had taken him by storm—Schopenhauer,
Nietzsche. Wagner, Ibsen. The "life-illusion." Free love. *Der Einzige
und sein Eigentum*. The superman. Richard Strauss. Oscar Wilde.
Dostoevsky. Strindberg. *Jugendstil*.

Everything he saw at home was like in Ibsen's play. Worm-eaten,
lying, suffocating. His dull, vegetative love for his parents turned
instantly to revolt. His whole generation was in revolt. All fathers
and mothers were saturated, overfed, hypocritical pharisees. He told
them so, and there were bitter words. Mama wept helplessly; sob-
bingly she crept to her bedroom, and then there was an unpleasant
and reproachful smell of Hoffmann's drops.

Back at the university Emanuel plunged into his studies and spent his leisure hours with his new friend, Max Lilien. They went for long walks and had long arguments, while the soft and lovely landscape slipped by them unobserved. Lilien was a Socialist. Emanuel tried to read Marx's *Das Kapital,* but he quailed under its long, dry and dogmatic sentences. It came to life only when Lilien interpreted its ideas, for Emanuel loved this first real friend he had ever had.

Max Lilien was a sturdy fellow with flashing eyes and an ascetic face like the monk's in Giorgione's "Concert." He was a man of burning enthusiasm who was always upsetting beer jugs, scattering ash about, affronting people and treading on ladies' dainty shoes; an ill-groomed, comic, angular person, hard and transparent as a jewel, a Socialist at a time when Socialism was almost a crime. "All Socialists are curs," the Kaiser had said. Emanuel understood nothing of politics; his bent was to music and away from facts. Somewhere in the world things went on and people fought and died, but it had nothing to do with him. The Boer War came, and people sided with the Boers. Then the Russo-Japanese War—and people sided with the Japanese, that little, unknown nation of which up to now scarcely anything had been heard. But all this was sentimentality, not politics. Nouveau art became Japanese. Lafcadio Hearn wrote his sentimental books about Japan; then they were forgotten again. Lilien picked a fight with a policeman, he spent three days under arrest and emerged from the adventure as a martyr in miniature.

Suddenly Emanuel's father died. He was quite well in the afternoon, but in the evening he got up from table, excused himself and went to bed. When Mama went into his room he was already dead. Emanuel attended the funeral in a daze. Mama hung sobbing on his arm and Uncle Paul's. Emanuel found it hard to realize that this little old Jewess was Mama, his mother, whose beloved perfume and tender good-night kiss he remembered from childhood days. His father's death was like a blow over the head. He sat in embarrassment while the will was read, clothed in black in the midst of black-clothed relations who awkwardly cleared their throats.

It came out that there were almost no assets in money, there were even a few debts. The house was mortgaged, and when it was put up for sale its value had declined, for it was old-fashioned and had no bathroom or electric light. The paintings too for which old Hain had paid large sums were worth very little; there were landscapes with waterfalls, fat, beer-drinking monks, a cat playing with a ball of wool, a solid portrait of Mama. Impressionists had become the rage: there was a lot of talk about *"plein air,"* and a new school of painting was already following on the heels of the Manets and Monets, people who painted confused, ugly pictures and called themselves Futurists. When it was all cleared up and Mama had gone to live with her son-in-law, who had taken on the business and the responsibility of providing for her, there was just enough money left to enable Emanuel to complete his studies without waste of time. The security in which he had grown up had begun to crumble. The twentieth century began to grow up: motorcars, uncomfortable and dangerous vehicles, were seen on the streets. There was an exhibition of the first motion photographs; some stubborn cranks promised a dirigible airship, and psychologists had discovered something called the subconscious.

For the first time Emanuel knew what it was to be embarrassed for money. He had a serious discussion with Uncle Paul, then he worked harder than ever for his degree. It appeared that he had some talent for the profession his family had chosen for him. He graduated *summa cum laude,* spent the required time as an intern, walking the surgical wards of the municipal hospital, then he joined Uncle Paul in his practice. The first case he had to deal with was his sister's servant, who had an abortion. He stood bewildered in the stuffy garret where the girl writhed on a blood-soaked mattress, and only the thought of Max Lilien restrained him from handing her over to the police. His sister never forgave him. Emanuel did not love his sister.

He told Lilien all about it later, not without pride, for the girl had got better and found another place. Lilien listened absent-mindedly. "There ought to be municipal bureaus to give advice in sexual matters, and municipal birth-control centers," he said dreamily; it sounded entirely crazy. He was on the staff of a free-thinking newspaper, and Emanuel spent every Wednesday evening with him playing sonatas. Max Lilien played wrong notes with great enthusiasm and snorted through his nose whenever he came to a cantilena.

When Emanuel was thirty-one he fell in love with Irene von Stetten. He had had various love affairs before this: there were secret rendezvous with a married woman in a private room of a smart restaurant patronized by the world of fashion, an affair with a young milliner, which went on for nearly two years until she got engaged, and a passing and ardent liaison with a young actress in the Stadt Theater. But this was something different. It bowled him over in a moment, thunder, lightning and annihilation. "You've got it this time, Mani," Uncle Paul told him, good-natured and experienced. As he got older he handed over more and more of his practice to his young partner, and it was at the house of one of his patients that Emanuel met Irene. Lieutenant Colonel von Stetten had come back from the Franco-Prussian War in 1871 with rheumatism and had never been able to get rid of it for the last forty years and more. The doctor's visits were more a way of passing the time and keeping him in a good humor than a real treatment. Uncle Paul had for a long time given up prescribing medicine for the pains in the old retired soldier's left side. But Emanuel, inspired by the ambition of a young doctor and pride in his new methods, paid him daily visits, applied electrically heated pads, ordered massage and put him on a diet which the colonel kept with Spartan courage.

Irene von Stetten, his daughter, was twenty-one and very beautiful. But it was not her beauty that carried Emanuel off his feet. It was the wonderful vitality that radiated from her, and a transparency for which he could find no words. He was happy when she entered the room, it went dark when she left it. When he gave her instructions for the colonel's treatment in the dark hall of their small flat, his heart beat so loudly that he was ashamed. Irene laughed softly. For three weeks he had not the courage to kiss her. Irene was everything he meant by a lady. She was tall and slender, noiseless and yet lively, she was not prudish as most girls were, her hair was blonde with a dull sheen like tin, she was of good family and yet poor, she had a boundless capacity for joy, in fact she was in every aspect the fulfillment of a desire he had never even known until he saw her. "The girl has breeding," Uncle Paul said with the complacency of an old bachelor who had been a connoisseur of wine and women in his day.

The sky did not fall nor did the earth open nor did Irene box his ears when Emanuel took her in his arms. She clasped her hands behind his neck and not only received but returned his kiss. "At last," she said with a deep sigh.

From that day onwards they met both secretly and openly; they went to the theater together, chaperoned by old Frau Geheimrat Schönchen, made expeditions and went for long walks, visited exhibitions and danced. It was only when Emanuel spoke of their marrying that Irene drew back. They had many quarrels over this question and many reconciliations; once they discussed it at length.

"It's impossible because of my father—and don't ask any more," Irene said. "I have talked to him about it and it's impossible. I should love you even if you were a Hottentot. But my father can't get over your being a Jew. Let's forget this stupid business of marrying— we're very happy as we are. Aren't we?"

Emanuel had left his uncle's house some time before and taken a small flat of his own, and there they could see each other undisturbed and belong to one another. When he held Irene in his arms, it seemed as incomprehensible as ever that she loved him almost as much as he loved her, and now she called him a Jew. His face burned and then became cold as ice.

"But I'm not really a Jew," he said stubbornly.

"No—not really," Irene replied with a smile. "Not for yourself, not for me either. But for my father you'll always be a Jew. You don't know his sort."

They kissed each other, and neither of them observed that Emanuel had denied himself instead of standing up for himself.

Irene often talked of becoming a nurse. She felt a vehement urge for activity and independence, and this was a profession open to ladies. But one spring that bloomed more luxuriantly than any before, she forgot all about it again. The fruit trees along the Bergstrasse were a snowdrift of white and red petals with the almost carmine patches of the vineyard peaches in between. A little later the lilacs were out, clouds of purple trusses in the parks and gardens of Frankfort. The whole air smelt of lilac and then of June and roses, the whole world was drunk with the heavy luxuriance of early summer. There were so many cherries that the market women in the old town were selling them for twopence the pound, and boats laden with fruit followed each other down the Main. In July a storm cloud blew up and darkened the whole of Europe, and old soldiers like Colonel von Stetten sniffed the air and prophesied war. The younger people did not believe it. There were wars in Africa and Manchuria but not at their own door.

On the second of August war was declared.

Enthusiasm, jubilation, speeches, flags, flowers, drunken men in the ditches. "I know no parties, I know only Germans," the Kaiser said. The first troops were called up and sent to Belgium. In three weeks we shall be in Paris, in six weeks the war will be over. Germany looked round for friends. The English, blood relations and cousins? The Italians, allies by oath and treaty? Perhaps the Japanese, that energetic race in the East, whom they respected and had supplied with arms and drill instructions?

Suddenly the Germans were alone; they could not explain to themselves why, they understood nothing of politics, they trusted their leaders and their newspapers. The youthful regiments marched singing to their death, and their heroism was acclaimed on all sides. The older soldiers, the reservists, took the field calmly and deliberately. If there was work to be done, then it should be done. New victories were announced daily on the kiosks, and the church bells rang for ever new victorious battles. Soon the first casualty lists came through; the first mothers were seen in mourning, smiling through their tears and proud of their fallen sons.

Dr Emanuel Hain, a lieutenant in the reserve, joined his regiment. But first, in the exuberance of feeling that marked the outbreak of war, he was able to overcome the old colonel's opposition. "I know no parties," the Kaiser had said, and Emanuel was now an officer too. Hasty war marriages took place by the thousand. Emanuel and Irene were only one of thousands of young married couples who parted after one night together. In the gray of dawn Irene stood on the station platform, waving to Emanuel. "To Paris," was scrawled on the train in chalk. Max Lilien was a soldier too, a volunteer and as enthusiastic as the rest. Irene joined the Red Cross for home service. Emanuel was sent to Belgium, first to the base and later to the front.

So much has been written about the war that there is no need to repeat it here. Dr Hain had his full share of it all, of victory and defeat, of attack and retreat, of dirt and blood, of enthusiasm and fatigue, of assault and exhaustion; enough of rain and snow and mud and sun, of the never-ceasing, never-ceasing noise of the guns. As he was a doctor and worked for three years in field hospitals just behind the front line, he saw all the refuse of battle, his own and the enemy's; they were picked up from the battlefields and thrown into the hospitals as offal is swept up from the floor of a slaughterhouse. Dr Hain forgot how to pity the dying; he needed all his pity for those who remained alive. The ceaseless stream of surgical cases gave him endless opportunities of practice, and thus he became an excellent surgeon. He learned to choke back his pity and to perform desperate operations on desperately mangled cripples who implored him for God's sake to let them die. He was too tired to think; nobody thought as long as the war went on.

He was just about to operate on the shot, mangled entrails of a Hessian sergeant major, when his hospital was shelled. He finished the operation, not out of bravado, but with the instinct of a doctor who cannot bear to leave a cavity open. His orderlies loaded up the casualties and fled, but he went on fixing clips, extracting splinters and finally stitched it all up. He had scarcely done, when a shell hit the building and buried him and his patient. The man died, and he himself was only rescued two days later. He was given the Iron Cross of the First Class. It was a senseless distinction for one of the senseless acts of gallantry of which the war was made up.

He met Irene in Brussels. His longing for her had been so intense that she had ceased to be a real person, a girl, a woman with eyes and small breasts and warm hands: she had become merely an idea, an imaginary being, like the ghost of a dream he had once dreamt. Now she was there, Irene, his wife. Her mouth, her smile, her eyes, her whole self. Brussels at that time was a rather crazy city. The women of Belgium were in mourning, the inhabitants made themselves as invisible as they could, and there was a black background of hatred to be seen in every face and every movement. Men and officers were sent to Brussels from the fighting line for a few days and then back to the front again. Leave there was an almost certain sign that they were destined for a new offensive. There were banquets and dinners to celebrate meetings and partings. There were theater companies and cinemas for the soldiers and bevies of women had descended upon the hotels; there were cocottes for the officers, prostitutes for the sergeants and low brothels for the men.

The two lovers met in the turmoil of this town. Their union was profound and impenetrable, a primeval forest. A child was born of that night, a son to whom Irene gave birth when famine had already laid hold of Germany. She was brought to bed between sheets made of paper, and the new-born baby was wrapped in paper, for there was no more linen left. The flood of woolen things which had been lavished on the soldiers in the trenches during the first year had long since rotted in those very trenches. All that was left was "Ersatz." The troops wore boots of leather substitute which went to pieces in the mud. Their uniforms were made of substitute material which fell to bits. The country ate substitute and then even substitute gave out. The soldiers who were sent to the front were substitute too, very old men and very young children. Those who stayed at home were weary and apathetic from undernourishment, too weary to feel even disaster very acutely. There was no more hope of victory, only of peace. Every month a new peace rumor flickered up and then died away. The men who came on leave or were finally disabled said nothing. This silence came between those who were at the front and those who stayed at home, between the army and the civil population, between mothers and sons, husbands and wives; it formed an abyss, an estrangement that could scarcely be bridged.

Then America entered the war, and the last spark of hope was extinguished.

Dr Hain came twice to Frankfort in the last two years of the war to see his wife and child. Roland, the child, seemed to flourish, but

Irene grew thinner and more transparent. She had a desperate and uncontrolled way of caressing the boy which almost frightened Emanuel.

The doctor had one more opportunity of showing his courage. It was in the last days of the war, just before and after the armistice, when all discipline had been thrown to the winds. The story was never told—and so he received no decoration for it. With the help only of his sergeant, Heinrich Planke, he transported fourteen badly wounded men to Germany right through the mud and rain and confusion of the roads, right through rebellion and mutiny, right through the horrors of a beaten army in revolt. When he handed over his wounded men in the railway station at Wiesbaden, a soldier stepped up to him and tore off his officer's shoulder straps. Sergeant Planke gave the man a punch in the face and knocked him down. This was the end of the war for Dr Emanuel Hain.

The country was in chaos—a German, that is to say, an orderly, deliberate and organized chaos. Barbed wire and barricades, a little shooting in the streets, then calm. Hastily assembled committees of workmen and soldiers kept order. Dr Hain reported and put himself at their disposal. He felt no hostility for the new rulers; he knew too well what they had suffered and endured. A bearded man with a deep scar across his forehead threw himself upon him, kissed and hugged him. It was Max Lilien. "Comrades," he shouted, "this is my friend—we lived together, we dreamed of the future together and recited Karl Marx—isn't that so, Mani?"

Dr Hain made no protest, and besides it was more or less true. He consented to join the committee, he thought it right to stand by these inexperienced people and to see that the returning troops did not infect the country with too much vermin and sexual disease. He soon had his hands full with arrangements for disinfection and delousing. It was not from lack of character that he put himself at the disposal of the new regime. He was a Jew: he took the color of his surroundings.

On Wednesday evening Lilien paid him a visit; it was a happy evening, and they played the Brahms Sonata in A Major for violin and piano, both of them with clumsy soldiers' hands, but with much feeling. Irene brought in Roland to say good night. Lilien gazed at the child, amazed.

"He's the most beautiful creature I've ever seen in my life," he said in all seriousness. Dr Hain took the child in his arms and breathed the warmth of his silvery hair; he was so overwhelmed with tenderness that he could have cried.

Slowly everything settled down: the government, life in general—and Dr Hain's marriage. For the first time Irene and he could live for each other in a harmony beyond all expectation. As Irene had been a nurse, she could now help when he saw patients in his house, keep his instruments clean, listen when he talked about his cases. Her father lived with them; he was very old, very lost and utterly incapable of understanding the new situation. He had never got beyond Sedan. "The curs!" he would mumble. "Pack of cowards, scoundrels!" When the Treaty of Versailles was signed he had a stroke—not metaphorically but in actual fact. From that day he kept to his bedroom, a crippled, warlike skeleton who weighed heavily on Irene.

A new cleavage soon split up the already divided country; the humiliation of the dictated peace smarted and burned in the souls of many, and they despised the new government, which was so eager to make friends with the enemy that it swallowed every undeserved insult. Thy had fought obstinately and courageously and alone, but the conquerors showed no generosity towards the conquered; there were colored regiments in the occupied territory, and the German people, bled white and starving, had to grovel for the gift of peace. Half of the people had no love for their new liberty, a sickly liberty from the start—and the world outside Germany did nothing to put this liberty on its feet.

When Dr Hain joined the workers' committee, he had no thought of personal advantage; he was not an opportunist but merely a man who went with the current. Nevertheless, this connection got him a post in Berlin after Max Lilien had become a secretary of state. As head surgeon of the Charlotten Hospital he began on a career which soon put him in the first rank. "The Jew has pulled it off," many people said behind his back.

The Hains first rented and then bought a home in Grunewald, beautifully situated on a small lake, with a garden and a sandbox where little Roland could play. Chamber music was now played on the Wednesday evenings by musicians from the opera house instead of the bungled sonatas, and Irene wore a pearl necklace round her delicate neck. Best of all, the love between Emanuel and his wife did not seem to grow old and threadbare as love in marriage usually does. And so, blessed with work, success and prosperity, Dr Hain might have been called a completely happy man but for the ever-growing anxiety he felt over his son.

Roland grew more and more beautiful; he was such a perfect specimen that many people gasped when they saw him for the first time. Emanuel was attached to his child with a physical intensity of almost the same kind as attached him to Irene. But Roland remained distant and strange with him, and it seemed that his first two years of life without a father had made him solitary forever. From his birth he was afflicted with a nervous sensibility; he cried too easily and was afraid of all kinds of everyday things; for example, he could never be got to sleep in a dark room; he was sick with terror, became feverish and turned up his eyes as though in a spasm. Even a shaded lamp was no good: he demanded the brightest light, every electric lamp switched on, and he woke up the moment they were turned out. Emanuel would have preferred to be strict with him, but Roland's upbringing was the one point on which Irene opposed him. Roland was her child; there was always something going on between the two; there were whispered talks and suppressed laughter in the nursery, things were dragged about, bells were rung and clothing rustled over the floor, but as soon as Emanuel went in to share the fun they were silent and the playthings were guiltily pushed aside. Every one of Roland's meals required patience. Stories had to be told: a guardian angel, which was supposed to watch from a tree outside the window, was implored to look on; the Teddy bear had to share the meal, and Irene begged and wept and moaned before Roland could be induced to eat a mouthful. New antics began when it came to going to bed. As long as Roland was little no one understood him, but as soon as he was nine or ten years old and could express himself he confided to Irene that he was afraid of his dreams. "I dream such horrible things," he said, but more than this he could not be induced to say, and so Irene insisted on putting the big boy to sleep. She sat on his bed and he twined a strand of her hair round his finger. This was the only way he could go to sleep. Irene waited, with every light on, until he was fast asleep; only then was she at liberty to spend the rest of the evening as she liked.

Dr Hain sought the help of psychoanalysis but without much practical result. It is one thing to understand a condition and its roots but quite another to cure it. Also the one-sided mental processes of psychoanalysis seemed slightly disgusting to the surgeon whose knife made a clean-cut, exact job of things. And so he prescribed sport, cod-liver oil and fresh air.

"A war child . . . " Irene said. She thought of the night in hell's kitchen when he was conceived, the days of want while she was pregnant and the months of terror when he was born and suckled. Roland, however, was taller and stronger than most children born in those days of famine, and unusually good at all kinds of sport. He was the best athlete of his school, the fastest and most tireless swimmer on the lakes of the Grunewald, and a tennis player of whom the club professional promised to make a champion. Without needing to be taught, he drove the motorcar which his father acquired at that time, and at school he was the best at history, although he failed at all other subjects; yet he had an oddly skeptical turn of mind and wit, unusual in a child.

Dr Hain would have liked his son to have brothers and sisters, but apparently Irene had exhausted all her reproductive energy in this one beautiful and original child. At this stage in their married life it happened that Kurt Planke joined the household, a welcome playmate for Roland. Dr Hain's meeting with his sergeant occurred under strange circumstances. It was part of his duties to demonstrate operations for the medical students; thus, one morning, he was operating a rather complicated case of gallstone. Although this was purely routine work he took the same pleasure, whatever the operation, in his own accurate craftsmanship. When he entered the operating theater the man on whom he was to operate was already under

the anesthetic and covered with white cloths, which left only the
field of operation exposed. Hence he performed the operation without knowing who the man was. It was not until the next evening,
when he was going his rounds and came in due course to this patient's bed, that he recognized Heinrich Planke, his old sergeant. He
was weak and pallid from the aftereffects of the anesthetic and distressed in mind. Instantly the days of the retreat rose before the two
men—the comradeship and the dangers shared—and for a moment
they were both back in that other world, the man's world of war of
which those at home knew nothing. Planke was moved from the
ward into a room which he shared with only one other patient. Dr
Hain took personal charge of him and soon had his sergeant on his
feet again. "I feel as good as new," the Berliner said, and his good-
natured face of a sea lion soon got back its color. He was a so-called
social-security case, for as a worker in a rubber factory he came under
the new health-insurance laws. This was one of the new laws that
caused much unrest. The employers, who had to pay monthly contributions whether the men they employed were sick or not, complained of the imposition. The employees complained even more
loudly over the deduction made from their weekly wages. The sick
complained most of all, for they were profoundly convinced that
the doctors paid them very scant attention and would let them die
from pure malice.

It was five years since the end of the war, and yet Germany was
still shaken with convulsions. The fantastic inflation caused a catas-
trophic devaluation of money from one day to the next. Pennyworths
were paid for with billion-mark notes. A new and ridiculous class of
upstarts with no traditions came to the top, while the solid old middle class was destitute and lacked everything: food, coal, warmth,
rooms and respectability. At last its late enemies came to the help
of the crippled country and a policy of appeasement introduced better days. That Germany began to be herself again was shown above
all by the revival of the arts, for music and books and good drama
were more necessary to the Germans than bread. Berlin breathed a
freer air, and it almost looked as though a real democracy might
spring from soil manured with the blood of war.

But just at the very moment that seemed to herald prosperity a new difficulty arose: the country was too small and too closely populated with people who worked and produced more than was needed. The large factories, compelled to pay union wages, began dismissing their men.

"They've laid me off," Planke announced as soon as he was well again. "Out of work! What a mess!"

So it happened that Planke became the Hains's chauffeur. He moved with his wife and son into the chauffeur's cottage and helped in the garden in his free time. Kurt, his boy, was three years older than Roland, a sturdy fellow with large hands and vivacious eyes. The doctor did all he could to encourage the friendship between the two boys and often listened with a pleased smile when they were romping in the garden.

One Wednesday evening in July, when they played chamber music, and the warm starlit night air from the terrace streamed through the open doors, Max Lilien discovered Kurt Planke, who was then thirteen, hiding in the shadow of a beech, listening to the music with tense face and clasped hands. It was the second movement of Schubert's D Minor Quartet.

"Who ever's that boy?" the secretary of state asked. "He seems to be quite drunk with the music."

"It's only Kurt," Irene replied, shutting the doors on to the garden.

But Lilien wanted to have a look at the boy. He slipped out during the next movement of the Quartet, and sat beside him on the lawn, and after a while he began to talk to the shyly smiling boy. It soon came out that Sergeant Planke's son, the chauffeur's son, thought and dreamed of nothing but being a musician. Lilien dragged him into the music room and introduced him, who almost cried from embarrassment, to the musicians and guests, and amidst a clamor of questions and good-natured laughter Kurt sat down at the piano and played. He played his own rendering of a phonograph record he had made Roland put on for him over and over again: Bach's Prelude and Fugue in E Minor for the Well-Tempered Clavichord, played by D'Albert. The company listened with amusement to the strange performance, which was full of mistakes and wrong interpretations, of ragged patches, wrong notes and distorted rhythms, but all the same amazing in its naïveté and fervor. Kurt, his ears red, seemed long since to have forgotten his audience; he was completely lost in playing. When he stopped and there was an outburst of laughing applause, he started as though he had been playing in his sleep.

His mother scolded him later and begged Irene to excuse him. But the doctor and Max Lilien had meanwhile taken Kurt's destiny into their own hands, and after he had been given some auditions and put through his paces he ended up in the State Academy of Music as a pupil of the celebrated Professor Boskowitz. The professor was an eccentric with an enormous nose and elephantine ears which absorbed every tiniest nuance. "He sniffs with his ears," Roland said of him.

Kurt was soon devoted body and soul to his teacher. Roland was greatly annoyed at being left to himself again. Now that he was in the throes of growing up he was more difficult than ever. He went from bad to worse at school, and he had only one interest of his own —heraldry. Most of his time was taken up in learning all about the old families and names and arms of Germany. He also produced a number of abstract drawings, sinuous and geometrical designs which looked like nothing on earth. He colored them in faint, fatigued and sick water colors and hung them over his bed. Unreal as these compositions were, they seemed to have some mysterious principle of their own, and Irene was often lost in contemplation of them for minutes together. When he was asked about them, Roland announced without hesitation that they were pictures of his dreams. Dr Hain purloined two of these creations and showed them to the neurologists at his hospital. Nothing came of it.

"The boy gives me the creeps," Emanuel told his wife when, getting home late from the theater or a party, they saw the brilliant light of Roland's window stretching far across the garden. The trees stood motionless and silent in the light.

"Wait until he has got over puberty," Irene begged.

She went into his room on tiptoe; Roland lay fast asleep, stretched out and breathing regularly. His young face, cut so clear, beautiful, with the keen sweep of his fair hair, seemed tense even in his sleep. Sometimes Dr Hain could almost understand the strangeness between himself and this child whose blood and whole nature were so different from his own.

It was around that time that the doctor began to feel that he was growing older. He got up at six every morning, breakfasted alone, was driven to the hospital, operated from eight to twelve in the white light of the shadowless lamp, a recent invention; when he had done he pulled off his white linen mask, washed his hands, took off his rubber boots and smoked a cigarette, and another one and still another one. By the increasing number of cigarettes he needed, he could measure his exhaustion. He went the round of his patients, ate a hasty meal in a small restaurant, attended professional consultations, was called in for urgent and desperate cases, operated again, operated at every hour of day and night. There was no time to think, scarcely time to live. He had accustomed himself to doing with four hours' sleep, so that, at least at night, he might have time for a little music, a little of Irene, time to breathe and indulge his fatigue. When he went to the opera or sat listening to music at home, smoking incessantly, he could feel himself going to pieces. His back, his eyes, his shoulders were tired—round shoulders, bent Jewish back. The wrinkles that lined his face were Jewish wrinkles, engraved in the faces of a race that for thousands of years had blinked at the desert sun.

It so happened that the circle of friends the doctor collected round him consisted more and more of Jews. Max Lilien, Professor Boskowitz, the musicians and directors of the opera house, the actors, writers and journalists, the lawyers and the other doctors who came to the house—they all were Jews. Irene's friends came from the other camp—conservative families of nationalist leanings, discontented with the new regime. Impoverished people of noble birth and wealthy landowners, who came to Berlin for the "Grüne Woche," and their young sons and daughters who did not know what to do with themselves. Again the times wore a new mask: jazz, short skirts, short hair, woman suffrage, a plethora of woman students, birth control, relativity, flying records, Americanization, films, pacifism, speed,

speed, speed. The Spartacists of the revolution had become Communists after the Russian pattern which was rather unsuited to Germany. Parliament was made up of so many parties that none had an absolute majority. The German vice of quarrelsomeness split up the nation. Max Lilien left his party, resigned his post and became a Communist. Danger was in the air. But the dance orchestras still played in a thousand night clubs. Foreigners were shown these night clubs, as a specialty of Berlin, where homosexual boys dressed as women and monocle-wearing Lesbians amused themselves. The unemployment figures went up and miserable chains of beggars took their stand in the main streets of the city.

Emanuel and Irene had their first serious quarrel. He accused her of spoiling the boy, of ruining him by her weakness. She replied that he did not understand the child and that any appendectomy was more important to him than Roland's development. Meanwhile Roland's portrait was to be seen at every street corner. Von Ruding, the painter, a cousin of Irene's, had painted him, with his streaming blond hair, and made use of it as a poster for some national meeting or other: the Jew's son, the German ideal. Sometimes Emanuel felt afraid when he thought of the confused and blurred relations between his son and himself. He tried to talk to him. But the boy had an impish way of thwarting him. For days he would make a joke of addressing his father as professor. "How is the professor feeling tonight? How many corpses has the professor pickled today?"

Young Planke made good progress. He was a silent listener on the Wednesday evenings and was often present on other occasions, too. Professor Boskowitz had taken a great fancy to him. He discussed knotty problems of counterpoint with him, equally knotty problems of philosophy, and taught him chess. Sometimes Emanuel felt as if this son of a proletarian were more his own child than Roland was. The quarrel between him and Irene ended with Roland's being sent to one of the new country schools from which he came home only occasionally for week ends. It lasted only for a year and a half. One of the masters fell in love with the boy, he could not break the spell which Roland's weird charm had cast, and he shot himself. Scandal and catastrophe. Roland spoke of it as though it were something he had read in the newspaper, quite impersonally, quite unmoved by the aberration as well as by the tragedy.

Demonstrations in the streets. Communistic and Nationalistic ones. Anti-Semitism, kindled by a few muddled heads after the war, now received scope and a name. Its adherents had so far been laughed at for their absurd, barbaric and even bestial manifestoes and for their leader, whom many took to be insane. Suddenly a new party was in being, the National Socialist party, with representatives in Parliament and influence and a following in the country. A party, composed of desperadoes and fit for the desperate. Germany was on a sickbed, tossing from side to side, hoping that any change might relieve its agonies. No party promised such radical changes as the National Socialists and therefore none had such punch and such a simple idea at the back of it.

The Jews, who had grown their roots in the country for over a thousand years, who were entwined with Germany by a thousand links of common language, education and culture, who were scarcely aware that they were Jews any longer, pricked up their ears. The great-grandfather went from house to house with a sack on his back, they remembered. The race remembered the sufferings the individual had forgotten. There was danger in the air; they scented it with the experience of a hopeless race that had always lived in danger.

Dr Hain scented the danger. His son Roland had become a member of the Hitler Youth and was eagerly pressing on through the various stages in the career of a Hitler boy. The romantic and heroic element in it appealed to him. Enthusiastic and happy, he came home from their meetings and outings.

Despairing, whispered discussions between the doctor and his wife at night, in the darkness of their bedroom. "It can't go on! I must tell the boy he has Jewish blood in his veins. I ought to have told him long, long ago. I should have, if I had attributed any importance to it. It is important now, he must know it, he must!" the doctor implored.

"Impossible. Wait a little—I'm afraid. The boy is hypersensitive. He might kill himself. He might go out of his mind. Suppose the shock were too much for him? What would you do then? Wait until he is older and maturer and knows more of life," Irene replied desperately. They lay close together, and her head was on his shoulder in their accustomed closeness and intimacy. He breathed the scent of her hair, which for him always had the same youth and sheen.

"Will you stick to me, Irene?" he asked anxiously. He could tell she was smiling in the darkness.

"Don't be so silly," she said tenderly. All was well.

Then Max Lilien was shot by an assassin. It was the beginning of a series of political murders. The assassin put a bullet through his own head before he could be arrested. This act of suicide filled Roland with wild enthusiasm.

"That is real heroism—he paid with his own life!" he exclaimed. "Now we shall show the Jews at last!" He was standing in the window, framed against the background of the snow-covered garden, and he raised his arms like wings. Emanuel, wounded and aching with the loss of his dearest friend, started back, and an ice-cold shudder went to his very heart. Roland, who was sensitive, saw his father go white. "Sorry," he said with casual politeness. "I forgot you liked Lilien. Never could understand it."

We are Jews ourselves, I altogether and you half, Emanuel wanted to say. He opened his mouth but checked himself. Irene had come up behind him and put her hands on his shoulders as if to prevent it. The critical moment slipped by, missed and gone irrevocably. In the chauffeur's cottage Kurt could be heard playing the piano— Chopin's Polonaise, triumphantly, intolerably.

"You've still got your homework to do, Roland," Irene said. Roland left the room, whistling.

Dr Hain resigned his post as head surgeon of the Charlotten Hospital soon after Hitler came to power; he did not wait until he was ordered to do so. His private practice was a good one, and also he would still be called in for particularly difficult operations in the hospital. At home things began to alter. The atmosphere had changed; it was lonely, more secluded, anxious, and vaguely insulting. Roland went about like a sleepwalker, too much occupied with himself to notice anything. On the streets the tramp of marching demonstrators, on the radio the fanatic, shouting voice of the Führer, in the newspapers the resounding catchwords of the Third Reich; flags, banners, the swastika, noisy enthusiasm and secret criticism. Dr Hain felt like a tightrope walker whenever he sat opposite his son at table. For the first time there was something in which Roland was seriously interested.

The leader of his Youth Group, Erhard Gerhardt, a lean fellow with long hair, sometimes came to the house. "That Gerhardt follows our boy about like a dog," Irene said.

"What do you mean?" Emanuel asked uneasily; there was scarcely anything now that did not make him uneasy.

"I don't know—there is something doglike about him when he looks at Roland."

"Let us hope we're not going to have a repetition of that business at school," the doctor said anxiously.

Irene stroked his head. "You old raven," she said, joking at his pessimism.

One evening in June Roland was absent from dinner. "Where's the boy?" the doctor asked. Irene replied that he had gone out with three other youths. "When will he be home?" the doctor asked again. There was a strange uneasiness in the air that day.

"I don't know. They've gone to a meeting or something of the kind. Get on with your dinner, Mani," Irene said. "Roland is a grown-up fellow, you can't interfere with his comings and goings."

That's quite right, Emanuel thought. "I believe we're going to have a storm," he said. He pushed his plate away and lit a cigarette. His hand trembled. Roland did not come home. Twice during the night the doctor got up and went to Roland's room. The lights were not turned on, the bed was untouched. He could not sleep, but he laughed at his fears. The boy is having his first adventure, he thought. He's with a girl for the first time. Roland was nearly twenty years old and had never yet paid any attention to girls. Perhaps that was the source of the strange shine about him that attracted everybody, the inviolate and inviolable. The doctor tried to sleep. He had a difficult operation next day, a tumor of the brain, and he needed repose for his nerves.

Before setting out he went to the chauffeur's cottage. Frau Planke apologetically dusted a chair for him, but he did not sit down. "I must speak to Kurt," he said briefly and went to the boy's bedside.

"Roland went out yesterday with three other boys of the Hitler Youth, and he hasn't come home," Dr Hain said. "Have you any idea what it's all about?"

Kurt was wide awake in a moment and looked unusually serious. "I'll go and look for him immediately," he said, throwing off the cover.

"Telephone to the hospital and tell me what's up," the doctor said, quieted by Kurt's ready help and at the same time disquieted by his seriousness.

That day a whisper went through the town, news or the rumor of news that aroused fear and horror. The newspapers were silent as yet, but many people knew already that the Führer had carried out sentence with his own hand on enemies in his own camp. When the doctor got home neither Kurt nor Roland had come back. Irene walked up and down the room trying to smile.

"After all, the rascals are probably out on a hike or on one of the lakes with their foldboat, and we are worrying ourselves quite unnecessarily," he said cheerfully, and Irene eagerly agreed that it was very likely. They did not believe one another and avoided looking at one another. Time stood still.

In the evening Kurt came back with the news that no one in Roland's group knew where he was. "Let us hope it is nothing to do with Gerhardt," he added.

"Why Gerhardt?" Irene asked.

"They've had a scene," Kurt said dryly. "Gerhardt wanted to and Roland didn't want to."

There was a silence.

"Well, I'd better go," Kurt said.

"Good night, and thank you," the doctor said.

A day passed, two days, three days. The papers had now published full reports about the events of June 30. The list of the dead had appeared. There were whispers behind locked doors of hundreds more who had been punished or murdered. Gray clouds with metallic edges moved over the town, and the trees in the garden rustled suddenly and then ceased. Kurt practised at the piano in the chauffeur's house. "It's just like Sodom and Gomorrah, Doctor, 'pon my soul," Heinrich Planke said after reading the paper.

On the third day Irene came into the room in hat and gloves. "I can't stand it any longer," she said, though she still kept up the attempt to smile. "I am going out for a bit."

"Where to?" Emanuel asked.

"Oh—nowhere. Perhaps to Brandt," she replied. Brandt was a distant relation of the Stettens and public prosecutor under the new regime. Irene disliked him, the doctor knew. He went back to the window and gazed out into the garden, which was slowly growing dark. The telephone bell rang, and one of his patients begged him to come. Unbearable cramping pains in the stomach. Dr Hain was almost thankful to have something else to think about. Now it had begun to rain, heavy drops came down, and there was a smell of moist dust.

"Drive fast, Planke," he said when he was on his way back from visiting his patient. He felt as though Roland had meanwhile returned, happy and well, and that all his fears had been merely ridiculous.

"Has anyone come?" he asked at the door.

"Two young gentlemen brought a bundle. They put it in the young master's room," the girl said, wiping her hands on her apron. Emanuel went up quickly to his son's room. It was dark there, and he turned on the light. A sack lay on Roland's bed. The sack was damp with rain; long, large, dark brown. Even before the doctor touched that sack he knew what was in it. The room swayed with him and then stood still again. He walked slowly up to the bed. He took hold of the sack. The thing inside, limp and still warm, was Roland.

Some minutes followed of which Emanuel knew nothing. He had seen many dead, by the thousands in the war, hundreds in hospital; he had cut into living flesh without a tremor. He pulled himself together. He was unable to form a thought, that was a great relief. He stripped the sack off his child's body and, examined it. Rigor mortis had not set in yet. He found the wound on the head; the skull had been bashed in with a blunt instrument, possibly the back of a hatchet. The body was covered with bruises. The face looked arrogant, slightly surprised. Dr Hain washed the body, closed the staring eyes, dried his hands. He felt as though he were out of his mind. He looked for a sheet and spread it over the dead body. It's my fault, he thought, my fault, my fault, my fault. He turned out the light, for the white sheet was much too white. In darkness he sat beside the bed on which his child's body slowly grew cold and stiff.

The most horrible thing of all after that was that Irene insisted on having all the lights turned on, day and night.

"You know he was afraid of the dark," she said again and again. She did not cry, and she made no reproaches. But she offered him no consolation and accepted none. There were times when he thought she would break down, but she was made of a stuff that does not break.

"Our son Roland, aged nineteen, has met with a fatal accident," the obituary notice read. There was no complaint, and there was no trial. My fault, my fault, the doctor thought, my fault.

A week later the house was searched by the police. And a week later again Irene was rung up on the telephone by Brandt, the public prosecutor, who was a distant relation of hers and a favorite of the new regime.

"Information has been laid that your husband has been guilty of treasonable utterances against the State and that his house is in general a center of political disturbance. He is going to be examined the day after tomorrow by the Gestapo. You know what that means. For your sake I am giving you a friendly warning," the public prosecutor said and rang off before Irene could make any answer. She went into the drawing room where Emanuel was standing by the window with his violin, trying to play in order not to go out of his mind.

"You must pack a few things at once and get across the frontier," she said. The doctor still had the bow on the strings, and the last note broke in two with a ridiculous screech.

"Across the frontier? Where to? And what for?" he asked.

"I've just had a warning from Brandt. The Gestapo. That means prison. I don't want them to kill you, too," Irene said, it sounded almost childish. Emanuel thought it over for some minutes.

"Good!" he said at last and stood up. "Are you coming with me?" he asked. "Our passports are in order."

"No. I must stay here. I can't. Later on——" she said distractedly. "I can't leave Father alone," she added; it sounded much too sensible. The colonel, feeble-minded from old age, still sat about in a wheel chair and knew nothing of what was going on.

"Life means nothing to me—without you," Emanuel said.

Irene examined his face. "No—certainly not," she said, stroking his hair lightly with her hand. Tears rose to his eyes at this familiar and tender gesture, his first tears since the catastrophe.

"It will all come right," Irene said. "Just go and pack quickly. I'll follow you—soon. We'll begin afresh. But I can't come just yet."

She had walked away from him, and the room lay between them, wider and deeper than an abyss. There are things which no one can live down; the doctor knew it. Nevertheless, he obediently went and packed his trunk.

"Friedrichstrasse Station, Planke," he said. "I'm going away for a few days." His chauffeur looked at him inquisitively and sympathetically. At the last moment Kurt came up and held out his large hand. "Auf Wiedersehen," he said. Dr Hain went weak as he felt the warm touch of Kurt's fingers. "Perhaps auf Wiedersehen, Kurt ——" he replied.

"Shall I come with you, Doctor?" Kurt asked. "I'd love to get away from here."

Emanuel only shook his head. The car drove out through the drive gates. His home remained behind. The last he saw was the glaring, lighted window of Roland's room. Then Irene too was left behind on the station platform with a smile glued on her disconsolate face.

That same night Dr Hain crossed the frontier. His passport was in order, and he was allowed to take fifty marks with him. Behind him lay his life in ruins, before him lay the great nothing. On a rainy morning he reached Paris.

III

Kurt Planke

KURT SPENT THE FIRST SIX YEARS of his life in his grandparents' fisherman's cottage which stood on a low hill just behind the sand dunes along the coast of the Baltic Sea. His mother, Anastasia Dreggsen, had become a housemaid in Hamburg, as the monotonous life at Hilligenlei was not to her taste. When she was in the eighth month of her pregnancy she went back to her parents and had her child in the hospital in the county town, left it with her parents and returned to Hamburg. She was a good maid and earned forty reichsmarks the month. Of these she put twenty-five into the savings bank, sent ten home for the keep of her boy and kept five for herself. Heinrich Planke, the father of the child, worked in a rubber factory and promised to marry her as soon as they had saved five hundred marks between them. Before they had succeeded in this, the war broke out. Planke forgot that he was a Socialist and joined up with great enthusiasm. He married Anastasia on his first leave, and thenceforward she received part of his pay. Nevertheless she stayed on with the family she served.

The old fisherfolk in Hilligenlei were angry at first about the illegitimate child. "What will the neighbors say?" they asked. But the nearest cottage was more than a kilometer away, and girls who went to the big town usually had children. When Anastasia announced her marriage in a labored letter and sent twelve marks instead of ten on the first of the month, the old people began to think that it was all for the best.

The piece of ground on which their cottage stood and where they grew potatoes was not their own: it was part of the large Einstam estate. But the fishermen were given land and cottages on a leasehold that made them almost seem their own property. They paid fifty marks rent a year, and the men were bound to help on the estate at harvest time. Though serfdom had been abolished for over a hundred years, the Dreggsens still felt they belonged to the estate. This did not suit the sons and daughters of the fishermen along the coast of Schleswig, and they migrated to the towns, the factories.

Kurt grew up with the dark, rhythmical pounding of the waves in his ears and the far horizon in his eyes. He lived in a wide, open vastness. There was nothing to stop the eye—only the sea without and the dune grasses sifted by the wind. A large swamp, full of berries and with the bitter smell of peat, stretched between the cottage and the village. He wore his grandfather's patched trousers cut down to fit him and lived on blue skim milk and potatoes and never knew they were poor people. While the whole country suffered from starvation, the fisherfolk still had something to eat. They caught crabs and shellfish, gathered bilberries in the swamps, and when food got scarce they fell back on the despised sort of mushrooms they called toads' legs which grew by the million on the sheepwalks of the estate. It is true they had to slaughter their pigs by order of the government before the war had lasted even a year, although there was no rhyme or reason in it. Kurt was six years old when he tasted meat for the first time. He spat it out and started to cry, for it had the stink and taste of death.

He was horribly homesick for the Baltic Sea when the war was over and he was suddenly sent off to Berlin to two strangers who called themselves his father and mother. It took him some time to get used to them, for they spoke a strange dialect he could not understand at first. They lived in an interminable row of houses called Keglitzstrasse, one house just like another, and each one containing fifty or sixty small flats for workmen's families. The buildings had six stories, a first yard, a second yard. There was coconut matting for the stairs of the front block, linoleum for the stairs of the next one, and bare wood, which was soon worn down, for the block in the rear. Kurt grievously missed the smell of the sea, the untrammeled wind and raging of the ocean, the stories he made up as he lay on the shore, the songs he had valiantly roared out against the roar of the breakers. He went about looking for a scrap of earth, but there was none in the Keglitzstrasse. It was smothered beneath asphalt and the paving of the street. At seven in the mornings the sirens sounded for all the factories and the men stuck their pieces of bread in their shirts and went off in somber twos and threes. The whole building smelled of cabbage and the detested turnips, the cattle fodder which human beings had to eat in the war; the smell clung to the walls and could not be got rid of.

The search for earth, air, plants, for something he could not describe, took Kurt on longer and longer wanderings about the district. As he was stronger, taller and more fearless than the town children, he unexpectedly became the leader of a band of small boys. The children of the street were divided into Communists and Socialists, just like their fathers. They had glorious street fights and a perpetual state of war. Kurt was a Socialist, as Heinrich Planke was, too. He became a great fighter and shouter. When bread got scarce and the bakeries closed their doors, he was one of the band that broke in and plundered. He proudly produced half of a stale white roll. His father gave him a box on the ear and ate up the bread.

Kurt was such a stranger to his parents that his father quarreled with his mother about him. "That boy's none of mine," he shouted at her. "You've been making a fool of me. Anyone can see the rascal's not mine." Kurt heard his mother crying in the kitchen while the potato pancakes burned on the stove. He badly wanted to know whether his father was his father or not. He did not like his father.

After leaving the factory and moving to the Grunewald, Heinrich Planke gave up his leanings to social democracy and became an out-and-out reactionary. He changed, almost without noticing it, from a proud member of the War Veterans' League into one of the new Brown Shirts. There they had beer and music, and speeches that made the blood tingle in your veins. Heinrich Planke began to hold himself more erect than he had for a long time past, wore a new uniform and hung the mustached photograph of the Führer on the wall. There were scandalous trials, graft, corruption; there were unemployment, an increase of crime, much need and poverty. "It's the Jews," Heinrich Planke said, embittered, "the Jews are at the back of it all. They ought to be poisoned like rats, the whole lot of them."

"First eat your sandwich, Papa," said Frau Planke, regarding her belligerent husband uneasily.

Kurt left the room, banging the door loudly behind him in protest. Once he too went to one of the meetings which his father attended with fiery enthusiasm. He found the proceedings interesting, even exhilarating, but at the same time utterly repulsive. The uncouth threats against the Jews embittered him, and he decided once more that he could not really be his father's son.

There was another boy in the house of his father's employer—Roland Hain. He and Kurt sniffed at each other for a few days like inquisitive and distrustful puppies. Roland was standing outside the lowly chauffeur's cottage and pretending to take an interest in the buds of the fruit trees on the espaliers. Kurt turned on the radio and opened the window. A Haydn symphony came surging and stamping and singing and dancing out. Kurt, who could never hear music without a pleasant, almost embarrassingly sweet sensation in the pit of his stomach, looked expectantly at the young master outside; but Roland behaved as if there were no radio. Just as Kurt was going to shut the window again in disappointment, Roland put his hand against it. "Leave it alone," he said hostilely. "Take your paw away," Kurt said. "I shan't," Roland said. The shutting of the window had now become an affair of honor which had to be settled. Kurt slammed the window and pinched Roland's hand in it. In spite of the pain Roland's face gave no sign except that his strange eyes went dark with rage. When Kurt, taken aback by his own brutality, opened the window, Roland slowly withdrew his hand, which was bruised purple. Then he bent down, picked up a stone and hurled it through the windowpane. Frau Planke came running in at the crash, the radio was turned off and there was an uproar which reached the ears of Dr Hain himself. It was an odd beginning to a friendship which was to influence Kurt's whole life.

Roland was cleverer than he and of a finer grain and rich. He, on the other hand, was stronger and knew more of life and could easily have knocked down the younger boy. As soon as his physical superiority was established he appointed himself the boy's protector and elder brother. They went to the same school even if they were not in the same grade. Roland learned Latin and Greek, and Kurt chose the modern and easier classes, English and French. They joined the same troop of Wandervögel, Roland with a sleepy enthusiasm and Kurt only to be there to protect him. The behavior of these girls and boys, with their pennants and flags, their lutes and songs, seemed to him utterly childish and absurd. Roland had got a great influence over him through the victrola they had in the large house. Kurt begged for particular records again and again as though they were forbidden poison: Arthur Schnabel's Appassionata, Nikisch, Beethoven's Eroica, Bach's Toccata and Fugue rolling out from the organ, player unnamed. They smoked their first cigarettes together, while the needle followed the fine spiral grooves from which the slow movement of Schumann's Piano Quintet blossomed.

"You're a drunkard," Roland said, with gentle mockery. "You get yourself drunk with music."

"And what do you get drunk on?" Kurt asked indignantly.

"I? Wouldn't you like to know?" Roland replied, retreating again into his arrogant reserve. When his parents were out he allowed Kurt to pick out tunes on the piano. All the notes there were in music were in the white and black keys; all the music, constricting your heart like a burning chain, arousing your nostalgia and yet stilling it, was concealed in the black wood of the piano. Kurt tried to draw it out with his awkward and clumsy fingers. There was a law and a principle in every piece of music, he felt, and by the time he was fourteen his most ardent wish was to learn these secrets and be a musician. It was not until he entered the State Academy of Music and began to study that his life had an aim and meaning.

Yet music, which had so far been a vague delight, unattainable as a dream, now receded further from him the more he strove to overtake it; a barricade of endless and tedious finger exercises had to be overcome, a thicket of theoretic rules and laws, which became a torment to Kurt's slow wits. He had large heavy, leaden hands, the legacy of his proletarian father and mother. He had to work harder than any of his quick-minded fellow students, and yet he achieved less. Nevertheless his whole life was in music. The galleries of the opera houses and concert halls became his home. He gave himself over entirely to his professor, Simon Boskowitz, a fanatical Russian Jew. To him the whole universe now seemed to pivot around one point: the Etude, the Sonata he was just studying. It was odd that all the people with whom he was in close contact, all who showed him kindness, were Jews. The men who paid for him to study music were Jews. His piano teacher, the inexorable, black-haired and sonorous Simon Boskowitz, was a Jew. Most of his teachers, his friends and fellow students were Jews. Dr Hain, who had given his father a job when he was sick and out of work, was a Jew, too. "The doctor? Don't be a silly fool," Heinrich Planke shouted back when Kurt brought this up. "He's all right. He's no Jew. I was in the war with him, and he got the Iron Cross of the First Class. D'you think a dirty cowardly Jew'd get that?"

Kurt had his doubts. "Tell me—are you really Jews?" he asked Roland in the school yard.

"Something wrong with you?" Roland said and described a circle on his forehead.

The man to whom he felt most deeply indebted, Max Lilien, was not only a Jew but a Communist. Although he was no longer young he always seemed to be aflame, blazing with enthusiasm, and it was he who had made it possible for Kurt to study music. He unobtrusively kept his eye on him. He invited him in, talked to him, lent him books, introduced him to other young people, painters, authors, journalists and working men. There was little talk of politics between them, and Kurt was grateful for that. There was too much of it in the air in any case, Kurt did not want to hear about them. Everything political sounded as false as a harsh discord. Parliament consisted of so many conflicting parties that it was practically paralyzed, while discontent spread through the country. The meetings his father attended were now usually broken up by Communists and everything ended in a mighty fight. The police had plenty to do. In the industrial quarters some shooting occurred, but in Grunewald you were not afflicted by it.

The Youth Group, too, to which he and Roland belonged had gradually changed and became a Nazi formation. If Kurt still stuck to it, he did so for special reasons of his own. The Wandervögel

groups consisted of youths and girls, and these young people behaved as they liked on their outings, in the youth hostels, the tents,
in the woods and on the banks of the streams. Nothing was said
about it: it simply happened. Kurt from early years had an eager
longing for women, not for any woman in particular but for the
whole sex. Prostitutes did not attract him, and he had no money to
spend on them. The affairs with the girls of the Wandervögel groups
were lax and irresponsible. It was as primitive and satisfying an arrangement as the communal sleeping quarters of young natives on
remote and savage islands.

Besides this, Kurt still had the feeling that he ought to protect
Roland, and even if he sometimes thought of leaving those circles
he never had the energy to carry out his resolve.

One day he had a dispute with Max Lilien. He went to him to borrow some books and came on him packing his suitcase. Kurt could
not help noticing how careworn and disheveled he looked. "Where
are you off to?" he asked.

Max Lilien shrugged his shoulders. "Munich probably," he said
after a pause. Kurt went to the upright piano against the wall and
mechanically opened it.

"A little Bach wouldn't be amiss," Lilien said as he shoved some
socks into his bag. "It puts your thoughts in order to hear Bach."

Kurt disregarded the request; he struck a few aimless chords and
then shut the piano again. "I've been playing like a swine," he said
petulantly.

Lilien came to his support at once. "Boskowitz is pleased with you,
my boy," he said, clapping him on the shoulder.

"Boskowitz doesn't know what's going on," Kurt grumbled.

Max Lilien looked at him. "What's going on?" he asked kindly.

"Nothing," Kurt said awkwardly. "Nothing's going on. That's just
it. It's everything, you see, the whole muddle one lives in. What does
it all mean? What's going to become of us? Nobody knows what's
the point of it. We learn, we study, we practise, we sweat, we want
something, and all the time we know it's idiotic. It leads nowhere.
Unemployed, and still more unemployed. You talk about Bach.
Who wants to listen to Bach when everything's going to pieces?"

"That's just the time," Max Lilien said consolingly. "That's just when they do need Bach. In the war, for example—all the concerts were crowded out——"

The mocking look with which the boy sized him up brought him to a stop. Idealist, Kurt was thinking contemptuously. He scrutinized the fiery eyes of the older man, his pure silvery curled hair, his impotent hands of a dreamer.

"It's a fine world you're handing on to us," he went on, continuing his litany and finding it almost insuperably difficult to express his meaning. "A scrap heap—a heap of dirt—what shall we do with it? What is there for us to believe in?"

"You all flirt with the notion that you are the 'lost generation,' " Lilien said rather impatiently. "You have your problems, granted. Do you suppose we had no problems when we were young?"

"It's all such a mess," Kurt said without listening. "Everything— the whole rotten show. All that whoring around with the Wander-vögel, for example. Sometimes it makes you sick, really——"

"Why don't you leave them?" Lilien asked.

Kurt only raised his hands and let them fall again apathetically on the lid of the piano.

"Are you a Nazi?" Lilien asked.

"What an idiotic question," Kurt answered, rudely in order to carry conviction.

"You are not a Nazi, then," Lilien said. "Are you a Communist? Neither. Then what are you? You're nothing. I'll tell you what's wrong with you, my boy. You have no aim. You have no ideal that makes life worth while."

Kurt looked mockingly at his friend's agitated movements as he casually and clumsily crammed things into the bag.

"Must one be anything? The one or the other? Is there no alternative in the world but Nazi or Communist? You weren't always Communist yourself," he went on sullenly.

The blood rushed to Max Lilien's face. The deep scar in his forehead, which he had brought back from the war, went red. The boy had touched him on a sore spot, the most sensitive, sorest spot in Max Lilien's spiritual make-up. For years he had been a representative of the Social Democratic party until, disgusted by the weakness, the unprincipled jobbery and corruption, the bourgeois leanings of his fellows, he had gone over to the Communists. He had many enemies in all camps and did not belong wholly to any.

"If I have a conviction I stick to it whether it makes things difficult for me or not," he said loudly, as though to shout himself down. "I expect the same of you. Anything else is washed-out and spineless and unworthy of a young fellow like you. Why don't you join the party? Then you would quickly find a meaning in things."

Kurt opened the piano and began to play. He played something utterly senseless—a Czerny Etude: En carillon. "Partisans are born, not made," was all he said.

Max Lilien shut his bag. It was the last Kurt saw of him. He was shot in Munich railway station.

"What a horrible business politics are," Kurt said to his teacher, Simon Boskowitz. His eyes were red and his lips swollen with weeping, and it gave him a childish look, but he did not know that a night spent in tears had left its mark on him.

"We have to fight, Florestan, we all have to fight," the professor answered emphatically, calling him by the name he took from Schumann's Davidsbündler, as he only did on very special occasions. A few days later Kurt went to Bülow Platz to enroll himself as a member of the Communist party at Liebknecht House. The stairs were crowded, the whole building buzzed with activity; doors were hurriedly opened, young men rushed out with papers in their hands, an intense look on their faces, and the slogans on the walls—"Proletarians of all countries, unite"—instead of enthusing Kurt only aroused his mockery. Finally he found himself in a room smelling of beer and cigar butts and announced his intention to a man seated at a desk. He was inspected and interrogated, and other men were called in to assist. Something about him did not please the party bureaucrats. Perhaps they took him for a Nazi spy, perhaps they detected a lack of fanaticism. He wanted to be a Communist, like someone who might lay a wreath on a grave. He showed the convinced and earnest letters Max Lilien had occasionally written him and they were read with respect and a dry sort of emotion. Finally a document was put before him which he signed unread. Handshaking. Shoulder-clapping.

"You know it's not altogether safe to be a Communist in Germany these days," a clean-shaven young man remarked, whose eyes looked as though he never had enough sleep.

"It would be difficult to overlook that," Kurt replied rather ironically.

He was ordered to attend some meetings which were the exact counterpart of the ones he had attended with his father. He was neither elated nor convinced. He marched in a demonstration that ended in a street fight. He beat up a man who was stouter than he but not so strong, and who kept on shouting: "Germany, awake." It all amounted to nothing. Max Lilien lied to me, he thought. It's no good joining a party. It only makes everything more senseless. He soon grew slack about his duties to the party. Music, he thought, music is better than all politics.

One night in February, after a performance of the Johannes Passion in the old Singakademie, he was walking slowly home as it was early and all the busses were full. He often did, particularly when he was so wrought up with music as he was at that moment. Mentally he went over the music he had heard, conducting it at the same time cautiously and rather shamefacedly—for fear of attracting attention. He passed through the Brandenburger Tor, reached the Tiergarten and, as it was a fine night, he strolled on along the side avenues, still lost in the music that echoed in his head. When the sky overhead grew red and fire engines raced along the main avenue with hysterical clanging of bells and people began running all in one direction, he woke with a start. The Reichstag was on fire. Kurt joined the throng and ran towards the fire. Police formed a wide cordon round the scene. The people stood mute and black, looking up at the blazing barrel roof; here and there men pushed their way into the silent throngs shouting, pointing up, clenching their fists. "It's the Communists. Down with the Communists! The Communists have done that," they shouted, and after a few minutes they had got the crowd pretty well worked up. Agents provocateur, he thought to himself. It occurred to him then and there that the fire had a political meaning. An elderly man who was standing next to him put his hand, tattooed with an eagle, to his mouth and muttered: "Communists? Rubbish. You'll soon find out who set fire to the Reichstag. It 'll open your eyes, my boy." He spat, hitched up his trousers as sailors do and pushed his way out of the crowd.

Kurt went on home feeling depressed. He waited. Nothing happened. There was no fight, there was no revolution, the Communist party was dissolved. Arrests, executions, and then a frightened, apprehensive silence.

Kurt practised resolved-diminished-sevenths for hours together. His touch had suffered during the brief political episode. Now he plunged back into music. Ever since they had shot Max Lilien he had felt utterly lost and alone. He talked the cynical jargon of his generation, which shunned feeling and sentimentality, and tried to imitate the dry wit of his teacher, but he felt inwardly that he was soft and vulnerable.

Soon after the country had embarked on its new course, Professor Boskowitz resigned his post. "I would rather sell shoelaces in Haifa than give concerts in Berlin," he said. Kurt tried not to show how hard the blow hit him.

"I feel like a cake that has been taken out of the oven before it is baked," he said as lightly as possible. He had last been learning the D-minor variations of Mendelssohn; he was no musician as yet; he was a student without a teacher. He practised endlessly on the piano at home, the piano for which Max Lilien no longer paid the installments. Most of his fellow pupils followed Professor Boskowitz abroad. "I don't quite know what to do with myself," Kurt complained to Dr Hain, who had helped to pay for his lessons. The doctor listened absent-mindedly.

"I don't know what to advise you," he said. "You are a pure Aryan. You have nothing to worry about."

Kurt, whose ears were sharpened by music, understood what lay behind his words. His friend Roland was not a pure Aryan, and what was worse he did not appear to know it. Roland went his own way, it seemed as though something had at last filled the void of which he often used to complain. "There's no sense in it all," had been his motto before. Now he was busy and important.

In May a few of the young people went on a three days' hike into the Spreewald. Roland begged Kurt so urgently to go with them that he rather unwillingly joined them, half out of anxiety for his young friend and half attracted by the prospect of being with one of the girls. In a cloud of gnats they glided in flat-bottomed boats along the narrow, tree-bordered canals and sang the new songs. Kurt sat silent meanwhile and smiled ironically over the pure Aryanism which they were disseminating in those purely Slav villages.

At night they encamped in a meadow, and Kurt spent an hour with a girl called Trude Heilig, with whom he had had an occasional relation before. Her blood was heavy and hot and hungry with youth, and she willingly gave herself to him in the moist tall grass, while the frogs sadly croaked and the large gnats sang their high-pitched song. As he passed through the sleeping camp to get back to the tent he shared with Roland, he overheard subdued voices in the tent of the group leader, Gerhardt.

"Very well, my boy, as you like. But the consequences are on your own head," Gerhardt was saying, and then the flap of the tent was opened and Roland came out. He did not notice Kurt, but after walking a few steps he stood still and looked up into the sky with a peculiarly sad and arrogant expression. The swastika pennant waved limply and drowsily in the night wind from the top of the tent pole. When Roland walked on noiselessly over the mossy ground, Kurt caught up with him. Neither of them spoke, and they went on in silence to their tent. Roland undressed in the darkness, then stood naked outside the tent for a moment, again looking up into the sky in the same serious, solitary, mournful way. The dim light of the misty moonlight night between the sparse trees of the clearing was white on his slender boyish body. Kurt, already lying down on his blanket, looked at him in some surprise, but he was satiated and drowsy and released after his love adventure.

"Have you had a row with Gerhardt?" he asked. Roland shrugged his shoulders, came back into the tent and lay down on his blanket.

"If you like to call it a row," he said.

"What did he want from you?"

"It doesn't need an extraordinary gift of penetration to guess that," Roland said arrogantly. "They all want the same thing, girls and boys alike. It's vulgar."

Kurt said nothing. Roland turned over, was soon asleep. Kurt listened to his breathing for a time, then fell asleep, too.

It was only after Roland's death that he remembered the cold and lonely tone of Roland's voice in the dark tent. He too belonged to the postwar generation, which was not surprised by homosexual love. Perhaps it was a legacy from the man's world of the war; or perhaps it was an overpeopled country's weariness of reproduction. Some found it funny, some tragic, some interesting, and many snobs took part in it as the latest fashion: as soon as science took up the problem it was removed from the moral to the medical sphere. The purge of June 30, the secret execution of uncounted men, the fanatical persecution of those that were left, all came like a thunderclap. Again Kurt felt his gorge rise and had that same taste of corpses in his mouth as he had after the war when he ate meat for the first time. Group leader Gerhardt had vanished, too.

A strange restlessness took possession of Kurt; he felt a pressing need to know, to explain to himself and find out how it all happened, why Roland had been killed and who had done it. But he discovered nothing. Silence closed over the dead like a deep, black water.

Bit by bit the world in which Kurt Planke was at home fell to pieces. It began with the assassination of Max Lilien; then Professor Boskowitz went into exile, his circle of friends were scattered, books were burned and banned, even music was different, even the language itself. Roland was dead and Dr Hain had fled. For a time Roland's room was brilliantly lighted up all night long, then the house was sold at a price which made the sale look like a confiscation. An ancient skeleton, Lieutenant Colonel von Stetten, was taken in a wheel chair to the taxi and driven off. It was said that Roland's mother was in a sanatorium and not quite right in the head. The Plankes left the chauffeur's cottage, the piano was taken from them and vanished in a furniture van. Kurt sat there oblivious, with idle fingers which slowly grew numb. As Heinrich Planke, his father, had entered the party at an early date and was in its good graces, he succeeded in getting a job in a factory again. True, it was in a chemical factory and he could only be taken on as an unskilled worker. Wages had fallen and all sorts of taxes had to be paid. Nobody knew whether the workers were contented or not, for nobody dared speak his mind. Everybody was afraid of everybody. But many who were nothing before were now something they could be proud of— they were Germans, Aryans. A humiliated people was given back its pride. A craving, deeply rooted in the German nature, which the democratic era had done nothing to satisfy, was now appeased—the craving for pomp and splendor and grandeur; for sharp commands and orders; for discipline and submission; for big words and resounding speeches; for being put into uniform.

Kurt often wondered why he could not fall into line and be content and enthusiastic like the millions. "You've been around with Jews too much," his father told him. That's possible, Kurt thought. He sat in the kitchen of their small working-class flat, feeling lost and unhappy. His mother nagged him as a ne'er-do-well. He joined the musicians' union in order to be registered for employment, but he did not get a job. If he had had the money he would have left home, but he had not a penny. He went to the museums and the aquarium on free days simply to pass the time. He stood looking at blue fish from the South Seas while scraps of piano music he had played went through his head. On Sundays too he went into the Catholic churches to listen to the choir and the organ.

Then one day he was arrested after a visit from the police, who searched his cupboard and found letters from Max Lilien as well as banned books which he had not been able to return after Lilien had been shot; all this went to prove that he had been a Communist. His mother wept and his father abused him. Heinrich Planke had never really been able to convince himself that the changeling was his own child.

Kurt was under arrest for three days. Every night he was roused from sleep and interrogated. They wanted to get names and addresses of suspicious characters from him: there were Communist pamphlets passing from hand to hand—where did they come from and who distributed them? As he had nothing to confess, he was roughly treated. They did not beat him up, but they had a very thorough system of mental torture. On the third day he was taken before another inspector, who kindly offered him a chair and a cigarette, which Kurt inhaled as though famished, and skillfully cross-examined him. His nerves felt like a jelly, cold and shivering.

"We'd be very glad to treat you well if you'd do the same by us," the inspector said. Kurt grinned obligingly and feebly. He was offered a scholarship in the State Academy of Music on condition that he would inform them of any suspicious or seditious word or speech, whether of pupils or teachers.

"I don't know whether I am clever enough for it," Kurt stammered.

"It would be too bad for you if you weren't," the inspector said. Kurt was released and ordered to report in two days' time.

Kurt went straight from the prison to Frau Irene Hain's flat. Her new address had come to his mind with extraordinary clearness. All he did now had a peculiar clarity and transparency. During the last seventy-two hours he had never been allowed to sleep for longer than ten minutes together, perhaps that was the cause of the sleep-walking perspicuity in which he acted.

Frau Hain and her father now lived in the rather new and cheap quarter behind the Preussenpark. As Kurt passed along the benches in the park he saw the freshly painted yellow ones which were marked "For Jews." The flat was in the back block, and Frau Hain opened the door herself. She had only recently left the sanatorium. With an emotion he could not conceal, Kurt recognized the old furniture squeezed into the small room. Frau Hain looked the same as ever, and the peculiar clear-sightedness with which Kurt was now endowed showed him Roland's beautiful face shining out ghostlike from hers. He told her briefly but rather breathlessly that he wanted money in order to get out of the country. "Where are you going to?" she asked with a smile. She smiled all the time, and that too had something ghostly about it. "I thought—Paris," Kurt said. "Professor Boskowitz is there, I believe—and Doctor Hain——"

She continued to smile and look at him in thoughtful surprise. "Why do you want to go away?" she asked.

"The concentration camp——" was all he said.

She stood facing him for another moment and then turned round. "I'll give you my husband's address," she said. The colonel, who was sitting in the room in his wheel chair, tapped impatiently on the arm of it. "My husband will be glad to see you. He was very fond of you," Frau Hain said as she wrote down the address. "He is getting on very well in Paris, I believe." She put the sheet of notepaper in an envelope and took five ten-mark notes from a locked cashbox. It was all he would be allowed to take.

"Is your passport in order?" she asked.

"Absolutely," Kurt said, almost taken aback by his own clearheadedness. "I took it with me when I was arrested, just in case——"

Frau Hain again looked at him thoughtfully. "You can be thankful they didn't take it away from you," she said as she put the money into the envelope. "And listen, Kurt, tell my husband I'm quite happy and I look well—I do look well, don't I? Tell him that, please. I hope you will have a good journey," she added with absent-minded politeness.

When he was in the street again Kurt wondered whether to go and say good-by to his parents. Better not, he decided. His life during the last year had been so dislocated that his sudden trancelike flight seemed to be a logical consequence of it. 37 Rue des Acacias, was scribbled on his note. He went to the Zoo station, bought his ticket, waited two hours in the waiting room, ate two apples, mechanically read the arrival-and-departure board over and over again. For the first time for many years his brain was entirely silent, empty of melodies. As soon as he was in the train he fell asleep. In his dream he was a child again, the great voice of the Baltic Sea sang aloud, he looked for mushrooms in the sheepwalks where they used to grow in thousands but he could not find a single one.

Paris has ever been the haven of refugees, of immigrants, of political suspects, hospitable to all who love freedom and suffer for it. Paris received them without making too many difficulties, set up a few charitable committees, dealt with the first rush of immigrants, hospitable and sympathetic without for a moment interrupting its everyday life. It had received Russians, Armenians, Hungarians, dethroned kings, disgraced Chinese generals on leave, free-thinking Italians fleeing from Mussolini, reactionaries and rebels, political refugees from every unsettled country. Now it was the turn of the Germans. They took up their abode in cheap little hotels, in garrets of the Rive Gauche, but also in the smart new houses in the streets beside the Champs Elysées where wealthy immigrants temporarily offered shelter to poor ones. They were sharply divided into two camps: those who had got their money out of Germany in good time and those who lived on the fifty marks a month which was all they were allowed then, or on the charity of others.

The thing which inwardly consumed and rotted all these people was their enforced idleness. They were all used to working, but France refused them permission to work. France had cares enough of her own in the way of unemployment and sudden outbursts of disorder in the streets. She could give foreigners shelter, but no more. These Germans sat on and on in the cafés, lingering out the hours with a cup of coffee and becoming callous to the hints of impatient waiters. They talked politics and philosophy. All these Jews and Communists were bitterly homesick for Germany. Every day there were new stories about "him." They exercised their wit in order to find some relief in their misery. They forged plans, hammered out ideas: something would have to turn up, it could not go on like that. Every exile had some little private hope which kept him alive.

Kurt found Dr Hain in a ghostly flat in the Rue des Acacias. The furniture was all in covers, the chandeliers were in large linen bags, the air smelled of moth balls and the floor boards were bare. It only made it worse that all this shrouded glory bespoke a certain elegance and splendor. Dr Hain occupied a corner of the large kitchen, into which he had dragged a sofa. Unwashed cups stood on the kitchen table, the bed was unmade, the pillow had no pillowcase, and Dr Hain was walking about in downtrodden bedroom slippers with an old dressing gown over his pajamas. "The woman who looks after me has left me in the lurch," he said.

Kurt pretended to believe the barefaced lie. "Could you put me up for a few days, Doctor?" he asked. "You are the only person I know in Paris and I cannot go back."

He was shocked to see that the old man's face began to quiver, then he understood that he was crying. He himself had had a severe blow when he learned as soon as he arrived in Paris that Simon Boskowitz had died in Zürich. In Germany nothing was known of the fate of the exiles.

Kurt started putting the cheerless kitchen to rights.

"The flat belongs to a former patient of mine," Dr Hain explained. "The Menolescus are at Cannes. It is a great saving for me to be able to live here in the meantime."

Madame Menolescu's portrait in oils hung over the drawing-room mantelpiece, an exuberant woman draped in green and holding a fan. Before the war, when the portrait was painted, she had been young and beautiful. "Is she French?" Kurt asked for the sake of saying something.

"No, Rumanian," Dr Hain replied. "She has a very beautiful daughter who is learning to dance here, that is why they have come to live in Paris."

"When are they coming back?" Kurt asked. "I don't know," the doctor replied. It made Kurt uneasy. Whenever the doorbell rang he started. Where are we to go then? he thought. Where?

Every day the doctor expected a letter from his wife, but there arrived only one in a fortnight. "She's getting on very well," the doctor announced. "She is going to pay me a visit as soon as I have a flat of my own. She writes so bravely," he said, looking up from the letter at Kurt. "She can't say all she would like, owing to the censorship," he went on. "You have to read between the lines." He sat down at once to write an answer, but he tore up many sheets of the cheap paper he had bought for the purpose. He told her that he was getting on well, very well indeed, and that he was expecting her shortly. "Professor Lafitte, you see, an old pupil of mine —you remember him?—is doing all he can to have an exception made in my favor and to get me taken on to the staff of Saint Antoine Hospital. It will probably be decided this month."

The decision took the form of polite regrets. Dr Hain informed Kurt of this with a brave smile. "There are still hopes at Rouen," he said optimistically. "I have good prospects of starting in a practice there. I only need the prefect's good word. . . ."

Kurt was surprised sometimes that the doctor lived on. It was all so utterly hopeless and pointless. When a week had gone by without a letter from his wife he seemed to crumble away to nothing, and then a letter came and with its pretense of cheerfulness pumped fresh strength of life into his failing energies.

Gradually Kurt realized that only this one thing kept the doctor alive: the hope of being able to offer his wife a new life in another country. Every Wednesday evening he went to the Rue d'Université where, in a stable which had been converted into a studio, he played chamber music with a Russian, a Belgian and a German. "I've given up smoking," he said, "but I simply cannot get on without music." Kurt accompanied him on two occasions, but he could not endure the sawing and scraping of the four enthusiasts.

He occupied Madame Menolescu's dismantled bed; the head of it was paneled in gleaming satin which exhaled a stale and faded perfume. When he woke in the night he saw a light in the kitchen and heard a montonous muttering. He got up and tiptoed in: the doctor was sitting on his sofa and studying French from a medical handbook. Kurt softly closed the door again. He himself picked up the language by ear. He talked to everybody, to the postman, the concierge who swept the stairs, to the people at the grocer's where he bought the potatoes for their frugal meals, to the waiters at the café to which the doctor sometimes took him. In this way he learned a clipped, colloquial sort of French which sounded funny enough in his North German mouth.

There was a piano in the drawing room. It was locked. Kurt got into the habit of going for long walks in the outer boulevards. Once more the need of women oppressed him, but he knew none and he had no money. He walked and walked to tire himself out. But the streets were full of girls who looked at him, girls with sex, all mouth and breasts and thighs. He walked in a red mist, he suffered from dizziness and headaches, he didn't know what happened to him.

One day a telegram came from Madame Menolescu and within an hour they arrived: Madame, her beautiful daughter Elaine, a French maid, a Pekingese called Fo, trunks, flowers, laughter, greetings, perfumes; carefree lively people. Madame kissed the doctor, and when he introduced Kurt as his foster son, she kissed him, too.

"What a good thing you are here to keep our poor doctor company," she exclaimed. "He has told me all about you. I know it all. You are the virtuoso. How charming, he's blushing. Just look, Elaine! You need not mind a kiss from an old woman."

Madame looked younger than her portrait of twenty years before. She had soft hair, bleached platinum blonde, the firm slimness of a woman who massaged and did exercises and perspired and starved, large eyes and a well-cared-for skin. "I'm as brown as a gypsy," she said as she looked at herself in the glass. She fastened a bunch of flowers under her chin to hide the danger spot where age begins to show.

Suddenly the flat was full of air and light and noise instead of being the vault it had been before. The windows were thrown open, the covers taken off; there were flowers in the vases, the table was laid. The maidservant was sent down to the cellar for champagne. The telephone rang, the dog barked, Elaine played a waltz, Madame went to the kitchen to make her celebrated *omelette aux fines herbes*. Dr Hain packed his suitcase, the smart, expensive suitcase which had survived the days of his prosperity.

"We will now take our leave, madame," he said, going to her in the kitchen.

"Leave? But where are you going?" Madame asked.

"To a hotel," the doctor said.

Madame looked at him thoughtfully for a moment, a wooden spoon poised in her hand. "Nonsense, Doctor," she said. "I shan't let you go. You saved my life, monsieur—and do you think I am going to let you go to a hotel now? Besides, we are glad to have men about the house. Elaine—" she shouted into the drawing room, "aren't we glad to have some men about the house?"

"Oh, frantically," Elaine answered icily, without breaking off her waltz. They ate and drank to better times; Dr Hain had a silver cigarette box in front of him and smoked without ceasing. Madame miraculously produced another room; it was really a servants' room under the roof, but nothing was said about that. Furniture was dragged upstairs, the concierge worked asthmatically, Madame swept through the flat commandeering vases, mirrors, books and chairs and had them carried up. At last she surveyed her work and seemed contented. Out of the goodness of her heart she begged Dr Hain's forgiveness for having nothing better to offer. "I am not such a nice person as Margot," she said, laughing. Margot, she explained, was a little cocotte, who did not actually walk in the streets but had certain haunts where she picked up men. Among these men had been a German, who came regularly to Paris and regularly spent a night with Margot. Then came Hitler and Margot got a letter: "Dear Margot, I have got to leave the country, I have a wife and two children, I can only take very little money with me. Please tell me where I and my family can live."

Answered Margot: *"Mon pauvre chou,* as you know I have three rooms and I only need one. I think that you and your family can live with me as well as anywhere else. When you have money again you can pay me back."

"And so," Madame concluded, "the whole family, bag and baggage, live with Margot, and the wife has no idea how it all came about."

Madame radiated irresistible warmth and good spirits, and although Kurt only understood half of what she said in her fluent French, he enjoyed himself and never took his eyes from her mouth. The champagne went to his head, and he stood up and made a speech. Madame laughed herself sick at his argot, and even Elaine produced a pale smile. She was as cold as her mother was warm, a cool, white-skinned, dark-eyed beauty.

"Like a moon goddess," Kurt said in a haze of champagne.

"Bébé is getting lyrical," Madame laughed. "Off with you to the piano, Bébé, and play us something beautiful."

"What am I to play?" Kurt asked Elaine, who sat down beside him on the piano stool.

"The Bolero, Ravel," she said. He had heard the piece but never played it. His fingers were out of practice, but as he was drunk he played. After a while Elaine got up and glided into a dance through the room. He could not see her, but he felt her in every nerve. Madame had an inspiration.

"We must dance now that the carpets are up," she cried out in delight. In a moment she brought in the victrola, whipped up friends on the telephone, and the evening ended in an orgy of tango and tiny sausages, which appeared from nowhere towards midnight.

"I've never been so gay in my whole life," Kurt confided to the doctor when they went to bed in their newly furnished garret. He dreamed feverishly and confusedly of both the Menolescu ladies, who were melted in his dream into one—Elaine who was beautiful, and Madame who danced the tango as well and with as much gusto as she did all else.

Kurt wanted Elaine, and a. few times he tried to kiss her. No objection and no response. If the word love had been in his vocabulary, he would have known that he loved Elaine. Nevertheless, by the end of the week he had become the lover of her mother.

"Those who love me call me Gucia," she said the very first day, and so they were Gucia and Bébé to each other. She took possession of him lightheartedly and unhesitatingly, and he submitted with good grace. She had a good amount of mother in her, it soothed the lost boy. She showed him Paris; they drove about the town for hours in her roadster and out to Fontainebleau and Versailles. They ate in hidden restaurants known only to gourmands, danced in the artificially bohemian night clubs of Montmartre; they went for more distant expeditions too and spent the night in ancient little inns meant only for lovers. As he had only his one worn suit, Madame took him to a tailor, ordered suits, chose the patterns, sat watching while he had his fittings and drawing attention to what she liked about him.

"Monsieur has broad shoulders, he does not need any padding," she informed the fitter. "Monsieur has narrow hips, the trousers must fit well." In return, he had to go with her when she chose her dresses. The ladies of the dressmaking establishment treated him with scant courtesy, the young lover of an aging woman, the kept gigolo. When they went places, Madame slipped her purse in his hands. "Please take it, Bébé"—and he paid the large bill with lowered eyes. Later she made him out blank checks. "Please, Bébé, get some money from the bank for us—whatever you like. That is simpler," Madame said.

As Kurt had never had any money, he did not know how to deal with it. He bought her flowers and presents with her own money and gave much too large tips. Gigolo, maquereau, the waiters thought behind his back. On the faces of the maid, the concierge and the fat cook he caught the same expression of amused contempt. Even Fo, the pet dog, looked down on him. Only Elaine seemed to notice nothing, and Dr Hain was too much engrossed in preparing for the medical examination in French he would have to take in case he got permission to set up in Rouen.

One night they were dancing in a bar whose walls were lined with mirrors. Kurt was pleased with the sight of himself. He wore his new dinner jacket with broad shoulders and trousers fitting tightly to his hips. There were pearl studs on his shirt front and a platinum watch on his wrist—presents from Gucia. His smooth hair shone with brilliantine and his face looked pale owing to the powder Gucia had made him take to using. He had a dark red carnation in his buttonhole and a sapphire ring on the little finger of his left hand. The date of their first night was engraved on the inner side.

Unexpectedly he caught sight of Gucia too in the mirror. He had often observed that she wilted in the course of the evening; particularly when she had anything to drink, puffy little bags appeared under her eyes. Her shoulders drooped and she aged years within a quarter of an hour. Now that Kurt suddenly encountered himself in the mirror and saw himself, a good-looking gigolo with his arm round an old woman, he had a shock. He woke up and came to himself for the first time in many weeks. It's nobody's business if I'm fond of a woman who is older than I am, he thought all the same. But he saw himself in the mirror as others saw him. Small and cool, a shiver crept down his back.

He had a serious talk with Dr Hain. It was not easy to shake him from his studies, for he worked with a fanaticism that shut out all else. The rims of his eyes were dark red, the veins stood out on his hands.

"It's no small matter for an old fellow like me to cram for examinations all over again," he complained absent-mindedly.

Kurt told him what was on his mind. Madame was very kind to him and meant it all for the best, but she did not seem to know the right way to go about it. He earnestly begged the doctor to talk to her. He did not want any presents, he wanted to earn something by his own efforts, however little it might be. And he wanted to work, to practise the piano and have time to himself. "I'm a musician, after all, and that she can't see," he said pleadingly.

"Tell her yourself," Dr Hain said, feeling put out.

"I can't."

"Why not?"

"I can't tell you."

Dr Hain gave him a searching glance and spoke to Madame that very evening. She was touched and enchanted. "How charming! Bébé wants to work! What a fine boy you are, and what a stupid old woman to drag you off to night clubs instead of leaving you alone with Beethoven. But that is all over now. From now onwards we will be very serious people," she cried and threw her arms round his neck, pulled his ears and rubbed her nose against his.

Work was found for Kurt with surprising speed. La Serginskaya, Elaine's teacher of dancing, was looking for a pianist, it appeared. She had to get up a ballet for a revue and gave lessons from morning to night, and the musicians' union, for once, had nothing to do with the filling of this post. All over the world by this time the doors to work were bolted and barred: there were unions and guilds, some of which were closed to new members while others did not admit foreigners, and Kurt had run his head against many a stone wall during his first weeks in Paris. Now here he was in the Serginskaya School of Dancing. It smelled of the sweat of many girls, and the work was monotonous. One, two, three, four, and, one, two, three, four, it went on for hour after hour.

The girls in their scanty shorts treated him not as a male creature but as a vegetable. They came half dressed and unconcerned out of the improvised dressing room, ran their fingers through his hair, steadied themselves by his shoulder, made him tie the tapes of their dancing shoes, do up their buttons and hold their lipsticks. Elaine was one of them, and his longing for her, which had died down in Madame's bed, woke up again.

As his fingers had got stiff, he practised for hours in the drawing room. Madame was deeply impressed. She crept about on the tips of her toes, cast admiring glances at him and sat down near by with her eternally unfinished embroidery.

"I'm being as quiet as a mouse," she hissed in a piercing whisper. The consideration she showed grated and screeched in his ears. He banged the piano shut.

"I can't work like this," he cried, all on edge. Instantly the tears streamed down Madame's faded cheeks, and she crept out on tiptoe and returned to her bedroom. Kurt had to follow and console her.

With the first money La Serginskaya paid him, he took a room of his own, if the hole deserved the name of a room, in a small hotel near the Gare Montparnasse. It was all up with his practising again. Ever since he had had work Madame had been displeased with him. "You have become as boring as a husband," she complained.

In the background of the distraught life he led there was Dr Hain tormenting himself to death. No, he had not received permission to practice in Rouen, and now he was corresponding with the university in Jerusalem. The answer was studiously polite. Palestine had admitted all the immigrants it had room for. The Promised Land could not do with any more doctors or intellectuals of any description. Tillers of the soil were what was wanted there. The committee hinted that there was no call whatever for baptized renegade Jews of Dr Hain's description. He had lately begun working at English, the whole of medical science in English. He was fifty-three and looked an old man. In America, so they told him in the cafés, in America it was easy to make a fresh start. At night Kurt had to sit in his attic room and put him through the simplest questions on organic chemistry as if he were a schoolboy. The doctor had tacked an encouraging letter from Irene to the sloping wall above his bed.

The Serginskaya School of Dancing prepared for a dance recital with a paying audience. Elaine was practising something called "The Dance of the Pearl Diver." She asked Kurt to work with her. The drawing-room carpet was once more rolled up and Kurt played bits from Bizet's *L'Arlésienne,* while at his back he heard the heavy breathing of the girl as she danced, heard her land after every pirouette with a little dull thud on the floor. There was a tension between them, a wire charged with electricity. One evening they both exploded. Kurt overpowered her and kissed her; he had striven long enough to hold himself back. Elaine did not slap his face, she did something much worse. She turned round and spat loudly and deliberately on the floor. Kurt went cold to the roots of his hair.

"Why are you so beastly to me?" he asked with a blanched face.

"Considering my mother keeps you, you might at least have the decency not to betray her in her own house," Elaine cried. Suddenly she burst out sobbing and, rolling herself up in a little bundle of misery, she cried her heart out. "It's always the same thing—every one of her gigolos tries it on with me—but I am not like my mother."

Kurt crept away, besmirched from top to toe as if he had fallen into a muddy puddle.

Next day there was a row in the dancing school. "Don't go to sleep," La Serginskaya shouted at him. "You're useless, you only spoil everything."

"If I don't give you satisfaction I can stay away," Kurt said. He felt inflamed inside from all the humiliation, as if he had swallowed a packet of needles.

"All the better," the enraged dancer shouted. "I've had enough of the whole affair long ago. If Madame Menolescu wants to provide you with money, let her pay you directly instead of arranging this farce."

The ballet girls stood in transfixed poses their hands gracefully resting on their gauze skirts. Kurt took his coat and marched out with as much dignity as he could summon in his misery. For a few days he kept away from the Rue des Acacias, then he had it out with Madame.

"I know you mean it for the best," he said, feeling rather sorry for her. "But you have got me in the dirt so deep that I don't know how I shall ever get out again." Madame consoled him distractedly. She had a new favorite, a pale, dark, melancholy Russian from the ballet school.

A few days later Mr Menolescu turned up in Paris: a short-winded, energetic, little gentleman with a mouthful of gold fillings. "Le pauvre chien," Madame had always called him if she ever mentioned him at all. The pauvre chien quickly broke up the establishment and took his wife back to Bucharest. It all burst like a soap bubble of cheap and too scented, too pink soap.

Dr Hain migrated with all his books and all his cares to Kurt's tiny room. For weeks after, Madame's scent clung to Kurt's hair, to his linen, his little suitcase and his monogrammed silk gigolo pajamas. Then that too vanished. Sometimes he even had a faint longing for Gucia. Or perhaps it was for Elaine.

Nothing came of America for Dr Hain. You had to produce money in order to enter the country and people to give you affidavits, a financial basis. Exhausted, the doctor laid aside his English handbooks. For a few weeks they had no idea how to go on. But there were the letters from Berlin. There was the fixation that kept Emanuel Hain alive: to be able to offer his wife a life once more. It was as though he had to make up for his guilt in being a Jew.

Some of the exiles had found jobs for themselves: they baked German cakes and sold them to other Germans who had a little money; they addressed envelopes, they even started magazines: they made wurst, tea-cosies, book bindings. They were Germans, perseverant and industrious, and they did not give in.

My profession? Gigolo, Kurt thought. He had gone to the very bottom. The pale Russian from the ballet school laughed at him as he met him in the street. He took him to a night club where dancing partners were wanted. There were many lovely women tourists in Paris, they all had a passion for dancing and many of them gave their partners tips. This was how Kurt and Dr Hain lived for some time.

A former patient of the doctor's, an Englishman, wrote to him from Shanghai. You could go there if you had ten dollars in your pocket. You could practise as a doctor without having to pass an examination. The Englishman wrote with gratitude and respect and asked Dr Hain whether he would not like to migrate to Shanghai. The letter rang through their Parisian gloom like a clarion call. Emanuel Hain wrote to his wife, and she answered at once. Yes, she had the courage and she would follow him to the end of the world, and she would be particularly glad to go to Shanghai, for it sounded like a paradise of liberty and freedom. Dr Hain revived. He showed her letter in cafés and talked of nothing but this new prospect.

"I have had an invitation to settle in Shanghai," he would boast with childish pride. Nobody believed him.

"Well, if you've such wonderful prospects, why don't you go?" the careworn Germans in the cafés asked him.

"Why? The passage money," Dr Hain replied with a shrug of the shoulders which was resigned and very Jewish.

Kurt sold his pearl studs, his platinum watch, the sapphire ring, his dinner-jacket suit, everything he possessed. As there were still thirteen odd hundred francs lacking before they could pay their passages third class on a small Messageries Maritimes boat, Kurt did something rather desperate. He asked an Australian, with whom he danced, for the money. She was very thin and no longer young, and her French was of a pitiful vulgarity. But Kurt confided in her. He offered himself to her. He tried to prostitute himself. Mrs Adelaide Wilkinson did not give him the money. A little whore who came sometimes to the night club had been observing him. She was good-natured and generous, particularly when she was under the influence of cocaine. She took pity on him and gave him the money in a dry, almost unfriendly way. "Send me a postcard and a little Chinese baby, *petit chou*," she said.

They went on board in a fever of hope and joy and with renewed vitality. Before they started, Irene Hain came to Paris for three days. She did not tell her husband how difficult it had been to extort permission for the journey. "As soon as I have ten patients, you'll follow," Dr Hain said. "In two months, then," Irene said with her frozen smile. Her white handkerchief waving through the smoke of the departing train was the last Kurt saw of Paris.

When they reached Shanghai their English patron was already dead and buried. An accident at polo, a bad spill, a smashed skull—a poor joke of Fate. The nothingness in which the exiles lived became black and dense and impenetrable as never before. The foreign city swallowed them up.

IV

Jelena Trubova

RUSSIA WAS BURIED under thick layers of oblivion. All that Jelena could remember was the prismatic lights in a luster chandelier. When she lay in bed as a child with a sore throat and a slight temperature, the luster chandelier was there to keep her company. It hung down from the center of a plaster rosette in the high ceiling, flies buzzed round its branches—for in Jelena's eyes the chandelier had branches and was alive like a tree in the park—and the sun made stiff little rainbows out of the luster drops. When Papotschka paced up and down overhead, the crystal drops began to swing gently and shone with white and colored sparks which made reflections flit like living things over the ceiling. The Njanja came in on tiptoe: "*Polostchy tri ahsa, golubushka,*" she said. "You must gargle three times, my little dove."

Jelena unwillingly gargled with the purple-colored antiseptic. Then there was Grischa, her brother, in his little uniform; he came for the Easter holidays and they all embraced and kissed one another: *Christos woskrese.* Christ the Redeemer is risen. He is risen in truth.

"*Parlez donc français, mes enfants,*" Mamotschka said.

One night Jelena was snatched up out of bed and wrapped in a woolen cloth like a peasant's child. She never forgot the kitchen smell of the scratchy wool next her face even when she had forgotten everything else. The flight left only a chaotic blur on her memory. Tumult, noise, a never-ending, never-ending journey in over-crowded trains.

In a corner of a desolate station the Tschirikows picked her up. As Mrs Tschirikow told her the story a thousand times, Jelena could not help knowing all about it. "In a corner the child was put down all alone, asleep. 'Where do you belong to?' I asked when she woke up. 'Home,' she said. 'Where is home?' I asked. She didn't know. She didn't know how old she was, nothing. 'What is your name?' I asked. 'Jelena,' she said. 'Jelena what?' I asked. 'Jelena Feodorovna Trubova,' she said quite distinctly. She knew her father's name and everything. 'Where are your parents?' I asked her. She turned away and did not answer. 'Is Grischa dead, too?' she asked later on. It made my heart turn over. Is Grischa dead, too? And there the child all alone, a lovely child she was, with curls, she looked like a princess in her rags. When I undressed her for the first time I found a few pieces of jewelry tied in a little bag round her waist, a bracelet and two brooches. Old-fashioned and not worth much, I sold them in Constantinople. For the sake of God's mercy I kept the child—and what thanks have I had, I ask, what thanks?"

Madame Tschirikow was a good-natured woman as long as you admired her for her good nature; she made sacrifices as long as you noticed it and made a great fuss about it. She could not suffer from a headache or a gnat bite without making a parade of her silent martyrdom before the whole family. Monsieur Tschirikow, a small despondent gentleman, had been a second-rate journalist; he might perhaps have been able to alter his opinions and put himself at the disposal of the new regime, but he was too afraid of the Bolsheviks. Out of fear he carried out the heroic enterprise of fleeing all through Russia, from Saint Petersburg to Odessa and from there on to Constantinople. The Tschirikows had three children, the boy was called Grischa as Jelena's brother was. There were many White Russians living in Constantinople in a tumble-down house built of wood with funny stairs and latticed closed-in balconies. The vermin in the walls mingled with the vermin the refugees had brought with them in their clothes. They cooked on numbers of primus stoves and quarreled about the prominence of the various odors. Jelena felt distinctly that she was different from the other refugee children, quite differ-ent from the Tschirikows' children, for example, who had black hair and hooked noses and could not speak French.

Just as at the beginning of the war people thought it would be over in a few weeks, or a few months at most, so they took their present plight for only an unpleasant interlude. The men of the little colony brought back consoling rumors from the cafés and the streets every day: the White Army was advancing, the Reds had suffered a crushing defeat: patience for two weeks more and they would all go back to Saint Petersburg, patience for two more months, patience, patience. Each family had brought with it a little money or jewelry, and on this they lived. It was only an interlude, just a bit more patience. At night they sang Russian songs and all had tears in their eyes, for they loved to weep and their homesick souls were always full to overflowing.

Jelena detested her benefactors from the moment she set eyes on them. She hated the high-laced, yet soft breast to which Madame Tschirikow had squeezed her when she decided to adopt the for-saken child. She hated Monsieur Tschirikow's tobacco-stained fingers and the red glow and the smoke of his cigarette at night in the room where they all slept—six of them, the parents in bed, the chil-dren on the floor. Most of all she hated Grischa, whose voice was just breaking and whose face was covered with pimples which he tried to squeeze, putting his tongue in his cheek and turning his head this way and that in front of the broken looking glass which was common property. Russia retreated further and further from Jelena, became at length the rainbow gleam in a swaying crystal.

She horrified the Tschirikows when she insisted on going to a Turkish school, but she carried her point. She already knew the easy letters of the French language fairly well, now she learned the Turkish alphabet. Grischa tried to show her what Russian writing looked like, and at last she mixed up all three alphabets and lan-guages together until the Tschirikows laughed at her. Jelena hit out in exasperation and broke one of the elder Tschirikow girl's precious teeth. Monsieur Tschirikow, urged on by his wife, set himself with a sigh to spanking Jelena. For the first time Jelena heard the tearful:

"In the name of God's mercy I picked her up, and what thanks have I had, what thanks?" Jelena was so embittered that she did not utter a sound during her chastisement and refused afterwards to promise amendment. "I am glad I knocked out Vera's tooth," she said on the contrary, as soon as ever Monsieur Tschirikow in exhaustion had put down the leather strap which otherwise he used for stropping his razor. Jelena had a deep conviction that she was of finer clay than the Tschirikows, that she was not going to suffer humiliation at their hands. She somehow contrived to get possession of a heavy old revolver and announced that she would shoot the first person who tried to insult her again.

Sometimes she disappeared for half a day and hid in the Turkish cemetery on the Bosphorus, where the rose trees rambled from gravestone to gravestone. There she crouched, bent double with weeping; she felt such an insuperable longing for Papotschka, for the smell of brilliantine in his silken mustache, the long-lost sense of security in his arms. As she knew nothing of her origin, her family and her past, she began to make it all up for herself. She soon evolved a whole house from the gleaming crystal lusters, a palace with many servants and an escutcheon over the gateway, such as she had once seen on a walk in Tsarskoye Selo. Grischa became a page of the Czar's, Mamotschka a princess, Papotschka a prince. When the Tschirikows announced their intention of adopting Jelena, the orphan child of unknown antecedents, she raged and pointed her revolver at them and threatened murder and suicide. "That's all the thanks . . ." Madame Tschirikow exclaimed once more.

When it came out that the situation in Russia was not an interlude but an end and the beginning of a new state, the world began to concern itself with the Russian refugees. Attempts were made to absorb these people who were so unpractical but so full of feeling, to parcel them out and distribute them throughout Europe. There was an English committee in Constantinople to which they were invited to report themselves. The League of Nations made out new passports which at least enabled the Russians to go from one country to another. Jelena was a problem for the well-meaning but rather thickheaded young English major, for she had no papers of any sort.

Her age was made out with some trouble to be eight or nine. If she had been any older one might have accused her of flirting with Major Alden. In any case she went back to him next day, alone and secretly, and confided to him that her passport ought not to be made out simply in the name of Jelena Trubova but with the title of Princess Jelena Feodorovna Trubova.

The officer was amused by the child. As it was getting dusk before she made up her mind to go home, he accompanied her, for the streets in his opinion were not too safe. Jelena treated him to a highly colored and detailed account of her childhood, the splendor of her parents' princely mansion. Alden believed every word of it, for he was too unimaginative himself to be able to lie. Jelena felt happy and exhilarated, although she did not know at that time that lies were her native element. She tried to keep step with the officer's long strides, and the feel of his large warm hand in which her little one was clasped gave her for the first time the old feeling of safety and protection. "I have taken the liberty of bringing the young lady home," he said politely as he handed Jelena over in the Tschirikows' untidy room. Madame had divided the space up with trunks and curtains of blankets, and a smell of cooking rose from the primus stove. At the last moment Jelena drew the major down and, putting her arms tightly round his neck, kissed him on the mouth. His mustache had a clean smell of brilliantine, and he understood French.

In Belgrade Madame Tschirikow set up as a dressmaker, in Budapest Monsieur Tschirikow was a supernumerary waiter, in Vienna they opened a beauty parlor. "In Russia I had my own house and four servants," Madame told her clients while she rubbed cream into their faces. It was not true, but it was the same with all these Russians: their native land shone brighter the further it retreated, and the past became more and more gorgeous as the present grew drearier. There was an unspoken understanding between them all to honor each other's pretensions of having been something great and important in Russia, in the old days. They massaged their clients' faces with their beautiful soft hands, inheritance of all Russian women, they put on rouge and let them in on some of their beauty secrets. Soon there was not a beauty parlor in Europe which had not a Russian among its assistants.

Jelena added German to the French, Russian, Turkish and Hungarian which she had already acquired. She was much too tall for her age, much too beautiful for a schoolgirl. She was the top of every class, if she ever failed in one of her school tasks she burned with rage and shame; she could not have borne not to be the tallest, the most beautiful, the cleverest. As she had made herself a princess it was up to her to show that she was better than anybody else. Out of the lie came the ambition that decided Jelena's whole destiny.

It was in Vienna that Grischa Tschirikow began to learn the violin and his master made much of him. Monsieur Tschirikow worked for an obscure magazine which the Russians brought out. In the kitchen Madame concocted a face cream, insisting that Pavlova always used it. Jelena strolled about in the Kaerntnerstrasse, looking into the windows of the smart shops; not a detail of the dresses displayed there escaped her. She turned the back room which she shared with the two Tschirikow girls into a workshop where she made dresses for herself and the family, later for some of their Russian acquaintances; the work was scamped but the dresses had great chic.

She left school with a scant education at fourteen, went as an apprentice to a large dressmaking establishment. At fifteen she was taken from the sewing machine and employed as a mannequin. The buyers from the provincial towns made clumsy advances to her. Jelena pretended not to hear. "She is a Russian grand duchess," the head saleswoman whispered to her clients.

Jelena was tired and fed up when she got home at night. Madame Tschirikow reported in a suffering voice of all the trials she had been through that day. When the washing up was done, Grischa retired with his music stand and his violin to the kitchen in order to practise undisturbed. The thin singing notes came through the old-fashioned glazed door. The two Tschirikow daughters took the samovar apart and polished it. Monsieur Tschirikow laid out a game of solitaire, groaning to himself when it did not come out. Madame sat with a basket of silk stockings for darning. "The devil himself must have invented these short skirts," she said bitterly. The basket remained untouched in front of her. She put her hands in her lap. "I can't go on——" said Madame Tschirikow in dramatic resignation. The two girls started quarreling. Grischa put his head in at the glazed door. "I can't concentrate with a noise like that," he complained.

The Tschirikows always lived in too confined quarters and were always short of money. Madame made debts to pay other debts. Monsieur Tschirikow embarked on a venture from time to time; he invested two hundred Austrian schillings in an enterprise of one of his Russian friends. Nothing ever came of these enterprises. Jelena sat silently among them, she didn't belong here. She meticulously manicured her nails, sewed a new trimming on a blouse, arranged a veil on her hat.

Suddenly Madame had her attack. It was a mysterious pain in her back which no doctor could explain or even locate. She leaned groaning on her husband and, followed by the pitying looks of her daughters, tottered into her bedroom. Jelena was told to prepare the bags of hot bran which seemed to be the only means of alleviating her pain. "What a fuss!" she said in disgust. She hated being left alone with Grischa in the kitchen, for Grischa had recently fallen in love with her.

"Why not try shaving?" she said in the jargon of the mannequins when he put his face near hers.

"I shave twice a day," Grischa assured her, and it was the truth. Nevertheless his cheeks were always rough and blue. "A strong growth is the sign of a strong temperament," he said with ruffled pride, as he put the violin under his chin again. "You don't know what's inside of me," he said as he began to play.

"I've no wish to know," Jelena replied.

The kitchen was pervaded with the repulsive smell of hot bran. Jelena filled the bags, which were made out of Monsieur Tschirikow's old socks. Even her fingers were nauseated, each one separately. Grischa put down his violin and tried to take hold of her as she left the kitchen. She pushed him away. "What's the idea?" she yelled at him, suppressed, in case they were overheard in the bedroom. Suddenly her face was covered with tears which streamed out quite against her will.

"For God's sake," Grischa exclaimed. "For God's sake, Jelena, what is it? What is wrong with you?"

"Leave me alone—I'm so unhappy," she murmured as she shut the door behind her. Grischa took up his violin. If you weren't so heartless you'd be happier, he thought.

Jelena was not sure whether she was sixteen or seventeen when Herr Leibel, the head and owner of the dressmaking establishment, took her with him to Paris. It was warm September weather, and Herr Leibel was going to Paris to look at the new models and make purchases. "You have good taste and understand our customers, Leni. You can be of use to me in Paris. It 'll be worth your traveling expenses," he said, very businesslike. But Jelena knew exactly what this invitation meant. "I'll think it over," she said, although she had quite decided to go.

"You will want me to be well dressed. I must represent the firm in a decent manner," she said two days later. "Now I only need a handbag, but a good one, I have a cheap one myself," she said the day before they started. "I'm not sure yet whether my foster parents will let me go," she told him, although she had not the least intention of telling the Tschirikows anything at all. Thus she managed to keep the Old Man, as Herr Leibel was called in the shop, on tenterhooks and to have herself equipped with a complete trousseau before she consented at the last moment to accept the invitation which any of the other mannequins would have jumped at.

Herr Leibel was a man in his fifties, who wore well-cut clothes and prided himself on a resemblance to Menjou, the latest screen lover. He had got this flattering impression by looking at himself frequently in the mirrors of the showrooms, which were all specially made to give slim, elongated reflections of the clients. He had an unerring instinct for quality and was in this respect a true Austrian. Quality in materials, dresses, wine, food, perfumes, women. Jelena had quality in the highest degree, she was A1, créme de la créme. The girl was so beautiful, so ladylike, so sure of herself that Herr Leibel, although he had always considered himself a great ladies'

man, was somewhat embarrassed when she submitted to his wishes
without difficulty. But Jelena had calculated the Old Man into her
schemes long before he felt those disturbing sensations which now
had landed him in a Paris hotel with an unlocked door between her
bedroom and his. Herr Leibel belonged to that most commonplace
variety of married men, the ones who at home are the best of husbands and fathers, but drop all restraint on their trips; whatever
happens outside the domestic circle is after all of no importance.

"I love my wife," he told Jelena as she sat on his bed, undressed
and ready. And Jelena, with a cold amused smile, replied: "Of
course; I am quite aware of that."

She wanted to get away from the Tschirikows, away from Grischa's
intolerably sentimental declarations of love. Anything was justifiable
that would get her into a life of her own. The next morning, as she
luxuriated alone in her bath, Jelena wondered why so much fuss
should be made of so simple a matter. As for Herr Leibel, he felt
slightly chilled and disillusioned as he put on his highly recommended Gentila belt, the corset for well-dressed men. What they
say is quite right, he thought, perfect beauties are no good in bed.

The affair was tactfully and quietly conducted to its conclusion.
Jelena hinted that it might be pleasanter for Herr Leibel if she did
not return to his establishment and under the eyes of his wife. And
the Old Man offered hastily to leave her with enough money to live
modestly in Paris for three months.

"By that time I am sure to find something," she said vaguely.
She even accompanied him to the train, pressed his hand, politely
brushed her lips against his smoothly shaved cheek which smelt
of the best lavender water. She had sent the Tschirikows a telegram
before leaving Vienna; now she wrote them a fairly lengthy letter,
painstakingly writing in Russian, thanking them and saying that
she no longer wished to be a burden on Madame. Best wishes to all
and particularly for Grischa's future.

And now she was alone in Paris, a young woman, striking like
a poster, tall and long-limbed, with red hair, a white skin, a large
red mouth, oblique green eyes. The things men whispered to her
on her first walk were enough to fill a pornographic volume.

The first step in her career was amateurish and mistaken. The only thing that survived her liaison with the painter Pierre Colin was some experience and a new name. "All that *chichi* about a Russian grand duchess is no draw any longer. A stale cliché, fit only for comic papers," Pierre told her. It cost Jelena a lot to drop the lie which had grown to be a part of her. She now called herself Hélène Renard, it suited her red hair; Ponpon for Pierre's private use. She took up with him because he had the stamp of genius, or at least Jelena thought. She understood just enough of art to be easily taken in, still less of human beings; for she did not regard them with any feeling, but as arithmetic problems to be worked out. Pierre thought a great deal of his abilities, prophesied a great future for himself. He was the leader and center of a circle of young artists who proclaimed him as the founder of a new school. Somebody said jokingly of him that he would have to count Jelena's hairs before he could paint them. The new style, surrealism, was anathema to him, and he painted tiny pictures with microscopic accuracy. In spite of this everything in them was askew and out of drawing. Jelena figured on sharing in his fame as his model and friend. As she still spoke French with the easy Parisian accent she had learned in her childhood, she was gladly admitted to the circle. She quickly adapted herself to her new surroundings, and the wit of these artists appealed to her. She knew that Pierre made use of her; he showed himself off in her company, tormented her with endless sittings and finally borrowed money from her—the last remains of Herr Leibel's funds. The best that can be said of Jelena's feelings for Pierre was that she did not dislike him. It was only when she realized that he met with nothing but failure, that his pictures were rejected on all hands, and that he had absolutely no future whatever that she began to find him unpleasant and ridiculous. Meanwhile Pierre had fallen passionately in love with her, and it was no easy matter to get rid of him.

Paris was full of Americans, the Parisians complained that their city was Paris no longer. Nevertheless many of their industries lived on the dollar, the great fashion houses designed their models to suit the louder American taste. Jelena bestowed her society on an American businessman for a whole week and found him quite amusing.

At the beginning of the next season she got herself a job as a show-girl in a large revue. Nude girls wholesale were the vogue. Those whose breasts were fit for exhibition got twice as much as the others. Jelena stuck out almost embarrassingly among all the wide-hipped, short-legged French girls. With an enormous structure of artificial grapes on her head, which she steadied with raised arms, she slowly walked across the stage and waited for the overtures of some millionaire. They never came, for the average man is afraid of real beauty. The little dolls all around her had their *petits vieux,* but nobody waited for Jelena at the stage door.

When she had been two years in Paris she saw Grischa again. First there were the posters, then the advance publicity in the news-papers, then Grischa himself, Grischa Tschirikow, the virtuoso of the violin, the new discovery, the youthful celebrity. Jelena, who seldom wept, now wept for rage. She had put her money on the wrong horse, on the fraud, Pierre Colin, instead of on the genius, Grischa. With his smooth and gleaming hair brushed back, his blue cheeks powdered white, his eyes shut, and wearing a smart, close-fitting dress coat, Grischa played his program, and the audience was beside itself with enthusiasm. After the recital Jelena joined the rest who crowded into the artists' room and flung her arms round Grischa's neck according to the old Russian custom. "I am married," Grischa said at once and introduced her to a thin, large-eyed Russian, who was obviously expecting a baby. Jelena with a prac-tised glance sized up the dress, the fur coat and the rings of Grischa's wife. She could not disguise from herself that everything she had done up to now had been a mistake.

On that bitter night she became even harder than before.

Not long afterwards Jelena fell sick and lost her job in the revue into the bargain. She had often before had sore throats and tem-peratures. Now streptococci, chainlike, malignant bacilli, swarmed into her blood and she nearly died. She lay in bed sizzling with a high fever, there was a continual buzzing behind her forehead, and whenever she opened her eyes she saw the luster chandelier, swaying and turning; a dizzy rainbow came down above her head and choked her. Emaciated and weak, she started to live again. The concierge, who knew how much rent she owed, shouted at her without consideration or pity on the stairs, showing the lack of amiability of which the amiable French people are capable when money is at stake.

Jelena conceived a new ambition: she was going to be a singer. In the tumult of admiration and congratulations at the end of Grischa's concert, she had got to know Madame Cernofska, a dramatic woman of enormous circumference. Madame Cernofska claimed to have been prima donna of the Imperial Opera in Saint Petersburg and displayed a photograph on which Chaliapin had written: "To my dear friend the great artist, Marfa Cernofska." This woman, who took everything Russian to her large bosom and embraced it with fanatical love, was the only friend Jelena had during her illness. From time to time La Cernofska came panting up the narrow stairs to Jelena's room, bringing soup she had made herself, cold Pirogge and once even a tiny tin of caviare. Then she discovered Jelena's voice and began giving her lessons. Jelena worked hard at her singing. The Cernofska asked no payment for the lessons; nevertheless Jelena had to live until she was ready to launch out on the great career that Madame prophesied for her. Meanwhile she dropped her French name again and resumed her rank of a grand duchess.

That spring Jelena added Japanese to her other languages, for she had to have money in order to live. A young Japanese prince, whose spectacles made him look like a small, frightened schoolteacher, was her first Japanese friend. He appeared to be provided with an inexhaustible income and had been brought up to spend money on women. Prince Hayashi treated her with great courtesy, and his greatest delight seemed to be to dress and undress her, to use her as a clothes tree for an endless succession of new dresses. He transferred the fetishistic passion of the Japanese for the beautiful kimonos of the geishas to the Parisian dresses which they selected together during long sessions. Jelena swapped her French against Hayashi's Japanese. She had a perfect ear for languages and soon learned to employ all the little flourishes which in Japan distinguish the language of women from that of men. In Hayashi's company she refined her taste, and his imperturbable calm and politeness did her good. Prince Hayashi had the hard pride of a feudal Japanese and at the same time the inferiority complex of his race when confronted by Europeans. He was the pleasantest of all the men Jelena knew, for he not only did not expect any demonstration of feeling from her but would even have thought it bad manners if a paid woman had shown any emotion.

The months passed in a twitter of mutual compliments. Then Hayashi was suddenly summoned home. The head of his family, a member of the Cabinet, was shot by an assassin. Jelena was left behind and became the mascot of the colony of Japanese students. They all looked alike and behaved exactly alike, for they had a strict code of manners. Jelena scarcely observed that she was handed round from one to the other, twittering, beautifully dressed, treated with respectful care like a precious inherited toy. When the war in Manchuria broke out, the Japanese all vanished and Jelena was left with a small bank balance, a silver-fox fur, and a stiff kimono of antique, silver and green brocade.

Nothing came of her voice. A few auditions elicited only discouraging remarks and an entire lack of interest. Madame Cernofska's kindness cooled off. Jelena worked this new rebuff into her being; she became like concrete from which everything rebounded. She had never yet loved anyone in the whole of her life, not anyone and not anything. Flowers pleased her only when they were expensive, violets in autumn, lilies of the valley in winter, orchids to pin on her silver fox. In jewelry she considered neither the shape nor the setting but only the value of the stones. It was the same with people: she took no interest in them for themselves but valued them only according to what use they could be to her.

And yet Jelena was a Russian, and somewhere within her the soul of that boundless country must have been hidden. Feeling lay deep within her, submerged and petrified. It was one of Jelena's peculiarities that she never dreamed; the whole dim and indeterminate twilight world of dreams was unknown to her. She had sleepless nights, and she had them at ever shorter intervals. But when she slept she slept so soundly that if she dreamed at all she forgot all

about it the moment she waked. And yet she was puzzled sometimes when she found her eyelashes and cheeks wet in the morning,
as though she had been crying in her sleep.

When Jelena was twenty-two she turned her ambition abruptly
in a different direction like a sail to the sun. She was weary of brief
liaisons. She had enough of dropping or being dropped. The French
family and the French house were impregnable citadels: their gates
barred, their drawbridges raised. The demimonde in which Jelena
lived became dingier from year to year. Men had giving up ruining
themselves for cocottes. All women wore the same panoply of seduc-
tion: paint and powder, dyed lips, dyed hair, silk stockings, gossamer
lingerie, dresses that clung like a sheath of gleaming skin. All women
moved in the same way, spoke the same jargon. As they were so
openhanded their value declined. Virginity was no longer precious,
vice had lost its mystery and lure. Jelena decided to get married. A
good marriage—that is to say, marriage with a rich man—seemed to
her a better career than any other. But the transition from her present sphere into that of daughters and brides was not so very easy
to arrange.

She saw in the newspaper that Baroness Meyerlink of Vienna was
staying at the Hotel Athéne. Jelena remembered the baroness well,
for she had displayed dresses to her as a mannequin in the Maison
Leibel. She was a gray-haired, powdered woman with rococo dimples
and podgy hands; she was always in a hurry, she sat on a thousand
committees, arranging bazaars, flower carnivals, tombolas in aid of
charity—in fact, a busybody. She was an amusing and kindly woman
of the world who always bought dresses of the color of parma violets.
Jelena sent flowers to her hotel: "An old admirer takes the liberty
of sending you warm greetings, Jelena, Princess Trubova." She
called her up next day on the telephone. "You won't remember me,
Baroness. You knew me only when I had fallen on bad times—but
I have thought of you so often."

"But of course I remember you, child. You were the white ele-
phant of the Maison Leibel . . . "

The result was that Jelena was invited to lunch, and she looked
very ladylike in a black dress, with white gloves and her silver fox.

The baroness proudly basked in all the glances which paid their homage to Jelena's beauty. "And life is kind to you, child? But I need not ask."

"I have had a small legacy," Jelena said with reserve. "My uncle, the general, has died. I live very quietly in Paris. I am rather lonely sometimes."

The baroness was on her way to Torquay. "What a coincidence," Jelena said with a smile. She too was going to Torquay and also to the Hotel Imperial. How charming! Then they would see some more of each other, the baroness said, genuinely delighted. She had a weakness for everything beautiful. "So it's au revoir very soon! Au revoir!"

Jelena had to strain every nerve to get the money for the journey and her stay in England. She was a genius at dressing herself well for very little money. She was received into Baroness Meyerlink's smart and lively set when she arrived at the Imperial Hotel, Torquay.

On the tennis courts she came across Major Alden again. She recognized him at once. He looked younger than he had at Constantinople, for he was clean-shaven. "We're old friends," she said when he was introduced to her. He went red and looked embarrassed. He still smelled of lavender water. For a moment it all came back very clearly to Jelena—the dry dust in the streets of Pera, the sparse lamps, her little hand warm and safe in his big one. "I once gave you a kiss—in Constantinople," she said with a smile, and Alden went redder than ever. Then it came back to him: "The princess was the most charming child I ever saw," he said. "No one would believe that who saw her today," a gallant and elderly gentleman joked. The baroness thought the encounter and the whole story charming, and there was a celebration of it that night.

"And how have you got along all this while?" Alden asked when they were dancing together.

"Up and down," she said briefly. She had no wish to lie to him. She suddenly felt tired, soft and pliant. She tried to find words for this unfamiliar feeling. "You remind me of my father," she said reflectively.

"That concerns only the psychoanalyst," Alden replied. She let the remark pass.

"You're the first Englishman to dance a good tango," she told him later in the evening.

"A dubious compliment," he replied as she sank into the hesitating and dragging rhythm of the dance.

"Why dubious?"

"Men who dance the tango well are generally gigolos."

"The exception proves the rule."

"Thanks. How long are you stopping here?"

"Don't talk. Dance," Jelena said.

They danced on in silence to the end of the dance. There was applause from the party at the table when they rejoined it. Jelena was surprised at herself. There was a new and unknown thawing in her. She wanted to sit beside Alden, talk to him, dance with him again. When he was saying good night to her and putting her evening cloak round her shoulders, she waited for some secret sign or mark of tenderness—but none came. As she fell asleep she was already looking forward to seeing him next day. He had promised to coach her in her forehand drive.

Jelena had already picked up a smattering of tourist English in Paris: now she applied herself energetically to the study of the language. There is an old saying that only the first four languages are difficult. It took Jelena only two weeks to speak with the same accent as Alden. "Pure Cambridge," said Lord Inglewood, the elderly gentleman who could not help making flattering allusions to Jelena now and again. Baroness Meyerlink, who was a born matchmaker, had drawn Jelena's attention on the very first day to the fact that Lord Inglewood was still a bachelor and one of the wealthiest men in England into the bargain. "South African diamonds," she whispered to Jelena. The baroness combined a disarming naïveté with a great knowledge of the world. Her instinct told her that Jelena was on the hunt for a husband, and it amused her to give her a helping hand. "Our little princess looks as charming as ever," she remarked to Lord Inglewood. "She ought to be presented. A little accession of beauty would do Buckingham Palace no harm." Inglewood, who was shortsighted, fixed his eyeglasses whenever Jelena came into view. But Jelena ignored him.

If anyone had told her she was in love with Alden she would have laughed. Love did not enter into her scheme of life. With an indulgent smile she allowed herself a little sentiment; and the walk at night through Constantinople lingered in all she said to Alden. She was drawn to him, perhaps, because he had known her when she was still near to Russia, still undiluted and unspoiled. She told him one day about the luster chandelier. Next day he brought her a luster drop he had picked up in an antique dealer's. It was the first present Jelena valued for reasons other than its worth in money. She was missing her opportunities after all the trouble she had taken to get into good society under the wing of a real lady. She let herself drift with the current—for the first time in her life. She was following her inclinations instead of her advantage and spending every moment she could with Alden. It was a luxury, a greater and more costly luxury than ermine and diamonds.

It was obvious that Alden loved to be in her company. Nevertheless he was reserved and kept his distance. It's out of respect for me, she thought; it's his English upbringing, she thought again and laughed. The season drew on, Jelena's money ran out. She had no idea what was to happen next. I have got so used to Frederick, she thought in excuse.

He too seemed to be preoccupied, uneasy, tongue-tied and distraught. Jelena welcomed these indications and laughed to herself. One evening after a dance he took her down the narrow cliff path to the beach where the warm summer wind caressed her thin dress.

"I have been wanting to ask you something for a long time, Helen," he said, speaking hurriedly. "Will you—would you consider marrying me?"

"I don't know what one says at such moments, Frederick——" she said rather breathlessly.

"Wait a bit," he said. "I have something else to say." He threw his cigarette down on the sand, lit another. His hand trembled, Jelena felt a deep pleasure at his agitation.

"You are very beautiful, Helen, and you have been very good to me," Alden said. "And you have not tried to deceive me as you have the others. I appreciate that very deeply. Naturally most of the people here take you for a gypsy, Helen, even if they don't let you see it. The world has become very small, and tolerant too, up to a point. Please don't say anything yet, Helen."

He gripped her arm to stop her speaking, and she kept silent. She felt unutterably duped and ridiculous.

"You were not born to be an adventuress, Helen, and it has occurred to me that you might make concessions in return for being given your proper place in society. This sounds more brutal than it really is. I don't want to go into it at great length. So just listen to what I have to say. I have got to marry and very soon. My family is very conservative and very religious. I must marry in order to give the lie to certain rumors which have come to the ears of my family. Do you understand me?"

"Not quite."

"I hoped you would understand me. You have a lot of experience, that is why I turn to you. I cannot marry an inexperienced girl of a county family. I—won't you help me, Helen?"

"Yes, gladly. But how?"

"I have—no interest in women. I love a young man and I could never part from him, never. What I offer you is a good name and a very, very sincere friendship, my gratitude and protection—if you choose to call it so. Nothing very splendid, I grant! I have fifteen hundred a year. What I would have to ask of you would be a little understanding, and consideration and tolerance. Do you think you could, Helen?"

They walked up and down along the shore, up and down, and the silence that followed his question grew longer and longer.

"Give me a cigarette, too," Jelena said at last. He searched her face as the flame of the match flared up. She inhaled the smoke.

"Yes," she said.

Something died that had begun to live. Something that was about to open shut up again. Something that had grown soft in her became utterly stony. She became a competent Mrs Alden, as she had been a competent schoolgirl, an outstanding mannequin, a first-rate show girl, a perfect mistress for Japanese students. Whatever Jelena did she tried to do to perfection—only she did always the wrong thing.

Dower House was in Hampshire. It was smothered in ivy, rather damp in the corners of the room, of a gentlemanly discomfort, with large open fireplaces in every room, fine old silver, eccentric but fanatically loyal menservants, who were all rather hard of hearing, and an atmosphere that smelt old and seasoned, oppressive with comfortable boredom. Jelena, Helen Alden, became even more reserved and arrogant than the rest of the family. On Sunday she went to church with her mother-in-law and her unmarried sister-in-law Mabel. At night there was bridge, or else dreary articles of clothing of scratchy gray wool were knitted for charitable purposes. The Aldens visited the neighborhood and the neighborhood visited the Aldens. In London Frederick had a little flat in Duke Street and vanished there at tactful intervals.

"Would you like to meet Gerald?" he asked her once.

"I think it in better taste not to," Jelena replied. She felt as if she were dead and buried, and her hands were now always cold. I shall get a divorce, she thought when the gray mists of the second autumn descended over Dower House. She had destroyed her feeling for Frederick with such violent rage that now even ordinary politeness seemed painful. She might have been able to help him if she had tried to be kind to him instead of correct. As it was, she could not see that he was unhappy and never noticed that he went about with a more and more hunted look and broke matchsticks by the hundred as he stared into the fire. She knew nothing of the blackmail he was the victim of and the scandal that threatened him. She did not know that Gerald, a pretty, insignificant little actor, had given Frederick up and if she had known it she would only have been glad.

Before October was over, Frederick was dead. A shooting accident, it was said. He died as discreetly as he had lived. The property went to his younger brother, and Jelena was left with a modest income paid her under a life-insurance policy.

What a farce, she thought. Now I am the widowed Mrs Alden. She was twenty-five years old.

Lord Inglewood was a friend of the family and twenty years older than Frederick. He came over for bridge every Wednesday evening, for his country place, Inglewood Hall, was in the same neighborhood. After the funeral he rode or drove over on other days too to keep Helen company. He had given her away at her wedding and felt himself responsible. Jelena found him unutterably boring, smothered her yawns, made polite replies. Inglewood was a die-hard and was up in arms at any mention of change or progress. He felt with bitter exasperation that England's power and prestige were on the wane. His blood pressure was too high.

"Instead of sticking up for ourselves, we bargain and haggle as if our ministers were greengrocers," he growled from behind the newspaper.

The good old times when England joyfully and thoughtlessly pocketed one colony after another were over. The dominions were becoming independent, and the troubles in India never ceased. Lord Inglewood was one of those men who write letters to *The Times*. He collected arms, shot quail and was keen on growing tulips. He entertained Jelena by yarning on about his joys and sorrows until she wilted and went pale. It was not until she decided to marry him that she cheered up and came to life. She was twenty-five years old and Lord Inglewood sixty-five. It was a simple conclusion that his wife would be his widow and heir within a reasonable time. It was the coolest stroke of calculation Jelena had embarked on up to now and the most successful. Lord Inglewood was to some extent a lonely man. His younger brother Edgar had been killed in the war. He had brought up the two surviving nephews as his sons, only to experience bitter disappointment. Clarence, the elder of the two, had lately become a Labour Member of Parliament and developed into what Lord Inglewood called, in a voice that trembled with rage, a filthy Red. His speech about the abolition of the House of Lords had attracted great attention and so exasperated old Inglewood that he nearly had a stroke. Bobbie, the younger, a good-looking fellow, after being dragged with difficulty through school, had spent two years at Sandhurst, but soon gave up the army as a career and now divided his time between clubs, night clubs and bars. What particularly annoyed Lord Inglewood was that Clarence would inherit the property if he himself died without a direct heir. The idea of Inglewood Hall in the hands of that filthy Red was more than he could contemplate without damage to his liver. It was for this reason that he eagerly caught at the idea which Jelena hinted at when she observed that they were both lonely and disillusioned people, who might well console one another. Now that he was in love with his friend's beautiful widow he felt younger and more vigorous than for a long time past. His cultivation and cross-breeding of tulips provided him with flattering comparisons, he hoped that union of his maturity with Helen's youth and beauty would produce an heir and bring peace to his mind. Jelena, Helen Alden, as she was now called, clenched her teeth and marched on to her goal. She was ready to put up with the capers of her aged lover with a good grace in order to become Lady Helen Inglewood and the heiress to the Inglewood millions.

It was raining as usual for Goodwood races. Lord Inglewood caught a cold and went sneezing to bed, coughing and feverish; pains in the chest supervened, his breathing became difficult. The doctors still called it bronchial catarrh when his lordship was already dying of pneumonia. The funeral took place three weeks before the date of the wedding.

Helen was petrified for a time and only woke up when the will was read in a shaky voice by the old family solicitor. It had been made at the time when Clarence joined the Labour Party. Inglewood Hall went to him, and also the title, which would put an end to his career as a Socialist. Everything else with the exception of a few small legacies was left to Bobbie Russell—"My younger nephew, who, though a worthless member of human society, is at least not a radical," old Inglewood had inserted in his rage. As the will had been drawn up before his engagement to Helen, her name did not appear. Her bitterness against the dead man knew no limits. She accused him of dying out of sheer malice. The sight of the heirs filled her with hatred and envy.

When Bobbie Russell was offered a whisky and soda he declined.

"On the wagon," he said. A little later he helped himself with a trembling hand and soon repeated the dose. By nightfall he was completely drunk, though perfectly correct in his behavior; his sandy hair was brushed smoothly back, his clothes were faultless, he was polite and quiet and only rather too rigid and stilted in his bearing. He felt wretched in the morning and began the day with whisky to give himself a lift. He felt better after a ride on horseback and made up his mind to give up drinking. "Thanks, but I'm on the wagon," he said in the club. Like all habitual drinkers he imagined he could stop when he wanted. But he never had wanted. When he was sober he felt despondent about himself, empty, meaningless, hollow, but as soon as he had had a few drinks he felt bright, amusing, in agreement with everybody. The decay of an old family came out in this well-brought-up and good-looking young fellow, and he only felt alive when he was fuddled. He had, too, a leaning for low life. He was fond of expeditions to Limehouse and the Docks; slumming, it was called euphemistically, and it was considered a smart fashion, but in Bobbie's case it went further than mere curiosity. He spent whole nights with drunken sailors and old dockside prostitutes, drinking and fighting, coming home with a black eye. In the early hours he began throwing things at Potter, his man, who said nothing about it for his own sake and his master's. When Bobbie got beyond all bounds, as sometimes happened, his anxious friends called in the old family doctor, and he was put away in a nursing home. It was owing to one of these cures, which could not be interrupted, that Bobbie was missing at his uncle's funeral and at the reading of the will. He put in an appearance three weeks later to offer Helen his condolences. He was a quiet, well-mannered, handsome young fellow, a year younger than herself, assuming that the age on her passport was correct.

Bobbie took an ingenuous and almost idiotic pride in his cure, and so far from making a secret of it, he loved talking about it at great length.

"They have a damned good treatment there," he would say. "You're packed up good and proper just like those things in the museum—mummies, don't they call them? After you've been packed up like a mummy every afternoon it's marvelous how you lose the taste for drinking. You can offer me the best whisky you like this moment, I'll say no, thank you. Just try it on if you don't believe me."

But Helen did not attempt the experiment. She inspected the young man and sized him up. And in spite of his lack of culture, the utter vacancy and weakness behind his correct façade, she decided to marry him. I can't afford to let an idiot like that get away with five million pounds, she thought.

It was the elder brother who had the title, but Helen was content to marry the money and take the Honourable Bobbie Russell in the bargain. I can do what I like with him, she reflected. She felt strong enough to inoculate Bobbie with her own ambition and push him. As Helen wanted to marry Bobbie, she did so after a decent interval for mourning. But it seemed that this exploit exhausted her influence over her husband. He was like a cracked vessel that wouldn't hold water, a broken tool that wouldn't function, a ruined machine that wouldn't go.

He had been cured of drinking and for a time he proudly refused whisky with the air of a tightrope dancer doing his most intricate trick. Then Helen noticed a flickering light in him, a strange increase of self-reliance, and she discovered that one of his friends had introduced him to cocaine. Helen intervened before he became an addict. Fortunately he had a horror of injections, so that there was no danger of his becoming a morphine fiend. On the other hand, he complained a great deal of headaches and began swallowing quantities of aspirin, pyramidon and other common medicines. He consumed them by hundreds and got a certain benefit from them. When the doctor limited the consumption he took to drinking again.

If Helen had any heart or feeling she could have rescued him; but then Alden need not have shot himself and her life of ambition would not have been a series of successes that were really defeats. But Helen had no heart, or if she had, it was too petrified, too deeply encased in her. She gave up hoping anything of her husband. At first she took great trouble to keep up appearances. When Bobbie took openly to drink and even began sniffing cocaine again, when disillusionment and vacancy took the upper hand, when she hovered between gilded despair and dreariest boredom, she took to traveling.

In his lucid intervals Bobbie was devoted body and soul to his wife; when he was intoxicated he was possessed by somber rage and jealousy. He followed her round on her travels like a dog. He insisted on sharing her room. Sometimes he wept for hours on her merciless shoulders, at other times he beat her. Helen Russell, one of the wealthiest women in Europe, beautifully dressed and hung with jewels, so painted and got up that she looked like an idol, traveled restlessly from place to place with her husband at her heels. Paris, Monte Carlo, Salzburg, Warsaw, Budapest, Nice. The two of them could be seen wherever care could be drowned, wherever you need not listen to your own heart, wherever drunken gentlemen in evening dress caused no comment.

A gray-haired Englishman came up and spoke to her at Le Touquet as she was leaving the chemin-de-fer table. She was wearing a white evening dress and her emeralds, and she had green paint on her eyelids. "You are fond of gambling, Mrs Russell," he remarked. "I have been watching you. I had the pleasure of being introduced to you at poor Inglewood's funeral."

"Yes, I remember," Helen said. Captain Cyril Sanders was a big noise in the secret service. "Yes—I gamble. Life's boring."

"Quite so," Sanders said. "I hear you are going on a world tour with your husband. Perhaps it might be more exciting if you had something to do?"

"How do you mean?" Helen asked, looking at the rings on her fingers.

"Oh, nothing much. You're a woman of the world, you speak many languages very well, you know your fellow men. Just send me a little account now and then of anything that strikes you as interesting—or of importance to England," he added.

"What do I get for it?" Helen asked, for she could think only in figures.

"Oh, just the fun of the thing, the gamble, a spot of excitement, a little bit of danger possibly. I always took you for an ambitious woman. You could be of use to us, even if your husband has no desire to serve England."

Helen considered her reply. She had always supposed that the secret service swore in its agents and spies behind locked doors and with the blackest rites. She picked up the train of her dress.

"Very well," she said. "Perhaps I'll send you a picture postcard now and then—if I get too bored."

With husband and dog, lady's maid and manservant, with eighteen pieces of luggage and escorted by a drunken send-off party, she went on board the *Victoria*. Bobbie's pupils were like pinheads. She searched his luggage, his bed, his trouserpockets. She came upon the white powder concealed in a toothpaste tube and threw it out of the porthole.

V

Lung Yen

THE DRY RUSTLE OF BAMBOOS accompanied Lung Yen's childhood. The ancestors' house stood on the saddle between two hills just outside the Village-of-the-Clear-Mountains, its whitewashed walls surrounded by fields. The roof was thatched and tightly bound in with string round the eaves so that it had a gentle upward sweep like a boat. Sun and rain had bleached the straw to a silvery gray, the shadow of the bamboos moved to and fro on the walls of the house. The pear tree bloomed white in the spring, its leaves were fuzzy at first and became shining like satin as they grew up. In autumn the large round fruit dropped with a pleasant thump into the grass. Beautiful clouds drifted over the sky above, and as many ducks quacked in the pond as Lung Yen could count on the fingers of one hand. The Old Man, the honored grandfather, came out of the house, carefully carrying the bird in its little bamboo cage. The golden bird was called Ying, and he had a voice like the flute which the beggar played in the market. Sometimes the Old Man took the bird down to the canal and sat down on the bank's edge, and the honored bird as well as the honored grandfather looked contentedly at the boats as they glided past. Sometimes too he took it into the sunshine and strolled along the dikes between the rice fields, and then Ying began to sing with all his might. But generally the Old Man took the cage to the high bamboo pole which stood near the house and on which the Heaven's Lantern was hung on feast days; he hoisted the cage up to the mast-head until it looked a tiny object in the sky and the bird broke into loud jubilation. The larks above the field at morning could not sing more loudly or more beautifully than Ying.

Lung Yen first saw the world from his mother's back. Firmly tied in a cloth, he accompanied her wherever she went as though a part of her. When she was cooking she put him down beside her on the floor in a nest she made for him of old, padded garments and he gazed at the steam that rose from the built-in pots. When she went to wash clothes at the canal, she took him up again. Clop-clop-clop went the wooden beater with which she beat the dirty clothes, and slop-slop went the water as it spilled slowly over her busy hands. When she worked in the fields she sometimes laid him down at the edge of the field, but if he cried he was soon back in his warm nook on his mother's back. When another child was born and, worse, a sister, who squeezed him out and took his place, Yen felt deeply hurt. His mother squatted at the edge of the field and fed the useless little girl. Yen, who could now stand, waited impatiently with his mouth open until his turn came for what was left in his mother's breast. His father, after his work was done, took him on his knee and advised him to be tolerant. He consented to teach the little girl to walk as his elder brother had taught him. He tied his belt under her shoulders and dragged her about until she was able to move her fat legs for herself. Then for a long time no more children were born.

The fields of the Lung family had had good harvests for three years, and for that reason the children were fat and so were the hens and the eleven little pigs which the sow had littered. The father took them to the town one after the other, sold them in the market and brought many good things back instead, tea and bean curd and blue cotton, enough to make new clothes for the whole family. The Old Mother kept an eye on her daughter-in-law and bade her make moon cakes of rice, which were set out for the honored spirits of the ancestors, so that they too should have their share in the prosperous years.

Lung Yen was a happy child even though his place in the household was not particularly eminent. He was, in a word, the younger son of the younger son, and that is not much to boast of. But he belonged to the Lung family, peasants and respected people, who had lived in the village for eight generations. The Old Man, the wise grandfather, even sat in the Council of Village Elders. They owned five fields of good dark, patient soil, which had served all the Lungs and still went on yielding crops. Here and there old grave mounds rose from the fields, shaded by cypresses on whose branches the spirits of the forefathers could rest. The men of the family guided their buffaloes carefully round the graves when they were plowing. At the feast of the ancestors they all went from grave to grave taking offerings of food and incense, bowed three times to the ground and entrusted their mute wishes to their forefathers for fulfillment.

There were many of them living under the thatched roof, at night the house was loud with coughing and snoring and an occasional shout of one who was having a bad dream, also with the grating noise of a buffalo rubbing its side against the clay wall. There were the patriarch and the grandmother, their first-born, Yen's uncle, and his wife, who was slow at work because she came from the town and had bound-up feet. She had brought a little money to the family at a time when house and fields were mortgaged. She had three children, the clever elder son, Lung Fu, a daughter and a small younger son. Then the house also contained the young uncle, the youngest brother of Yen's father, who was jolly and clever with his hands; it was he who mended the roof, made a chair for the Old Woman and always won at the finger game. A year before Yen was born, the cultivation of poppies for making opium was suddenly forbidden by decree of the Emperor. The peasants fell into debt and want; the edict allowed only three years' grace before changing the fields over to other crops, and anyone who disobeyed it had either to bribe the officials in the yamen with silver or else to suffer the penalty. Many heads were cut off and impaled on the town wall. But in spite of the edict the foreign devils went on bringing dear opium into the country from the countries behind the four seas, and many who fell a prey to the Foreign Dirt sank into disgrace and destitution. Yen loved listening to the stories of the old days when the mandarins used to pass along in pomp with stiff girdles and peacock feathers or coral buttons in their caps, and the scholars pilgrimaged to the solemn imperial examinations. But Lung Fu, his cousin, his uncle's eldest son, laughed at him. "Stories to put children to sleep with," he said. Lung Fu went to the village school, where he learned reading, writing and arithmetic. He was of great use at harvest time, and it was astonishing too to see how he held up one of the newfangled newspapers and labored through it with moving lips and then told the listening family all that was happening in the Middle Kingdom.

Sun Yat-sen had seized·power. They said he was a greater man than Confucius, whose teachings the country had followed for nearly two thousand five hundred years. Three years after Yen's birth, the provinces had claimed their ancient right of deposing a ruler who did not rule virtuously, and since then the Manchu Dynasty had ceased to exist. Unfortunately the officials had not only not become better but, if anything, worse. "If you want to keep your buffalo, avoid the yamen," the Old Man said. It was from his grandfather that Lung Yen received his education in life and, beyond all, politeness, which was worth more than money. The Old Man tried to imprint the four cardinal virtues in him, and sometimes they smiled surreptitiously among themselves when Fu, the schoolboy, the first-born, the learned one, was loud and forward and used rude expressions.

These first years of Lung Yen's life were as calm as standing water in which everything was reflected. Sometimes he went down to the canal and watched the fishermen making their cormorants dive. The birds that were idle sat chained to the edge of the boat jealously beating their wings, while their fellows fished with their long beaks. The fishermen took the large fish, but the birds were allowed to swallow the little ones. Boats with rust-brown sails glided past, a white heron rose from the edge of the rice fields. The creaking of the coolies' wheelbarrows came from the narrow, stone-paved tow-path, answered by the deeper monotonous sound of the water wheel driven by a buffalo cow as it plodded round and round. Red dragon-flies hung motionless in the air and then suddenly darted away. The willows drooped their branches gracefully over the water in curves very pleasing to the eye. A mother followed by three children came tripping down the paved slope to the water with two water jars over her shoulder on a bamboo pole. My mother is strong too, Yen thought contentedly. She has large feet on which she walks firmly, and a large kind face you can trust. It was thanks to her that there was never any quarreling in the kitchen, for she served the Old Woman respectfully and willingly, as though the modern ways had passed her by.

Sometimes Yen went on long wanderings as far as the little town Fukang, whose gray walls could always be seen on the horizon. A thin blue mist hung all the time over the rice fields, it was only in late autumn that hills and trees were clearly outlined. The road to the town led over a highly arched bridge, there were always a few people sitting on the stone coping and looking down into the water. Old men, such as the honored grandfather, sat there with their birds or smoked their long pipes with tiny bowls. It was cool beneath the town gateway, and Yen's heart beat whenever he ventured so far afield. The beggars and sellers of chestnuts and fruit sat within the archway, which was high and vaulted. A few Little Men, ricksha coolies, lounged between the wheels of their vehicles. They made fun of Yen and called out to him: "What is it that walks on two legs and has no teeth?" He quickly shut his mouth to hide the gaps in his teeth and walked on hurriedly, though he did not forget the dignity the Old Man had impressed on him. "Dignity is a better cloak than silk," the proverb said. His way took him past the Children's Tower and he breathed cautiously, for the smell there was not nice. The tower was not so much used as in the early days of which his honored grandfather told him, but nevertheless there were always a few unwanted little girls to be cast in there, or boys who seemed likely to die before they got their first teeth. It was of the utmost importance to prevent their dying in the house of their parents in case their unreleased spirits might haunt it. Yen could sometimes actually feel the spirits that hovered about the Children's Tower tweaking his nose or sending cold shivers down his back. He hid his face in his hands and ran past the perilous spot, pursued by clouds of big blue flies and the barking of the dogs who besieged the tower and its small, decaying corpses.

Within the town walls were the teahouses, the outdoor kitchens with their savory, warm smell of leeks and fat and the street where the beautiful singsong girls lived. There was a letter writer there too, a learned man of the old days in a mandarin cap and spectacles and next to him a soothsayer who could read the lines of the hand and the face.

But it was not this that drew little Yen to the town. It was the marvels that grew up before his very eyes as he himself grew older and bigger and wiser. It was the new foreign-looking houses with straight roofs and far too many windows, in which the sunset was reflected, and the shops of the foreign devils that attracted his bewildered eyes. Young people in Western clothes stood about in the street, smoking cigarettes. Yen sometimes picked up a cigarette end and smoked it then and there. It brought an acrid, bitter saliva into his mouth, made him dizzy. Nevertheless the longing for that acrid bitterness and that dizziness haunted him. To tell the truth, the prospect of finding a cigarette end was one of the chief motives of Yen's excursions to the town.

The yellow dusk had scarcely died away and the shadows fallen on the streets before all the lights went on with one accord—in the squares, at the corners, in the stores, even in the dwelling houses. It was the power of lightning that lit all these fiercely white lamps, as Yen knew from his cousin, who was older than he was. He stared open-mouthed at the marvel which the foreigners had brought to China out of the West. From the bottom of his heart he envied the young men as they rode along on bicycles, more swiftly and smoothly than the boats on the canal. But most exciting of all was the place where once every day the fire wagon stopped snorting in its strength, an angry and portentous beast that had forced its way through the town wall. Yen could reckon from the position of the sun when he had to be at the station to see this spectacle. There were many people there already, crowding against the railings to watch the arrival and departure; even women were among them, with children on their backs, and even young girls of good family, for manners were getting looser from day to day. Yen returned to the house of his ancestors with belly and head chock-full of new experiences. "Your worthless younger son has declared that he wishes to go to the school of the foreign devils," his mother announced to his father. His father looked at him over the edge of his rice bowl, for he was just eating his supper. "Swans do not come out of ducks' eggs," was all he said.

Buffalo calves learn to plow by being harnessed beside their mothers. Lung Yen followed his father and his uncle into the fields, learned how to till them. At first he had only to see that the ducks came home at night. Next he was set to drive the buffalo round and round at the water wheel so that the fields had enough water. Later he watched while planting went on, although he was not yet skilled enough to take a hand in it. The day when his father put the plow shaft in his hands and he tried, trembling with excitement and exertion, to drive a furrow in the muddy earth, his first crooked and faulty but proud furrow, he felt himself a man at last. He was Lung Yen, a farmer's son, who came of a long line of farmers, a fourteen-year-old boy with short cropped hair but for one long black forelock over his forehead, brown-skinned, with the muscles beginning to swell and harden on his arms, the younger son of a younger son, born in a time when everything was changing as it had not changed for a thousand years. On New Year's Night it was the old custom to affix the pictures of the warrior keepers of the gates to the door of the house; the village resounded with rockets and the family ate flesh and dumplings and sweetmeats and the ancestors too had their share of the feast. Mottoes were hung on the doorposts—"Gentle winds and rain in due season." "Peace in the land and contentment among the people." They were still hanging there when the evil day came and war had spread havoc far and wide.

If Yen had not been a child he would have known more of the disturbing and menacing signs that preceded the invasion of the country by soldiers. Large taxes were extorted from the peasants, taxes that could not have been paid if the gods had not sent particularly good harvests. But now it was winter, eight-coat weather, cold indoors and colder still out of doors, provisions almost spent, and in the mornings there was a thin, gray sheet of ice on the duckpond. Nobody was in a position to pay three years' taxes in advance, as all were required to do. Yen's uncle and father took everything from the home which could be spared and carried it off to the town to the pawnbroker. They got eighteen taels for the lot, and they had to pay a hundred of the pierced cash pieces a month in pledge for them. Lung Fu did a complicated piece of reckoning. "Twelve per cent a month," he said. The honored grandfather sat and said not a word, as though he had heard nothing and had never noticed that the brass candlestick, the most valuable article in the house, was missing from the altar of their ancestors.

Every day there were fresh-printed notices posted on the town gates, and a group of people was always standing there; one or the other of them, who could read, explained what it was the government wanted. There was a movement throughout the whole province of Kiangsu to get justice for the poor, while at the same time the war lords were extorting the last coin and the last grain of rice. The elders of the village considered sending a deputation to the yamen to ask for respite in the matter of taxes. But the simple folk still had the respect and fear of the official class in their very bones, so the project came to nothing. "Go to the yamen," the Old Man growled, "and you will get a cat and lose a cow." The foreigners' stores in the town was looted. There was a persistent rumor that the foreign devils had only put through the decree against the cultivation of opium in order to make more on opium of their own. The government had taken a desperate step: they had bought all the foreigners' stocks of opium and burned them, burned the taxes extorted from the life blood of the people. Nevertheless—and how could this be?—there was more opium in the country than ever, and the evil, which had died down for a time, now shot up again on all sides. In the City-by-the-Sea, Shanghai, anyone could smoke as much opium as he could pay for.

Students now arrived in the town and even in the villages, young men of the better families, who had studied in the countries of the foreigners. They made appeals to the pride and dignity of the men, promised the women an easier life of it. The Japanese had long since established themselves in Shantung, the brown dwarfs, the despised and hated upstarts who had to be fought. In the West, in Russia, a country nearly as big as China, the Emperor had been deposed and there were new laws which aimed at giving the peasants, the poor people, the Little Men there, new rights of their own. The villagers listened with dazed and unresponsive faces to the speeches the students made. Their new leaders had nothing of the politeness and elegance of their former oppressors. They did not quote the classics and they were not arrogant. They meant well, but their residence in foreign lands had made them look almost like foreigners themselves. They spoke the language of China, but they had harsh voices and they made use of new, unfamiliar words—Communism, Nationalism, the New Party. They besought the peasants to send their children to school, not to spit so much and to unite throughout the country against the great landowners and the usurers. They talked of a new and just partition of the land, the cancellation of all debts. "Young dogs bark the loudest," the Old Man said; he sat shivering in the cold house; they had pawned his little coal stove for warming his hands, and he coughed obstinately and spat more than ever.

Then the soldiers came and there was war between the provinces of Kiangsu and Chekiang. "One war is worse than three swarms of locusts," said the Old Man, and he was right as usual. "A dog in peace is better than a man in war," said the village. It was not regiments but hordes that invaded the country, savages without one of the four virtues but riddled with evil and vices. They trampled down the fields as if they knew nothing of seedtime and harvest. They showed no respect even for the graves, they took possession of the houses with as little ceremony as a herd of wild buffaloes. They tore the doors from their hinges, slept on them, so that the cattle escaped from their sheds and the wind blew through the rooms. They violated the women, and every family who could afford it sent their daughters far away to relations who lived in quieter districts. Yen's father went for a soldier who laid hands on his brother's daughter.

The soldier felled him and stamped on him. From that day blood ran from his bowels, and he died soon after in great agony.

The soldiers, bad as they were, were openhanded when they had plunder or got their pay—which was not very often. They threw coins to the children and laughed as the children scrambled for them, they brought wine into the houses where they were billeted and shared their food and drink with all. But the war lords needed money to pay the soldiers. It was amazing what taxes they invented in order to drain the province dry. There was a tax on each little pig of every litter, until at last the peasants prayed to the goddess of fertility for barrenness. There was a tax on every son of the house, a tax on weddings and funerals, a tax even on the incense offered to the gods to induce them to send the soldiers out of the country.

The war went this way and that. There was much extortion and little fighting and whichever side won or lost the people had to pay. "Soldiers are wolves in victory and tigers in defeat," said the honored grandfather. The children sat by the hearth sipping hot water from their bowls while their mother tried to make them believe it was soup. "We must grow poppies again," the young uncle said suddenly. "He who smokes the Foreign Dirt feels no hunger." Yen's mother was groaning in the next room. She was giving birth to a child in all this misery, Yen's aunt was helping her. It was another little brother, who cried all night long. He ought to have had a little cap and shoes with tiger faces, but the Lung family was too poor even to dress up their sons properly.

The bitter jest of the younger uncle came true, for the war lord who ruled over the neighborhood ordered half a mo of poppies to be grown on every mo of ground. His own men harvested the poppies in place of a tax, and the peasants could see there would be no rice to keep them alive.

This summer was the first time Yen saw a field of poppies. The men had sown the best land, which sloped gently to the canal, with them; but first they sowed clover, then the purple-flowered clover, humming with bees, was plowed in to make the ground fertile after all the ravages of the hordes of soldiers. Now the poppy flowers swayed on their tall stalks, and when the wind passed over them it looked as though a hand stroked a large calm face. There were black shadows in every flower, just such shadows as opium threw on the eyelids of opium smokers. A drowsy scent hung above the field, and Yen's dilated nostrils went questing after it.

He had grown into a big fellow during the years of war and began to think of girls. When the time came to tap the poppyheads in the poppy field he went at it with a will. He made the incisions with a small knife, and next morning he rolled up the sticky juice in the dried petals. He secretly tasted the raw, resinlike stuff, and it gave him the same sensation as when he had smoked his first cigarette end. There was a mist before his eyes, his stomach heaved, he swallowed convulsively. Then he fell asleep close up against the emaciated buffalo's side in the shed, which had straw stuffed into its gaping walls.

At this time many people fell sick of the hot-and-cold sickness, against which neither the old nor the new medicines seemed to be of any avail. Cypress branches were burned outside the doors of the houses and at the outskirts of the village, but it did little good. The plague ran through the whole district and got so bad that coffins ran short. "You can throw money down in the street and no one will pick it up—people are so afraid of contagion," Yen's mother sighed.

Yen too fell sick of it and suffered agonies such as he would not have believed he could bear. He lay still and silent, doubling himself up when the pain was too bad, and he was thankful for the respite when he lost consciousness for a time. The grandfather, the honored patriarch, died, and so did the little sister. But Yen recovered. As the family had now to provide for a funeral befitting its station, Yen's uncle went to the town and humbly addressed himself to a rich man. He mortgaged the house and the fields, as was only right when it was a question of burying a father, and all the relations of the family whether close or distant gave their approval, since he was fulfilling the filial duty.

Thus the Lung family became quite impoverished through no fault of its own, as was the case with so many others. The men were not drunkards nor did they spend their money in teahouses or on the sort of girls who were as beautiful as butterflies but who sucked money as bees do honey from flowers. The women were industrious and thrifty and as peaceful as women could be who had to cook on one and the same hearth. Even the children did their bit for the honor of the family, from Lung Fu, who was a master at figures as well as at reading and explaining all the many new regulations, down to Yen's little brother, who very soon herded the buffalo. The younger uncle was hit the hardest, for he had been betrothed for a long while to their neighbor's daughter, and now that the family was destitute he could not think of getting married. "Maskee—it can't be helped," they all said submissively, and they even enjoyed the funeral and the lavish fireworks and the feast they gave for their friends and relations.

During these months the bitterness among the inhabitants of Kiangsu rose to such a pitch that it roused them from their customary placidity and submissiveness and they began to wonder whether there was any just reason why the poor should have paid century after century for the luxurious and sinful lives led by the rich. The young men met in a tailor's cabin and listened to the talk of the men who came from the large cities, from Canton and Hankow, to put fresh heart into them. Lung Fu, Yen's elder cousin, often attended these secret meetings and told Yen about the New Party. Yen was inquisitive like anyone else and went along with Lung Fu to the next meeting. He did not understand all that was said, no more did anyone else. They listened with a dazed and sleepy expression on their faces, only the muscles of their temples contracted now and then as they remembered how they had been humiliated, insulted or plundered. But Yen understood at least that things ought to be different, different and better. The speaker pleased him, too. He was a young man with delicate features, a narrow chest and the long, thin, backward curving fingers that showed he came of a great family of learned men.

"What is the honored gentleman's name?" Yen asked his cousin.

"He is Chang Yutsing, the friend of the Little Men," was the reply. "His father is Chang Bogum, the richest man south of the great river," another man put in.

They all pricked up their ears, for every man in the whole province knew the wealthy Chang by name, and many stories were told of his highhandedness, his ruthlessness, of the numbers of his concubines, the splendor of his estate at the Western Lake near Hangchow. Yen scrutinized the speaker and could not believe that he was the son of that mighty man. "I'd like to know how many picul of rice he could carry," he thought half contemptuously and yet with a feeling of awe, for though Chang Yutsing looked weakly, his narrow chest and stooping shoulders were those of a scholar whose station was far above any menial task. Yen could not forget his face for a long time after, and he took note also of some of the things he said. But respect for his uncle, who was now head of the family, prevented him from trying to put into practice any of the reforms which were preached in the tailor's cabin.

Now that poverty had come to it and the voice of the patriarch was silent, who with weight and wisdom had advised thoughtfulness and tolerance and the practice of the four virtues, and the children had grown to be young men and girls, a spirit of unrest vexed the Lung household. A hungry man does not see the moon, an old poem says, and it is true that the joy of life left them and even the children no longer laughed now that they suffered from hunger and there was quarreling and discontent.

Lung Fu had a serious talk with Yen, a talk that altered Yen's whole life.

"Yen, my elder brother," Lung Fu said, and the polite address was meant to take the edge off what he had to say, "the rice bowl is empty and there are too many hungry bellies in the house of our ancestors. I know that my father thinks of selling his daughters. I have tried with all respect to dissuade him from it. What do you say about it?"

"It is so," Yen said after he had thought it over from all sides. "It would do great harm to the family if the daughters were sold." Both of them avoided mentioning the most important aspect—the loss of face the family would suffer if it took this desperate course. "Better times will come, the debts will be paid and the fields set free. But if the girls are sold it is irrevocable," Yen said sadly.

"I can read and write and reckon figures," Lung Fu said. "I will go to the town and engage myself to a merchant. Wong, the tea dealer, has often promised me a bowl of rice, for he is a relative of my mother." He waited a moment before adding: "And what will you do?"

Yen saw that his cousin intended to earn money, to pay the debts and set the family up again. He too would have liked to go to the town. "I am strong," he said. "I can carry loads. I will ask Elder Brother for his advice." His cousin stole a look at him and then dropped his eyes. Carry loads—that meant falling out of the peasant class into the coolie class. "We must find a way," Lung Fu said.

As Lung Yen's elder brother and also his uncle, the head of the family, agreed that he should go, he went to the town and was no longer called by his family name but just Yen the water carrier. "I have a position in Mr Ling's store," he told his family. But he did not say that all he did was to carry great pails of hot water to the houses of people who allowed themselves this luxury. Ling's store was in the Street-of-the-Rising-Moon, not far from the town park which was situated where a part of the old town wall had been torn down. Yen loved his work in a way. The town did not smell the same as the country, people were quicker and livelier, the noise was cheerful. The young salesmen cried out their wares in the street of the cloth dealers and tailors, the oil seller with his barrow, on which he had his enormous earthenware jars, had his loud call, the seller of bean curd rang his bell, the man with his itinerant kitchen on a pole over his shoulder clapped two bamboo poles together, the sellers of chestnuts, mangoes, sugar cane, rice and a hundred other things, each one had his own shout and cry. Pouring with sweat, Yen ran among them, pushing children aside and jostling smart gentlemen and their chair bearers, for the moment he got out of his regular trot his wind gave out and he felt the weight of the load on the pole over his shoulder. The tea vendor's shop, where his cousin worked, was elegant and quiet behind its glazed doors. Beautiful girls, too, came in to buy sweetmeats, sugared lotus kernels and candied oranges from the provinces south of the great river. But Yen's work was rough, he had to forget the politeness the patriarch had taught him if he wanted to get on with it.

One of the houses at which he had to deliver hot water morning and evening was inhabited by foreign devils. It was a large house and had four courtyards in which there were goldfish ponds and flowering bushes and it had red painted pillars along the narrow outside galleries. The foreigners had rented the house from a family which had come to grief through opium and gambling and left the town, as they could not pay their debts and had lost face. When Yen met the foreign lady for the first time, he was rather afraid, for she was indescribably hideous and ghastly, with wild red hair and whitish eyes such as only the blind beggar in the market had. The gentleman looked like a corpse and, what was worse, stank like one. But when the lady spoke to him she had a friendly voice and he laughed to himself, for she could not speak properly. What she wanted to say was "Pour out the water." Instead of that she said: "Strike off your water." Yen told this story again and again at nights in Mr Ling's steamy shop where he slept on the ground with the other water carriers. As the foreigners seemed too stupid to learn the language, Yen set about learning a little pidgin English. It sounded like the croaking of frogs, but at least it was easy. He soon learned to read a few characters also and was able to decipher the names carved in wood on the doors of the houses and the names of the streets. He observed that there were several foreign devils in the town, but they looked so completely alike that he was never quite sure whether he was meeting many different ones or only a few over and over again.

He visited the family in the village before the next New Year's feast, that dreaded day on which all debts had to be paid off. It was possible to pay a small part of the debts with his and Fu's assistance and thus show the creditors that they were honest people with good intentions, and the family kept its face. Yen was eighteen that summer, and his uncle spoke to him and told him it was his duty to marry and beget sons, so that the chain of life should not be interrupted. Yen dropped his eyes, for he knew a girl who pleased him well, but it was not the girl Wong Sing, to whom he had been betrothed in his childhood. It was odd about Wong Sing. There was a rumor in the village that she had been raped by one of the soldiers and left with a sickness, but no one was so unkind as to find out whether it was true. Yen had occasionally seen Wong Sing in the village street or at the edge of the fields and she pleased him less and less. She squinted and she had large heavy breasts under her blue jacket, just like a lazy old woman. Yen grumbled to himself over this girl to whom he was betrothed. Why should I eat what another has spat out? he thought to himself. Every man is free to choose a wife to please him. This latter sentiment was one he had heard at the meetings, and he knew young couples in the town who had married without paying the slightest regard to the wishes of their parents.

Jasmin was the name of the girl whom Yen liked, and she served in the house of the foreign devils. Mr Lee was one of these devils, a doctor of the new medicine who came from the Western countries. He and his wife had taken Jasmin into the house when her parents died of the plague. But she was no slave and was not treated even as a servant but rather as a child of the house. Yen found her confusing altogether. She was always there when he poured the steaming water into the foreigners' tin tub, and she spoke to him, without shame, as only the girls in the teahouses did. That was because she had been brought up in the ways of the foreigners, and at first she alarmed Yen by her cheekiness and freedom. It was many days before he took courage and made her any reply, since he had been brought up according to the precepts of his old grandfather. "Have you eaten?" he asked her and, as she pleased him so well, he added: "Have you eaten anything good? Did your meal please you?" But after giving vent to his feelings in this fashion he quickly swung the pole and its empty water buckets over his shoulder and trotted off.

His first conversation with her left him with a great restlessness in his bones. At night when he had eaten his rice he returned to the narrow street where the foreigners lived, the Lane of Peace was its name. He leaned for a few minutes against the wall behind which Jasmin was sleeping. A round moon hung in the sky like a large yellow lantern. Yen sighed as though he had eaten too much and went home to the wet premises of the hot water shop. He rolled himself up in his blanket behind the large built-in copper cauldrons and tried to sleep. But he heard the mosquitoes humming and even the gong of the night watchman beating the second watch before he could close his eyes.

Next day he lingered in the market, making long and careful search and at last for two cash he bought some sesame cakes wrapped in red paper as a present for Jasmin. He was now used to her not being dumb and humble, and at last she pleased him better than any other girl he had ever seen, and much, much better than Wong Sing, whose squinting face was dead, whereas there was life in Jasmin's.

Yen saw the girl every day, and she always looked clean and neat. She wore one of the narrow new-fashioned dresses which were slit at the side so that only a little piece of her trousers was to be seen. She could read and write; she knew how to work the abacus with lightning speed, and she spoke English too and tried to pound a little Chinese into the great wooden, disorderly head of the foreign woman. She had been converted to the religion of the foreign devils and often talked eagerly to Yen about it. There were many Christians in the town and some even in the village. It was said that the foreigners paid you well with rice if you prayed to their god. The picture of this foreign god was hanging on the wall, and it was quite enough to give you a fright. He had an emaciated body, he looked like a man who had smoked too much opium, his face instead of expressing the calm you would expect in the face of a god was distorted by a grimace of uncontrolled passion. "It is easy to see that this god has no power even over himself. How can he have power over other gods?" Yen said to Jasmin.

"He loves the poor people and helps them," she replied earnestly.

When Yen had poured the water into the tin tub and received his coppers for it, Jasmin contrived to be standing at the Moon Gate in the back courtyard by which he left the house. There they talked together for a minute every day until the old amah called for Jasmin. She told him that her parents had been poor and that she too was as poor as a stalk without ears. She also told him once with downcast eyes that she was ashamed to live in the house of the foreigners and to be dependent on them, since it was said on all sides that the foreigners had no business in the country and ought to be driven out.

Yen told her in return that he was no coolie, but had only taken up the lowly job of a water carrier in order to help his good and honorable family to pay their debts. Jasmin praised him for this; and if Yen had ventured to look directly into her face he would have seen by the shine of her eyes that she was moved to tears. The amah came wobbling along on her bound feet and abused him. "Son and grandson of a turtle, what are you doing here still? Get on with you, worthless one!" Yen took up his buckets and trotted off obediently.

One night when he had delivered the second supply of water and passed through the Moon Gate into the narrow lane outside, he heard the light shuffle of soft soles behind him.

Looking round, he discovered that Jasmin was following him along the moonlit lane, keeping her distance almost as though she were his wife. He pretended not to see her and walked on. He put his pole and buckets down in Mr Ling's shop and peered through the crack of the shutters which had been put up for the night. Jasmin was walking slowly up and down the street with a basket in her hand as though she were shopping. Yen hastily washed his hands and face and rinsed his mouth, but he ate nothing because his stomach had suddenly gone small from excitement. When he went out and set off towards the town wall, Jasmin followed him at once. He traversed the new park, crossed the canal by the high-arched stone bridge, which had been there since ancient times, and sat down in the grass on the other side. Soon he saw Jasmin coming over the bridge. When he looked across at her she walked more and more slowly, and after a while she sat down a distance from him. There they sat, the two of them, looking at the moon which was rising above the horizon through the silver haze above the rice fields. It was a warm, light night, the crickets chirped, the cicadas drummed, the frogs croaked in the rushes at the edge of the canal, a nightingale sang far away in the willows. Yen felt happy and content and in tune with the ten thousand things of the universe, of which he was but one. When he looked round at Jasmin she was sitting with her hands folded in her lap, smiling softly with downcast eyes and her unusual, silent humility made his heart resound like a gong. After a time she got up and he followed her along the canal. There was a little shelter at the side of the road where porters and travelers could rest. Jasmin stood still in its black shadow and Yen caught her up. His flesh began to burn. He groped for her and took her.

A few weeks later Jasmin told him she was pregnant. I shall take her as my wife, she will be a good wife for me, he thought often during the following days. He lifted the large wooden lid from the copper cauldron and poured water over his body and washed himself clean. And he saved his coppers for the day when Jasmin would bear his son. And again Yen thought: If I am to beget sons and sleep with a wife, why should it not be with one who is dear and pleasing to me and wears clean clothes and can read? But he was afraid of speaking to his family about it because he knew well that Jasmin did not fit into the house of Lung, and also there was his betrothal to Wong Sing.

One evening after his work there was much courage within him, so he crossed the bridge and walked along the canal as far as the house of his ancestors, which stood to one side of the village. The dogs knew him by his smell and did not bark, and neither robbers nor soldiers nor spirits interfered with him on his way.

The house was dark and they were all asleep. He called out softly to his mother, and she heard him at once and opened the door. Hunger and care had greatly aged her, and as soon as Yen looked into her wasted face his courage deserted him and he did not open his mouth. There is still plenty of time to tell them the news, he thought to himself. He merely gave as the reason for his late visit that he wanted to inquire how the honored family was, and the lamp was quickly extinguished. Yen lay down to sleep beside his young brother. Next day, however, he spent five coppers on incense and took it to Jasmin. "You must offer it to your god, and it could not do any harm if you offered incense or spirit money to the goddess of mercy in the temple of Confucius as well," he told her. All day long the thumping of the press could be heard as it stamped money out of silver paper for the gods, and the pious burned it as an offering, and the smoke was pleasing to the gods.

When Jasmin's womb began to grow big and first the amah and then her foreign mistress discovered she was with child, there was a great clamor and consternation. Jasmin was thrown into the street, and when Yen came to deliver the hot water he was greeted by the most horrid abuse he had ever heard in his life. But what was worse was that the foreign devils broke his rice bowl. Mr Ling, the purveyor of hot water for whom Yen worked, had become a Christian, and that was why the foreigners bought his water. Dr Lee, the thin, long man with hair that looked like a flaming torch, went to him in person to demand Yen's dismissal. Mr Ling bowed his consent. "The foreigners do not know moderation, my son," he told Yen in excuse when he dismissed him. It was small consolation in the troubles that now heaped themselves on Yen's head. He gained new courage by attending a meeting of the New Party and walked out to his village immediately afterwards to consult his family.

Yen's mother wept silently. His quarrel with his uncle and his elder brother made all the more noise. His belly was still full of the liberty and revolt which had just been pumped into him, and he poured it all out for the benefit of his horrified family. "Who is going to pay Wong Sing's family the compensation they will demand for the insult?" his uncle shouted again and again. "Wong Sing is not worth three cash," Yen shouted back in scorn. "She is sick and rotten and she has gone with the soldiers; she has squinted with her eyes at them and I will pay what she is worth."

The unkind and hateful way he spoke about the unfortunate girl to whom he was betrothed only made things worse. It soon came out that Wong Sing's family in fact required thirty taels compensation. The matter came before the village elders. Yen's family lost much face, for they could not even pay the eight taels agreed upon. In order to recover their face they loudly and publicly disowned Yen and cast him out of the family. It was as though the sky had fallen in upon him.

Yen's son was not born in the house of his forefathers but in the foreigners' hospital. As Jasmin was now a married woman she was taken in there when her time came, and Dr Lee himself took charge of her and looked after her well. During this time Yen did the meanest work there is. He collected the great jars containing human dung and night soil and carried his stinking burden to the fields, on the edges of which it was collected in little sheds. The smell of his work clung to him when he went to the hospital to see his son. He was a fine strong boy with a thick head of black hair, and even on the third day he tried to laugh. They called him Seileong.

When the foreign doctor saw Yen's humiliation he offered to take Jasmin back into his house again with her child. She would have food and shelter and be able to make herself useful. In return Yen would have to agree that his son should be baptized and brought up as a Christian. Yen gave the matter deep and earnest consideration.

"Will it do the son no harm?" he asked Jasmin again and again. She smilingly shook her head. She seemed to be relieved and glad that Dr Lee had made peace with her. One evening when Yen went to see her the foreign lady was sitting on her bed with his son on her lap, tying a little silver cross round his neck. "It's to ward off evil spirits," Jasmin told him, and Yen was content. When she left the hospital and returned to the foreigners' house, Dr Lee employed him as chair bearer to the household. At night he was allowed to sleep with his wife in a tiny room with his little son close by his side. By day he hung round with the other coolies in the yard, waiting to carry his master or his mistress. He scarcely noticed that he, too, had been baptized a Christian.

There were times when it came home to Yen with great bitterness that he no longer had a family, that anyone could call him a stray dog. He had got used to the petty arrogance of the town dwellers towards the stupid peasants, but in secret his heart longed for the fields. He missed the smell of the earth, the peaceful sound of the buffalo chewing the cud, the dull thump of the ripe pears in the grass, the whisper of the wind over the dense rice haulms.

In September, when the noise of the threshing of the rice sheaves could be heard even in the streets of the town, he grew very restless. "I am not a coolie," he sometimes muttered to himself at night when he could not sleep. He heard the night watchman's gong, watch after watch, the barking of the dogs, the busy pounding of the press stamping out money for the spirits. "I am not a coolie," he muttered with his lips against his son's little warm, black head. Jasmin comforted him as well as she could. "He who is carried in a chair is a man, and he who carries the chair is a man also," she said. It was a good old saying.

Secret meetings in peasants' huts, in garages by night and openly at street corners. Exciting speeches of agitators, oppression from above, where war lords and unscrupulous officials ruled, sheer, naked destitution down below, among the simple people. Unrest broke out anew, fresh hordes overran the country—soldiers or bandits, it was hard to say which. There was war again in the South, and it drew nearer; it was not thunder or tempest that made the windows rattle but the distant noise of guns. The magistrate was sorry they had had the town walls torn down. The light, foreign discovery of the power of lightning, failed, and suddenly the streets were dark; there was not even a moon, the only light came from the tiny swaying ricksha lanterns. It was the very night for looting and plundering. There were tall poles along the country roads connected by wires by which the officials of the yamen could send out news. Sometimes you could hear the wires hum, but you could never catch the words. Two days later the soldiers were there—not the ragged private armies the war lords got together, but clean little men with rifles and Western uniforms who marched and bore themselves exactly as the foreigners did. It was said they had been drilled by the foreign devils, and no one could say whether these regiments of the Kuomintang meant them well or ill. New orders were posted on the gates, drummers went through the town proclaiming that law and order would be maintained. At dawn sixty-four people were strangled in the prison yard. The town was dumb, and not an eyelash quivered when the sentence was carried out.

Suddenly the sky went dark with smoke, then yellow and red with the reflection of flames. Fire had broken out near the northeast gate of the town where the last bit of the wall was still standing. Some people thought that a boy who was used only to the cold light derived from lightning had let his lantern fall into some straw, but most people were of the opinion that robbers had set fire to the town in order more easily to plunder it. Others again, to whom the wind carried the latest news, whispered that adherents of the government had planned the fire to smoke out the soldiers of Kuomintang. How-

ever that may be, the fire took hold and spread from quarter to
quarter, eating its way along the streets, leaping the thatch of a
poor man and taking firm hold of the timbers of a large house. The
acrid fumes took away the breath and blinded the eyes of those who
tried to get it under control. All the time the foreign-sounding bugles
of the soldiers rang out, and the confusion was endless.

That night Yen had helped to carry the doctor to a sick man who
lived on the outskirts of the town. He fell asleep while waiting for
him and was awakened by the noise, the smoke, the reflection of the
fire and the shouts of people running. He stood there open-mouthed
without understanding what had happened. "Fire, fire! They have
set fire to the town!" the people shouted, hurrying past with bundles
and children. A donkey that ran with the crowd uttered a loud doleful bray. "Where—where's the fire?" Yen asked in dismay. The sky
was red, and the wind blew the smoke from the east where the Lane
of Peace was. "On the east side of the town," an old man, who was
clutching his bird cage to his breast, called out. Yen forced his way
against the crowd of fleeing people. He forgot that he ought to wait
for his master; he thought only of his son, of little Seileong, who was
perhaps in a burning house.

He ran on through clouds of smoke, between the crackling of
flames and the crashing of house walls. The sheds of the poor, built
only of matting, blazed furiously. Yen hurried on, wiping the tears
from his smarting eyes. He reached the Lane of Peace, found it in
flames. There was a chain of fire fighters passing buckets from hand
to hand at its entrance. The bugles of the soldiers could be heard
once more amidst the crackling and roaring and clatter of falling
masonry. High above, the flames were blue against the dark and
lurid night sky. Yen fought his way on and reached the house. The
walls were still standing, the gateway was open, he rushed in. He
had only one thought—his son.

The yard was seething with a black crowd of men, the house was
not yet alight. His mistress was standing quite alone on the threshold with a lamp in her hand. As the mob swept past her she gave one
loud cry. Yen rushed on; he had no thought of helping his mistress;
he had to reach the second building and the room on the top floor

where Seileong was sleeping. As he hurried past the door he saw that his mistress was lying on the ground as the mob crowded in and trampled over her body. He could not help himself—he ran on. He reached the second building and the room. It was empty. He stood panting for a moment in the empty room. And now at the rear, near the kitchen, a flame shot up and a confused outcry greeted the hissing of the fire, which had caught hold of the house. Yen fell rather than ran down the stairs. He did not know where to look for Jasmin and the child, but he hoped they had been rescued. As soon as he reached the yard he was wedged in with the cursing, shouting, stampeding crowd, and he saw that there were soldiers too pushing their way through it. The furniture in the house had been over-turned, the chests forced open. Some of the soldiers were dragging out the wretched plunder even while flames caught hold of the room.

Yen made his way back once more to the threshold. He wanted to ask his mistress where Jasmin and the child were. But one look at the trampled body told him that she was dead. He turned away and found himself next to a man whom he knew, though he had never spoken to him. It was Kwe Kuei, the head of the thieves' guild of of the town. He was a tall man with a wild, lean face, which was as bearded as that of a devil. "Quick, the roof is going to crash," Kuei shouted in Yen's ear as he pulled him away from the threshold. Yen shut his eyes. Behind him there was a loud roar, the glowing timbers fell in and covered the scene of desolation.

It seemed to Yen that he could hear a faint whimpering through all the tumult. In the yard, where he now was, he was wedged so tightly in the crowd that he felt his ribs would cave in. Those who had reached the large street gate suddenly surged back, those who were still in the yard surged forward with loud shouts and curses. Yen was pushed backwards and forwards until he no longer knew where he was. His eyes were so singed and smarting that he could no longer keep them open.

It was not until he reached the street that he understood too late why the crowd had surged back into the burning courtyard. There was a cordon of officers outside with stern impassive faces, who were arresting all looters, whether civilians or soldiers. Any who resisted were felled with a blow from a rifle butt or else instantly shot. The rest were taken by the soldiers to the prison near the yamen. Yen was among them. He was taken prisoner, he did not know why. He submissively clasped his hands and waited to see what would happen to him. From time to time a few people were taken out, then shots rang out in the prison yard. When Yen reflected that he would have to die before sunrise he was tortured at first by great fear. But soon he felt as if he had left this world of his own will, as he had that time when he was sick. Just as then he had no longer been aware of the pain, so now his fear passed and he became quite empty. Only his belly pained him as if he had eaten uncooked rice. There was a priest of Buddha with shorn head and begging bowl crouching among the prisoners, telling his beads and muttering without ceasing. A woman lay on her face on the ground moaning. Whenever Yen shut his smarting eyes he saw flames and the foreign lady on the threshold and his son's toothless, laughing mouth. Kwe Kuei was squatting next him against the wall. When the woman's groans got louder he took something from his sleeve and gave it to her. "Eat it, Mother," he said. "It's good when you're in pain."

Yen woke from his dazed condition and looked on inquisitively. The woman chewed and swallowed, and after a few minutes she stopped groaning. The shots were heard again and again outside. "Perhaps they'll just leave us here to burn," said one of the soldiers who were under arrest. The air was hot and laden with acrid smoke. A fresh wave of fear swept over Yen. He looked at Kuei, who was now chewing too, with a dreamy smile. He had the marks of the opium eater on his ravaged face.

"Give me some, too," Yen heard himself saying suddenly as he held out his palm to Kuei. The town was burned down, the fields were mortgaged, the house of his forefathers oppressed with hunger, Yen disowned and a prisoner. He felt that the burden was more than he could bear.

A little speck of blackish paste lay in the hollow of his hand. Kuei's wild devil's face was smiling at him. He muttered his thanks and put the opium into his mouth. Its bitter-sweet taste made his gorge rise for a moment, then he chewed the gummy stuff. He was no longer afraid, his sorrow vanished as a cloud at evening. He became light and in harmony with all things, as he had that night when he made Jasmin his own. His brain was clear as it had never been before; it seemed to him that there were a hundred ways of making his escape and getting to his son. He saw his son, he could already walk and talk. Rice fields, poppy fields, white flowers on swaying stalks waved about him, the pear tree blossomed again, the wind rose and scattered a cloud of petals. I will go to school and learn to read and write, Yen thought. He raised his arm, and his hand drew firm lines as if he already knew calligraphy. The woman who had been lying on the ground laughed aloud. The rifles rang out in the yard. The next lot was taken out.

It was Chang Yutsing who saved Yen's life. He was one of the officers who were dealing with those guilty of arson, thieving, looting and rioting and who let off any who had the means of bribing them. Chang Yutsing was unbribable, but he recognized the peasant's son who had been among his audiences at his earlier secret meetings. "Are you a relation of Lung Fu?" he asked. Yen, who was still buoyed up by the gentle waves of opium, proudly acknowledged that he was a cousin of Lung Fu, an unworthy offshoot of the honorable Lung family and father of Lung Seileong.

Chang Yutsing, after a brief interrogation, enlisted Yen in a labor detachment which was employed in transport and in the making of roads and the building of bridges. Yen woke up next morning in utter wretchedness. No more opium for me, he vowed. Chained to the thief and outcast, Kwe Kuei, he dragged himself along in sun and rain, dust and mud, digging trenches, hauling sandbags, carrying loads. Often beaten, never paid, seldom fed, shoveling and toiling, he found his way at last to the City-by-the-Sea, Shanghai.

At first he thought the houses, which were higher than the highest pagodas, would fall on him. His ears were deafened by the noise of the traffic and the crowds in the streets, his sense of smell was blunted by the stink of the vehicles called stink carts, his eyes were inflamed by the gritty dust of the paved streets. When the war raged fiercely in the streets Yen often thought that he was alive no

longer, that he had died during one of his opium bouts and had
been thrown into that hell of whose terrors Jasmin had sometimes
told him. Officers, revolver in hand, forced him to build barricades.
Fire in front of him and fire behind him, collapsing houses, dead
bodies in the streets. Yen came upon five dead children in a doorway, then he thought of his son. He did not think of him as a real
person; he thought of him as a dead man might think of the living.

But that too passed over. "Are you coming with me?" Kuei,
the robber and outcast, to whom he had been chained when they
marched along the road, asked him. "Where to?" Yen asked.
"Opium," Kuei answered. "Money?" Yen asked. "Enough to buy
a smoke for both of us," Kuei said. Yen was grateful to him. The
Great Smoke was the one thing left to wish for; the calm, the clarity
of mind, the release from pain after the first few puffs. People are
right, he thought, when they say that nothing but the Great Smoke
makes life bearable.

He learned much in the city and forgot all he had known before.
He worked in a cotton factory at Pootung. He was a bad and un-
disciplined worker, and he sorted cotton twelve hours a day for
a miserable wage. Here too there were agitators, riots, revolt and
rebellion, strikes. The cotton fibers got into Yen's lungs. He spent
his earnings in opium dens. His clothing was saturated with the
ineradicable smell of opium, his wasted face bore its marks. When
the workers went on strike and he earned nothing, he nearly died
of the craving for opium and the agony in his innards. His chest
caved in. He took the place of a ricksha coolie who had collapsed
and died in the street. He was still young and could run at a regular
pace and thrust the other coolies aside when a customer appeared.
Some days he earned sixty coppers and on others five. Out of that
he had to pay the firm from whom he hired his ricksha, the policeman—the tall and fearsome Sikh at the corner of the street—the
Number One hotel doorman who allowed him to wait for fares
outside the hotel, the guild of ricksha coolies and several other
people too on whom his living depended.

When he had twenty coppers in his belt he ran out to Chapei,
through streets which had been shelled in a new war and were being

built up again; he turned into ever narrower and shabbier lanes until he reached the opium den Kuei had bought himself with stolen money. On a dirty bunk, rolled in a torn mat, the coolie Yen was once more attuned to harmony with the ten thousand things of the universe.

When Lung Yen was twenty-six years old he began to cough blood. Foreign doctors had set up a clinic in Chapei, and there coolies were examined and given medicine for nothing. The Number One doctor, Mr Hai, compelled him to register at one of the offices for the suppression of opium which had been set up in all districts of the city. He was given a year's grace in which to cure himself of the vice. If after that he was caught smoking opium again he would be handed over to the law and executed.

Lung Yen, descendant of farmers, grandson of a village elder, unworthy son of the honorable family of Lung, disowned, abject and astray, a sick coolie in the pitiless streets of Shanghai.

VI

Ruth Anderson

It HAD RAINED in the night. Early in the morning the wind changed, the streets were coated with ice. When Mrs Anderson went down the two steps from the front porch to take in the newspaper and the milk bottle, she slipped and fell down. That was the reason why the twins were born four weeks too early. One of them died the same day, but Ruth was put into an incubator and hatched with the greatest care. She only weighed four and a half pounds when born but she was as perfectly proportioned as a little doll. Jack Anderson was never done marveling at her little toes, her fingernails, her eyelashes, at all the dainty and enchanting perfection of his little girl. He was twenty-four years old when she came into the world and he took complete possession of her from the start.

Anderson's grandfather had emigrated from Sweden and had first been farmhand and then son-in-law on a farm in Minnesota. His father was foreman in one of the big flour mills in Minneapolis. He himself had been to high school, where he particularly enjoyed the printing class, and later he was taken on as a boy in Galing & Co.'s great print shop in St Paul. He fell in love with the sandwich girl in the corner drugstore and married the black-haired, quick-minded creature before he was twenty-two. Up to then he had hoped to work himself through some junior college; but when he emerged as a husband from the whirlwind of love and quick marriage, he speedily and utterly renounced his grand plans and was glad to get a job as typesetter on the *Morning Herald* in Flathill, Iowa, at twenty-three dollars a week. He could never quite get rid of the Swedish solidity in his blood and when he was absent-minded and had not heard what his wife said to him, said: "Vass, vass?" instead of "What."

Flathill was a town of just under thirty thousand inhabitants but with enough pride and ambition to do for a million. Its red and gray houses nestled among green and yellow fields. The edges of the town were frayed and ran on into the endless stretches of cornfields that surrounded it, dotted with gasoline stations, grain silos and a few factories. Watson's factory of tractors was the largest of them, and Watsons were the most important people in town. There were churches of all denominations. The Catholic one displayed a modest attempt at Gothic, but so did the Jewish synagogue with its stained-glass windows. There were three skyscrapers in the center of the town, and a square park in front of the county court, where every celebrity who passed through the town had to plant a tree. There the trees stood, each with its compact little shadow beside it, growing much slower than the town. As for the celebrities, they belonged to various categories: there were the gray-haired gentlemen and elderly ladies with floating sleeves who gave lectures at the Woman's Club; there were violinists and second-class singers who gave recitals in the municipal auditorium to fill up gaps in their itineraries; there were renowned preachers who came to ginger up the faithful, and there were politicians who turned up, in clouds of brotherly love, smugness, optimism and earnest conviction, to speechify whenever a judge, a senator, a deputy or a new president of the United States had to be elected. There was a main street of respectable length, Commerce Street; the stores, which were lighted up all night, were all collected here, and also the three skyscrapers of Flathill. A fourth, which was to accommodate a branch of the Bank of America, had, with an ear-splitting noise of automatic drills and steel girders clattering one upon another, risen to the tenth floor so far. On Saturdays, when the farmers invaded the town, there was not enough room in Commerce Street for all their old motorcars, which were parked in long, uninterrupted rows against the sidewalk. The Grand Hotel of Flathill likewise was in Commerce Street and its Marble Hall was the meeting place of the Elks, the Rotarians, the Kiwanis; three hundred bedrooms with baths, three dollars each. In the next block there was the Colony Club, where the gilded youth of Flathill met, particularly on Friday and Saturday evenings. Jazz orchestra, dinner and dancing, one dollar, two floor shows nightly. The floor shows consisted of the appearance of the eight Coloniettes in various changes of scanty attire, of the frenzied wisecracks of the master of ceremonies at the microphone, and of the Blues which his wife, called Alabama Lily, sang in a raucous voice and with an assumed Southern accent.

The smart set of Flathill did not patronize the Colony Club, or at least not officially; they assembled every Saturday evening in the Country Club, where even during prohibition there was always something to drink, and danced until one o'clock. The club and the golf course, which had been scratched out of the farm land of Iowa and suitably laid out, were on Watson Heights, the smart residential quarter of the town, named after the patrician Watsons, who had lived there for thirty years. Their first house, a farm, had been built on this almost unnoticeable mound when there had been nothing around but corn. Now Watson Heights was the high-class part of the town, with neat homes in pretty gardens, with tree-lined streets, along which the children of the smart families' chauffeurs went roller skating.

It looked quite different in the eastern part of the town—in the suburb of Newflat. Newflat was dominated by the great factory where the Harmony Toilet Seat, known and in use throughout the country, was made, and by the huge gasometer behind the station. There were derelict lots where used cars were sold for the benefit of the farmers, the streetcar depot, the starting place for the transcontinental busses and again some factories, bean fields, building sites, schools and the prison. Newflat was a little town in itself, with its own main street and department stores and hotels. It consisted of twenty-four numbered streets, crossed by six boulevards known likewise only by numbers, in strong contrast to the flowery quarter of Watson Heights, with its Hyacinth and Magnolia streets. Where these twenty-four streets of Newflat joined up with the marshy corner of Flathill there was a small Negro section of patched wooden sheds on posts and a chemical fertilizer factory, which worked night and day and pervaded the whole district round with an odd chemical smell.

The Andersons lived in Fourteenth Street, and when the wind came from the east they got a faint whiff of it. When it was in the west they could hear the bell on the town hall clock and the noise of trains shunting in the station. In fact it was Jack Anderson's habit to wake when the 5:23 milk train was being unloaded.

They lived in a bungalow, which looked exactly like all the other bungalows in Fourteenth Street, and they lived just as all the other people in the street did. Two steps led up from the little front patch to the porch, where an old rocking chair stood. The porch opened straight into the living room, which contained a gas stove disguised as fireplace. They had two small bedrooms with a bathroom in between, and a kitchen, parted as to give space for a so-called dinette. In winter it smelled of gas and baked apples. Mrs Anderson did the housework in flowered cretonne dresses, her curls protected by a veil, in high-heeled shoes and wearing gloves. Her husband helped her, as all American husbands do, by carrying the garbage can, pushing the pram, drying dishes and sweeping out the porch. Throughout his entire life he considered his wife a much finer and higher being than he was himself.

Ruth, though small and dainty, was a strong and healthy child.

By the time she was two she developed a passionate attachment to children even smaller than herself, and as soon as she could speak she clamored urgently for a live little doll. Mrs Anderson had no desire for a second child: her difficult delivery had been enough for her. So Ruth had to carry, wash, feed and console all the babies in the street. She only liked dolls when they were sick, and for that reason she smashed them as soon as she got them, in order to be able to bandage them and make them comfortable. Her greatest joy was a menagerie of sick and vermin-infested animals she brought home with her. Mrs Anderson scolded her laughingly for the collection of blind kittens which had to be rescued from drowning, not yet housebroken puppies of dubious descent and half-fledged birds with broken wings. Once she even brought a frog home with her and bathed it in hot water, remarking, "The poor thing feels cold."

There was a little motor concealed inside Ruth's mother which turned out desires day and night. A permanent wave. A new handbag. Patent-leather shoes for Ruth. Frilled curtains for the kitchen. A bottle of eau de cologne. A gas cooker with four burners. A second-hand refrigerator. A fur collar for her old winter coat and then it would look like new. A radio. An automobile. They paid and paid, installments, interest, they paid to the financing corporations, they paid too much for things, but Mrs Anderson got what she wanted. Jack Anderson struggled on although he knew that he could never get above the twenty-five-dollar line. His money never went round, they were always in debt. Jack Anderson had secret leanings to Socialism; he was an enthusiastic member of his union and he sometimes read the Red publications which his Red friends thrust upon him, but he soon put them down. They only spoiled his temper and made him discontented when he was quite contented in reality. When Sacco and Vanzetti were convicted he was greatly wrought up, and he also signed all the petitions for the release of the innocent but condemned labor organizer, Mooney; but there were not the makings of a Socialist in him, particularly when he began thinking of his Gothic alphabet, for it meant much more to him than the union. In any case his little excursions into politics had to be concealed from his wife, for Hazel Anderson was a capitalist, although she did not happen to have any money. She was a society lady without the society. She knew everybody on Watson Heights; not an engagement, not a divorce or a single detail of any little scandal that went on in those select circles escaped her. She imbibed, as parched earth imbibes water, those columns in the newspaper which gave advice to women in judicious doses about matters of conduct, life, dress and taste. "Show personality in your salads." "Housewife, what do your hands look like?" "Individual hairdressing at moderate cost." "Charm is the password to any society." Hazel Anderson cooked in gloves, she rubbed cold cream from the ten-cent store on her face before going to sleep and bought an artificial gardenia for her buttonhole. She tried her charm on herself all alone in the kitchen and practised easy manners spiced with personality. Sometimes she dressed up Ruth and herself in all their finery and took the bus to Watson Heights. She took her pretty little girl by the hand and walked along the smart and pleasantly winding streets, Magnolia Street, Carnation Street, Daffodil Street. The streets in Newflat were as straight as a die. On one of these occasions she had an encounter with old Mr Watson, the great man, the King of Flathill. Mr Watson was emerging from his garden gate to take his dog for a walk, as any other man might. The dog, a young red setter, must have divined Ruth's love of animals, for he ran yapping up to the little girl, and Ruth at once put her arms round his neck and lavished on him all the vulgar pet names current in Fourteenth Street. Mr Watson called out: "Duchess, come here at once." Duchess did nothing of the sort but licked Ruth's face and wagged her tail. Ruth was delighted and squealed with joy, whereupon Mr Watson went up to Mrs Anderson, took off his hat and said: "I'm sorry, that bitch has no manners." Hazel Anderson, trying to combine the gist of all her studies, said lightly: "It is our fault entirely. Ruth is simply crazy about animals." Mr Watson smiled kindly and said: "Just like me. Your little Ruth is a charming young lady."

"Thank you," Hazel said. "Come along, Ruth. Say good afternoon. What a beautiful dog! What is she called? . . . Duchess. What a good name for her!" Mr Watson patted Ruth, and Mrs Anderson patted the dog. Mr Watson stood there with his hat in his hand, his white hair blowing gently in the wind, until they had vanished round the next corner. Hazel Anderson often thought of that smart and successful encounter. She was convinced that Mr Watson had taken her for a lady and Ruth for a Watson Heights child.

Meanwhile Jack sat at home playing with his Gothic alphabet and smelling of printer's ink; his eyes were always inflamed, and he bathed them every morning with a solution of boric acid. Much to Hazel's annoyance, he had put up a sort of miniature bench in the corner of the living room. There he sat drawing until late at night by the light of a powerful lamp as he was accustomed to do. He got up again early in the morning to the clatter of the milk cans and made himself ready to go to the print shop.

"What are you always drawing, Jackie?" Ruth asked her father one evening. "Flies' legs, Baby, nothing but flies' legs," he said as he tore up a few sheets of paper and threw them away. Ruth clambered onto a chair, propped her elbows on his work table and her head in her hands and looked on. She was never tired of watching Jackie. A pot of weak coffee was simmering gently on the gas stove. From time to time Ruth, with an air of great importance, poured out Jackie another cup. Her mother emerged from the bedroom with her hat on her head and said: "Time to go to the movies."

"Okay," Jackie said. "Just another two minutes—I'm on the track of something good."

"Don't you ever want to take me to the movies?" Mrs Anderson asked. She was pretty and young and had had her hair curled. She turned on the radio and danced round the room. Jackie looked at her and then went on with his scribbling. "It's nothing," he said. "I'm just doing it for fun."

Two minutes later he had forgotten all about the movies. "Are you coming or not?" Hazel asked, putting on her gloves. She always wore gloves—to the amusement of the whole of Fourteenth Street. "Which is more important, going to the movies or making some money?" Jackie asked rather crossly. Whereupon Hazel merely said: "Why, I can just as well go with the Cobbs, but then you'll have to put the child to bed." Jackie nodded in relief. Ruth said pertly: "I'll put myself to bed." As soon as Mrs Anderson had gone, they spent a grand evening together, eating baked apples and playing which of the two could pull the best faces.

When the Andersons moved to New York, first to a little flat and later to their own house at White Plains, everything was different and Ruth crept into corners, too sad even to cry. All her broken dolls and sick animals were left behind in Flathill. The pedigree terrier she was given to console her was only an acquaintance and never became a friend, as all those disowned creatures did whom she had picked up in Fourteenth Street. She missed the other children and Jackie's work table in the corner and the evenings when she looked after him, making coffee and toast and turning the radio on and off.

Jack Anderson, relentlessly driven on by his wife, had pulled it off. He had evolved the Anderson-Gothic, a font that was at once simple, beautiful and individual. His seven years of labor, of casting about and casting away and then beginning all over again, had finally lifted him above the twenty-five-dollar level which otherwise would have been his lifelong fate. Jack was no businessman, but his friend Conwell was. Conwell, who had been through a business school at Indianapolis which described itself grandly as the "Commercial and Technical University of Indiana," Conwell, of the advertisement department, took up the Anderson-Gothic. At first nothing came of it. Then an offer was made by a printing plant in Chicago to buy the font for three thousand dollars. When Conwell had this proposition in writing he ran amok. Without heeding Jack Anderson's frenzied remonstrances he went and sold his old motorcar and Jack's as well. With the three hundred and twenty dollars arising from this dual transaction he bought a ticket to New York and put himself up there. After five weeks had gone by he sent for Jack Anderson and mailed him money for the purpose. He had sold the option on the sole use of Anderson-Gothic to an advertising agency for cash money. From that moment things began to happen and money poured in so fast it took Anderson's breath away. It ended with their all moving to New York, where Jack and Conwell opened an office; Jack designed lettering which Conwell disposed of to large firms for their advertisements. The Anderson-Gothic alone brought in a regular income which increased year by year. Some weeks they made up to four thousand dollars. The secret of their success was the streak of indomitable individualism in Jack Anderson, for in a country so standardized and uniform originality meant money.

The Andersons now lived in the right neighborhood among the right people. They had a garden with two trees and a rose bed. The porch became a terrace, and visitors entered a tiny hall instead of walking straight into the living room. The fireplace was not now a gas fire disguised but a real fireplace in which you could light a fire. They had two bathrooms instead of one, and a two-car garage.

Hazel Anderson had arrived. She had a colored maid in a white cap. She had her bootlegger, her bridge circle and belonged to three clubs. She had her hands manicured, she visited the theater now and again when there was anything on which her newspaper told her to see, she knew which perfume was in fashion and which actress. She induced Jack to take up golf, telling him he owed it to his health. And Ruth sat at the recently acquired piano with set teeth, trying to play with her left and right hand simultaneously and yet something different with each.

At thirteen she started upon powder box and lipstick, as all the other girls did, and the boys in class ceased to be punks and became suitors. One of them kissed her on the locker-room stairs, and for some days she felt a sense of her own importance. Then she forgot all about it again. "It isn't half the fun it used to be before we got on in the world," she confided to her father. She missed something, but she did not know what. So far the life of her street, the life of her class, the life of the others had carried her on; now she was slowly beginning to grow up, to feel that she was something apart, something different: Ruth Anderson, in fact. Then the day came when, clad in a tea-rose-colored evening dress, she took part in her graduation from high school. Now life could begin.

Now and then she stole a glance at her father. He looked tired. To have success meant that you had to be on the job at any hour of day or night. "Anything wrong, Jackie?" she asked him tenderly. He muttered something about low blood pressure and old age. Ruth reckoned it up. Her father was forty-one, too young to be old. Her mother had joined a fairly exclusive woman's club and ambitiously worked her way on until she was Second Corresponding Secretary of the Program Committee. She had an expensive fur coat, but she was no happier for it. She got thin, her face was lined. She never compared herself with those who were worse off than herself: she had eyes only for those who had more than she had. It was the same thing with most other people. Life had no charm except when there was competition. It was the same in business, society and love. The producers did all they could to stimulate demand, the consumers of goods were miserable if they could not buy things of which a moment before they had never even heard. It was an artificially fostered striving for possessions—but it was the lifeblood of the country.

Money was earned in hard work and easily spent. The consumption of tobacco and liquor knew no bounds. Prohibition had given alcohol all the importance of a forbidden thing. Gangsters, bootleggers and police were indissolubly intertwined. Puritanism switched to libertinage. There was much fun and little happiness. But all this was only a superficial fashion. Beneath was the simple, steady pioneer breed, neighborliness and decency, a deep reservoir of strength and enterprise and an inexhaustible fund of lively wit and good humor.

When Ruth went to college she had her first real bout with her mother. Ruth knew quite clearly what she wanted. She wanted to be a doctor and to study at Columbia University where the wonderful, incomparable Professor Albin was head of the medical faculty. She wanted to be a children's doctor and make little babies well; she would hold the little feverish hands in hers, feel their pulses and unerringly diagnose what they suffered from and make them well again. Tiny but obdurate she faced her mother, keeping back her tears at any cost and repeating again and again: "It's in me, I know it's in me, and if you don't let me study medicine I'll raise hell and you'll be sorry."

But Hazel Anderson could be pigheaded, too. She had long since consulted the smartest woman's magazine in all America about the college to send her daughter to. Flynn's College near Boston had been recommended. Flynn's had a long tradition of snobbery, the best English and school dances to which only young men in evening dress were admitted. Flynn's stood for high society and no education whatever. At Flynn's College desperate battles were waged about the most expensive evening dress, the wealthiest antecedents, the most numerous dates with young men of the same social standing and the largest orchid corsages. "I'll cut as good a figure at Flynn's as Chip at a dog show," Ruth wailed. Chip had been the ugliest, lousiest and mangiest of all the low-class curs that had ever moped around the little house in Fourteenth Street. Her mother replied in a steely voice: "I have decided to make a lady of you, and that's how they'll turn you out at Flynn's."

"She wants to make a lady of me if it kills me," Ruth complained to her father. Jackie did not look well; the big city did not suit him. Even in the composing room of the *Morning Herald* at Flathill there was always the wide unspent air of the open country, with its savor of sunny fields, its delicate summer scent of growing corn. As he complained of vague wandering pains, he had recently on medical advice had nine teeth extracted to ward off the danger of auto-intoxication from abscesses at the roots. He was no better for it. He sat forlornly at table, eating nothing, because his new bridgework made chewing troublesome. He let his hands drop and looked at Ruth sadly and quietly. "Baby," he said, "don't you know by now that your mother's a woman whom we cannot beat? What she wants, happens."

"Well, you'll see what will come of it if I'm put up with that snobbish crowd," Ruth threatened darkly.

"Just give in to her," Jackie begged. "Later on we'll go to Vienna together. I'm told that's where they make the best doctors."

Ruth was sorry for her father. She kissed him on the tip of his nose and said to comfort him: "You'll see, I'll soon be thrown out of Flynn's."

It never got to that. The crash of 1929 ruined Anderson. He had gambled on the stock exchange, like everybody else, in order to keep pace with his wife's growing expenditure. He had bought on margin and now came the crash. The boom was over, the war profits had gone up in smoke, Europe did not pay its debts, world markets were choked by overproduction that no economist in the world knew how to check. Coffee was burned, wheat dumped into the sea, cotton plowed into the ground again and unemployment increased as the means of production were perfected and one machine replaced three hundred men.

Conwell, with his head for business, had led Jack Anderson into speculative dealings he did not understand. Now he had to sell the house, the car, even Hazel's diamond ring, which he had given her on the twentieth anniversary of their wedding day. They gave up their too expensive office. In order to stave off the worst of his difficulties, Jack Anderson did a rather desperate thing: he sold his Gothic, from which he had drawn a regular income, lock, stock and barrel. Finally a magazine gave him a small job as designer of lettering. He was no longer young, his inspiration was giving out; all the headings he devised looked alike, and there were so many looking for work that salaries fell. Twenty-five dollars a week. "Just like a roller coaster," Jack said to Conwell. "Up and down—it makes you sick."

Back to a little house again, in Jamaica suburb, in a wrong neighborhood among the wrong people. Once more they tumbled straight from the porch into the living room, and there was not even the semblance of a fireplace, just a gas stove; the bathroom was dilapidated and cheerless and pervaded by the smell of gas; no maid, no luxury, no smart bridge parties.

Hazel Anderson now showed the stuff she was made of. She did not complain or reproach her weary husband; she did all that had to be done and gave up all that had to be given up; except that she took up with Christian Science. It did her good and kept her quiet. She read the *Monitor* and went to a service every Tuesday, from which she returned bathed in tears but always greatly elevated. Ruth had abandoned Flynn's College, and she was not the only one. She was neither puffed up nor cast down, and she appeared to greet the return of poverty as a stroke of good fortune as far as she herself was concerned. "I could get a job as children's nurse and save up enough to study medicine," she confided to her father. "Vass?" he asked absent-mindedly. She stroked his thin, fair, Swedish hair

and asked: "How would you like a baked apple, Mr Anderson?"
When he fell asleep at night over his lettering she took the pencil
carefully from his fingers and led him into the cold little bedroom.

Jack Anderson died of a simple operation for appendicitis. The
doctor announced that he had "used up his reserves." "Keep your
chin up, Baby," Jackie said to Ruth. "Look after Mother . . ." He
was given a bit of morphine and never came round.

Grief for the loss of her dearly loved father made a woman of
Ruth at once. They gave up the little house. Mrs Anderson moved
into cheap lodgings and fell back on Christian Science to take her
mind off the disaster. As Ruth had not and never would make
enough money to study medicine, she quickly made up her mind
to be a hospital nurse. She went to the Nurses' Training School of
the Urban Hospital. "It's nearly as good as being a doctor, in some
ways even better," she told her mother. "It's heaven after Flynn's."

The girls lived in an old wing of the hospital, four to a room.
Stiffly starched blue uniform, strict discipline, the solemn oath repeated each morning like a prayer: "I solemnly pledge myself before
God and in the presence of this assembly to pass my life in purity
. . . I will abstain from whatever is deleterious or mischievous . . .
hold in confidence all personal matters that come into my keeping
. . . aid the physician in his work and devote myself to the welfare
of those who are committed to my care."

Cramming, learning by heart, the never-ending learning by heart
of incomprehensible words and sentences. The four of them said
their lessons over to themselves, prompted each other, heard each
other, then forgot again. Gradually it dawned upon them that all
they learned by rote had a meaning. The unfamiliar words, the
strangeness of it all, the classes, the difficult, advanced subjects. General medicine, anatomy, bandaging, disinfection, psychology, first
aid, pharmacology. The first manipulations, the fear of the doctors,
the fear of examinations. Giggling, gossip, jealousy, striving, small
but glorious and unspeakably important successes.

They learned bandaging on a dummy called Ali Baba, they gave
oranges injections, they bathed artificial babies. They grew cynical
and made jokes over Johnnie, the skeleton, as generations of proba-

tioners had before them. Their hands got rough and coarse, their backs ached, their nerves were frayed by pity for the sufferers and annoyance with the insubordinate, by dread of making mistakes, dread for hopeless cases. The first corpse, the first operation, the first confinement. Ruth learned to be as little nauseated by the sick as by the wooden Ali Baba. She learned to take birth and death as ordinary and natural things and not to let them agitate her. She was praised and scolded, made friends and enemies. She fell for Professor Boerner, the surgeon, who spoke wretched English, was sixty-four years old and never without a most unhygienic deposit of cigar ash on his waistcoat, whereas she thought nothing of young Dr Synge, who had fallen in love with her. She got so used to the smell of disinfectant in the highly polished hospital passages that she no longer noticed it. She could prepare the trays in her sleep that were needed when bandages were changed. The containers of gauze, sterilized pincers, sharp and blunt scissors, scalpel and syringe. The test tubes, ointments, the mercurochrome, benzine, peroxide, the bowl for waste. She dealt with bedpans as if they were nosegays of violets. She made beds, innumerable beds and ever more beds, in which serious cases lay motionless and smelling of sickness and pain. She recovered in rare moments of self-divination her belief that she had it in her, that her patients smiled when she came into the room, that the sleepless fell asleep if she sat for a moment by their beds at night, that the mother of a stillborn child stopped crying out when she spoke to her. Ruth's great bugbear and her mortal dread when it came to her finals was theory. She always knew what to do when she was faced by a sick person, but words meant nothing and would not get into her head, or, if they did, they took leave of her again with the utmost volatility if she gave them a chance. She murmured questions and answers over to herself before she fell asleep, in her bath, while dressing and brushing her teeth. It seemed a miracle when she got through.

She was put into the maternity wards, and she was glad. Although her duties consisted chiefly of fetching and cleaning bedpans she was happy among all the pregnant women. It gave Ruth a wonderful, warm feeling of joy to carry the warm and bundled babies in and out, to wash the mothers' nipples with alcohol and see how vigorously and cleverly the newborn infants sucked. They had babies of all shades and colors. There were white babies, light- and dark-haired, in the large ward; yellow and brown, thick-lipped Negro babies in the little ward and even little Chinese and Japanese creatures with slit eyes and black hair above their wrinkled foreheads. There were Italian mothers with wide breasts, excited, superstitious Mexican women, Jewish women, regular customers who had a baby every year and timorous girls who were having their first. Ruth admired each one for performing the miracle of producing anything so sweet and captivating as those babies.

Meanwhile her savings were exhausted, and Ruth was a long way from being able to support her mother. "Keep your chin up, Baby. Look after Mother . . ." She had no idea how she was to do it.

Suddenly the news went through the hospital that experienced nurses were required as stewardesses for a large fleet of air liners. Although Ruth had never flown and had to overcome her horror of being tossed about high in the air, she applied for the job. Twenty-seven dollars a week. Three new pairs of stockings for Mother. A new hat for Mother. A handbag at a sale for herself. An evening at the pictures and dinner at Schrafft's, for them both.

The stewardess had to be slender, pretty, young, charming. Ruth got the job.

They gave her a jaunty cap, told her to be measured at a good tailor's for a smart, light gray uniform. Mrs Anderson began to dream of better days. Ruth's figure became even slighter, for her duties in the air were trying, but she loved them.

One February evening when Ruth had put in nearly a year with the air line she met Frank Taylor. It was the most thrilling evening of her life. Flight five, the airplane from Crane to Brentford, took off at four-twenty in the afternoon in moderate weather. Visibility one mile, ceiling seven hundred feet. First pilot, Ed Warner, co-pilot, Bob Spencer. There were seven passengers, and as it was cold Ruth went round tucking one after another up in the check rugs provided for the purpose. After three quarters of an hour they ran into fairly bad weather and two of the women passengers went green.

Ruth adjusted their seats at a better angle and began talking to the elder of the two, for she knew that the great thing in airsickness was to distract the sufferer's attention. She still got racking headaches herself when the airplane bumped about as it did now. A stout man in the front seat who had so far been smoking cigars now unobtrusively and shamefacedly began to spit into his little paper bag. Warner climbed and rose above the clouds in search of better weather, but at three thousand feet they ran into a hailstorm. Ruth handed cigarettes round, smiled at her passengers, brewed coffee. The aroma made it seem more homely in the cabin; two businessmen who had often made the trip with her produced cards, began to play.

The young man who was on the list of passengers as Frank Taylor had settled himself down at once and shut his eyes. He refused rug, cigarettes and coffee, and Ruth smiled to herself: it always seemed funny to her when strong young fellows like him felt sick in the air.

"You should drink some coffee. You don't know how it helps," she said, holding onto the arm of his seat, for it was very bumpy at the moment. Without opening his eyes he smiled rather mockingly and asked: "Helps what?"

Before Ruth could reply, all the small articles of luggage shot out of the racks and a woman screamed, but next moment Ed Warner straightened the machine out again and all the passengers put on forced tense smiles. The shaking caused Mr Taylor to open his eyes. He looked at Ruth attentively. "Aren't you ever afraid?" he asked gravely. She shook her head, laughed. It had been dark for a long time, the lights were on. Ruth returned to her tiny kitchen, unpacked the box of sandwiches. When she looked out of the window she saw nothing but opaque darkness on which the light from the windows fell as though on a compact surface, a sheet, a soft and yet rough expanse. As a rule the lights of small towns and villages were visible below, but now nothing was to be seen but the fog or snowstorm through which they were flying.

Ruth served the so-called dinner. It was now dead calm, the passengers had begun talking together. Mr Taylor alone refused to have a sandwich, kept to himself. Ruth brought a rug, put it over his knees without asking. He jostled about with his knees but finally made no further protest. He had a handsomer face than any passenger Ruth had yet seen.

They were due to land at Brentford at 6:40. Ruth looked at the time and went the round, strapping her passengers tight. "What's up now?" Mr Taylor muttered.

"We're just going to land," Ruth said. He sighed deeply as though asleep. But they did not land. Instead they climbed again, banked steeply and circled round. The little light sign in front called her, Ruth went forward and opened the door leading to the cockpit. "What's the matter?" she asked in a low voice through the crack.

"Nothing's the matter," Spencer said. "We can't land."

"Okay," Ruth said. She shut the door, turned round and surveyed the passengers. The two who had often made the trip had put on their hats and snapped the catches of their attaché cases. "Late?" one of them asked. "A minute or two," Ruth answered. The light signal. "Yes?" she asked. "We've lost the radio beam. Keep them quiet," Spencer said. "How long will it be?" Ruth asked. "Ask me another," Ed Warner replied. When she turned round she met Taylor's eyes, and it seemed to her that he knew what the pilot had said. She went round and unbuckled the straps. "We're a little behind time," she said brightly. Then she went into the kitchen, heated up all the coffee there was left over.

"Coffee? Cigarettes?" she asked, going the round of the seats with a clink of cups and saucers. It was not very easy. The airplane leaned right over each time Ed banked to fly a fresh loop.

"When are we going to arrive?" the elderly lady asked.

"In a few minutes," Ruth told her.

"Coffee?" she asked Mr Taylor. He waved it away with his hand without turning his head. He was looking out at the compact screen of darkness illumined by the light from the windows.

Twenty minutes, thirty minutes passed in this way. The passengers were getting restless. Ruth felt they would get into a panic of shrieking and praying the moment she stopped smiling. The elderly lady bit her nails, the man who had been ill asked hoarsely for a glass of water. They all stared out of the windows where nothing whatever was to be seen. The light signal. "How are the Rabbits getting on?" Spencer asked.

"Everything okay," Ruth said as cheerfully as she could.

"Like to know where we are?" Spencer asked again.

"Yes," Ruth replied.

"So would I," he closed the conversation. She slowly and thoughtfully shut the door. Ten more minutes went by. They all knew by now that the airplane must have got out of its course. But they behaved well; they sat with forced, expectant smiles on their faces, holding tight to the arms of their seats. The light signal.

"The emergency airport," Spencer said. "We can see the lights."

"Kingston?" Ruth asked in relief.

"Hold onto everything," Ed Warner said grimly. "I'm going down."

Ruth quickly strapped all the passengers in. "We're going to land," she said reassuringly. The engines stopped, and they glided down through the dense layer of nothingness. The passengers held their breath. Suddenly the engines started up again to take off the shock of landing. But it was already too late. The white wall of a mountain rose from the fog; it was above and below and all around them. The shock with which Ed Warner pancaked the machine on the ground threw them all over the place. The lights went out next moment, and in the dark there were the clatters of broken glass, the screaming of women and the cursing of men.

Ruth flung herself against the door to open it and let the Rabbits out. With rage and despair she found she had not the strength for it. But now in the darkness she felt a man beside her pushing against the door and through the shouts and screams and groans she could hear him panting with the exertion. The door gave way, together they fell forward into the icy air.

"Hurt yourself?" Taylor asked as he lifted her from the snow.

"No. What about you?" she replied as she began pulling her passengers out of the crumpled plane. Spencer came up with a torch; he was gray in the face. "Ed's knocked out," he told Ruth. It took some time to get all the passengers out. Nobody was badly hurt.

Ruth tried in vain to get her first-aid equipment out of the battered cupboard on the kitchen wall. There was a strong smell of oil which was pouring out onto the snow from the burst tank. Ruth emerged again and looked about her. They had landed on the slope of a thinly wooded mountain. The air was clear there and very cold. Every passenger's breath hung in a cloud before his face. The fog was suspended far above and cast a feeble light on the snow. Spencer sat on the ground holding Ed Warner on his knees as if he were a little child. Ruth quickly picked up a handful of snow, rubbed Ed with it to bring him round. He looked about him in a daze, then a broad grin spread over his face as he grasped the situation. "Damned if we didn't make it after all," he said, then he laughed. Spencer laughed too, so did the passengers. It was a nervous and hysterical laughter but one of real relief after the fright they had had. Only Ruth looked gravely from one to another as she began to search them for injuries.

Ed Warner could not stand up. It seemed to Ruth that his left leg was broken above the knee. "We want a splint," she said. Taylor was already breaking branches from a tree, and Ruth tied them with her leather belt to form a splint. Amid shouts of laughter and everyone's compliments, one of the two businessmen produced an unbroken bottle of whisky.

"The very best medicine, costs me three dollars a bottle wholesale," he said as he regaled the ladies. All of them had slight injuries, but now that they were out of danger they all behaved with conspicuous courage. Ruth washed and dabbed cuts and scratches. She did not know that blood was trickling down her own face. She heard a painful coughing and looked round. Taylor was leaning against a tree holding his sides as he coughed. "Are you hurt?" Ruth asked. He shook his head, tried to get his breath. "It's nothing, it's nothing," he said. "It's only I can't get my breath."

Ed Warner behind the machine was shouting at one of the women who had taken out a match to light a cigarette. "We're swimming in gasoline," he roared at her. "Do you want to blast the little that's left of us?" Taylor handed Ruth the whisky bottle of which there was just a drop left. She swallowed it thankfully, for she was now feeling a little dizzy. "Who's going to go and look for the nearest house?" she asked.

"You stay—I'll go," Taylor said. He bent down, picked up a handful of snow and carefully wiped a little blood from her face. "Thank you," she said in surprise, smiling after him. His black shadow vanished between the scattered, white trees.

It got still colder. At first they had Spencer's torch until the little battery gave out and left them in darkness. The two businessmen told their whole stock of old jokes to keep the company awake. Ruth was grateful to them. Ed Warner had begun to curse softly, and his curses passed gradually into a sort of profane groaning. Bob Spencer prevented some of the passengers from setting off to look for help on their own; he took command, ordered them to wait for the help Taylor had gone to seek.

After two hours that seemed an eternity he came back and helped Ruth to escort the Rabbits to the two horse-drawn trucks which were waiting on the highway below. From time to time he stopped and held his sides to suppress his coughing.

When they got to Firdale at about midnight, it turned out that he had three broken ribs. Ruth assisted the country doctor, who in a state of drowsy agitation taped Taylor's capacious chest, put a proper splint on Warner's leg and treated the trifling wounds of the other passengers. Ruth was a little faint from loss of blood and fatigue, and he praised her grumblingly as she assisted him.

Ruth and Taylor awaited the arrival of the morning train in front of a fire in the inn, and the rest occupied the few available beds. After a while she fell asleep, and he drew his chair up to hers and pillowed her head on his shoulder. He marveled how lightly she lay there asleep. Later he too fell into a dreamless sleep, leaning against Ruth. When they woke they were so twined together that they had to sort themselves out, laughing as they did so in the red glow of the smoldering fire.

"What's your name, by the way?" Taylor asked.

"Ruth."

"Mine's Frank."

"Pleased to meet you," Ruth laughed.

Thus it was that they skipped weeks of getting acquainted and were friends right away.

Ruth's photograph in cap and uniform was in all the papers. "Heroism of an air hostess," the caption read. Mrs Anderson bought herself an album in which she pasted all the clippings. But she would not on any account hear of Ruth's returning to her post. Ruth made little protest. It had been a severe shock to her nerves, and she trembled and felt dizzy the next time she got into a plane. She ran around New York looking for a job. Finally she found a position as reception nurse with a certain Professor Richards, who performed sensational and lucrative cosmetic operations and paid her thirty-five dollars a week. That was a lot of money, but Ruth did not like her work. "Next lady, please. . . . Next lady, please. . . . The professor can see nobody, he is operating on Mrs Vanderbilt. . . . You look marvelous—twenty years younger since the operation. . . . No, I'm sorry, the professor cannot make a nose under a thousand dollars." Washing instruments, putting magazines in the waiting room, telephoning and telephoning. Making out bills, noting down addresses, bookkeeping. The flattering of wealthy patients, the shooing off of poor ones who were convinced that a different nose would put the world at their feet and could not pay for one. Professor Richards was a misogynist and no wonder! Sometimes he was rude to Ruth, at other times he pestered her to let him operate on her. He badly wanted to have a receptionist whom he could use for the benefit of timid clients as a demonstration of his power to rejuvenate without leaving the trace of a scar. Ruth began to ache with longing for the maternity wards and sick babies. But thirty-five dollars a week was a lot of money.

Ruth saved up, and after four months she could pay the first installment on a small car which she shared with her mother. Mrs Anderson changed over at this period from Christian Science to astrology. She refused to live with her daughter any more, as the stars were against it. Soon after, she announced with a certain embarrassment that she was engaged to marry a certain Mr Lonsdale, a man with a scanty mustache and an exaggerated English accent.

Ruth threw her arms round her neck and wept. If she had not been so deeply in love herself she might have felt annoyed. But just at that time she was far too deeply engrossed in her own blissful preoccupation. Her mother married and went to England with Mr Lonsdale to be introduced to his family. She looked thin and distinguished when they said good-by, and even the too vividly carmine cheeks she had lately taken to gave her the air of a duchess. So at least Ruth thought. Then several picture postcards arrived and finally the announcement that Mr Lonsdale had decided to remain in his native land, where astrology was just catching on.

Ruth lived at the Nightingale Club, and went on living there although Frank would rather have settled her in a little flat of her own. She chose this respectable home for hospital nurses partly as a protection against the strength of her own feelings, for she had so completely lost her head since she got to know Frank that she would have drowned or gone up in flames but for this restraining influence and her fear of the gossip in the Nightingale Club.

At first she met him every week, then nearly every evening. By degrees it came out that he had only just emerged from an unhappy marriage and was still shattered by it. Ruth teased him and quarreled with him a lot of the time to prevent him from seeing too clearly how madly and desperately fond of him she was. She thought him handsomer, stronger, cleverer and more wonderful altogether than she had ever imagined a man could be. The air of mystery and unhappiness that surrounded him during the weeks before and after his divorce made everything even more beautiful.

After spending the whole day encased in her white nurse's uniform, Ruth thawed out at night and became prettier and prouder every day. She bought herself clothes to please Frank, took great pains to rid her speech of all traces of Iowa and Fourteenth Street. She tried to recover what little varnish they had superimposed upon her at Flynn's College. She subscribed to a lending library and read in the intervals of her duties during consultation hours. Sometimes Frank was quite close to her, sometimes he suddenly became a stranger. His mood changed abruptly: one moment he was exuberantly merry, the next silent and embittered. She did not really know him. She did not really understand anything about him. When she discovered that he was poor and out of a job she was greatly disillusioned for three whole days. Then it occurred to her that Frank was unhappy, weak, helpless, forsaken, a stray dog, a broken doll, a chilly frog. Before, she had admired him. But now at last he really belonged to her, and she began to take him in hand with energy. Chip, she called him tenderly, Chip, the beloved, never-to-be-forgotten mongrel of Fourteenth Street.

Frank was a chemist; so much she knew. He had been in his father-in-law's business and given it up when his marriage went to pieces. Now he had a few weeks' work on and off or else nothing at all. Ruth knew now that it was his desperation that made him want to go out, to dance, to drink, to escape. Distraction was the sovereign cure in America, alcohol its medicine. Sometimes he talked of great prosperity, hinted at a legacy, prophesied that he was going to make a great invention. But he was not like Jackie who had bent over his table for seven long years in his shirt sleeves working out the Anderson-Gothic. Frank was inscrutable. At bottom she knew only one thing for certain: that she loved him and that he needed her. Often she was jealous over another woman, but she never said so. Finally she left the Nightingale Club to be of more help to him and moved into a little flat where they could be alone together as he wished.

One night after a heavenly dance together, when they were both a little tipsy, he spoke of marrying her—that very night. But at the last moment Ruth drew back. "Not until you have a job," she said, summoning all the common sense she could command. They did not get married, and Frank felt hurt for long after.

It was more than a year later before he found a job with the Eos Film and Foto Company, Shanghai. Fifty Shanghai dollars a week. When he told her about it Ruth at first thought he was joking. But he showed her the letters and began packing his things. "I'll take a look at the mess, and if I should like it I'll cable you to come out," he said lightheartedly. Ruth smiled pluckily until the bus, which he took for cheapness to Vancouver whence his boat sailed, carried him off. She grasped his hand tightly, ran as far as she could beside the huge, gray bus. A whiff of gasoline from the exhaust and then Frank was gone.

He wrote her nice letters. I love you—today more than yesterday, tomorrow more than today. But it was nearly three years before the cable came, summoning her to join him. It felt odd to leave America, but Frank was more to her than her native land. She gave in her notice, hurriedly found another nurse to deal with Professor Richards' clients, wrote to her mother, bade farewell to Jackie's grave.

All the boats for the East were crowded. She had long ago saved up for her passage. She bought her railway ticket and sailed on the only boat on which she could book a passage. It was a fast and clean Japanese boat called the *Kobe Maru*.

VII

Frank Taylor

WHEN FRANK WAS SEVEN YEARS OLD he heard a bird sing for the first time. There were no singing birds on the Hawaiian Islands where he was born, apart from a cheeky blackbird with a yellow beak which had a scolding cry and invaded the veranda to forage for the breakfast crumbs. Daddy and he arrived in the evening by boat at San Pedro, where a severe old lady, who had to be called Grandmother, met them with a funny old car and drove them to her white-painted frame house in Los Angeles. Little was said. "Hello, Henry," said Grandmother. "Hello, Mam," said Daddy. "This is Sonny, Mam."

"Hello, Sonny. How brown he is, Henry!"

"It's the sun," said Daddy.

The guest room where Frank was to sleep by himself was on the first floor. He had never slept by himself before. "You can have Father's room," Grandmother told Daddy, and he had remained below. Grandmother took Frank into the guest room, put him under the shower and washed him.

"Where's your nightshirt?" she asked.

"I always sleep with nothing on," Frank said. Grandmother opened her mouth, said nothing and shut it again. "Don't you say your prayers?" she asked as he was slipping into bed. "Oh yes," he said hurriedly, for he often forgot all about them. He knelt up in bed and muttered rapidly: "Dear God, protect this house and all who are in it, Daddy and Mamo and Puolani, Amen."

"Who is Puolani?" Grandmother asked.

"My pony," Frank said, with a feeling that he might soon begin to cry.

"You don't pray for animals," Grandmother said as she turned out the light. Then she bent over him in the dark and gave him a hard, frigid kiss on the forehead. After that there was only the light of a street lamp and the shadows of the curtains, which waved slowly to and fro at the open window. Frank shut his eyes tight and soon fell asleep. He woke up in the middle of the night, for a bird had started to sing on a tree outside the open window. Frank sat up, clasped his hands, listened in amazement. The bird sang loud and very fast, it sounded as if it were all alone in the dead of night. Suddenly Frank was overwhelmed by the whole surging weight of homesickness for his mother and all he had left behind, and he lay with his face buried in the pillow and began to cry noiselessly while the bird sang on and on. In the morning Grandmother surveyed the moist pillow, and after a while she said: "You'll soon like it here, Frank—once you've been to school."

Frank Taylor's grandfather had come from Vermont. As a young man he had gone out to Hawaii as a Methodist missionary and preached the Word of God in the Kona district. He returned to Wheelston, Vermont, for his first vacation and brought back a wife with him. Later on he was transferred by his Church to Hilo and later still to Honolulu, or rather to a little settlement some eight miles outside Honolulu inhabited by the laborers of a large sugar plantation. There was a little wooden Methodist chapel next to the school, and Pastor Taylor took charge of the souls of a multicolored and multilingual community. Henry, the only son of the minister and his wife, was a frequent visitor at the planter's house, for there was no other white playfellow for the planter's children. As Henry was a quick lad and eager to make his way, Mr Hancock decided to pay for his studies in America and saw to it that he went to Yale; when he came back, Mr Hancock took him on in the office, and after marrying Mr Hancock's daughter his promotion was rapid. Finally he was appointed as manager to develop the export of raw sugar to the refineries in America.

Frank's mother, the lovely and merry Mamo for whom he was at first so homesick, was of quite different blood and stock. Many of the island families had a dark spot in their past, and very little was made of it. Their first progenitor was an English sailor who in the sixties had gone ashore in Honolulu and drunk himself blind on the native drink, okulehau; he came to blows with two or three lusty young natives about a girl, was thrown downstairs in a brothel and broke his leg. When he came to himself his boat had sailed, so this Joe Porter remained on the island. Later he married a native girl of royal blood who brought him a large property, which he planted with sugar cane. Thus the blood of adventurers and natives was mingled in Frank Taylor with that of stern and pious ancestors just enough to prevent him from being a typical hundred-per-cent American.

Frank knew nothing of the uproar and scandal that had preceded his parents' divorce. He did not know that his father had forgiven his mother time and time again and only gave her up when he found her in the arms of a young assistant on the staff of the plantation's experimental station; that he was therefore given custody of his child and left the island disgusted by its loose morals, its enervating softness and its climate, which undermined the white man's physical and mental energies. Frank was uprooted from its tropical soil before his roots had taken firm hold. At first he interspersed his speech with a few Hawaiian words, and his grandmother, the missionary's wife, understood him, for she was used to them herself. But as soon as he went to school and was laughed at by the other boys he soon gave it up. He wanted to be like the others and not to attract attention. His memories of Hawaii soon faded away. At last nothing was left but a bright but blurred vision of snow-white coral sands and black lava, white-crested breakers that rolled shore-wards with brown exultant bodies on their backs. Gigantic trees, a profusion of large flowers, the house on the hill with the shadowed rooms behind the veranda that ran all round. Fong, the Chinese cook, who made Mamo laugh because he wrote Chinese poems in the kitchen. The smell of curry which always clung to the walls of the dining room. Pineapples, cold, cut in dice and served in a large yellow flower as a cup. Long rides on his pony, Puolani, among the interminable sugar plantations. The acrid smell when the leaves on the tall stalks were burned on the fields. Clouds that never left the sky, rain at all hours and then sunshine again, great stars just above the garden. Coconut palms in the wind, music and company in the garden while Frank was supposed to be asleep upstairs. His mother's laugh, which he could distinguish from anyone else's. His mother's perfume, her white skin, her warm hands, her laughter; the way she rode, the way she swam, the way she bit his neck and his ears when they played "little horses," the names she called him by: honeydrop, little fish, *laipala liilii*—all this gradually fell away until at last it went beyond recall.

His grandmother was right. After a time he liked it here, it was nice at school, he made friends and was much admired for his strength and tanned skin and was a favorite with the little girls in his class and still more with the boys. Soon after his grandmother's death his father married a lean woman, who had a strong-minded expression about the chin which Frank did not like. Her name was Mrs Henley, and she was a widow with an eight-year-old daughter. "Call me Mother," Mrs Henley told him. "Very well, Mrs Henley," Frank said. "Have you brushed your teeth properly, Junior? . . . Have you washed your ears? . . . What's that dirty mark on your trousers? . . . If you say 'lousy' again, I'm afraid I shall have to take away your dessert, Junior. . . . When you go to the baseball game you really might be a little gentleman and take Dot with you, don't you think, Junior?"

"Very well, Mrs Henley—I mean, Mother."

The town grew and grew and they moved to Eighth Street, near Westlake, where people went rowing on Sundays. There was a lot of talk at home about something they called the Bonus. Everything, from Mrs Henley's new evening dress to the gold braces for straightening Dot's teeth, depended on the Bonus. Daddy was employed by the sugar refinery of a firm which was in competition with his former father-in-law, the Pacific Sugar and Molasses Company. The glamour and prosperity of the house on the hill at Oahu were things of the past, but all the same they were well enough off. "My mother was one of the Stanwicks," Mrs Henley used to say, and it sounded as if she were descended straight from the Plantagenets.

Meanwhile Frank was taught at school that America was the best country in the world, California the best state in America and his school, the L A L H I , the best in Los Angeles. All this, together with the fact that his football team beat that of S M F H , 9–0, gave him a pleasant feeling of superiority and made him tolerant towards other people who had not his conspicuous advantages in life.

When Frank was eleven he had a dangerous mastoid. It was the first occasion on which a quarrel troubled the studied politeness of Henry Taylor's second marriage. "I can't take the responsibility— if anything happened to the child—after all, she is his mother— I should reproach myself ever after," Henry whispered anxiously, and at last Mrs Henley gave way on condition that he was out of the house, even out of the town, on the day when his first wife came to see her son. He agreed to this; perhaps he himself was afraid of his love for Mamo which he had buried so deeply within him. Mamo took the first possible boat and there she was at the door, giving the colored girl her card. Her name was now Mrs Lester Ingram. She breathed gently into her veil, for it was very cold in California in winter, and she gazed in surprise at the exhibition of tidiness and middle-class respectability called Mrs Henley's parlor. There was a smell of waxed floors, an opulent but empty flower vase stood on the table, the piano looked as if it were kept locked. Mrs Henley wore a stout net over her hair. She had just come from the hairdresser and had to preserve her fresh waves. The meeting of the two women was conducted with exaggerated politeness. Mrs Henley called up the hospital and announced Mrs Ingram's visit.

Immediately Mamo was on the way, Mrs Henley called up her husband and warned him in a tremulous voice not to go near the hospital and then began packing his suitcase. She threw open the windows to expel the first Mrs Taylor's much too pungent perfume before her husband came home.

The nurse who was knitting beside Frank's bed went out on tiptoe when Mamo bent over the child. Frank was unconscious, his lips were cracked and parched with fever, he tossed his head to and fro. Mamo's tears rained down upon him, she deluged him with them as she had when she said good-by to him. At night she sat by his bed gazing at him. He has grown a big boy, she thought, laughing and crying at once. The tears kept running down into her mouth, she had to lick them away. Once Frank opened his eyes and moaned piteously. "Liapala liilii, my little pink fish," she whispered eagerly. She laid her face on his hands, but instead of kissing them she gently bit each fingertip as in the game of "little horses." The child shut his eyes again, but he smiled.

Mamo stayed at a hotel, but she visited her son every day. She sent Mrs Henley flowers, she bought her little daughter a doll, but she could not break down the barrier of politeness, which was as common and inflexible as cast iron. When Frank was out of danger she wept torrents of tears once more, not by his bed but alone in her hotel, and then returned to Honolulu. But first she bought herself some new clothes, for there was a larger selection in Los Angeles than on the island.

Frank knew very little of his mother's visit, for he had been delirious most of the time. All that remained with him was the feeling of something warm and good as after a happy dream. But now Mamo had plucked up her courage; letters arrived now and then for her son, and Henry Taylor could not bring himself to forbid this correspondence, which went on behind Mrs Henley's back. Mamo told him how Fong's poems progressed in the kitchen, of the enormous frogs which had been introduced to combat a sugar parasite and now jumped about in hosts all over the veranda, and about the foal Puolani had had.

At Christmas a parcel arrived for Frank and Dot, ukuleles and sugared nuts, grotesque Japanese dolls, Chinese silk-embroidered pajamas, whole boxfuls of amusing exotic things. Frank carried the letters about with him as if they were love letters and regarded the fact that he had a mother of his own in the light of a mysterious and secret love affair. Also he sat down and answered her letters in a clumsy, schoolboy way:

DEAR MAMO:

Thank you for the lovely presents. I am only two inches shorter than Daddy now and he says I shall soon leave him behind. I often go swimming in the sea with my school friends but the waves are too flat here and you can't do any surfing. There's an amusement park and a water chute which is good fun. As soon as I've left school I'll come and see you in Hawaii.

or else:

DEAR MAMO:

I'm quarterback now in the school team and last Friday we beat the H.H.S. seven to three. I made a touchdown, pity you weren't there to see. The silk shirts you send me are beauties, but Mrs Henley says I must keep them for going to parties in. The boys here don't wear silk shirts. But I like them very much. With a hug from

Your big little Fish.

And:

DEAR MAMO:

I am writing from the summer camp where Daddy has sent me. It is in the Sierra, nine thousand feet up and there are tall trees, not like the ones in Los Angeles which you have to buy and plant but real, full-grown ones. We sleep in tents and at night we sing round the campfire. I went on a pack trip too, we rode on horseback for three days and slept in sleeping bags. Daddy says, if his Bonus turns out well he'll perhaps buy a cabin in the mountains and then we can always be among the trees at week ends. There is even a river here, it's dried up now but up to June there is water in it. I remember a waterfall I saw when I was little. Only three more years of school and then perhaps I can come to Hawaii.

And a cable:

VERY UNHAPPY STOP CANNOT COME AS FATHER SICK.

Henry Taylor first became aware of his gastric ulcers just as Frank left school. Mrs Henley's mania was diet, and as new diets came to the fore every month in America her life was never devoid of interest. A procession of colored cooks came and left again, insulted and annoyed by the demands that were made upon them. Raw foods, saltless foods, protein-rich and proteinless foods, butter-milk diet, banana diet, tomato diet. For a week there was nothing but unsalted vegetables cooked without butter and the next week nothing but gory steaks. And now Daddy was sick and dietitians took him in hand. But he was still in pain, lost weight and could not work; a substitute was found for him in the Pacific Sugar and Molasses Company, at first only temporarily and then permanently. Henry Taylor lost his job or threw it up. He became an insurance agent, since thus he could work when he felt able to and leave off when his attacks came on. As a side line he gambled on the stock exchange, as everyone else did, in order to make up for his dimin-ished income. Frank could not go to Yale, as had long been planned for him. Instead he attended the state university in Los Angeles and stayed at home. As a consolation his father gave him a relic of a car. Frank painted it bright green and drove to the university with great pride.

Mrs Henley set her teeth and courageously economized; she went into the kitchen and made mashed carrots and spinach for her husband with her own hands. "My mother was one of the Stan-wicks," she informed her cook. It was owing to Mrs Henley and her social ambitions, which embraced even her step-son, that Frank finally got as far as joining his father's fraternity, the very eligible Sigma Alpha Epsilon.

At high school he had been a general favorite—"the great hope of the football team"; he wrote entertaining little items for the school paper, and the girls gave him the eye, handed him notes and drew hearts inscribed with his initials in their copybooks. At the university he was a nonentity, a razzed freshman, a chemistry student who had to go through the most boring elementary stages, a nobody who had to show first what he was made of. He had decided on chemistry not because he had any marked talent for it but because his father considered there were prospects in it. Also the explosions and experiments in the school laboratory had afforded him some slight amusement. Every Monday he put in an appearance at his fraternity, where he had his corners rubbed off and was roped in for the Friday dance nights. He danced stiffly, holding his partners carefully at a distance, as they made an extremely fragile impression on him.

Ever since the word "sex" had been declared eligible for polite society there had been a great deal of talk about it. Three sections of the university paper were devoted to it: advice for lovers was one, campus gossip was the second, and the third was earnest and defiant—free love, companionate marriage, sexual diseases and how to combat them, what is birth control? The question mark was superfluous in the case of most of the young people. Frank was too shy or too arrogant. He had no girl of his own. He looked at girls, observed that they had pretty figures, found them provocative but thought of none in particular. He waited, he did not know for what.

Football was more important than either his studies or sex. It was a great blow to Frank for a time that he was not chosen to play for the university. He had to resign himself to sitting with the cheer section at the games, studying the card of instructions, howling the university cheers, turning his cap inside out, waving blue, green and red sheets of cardboard, relapsing into gloom if his own side lost. When he was a junior, in the third year of his university career, he achieved the position of cheerleader. He had pep and a sense of rhythm and what the other boys called personality. He stood with two others in front of the section and led the outbursts of cheering to ginger up the team. He practised them under the cold shower, and once by a stroke of genius he even invented a new cheer which was approved and adopted.

He accompanied the team to San Francisco and even to Seattle. After the match conquerors and conquered got drunk on the booze they had brought with them, and then they raised every sort of hell. Frank had his first drink and his first love affair on these occasions.

It occurred to him later that his experienced fellow students had greatly exaggerated the delights of both.

It was a point of honor with the girls to make their friends spend as much money as possible, for by that their love could be measured. A boy with an automobile was better than one without, and a boy with an expensive automobile was highly favored, while one who had only a cheap one was merely tolerated. The flower corsages their boys had to present, the places where they were taken to dance, the price of the dinner they were given were all reckoned up and weighed, not for their own sake but as symbols of a greater or less degree of devotion. It taught men to lavish money on women and the need to earn it. It taught the girls a thoughtless egoism and to treat love as a sport.

There was something in Frank Taylor, a softness or a hardness, that kept him apart from this traffic. His missionary blood gave him a distaste for love affairs in cars, which were the customary thing; and the legacy of sentimental romance he inherited from his mother made all this love-barter seem somehow too narrow, too cold, too calculating.

When he was twenty-one and of age he went to Hawaii. He took a passage in a cheap cargo boat—he had earned most of the money for his passage himself. He had made a hobby of photography. He photographed boys and girls, the campus, the football team, the dramatic class. He developed and printed industriously in the university laboratory at nights, not only his own films but the snapshots taken by others, for photos were the rage. In this way he made sixty-four dollars. Mrs Henley wept when he carried his point and set off; it was an odd and unconvincing spectacle, like a fountain in the desert. A hectic exchange of cables between him and his mother preceded his departure.

They sighted the island at six in the morning. The mountains rose up in trailing flannel nightshirts of cloud. An orchestra was playing "Aloha" on the pier, not for the little cargo boat but for a large luxury liner that was just steaming out. *Aloha, aloha nui.* Frank had a lump in his throat. A woman who was as fat as a soft white cushion threw her arms round his neck and smothered him in garlands of flowers. Her eyes were young, and she laughed and cried and took his hand and bit his knuckles to hide her tears.

Mamo?

Mamo.

A large gray automobile, a Japanese chauffeur and a pleasant-looking gentleman with a wreath of feathers round his wide-brimmed straw hat. "My husband," Mamo said. "My son." When she got in, the automobile was full. The two men took the pull-down seats facing.

It was quite different from what Frank had imagined: American streets with drugstores, bars, streetcars and many, many automobiles; streets surging with crowds made up of every race and color, a paradise of tolerance and good temper. They did not drive to the house on the hill but out to Waikiki past the big hotels, through garden streets, and then turned into an avenue leading to a house whose garden fell to the shore. The sea and its white-crested waves could be seen between the bent gray trunks of the palms. Mamo talked the whole time in her deep, husky voice and never took her hand from Frank's shoulder; now and again she gripped it tighter, shook him affectionately to emphasize what she was saying. Frank, who was accustomed to Mrs Henley's dry restraint, was overwhelmed at first by his mother's effusiveness. He remembered Mamo as a young and slight woman who rode like the devil and swam like a fish. She joked herself about her corpulence, and as she laughed and talked she became younger and thinner until at last she was just as he had dreamed.

A white-haired Chinese in a white suit came out onto the terrace and made a low bow. "*Aloha,* master, Missy velly much glad. *Aloha!*"

"Fong!" cried Frank and shook the old cook's thin hand.

"It's Fong's fault I'm so fat," Mamo said, and again tears trickled down her laughing face.

"The rain of Wai Alealea," Mr Ingram said, smiling. "It comes every quarter of an hour, and the sun shines at the same time."

Mamo watched while Frank undressed and had his shower, she fed him, she gazed at him, she cross-examined him, she groped to find out what sort of man he was. She put him to bed and sat

beside him, she watched him as he fell asleep. "You sleep with your
knees to your chin. Do you know what that means?" she asked
him at breakfast on the terrace. "It means you're homesick for
the womb," she went on, answering her own question as she handed
him a papaya. "Maybe so," Frank said in confusion. If he had been
longing for a mother without knowing it, he had certainly got her
now in full measure.

Sun, swimming, surfing, loafing, dancing; sky, clouds, moon,
shooting stars, the murmur of the sea, the morning wind, the
sunset, sand, shells, palms, flowers; scent, glamour, happiness. Mamo
showed off her handsome son and gave feasts for him. "You can
see he belongs to the islands," everybody said. He was tall and
strong and had a golden brown skin. "He takes after me," Mamo
said proudly, although she was never seen without a Japanese paper
umbrella to keep her complexion white.

Color played a smaller part in Hawaii than anywhere else in the
world. The whites, the *Haule,* were mixed and intermarried beyond redemption with the native population. The Chinese, Portuguese, Koreans, Filipinos, who were brought in in shoals, because
the Hawaiians were not fitted for work on the plantations, mixed
and mated regardlessly and wonderful examples of humanity resulted
sometimes. Only the Japanese kept to themselves and formed a
nice, decent middle-class, honest and industrious, cleanly, frugal
and obliging. They ran stores and hotels; they were excellent
craftsmen and made the best foremen on the plantations; their
pretty daughters went to the university or into service in the houses
of the wealthier *Haule*. They got on quite well with their deadly
enemies, the Koreans and Chinese. The old had their faces turned
to Nippon, the young were already Americans.

Dances at the club right on the sea, dances on Mamo's wide
terrace to Hawaiian music, lighted by the flickering pitch torches
of the fishermen; dances under the giant old banyan tree of the
big hotel in Waikiki. Mamo gave Frank a white dinner jacket,
his cramped style of dancing gave way to a new ease and suppleness.

One night when the moon was full and large and yellow, he fell
in love with Chummy Page. The Pages were staying in the hotel

and often came to the Ingrams'. Mr Page had something to do with oil, and the Pages had been two years in the social register. Chummy had a fine, coppery skin, blonde childish hair, she wore no stockings with her evening dress and danced marvelously and insatiably. When Frank told her anything about himself, his chemistry or the touchdown in the famous match against Stanford, she listened breathlessly and opened her eyes on his as no one in the whole world ever had. When he told her in a choking voice that he loved her, her eyelids fluttered like a butterfly's wings. He led her away out of the dance, his emotion almost suffocated him, he took her down to the sea, lifted her in his arms, carried her across a little stone breakwater, put her down in the black shadow under a palm. They kissed breathlessly. She had tiny silver shoes and a dress woven of moon dust. Frank could find no words to express how bewitching and enchanting and wonderful she was. "If you only weren't so damn beautiful," he complained, and that was all he could make of his declaration of love.

Mamo watched the two children with amused and fascinated eyes. Like all women who have had their share, and more, of love, she liked to do a little matchmaking. She sent the two into her greenhouse to see her orchids or out in the outrigger canoe to wait for the big breakers to race them back to the shore. She kept the Pages chained to the bridge table to leave the two young people their liberty. And when Frank at last had to leave again, she surprised him by giving him a first-class passage on the boat the Pages were were also leaving by.

Aloha! Aloha nui! Music on the pier, paper streamers, Frank holding one end and Mamo down on the pier the other. It tautened, it broke; the ship trailed a bright train of paper behind it through the water, and that was their good-by. Chummy was smothered in flowers to the ears, and Frank gave her his own leis into the bargain. As they steamed past the bare cone of Diamondhead they threw two of them into the water; that was their promise that they would return.

For six days longer the intoxication went on, with dancing on deck and star-gazing on the boat deck, with the strains of Hawaiian music and all the exuberance of feeling for which Frank had been waiting when he kept away from the girl students.

Mrs Henley was standing on the pier at San Pedro with a face of conscious rectitude. "Your father could not come. He is in pain," she announced. Frank introduced her dry parchment person to the Pages. While the luggage was brought ashore she hurriedly dived into her past for common acquaintance. "My mother was one of the Stanwicks," Frank heard her saying very soon.

"The San Francisco Stanwicks?" Mr Page asked, as though raising his hat. Mrs Henley avoided a reply, for her Stanwicks were only the South Bend Stanwicks. She whispered excitedly to Frank when they were driving away: "They are the Consolidated Oil Pages. First-class people." Father was lying in bed in the house in Eighth Street, and his lips were white. It seemed as if the blood trickled away from him month by month in great pain and in spite of the diet cure.

The Pages owned a house in Pasadena, where they usually spent some of the winter months; apart from this they lived on Long Island, where wealthy people in the social register properly belonged. They were staying on for a week in the West to see old friends, a single week, a farcical seven days. Neither Frank nor Chummy could imagine being parted. He called her up, took her off to play tennis. But they did not play tennis: they drove instead in his fifty-dollar car to the register office and the justice of the peace and got married. They called up their respective parents from the drugstore at the corner, told them the news and rang off before either party got breath to reply. Then they drove on to Santa Barbara. Chummy laughed till she cried over the way Frank had to coax his car to keep going. He still had twenty-four dollars. On this sum they could spend a week in some inexpensive inn or two days in a smart hotel. They chose the hotel. They did not give a thought to what was to happen after that. They had nothing in common but their youth and the memory of their dances under the banyan tree, but that was enough to carry them on through their wedding night.

Father Page, a fine gray-haired man with puritan lips, became

quite unpleasant. "Young man, if you imagined this was the way
to feather your nest you made a big mistake," he shouted. Frank
flushed to his ears and shouted back that he only wished Chummy
hadn't a nickel and that he wouldn't dream of accepting a cent from
Mr Page. Mrs Page had retired to bed with a migraine. Chummy
squeezed out a tear or two, flung her arms round her father's neck
and said: "Pop, how was it when you married Mom? Have you
forgotten?" Thereupon Pop relented, and the night ended with
much illicit whisky and a little soda water. Elopements of this
description were as customary in America as the forcible carrying
off of wives among many tribes on the Amazon. Pictures of the
young couple appeared in the papers on the society page, and the
text told of a romance begun beneath the palms of Hawaii and
ending in an elopement. Mrs Henley showed the cutting round
among all her acquaintances.

Chummy did not return to her exclusive college in Massachusetts,
but lived with Frank in two rooms in one of the many comfortable
apartment houses which were springing up in Hollywood to accommodate all the people whom the movie industry drew there. A
compromise was come to. Pop gave his daughter a monthly allowance to keep her from want, and Frank went back to the university
to finish his course in chemistry. All his professors were astonished
by his sudden ardor and the fanatical engrossment with which he
devoted himself to the study of chemistry; but it was not possible
for him to make up for the years he had wasted as cheerleader.

Chummy sat at home with nothing to do. The management kept
the rooms clean for her and a little grinning Filipino brought her
breakfast in bed. At nights she went to some restaurant or other
with Frank. She was bored. She sat in front of the looking glass
and tried six different ways of painting her lips. She read a book
and was more bored than ever. She called up acquaintances—reckless
young married couples. She took out the little automobile Pop
had given her for a wedding present and drove to tennis, the hairdresser or a cocktail party. She bought clothes merely from boredom
and sent her father the bills. She ordered two cases of whisky and
gin and let her bootlegger wait for payment. She made a habit of

having a drink before Frank came home so as to be in a good humor. Sometimes he was out for half the night, and she was jealous, for the university was humming with pretty girl students. Frank took photographs by day and developed the films by night. He produced illustrations for the university annual and sometimes sent in photos to the newspapers. In that way he earned a little. On Fridays and Saturdays they went dancing, as all the other young couples did, for at the week end Frank could have his sleep out. He made love to her, kissed her in the automobile on their way home, carried her to bed in his arms, made jokes, called her his ball-and-chain and his worst habit, and it all ended in an embrace. In the middle of the night Chummy put her hand out to him, but he had got up again. He was sitting in his pajamas in the next room with the electric coffee machine beside him, working. He was a virtuous and industrious little married man and there was little left now of the glamour and exuberance he had had for her in Hawaii.

Frank too looked at Chummy and found she was no longer made of moon dust as on the beach under the palms. He had read the starry nights into her, the scent of the night-flowering cereus, the gentle sea, all the soft bloom and enchantment of the island. By degrees he discovered that he had fallen in love not with the girl but with the surroundings.

Chummy had a fixation: she was not going to have a baby, not on any account. "It would spoil everything," she said. It was an obsession; it made her hysterical whenever he approached her. He too thought they were not old enough to be parents. There were students who had children, but it was a bit funny and was generally kept secret as far as possible. He had defended the frank articles on birth control in the university magazine, but in practice, in the innermost core of his own experience, it was another matter. It took away from the spontaneity, the mystery; it made them both nervous and self-conscious. They often quarreled now without knowing why.

When Frank was working for his finals he had no time for Chummy, and she was annoyed. She had been accustomed from her early schooldays to playing off her admirers one against another. The technique was as old as the United States, as old as the world perhaps. Out of defiance she began flirting with one of her tennis partners; wilfully she let him kiss her and take her out. Frank was not jealous as she had expected; but his self-esteem was wounded.

Then their marriage crumbled, as a mountainside where first the loose stones and lumps of earth loosen and roll down, until at last it becomes a landslide. They quarreled by day and were reconciled at night. Their wrought-up embraces left an unresolved discord behind. Chummy drank—just a little; she flirted, ran up debts, had to tell lies, got involved in feminine intrigues and began to regret being married to a man who had no job and no money. Frank slaved away, but he felt hampered; a student had no business with a wife, a student ought to be unencumbered. Sometimes he longed for the days when he had only dreamed of women instead of having one of his own. Their marriage was a legalized love affair and had no more permanence than such affairs had.

Early next winter the Pages arrived in California and occupied their house near Pasadena. The young couple pulled themselves together and put up a good imitation of a happy marriage. Frank had now done with the university and for some months had been looking in vain for a job. It was the same thing with the young all over the world. They learned, they worked, they studied, passed examinations, crammed themselves with knowledge, and all the time they knew that there was no point in it and that there was no room and no future for them. He smoked a lot because he was restless and uneasy, and every evening he needed a few cocktails to cheer him up. Cheap whisky was poisonous, and good was beyond his means. When he went dancing with Chummy he now always had to have a flask concealed in his pocket. Secretly he poured gin into the soda water to put him in the right mood. "Give me a drop, too," Chummy said every ten minutes.

Pop took his nervous son-in-law in hand and had a serious talk with him as one man to another. The upshot was that he found a place for him in the management of the Los Angeles branch of Consolidated Oil. He was provided with a room, a desk, charts with curved statistics on the wall, a stern and sour secretary and the title of assistant manager. Every Saturday he found a check in a blue envelope on his desk. He understood nothing of oil and nothing of business. He knew it, and so did everyone else. He read the newspaper, did crossword puzzles, smoked many cigarettes and was thankful when anyone came to read a letter to him or pass the time of day. At office meetings he had only the haziest idea what was being talked about, and when he was asked his opinion he agreed with the last speaker. It took all the guts out of him and he felt like a worm-eaten apple.

"You must get in with the right people, young man, and then you will make your way in the world," Pop preached at him. In his benevolence he installed the young couple in the house at Pasadena before leaving again and decreed that they were to live there and represent the family. It was a whale of a house. Garage for five automobiles, an artificial waterfall with floodlighting. Many large and marvelous brand-new "antiques." Church windows and an out-of-tune organ in the drawing room. Gobelins in their bedroom. A huge Italian Renaissance bed, into which wormholes had been shot from a shotgun. The new battlefield of the Taylor menage.

When Frank came home at night he found a number of guests who were obviously enjoying themselves. He went around pouring out cocktails for people he did not know.

"Who's that tall good-looking fellow who's just come in?" one of the company asked.

"Oh, that's my husband," Chummy said. "Come along, darling, and make your bow." A zero with no figure in front, people called him.

Now and then they discussed matters quite calmly and decided that it would be best to be divorced, but nothing came of it. Frank was almost certain that Chummy was unfaithful to him. He asked her about it. She wept and had a chill. "Do let's be civilized," she begged with flickering eyelids. "I can't help it if another man takes my fancy now and then. After all, we are modern people." It ended with Frank begging her pardon.

That winter his father died. It was only in the last few weeks, when pain made him cry out like an animal, that Mrs Henley could bring herself to call in a proper doctor. By that time it was much too late. Blood transfusions, a desperate operation for cancer, which Henry Taylor did not survive. Frank felt numb and frozen: he had been estranged from his father for a long time past. Shortly after her husband's death Mrs Henley came in for a stroke of very good fortune. She owned some land in San Fernando Valley which had once belonged to a ranch and had since been almost valueless. A movie company now wanted to establish itself out there. Mrs Henley got a good price and moved to South Bend, where there were still really good people left. Ever since the movie industry had spread itself all round Los Angeles the town had grown by leaps and bounds and taken on a tone that was not pleasing to people like Mrs Henley.

Late one night, a month after this, the telephone beside the Renaissance bed rang. Frank felt for the receiver in the dark without opening his eyes and almost fell asleep as he held it to his ear.

"Western Union speaking," he heard. "A cable for you. Shall I read it?"

"Go ahead," Frank muttered with his eyes shut.

"The cable comes from Honolulu. It reads: 'Mamo M-A-M-O fatal automobile accident stop our loss irreparable stop signature Lester L-E-S-T-E-R.'"

"Yes?" Frank said.

"Shall I read it again?" the telephone asked sympathetically.

"No, thanks. It's all right," Frank said.

He put down the receiver, sat up and turned the light on. Chummy came in from the next room, stood still in the doorway. She had recently moved out of the Renaissance bed. "Was it for me?" she asked. "Who were you speaking to?" He looked at her absent-mindedly. She was wearing a thin, tea-rose-colored nightdress, her face shone with cream.

"No," he said. "It was for me." He turned out the light again. He wanted to cry. But the only place where he could have laid his head and cried was Mamo's large, soft white shoulder.

In the third year of his married life with Chummy something went wrong with Consolidated Oil. And not only oil, everything was under the weather throughout America and throughout the whole world. The goddess of prosperity, the adored idol of America, hid her face. Panic on the stock exchange, disaster, depression, unemployment. Frank Taylor, the ornamental appendage, got the sack. He went around looking for work, as did millions of other young men. The little he knew of chemistry was no great recommendation, and he had forgotten half he ever knew. He hawked his best photographs around the newspaper offices. He wrote letters, he pulled every string left him from the old Sigma Alpha Epsilon days, he telephoned and urged his claims for all he was worth. For three months he did not earn a cent, and nevertheless life went on as before in the Pages' pseudo-Spanish castle. At last he got a thirty-dollar job in the laboratory of a small movie company where a Sigma Alpha Epsilon brother was director.

As this was the first real job of his life, his crippled self-esteem revived. Chummy was away a lot at this time. She had developed into a good tennis player and traveled with her tennis friends from one tournament to another. A small array of tasteless cups was exhibited on the sham rococo writing table in her bedroom. Frank dismissed the domestic staff and shut up the huge empty house. He retired once more to an apartment house and waited there for Chummy's return. There was thunder and lightning. She packed her trunk and left for New York. It was an open breach. "My wife is visiting her parents," Frank tactfully told acquaintances who asked after her.

A queen sat down at Taylor's table in the commissary of the studio. Sho wore a white, gold-embroidered First Empire dress with a train, and her face, in spite of the yellow grease paint, was beautiful. "As usual—caviare and champagne," she told the waitress. After a time a plate of thick bean soup appeared and, vulgarest of all drinks, a sickly green fizzy liquid called soda pop. "No drinks in this joint," the queen remarked to Frank. She sighed, put her elbows on the table and began upon her soup. She had a thick, drunken sort of a voice and the commonest accent he had ever heard in his life. "You an actor, too?" she asked after she had taken a good look at him. "No —I work in the lab," Frank replied. Her eyes went on a pleasure cruise up and down him. "With your looks?" she said, and in spite of her impudent way of making advances Frank felt a pleasing warmth down his spine. The queen wiped her brow with her table napkin, gave a touch or two to her paint and patted him on the head as she went off. "So long," she said.

Punk was a student of men, in her way. "What you want is booze," she said when their acquaintance was still young. "You look like chewed string, man. Get drunk and everything 'll be okay."

Frank Taylor got drunk and everything looked okay. Life turned on alcohol for Punk. "I've time tonight," she said. "How about it, kid? You bring the whisky and I'll see to the rest." She lived in a shabby apartment house in a side street off Hollywood Boulevard. The rest consisted of a bed, which Punk 'let down with a bang from the wall. "Good luck!" she shouted with joy. "Monday! Clean sheets! Generally the stinkers forget all about it."

But she was a hearty wench and beautifully made, and she made no fuss about so simple a pleasure as sleeping together. "Tonight I'm busy building up my career—but tomorrow," she would say while she was painting a large, dark red mouth on her face. Punk was the stand-in of a film actress who had not got very far herself. What Frank enjoyed in her society was the relief of a man who has been wearing tight shoes for hours and at last can take them off. There was no mention of love between them, but they laughed a lot when Punk opened out with her cutting comments on the big guns of the studio.

One night, when Frank Taylor was leaving Punk's room, two men rose from the green plush sofa which suitably adorned the entrance hall of the building. A dim light was on there all night, and the outer door was always open for late visitors, as in all apartment houses of the sort.

"Mr Frank Taylor?" the taller of the two asked, stepping close up to him. Frank took a step back, for he knew he smelled of whisky and looked untidy. "Yes, what is it?" he asked, his mind a blank.

"My name is Steuber. I am a lawyer. Your wife has instructed me . . ." the fellow said.

Frank lit a cigarette to steady himself. The shabby hall with its Spanish pretensions, the plush sofa, the letter boxes on the wall with the names of the tenants on them, the murky smell, the whole impossible, unappetizing situation . . .

"Can't we discuss this matter somewhere else?" he suggested, opening the street door. But one of those rare but murderous torrential rains of southern California was coming down at the moment.

"During the last three weeks you have spent four nights with a girl named Miss Katharine Green," the lawyer read from a document which he held under the feeble light. "Detective Morgan here has kept you under observation."

Detective Morgan made a quadrangular bow. He had the broad shoulders and the laced-in belly characteristic of his profession.

"Is that correct? I think it will simplify matters for all concerned if you agree that that is correct," Steuber said in the tone of a nurse administering a bitter pill.

"That is correct," Frank said and then cleared his throat. Can't we be civilized? After all we're modern people. He recalled her words, but it did not appear that Chummy's civilization counted for much. He swallowed his bitter saliva with the smoke of his cigarette.

"It is purely a formality—it simplifies the divorce," the lawyer said. We're men and we understand each other, the expression on his face implied.

"Good night," Frank said, and it sounded like an insult. He opened the door, stepped out into the rain. It was almost a pleasure to be soaked to the skin.

That night of the forced landing when he got to know Ruth Anderson, Frank Taylor had about touched bottom. The affair had been blazoned abroad in the papers. Punk showed him the door. She had had an unpleasant scene on his account with the director, the Sigma Alpha Epsilon man, on whom the edifice of her hopes rested. For the same reason Frank lost his little job. He left for New York, where he had two or three meetings with Chummy, in the course of which they both behaved like cannibals. The raw flesh hung in shreds by the time they had said all they thought of each other. Father Page treated him as if he were a leper, although it was known to a wide circle that the old gentleman kept a girl in a penthouse in Seventy-second Street. Frank's life was in ruins when he got into the airplane. He had not even enough money for the journey. A friend in his useful fraternity, who was connected with the air line, in some way had wangled a free trip for him on the pretext that he was a press photographer. Frank felt a grim pleasure when they ran into stormy weather and the bus was wrenched up and down. I only hope the whole damned show comes down in flames, he thought again and again. A crash and it's all over. There's no sense in being alive at all. It would be grand if my free trip included a funeral with all honors.

The stewardess's attentions exasperated him. Thanks, I always change my own diapers, he thought irritably. Coffee? No, thanks. If it were poison . . . That was a good bump but not enough to put us into a nose dive. Here she comes again. It 'd do you good. What for? A fine mess I've made of life. If only I could go to you, Mamo . . .

She brought him a rug and tucked him up. She had pretty brown eyes. Motherly eyes, he suddenly felt. She looked kindly at him and tried to cheer him up with a smile. She was as slight and small as a child, a mere girl, but she had motherly eyes. "We're going to land," she told him. Pity, Frank Taylor thought in black despair. Best if we were never to land.

His suicidal mood vanished the instant real danger threatened. He looked out anxiously into the foggy night through which they hurtled. Suddenly he wanted to live, with strength and determination he wanted to live; instantly it seemed to him that he should have missed the best of life if that idiotic plane crashed. He suddenly felt the simple, universal, blindly human fear of death. The girl came, strapped him in. She wrapped the rug round his legs as if they were something fragile.

"There may be a slight bump," she said with a reassuring smile. He followed her with his eyes as she made her round and attended to the passengers. She was the personification of calm and clarity and cleanness. He never took his eyes off her; when the engines stopped and they came down, her lips suddenly went quite white, but she bravely went on smiling. He had never seen anything so moving as that blanched but reassuring mouth. He felt he must take hold of her and clasp her head to his shoulder to prevent her seeing; protect and help her so that she should not need to be brave all alone. All this swept swiftly and blindly through his feelings for the second or so as they went down. Then there came the crash.

It was the crisis of his life. As he helped her to force the door open, as he ran, feeling the pain of his broken ribs, along the endless dark mountain road in the icy wind to the nearest habitation, he knew at long last that he was a man again, that he could hold his own in the world. He grasped at Ruth, held fast to her.

"I need you," he told her a thousand times. "You are necessary to me. I shall never give you up, as long as you don't give me up."

She told him about her childhood, and it all fitted in. "I'm your sick cat," he said. "I'm your poor cold frog." They went for walks on Sundays through the streets of New York. He held her hand tight in his coat pocket. It was warm in there, a little home with her hand in it. For a time he even had a job: he put records on the phonograph in the music department of a store at Christmas time, when extra assistants were taken on. It lasted only three weeks. But for Ruth, he could never have got through those months of unemployment while he was passing through the torture chamber of divorce. His ribs mended, but it hurt him to breathe for some while longer. Yet in his inner mechanism a spring had been broken that would never mend. Ruth was not made of moon dust, and he knew that what he felt for her was not the intoxication of Hawaii. He was damaged, and she had the power of healing. He handled her with care, for he was acquainted by now with some of the sunken reefs between a man and a woman. He knew that he wanted Ruth for good and all, and he was prepared to work for that, to wait for it. He would gladly have laid his head in her lap and rested, but there was nowhere they could be alone. Ladies were not allowed as visitors in the small hotel on Second Avenue where he lived for four dollars a week. In Ruth's hostel, fancifully called the Nightingale Club, males were tolerated only in the parlor, where there was always a bevy of girls sitting round the imitation-marble fireplace. They did not possess that refuge for all American lovers, an automobile. Sometimes they took a taxi, but it poisoned all his caresses to know that Ruth would pay. So they walked round and round the block where Ruth lived, sat in dark movie houses, on bus roofs, on benches in Central Park or Riverside Drive and held hands.

He kept himself afloat by occasional work of odd and highly varied kinds which had nothing whatever to do with chemistry. He had evolved a complicated but workable system for the weeks when he earned nothing at all: he went the round of those of his friends who might lend him money. Whatever his difficulties, he never pawned or sold his camera and photographic equipment. Sometimes he made a scoop and planted a few pictures on a magazine. He had a certain talent for broad posterlike effects. Ruth frowned as she puzzled over what could be made of this gift of his, but in spite of all their hard thinking they could not hit on anything.

"Poor kid," he said. "You've let yourself in with a bum." Ruth laughed at him. "You're a genius," she told him. "Don't you know that all geniuses have to suffer at the start?"

One day a miracle happened; not one of the great miracles of the world, but all the same a miracle of a satisfactory size. Mrs Henley wrote to him for his birthday, saying she had bought a ticket for the Irish Sweepstakes and had written his name as part owner, as a present. "A thousand good wishes and may the blessing of heaven go with you, dear Frank. Dot has made the acquaintance of a *very* eligible businessman." Frank tossed the letter aside and consigned it to the same category as he did diets and nature cures. One day a hundred and thirty-four dollars arrived for him in tangible form. That meant a winter overcoat, two pairs of shoes, a yellow filter (the old one was broken—a great catastrophe), and a gala night with Ruth in celebration. The dream of an exposure meter Frank put resolutely from him. Instead he went out and bought two theater tickets, sent Ruth three gardenias to wear on her dress and called for her in a taxi. For one night he played at being Mamo's son again, the spoiled son of a large house, who had inherited the lavishness of his Hawaii ancestors. They sat solemnly side by side with a sense of great importance, Ruth in a long coral red dress, which he thought charming, and he in a new tie, new shoes and an old suit pressed as new. The play they saw was tedious though famous, but this did not at all detract from their pleasure. The only thing that mattered was to go to the theater as people did who had jobs. He took Ruth out beforehand to a dollar-fifty dinner, and after the theater the evening began to be really *great*. They went to one of the bars which shot up in great numbers immediately after Prohibition was repealed, and Ruth became extremely full of feeling after a Manhattan cocktail. They migrated thence to the "Hawaiian Paradise" in Forty-second Street, where there were two scabby palm trunks with large green crumpled paper leaves and three men with paper leis and ukuleles to evoke a carefree and dusky South Seas atmosphere. It was quite enough to infect Frank with a sentimental homesickness for his islands. "I want to go back to my little grass shack in Keola Kekua, Hawaii," he sang in a transport as he danced with Ruth beneath the paper palms. After a while he was aware, in the subdued light, of eyes fixed upon him, and when he looked he found they were Chummy's. Chummy, his wife, rather drunk, in an ermine cloak, with diamond bracelets from wrist to elbow, Chummy with an escort in tails and as drunk as herself. Frank felt a strong inclination to cause a regrettable scene. Just as well I'm not drunk, anyway, he thought as he put the idea from him. He gripped Ruth so tightly that she asked: "What's up, darling?"

"We'll go right now and get a marriage license," he said grimly. They danced close past Chummy. Chummy waved and her bracelets glistened. "Right now, at once?" Ruth asked, laughing. "Straight away—tonight," Frank replied grimly. Ruth merely shook her head. "Why not?" he asked obstinately. Ruth thought it over gravely as she danced on. "When we marry I want to have children," she said, and it fitted in so ill with their surroundings that Frank burst out laughing. But Ruth would not be put off. "Fifty dollars a week and a little house out of town somewhere," she persisted. "It needn't be a smart neighborhood. And a little garden of our own and a dog and a cat and a child—or two. That's what I mean by being married."

The three wreath-hung men played "King Kamehameha" as an accompaniment to her proposition. Frank felt a constriction about his heart as Ruth depicted the future. A suburban house, a baby carriage in the hall, cheap furniture on the installment system. He mutely helped Ruth on with her cloak, put on his new coat and left the "Hawaiian Paradise" without another glance at Chummy. He took Ruth home in a taxi, and that left him six dollars and forty cents. They were no nearer marrying after all.

Finally it was Lester Ingram, Mamo's kindly second husband, who found Frank a job, a job of a vague description in the Shanghai branch of the Eos Film and Foto Company. Ruth smiled as bravely when it came to their parting as she had that night in the airplane. It was snowing a little as Frank got into the large coach which was the cheapest way of reaching Vancouver, where he was to embark.

He went third class and by the northern route, which avoided Hawaii. He shrank from seeing the island again where he had been born and where Mamo had died.

VIII

Yoshio Murata

THE OUTLINE OF A PINE BRANCH outside of the window's dim, white, paper pane. Whorls of needles encircled the gnarled branch which, forging out into many horizontal twigs, threw its picture through the transparent paper. Once in a while there was a gentle gust of wind, the branch came alive and stirred. In the middle of the room there was a square pit filled with glowing charcoal and ash. The iron kettle, suspended from the ceiling, began to sing, gently at first and then more loudly. Grandfather, kneeling on a cushion at the time-polished wooden edge of the pit, began to set out the paraphernalia for the tea ceremony. His hands moved slowly and peacefully among the smooth, gleaming vessels, putting powdered tea into a deep bowl, pouring water on it out of the old ladle, stirring the liquid with the bamboo stirrer until it was thick and foamy.

Yoshio, very small yet, knelt gravely and politely opposite his grandfather, with the palms of his hands resting on the matting that covered the floor, as he had been taught. But after a time he found the ceremony tedious, and he edged nearer and nearer to the wall in which the window was. He struggled hard, but the temptation was irresistible: he stretched out his forefinger, poked it through the paper, and it made a pleasing little pop as it burst. Grandfather, in his dignified gray kimono, scolded him smilingly, for the cold air blew in through the little round hole. Then Mother came and moved the screens in front, and window and pine branch vanished. The old Baaya appeared, kneeling in the doorway of the sliding door which led to the interior of the house; she bound Yoshio firmly to her back and carried him off. Grandfather was left alone again.

Little Yoshio saw a great many things when the Baaya carried him for a walk on her back. The village of Kamioka stood on a gently rounded hill, clothed here and there with feathery bamboos. There were many fine trees, pines and maples, which in November burned like fire on the hillside. There were clouds, towers of straw, neatly built up by the peasants, gray steps up to the Temple, in which there was the altar with many foxes, and gaily dressed processions on feast days. There were also bicycles and a few automobiles. Yoshio was born in the thirty-seventh year of the Meiji period, called the Period of Enlightenment. At the Feast of the Boys in May his parents gave him a modern uniform and a rifle that went plop-plop, and from Grandfather he received a little samurai armor with a helmet and two swords, which looked very dangerous, although they were only made of bamboo and tinfoil. A gigantic, beautifully painted fish made of cloth with gleaming scales was hoisted up to the tall pole behind the house as an emblem of good fortune for the only son. The fish filled out with wind, rose proudly up into the air, hovered there in a horizontal position. There were houses with five or six fishes, envied houses with many sons. Yoshio's mother sometimes looked across at them with a sigh, and her face was troubled, although she never ceased smiling, as good manners enjoined.

Grandfather also had two swords, a long one and a short one. Before the Feast of the Boys he took them carefully from the drawer in the wall, unwrapped them from their silk wrappings and polished them until they shone. Yoshio knelt expectantly and reverently beside him, listening to the old stories which the sight of the now idle samurai swords called up in the old man's memory. He told of the battle of Ueno, which had been fought where the beautiful Ueno Park in Tokyo spread now. The revered grandfather had himself fought at this battle when he was twenty-five years old, and his revered father, Yoshio's great-grandfather, had fallen there. The family belonged to a clan whose head and chieftain had been a loyal follower of the Tokugawa, the mighty Shoguns who had ruled the country for two thousand and sixty years. All that time the emperors of Nippon, the descendants of the sun goddess, Ama-Terasu-O-Mi-Kami, had sat idle and sacrosanct in their palace in the ancient city of Kyoto. After the imperial troops had defeated the partisans of the Tokugawa it was their chieftain's duty to commit hara-kiri, or *seppuku*, as the grandfather called it, using the more elegant Chinese word. In order to save his life and at the same time to clear his name of the disgrace of defeat and of rebellion against the divine rulers, three of his officers disemboweled themselves in his stead. One of them was Grandfather's brother, Great-uncle Kitaro. The glamour of chivalry and heroic self-sacrifice clung to his memory, and his grave was still a place of pilgrimage, where people bowed before him. Yoshio too, as he stood beside his grandfather before the shrine of his ancestors, made a particularly low bow in memory of his great-uncle Kitaro. The son of the rescued chieftain, however, whose name was cleared and who was honored by the Emperor as the offshoot of a gallant foe, had been given ministerial office. Yoshio dimly grasped that his grandfather had kept on being a samurai, although the Emperor had abolished the old ranks of nobility and replaced them by new ones. And he learned in early years what the grandson of a samurai who had fought at Ueno might not do: he might not cry when he was hurt, he might not run away when he was afraid of a neighbor's great noisy dog, he might not do or think anything that could stain his honor, the honor of a four-year-old child. Yoshio was firmly resolved to become as one of the forty-seven ronin who came up again and again in his grandfather's talk, the masterless men, the forsaken ones, the "men of the waves," who for long years held themselves in readiness to revenge the death of their prince and who paid the penalty by committing hara-kiri when the deed was done.

Yoshio bravely swallowed back his tears while he listened to all this, for he was deeply stirred, and self-control was the virtue most insistently demanded of him. Before the Feast of the Boys the two swords and the helmet, which had been handed down in the family for generations, were solemnly deposited in the niche in the large room, and Grandfather instructed the child to bow low before them. As soon as the feast was over they were put back in the wallboard, and Yoshio sometimes surprised the old man as he unwrapped the swords from the silk cloth and looked at them. A fine fern was inlaid in the hilt of the handle.

When Yoshio Murata remembered his grandfather in later years, he felt that the old man must have been very lonely, a survival from a time which to the enlightened and progressive children of Meiji seemed almost comic. He always had his frugal meals alone, for he could not accustom himself to the newfangled ways which permitted children and even women to eat in the presence of the head of the family. As he grew older he spent half the day arranging flowers in a vase according to the classic rules and symbols which represented the sky, man and earth in hundredfold meanings and moods. He himself carried the vase to the niche and selected the hanging scrolls that suited it. Sometimes it might be a landscape, sometimes the sketch of a bamboo branch, sometimes merely a few words of choice calligraphy. Yoshio's mother, the old man's daughter-in-law, was a little annoyed and jealous when he took on himself to arrange the flowers, for she too was skilled and educated and knew how to set the flowers. But Grandfather did not like her way of doing it according to freer and modern rules; once she put out a flat Satsuma bowl with only three autumn-tinted maple leaves floating on the surface of the water, and Grandfather was cross. "What does that signify?" he asked several times. "Would the honorable daughter have the goodness to explain to a stupid old man what it signifies?" Yoshio's mother knelt before the old Murata and murmured humbly that the three faded leaves were intended to express how she missed her husband who had journeyed to the North on business. Grandfather made no comment on this unsatisfactory answer, which was of much too personal a nature; but from that day onwards it was he alone who arranged the vase.

Grandfather showed the slyness and stubbornness of an old man in the care he took to imbue his grandson with Bushido—the ancient and unpractical samurai code of honor, which enjoined on him never to tell a lie, to despise manual labor and to regard money as an unworthy thing. It was hand in hand with Grandfather that Yoshio first went out on the days prescribed, to admire the cherry blossoms, the peonies, the chrysanthemums, to listen to the crickets, which they bought in little cages and set free towards evening in the gloaming of a bamboo thicket, and to gaze at the moon on a particular evening in autumn. He slept with Grandfather in the little six-mat room. At night the Baaya took the quilted mattress from the cupboard, spread it on the matting and put a little pillow for Yoshio and a hard neckrest for Grandfather; then, when the electric light was turned out, Yoshio felt utterly safe and protected with the soft, regular breathing of the old man so close beside him.

Grandfather often took him with him to the public bath too; their house was small and primitive, almost penurious, and it had no proper bathroom. So at least Grandfather said; but perhaps the long talks with other old men in the public bath were a pleasant way of passing the vacant hours of old age. Men and women politely drew to one side when he sat on the narrow plank in the hot water, and Yoshio learned how to behave and to avoid impolitely touching another bather. He loved the warmth of the water and the soapy steam in the first room, where strong, naked youths rubbed him down before he was allowed to enter the bath. In the cold of winter it was particularly pleasant to stay for hours in the bath and to come home heated all through, for the little charcoal braziers made it very little warmer there than it was outside. Grandfather gossiped in the bath with the other men about village affairs and the price of rice and fish. The women sat there quietly and decorously, trying to take up as little room as possible. Yoshio's mother never went to the public bath: she bathed at home, and the Baaya was permitted to warm her old bones in the warm water at the same time. Cleanliness and decency were as much a matter of course with Yoshio from the first day of his life as the air he breathed.

Yoshio was a soft and timid child and cried very easily. Stories could move him to tears and sometimes too he was moved to great pity for himself. It was apparently his fate that all the other boys with whom he played in the road were older or at least stronger and taller than he. Many already went to school and wore trousers, jackets and caps of the modern fashion. They did not find it beneath them to make jokes at Yoshio's expense, to which he could not submit without loss of honor. Therefore, although he hated and feared fighting, he was always mixed up in fights. His nose bled easily, and he felt nauseated by the sticky blood that ran down over his kimono and his child's pinafore. When he came home, pommeled, pale and sick, Grandfather only laughed at him. The Baaya took him into the kitchen, washed him with warm water and comforted him. When he was in a particularly bad way she burned a small quantity of a strange herb on his skin, and after the pain and fright caused by this proceeding he felt quite well again. The Baaya, too, had a fund of funny stories that made him laugh; she picked them up from the storyteller when she went marketing, and although she mixed them all up together so that the ends and beginnings did not belong, this only made them all the more gay and entertaining. When she told him her favorite story about the wet nurse O-Sade, who died for the baby at her breast and was born again as a cherry tree, Yoshio had difficulty in choking back his tears. But the most beautiful of her stories was about Momotaro, who came sailing down the stream in a peach and was brought up by the old fisher folk, until he went out and conquered the Island-of-the-Demons with the aid of the dog, the monkey and the pheasant. A Momotaro doll with a round jolly face and a look of courage and strength was displayed in the house at the Boys' Feast, Yoshio's Feast. But Yoshio did not look like Momotaro. He secretly looked at himself in his mother's little dressing mirror. He knelt down in front of it and gazed unhappily at his thin arms and his face, which would not look round like a peach but only long like an egg.

Yoshio's father, Toson Murata, Grandfather's son, was made of different stuff altogether. For the samurai view of life he had only a good-natured, politely veiled pity. He was a genuine child of the Meiji, and progress was the word that was oftenest on his lips. It always sounded like a fanfare, a call to arms in unknown battles. Technical knowledge, machinery, electricity, automobiles were the things he reverenced, and he had only contempt for the Old Japan. The day when England purchased the patent of a Japanese machine, invented by one of the engineers employed in Toson's cotton factory, was celebrated with an orgy of joyful anticipations. "Just wait, just wait," he exclaimed to his father and son. "It has taken us forty-five years to catch up with England. How long will it be before we are far in advance of all the countries of the world?" Toson was a huge, strong jolly fellow. It was very clear that he was not afraid of anything, and he did not need Bushido to give him courage. When he came in, the little house seemed even smaller than before, as though it were too tight a garment for the honorable father, the boisterous stranger, the pampered guest. Every time he arrived from Tokyo, Yoshio was dressed up especially clean and elegantly, to go to the station hand in hand with his demure mother in her dark clothes. The station and all the strangers who were waiting for the train never failed to excite him. They made low bows, with their hands on their knees, when their relations departed or arrived. There were lots of vendors, boys with newspapers, men with wooden boxes of hot rice and sweetmeats, women handing tea in funny little teapots to the passengers. The smoke, belched out of the engine, had an ugly smell and made him cough. Mother, smiling politely, bowed to his father, and he picked Yoshio up and swung him high in the air. When he arrived he was a foreign gentleman in a hat and modern clothes; but once at home he soon made himself comfortable in a kimono and white linen stockings. Yoshio was allowed to have his meals with Father and Mother, but he must speak only when spoken to.

The revered grandfather died just before Yoshio entered school. They moved to the great town of Tokyo, which Grandfather had obstinately called by its old name of the Tokugawa days—Yedo. Yoshio felt very sad and desolate, but since his grandfather had impressed upon him in season how unfitting it was to show sorrow, he smiled bravely all through the funeral ceremonies. Also the preparations helped to distract him and were so engrossing that there was a great deal of pleasure mixed with his grief. He made the jump out of the medievalism of the village into the modernity of the great city easily, almost without knowing it.

Until he went to school Yoshio wore bright-colored kimonos, bright because he was a child, but yet not brighter than was becoming for a boy. Now he learned to wear trousers, shoes and jacket. He liked going to school, because he was given a little soroban and a black slate on which he could write with white chalk. The limy smell of the chalk was indissolubly bound up with his new life. Grandfather·had always written with brush and ink which had to be crumbled first and diluted in water. It had smelled different and looked different. Only when Yoshio could read, his very own life began, for it was his destiny to be one of those people to whom the marvel and charm of the printed word meant more than the thing it attempted to describe. The first words he was able to decipher were the scrolls of calligraphy hanging in the niche. "Fall down seven times, eight times stand up," it might be; or: "Your life lasts but a short time, but your reputation lives forever." All these mottoes, which his father himself selected, preached courage and endurance. On the paper of the sliding door leading to his bedroom his father with his own hand had painted a rude fist. "Do you know what that fist means?" he asked Yoshio. "It reminds me that I will get what I want and keep what I have."

At such strong talk, Yoshio's little heart was filled with timorous admiration. He tried clenching his own little fist; it was puny, he could feel little strength in it. He read and read. There were books crammed with stories of heroic deeds and self-sacrifice, and Yoshio dreamed of rescuing children from burning houses and of stopping the Mikado's runaway horse, or at the very least the horse of a great general. His father did not think much of such reading. He subscribed to a children's magazine for him, full of riddles, prize competitions, technical diagrams and descriptions of the West. A story about a Japanese boy in America gave Yoshio his first longing to see that foreign land. He besieged his father with questions about it. Toson Murata had been in San Francisco as a young man, to study, as he called it. As in the case of so many of his fellow countrymen, sons of good families, his studies had consisted in working as a servant in an American household; it was the cheapest and simplest way of getting to know the nature of foreigners. He had brought back from America an unreasoning admiration for everything foreign, American and new. Two of the rooms in the house they now occupied were furnished in the Western style, and there he received business friends and important visitors. There was a strident, agitated telephone in the house, and soon he bought a phonograph, which disgorged foreign music from a large iridescent horn. Yoshio listened at first with dazed astonishment and later with sheer delight.

At first he got pains in his shoulder blades at school from having to sit on a bench. But after a time he got used to it, and when the master told them that sitting on benches and chairs would make them grow as tall as Englishmen, he took to it with enthusiasm. Later, when he paid his grandmother on his mother's side a visit and had to kneel in front of her, resting the palms of his hands politely on the matted floor, he soon began to ache in every limb.

This grandmother whom he saw for the first time after coming to Tokyo was a serious and strict lady, the honored and respected mother of many sons. She too came of a samurai family, and it was said that in her youth she had been taught to fight with a halberd like a man; but Yoshio did not dare to ask her about it. This grandmother in her dark gray kimono, her gray, smoothly oiled hair tied in a knot on her neck, had in her possession a treasure, which Yoshio was sometimes allowed to take out of its drawer: an album of photographs. In it, she and her friends were to be seen in the full and elaborate dresses that were the foreign fashion in the eighties, sitting on chairs of turned mahogany and coyly propping their elbows on tables that were turned likewise. For when Grandmother was a girl everybody who was anybody had fallen in with the modern fashion, and sometimes Yoshio succeeded in enticing from the old lady tales of the foreign dancing lessons and balls in which she had taken part in her youth. It sounded as if these dances had been a severe penalty and a painful tribulation. But after Tsushima and the victory over the Russians a fresh wave of national consciousness had arisen, and Grandmother's generation went back to the beautiful soft and pleasing kimonos and to the strictness of the old manners in which Yoshio's mother had been brought up. When he visited his grandmother he had to leave his shoes outside the door and on his knees receive the rice cake she held ready for him.

Four of her seven sons shared with Yoshio's father in the ownership of the cotton factory into which he had married. Since Toson Murata had entered the firm it had expanded remarkably and the family grew ever wealthier. It was a period of great progress and prosperity throughout the country, and Yoshio's gigantic father took all he could and held all he took, as the fist on his door promised. One uncle had married into a noble family and taken the name of his wife. Two were abroad as importers of Japanese articles of extreme hideousness which were manufactured solely for that purpose and to suit the market. Yoshio's mother was the only daughter of the Sato family, and her ambitious mother had married her at an early age into the old and respected samurai family of the Murata. Yoshio's father had brought new life, energy and dauntless enterprise into the firm, and his brothers-in-law were glad to leave the management of the factory to him.

As he grew up, Yoshio felt as if his father had kept all his strength to himself and given none of it to the son. Much reading ruined his eyes, at twelve he began to wear spectacles. The moral tales which formed part of his school curriculum began to bore him, and he and his friends made merry over them. Nevertheless, he could not help their leaving an impression behind and having a lasting influence upon him. He went on to the grammar school and began learning Chinese, the four books of Confucius, learning by heart, endlessly and miserably, things that meant nothing to him at all. He plunged into English, which was the key to the entire world. It was a long and severe ordeal before he grasped the structure and principles of a language so radically different from his own. Only in the last two years he began to feel at home with its pliant and simple words. All students of it found the same thing: it was not the difficulty but the unfamiliar simplicity of the new language that troubled them. Their own books were written in a manner which had no connection with their daily speech. It was only by degrees that writers arose who struggled for a reform of the written language. Once Yoshio was familiar with English, he learned French without much difficulty, for it seemed to him that it was almost the same language.

The door of a new world of books was now opened. Shakespeare, Tennyson, Browning. Walt Whitman, Shakespeare, Shakespeare, Shakespeare. At sixteen he discovered Tolstoy and Dostoevsky in clumsy, Japanese translations. He swam in Russian melancholy for a time. He copied out a few poems on thin gold paper and pasted them up on the wall of his bedroom, poems in Japanese, Chinese and English:

> Halting before my mirror, when
> My own reflection I behold
> It is like meeting with an old
> And unknown gentleman.

And this one which he loved the most:

> Of twenty thousand warriors, life and sword and shield,
> Nought hath remained but the summer grass
> Growing over the old battlefield.

And Li Tai Po, who sang twelve hundred years ago:

> The fields are chill; the sparse rain has stopped;
> The colors of spring teem on every side.
> With leaping fish the blue pond is full;
> The flowers of the field have dabbled their powdered cheeks;
> The mountain grasses are bent level at the waist.
> By the bamboo stream the last fragment of cloud
> Blown by the wind slowly scatters away.

Yoshio felt proud to the depths of his being that Asia had made such poems at a time when England was a wild and barbarous island

and America an undiscovered continent in undiscovered oceans. Nevertheless this too was beautiful, and he pinned the poem up beside the others on the wall:

> In the swamp in secluded recess,
> A shy and hidden bird is warbling a song.
> Solitary the thrush,
> The hermit withdrawn to himself, avoiding the settlements,
> Sings to himself a song.
> Song of the bleeding throat,
> Death's outlet, song of life (for well, dear brother, I know
> If thou wert not granted to sing thou wouldst surely die).

Just before he entered his seventeenth year, he and a few of his school friends visited Yoshiwara, the love market of the city, lane after lane, house after house. One dressed for such expeditions in the old style, wearing a dark kimono and leaving one's wooden sandals on the step outside the house. A laughing god of happiness with fat, naked belly, stood in the entrance beside a beautifully formed dwarf pine. Dignity and decency prevailed here, too. The girls were painted white down to the neck, gaily dressed and well mannered. Although they were only poor farmers' daughters they tried to behave like elegant geishas. They twittered and laughed, quoted little sentimental ditties, paid compliments and told jokes. Yoshio drank more rice wine than he could carry, for he was a little afraid of the girls, particularly when they slipped out of their garments and offered him their smooth childish bodies. Next morning he did not feel very well. It never came out whether his father heard anything of this expedition. But soon afterwards he took Yoshio with him to a banquet given for business friends who were passing through, and here the boy met the geisha Aki Hanako, who encouraged him to see her again. Only many years later he realized that his father had arranged this encouragement and paid for it. Aki was a charming and experienced woman about thirty years of age. After she had met Yoshio a few times in a teahouse and talked to him and danced and sung for him, she condescended to initiate him into the rituals of love. As he was only a schoolboy, even though the son of a rich father, many of her subtleties were lost upon him. Yet he was very much in love with Aki Hanako-san for some weeks and visited her whenever she allowed him to. But once when he met her in the theater, where the most beautiful geishas of the town in their smartest kimonos were kneeling in the matted boxes, she behaved as though she had never seen him before, and he felt hurt and ashamed.

The theater took complete possession of him at this time, as books had earlier. He pasted up the photographs and arms of his favorite actors on his wall beside the poems; he had to choke back his sobs, while the tears he could not keep back poured down his cheeks, when it came to the great *seppuku* scene in the classical drama *Chusingura*. He reeled out of the theater, intoxicated with romantic enthusiasm for the heroic death of self-evisceration. But above all he loved a certain Kenzo Arai, who represented the seventh generation of his actor family and played young girls with such wit and grace that Yoshio was enchanted whenever he saw him.

During these years when Yoshio was growing into manhood he drew nearer to his father, who up to now had seemed to him only a loud-spoken, dominating visitor in the house. It was now a standing joke between them to converse in English. Toson Murata could still recall a few fragments from his days in San Francisco. "How are you?" "Yes, yes, excuse me," he would say by way of greeting, and Yoshio made a polite and delighted reply. He often visited the libraries and spent a great deal of his time at the well-stocked book counters of the new American-style department stores. The poorer students stood there in rows and read the expensive books which the store put at the disposal of those who could not afford to buy them; long rows of students with eyeglasses, book addicts and greedy readers, as Yoshio was. He had now discovered Proust, Wedekind, Oscar Wilde. . . .

Unwillingly he took part in the sports insisted on at school. Toson Murata observed his son's poor posture, his aimless gesticulations. One day he took him to the best judo master in town. He himself was an excellent fencer and rather proud of it. He had a fencing instructor for the young hands in his factory and had them taught wrestling and judo also. When a festive competition took place in the large hall of the factory, he loved to challenge a sturdy young champion and beat him. He was in radiant spirits for days after one of these matches.

At three in the morning Yoshio had to get up in the dark house, to go off with an empty stomach to the judo school. It was quiet in the cloakroom where the boys put on the regulation white trousers and jackets. Yoshio fastened his beginner's black belt and went into the hall. His bare feet were cold and numb. The place was very large and emanated composure and self-discipline. Before and after each fight there was a strict ritual of greeting and thanks. The fight itself obeyed strict rules. At first Yoshio suffered from the fear that overcame him on all occasions and which he was not allowed ever to confess to anyone, not even to his mother, not even to himself. But as the art of judo gave the weak power to defeat the strong, he soon grew to like it. He became an enthusiast, a fanatic, and at last won the privilege of wearing the red belt, which only the best fighters might wear. It was the only counterpoise to the bookish life he led. His education also included expeditions with his class to the celebrated temples and palaces of his country, and they filled him with pride and admiration for Dai Nippon. Such were the influences that formed the young Japanese and made him exactly like all the other young Japanese. Of delicate taste and a ticklish sense of honor. Uncertain and diffident of themselves and therefore proud to the verge of hysteria in face of the outer world. So tied and bound by a thousand laws and conventions that no room was left for individuality.

Everything was predetermined and laid down: in character, way of life, relation to parents and friends and to the divine Emperor. In the manner of greeting, thanking; in bearing and in movement. The cloth in which he wrapped his schoolbooks might only be knotted in a certain, fixed way. A present had to be tied up in such and such a manner and acknowledged in such and such a way. You looked at the moon at a certain day in autumn but not in spring. The color of the kimono was prescribed according to age and the month of the year. The way a geisha dressed her hair was unalterable. A geisha's servantmaid had to wear a red handkerchief in her obi. The ox had a blue and the cow a red bridle. Even the man who committed hara-kiri was not permitted to fall sideways: the dying man was bound by rule to fall on his face. Hundreds and thousands of such regulations ruled Yoshio's life and everyone else's life, so that at last it became like a game in which only certain moves were allowed which everyone knew and waited for.

Soon after Yoshio Murata entered Waseda University, the great earthquake took place.

His father had taken him that day to the factory to attend the ceremonious distribution of prizes to the workers who had done the best work. Toson Murata, in spite of his passion for progress, conducted his cotton mill on good old feudal lines. He was the father of his workers as the Emperor was the father of all Japanese. He hired the half-grown children of the poor on long-term agreements, and they lived, ate, slept and passed their days in specially built houses on the factory premises. They had no liberty whatever, they worked hard and were poorly paid. Nevertheless they were contented and attached to the factory as students to their university. Their sleeping quarters were spotless, the floors were laid with matting and they got better food than their parents could give them. The girls saved small dowries, the boys became good skilled workers. They got on, and the most talented were put into the technical department, where engineers were employed in improving the plant. There were lectures, there was a small shrine for the pious young people, who came from the country, and reverence was paid daily to the Emperor and the gods. Toson Murata was honored by his workers as an immensely rich and benevolent father, and if anyone had told him or them that he exploited them, both he and they would have laughed outright. They were in fact well looked after and protected from the insecurity and the ups and downs of general economic conditions. After the World War Japan had a critical time. The other countries restricted Japanese exports to the utmost of their power. By high tariffs and in every possible way they endeavored to squeeze out the competition of cheap Japanese goods. Unemployment and destitution would have swept through the country but for men like Toson Murata who kept their workers going and took the burden of the hard times on their own shoulders. Neither his employees

nor his family knew anything of his acute anxieties, the disappoint-
ments he had suffered and the desperate efforts he had made during
the last two years. Smiling and gigantic, he sat in the seat of honor,
as the men in their clean short coats and the girls in their light gray,
red-patterned kimonos, all with the Murata fern crest on their backs,
filed into the hall.

The niche behind him on the dais displayed the vase of flowers
and the kakemono. Yoshio sat beside him together with the brothers-
in-law and a few guests of honor and a representative of the government. The hall was large, a two-hundred-mat hall, and all round it
were hung banners inscribed with edifying mottoes. The workpeople
were drawn up in ranks, the men on the right with the oldest hands
in front, the girls on the left, expectant smiles on their good flat
faces. Toson Murata stood up and made them three low bows with
his hands on his knees: "Honorable workers," he addressed them,
and his deep, rich voice reached the farthest corner of the hall.

It was in the middle of his speech that the earthquake began. The
hall swayed, shook spasmodically and reared up; the flower vase fell
over and broke, the paper inscriptions fell rustling from the walls.
Some of the workpeople screamed, others were mute as stone, and
all surged towards Toson Murata as though they looked to him for
protection. A tremendous subterranean roar like a deep roll of thunder drowned the noise and confused tumult. Toson Murata just had
time to bow to his guests in imperturbable politeness and to murmur
excuses before the walls caved in. The human beings there were like
tiny insects on the hide of a gigantic beast which tried to shake them
off. Yoshio never knew how he survived the crash of the building,
whether he lost consciousness for some minutes or whether it was
his father who had dragged or carried him into the open.

For days a pall of smoke and fire hung over the city, and at night
the sky was a dark, lurid red. Weeping children looked for their
parents, and half-naked women dragged their goods and chattels
through the flaming streets. Ghastly rumors spread abroad, bands
robbed and plundered, and as no one would believe that Japanese
were capable of such crimes the blame was put on the Koreans. In-

numerable people perished in the burning ruins of their homes, and the danger of famine hung over the town, as the neighboring villages too and the port of Yokohama were destroyed. After a few weeks order was restored, however, and the people began quietly and patiently to build up their town again with the industry of ants. Their hard life on those pitiless islands had bequeathed to them an age-old inheritance of tough resignation and endurance of suffering. Many farseeing people—and Toson Murata was one of them—were secretly delighted at the destruction of many unsightly and antiquated quarters of the town; a new, enlarged and modern Tokyo sprang up, and the building of it gave a tremendous impulse to industries which had been stagnant. Many habits and customs were swallowed up in the earthquake together with the old quarters of the town, and life was never the same afterwards.

The earthquake did not cause the death of anyone in Yoshio's family; on the contrary it presented him with a new brother, called Kitaro, like his famous forefather.

Kitaro's mother, Sumi, had perished in the earthquake. She had previously been a celebrated geisha, whom Toson Murata had often engaged when he had guests whom he particularly wished to honor and entertain with charm and taste. So it came about that he often saw this beautiful, decorative and educated woman; sometimes had had to take her into his confidence, when the object of one of these banquets was to put through an advantageous business deal. As often happened with men of his age and class, he fell in love with the geisha; he got so used to her that he could no longer bear the thought of her being at anyone's disposal. He bought her a little house in the Tsukiji district and established her there as his concubine. It was a secret hidden from nobody, probably not even from Yoshio's mother. Yoshio himself had often heard whispers about it, and although he loved his mother and was greatly attached to her, it seemed to him quite right and natural that his father, who was so large and hearty, should have something more from life than his work in the factory and his quiet home. But the cozy little street had gone up in flames; the delicate woodwork of its houses, the paper windows and sliding doors were all burned, and many of the charming little women dwelling there were dead. Here and there a stone lantern, or a bronze crane rose from the wreckage over which the charred trees extended mournful branches.

Kitaro was seven years old when Toson brought him home to his wife to be adopted. A strong and remarkably beautiful child, who seemed to have inherited all the strength of his father. He had a round face, beautiful eyebrows, delicate nostrils and full lips with rounded corners, like a childish Buddha. Momotaro, Yoshio thought, when he saw him for the first time. To Yoshio there remained always some glamour about this young brother, the child of the geisha, the dead mistress. Kitaro was an amiable, well-mannered creature, and as soon as his grief passed he radiated light and laughter through the house.

One day Toson Murata's hair was gray; although he had never been a great student or scholar, he now bought himself a pair of horn-rimmed spectacles. He sat at home in the evenings, talking to his two sons, and the way he looked to his wife for comfort and consolation for the loss of his mistress was almost childlike. Yoshio's mother had taken to Kitaro at once, and they all did their best to spoil the lovely child. Only the old Baaya grumbled sometimes, for she had carried Yoshio's mother on her back and was jealous on her mistress's account of the geisha's child.

Yoshio studied national economy at the Waseda University at his father's wish, but he did not on that account give up his favorite studies, literature and philosophy. Of learning there was no end. Spencer, Kant, Schopenhauer; Goethe, Thackeray, Maupassant; Bergson, Valéry, André Gide, Nishida, Emerson, Nietzsche; foreign politics, Lao Tse, Li Tai Po; accounting and statistics, Buddhism and Christianity, Renan, exports and imports—all these rushed in upon Yoshio, lodged themselves in his head and left him little time for sleep. The lenses of his eyeglasses had to be strengthened every few months, since his eyes grew more and more shortsighted. This was a great advantage, for it helped him to get out of military service. The government had attempted to introduce military training into the university, but the liberal-minded students went on strike and after a time the order was rescinded.

Waseda was for liberty and progress; even clumsy translations of the writings of Trotsky were passed from hand to hand. A few Chinese students, quiet, polite, thin young men, though looked at askance owing to their backwardness, nevertheless introduced Communistic ideas, which were eagerly discussed in the cheap little eating shops in the neighborhood of the university. A bohemian poverty and unkemptness were the fashion with the young, and sons of wealthy fathers, such as Yoshio, were ashamed of their origin. He went about in worn-out clothes in order to escape notice.

At home Yoshio now shared his eight-mat room with Kitaro. They bathed together before dinner, and when Yoshio sat up over his books the regular breathing of the sleeping boy was a peaceful accompaniment to his thoughts. When in a vivid dream, his young brother kicked off his coverings, he carefully covered him up again. When awake, Kitaro was full of pranks and boyish secrets. Sometimes he told about his grandparents, hard-working but poor farmers who in a year of locusts had had to sell their daughters. He had made a sort of ancestor shrine for himself in a corner of the room to honor the photograph of his beautiful mother, and made his reverences before it. He was a storehouse of poems and little geisha songs and memories Yoshio could not share. Sometimes his little brother seemed to him older and stronger and more confident than he was himself. When the boy fell sick, Yoshio was greatly distressed; in order to distract him he brought their grandfather's two samurai swords to him in bed. The sight of them excited Kitaro so much that his temperature went up. From then onwards Kitaro's education presented no difficulties as long as he was allowed to have the two swords to play with for half an hour.

When he was twelve years old he entered the Imperial Military Academy. It had been the dead geisha's wish that her son should become an officer. Toson fulfilled his dead love's wish now which he had refused her while she lived. He had grown old and soft and presented altogether the sad spectacle of a toothless lion. He became dependent on his wife. And for Yoshio's mother all the little pains he complained of were a delight. She tended him and warmed him and made him poultices and boiled herbs for him and counted drops.

Conscientiously she administered all the medicines the doctor prescribed and to be on the safe side mixed in the charred and
powdered bones of animals, by whose efficacy the Baaya swore.

Yoshio was preparing with smarting eyes for the ordeal of his final
examination. The room was empty and silent; Kitaro had vanished
and appeared only on rare feast days in a blue cadet's uniform, shining with the polish of discipline and drill.

The first time Yoshio slept in a bed such as foreigners affected was
on the ship which took him to America after he had got through
his examination. He had a bad night, high above the familiar floor
and covered by a quilt which continually slipped off and fell down.
It was a Japanese boat equipped in the foreign style, and the passengers were a mixed company of Japanese, Chinese and Americans
with a sprinkling of Germans, Siamese and Koreans. Each nationality kept to itself, for each had some grudge against the others. Yoshio
shared his cabin with a man who announced that he owned a business in Dallas, Texas. "I am an American citizen," he announced on
all occasions, and as he said it his Japanese face contracted in a
network of fine wrinkles. He had a Japanese wife and four children
in Dallas, Texas, and they raised and sold flowers. He had bad manners, sucked in his breath in his middle-class politeness, and spoke the
worst and most corrupt Japanese Yoshio had ever heard. It deeply
grieved him that the reputation of Japan in America should suffer
from such a common and uneducated man. The law that forbade
Japanese immigration into America was an open, smarting wound
in the self-esteem of every Japanese. When it was enacted, a man,
who remained anonymous, had committed hara-kiri in front of the
American embassy in Tokyo out of wounded honor and in order to
draw the attention of the foreigners in the manner of his country to
the mistake they had made. The sight of his vulgar cabin mate
convinced Yoshio that he too could not tolerate it if foreigners,
whether individuals or nations, got a bad impression of his country.

At the customs examination in San Francisco it was borne in upon
him that he did not understand a single word that the official addressed to him. For fourteen years he had studied English, a poem
by Walt Whitman was pasted up on the wall of his bedroom at

home, and yet he did not understand the customs officer. It was his first painful and humiliating disillusionment on foreign soil. There he was, in America: Yoshio Murata, a serious, smiling little Japanese, a lover of literature who could compose poems of seventeen and of thirty-one syllables, a bewildered philosopher in spectacles, armed with a camera. He knew the statistics of the trade balance between Japan and America by heart, and he could quote Spencer by the page, which was more, probably, than the customs officer could do. But that was no help to him. None of the rules by which he had zealously and studiously lived so far counted for anything outside Japan. His first days were beset by unexpected difficulties and struggles with insignificant and obstructive objects. Doors opened the wrong way, keys turned in the wrong direction, windows would not open, and when he had got them open, would not shut again. Elevators did not rise sedately as in Japan, but shot up so fast that he felt as if his stomach were still at the fourth floor when he was already emerging on the twelfth. When he embarked upon his polite and elaborately prepared remarks, he saw on every face the same look of smiling and indulgent impatience. The hurry people were in was incomprehensible, and Yoshio soon discovered that for all their hurrying nothing of importance awaited them. At bottom they were lazier and slower than the Japanese and only made a show of a constant and feverish activity. What surprised him most was their amiability and good temper and the ready helpfulness which everyone put at his disposal.

They all behaved as though they were devoted and dyed-in-the-wool followers of Confucius. For a time Yoshio put this unusual benevolence down to Christianity, but then he found that religion played no larger part in America than in Japan. The women of the middle classes and the farmers' wives and daughters went to church, as in Japan they went to the shrines of Buddha and the Shinto gods. Everybody wore a witty little mask and talked clipped, smart phrases as though afraid of being silent or in earnest. Yoshio had letters of introduction to many businessmen with whom his father had business relations, for the cotton which he manufactured in Tokyo came from the United States.

Yoshio was not one of those who went on pilgrimage to America as to the Promised Land, who expected miracles of perfection and achievement and for whom the West held the promise of a new birth. But though he had not expected much he was haunted by a sense of disappointment. Houses, machinery, newspapers and streets were really much the same as at home. The youth of Japan was familiar with movies, drugstores and soda fountains, with clubs and libraries; even jazz night clubs with hostesses and entertainers had recently been introduced in Tokyo. Japan had so carefully imitated the West that there were no surprises left.

Yoshio was most struck by the mechanization of labor. There was no handicraft in America, only mass production. He longed for the little shops of the potters, weavers and lacquer workers, the armorers and lantern makers. At first he found it difficult to distinguish one person from another, for they all looked alike; their legs were too long, their heads too small, their eyes too staring. But after a few months he got used to the American physiognomy, and now he could detect finer shades of difference than Americans could themselves. His slant eyes took in more than theirs did. Accustomed as all Orientals are to using their eyes, he soon collided with the ugliness of the Western world. Japan, his native land, now that it was far away, grew clearer and more beautiful every day. Even the moon did not look the same as at home, even the flowers. What chiefly shocked Yoshio was the freedom and impudence of the women. Sometimes he exchanged a fleeting look of scorn with other Japanese when he observed how the women domineered over the men. Literature had somehow given a false idea of what passed for love there. The women were shrill, ill mannered and almost repulsive in their emancipation; so at least it seemed to this young Japanese. "The servant girl of a poor whore in Yoshiwara has more delicacy than women of society have here," he confided to a Japanese friend, who merely shrugged his shoulders, for he had friends among the American girls. By degrees Yoshio got used to the quick and witty battles between the sexes, the smart repartee, the lunge and parry; when he saw an American girl cry for the first time—one of those hard and loud-spoken creatures in distress—he was helpless with pity and astonishment. In Japan women smiled if they were hurt.

He stayed in the States for over a year, but to the end he was revolted by the utter lack of reserve and the way they all blabbed out their inmost secrets to the first comer. And it was a painful and incurable wound to his pride when he realized that the Americans never regarded him as one of themselves. There were restaurants, and they were in the majority, to which a man of his race was not admitted; and there were glances and little, almost unconscious gestures which quivered in his sensibility like poisoned arrows and left a festering price. Why was it? He puzzled over it by himself and often discussed it with his Japanese friends. "Why do they not accept us? We are of an older, finer race; our emperors are descended from the gods" (for no exercise of his educated, critical faculties could eradicate this belief), "our implements and houses are simple and dignified, our behavior is better, we are cleaner and better cared for than many of them are; we get more done, and though they had the start of us by centuries we have overtaken them in a few years. What proof have they of their superiority?"

"Guns," his friend answered. "Warships, poison gas, bombs."

"We have them too," Yoshio said unhappily. He was no friend of the militarists at home, and it annoyed him that their arguments sounded convincing in America. He loved peace, both by nature and conviction. He thought of the poem on the wall of his room:

> Of twenty thousand warriors, life and sword and shield,
> Nought hath remained but the summer grass
> Growing over the old battlefield.

He left the West and traveled for a time through the Southern States, and to please his father he inspected the cotton plantations there, although he had made up his mind not to go into the Murata cotton mills. He went to the East and struck thin but tenacious roots in the asphalt of New York, which seemed to him the very navel of the world. He went to the New England States and visited cotton mills which were antiquated compared with his father's; he had a look at Vermont, where America was at its oldest and most genuine, with its farms, meadows, trees, and Maine, with its lakes and its sea coast and sea winds.

In mortal dread he started on an affair with one of the dancers at a night club in Harlem. She treated him as if he were a funny little doll. She was quite young, and her limbs were extraordinarily flexible and her skin was fairer than his own. Nevertheless she was a Negress. She was exuberant and unbridled to a degree that alarmed him, and although the longing for her haunted him for a whole week he drew back in fright.

He made the acquaintance in a Japanese restaurant of a certain Mr Isamu Ikeda, who was correspondent of one of the big newspapers in Tokyo. Ikeda did his best to be American, but the Japanese in him always cropped out: in quotations of a poem of the eighth century, in the way he treated his Mexican wife, and in the bold sweep of his calligraphy. When Ikeda went down with pneumonia Yoshio wrote two of his articles for him. Wrote them in the sweat of his brow and with great delight and henceforward he called himself a journalist. By way of thanks Ikeda did in fact put him in touch with a small monthly review of modern tendencies, published in Osaka. Yoshio, who had so far eddied about uncertainly like a kite with a broken string, now got some sort of direction.

He felt restless and uncertain of himself, as all people must who fall between two different civilizations. He did not rule his life, he was ruled by it. He knew neither want nor cares. He was no fighter for progress like his father and no keeper of the past like his grandfather. He had no religion, for Buddhism was too antiquated and fossilized, Shintoism too vague and primitive, and Christianity, to which he adhered in name, though it had some freshness and novelty, was too humdrum and limited to appeal to him. He had no fixed aim, no ideal to inspire him, no views for the future. He was the outcome of a disillusioned age and of a country in transition.

He was proud of Japan and considered it the finest, noblest, most beautiful, most lovable country in the world. But everyone he knew thought the same of his own country. Everywhere there were mountains and valleys, forests and meadows, towns and highways, houses and gardens and the same human beings. The nationalistic arrogance in which he had been reared wore off the more he saw of the world. As a state, America took an uncompromising, almost hostile attitude toward Japan, and the papers uttered warnings and war cries every morning; he could not understand how it was that at the same time individual Americans treated him, an individual Japanese, with kindness and friendliness. Unconsciously he was penetrated by the foreign atmosphere, with the Okays and whisky-sodas and the universal handshaking in place of the polite and distant bow.

"All the people here seem to be obsessed with the idea that time passes, whereas it is they who pass and time goes on," he wrote to his brother Kitaro. Kitaro replied with an old Buddhist saying: The life of man is like morning frost on the roof and like a candle flame in the wind.

He left America in a new and ill-fitting suit. Another boat, another arrival: Europe. France was easier to understand because it was old and had a past; not a past of thousands of years, like Japan; only a brief and recent past, which all the same lent a little dignity to things. Maupassant and Gide had given Yoshio some idea of Paris, which now proved out of date. New York had accustomed him to the appearance of Western women; now he discovered their beauty. Oddly, it was the paintings of Renoir that first initiated him into the beauty of their white and rosy flesh, and he began to feel a faint tremor of curiosity about them. Some other Japanese introduced him to a girl, Jelena Trubova, who pretended to be a Russian princess; but Yoshio's quick though shortsighted eyes detected signs of poverty and shoddiness in her. She talked French to him, although she had picked up a smattering of Japanese from his predecessors. Jelena was more or less a permanent feature of the little Japanese colony, and her first friend, a Prince Hayashi, had broken her in to the ways of his fellow countrymen.

It was Yoshio's first affair with a white woman, and it was destined to be his last. His pride and self-esteem were flattered when he found that Jelena seemed pleased with him and his caresses. When he held her in his arms it was not only a woman but the whole wide world of foreign arrogance that he embraced. Soon he became so ac-customed to her white skin, her dark red hair, and her blue-green eyes that the dark-haired Japanese girl students, polite and anarchistic, who belonged to their circle and met in a little café near the Place Vendôme, no longer pleased him. He sat in the chaise longue in his furnished lodgings and watched her as she moved about the room. When she was at a distance from his shortsighted eyes she became a lovely cloud in motion. When she came nearer her scent and warmth were like a breeze in summer. Yoshio had secretly begun composing poems again, little poems of seventeen syllables. He tried in his mind to get the syllables into the prescribed measure, five, seven, five.

> The hand of my friend
> Warms and cools like summer's breeze
> From Fujiyama.

"If we could get a few mushrooms I could make a mushroom omelette, with sour cream, Russian, you know, *chéri,* and then we could dine at home," Jelena said, interrupting his thoughts. She was making up in the little mirror he had hung up for her. "You are perfect, Jelena-san," Yoshio said, and at that moment he believed it. Jelena was not only beautiful and charmingly unhysterical: she was also practical. She was careful with his monthly allowance, which had fallen off since the Depression; she bought things for him, saw to his wants, cooked dainty little meals. She counted his linen when it came back from the laundress, kept his ties in order. She went with him to a tailor, and for the first time Yoshio had a well-fitting European suit. He felt more self-confident in it and became almost vain, for Japanese were considered interesting in Paris. He could discuss politics, plays, books and picture exhibitions with Jelena. She was nearly as well educated as the elegant geishas of his native land, and he felt at ease and happy in her company. She read French poetry aloud to him, Verlaine, Maeterlinck, Rimbaud. "Le Dormeur du val."
. . . *Les parfums ne font pas frissoner sa narine; il dort dans le soleil, la main sur sa poitrine tranquille.* . . . Since she had taste it was a pleasure to give her beautiful things. He wrote to his mother and asked her to send him an old brocade robe such as the ladies of the Imperial Court of Kyoto had worn. As he was a Japanese his amorousness was as much for the beauty of the dress as for the

woman within it, and the day on which Jelena put on the stiff, light green kimono embroidered with silver thread was the apogee of his love.

They made little trips together, to Brittany and Normandy. Yoshio felt happy and well cared for and even protected because he was in the company of this beautiful, amiable and white-skinned woman. He learned that peasants are the same all the world over. "There is less difference between a Japanese and a European peasant than between a Japanese peasant and a Japanese bank manager," he wrote in an article for his magazine. "America has farmers who do their work with machinery and drive to the movies in cars, but no real peasants. Perhaps that is the reason of the strange desolation of the States, a vacancy that makes even the most beautiful landscape meaningless." In France his eyes found pleasure again in the things they saw. Poplars along the roads, old trees in the squares of country towns, crooked streets—he loved it all and felt at home. The moist, rainy atmosphere of Paris brought out tints and colors, each of which Yoshio could describe in his own language, even though European languages were too coarse to give them their due.

He left Jelena with feelings of gratitude and regret which it was not allowed him to show. In his rather stiff hand he wrote on a scroll for her the old proverb:

Meeting is the beginning of parting.

She laughed when he put all his tips in little narrow envelopes, according to the Japanese custom. For the last time she took off his spectacles in the gently humoristic way he had loved, became a blurred cloud and gave him a parting kiss on the platform of the station, in front of all the people there. Yoshio was so much ashamed and vexed by the scandal of it that it helped him to get through the parting. It was not until he was deprived of Jelena that he knew how much she had meant to him.

Italy bored him by its superlatives. The sky was too blue, the cypresses too picturesque, the statues too large, the pictures too perfect, the Raphaels too beautiful. They cannot keep anything back, he thought in amusement as he looked at the Tintorettos in the Palace of the Doges in Venice and their barbaric riot of colors and figures. Oh, for a bamboo branch by Yosetsu! he thought longingly. The discipline and cleanliness imposed by Mussolini did not seem to suit the taste of the inhabitants and made him laugh. His was a country where the same word meant clean and beautiful: *kirei*.

He went to Germany. Many things seemed like at home. The cleanliness, the seriousness, the thoroughness with which they went about everything, the respect for handicrafts, the search for simple lines, the poverty and frugality of the land and the people. He even found the way political murders were taken for granted very Japanese. "Only Germans, from whom we have learned so much, are as unpopular throughout the world as we are. Do industry and thoroughness make for unpopularity?" he innocently asked in a letter to his father. "Or is the world afraid of the capable?"

There was a Chinese restaurant in Berlin next door to a Japanese one, in Kantstrasse. There had always been strained relations between the students who patronized them. When news of the outbreak of hostilities in Manchuria was published, they came to blows. Yoshio felt his childhood's fear of physical encounter; but honor demanded, as it had then, that he should play his part. He seized a great, heavy Chinese and threw him down on to the street with a judo grip. The man knew nothing of judo and so he fell clumsily and bruised his head. The police arrived on the scene, and Yoshio spent the night under arrest. His consul intervened and he was released. Just as Berlin was ceasing to please him, a cable arrived from his mother. She begged him to come home instantly as his father was sick. There was nobody and nothing to bid farewell to, so he left at once for Moscow to board the Trans-Siberian train. He stayed four days in Moscow and cautiously sniffed that city's dry and bitter air. He saw with a certain satisfaction, the poverty, the dirt, the hunger and lack of freedom there; he had disavowed his brief flirtation with Communism ever since its adherents in his own country had been persecuted. He was slightly appalled by the crude outspokenness of the anti-Japanese posters which had shouted at him from the moment he crossed the frontier. He caught a chill driving in one of the few open droshkies, and the rest of the journey, with all its interruptions and difficulties, was drowned by a high fever. Mukden was already occupied by his countrymen, and the South Manchurian railway was under fire. The train waited for hour after hour in tiny Siberian stations; there were weak tea and sour pickles, food became scarce, the heating failed, the Siberian autumn gave way to an early winter, and still Yoshio traveled on and on. His mother was waiting, his father was sick. He decided to proceed by way of Peking and Tientsin. The North of China looked impoverished and sleepily hostile. He still had a temperature; he scratched the bites he had got from bedbugs in the train and spent the hours half asleep and half awake.

He looked out of the window of the train. A mild autumn sun was shining, and the train arrived punctually at each station; he saw two schoolgirls, each carrying a tiny brother on her back, and each bowed to the other with great earnestness and dignity. Then Yoshio knew that he was back in Japan.

A slim officer was there to meet him in Tokyo station: in order to avoid being welcomed by a crowd of friends and relations, he had informed Kitaro alone of the time of his arrival. Yoshio, still rather weak from fever, was moved to tears of joy at seeing his brother again. Kitaro too, in spite of his smart uniform, was not ashamed to weep.

The square in front of the station had a look of Berlin, since the younger architects had caught the style of flat roofs and horizontal lines from Germany. Small women in bright kimonos hurried across the square among automobiles and trams, their knees pressed together and pigeon-toed in order not to lose their wooden getas. No, Tokyo was not the most beautiful city in the world, as Yoshio had often thought in his homesickness and his longing to see it again; nor was it the cleanest. It was a metropolis like any other, with stores, advertisements, traffic policemen, traffic jams, newspaper boys, dust and all the crass ugliness of the twentieth century. Most people went about with strange, black masks or rather muzzles tightly fixed in front of their mouths by means of straps fastened behind their ears. It looked ridiculous and horrible. "In case of infection—there is a lot of influenza about," Kitaro told him. Yoshio marveled at his countrymen's ingenious faith in nosebags. He marveled at the men he saw in European clothes but on high clogs owing to the rain that was beginning to fall, and at others who wore large cowboy hats with kimonos. He laughed at the hosts of oiled-paper umbrellas, which reminded him of a woodcut of Hiroshige. Girls in kimonos, powdered and painted so that their faces were as stiff and immobile as those of dolls. Women in Western dresses, all rather ugly with short, thick and rather bandy legs. The memory of Jelena came over him very forcefully.

Suddenly Kitaro laughed aloud and pointed with his finger. Yoshio looked through the window and saw a foreigner standing on the edge of the sidewalk, wearing Japanese dress. He stood there in all innocence, clad in a nightgown which he presumably took to be a kimono. To top it he had folded this suban the wrong way, befitting only to a corpse. "A foreign corpse in a nightshirt," Yoshio said, deeply amused and at once he was reconciled to the solecisms of his fellow countrymen. But Kitaro had stopped laughing and his face, as round as ever, wore an expression of hatred and exasperation which alarmed Yoshio. Meanwhile they had reached the fashionable part of the town and were being driven along the wall of the Imperial Palace, whose pines and wide moat were veiled in rain, and now they turned into the quieter quarter where his parents lived.

On the way Kitaro had told him briefly about his father's sickness and the operation he had undergone. The struggle against the trade depression of the last two years had taken much of Toson Murata's strength, and finally he had collapsed in great pain. Now that his gall bladder had been removed and he was out of danger, the doctors had allowed him to be taken home, and he was awaiting the arrival of his elder son with great impatience. The maple in front of the house was flaming red with Japanese November. The Baaya was kneeling on the wooden steps at the entrance, white-haired, brown-faced and wrinkled, and she murmured the formula of welcome as she took off Yoshio's shoes for him. Kitaro hesitated at the sliding door of their parents' bedroom and looked at Yoshio in questioning reproach. It was only when the young officer went down on his hands and knees before approaching his sick father that Yoshio remembered the act of reverence expected of him. The Baaya slid the door aside. His father raised his head from the padded head-rest;

his hair was white, he was a giant no longer, and as he smiled politely two tears rolled down the furrows of his face. A small gray-haired old lady, Yoshio's mother, knelt and laid her hand on his arm.

Yoshio found Japan in a fever of preparation for some danger, of armament, of readiness to fight, of nationalism and enjoying a new and hard-won prosperity. He felt with pride that his country was sound compared with the ailing nations of Europe. He had long talks with Kitaro, and he could not look at his young brother without a glow of happiness and joy. Now that Kitaro had got his promotion as lieutenant he slept at home again in their mutual room. He was a fanatical champion of the movement which aimed at bringing back the spirit and life of old Japan. He belonged to secret and public societies, blood brotherhoods which received their ideas and orders from an old and highly revered master and disseminated them through the army. Yoshio smiled at his brother's enthusiasm. It was, at bottom, Bushido, the law of the samurai, and its devotion to courage, loyalty and self-sacrifice, outrightness, sparse living and contempt for money. In new Japan it was called the war against and the contempt for capital and the capitalists. By an odd change of front the young were reactionaries and the old progressives, and the bitterest enemies of Communism were the most thoroughgoing opponents of capitalism. His father laughed at Kitaro, for Toson Murata belonged to a liberal age and he wanted neither war nor isolation, but trade, peace and barter. Kitaro got up and walked excitedly up and down the room while he defended his views. His gray military socks padded softly on the lined mats. He looked much too large and impetuous for the quiet and confined room.

"We shall see to it that the Western nations don't mix themselves in the affairs of the East," he shouted threateningly. "Asia for the Asiatics and Japan over Asia! It is our duty to free millions of Asiatics in China, India, everywhere from the tragic fate which has overtaken them of being slaves of the whites. We are strong and independent, and it is for us to look after this continent."

"If America boycotts our goods we shall lose more than we could gain by any number of wars," Toson said soberly. Yoshio was proud of his warlike brother, but he was on his father's side. He loved peace and hated war, though he knew nothing of it. Kitaro sought out fresh arguments and took some notes from his pocket, for he had no head for figures.

"Take Manchuria," he cried. "Do you know how many bandits there are in Manchuria? Three hundred thousand at the very least. Chang Tsolin and his son are no better than bandits. We have saved Manchuria from Russia by two wars, and by rights it ought to have been ours after the Russo-Japanese War. What civilization there is there, is due to our money and our people. Railways, coal mines, iron mines, all constructed and run with our money. How many millions have we sunk in the three provinces, and what thanks do we get? Only rebellion, murder and enmity. We need Manchuria and its products, and if it will not trade with us in friendship, then it must be subdued with the strong hand. I can hardly wait for the day when our regiment is ordered there."

His father looked at his agitated son with an almost pitying smile as Kitaro impatiently thrust his notes back into his pocket. Yoshio held his breath; he was uneasy on his brother's account.

"Your mother would not have let you join in a war against bandits," his father said almost tenderly. It very seldom happened that he mentioned Kitaro's mother.

"My mother would have made it her prayer that I should sacrifice myself for my country and the Emperor," Kitaro cried in a blaze of enthusiasm.

The sliding door opened with a slight grating sound, the Baaya brought in the small tables for the three Muratas' supper. A pleasant odor rose from the covered lacquered dishes, peace descended on the room once more.

Japan loved old China and hated the new. Beyond the Great Wall chaos ruled; there were destitution and plague, famine and corruption, civil war and brigandage and, what Japan feared most of all, the subterranean fires of Communism. The Chinese had shown since their two revolutions that they were incapable of keeping order in the country. When the Japanese maintained that China would be better governed and happier under Japanese rule they believed it—and had good reason to. "It is true that we are in the place of the man whose neighbor's house is burning and who has the right to put out the fire," Yoshio said, concluding the excited discussion on a staid and conciliatory note. There was one point in their political arguments on which all three Muratas were agreed: Japan needed an outlet for her population, and she could not brook opposition from the despised, dirty, backward Chinese.

Yoshio often felt colorless and washed out beside his brother, who seemed to have inherited all his father's energy, while he himself had only the weakness and softness and resignation of his mother. He could feel her affection for himself in her anxiety to serve him, in the expression of her eyes and more rarely in a fleeting touch of her emaciated fingers. Yet he was jealous of Kitaro, for only Kitaro could make her laugh aloud, and there was an understanding between them about many things of which Yoshio knew nothing. His young brother never entered the room without a word or two of admiration for the flowers arranged in the niche. She smiled gratefully when he inquired after her honorable cold, when he noticed she was wearing a new, beautiful and honorable kimono, or when he brought her some trifling present tied up in the proper way with gold-and-silver string. Sometimes he even induced his mother to play the koto. The thin twanging of the large stringed instrument, at which his mother knelt in earnest concentration, was empty and almost unpleasing in Yoshio's ears. They were accustomed to the resounding clamor of European symphony orchestras and to the rhythm of American jazz. Kitaro was more his mother's son than he, even though another woman had borne him.

But in the end it was Yoshio and not Kitaro who went to the war. Yoshio was sent to Manchuria by his paper, and Kitaro's regiment remained in Tokyo. It was winter when Yoshio arrived at Chinchow, which had just been taken, a winter so cold and cruel that the troops hardly knew how to endure it. Yoshio made his first entry into the close circle of war correspondents, an international, jolly, cynical, hard-boiled, quick, knowing and boyish phalanx of unshaven men, who played cards, drank beer, knew everything, took nothing seriously, and who taught Yoshio to distinguish news from lies and how to get it off in some way or other, by field telephone, telegraph or pigeon. He went gravely and soberly about among them without grasping their jokes and smiling politely when they laughed at him. While they played their interminable poker or dashed off their hair-raising cables, he sat at his typewriter and ground out pains-taking articles. He kept close to the fighting line to see everything for himself (report of an eyewitness). There was much maneuvering and little fighting. The men were in the last stages of exhaustion after the interminable marches, and their rations were not suited to the climate. Yoshio discovered, to his profound astonishment, that Japanese soldiers were no braver than Chinese. A legend crumbled in which, ever since his schooldays, he had placed firm and implicit faith. Chinese regiments might retreat after firing a shot or two to save their faces, but it was the generals, not the soldiers, who were disinclined to fight, and the generals had probably been bought. When the Chinese fought they fought as well as their opponents, and better, since they were badly equipped and badly led.

Once Yoshio saw thirty Japanese deserters marched into camp. They said in tears that they had been unable to endure the cold any longer and in their desperation had tried to get home. They were not afraid of dying, but they had not the courage to see the campaign out. They pointed to their frostbitten, gangrenous arms and legs, their inadequate clothing, their damaged lungs, and begged to be shot. Yoshio understood their brand of heroic cowardice: it was his own. Generations of Buddhists had implanted this indifference to death in the people but at the same time had made life of so little importance that the power to cope with hardships was sadly weakened. The campaign petered out after long months but, like a drizzling rain, never quite stopped. Yoshio returned home. He had seen the stiff and swollen corpses of men and horses and inhaled the smell of abandoned battlefields. His love of peace had been theory, but his hatred of war had become a reality. And the poem of the twenty thousand warriors was still on the wall of his room, and its painted characters had not faded. Although he did not know it, the real motive which took him to Manchuria and gave him strength to go through its horrors was jealousy of Kitaro. Kitaro talked—but Yoshio had been in the war.

Yet when he came home with frost-cracked lips, with his vitality lowered by dysentery, from which he suffered for a long time after, with his newly acquired, cynical pessimism and his passion for poker, he found that his brother in uniform still cornered all the glamour and that nobody listened to his, Yoshio's tales.

He got married a few months after his return. He had become something of what in Tokyo they call a Ginbura, putting in his time on the Ginza, where the bars were a blaze of light and the pretty girls paraded. There was an element of defiance in his dissipation, and his father only smiled over it. Now and again he visited night clubs and drank the Japanese imitation of Scotch whisky and spent the rest of the night with a Japanese imitation of an American taxi dancer. He was left with a headache and a bad mouth. Once he got Kitaro to introduce him to a beautiful geisha, but the only result was immeasurable boredom and melancholy. "They will soon be as extinct as the phoenix, the king of birds," he told his brother afterwards. A visit to a geisha was no adventure but a complicated ritual. He thought once more of Jelena with painful insistence. What he needed, he knew well, was a wife. And so he hastened to declare his willingness to marry the girl his parents had found for him.

His bride-to-be was eighteen years old; her father was the proprietor of an important liberal newspaper, and it was tacitly understood that Yoshio was to be given a post on it with a view to making his way. The honorable Hideko was a Moga, a modern girl. "She plays tennis well and can ski too," Yoshio's mother remarked at every opportunity. The first meeting took place on the tennis courts, and Yoshio looked away from Hideko all the time, since it seemed to him impolite to examine her as if she were goods on approval. She was shorter than he and pretty in a sleepy and withdrawn fashion. An automobile drive and a picnic in the country and a visit to the theater together followed. Hideko too was fond of symphony concerts. She played the piano and read French books. She talked eagerly about André Gide. She was complete in every direction: she was gentle and docile, modern and yet well brought up, as familiar with the arts of arranging flowers and preparing tea as with tennis racket and skis. It was not her fault that Yoshio found her boring.

He begged her to wear the kimono again for his sake. In modern dress she made him think of Jelena, and then Hideko pleased him no longer.

At his next visit she gave him tea in the old ceremonial manner. She was wearing a blue kimono with a large modern pattern of the bright red color of Japanese sealing wax. The nape of her delicate neck was revealed in a modest triangle, and she wore a broad gray obi, embroidered with silver cranes and fastened round her slender, sexless waist with a narrow bright red sash. Yoshio could tell she was agitated by the way the cups rattled in her fingers and she spilled a few drops of water out of the ladle. Dimly his earliest memory of his samurai grandfather rose up to remind him of the calm, the dignity and secure peace of the ceremony. He felt sorry for Hideko. He felt sorry for himself. As they knelt opposite each other they shifted the weight of their bodies from one side to the other, for the unaccustomed dress and attitude fatigued them. They were both uprooted and homeless; only they did not know it. Estranged from the old Japan; uncertain and awkward in the new one. They had two wedding ceremonies: first in church, since Hideko too was a Christian, and afterwards in the house of Yoshio's parents, where according to ancient ceremony they drank a bowl of rice wine together. Then they settled down in one of the new apartment houses in the center of the town. Bathroom, chromium furniture, phonograph, cocktails—and the flower vase with the classic arrangement of flowers in the niche before the beautiful old kakemonos. Yoshio was paid eighty yen a month, and as his father and Hideko's each gave them an allowance they were comfortably off. It appeared that Hideko's curiosity had been vividly excited over the indecent American habit of kissing, which had recently been censored and suppressed in foreign movies. Her awkward submission and desire to please were comfortable but without appeal. After a short time their married life was as monotonous as rain on a roof. Tennis in summer, skiing in winter, sometimes an evening among the throngs and shrill noises of Kamakura beach. Tickets for the symphony concerts, an occasional game of poker with other journalists. Yoshio was bored. Sometimes he felt great pity for Hideko, who did everything possible to make his life pleasant. It was as though his brief episode with Jelena had spoiled him for Japanese women. He threw himself wholeheartedly into his work, but he made very little headway. His articles were too thorough, too literary. As his fluent knowledge of English was greatly admired, it became his task to board ships arriving at Yokohama and to interview passing celebrities. He also wrote brief reviews of English plays and lectures that were given in Tokyo. At nights he labored at his long-winded articles in the noise and clatter of the editor's office. The apprentices in the typesetting room sang out the text, while they sought about among the ten thousand types in the type cases. Yoshio wrote on. He had no wish to go home. Thus the years followed one another.

Kitaro was restless and discontented. He muttered threats against the spineless ministry and the navy's poor showing. His samurai blood seemed to goad him on, as it did many of his fellows. The secret societies among the military party gained influence. From time to time a minister was shot: it was the ancient means of drawing the attention of the unapproachable Emperor to the fact that his ministers were following the wrong policy. Young officers opened their veins and wrote letters with their own blood, in which they vowed themselves and their lives to the welfare of Japan. Steady, sensible people smiled at such dramatic parades of heroism.

During one mild September, when a blue haze hung everywhere, Kitaro invited his brother to go on a hiking trip with him to visit Kitaro's grandparents. The old people lived in the village of Kitano Mura, about ninety miles from Tokyo. In earlier days the village had been on the great highway and thus had been rich and flourishing; but the railways had plunged many of these villages into isolation and decay; many of the people left, and those who remained were poor and backward. Yoshio thought he might be able to write a good article on the villages of the old forsaken Hur Road, and he was delighted to be off with his brother and to have a change from his daily life. They took the railway for a short way, then the old highway through the hills. The air was warm and soothing, the rice was harvested, the fields were flooded with an inch or two of water to prepare the soil for the plow. Pale clouds were reflected in the gleaming expanses. Mist came over at morning and night, and the crowns of pine trees rose darkly and sharply defined above it.

Shaven-headed monks meditated in little Buddhist monasteries in the folds of the hills; lazy carp swam in sun-warmed ponds; an abbot watched the shadows of a pine branch moving to and fro on a white wall. Young girls worked in small tea fields with large white sunbonnets on their heads; they greeted the travelers with smiles and neat little bows. Sometimes they saw a simple countryman writing a proverb in the last ray of sunset with bold sweeps of the hand that held the brush. Once more Yoshio saw the world as he had in early childhood from the Baaya's back, the beautiful clouds and trees, the chirping crickets, the storytellers, the stone steps up to the Fox Temple and the dignified old people whose faces grew kindlier with every wrinkle.

The houses in the villages through which they passed were simple and well kept, and the men shaded their eyes with their hands to have a better view of the travelers. The children came from school with their books, the women stood at their semicircular hearths in the gloom of the kitchens. The firewood was neatly piled up for winter in the yard, the buffalo cows, washed twice a day, were clean and shining. Sometimes a cuckoo called from the wood, a buzzard circled high in the air, wild duck flighted in triangular formation across the evening sky. There was peace and orderliness and gravity everywhere: the soul of Japan.

It was on this journey of theirs that Kitaro stopped abruptly and asked, "Do you love this country, brother?" Yoshio said in surprise that he certainly loved it.

"Do you love it as I love it?" Kitaro insisted, and Yoshio could not help smiling at his eagerness.

"I don't know how you love it," he replied, "but I have been deeply conscious every moment ever since we set out how beautiful our country is and how much it means to me."

"Yes—but do you love it enough to die for it?" Kitaro asked a little impatiently. It was a strange question.

"Of course," was all Yoshio replied.

Kitaro walked silently on, lost in reflection. Yoshio looked at him out of the corner of his eye and admired, as he always did, the clear lines of Kitaro's youthful face. Kitaro walked on with bent head as he said, "Your thoughts and my thoughts are enemies." Yoshio put his hand on his shoulder to pacify him, and they went on thus for some distance. "I am no soldier, if that is what you mean," Yoshio said a little later. "And I have seen war."

Kitaro stopped again and said slowly and clearly, as if Yoshio were a child on whose mind something had to be impressed: "If I die, will you promise to carry on what I have begun?"

"Shall I sign with my blood?" Yoshio asked with a smile. His brother's earnestness seemed to him funny.

"Do you promise?" Kitaro asked, ignoring his joke.

"I promise," Yoshio said quietly. "But why should you die? You are young and healthy."

Kitaro walked on. "You have promised," he said, and he drew in a deep breath of the moist mossy smell that rose from the bed of the stream flowing beside the old road.

They arrived that evening at the house of Kitaro's grandparents, and as the sun-tanned old people knelt down to welcome them, and as they ate in the matted room of the farmhouse, and as he drank in the clean, dignified and frugal life of the forgotten village, Yoshio felt again that he was going back, back, farther back even than his own childhood, back into the times before he was born.

He was burned brown by the autumn sun, and the skin of his face was peeling by the time he returned to Tokyo. He handed in his article, which, as often happened, was not printed. He soon forgot the strange conversation with his brother on the road and only remembered it again when Kitaro was already dead.

One dark snowy February morning Yoshio Murata drove sleepily to the office to arrange the day's work with the press photographer. It was too early for the subway, and he telephoned for a taxi. It was just before five in the morning, and an English boat was due in Yokohama at six. Yoshio and the photographer were going to drive there and go on board. The large office was empty and silent. The photographer did not come. There were only one or two night editors there, wearing green eyeshades and playing cards, surrounded by empty beer bottles. The printing press too had ceased for a time from its almost incessant rumbling. The morning edition had been got out the night before, and it was too early for the midday one. In the silence the telephone sounded doubly loud. One of the card players put it to his ear and held it there while he tried to find his tongue. A look of utter stupidity had come into his face. The others impatiently called to him to carry on with the game. "What is the matter?" Yoshio asked when the man still clutched the telephone as though his fingers were frozen to it. He opened his mouth, shook his head, but not a word came. At that moment the chief night editor came out of his room. He stood stock-still in the doorway. His face was white. "Revolution!" he said in a low voice. "The First Division. The Prime Minister has been murdered—they are all murdered——"

A belated typewriter stopped at the far end of the room. The card players were dumb and sat as though turned to stone. The chief night editor looked from one to the other. Suddenly they all began talking at once. Two reporters snatched up their hats and ran out. Yoshio's knees trembled feebly. "Shall I go to the boat all the same?" he asked idiotically. The chief editor made no reply. The room slowly filled with men—journalists arriving for the day's work, compositors, and the boys bringing the compositors' galley proofs. They were all talking and asking questions. "We have been told to wait for a statement by the official news agency," the editor said. In spite of the excitement there was a strange calm and taciturnity, for they were Japanese. Members of the editorial staff were now at every telephone, speaking in undertones. Yoshio despatched a boy to search the morgue for the reports of previous political assassinations. "This is the seventeenth minister the militarists have bumped off. They are lunatics," said an old journalist who had charge of the "Advice for Our Women" column. Yoshio applied himself to the slightly yellowed old reports, pasted on green cardboard. Then he took a sheet of paper and began a levelheaded article in order to be ready for all eventualities. Next, all the radios in the building began to talk, announcing that Captain Shiro Nonaka and his friends had taken steps to save the country by killing all those who hindered the imperial work of the Showa restoration and lowered the Emperor's prestige. Calm was advised and a better future promised. The trunk lines of the telephone and the telegraph cables were out of action. Lights were on throughout the building, for it was a dark day, and towards noon a snowstorm swept through the streets.

Yoshio read his article through, tore it up and put the pieces in his trouser pocket without thinking. He called up his wife to say that he was going to see his parents. After a long wait he succeeded in getting hold of a taxi and was driven along the almost deserted streets. Gray snowflakes fell densely through the chill air. Here and there an armed guard was posted: soldiers marched past: rifles were piled in the snow. Black and silent groups looked on at the revolutionaries with faces from which all expression had been sedulously removed. Even peasants, wearing their short quilted coats and with their legs swathed, had come in from the surrounding country to see the revolution. Students of the liberty-loving Waseda University, wearing the cap Yoshio too had once worn, stood silent and depressed at street corners, stamping their cold feet in the snow. Every one of the soldiers marching by had a cloud of frosted breath in front of his face. It was as if the snow muffled every sound.

Yoshio could tell by the fixed and exaggerated politeness of his parents' smiles how anxious they were. Hideko had come, too. Yoshio absent-mindedly stroked her smooth, short oiled hair, and she snuggled to his hand like a little animal. She had nothing to say. They all knew that Kitaro was one of the revolutionaries, but not a word was said; except that Toson Murata, the honorable father, remarked with irritation: "Stupid pups, playing at politics and ruining everything." The Baaya brought in the meal, and Yoshio noticed that she had been crying. The rims of the old nurse's eyes were red—a sad sight in her brown, wrinkled and mummied face.

Before nightfall troops were brought into the town to protect it against the revolutionary regiments. Yoshio, obeying his halfhearted journalistic instincts, went to the Central Station to watch their arrival. He was very keenly aware that day of being merely tolerated on the newspaper as a son-in-law, that he was in fact a parasite and that the whole staff knew as well as he did that he was no journalist.

Too unoriginal for a writer, too literary for a newspaperman. He had had no instructions, but there he stood in the snow outside the station, where the lamps were smothered in densely falling snowflakes, watching the troops as they fell in and marched off. Perhaps he hoped to bring off a big journalistic scoop as he marched beside them to the center of the town. It would, he knew, be a dangerous moment if they came into collision with the revolting regiments; but it was not danger Yoshio feared, but the vacancy in which his days were spent. He had lately begun to occupy himself with French books again. He collected a sort of cotton, woven by peasants and called Egasuro. He frequently went to the movies with his wife. He had meals with his parents, he attended concerts, he bought American phonograph records and expected them to make him sentimental. But they did nothing of the sort. He felt oddly withered up inside. He had schooled himself for so long to repress his feelings that they were now parched, dried up and dead. Many Japanese experienced the same thing.

The soldiers marched with rifles at the slope and frosted breath. The light of the street lamps shone on their bayonets. They were young men, strong, sturdy peasants who passively obeyed orders. The revolutionary troops also were of the same strong, sturdy peasant stock; it was very questionable whether either of them knew where their officers were leading them. Their discipline was based on complete confidence in their leaders.

The thought of Kitaro came over Yoshio with a stab of anxiety. At midday he had walked along the cordon which the third regiment had drawn round the massive bulk of the Imperial Palace. Barbed wire, machine guns, stolid guards, and the rest of the soldiers standing about smoking, laughing and unconcerned. Yoshio looked for Kitaro in vain. He had never admitted to himself that he was jealous of his brother, whom he loved. He did not know why he was marching along beside the reinforcements and why he wanted to be on the spot if danger arose: It was because Kitaro had helped to bring about a revolution.

There was no danger, nothing happened. The troops that had been drafted into the town marched past the soldiers of the rebellious Third Regiment in perfect calm and good order. Some of them even greeted each other with friendly and stolid smiles. Probably these were men from the same village. Yoshio walked more and more slowly until at last he was left far behind. He went on foot to the office to see whether his passing impressions could be of any use to the feature editor.

What had been taken for a revolution in the morning was now only called a mutiny and an abortive one at that. Rumors were going the round of the large office, telephones rang and typewriters clattered. The rebels, who had narrowly missed causing a civil war, were abused with great bitterness. Troops were now pouring in from all sides to punish them; warships were rushing to the scene, and the senior officers of the First Division began to repent of their rashness. Yoshio sat at his typewriter and began setting down his impressions in his laborious and methodical way.

The old office messenger came in and announced that two gentlemen wished to speak to the honorable Mr Murata. Yoshio hastily put on his coat and went along the passage to the waiting room in which visitors were received. A roll hung from the wall with a written motto: "Heaven and hell lie in man's own heart."

Two young officers in uniform made low bows to Yoshio, and he returned the salutation. The older of the two cleared his throat and said: "We have been sent to fetch you by your honorable brother, Lieutenant Kitaro Murata. The honored Kitaro begs you to be so good as to come to him at once."

"Where? Where is he?" Yoshio asked. His throat had grown dry at the formal address of these two strangers. "I thank you for the honorable message," he added more politely. "Is my brother—is he well?"

"He is," was the reply. More bows and elaborate politeness over precedence in leaving the room. "We have a car waiting, if you please," the officer said. They were little more than children in uniform and had the simple faces and large hands of peasants' sons.

It had stopped snowing, but a cold wind whirled up the powdery snow. Yoshio was politely ushered into a large, old-fashioned, brown automobile. They drove along in silence. Yoshio offered cigarettes to the officers and gazed vacantly at the two glowing dots as the smoke filled the car. He put out his own cigarette again at once, for it stuck to his lips, the smoke smarted in his parched throat. He was very worried over his brother.

They crossed the Nyubashi Bridge, once more passed the improvised barricades and barbed-wire entanglements; then the bare willows which hung down over the moat of the Imperial Palace glided past. It was covered with a dull sheet of ice in which the lamps were feebly reflected where the snow had been blown away. Yoshio took off his spectacles, wiped the misted lenses, put them on again. The Akasaka quarter, north of the Palace, was quiet and deserted and foreboding. The houses held their breath, the trees did not move. Now and then small parties of soldiers were encountered. Some of the houses were guarded. A shot rang out somewhere, or it might have been a tire bursting. The car stopped. The officers conducted Yoshio through a cordon of soldiers into a two-storied house. The lights were on, but there was no one to be seen. It was a modern house without mats, and Yoshio heard his steps echoing on the stairs. "If you will please have the goodness to enter," one of the officers said as he opened tall folding doors. Yoshio entered, and the officers shut the door behind him without coming in.

Kitaro was kneeling on the floor and writing with a brush on a piece of paper that lay before him. He looked up and smiled at his brother. "I thank the honored brother for coming," he said formally. He was already clothed in the white silk undergarment which could only have one meaning. Yoshio stood dazed for a moment, and then he too knelt down and touched the floor three times with his head. He was dizzy when he knelt erect again and looked at his brother. Kitaro's beautiful neck rose like a pillar from the garment of death. His face was almost transparent in its solemn joy. He put the brush down and folded the letter. "I beg the honored brother to take this letter to our revered parents," he said politely. Yoshio bowed his assent and waited. His heart was as small and tight in his chest as a clenched fist. It was a lofty room with large glass windows. A lamp high up on the ceiling diffused a hard light. There were a desk and a few chairs, and also some filing cabinets along the wall. There was a view of roofs through the window, and an electric sign stood out against the sky, advertising a Japanese beer. There was a glaring contrast between the young man in his white silk kimono and his surroundings. Yoshio now recognized with a quick stab of pain what it was that lay on the ground in front of Kitaro: the short sword, their grandfather's samurai sword in its silk wrapping. The much-scoured boards of the floor were bare and without matting. There was a cheap foreign carpet under the writing table. Not even mats, Yoshio thought; his thoughts flew away like clouds in a storm. The *seppuku* scene in the theater, at which as a young man his parched throat had choked back its sobs . . . Kitaro stretched out his hand and put it on the sword.

"I shot one of the honorable ministers," he said. He raised his head and looked at Yoshio, who knelt opposite him with the palms of his hands resting on the floor, for the time-honored attitude came to him of its own accord. Once more he touched the floor with his head. Suddenly Kitaro smiled, the rounded corners of his mouth took on a roguish look, he was a child again, Momotaro, the children's hero, who conquered the demons. "Brother," he said. "My honored brother . . ." and he smiled at Yoshio, a tender, light, almost mocking smile. But his lips went white, as though his blood had ceased to circulate, and he dropped his head.

"My brother will tell our parents that Kitaro made atonement," he said. Yoshio picked up the letter which was lying on the floor between them. The rustle of the paper as he put it in his pocket sounded as loud to him as thunder. Kitaro raised his head, looked piercingly into his brother's eyes. "Do you remember your honorable promise?" he asked. Yoshio merely nodded. The mossy smell of the stream beside the old road filled the large cold room. Yoshio heard his wrist watch hurriedly ticking, he saw the grain of the scrubbed floorboards with appalling distinctness, he heard the hoot of an automobile far, far away in the town.

"Kitaro begs the privilege of being left alone," his brother said with great gentleness. Yoshio felt his tears as a hard aching lump, not in his eyes but in his throat. Kitaro put his hands on the floor and bowed three times, touching the floor with his head. Yoshio returned the ceremonious leave-taking. His knees were stiff, his eyes unseeing as he made his way to the door which opened of itself behind him. The two officers were kneeling outside. "Allow me to take you to your revered parents," one of them said, supporting Yoshio with his arm as he staggered reeling to his feet.

During the next few days countless people came to congratulate Yoshio and his parents. Father and mother, both very old and desolate, knelt for hours in their reception room, bowing and smiling in acknowledgment of the praise of their dead son. "Man's life is as morning frost on the roof and as a candle flame in the wind"; Yoshio had written the saying himself in his impersonal characters, and it was placed on the kakemono that hung in the niche. A single camellia, symbol of early death, was in the vase.

Some of the other assassins shot themselves, and the rest were executed; Kitaro alone chose the proud death that gave sublimity to his atonement. His hara-kiri, heroic, senseless, unavailing and yet so full of glamour, made Yoshio all the more the mere shadow of his brother. *Seppuku,* his old grandfather had called it. People would go on pilgrimage to his brother's grave as they did to the grave of his ancestor. Yoshio was left with the promise he did not know how to fulfill. The February revolt did Japan great harm, and all condemned the instigators of it. Yoshio could do nothing but listen and wait.

Toast for breakfast, interviews in the port. Hideko's wearisome attentions. The bus, the office, the dentist. His small and slowly increasing bank balance, his efforts to make his way on the paper. Hideko gave birth to a dead child, a little waxen girl. Yoshio lost five yen at a football match when the Waseda eleven was beaten. The Baaya died and left him her life's savings, fifty-four yen. Once more, as he was drunk on rice wine, he wrote a poem:

> The autumn wind
> Plays on the broken flute.
> The rain beats on the torn paper
> In the windows of the forsaken house.
> Camellia blossoms
> Drop on the path
> Vanishing in the withered grass. . . .

When war broke out with China, Yoshio volunteered for military service. He was a bookworm, a journalist, a bespectacled civilian, he hated war and loved peace, but he had given his promise to his dead brother. They smiled at him, they did not give him a uniform. "You can serve Nippon better as a correspondent," they told him. He waited for further instructions. After several weeks they arrived. Yoshio was sent to Shanghai, where he was to receive further orders.

IX

Dr Yutsing Chang

THE OLD TEACHER looked at Yutsing through his spectacles. His forehead was as furrowed as a plowed field. "What does Confucius say in the tenth chapter of the Hsiao Ching respecting the duties of a son who is still a child?" he asked. As Yutsing only opened his mouth without making any reply, he began reciting them himself.

"A good son has five duties towards his parents. He must honor them in daily life. He must try—Yutsing, he must try . . . ?"

Suddenly the wisdom stored in Yutsing's six-year-old belly came to life. "He must try to make them happy in every possible way, particularly at mealtimes," he intoned in the singsong of the scholar. "He must pay them particular attention when they are sick. He should show great sorrow when they are dead. He must take offerings with all ceremony to his departed parents. If he has carried out these duties, then it may be said of him that he has done what a son can."

With his hands in his sleeves the boy swayed to and fro in time to the classic words. They came of their own accord, for he had learned them by heart and could think of other things while he recited them. Sinsong had promised him a kite, a yellow dragon with real eyes. The wind was in the west; you could tell it even indoors, and the trees in the courtyard waved gently. "The Superior Man ought not to be proud of the high position he occupies and not to show himself discontented if he stands lower than another. If he shows pride and arrogance as a high official, then he brings—he brings . . ."

The words died away on Yutsing's lips; he came back from the dragon he had been thinking of into the schoolroom again and stared at the honored person of his master. The old teacher tapped the table with his fan and helped him out of the rut in which he had been stuck fast: ". . . then he soon brings ruin on himself and his family. If he is discontented with his lowly station, then he may be led into evil-doing. And if he does anything contrary to public opinion, then he will be the object of attacks. If he does evil in this manner, then he cannot be regarded as a good son, even though he gives his parents good meals every day."

Scholar and teacher chanted in a duet without knowing what they said. They proceeded to the five penalties, and Yutsing's attention was aroused for the first time when the master began to tell the story of Wu Meng, who lived under the Chin Dynasty and was so poor that he and his parents had no mosquito nets over their beds. His parents have sunk in slumber. Myriads of mosquitoes attack them. At this, Wu Meng, a boy of eight years, pulls off his clothes and shouts out: "I do not fear you. I have a fan but I will not use it, nor strike at you with my hand. I will lie very still and let you eat your fill."

Yutsing, as he listened to the story, tried to impress the words on his memory in their right order; he began unconsciously to scratch the mosquito bites on his own thin arms under his sleeves. The old teacher recited on and on, and Yutsing grew sleepy and had difficulty in keeping his eyes respectfully open. The twanging of a lute came from the third courtyard, and a woman sang in a high-pitched nasal voice:

> "They who know me
> Share in the sorrow of my heart.
> They who do not know me
> Ask: Whom seek you?"

It was one of the worthy concubines of the high person, his father. Yutsing had seen them being carried into the house in a curtained litter. His father's concubines lived in a pavilion at a separate courtyard, so that Yutsing's honored mother did not need to see them when she walked in the courtyard in front of her own apartments. But Yutsing was curious to see the concubines; the gatekeeper had told him they were as beautiful as a dream. "Dreams are not beautiful," he had replied sensibly, for he often dreamt of foxes and ghosts and of women without feet who tried to strangle him. When he was small the Naimah had slept in his bed with him, and when he screamed she opened her clothing and took him close to her good brown body where he knew he was safe. When he began learning the Four Books his mother took him to task and told him that he was a man and ought not to be afraid. But his aunt, who slept in the same house, came and sat beside him and told him old stories and stroked his shoulders until he fell asleep again. Her hands were gnarled as pine branches, and her body was bent and strangely twisted. "The oar . . ." she said with a sigh. From his aunt Yutsing heard first about the life of the river folk and about poverty.

His aunt thought a great deal of him, so much that she collected his urine like precious medicine and rubbed it as a cure on her aching limbs. She maintained it did them good. She hung presents at his bedposts to bring him luck, and sometimes too a basket of fragrant Yileisan flowers. She lit the bitter, smoldering incense that drove away mosquitoes, and she knew how to deal with ghosts. Before the Feast of the New Year she went herself into the kitchen and smeared honey on the kitchen god's mouth so that during the following days, when he had a holiday and went to heaven, he should speak only good of the family there. Once when Yutsing was very sick and lay unconscious in his bed she brought back his strayed soul from the street by calling to it and showing it the way home with a lantern.

His mother knew as well how to proceed with the gods as his aunt with ghosts. With his hand in hers he visited all the many temples that stood round the edge of the Western Lake. He learned from her how to bow so low that his head touched the floor and to kneel down before his grandfather on feast days. Soon he knew how to perform the little services and politenesses due to the ancestors in the ancestors' hall. He lit the candles for them, burned incense and carried the bowls containing offerings of food to their altars.

He let off rockets in the outer courtyards with his cousins, who were older than he was; which in the first place was highly entertaining and in the second place drove away the evil spirits. They also taught him the finger game and some Shantung oaths which they had acquired in the days when they lived on the boat. But his best and most interesting friend was Sinsong, the son of his teacher.

Sinsong appeared bowing and waited politely until his father, the old teacher, released his scholar. "Have you made the dragon?" Yutsing asked eagerly as they crossed the courtyard. Sinsong's long blue robe raised the dust in little eddies from the stone pavement. He was twenty years old but not married yet, which greatly worried his father. He smiled to himself as he produced the kite from the woodshed near the kitchen. He had made it for the Little Master, and it was a large, yellow, marvelous dragon—with eyes. Yutsing shouted for joy. Sinsong, the younger teacher, as he was called, courted the friendship of the man-child, the Little Master, with many small presents and attentions. He had his reasons.

Yutsing had been given full permission by his father to go kite-flying with the younger teacher. Nevertheless he was unaccustomed to the crowded streets, and he held fast to his grown-up friend's hand. He was unused to walking, for he was usually carried in a chair, as became the son of a great house, and so he was soon out of breath. Again Sinsong smiled to himself, but he did not slacken his pace. "Your father can lift a buffalo, but you are out of breath if you have to walk two li," he said teasingly. "I am not out of breath," Yutsing said crossly, trying to get his breath. "Do you know why that is?" the young teacher asked. "Your father was a coolie, and so he has strength. You are weak and no more use than a candied lotus kernel."

Sinsong was the only person who told Yutsing home truths; nevertheless, the Little Master, the precious son of the house, was greatly attached to him and was proud of the privilege of his company. At last they reached the uncultivated land on the slope of a hill, and Sinsong ran cunningly against the wind to make the kite rise. Then Yutsing was allowed to try his hand, and when he was successful and the kite soared up to the clouds and the string tugged at his hand like a living thing, he was proud and happy.

"What have you been learning today, you little parrot?" the younger teacher asked. "Confucius!" he said, laughing. "That stupid same old babble. The more you learn the stupider you'll get. Confucius has put the men of China to sleep so fast they cannot wake up again."

Yutsing listened with a little shudder at such words.

"You must learn to think for yourself instead of blabbing out what you have learned by heart," Sinsong went on pursuing his design of re-educating him. "Don't believe any of that nonsense. What good did it do Wu Meng to let himself be bitten by mosquitoes? They did not suck any less blood from his parents. What do you say? Meng Tsung went out in the depth of winter to look for bamboo shoots for his sick mother, and heaven made them sprout from the ice because he was a good son? Heaven does nothing of the kind, Little Master, and if you rely on its help you will be in a bad way."

Yutsing heard these sarcastic and rebellious utterances with horror, feeling as if he were left without bed and roof. He tried to recollect what he had been taught. "The scholar's way is the way of humility and submission, and he takes every word of his master on trust," he said to confound the young teacher. Sinsong laughed aloud. "Well argued, my little scholar," he shouted. "But there is this also: 'If the father's commands are bad, the son must resist, and the minister must likewise refuse obedience to him who is over him.' This is the rule: 'Be disobedient if the order is wrong.' I will tell you something, and mind you remember it: our teaching is not good teaching. It is like the poisonous smoke of opium that clouds the brain and poisons a man with false contentment and brings him to ruin. But things will change, and soon, too."

No wonder Yutsing's sleep was disturbed after hearing such incredibly lawless talk.

Yutsing passed the days when his father arrived from Shanghai and took up his abode in the house, in a mixture of festivity and fear. He was given presents, a wooden horse, a hat such as foreigners wore, a gun which shot a cork if handled properly. His father laughed so uproariously that the written scrolls on the walls swung to and fro. He made a round target, and together they practised shooting in the inner courtyard. Mother wore her most beautiful clothes when Father came home and powdered her face white and had a jade butterfly in her hair. In a low and polite voice she told him all about the household affairs. Father made his voice as small as he could when he talked to Mother, and it did not escape Yutsing how polite his parents were to each other. Sometimes he sighed apprehensively. It is written: "To our mother we show love, to our high lord respect, but to our father we owe both love and respect."

In the evening and until late at night the sound of lutes and singing could be heard from the pavilion, the smell of sweet incense was wafted across and, from the loud guttural peals of laughter Yutsing could tell that the High Person was drunk. The younger teacher was sometimes drunk, too; he went often to the teahouses, but what he drank there was yellow wine, not tea. When he came home he stood in the first courtyard, where lanterns hung from their bamboo tripods to light the way for guests, and made speeches. "The Old Tiger in Peking is a silly old woman, bringing the country to ruin, and we are ruled by a lot of stinking eunuchs. It is not the wise man who is put in power, but he who buys his position with silver. The Middle Kingdom is rotten and stinks like a dead animal by the roadside."

The gatekeeper and the servants laughed and made fun of him, and at last one of them gave him a push as though by accident, and he fell into the little pond among the lotus flowers. Yutsing laughed until his sides ached.

His mother talked to him about quite different things when he sat beside her and she embroidered flowers on a piece of silk. He heard about his grandfather, the mandarin, the Superior Man who followed the Confucian ideal: respectful to his elders, kind to his servants, loyal to the throne, holding to the mean steadfastly and without arrogance. Even the memory of the deceased mandarin was a peaceful influence. Yutsing made a particularly low and perfect bow to the tablet on the household altar in the hall of his ancestors which bore his grandfather's name.

Grandfather had been executed soon after Sinsong's prediction came true and the provinces rose and cast off the rule of the Manchus. The younger teacher suddenly appeared with a rifle, from which, to make assurance doubly sure, a sword projected; and with it he fearfully and threateningly stabbed the air. It was not until then that the Chang household learned that he belonged to the secret society of the Elder Brothers and had helped to instigate the rebellion. There was shooting in the streets, and bodies floated in the lake among the stalks of the lotus flowers. One morning the yellow imperial dragon vanished, and the new white flag with a red circle and the ancient sign "Khan" blew in the streets in its place. Sinsong promised to protect the house which had shown kindness to him and his father; and in fact the rebels turned aside from its gates and left it unharmed. Yutsing's father calmly buried his hands in his sleeves and paid a polite and advantageous visit to the new masters in the yamen. Yutsing's grandfather, that noble man, was beheaded in the open market place together with five other imperial officials who refused to join the Revolution. The common folk, who had nothing against him, stood by and encouraged him, curious to see whether he would meet his death with dignity and keep his face even as the sword descended. This he did, and the story of his execution was told over and over again to his grandson. He was a spectator of the scene with the rest of the family, but it caused him to fall sick; he had an attack of fever which enabled him to hide behind the curtains of his bed and resign himself to the tender care of his mother, his aunt and his Naimah until the Revolution was over and the streets were quiet again. The younger teacher was now in the police and an important person. He kept his rifle and did not fly kites any more.

During the years that followed there was often shooting in the streets and warfare round the walls of the town, but no harm came near Chang and his great house, for the banker always knew how to keep friends with those who had the upper hand at the moment.

Life in his courts and houses and gardens kept to the even tenor of its way.

Thus Yutsing grew up, surrounded by the gentle scenery of the Western Lake, whose lovely shores were surrounded by the dwellings of the wealthy and great and by the temples of the gods. A thousand Buddhas were carved into the old rocks of Lingyin. At night boats sailed on the smooth lake, and there was eating and singing on board. In the mornings rosy mists lay over the landscape, and through them the tall Needle Pagoda pointed, as though floating in the air. Thus, many threads crossed and recrossed to weave the stuff of which Chang Yutsing was made up to the time when he went to St John's School at Shanghai.

His father's motive in taking him away from home and his family was ridiculous enough, although Chang Bogum was in a towering rage over it. One day when Yutsing's mother had left the house to pay a visit to the Temple-of-the-Cloud-at-Rest the concubines seized this rare opportunity of leaving their own court and pavilion and walking about in the other courts. There were four concubines in the household at that time, beautiful young girls whom Chang had picked up and bought in various places. They were intoxicated with the little scrap of liberty they enjoyed that afternoon, and their laughter and chatter echoed from court to court. They must have been bored to death in their pavilion in the absence of their lord and master. They threw grains of rice to the goldfish in the ponds, put the tortoises on their backs and left them sprawling, and whistled to the birds hanging in cages on the posts that supported the galleries. Yutsing fell into their hands as he passed in his long blue dress, holding his case of brushes, his paintbox and books discreetly under his arm. He lowered his eyes and tried to get by them to his room. But they joked so charmingly with him and also the upturned tortoises amused him so much that at last he began to laugh and forgot the dignity proper to an only son and a young scholar. It ended with the girls' taking the Little Master with them into their pavilion and playing with him as they might have done with a live, docile and excited doll; and when his aunt found him he was drunk and his face was painted with

white and red paint. As the concubines had given him his fill of
sweetmeats and rice wine, he was very ill all night long and repeatedly vomited in his bed. Next day his father arrived from Shanghai
and his mother complained to him. Yutsing's father, the High Person, went to the pavilion and gave the girls a good beating. Then
the child was packed off to Shanghai.

The shock of a foreign education coming on the top of his Chinese
childhood was so violent that Yutsing only bore up under it because he was a Chinese. The Chinese temperament is like water
that, however it is stirred and troubled, always returns again to its
level surface. Yutsing was a child and a Chinese, and he soon
adapted himself because not to have done so would have made life
difficult.

He learned English and he studied the Bible. "Our Father which
art in heaven"—that he understood easily. It was almost Chinese, a
family of brothers in Christ with a father over them. He took a
great liking to Jesus, who went about in white clothing and was
gentle and kindly to people. Jesus could bring the dead to life,
which was more than Confucius could or had even ever attempted.
Jesus and the master who told him about Him ran together in Yutsing's brain. The master too wore white clothes, in summer at least,
and was kind to children, and so Yutsing always imagined Jesus to
himself as the Reverend Thomas Warren, who taught them Scripture. Chang Yutsing was very pleased to be baptized and after some
persuasion took the name of John. As Americans put everything
topsy-turvy they had to reverse his name too and from Chang Yutsing he became John Chang. Everything there was different—clothes,
beds, prayers, the manner of greeting, the very essence of life. Books
were read backwards instead of forwards, the writing went from
side to side instead of up and down. The women wore long robes,
the men jackets and trousers, contrary to all decency. At home it
was impolite to shut a door, here you were not allowed to leave
one open. Worst of all was having to grasp another's hand in greeting instead of one's own, for it seemed to John very impolite as well
as unpleasant. Throughout all the later years of his Americanization
he never got over the discomfort and shyness of having to shake

another person's hand. He put aside paintbrush and paintbox as soon as his Chinese lessons were over and learned to write, first with chalk, later with a pen. He eagerly devoured the New Learning, the foreigners' learning, for he was the grandson of a scholar and born to be a student. After a while he began to have a great admiration for his foreign masters. He was astonished to find that barbarians, as they indubitably were, laid so much stress on cleanliness and good behavior and knew so much and could do so many things of which the sons of the Middle Kingdom knew nothing. His first journey on the railway impressed him above all, and he announced his intention of being an engineer and constructing such railways all over the country.

Henry Wong, the boy in the next bed to him and after a time his best friend, laughed at him. "They are devils and, what is more, stupid devils. Don't you let them take you in," he said. "We can easily learn what they know, but what we know they can never learn." And he began to reel off all he had against the foreigners. They had come into the country uninvited and undesired; they had introduced opium and made war on China to force her to buy their poisonous smoke; they had taken to themselves all that was of any use or value in the country—coal, minerals, the silver and copper mines and the railways; their warships lay in the great river with the menace of their guns; they had got the important towns on the coast into their own hands by treaties; they settled themselves down, with their own soldiers and rifles, warships, police, schools and courts of justice, as if they were no intruders but lords and masters of the country. It was high time China woke up and threw them out. They had enough room ·in their own countries, and China was not a colony.

John Chang was surprised at all this erudition, but Henry told him that his father had been one of the leaders of the Revolution and that he was now in Peking in Yuan Shih-kai's government.

"If you despise and hate the foreigners so much, why do you go to their school and become a Christian and even take the name they give you?" John asked.

Henry only laughed. "Christianity—that's only joss-pidgin," he said, contemptuously using the coolie expression. "We must learn what we need from the foreigners so as to use it against them." This was an illumination to John, and he began to look at his masters with a critical eye. He soon saw their failings and the funny side of them, and the composite portrait of Jesus and the Reverend Thomas Warren lost its magic and became merely silly.

A great war broke out in the countries beyond the great mountains, Russia, Germany, France, England and many smaller, less important countries. One day in school they were told that America and China were fighting on the same side against the same enemies. As there was always war in China the schoolboys received the news with composure. But when the war was over it was soon seen that Henry Wong was right. China had joined in the war in order to recover the province of Shantung from the Germans. Now the statesmen of the foreign nations in Paris came to the conclusion that the Japanese ought to have this rich province. "That shows what good friends the Americans are," Henry remarked to John, who was too much depressed to reply. For him, as for every Chinese, friendship meant a solemn bond. He was disillusioned. The Japanese, the brown dwarfs, were detested. They had already won a war against China, and the self-esteem of the Chinese had received a severe blow.

When the shameless Twenty-one Demands they presented to the Chinese were made known, all the rage and embitterment was concentrated upon the Japanese. The demands were printed on paper fans, so that they should be called to memory every time a fan was opened. The call for a boycott of Japanese goods was posted on the gates of Peking. Students and schoolboys invaded the stores and burned everything Japanese. As they did not know much about it, they burned Chinese goods as well, and the storekeepers suffered much loss. They wanted to damage Japan, but for the time being they damaged only themselves. Leaflets passed from hand to hand at school. It was Henry who smuggled them in. Boycott Japan! Down with the English Imperialists! Down with the rotten government! Students, workers, peasants, unite! There were pictures in the leaflets so that even the ignorant coolie could understand them. China—cutting Japan's head off with a great butcher's knife. The knife was the boycott. There was calm on the surface, on the politely inexpressive faces, but underneath the school was seething. John Chang went from one conviction to another. He had been born with a tooth in his mouth: he ought to become a leader of men. He did not know whom to lead or whither to lead them.

Often on Sunday his father sent his automobile for him. They talked, ate an enormous meal, went to the theater and had a grand time. After hymns on the harmonium and his English lessons it was a relief to hear the wooden clatter of the music on the stage and the actors declaiming. There were comic dialogues and marvelous fighting. Yutsing—for when he was with his father he became Yutsing again—feverishly chewed melon seeds; his head got hot, he laughed as though drunk and kept wiping his face with the hot moist towel that was tossed over to him to refresh himself with.

His father laughed when he started upon political questions. "He who is wise keeps quiet," he said simply. "When you come into the bank you will have friends of all sorts, Chinese, Japanese, American, English. Money speaks a language understood by all." John remained uneasy and dissatisfied. He had learned at school that hundreds and thousands of Christians had died for their beliefs. This had impressed upon him that a conviction was worth dying for. He was ready—only he had no conviction as yet. He was only feeling his way on into a new era.

Meanwhile Henry was caught reading aloud a down-with-the-foreigners pamphlet in the dormitory and expelled. "All the better, I'll go to Canton," he told John. "That's where the Master is getting ready for the next revolution." Everyone was grumbling and whispering that a new revolution was needed, for since the war lords had got possession of the provinces things were worse than under the Manchus. John, who had his arithmetic to do, envied Henry his expulsion.

The ideas that inspired young China seeped through to him by many different channels. Many a Sunday he forged a note from his father asking leave for his son to visit him, knowing well that B. G. Chang was away. The school was on the edge of the town, and he wandered about in the small streets of the suburbs and stood outside the open booths—for there was no Sunday for the Chinese—drank tea in a teahouse, listened to the older men arguing and to the speeches at street corners, until a policeman came along and dispersed the meeting with blows of his bamboo rod. John took a ricksha—his father always kept him well supplied with pocket money—and told the coolie to take him to the International Settlement. It delighted him to be able to read the foreign shop signs and even to catch scraps of the conversation of passers-by. The day ended with a visit to one of the new cinemas, where he sat breathlessly staring at the foreigners on the screen. He took a shameless pleasure in seeing how men and women talked to each other in public, embraced and caressed each other in a manner that was proper only in darkness and silence and in bed. He understood most of the captions and often laughed heartily to himself when a joke took his fancy. It was as though he had a boot in two continents. He did not belong to the foreigners, even though he understood their language and their ideas and had adopted their religion; but no more did he belong to his own people, for he was by now too far removed from their simplicity, their superstitions, their dirt and their contentment.

He was more clearly aware of this when the holidays came and he went home to the house on the Western Lake. As soon as he arrived at the station he encountered the younger teacher, Sinsong, in the uniform of a lower official and wearing spectacles of plain glass to lend him dignity. He examined the luggage of every passenger who got out there and levied a tax on many of them, a transport tax, in the name of the general who was in command of the district at the moment. When John Chang came up, he was just examining the passport of an Englishman with a grave and dubious air. "But I tell you my passport is quite in order," the Englishman was repeating in his own language with impatient annoyance. John smiled when he noticed that the teacher was holding the passport upside down; the top was the bottom and right was left and he was twisting his head in the desperate hope of being able to decipher the foreign writing if he got it in the perpendicular direction he was used to. John would have liked to come to his help, but that would have made his old friend lose face, and so he left the Englishman to curse and pay the illegal tax while the teacher put on the airs of a viceroy.

When everyone had left the station, he asked politely after his health. "I am very well and my rice bowl is full," Sinsong boasted; he stamped with his loud leather boots and patted his uniform to show off his great importance to the Little Master. John himself had put on his long blue robe of a Chinese student again for his return home and adopted quite naturally the bent and negligent carriage he had inherited from generations of scholarly forebears. He was Yutsing once more, the sole star and precious son of the house of Chang. He hailed a ricksha coolie, and as the man trotted with him through the town along the familiar, crowded, noisy, lively streets he talked to him about this and that.

"It is all worse than ever," the coolie said. "Before, when we still wore pigtails, they squeezed coppers out of us, but now it is silver taels." But he laughed as he said it, for he had a fare and would earn enough for his evening rice. Yutsing took a deep breath. The lake, the shores, the Needle Pagoda across on the hill, the newly whitened walls, the black double gates, the gatekeeper, fat and self-important as all gatekeepers were . . .

As soon as Yutsing was sitting with his mother again he wondered why he was full of unrest at school. In his mother's room there was such peace that you could hear it ring delicately like silver drops in a golden bowl. His mother handed him his teacup with her own hands, and he noticed that she had put on a beautifully embroidered dress to welcome him, as she used in earlier days to do for his father. But he saw too that she had plucked her hair from her forehead and wore a black fillet over it in the old fashion and that she was dressed in dark colors and no longer powdered, for she had grown old and wished to be honored on that account. He reckoned up her age; she could not be more than thirty. He thought of the American and French women in Shanghai with their forced and strident youthfulness and of the indecent films he had seen, and his mother seemed to him nobler and more worthy of honor than ever before. She asked him various questions, and he told her various tactful lies, for the truth would have been incomprehensible and wounding to her. He did not tell her that he had become a Christian and adopted

a foreign name; on the contrary he went with her to the house
altar and made his low kowtow, as he had in childhood, before the
spirits of his forefathers. And after a long, long time he felt contented and at peace again, and in his right place as a son and
descendant, and as a man and future father of generations to follow.

His aunt, who now looked just like a willow tree in winter when
it bends its leafless limbs over the stream, brought a vessel of hot
water into his bedroom, so that he could wash himself. She sighed
and made complaints after the manner of old women: the servant
girls ran into the streets like the bitches they were and the menservants made rebellious speeches in the courtyards. And no wonder, when every month a new general made himself master of the
town and authorities were authorities no longer. Yutsing heard her
loud, hollow cough at nights. There was coughing in all the courtyards of the compound and in all the buildings—he had never
noticed it before. A great leader would have to give them new
lungs, he thought as he fell asleep.

Next morning he paid a visit to the old teacher in his study. He
had become rather hard of hearing, and for that reason he shouted
as he talked to Yutsing. "I hope you have brought back a bellyful
of the foreign learning with you," he shouted ironically. "Empty it
out and let the humble young teacher learn something new, too."
And he called himself young from the excess of his modesty.

Yutsing sat down opposite him as he used when he had his first
lessons and painted a few of the foreign letters with the paintbrush.
The teacher looked at them with his head askew. "That's not difficult
to read," he said. "A moon, a man, a roof, a woman." He took the
paintbrush and quickly painted one of the letters three times over.
"Three women—there you have the sign for quarreling," he said
mischievously. Yutsing could not help laughing at this application of
Chinese hieroglyphics to foreign letters. He told the old man also a
little about Jesus, the Great Master of the foreigners, and the teacher
remarked casually: "Yes, yes, so I've heard." But he pricked up his
ears at the miracle of the feeding of the five thousand, for it was
remarkable that the Master was able to conjure a meal for five
thousand people out of five loaves and two fishes. It particularly

impressed the old teacher that twelve baskets of left-overs remained, and he said respectfully: "He must have acquired great merit to have been so highly favored."

"My uneducated son has been given the post of a customs official," he said another time. "It is no longer necessary now to pass the examination in order to be an official. It is enough to lick the spittle of a general and say it is honey." Yutsing could not help smiling at the old man's jealousy; he had studied for year after year without ever getting any farther. And so, as he smiled and talked and heard the familiar sounds and smelled the familiar smells, as he slept in his childhood's bed and was tended by his old Naimah, the house by degrees became his home again. When he went back to school after the holidays, he felt a stranger there at first; and the same process was repeated year after year.

Yutsing left school when he was eighteen, and his father took him home, but this time instead of the railway it was in his large new automobile. A servant sat beside the chauffeur and honked the horn for all he was worth to give notice that a great lord was coming; for though a master may be modest, a servant must boast of the glories of his master in order to have much face.

Before the journey was over his father had already announced his opinion that it was time for Yutsing to marry, and when they got home the discussion was continued in the presence of his mother. Yutsing had not yet had anything to do with women, for his education at St John's had made him rather shy of the subject. His father laughed at him. "The courtyards are full of slave girls," he said, "and you are the master." But Yutsing said quietly that he would rather marry, and his mother said: "The documents were signed twelve years ago, and Fong Yung will make you a very good wife."

In the stress of all his foreign education Yutsing had almost forgotten that he had been betrothed to Fong Yung since he was six. He remembered now that he had once run through the courtyards with a tiny little girl and played with her, but the memory had been buried under much else since then. His mother had sometimes mentioned her name in the holidays. "Fong Yung painted this fan for me"; or, "Fong Yung read the newspaper aloud to me, but I am such a stupid old woman that I did not understand half she read."

Fong Yung's father was a big landowner, and the famous Chekiang tea was grown on his land. He was a wealthy tea merchant, but he did not sit in his shop as the little people did but sold his tea whole-sale to the foreigners, who exported it throughout the world in their ships.

Yutsing's father was almost surprised that his son made no objection to being married in the ancient manner. The truth was that Yutsing gave way on this point because he had more important things to ask of his father, or if necessary, to extort from him, and he followed that old maxim of yielding a little to gain much. He only said: "I will not have a wife with bound feet," and old Chang looked at him mischievously as though to say: What would you know about women's feet? But his mother said reassuringly: "Fong Yung has large feet, and she wears clothes of the new-fashioned style, and she has been to the new school." And then after a while Yutsing muttered more shyly: "And I want to see her before I marry her." His mother merely smiled at that and made no answer. The documents had been signed, and the Chang family could not in any case back out of the marriage without mortal affront to Fong Yung's family. A few days later Yutsing's mother asked him to accompany her to the Temple-of-the-Purple-Cloud, and there he saw Fong Yung, who had gone there at the same hour with her mother to pray and offer paper money and incense. She was small and wore a silk jacket embroidered with pale yellow flowers and a skirt as the fashion was and shoes of the Western style with high heels such as the ladies wore in Shanghai. She looked down at her stick of incense and did not even by a quiver of her eyelids indicate that she had observed Yutsing Chang.

Yutsing was uncertain whether she pleased him or not. He begged his father to delay the marriage for a few weeks, and Chang agreed, for the soothsayers also thought that a certain day in the next month but one would be the most propitious. "I should like to travel a little with a friend of mine," Yutsing further requested.

"So long as his parents are alive, a son ought not to travel about the country. If he does travel, then it must be to some place in particular,"

Chang quoted, laughing to himself. "You have become a real American. They are always running about," he added with a certain pride in his son. As he spoke he remembered his own youth and the restlessness that drove him upstream and down, and he let the boy go. Yutsing telegraphed to Henry, whom he had lately met in Shanghai, to let him know that he was ready to join him. He nursed a secret hope that to travel with his friend might clear his mind about his future; for Yutsing was dissatisfied and confused in mind, as so many of the younger of his fellow countrymen were.

Confucius belonged to the past and was of no help to them. The Emperor as the father of the country, the governor as the father of his district, the father as head of the family, the family of more importance than the community, the community of more importance than the nation, and reverence for the dead of more importance than active life. For four thousand years China had believed that the learning by rote of these moral principles and the ability to compose a poem made the Superior Man and that manual labor was mean and degrading. The result was that the whole country was crippled and paralyzed and had to submit to foreign dictation.

Christianity, the teaching of the Great Master, Jesus: good teaching as far as it went, but nobody followed it. Behold the city of the foreigners, the Christians. Opium dens, gambling hells, brothels. Swindling and ruthless pursuit of gain, every Christian the enemy of his neighbor, and all of them China's enemy. Love your neighbor as yourself? The Christians were not such fools as to believe in so eccentric a precept.

Lao Tse, the great negativist, with his principle of Wu Wei, complete passivity? Every act leads to suffering: therefore do nothing. Yutsing was too young to retreat to a cave, to let his beard and his nails grow and to renounce the world. The religion of Buddha said very much the same, and the O-Omni-Padme-Hum jibbering of the orthodox priests was fit only for women and children.

The Revolution had failed and the Republic had become a bloody gambling table of the war lords. To come to terms with them and curry favor for your own advancement, as his father did, and many others, only meant plunging the country deeper in disaster. Yutsing

was not enough of a Christian to make common cause with the
foreigners and no longer Chinese enough to be satisfied with the
way things were going in China. He had read newspapers, listened
to speeches. Henry had written many rousing letters from Canton
and sent him pamphlets. Now Yutsing wanted to travel in his company, see with his own eyes, think with his own brain, and then
make up his own mind how he was to emerge from the tangle of
conflicting ideas. And so the two friends set out on their travels.

They traveled by train and by boat; they stopped in small towns
and villages; they went on foot too from village to village or were
carried in chairs to some temple where pilgrims were gathering.

His home on the Western Lake and his school had both really
been prisons where Yutsing saw only what he was meant to see.
Now at last he saw reality. He saw injustice and destitution, violence
and defenselessness, bribery at the top and oppression at the bottom;
he saw vice-ridden generals with their troops of women; the ruin of
girls in the villages, the public execution of the innocent; he saw dirt
and famine, floods in one place, drought in another and disease
everywhere, and saw the people, his people, a people who had lived
thus for four thousand years and still went on. He saw its patient,
indefatigable labor, its power to content itself on the meagerest diet,
to exist on the verge of starvation. For it was good to stay alive
and something even to be proud of. He saw it laugh on the slightest excuse and he discovered what a number of things it found
amusing. He saw its tolerance, and he came upon wisdom in the
most ignorant coolie. He saw the love with which people bent over
their children and the joy with which they gazed at the moon or
a willow or a bird; and he thought to himself: China can no more
be trodden under than water can be; whoever attempts it will drown,
and the water will be as before. China will be as before.

But this thought, however comforting, was not enough, for Yutsing had been born with a tooth in his mouth. Out of the endless
talks he had had with Henry one thing emerged with absolute certainty: All these people put their hopes on the New Party, on Young
China, on the new revolution which was to come out of Canton and
which the Great Master, Sun Yat-sen, had promised.

Yutsing returned home and, on the night before his wedding, he announced to his parents that he would not go into the bank, or seek a post under the government, or go to the university in Shanghai. He would not even go to America to study. He was going to Canton, the only place for a young man to go to.

In the quarrel which followed, his mother, although she spoke in a gentle voice and with great politeness, played the chief part, whereas his father was not so obdurate as Yutsing had feared he would be. It amused the banker to see that his son had a will of his own. The young, he thought, must have tall talk and excitement. It all dies down in time. He had frequently observed that the noisiest politicians soon calmed down and came to heel.

The wedding was celebrated in the usual manner. The guests had been arriving for days. They came by hundreds to honor the house of Chang and filled all the courtyards. The bride was borne to the gate in a gold-embroidered, red-curtained litter, followed by an endless wedding cortege and two bands each trying to outdo the other. Yutsing carried his bride over the threshold and marveled for one moment to find that she was as light and warm as the lovebird from which she took her name. Then all was drowned by the lavish hospitality, the incessant pouring out of wine for their guests and the pressing of food upon them, as was the bridal couple's duty; by laughter, clamor of voices, by music and innumerable skyrockets; by the interminable meal, and the jesting of the men and the whispers of the women wishing the bride a hundred sons. The smell of spilt wine and spiced foods penetrated even to the ancestors' hall and mingled with the scent of incense that rose to the fathers. At last Yutsing's head went round from fatigue and the wine he had drunk and the excited state of his feelings.

It was only when he was left alone with his young wife in their bedchamber that the thought of their strangeness smote him, and his flesh feared her strange flesh. The bed curtains were drawn back, and a flat bowl of fragrant Yileisan flowers was suspended from the canopy above the pillows. The room was full of their heavy scent.

The clamor from the outer courtyard, muffled by the distance. Closer by, the croak of a frog, from the pond below. From a belated boat on the lake, the rasping of phonograph music. Yutsing looked at the cup of wine on the table beside the bed, which he and Fong Yung were to share. He did not know what to say, so he asked shyly: "Are you tired, Fong Yung?" She shook her head and looked him full in the face for the first time. She was sitting on a low chair, and he was standing at the door which he had just shut behind him. She said almost vehemently: "I am sorry you have been forced to marry me. It means nothing. I ask only one thing of you: Do not leave me behind here in your parents' home when you go. Take me with you, and then we can be parted as soon as ever you like."

Yutsing was speechless at this unexpected pronouncement. He took a step back to the door, then said quickly: "I was not forced. I saw you and you pleased me." At this Fong Yung smiled at him as if he were a child in need of comfort and said more gently: "Perhaps I express myself badly. It is the first time I have ever spoken to a young man. But I consider it intolerable that we should be shut up in this room, like two . . . two animals who have to be mated."

Yutsing recollected the warmth and lightness of her body when he carried her over the threshold. "Why are you so unkind to me?" he asked. "I have done you no harm. I will do nothing to you that you do not wish." As soon as he had said it he saw that Fong Yung was wiping the tears from her face with her sleeve, and he knew that she was just as much afraid as he was. "Why did you marry me if you want to be divorced from me at once?" he asked. Fong Yung began to smile, and a dimple appeared in her chin. "To get away from home," she said candidly. Yutsing now sat down on a chair, too. He turned down the lamp, which had begun to smoke, while he took time for his reply. At last he said: "Fong Yung, I have made up my mind to go to Canton to study medicine. What do you mean to do after we are separated? Perhaps you will learn something too, as many girls do now?" "To Canton?" she said. The darkness of her eyes began to lighten as though a candle burned within their transparent depths. Suddenly she undid the two first buttons of her red wedding dress and felt in her breast, which was so small that it scarcely made the satin bulge, and at last brought out a small piece of silk which she had carried there, inside. It was something like a flag or pennant, whichever you choose to call it. She smoothed it on her knee and looked expectantly at Yutsing. A white star was embroidered on the dark silk. The star of the Kuomintang, the New Party, the star of Chinese youth. Yutsing went to her quickly and took the little flag from her lap and looked at it. "What does it mean?" he asked. Before he knew, they were sitting close beside each other. Fong Yung's dress was still undone. "We had a secret league at school—Blood and Iron, it was called," she murmured. Yutsing had heard of it already; it had cells in many of the places he had passed through. Cautiously and hesitantly he put his hand on Fong Yung's shoulder. She did not mind. She looked at him with her lips parted, and rather more confidently, but the tears still shone on her cheeks. Her fingers opened like the pale petals of a water lily. With a hot and almost frightened joy Yutsing grasped that he had found not only a wife but a comrade, someone who would stand by him and go wherever he went, as the wives of the foreigners did. He began impulsively stroking her shoulder and calling her in a whisper by that new name: Comrade, Tsung Tse, Same Ambition.

They felt their way on into the future: they no longer thought of the old way of marriage—in bed your master, elsewhere your guest; yet they were helpless how the new way of marriage should be begun. But as they were young, a man and a girl by themselves at night, they ended up in the large bed behind drawn curtains, in the scent of the white flowers, content and already a bit acquainted. When the storm was over and the cloud had burst, as the old books put it, Yutsing lay beside his wife and held her delicate hand between his. He had never before touched any woman's hand but his mother's. He took Fong Yung in his arms and drew her close to him, close to his skin as his aunt used to hold him when he was a child tormented by bad dreams. Thus they fell asleep.

They were two pampered, bewildered children when they reached Canton, but there they were forged afresh and struck in a new mold, given new ideas and aims and armed for battle. In Canton they learned how a revolution was hatched. Fong Yung, the small one, dainty one, soon glowed like white-hot iron. Yutsing followed more slowly in her tracks until he too was gripped by the spirit of the place. Fong Yung became pregnant and had the child removed from her by a Russian doctor. "We have no time to bring up children," she said. "This country must first be a place where people can live worthily." Sometimes Yutsing was shocked by the uncompromising vigor with which the girl students threw themselves into the work of revolution. Sometimes he was afraid of Fong Yung. Sometimes he was afraid for her.

Sun Yat-sen, a sick man, green in the face, gave his lectures. Chiang Kai-shek, his secretary, trained officers in his Officers' Training Corps and built up the revolutionary army. The town was full of Russians who brought their hangers-on with them, men and women of strange races and strange destinies. Russians organized the Rebellion. Day and night the presses printed posters, leaflets and manifestoes. Money was sent from Russia, money was squeezed from opium smugglers, brothel keepers and the ill-famed, notorious flower boats. But prudent men of good position and wealth made contributions too in order to stand well with the possible government of the future. In the shifting sand, to which Sun Yat-sen loved to compare his people, Yutsing and his wife were merely tiny grains carried along by the torrent. Fong Yung, in the short skirt of a student, carried out the dangerous tasks entrusted to her. Yutsing worked under Henry's direction in the propaganda department. He translated the Russians' poor English into good Chinese. He had inherited the fine style of his mandarin grandfather. Sometimes he was allowed to write the manifestoes himself. Occasionally he was sent out to address the workers, the porters and coolies. It was the greatest surprise for him and his like to discover that the New China meant to come to the help of these lowly people, too. Yutsing had always regarded them merely as animals. On the party posters were to be seen a student, a worker, a soldier, a peasant, a woman. Yutsing had no ideas of his own; none of the young students had ideas of their own; no one knew whither the forces behind the movement were carrying them. Sun Yat-sen's slogans were hammered into their brains: Unity, The rule of the People, Prosperity for All. Fresh slogans followed: Workers, unite! Down with foreign imperialism! Freedom for the peasants! Solidarity of the farmers and the canceling of their debts! Nationalism! Communism!

Assassinations, executions, shots in the night, smuggling of arms, torture of prisoners. Meetings, meetings, meetings. Sweat-soaked bodies of coolies in the tropical summer of Canton crowded together in halls, courtyards, garages and cellars. Their incessant coughing. The sore places on their shoulders where the chain poles galled them, the flies in the suppurating eyes of the old, their labored breath, their bottomless poverty, their slow awakening. Yutsing talked to them and got used to them. He never learned to love them, for the proud and weary blood of the mandarin was stronger in him than the proletarian blood of his father. But he learned to pity them, and he learned how to influence them with his well-chosen words.

There was no more question of studying. Yutsing and his wife had something else to do. They had missions of desperate urgency to carry out. Fong Yung fell sick with malaria. The fever wasted her, she got thin, the flame in her flickered, but she never stopped working. She went round prodding up the women, the dumb beasts, who bore and killed children without ceasing, who starved children, sold children, who consented to children being violated for a few coppers. If she succeeded in kindling a spark in their stolid faces, she exulted as gently and tenderly as a bird that is the first to wake in the morning.

Sun Yat-sen died. But the movement went on. General strike in Hong Kong, the first great blow to English imperialism, the first sign of the solidarity of the workers. The port was idle, the great English city paralyzed. Foreign guns and ships in the Pearl River. The first encounters between the revolutionary army and the northern government's forces. The first victories. One morning Henry lay in the gutter, dead, beside a bucket of night refuse.

Yutsing was ordered to Chekiang, his own province, whose dialect he knew. He went to the villages and small towns and addressed the farmers, who had fallen into the hands of the big landowners and usurers. Fong Yung remained behind in Canton, where she was needed. It was not until Yutsing was parted from her that he knew how necessary to him she was. Their hatred of the foreigner and the burning desire to help China bound them more tightly together than any love could have done. In Shanghai English police had shot Chinese students. Every university, every school in the country replied with an outburst of rage and indignation. The propaganda department made all the use it could of the incident. When the revolutionary army under Borodin and Chiang Kai-shek invaded the North, Yutsing and his wife were together again for a few weeks. When Fong Yung, a tiny, invalid soldier in uniform, was struck down with fever, Yutsing stayed behind with her in the inn of the little town of Fukang. He was sorry now that he was not a doctor; he knew too much to have any trust in the local medicine man and not enough to help her. Fong Yung lost consciousness, and he was afraid for her life, so he sent a note to the American mission and begged the hated foreign doctor to come to the help of his wife.

As the doctor bent over her bed, Yutsing was overtaken by a dim and gentle memory. The Reverend Thomas Warren, Jesus, the Scripture lesson at St John's. Though he was only twenty-one, Yutsing felt like an old man—the past lay so far behind, so much had happened since. Dr Lee's eyes were blue but not vacant and ghostly; they were the blue of the sparks the hammer strikes from iron. He had red hair that stood up from his forehead like a wind-blown flame and a small beard of a rather brighter red already touched with white. He had enormous feet, as all foreigners had, and large, firm, freckled hands. He came every morning and every evening for a week, and he made Fong Yung well again. It was beyond Yutsing to hate this quiet, charitable foreigner.

Fresh regiments were quartered in the town, and one night the sky was red with fire; in these unsettled times the rebel was always ready to break out with arson, rioting and looting. Some of them were executed, others were forcibly enlisted as coolies. The problems of the commissariat, the transport and supply of munitions and provisions were always a great difficulty in the advancing revolutionary army. It enlisted all the unpaid porters it could get hold of. Yutsing and his wife left the town and its acrid smell of conflagration, its charred timbers and its wretched inhabitants behind them and followed the army. They did not see the American doctor after the fire.

Meanwhile the revolutionaries defeated the armies of the feudal generals, established themselves in the villages and towns and continued their advance into the North. Chiang Kai-shek was a short, brown Cantonese who spoke the language of the simple people. He had little education but had worked his way up from the ranks to supreme command. Two great men had inspired him with their ideas and widened the outlook of the soldier's brain: Sun Yat-sen and Borodin.

Whether the students knew it or not, the Kuomintang and the Revolution were built up on and inspired by Russian and Communist ideas. Yutsing and his wife did not know it. They disseminated a faith and a hope based on the three popular principles enunciated by Sun Yat-sen. They never thought of the formulas of the sworn Communists. They saw that some people were too poor and others too rich. They wanted to help the poor against the mercilessness of the rich, for the poor were China.

When the revolutionaries established themselves in Hankow, Yutsing and his wife rejoined their comrades and waited for fresh orders. Although he had been born with a tooth in his mouth he had not become a great leader. He was just one of the thousands of young students who helped to create the New China, distributing leaflets, addressing meetings and talking at street corners, posting dangerous manifestoes in places where the war lords were still in power. Not one of them set much store by his own life. They never thought of danger but only of the goal and how to reach it. Yutsing, however, was no hero; he was a rather weakly, rather shy and rather too serious scholar, and courage was not expected of a man of his sort. But as a grain of sand among other grains of sand he was ready to die for China if it could be of any good.

In Hankow Yutsing became a coolie among coolies. In Hankow foreign ships loaded and unloaded, in Hankow men, women and children worked for twelve and fourteen hours a day in the foreigners' factories and on the Bund of Hankow were the foreign banks stuffed with the money extorted from the people of China. Yutsing and some of his companions mingled with the workers and coolies and while they shared their hard, degrading labor they worked for a general strike, a united front and rebellion. Yutsing, clothed in a coolie's rags, was ordered to work among the dock workers. His delicate scholar's hands were covered with burst blisters that laid the raw flesh bare. He sighed sometimes in the bitterness of his heart when he remembered his mother's family in which any menial task was considered a disgrace. He thought with a smile of his gigantic father who had been a coolie before him. He put the strap round his forehead and lugged his barrow along the quay until he felt the veins of his temples bursting. He struggled for breath and sang the endless, moaning chant of the coolies in order to control it. He learned to know what it was to have no breath in your body and the pain that stabbed from the overstrained heart into the pit of your stomach. When they knocked off work and squatted on the quay and had not earned enough for the second bowl of rice, he talked to the others.

At night he joined his wife. Fong Yung bathed his sores and blisters and complimented him on his strength. She herself was working in the poorest quarter of the town. Dysentery had broken out, and Fong Yung, whose large experience made up for her small knowledge, was trying to prevent the spread of the disease. The rest became the work of the men. The English had deserted the town. The banks on the Bund were shut, their steel shutters rolled down. Then work ceased in the factories. The broad river, almost deserted by shipping, looked as though it slept. It had been the same in Hong Kong. Just before Yutsing joined the army which was advancing on Shanghai, Fong Yung told him that she was once more pregnant.

They lay in bed together, and the darkness of the room was lighted up from the building opposite where printing presses were at work all night. The light from its windows shone through the mosquito net and threw a fine, reticulated shadow on the quilt. "Promise me a son," Yutsing begged his wife. She laughed softly as he put his hand on her body. "It will be months before he moves," she said gaily. Yutsing felt the warmness of her skin and that her body was still almost as slender and flat as a child's. "Promise me not to do away with the child in you this time," he begged urgently, for he had never quite got over what had happened in Canton.

"No." Fong Yung assured him earnestly. "So many are dying it is necessary that many were born." Yutsing fell asleep on her shoulder in the utter exhaustion of a coolie. It filled him with peace and contentment to know that a son was on the way.

The army of the Peking government had guns; but the soldiers of the Revolution had an ideal to fight for and leaders in whom they trusted, and so they were victorious. The fate of the Revolution was decided in Shanghai. The fighting there was sanguinary, the narrow lanes of the Chinese city went up in flames and were filled with the dead. The foreigners shut the gates that separated their quarters from those of the Chinese, and pinched their noses when the smell of corpses came on the wind. Yutsing had seen many dead, innumerable dead since the day when his mandarin grandfather had been executed. He had seen the dead lying stiff on the field of battle, black and charred corpses in burned towns and villages; he had seen the black-faced victims of torture and swollen drowned bodies floating in the rivers. He had got used to them and thought of them as decaying refuse, not as human beings. But it was in Shanghai that he himself fought and killed for the first time. And he did it because he was in despair—in so far as despair could find a place in the calm soul of a Chinese.

First there was murmuring and then an outcry among his companions. "Chiang Kai-shek has sold us." There had been splits and shades of conflicting opinion among the revolutionaries before now —Anarchists, Nihilists, Terrorists, right wing and left. Now it came to an open cleavage, and Chiang Kai-shek turned against his Russian abettors who had organized the Revolution for him. He had used them as long as he needed them; now he turned his back on them and on all the young Chinese who had been brought up in their ideas. Borodin had stayed behind with his men in Hankow. Chiang Kai-shek pushed on to Nanking: many foreigners were shot, and then the foreign warships bombarded the town. As soon as Chiang Kai-shek was victorious he turned upon the Reds who had been his friends.

Perhaps Yutsing had never known that he himself was a Red
He had been ordered to escort a lorry, loaded with hand grenades,
to a certain house in the old Chinese town. That night, while they
were unloading the bombs, the lane and the house were attacked
by Chiang Kai-shek's troops. There were women and children there,
weeping and sickly little boys, men of every age and condition: the
same mixture of races as in Canton—Chinese, Russians, Germans, two
Belgians, a French-Annamite half-breed. Yutsing helped to defend the
entrance to the house. He threw hand grenades as they were handed
to him, while behind in the darkness of the bombarded house the
dead and wounded lay in heaps and the cries of dying children
pierced the noise of the shooting. It was a wild, insensate battle.
Others of his comrades were taken prisoner at the North Station
and scalded to death in the steam of boilers. All that they could
hope for in their desperation—if they hoped for anything at all—
was to die fighting and so avoid being tortured to death. By dawn
four of them were still alive. There was silence outside. In the first
gray of dawn they saw the lane through the shattered windows
heaped with dead soldiers. Now that the shooting was over the rats
ran swiftly and eagerly among the dead. Yutsing's face was caked
with his comrades' blood, but he was unwounded. For some hours
after he knew nothing: he slept or lay unconscious in utter exhaustion. When he woke up, the other three had vanished, he was alone
in the house with the dead—men, women and children. Driven by
the fierce pangs of hunger, he climbed over the stiffened bodies and
through a hole in the wall into the lane. Outside, the sky was blue
and clear overhead and the early spring air was keener and more
penetrating even than the stench of death.

That day he succeeded in entering the French Settlement where
his father's bank was. The great man, Bogum Chang, was occupied
with an important meeting, and Yutsing had to wait in his office.
The contrast between the safety and security that was taken as a
matter of course within those walls and the horrors through which
he and his comrades had gone, plunged him into an extremity of
bitterness. He could taste the bitterness on his tongue, and it burned
and smarted in his eyes. When at last his father came in and looked

him up and down as he stood there in his tattered and bloody uniform, Yutsing found that his voice was parched with fire and smoke
and that it was only with difficulty that he could speak at all.

The father and son had not met for nearly four years, but Yutsing
had written regularly to his mother, and she had read the letters
to his father. The expression on his father's face made Yutsing
aware how dirty, war-worn and tattered he was. But Chang quickly
recovered himself; the look of horror and pity left his face, he
greeted his son with the time-honored greeting: "Have you eaten?"

Yutsing, however, had left all convention behind; he neither knelt
to his father, as would have been seemly after so long a parting,
nor did he even make him a bow. He moistened his parched lips
and asked with no polite prelude: "Is it true that you have made
common cause with the foreigners and bought Chiang Kai-shek?"

Bogum Chang gave no answer. "You look bad, my son, very bad,"
he said sadly. "Will you have something to eat or drink? Or a
smoke?" He pushed his massive cigarette box across the table to
Yutsing, who shook his head. "Answer!" was all he said.

Chang smiled. "It is not usual for the son to call the father to
account. But if you will have it, I am proud and happy to belong
to the group of men who are of the same mind as the General.
He is a capable man who deserves support. I was against him for
a long time, for I am only a stupid man. But I have become convinced that it will be of service to us all if Chiang Kai-shek governs
the country."

Yutsing deliberately inhaled the smell of blood which rose from
his uniform. "You have paid for the ammunition with which his
soldiers have shot at me and my friends. Remember that. If Chiang
Kai-shek had had me tortured to death, would you not have been
sorry you had given him money?" he cried. With rage and grief he
felt his voice break and the tears smart in his eyes. He was so tired,
so weak, so unhappy and confused. His father got up and, walking
quickly up to him, laid his heavy hand on his shoulder. "Do you
mean to say that you belong to the Communists?" he asked in
horror.

"Why not?" Yutsing cried out. "Why not? Shall I belong to the rich? To the foreigners? Look at this town! Its life of vice goes on, and what do you care for war or revolution and the dead and the poor? You are rich and unashamed, all of you, compradors, middlemen, profiteers, bloodsuckers! What do you know of the coolies? What goes on in your factories? They work till their hearts burst, they spit their lungs out on the streets, and still they do not earn enough to buy themselves a bowl of rice!"

Bogum Chang's red face went white; he looked frightful as the blood ebbed away beneath his copper-colored skin. He tore open his silk garment, and the little buttons shot across the room. He showed his son the scars on his gigantic shoulders, the white weal marks of his labors as a coolie. Yutsing took a step back, he expected his father to roar like a beast. But Chang restrained himself with an effort that made his fists quiver. He hid them in his sleeves. "You are green with youth," he said almost gently. "Green with youth, and you don't know what you are saying. You can make speeches, but work and hunger you know not. You do not know what the country and the people need. They need quiet and contentment, not bloodshed and famine. China is not Russia. It has had enough of blood and battle and death and sacrifices. I know nothing of politics and have not been to school, as you have. But common sense tells me this much: the Communists do not love us. They want to make a second Russia of China and to use our men for a world revolution. If you had not the brain of a monkey you would understand that."

"Quiet and contentment indeed! And you ask contentment of a people which has suffered and endured more, borne with more hunger and poverty than any other in the whole world. And you would rather have those who would come to its help murdered than your business interfered with and your swilling and guzzling——"

"Silence! I forbid you to speak another word," Chang shouted, losing control of himself. "You come here like a beggar, you put me to shame as your father in the eyes of my doorkeeper, famished you are, dirty and ragged, no better than a beggar. And you whine on like a beggar. You have no thought for your duty to your father or your family. You might have been a minister and been of use to the government and brought honor to the family; there is my bank here, which I have built up for you, that is where you belong, but you prefer to mix with beggars, you are a beggar yourself, and all you bring here is your stink——"

"A beggar, very well, and I would rather be a beggar than serve in a government bought by the foreigners. Better a beggar than a banker like you. You are criminals, you and your friends, criminals, thieves and murderers. You wallow in your filthy wealth——"

Chang raised his two fists and brought them down on his son's neck and shoulders. Yutsing tottered under the heavy blows, but he kept his feet. His nose began to bleed, he tried to snuffle back the blood. Bogum Chang turned away with a groan and sank back into the broad, carved chair at his writing table. Yutsing left the room without another word. He did not know where he was going, but his feet took him of their own accord back to the horrible lane whence he had come. It was cleared of its corpses. Even the bombarded house, into which he groped his way, was empty and strangely large and tidy. It gave Yutsing an uncanny feeling, and he dragged himself on and even ate at a street kitchen and paid for his rice and vegetables with the last coppers in his pocket. Up to now all through the years while the Revolution was being prepared, he had lived on his father without giving the matter a thought. Now that was over. He slept soundly and dreamlessly on the pavement of a narrow lane, in which there was a temple, among the huddled bodies of homeless wretches like himself.

When he woke in the morning he was in a poor way. He was stiff, his limbs shook, his teeth chattered with a feverish chill. It was a gray morning with a mist from the river. Yutsing found himself in a turmoil of people and noise. Fathers and children were even laughing, while the women, stolid as ever, rummaged in their rags and gave their breasts to infants in arms. A man in a white coat was threading his way among the homeless crowd, bending over children and giving them medicine and rice; two nurses followed him, one of whom had a huge stewpan of rice on a barrow and the other bandages and medicaments in a large black bag. Yutsing smiled in astonishment without knowing that he did so. The man was not Jesus, although he looked very like the Reverend Thomas Warren of St John's. It was Dr Lee who had looked after Fong Yung. "Doctor Lee!" Yutsing exclaimed involuntarily. The doctor looked up from the child, in whose little arm he had just made an injection, and recognized him at once. When the child had had its gourd cup, which its mother held out, filled with rice, the doctor came quickly up to him. Yutsing had involuntarily got up and was annoyed with himself because he could not stop his teeth chattering.

"What are you doing here?" Dr Lee asked as he felt his pulse. He spoke in English, not in Chinese.

"I might ask you the same question," Yutsing replied. Dr Lee kept his eyes on his watch while he felt his pulse. "The mission in Fukang has been evacuated for the time," he said dryly. "My house has been burned to the ground. My wife is dead. A stroke. The shock. Thank God my children are in America. Now I just do what I can."

Yutsing did not know what to reply. The doctor put up his watch. "You are feverish," he said. "Malaria probably. Here—nine pills a day. I can spare you only enough quinine for three days. We're rather short of medicines. How is your wife?"

"That I do not know," Yutsing said. He had been worrying over Fong Yung whenever, during these distracted and disastrous days, he had been able to think clearly of anything at all. Dr Lee had already passed on to the next group. The quinine pills grew warm in his hand.

He and a few companions got back to Hankow in a small boat. The town was vacant and still. The factories were shut, the foreigners' smart quarters deserted, the banks closed and the port dead. The printing press alone was busy night and day. The coolies were without work. Slips of paper were pasted on the telegraph poles on which was printed the one word—Hunger. Yutsing reported to the propaganda department, but there was little for him to do. After long asking and searching he found Fong Yung in a hospital which the foreigners had evacuated. Fong Yung was surrounded by sick children who lay mutely in their beds as if they were not in any pain. She was thin and wasted and transparent, and only the roundness of her pregnant womb showed beneath the nurse's uniform she had borrowed. To Yutsing she was like a drink of water on a hot day and like a hearth fire in winter.

The town was near to breaking point; there was the feeling everywhere of a general break-up and final liquidation. The strike funds were empty, the coolies unwilling and starved. Borodin was down with one of those attacks of malaria which had already put him out of action from time to time in Canton. Chiang Kai-shek's soldiers were advancing on the town. A rumor had reached them that the Christian general, who had spent a year in Russia, was marching with his troops to the rescue of Hankow. Telegrams went to and fro, messengers arrived, breathless and exhausted, to announce how far he had got and how large and well equipped his army was. Suddenly he chose the winning side and went over to Chiang Kai-shek. The news flickered through the foreign quarter, where the revolutionaries had settled themselves, through the Chinese town, reached the harbor and the arsenal. The printing presses in the building opposite Yutsing's room pounded breathlessly on. He hung about the propaganda office, but he was of no use. Later he went to the hospital to see Fong Yung, for he needed consolation. It came over him on that dreary and sultry and sweltering summer evening that every turn events took was only one more disaster for China, that it was in vain to make sacrifices for a country where each pursued his own advantage, where poverty and labor were despised and where wealth and a big face were the sole aim of all. He rang the bell at the hospital gate and collapsed onto the small hollowed-out flagstone put there for the benefit of women who wished to deposit their unwanted girl babies instead of killing them. He almost fell asleep in his weariness while he waited, ringing the bell at intervals. There were flashes of lightning in the clouds beyond Wuchang on the other side of the river. Finally, when no one opened the gate, he went back to the building which housed the International Delegation and played chess in one of the front rooms till morning.

He never saw Fong Yung again. When the Revolution collapsed and Chiang Kai-shek's soldiers entered the town, killing many and taking others away as prisoners, Yutsing lost all trace of his wife in the confusion. Friends urged him to flee, but he obstinately roamed the neighborhood in the hope of finding her. It was not until he learned that she had been tortured for three days and three nights and then strangled, that he too made his escape.

Fong Yung, nineteen years old, with her child's body and her heroic heart. She had embroidered a white star on black silk and concealed it between her flat little breasts, the star of New China, she had carried it in her hands and never surrendered. She was not violated, nor did the soldiers tear her bowels from her body and wrap her in them, as they did to others. They only tortured and then strangled her. The martyred blood of his wife parted Yutsing from the Nationalists in Nanking.

Seven months later, in the company of other refugees of Russian, Chinese or unknown breeds, he reached Moscow. The flight across the whole width of China, up rivers in boats, through mountains on donkeys, across deserts on camels, in trains crowded to the roof, through ever colder and more foreign lands; the friendship of Mongols, Mohammedans, Turkistanese and bandits of every description; the interminable forests of Siberia, the bitter, early winter of Russia; the foreign language, the foreign people, the inhospitable, incomprehensible foreign atmosphere—all this passed Yutsing by as if it did not touch him. As if he were only watching a man who achieved a senseless exploit, who had suffered much and lost still more. A man whose actions did not fit him and who lived a life that was not his own.

He came across many of his countrymen in Moscow. An official delegation had come for the celebration of the tenth anniversary of the Soviet Republic and stayed on. They were pressing round, rather pointlessly; nobody bothered about them; they shivered with cold and could not learn the language. "The Chinese experiment has not come off," a certain Sokoloff told Yutsing. It sounded as if China were not a country, inhabited by human beings, but a faulty chemical formula. Yutsing, the scholar, began to study the language and attended the Sun Yat-sen University which had been founded for people of his sort; he lived in unheated, crowded rooms allotted to the Chinese. He had no money, and the lack of it was no easier to bear in Russia than anywhere else. There was hunger on every side, only in the well-kept barracks of the Red Army was there enough to eat. Yutsing left the university, which slowly dwindled away, and worked in a factory that turned out lorries. There was much talk of politics, but little work was done. The ever-repeated slogans ceased to enthuse him; they began first to bore, then to exasperate him. The informer and the spy infested the workshops, and he felt that he was in chains. The Chinese were poor but free. The Russians were poor and not free. The more he saw the more he doubted. These people lived without wisdom like ants. The State was their ant heap; they knew nothing of the harmony and contentment of the individual which was the core and the heritage of the men of his own country. Power stations, dams, automobile works—but no happiness. Sometimes the machines turned against the men and ceased to work, and then it was not the machines that were condemned but the men. Many people disappeared and no one dared say a word. There were spies in every house and every family, and dynamite was less dangerous than having thoughts of your own. He attended a public mass trial, at which twenty-four men were condemned to death. For years he had lived, eaten, drunk and slept with death. It was odd that this little drop of foreign blood made him suddenly sick and tired; he felt that he could stand no more of it, that he could not bear to see another execution or hear another shot or have one more man beaten up for doing wrong. He pined with homesickness for China; there was so little laughter in Moscow. He was consumed with longing when he thought of the coolies' hearty laughter and their good-natured jokes. It is only we who know how to live, he thought and that "we" broke him free of Russia.

When he remembered those years later, it seemed to him that it had always been winter there, that no flowers had bloomed, no songs been sung. There was nothing but the Idea, and if the Idea could not make you happy there was no other happiness to be found in Russia. One day Yutsing broke through the trance in which his youth had been spent. One morning he woke and thought: All this time life has gone on on the Western Lake, the girls have been laughing in the courtyards, my mother has been embroidering on silk, my aunt has been burning incense, lotus flowers have been flowering on the lake, music has been resounding from the boats, lovebirds twittering in their cages, and the willows dropping their lovely branches over the water. He looked about him and turned away from the meagerness and inhumanity of his existence. He borrowed money for the journey and returned to his own country.

In return for the loan he had missions to carry out in the Red province of Kiangsi. There was still war in China. The Red Army was fighting against the Nationalist Army. Both armies lived on the country, and the peasants suffered. Both armies were better disciplined than they were when he had left China. Both fought in the Chinese fashion, according to which the weaker gave way without showing much fight—a wise and humorous strategy but for which China would long since have committed suicide in the course of her long history of civil wars.

Yutsing was offered the post of a commissar in charge of a small town in Kiangsi. While he was still considering whether it was his duty to take it on, an unpleasant incident occurred in a poor quarter of the place. The people had had it dinned into them for so long that an exaggerated esteem for the family and the reverence for the old were harmful that one day they began to make an end of their grandfathers and grandmothers on the ground that they did not earn the food they ate. A new campaign of enlightenment was called for. Yutsing declined the task with a smile. He might have been born with a tooth in his mouth, but he no longer wished to be a leader of men. I have come to the end, he thought. He gave thanks for the honor in well-chosen words and regretted with all the politeness incumbent on him that he was unworthy of the post offered him. He made his way home to the house on the lake as a pilgrim to a shrine. It was more difficult to get out of the Red territory than to enter it. Bus, boat, railway, chairs on bad roads, rickshas along the side of canals, disguises, perils, mortal dread, homesickness—and home at last.

Slowly he recovered his old self in the withdrawn but busy life of the courtyards and the gentle, almost humble care of his mother.

Once again he wore the student's long robe and let his shoulders droop forward as befitted a scholar's ease. It consoled him after long years in the strait jacket of a foreign uniform. He joked with his aunt who giggled like a girl. He paid the younger teacher a visit in the municipal offices and discussed the duties of a son with the old teacher, who had grown a thin and dignified white beard. He read the old books again and tried his clumsy hand at calligraphy. And he made a new friend who helped him to find his feet again—Liu, the son of a great family which had bought the neighboring property. Liu was a poet, a highly polished and mocking spirit, the possessor of a keen nose and cultivated palate. He invited Yutsing to select epicurean feasts, to drink tea of Luching, brewed with the water of the Old Dragon spring; to regale on fish brought alive to Hangchow from the Lung River; to an evening of music on the lute and a special fragrant incense; to smoke an occasional pipe of opium, which gave rare clarity to their talk.

Yutsing's father came from Shanghai for the New Year's feast, and his mother went as far as the first courtyard to meet him, tripping on her tiny old-fashioned feet. Yutsing in a sudden fit of vehement remorse knelt down and touched the ground with his forehead. His father quickly raised him up and gave him a fleeting and shamefaced embrace as if he were still a child. Not a word was said about the years of Yutsing's exile or the circumstances in which they had last parted. When they went together to the shrine of their forefathers, he saw with amazement that tears ran down his gigantic father's cheeks. He wiped them away with his sleeve as a coolie might the sweat from his face.

Yutsing was twenty-seven years old. The burden of all he had lived through made him feel as tired as an old man. He would have lived on as an old man if the Japanese had not come to Shanghai.

He had turned a deaf ear to the Manchurian war in spite of the loud and angry protests against the Japanese. The three eastern provinces were not really China; they had been the possessions of the Manchu emperors and had never really become a part of the Middle Kingdom, and Japanese rule could not be worse than that of the bandit general Chang Tsolin, who had so far ruled there. Yutsing was weary, too weary even to take sides. He chewed melon seeds and sunflower seeds and drank tea and played Mahjong with Liu and thawed the frost that gripped his heart. But when in 1932 the Japanese turned Shanghai itself into a battlefield and made war on China he woke up and took notice. For the first time for many a long year Chinese troops fought seriously and with courage and tenacity against a foreign foe; for the first time for many a long year war was not a deal, in which one of the opponents could buy the other or win him over to his own side by the offer of high position. For the first time a sense of nationality and national honor came into play. For the first time Yutsing saw the first green streak in the sky which is not yet dawn but is the herald of dawn. And for the first time he felt a glimmer of respect for the National government, which had killed his wife. His father came home for a few days. He was in radiant spirits and treated the war in Shanghai as a good joke or as a race meeting, where nothing mattered but putting his money on the right horse. When his father returned to Shanghai, his mother begged Yutsing to accompany him, as though the feeble son could protect his giant of a father. Yutsing was glad to go, not to fight at the barricades, for he was no longer a soldier, but to see with his own eyes and to form his own judgment about what was going on.

The town was in the throes of war, but this was nothing new, and its life went on as if nothing could disturb its shameless self-assurance. The night clubs were open; dancing, drinking, gambling went merrily on, the brothels and opium dens were doing a livelier trade than usual, relaxing strung-up nerves. Ears got accustomed to the noise of the guns, or else the noise of the city drowned it. Yutsing recollected a passage in the Bible, a book which had long since vanished from his mind. There was a Bible in English in every bedroom of the hotel in which he and his father were staying—an attention odd enough in that depraved city. He read with difficulty at first and then with a smile; the verses he had learned by heart as a boy came back of themselves to his scholarly memory. Sodom and Gomorrah, that was it. At night fire and brimstone rained down upon the town, the streets were darkened as a protection against bombing. There was shooting from the windows of Chapei, the Chinese were entrenched and barricaded behind doorways and they faced death with an indifference that to the foreigners was incomprehensible but which Yutsing knew well. "Better a dog in peace than a man in war," said the coolies and half-grown children who crept out whenever the shooting slackened and gathered up as booty whatever they could find in the streets in the way of empty cartridge cases or other by-products of battle.

One sunny winter day when a truce had been declared, Yutsing drove out to Chapei. He had his pass, for his father's name alone was a passport. They crossed a bridge over the Soochow Creek, and he had scarcely got out to make his way on foot between abandoned barricades when he was thrown to the ground by a terrific explosion. The Japanese had apparently thought better of the promised truce. A bomb had been dropped on a warehouse and destroyed it. When Yutsing picked himself up and found that he was uninjured, he ran in the direction of the explosion instinctively, without giving the matter a thought. The lane into which he turned was utterly deserted, as was the whole of that district, where only a few barricaded windows were employed for sniping. He came on a man who was dragging the wounded from the ruins of the warehouse and laying them out in a row in the middle of the street. He wore a grimy white doctor's coat, and his face too was black with smoke and dust. "Can you give me a hand? My stretcher bearers have run away. The ambulance is back there," he said hurriedly. Yutsing followed him across the ruins, which had begun to crackle and blaze. Together they pulled out one more man, who died as they laid him down. Something in the doctor's movements as he bent over the dead man dimly reminded Yutsing of somebody. "Dr Lee?" he asked abruptly. His hands were still trembling from the shock and fright of the explosion. The doctor raised his blackened face in a fleeting glance. "Have we met before?" he asked. Yutsing nodded. He gave a hand, and together they carried the wounded one by one to the ambulance, which was waiting in the cover of an empty garage.

A bomb splinter had torn off the leg of one of the wounded men. He held it convulsively in his hands and implored the doctor piteously to stitch it on again. "If you die I will stitch it on again, but if you live you can earn more with only one leg," Dr Lee said to console him.

It was the most kindly and sensible thing Yutsing had ever heard a foreigner say, and it was Chinese through and through. The wounded man had no great fear of death, but a mortal terror of going mutilated into the next world. But a cripple is sought out by every beggar's guild and can count on a regular income. It was this remark that induced Yutsing to accompany the doctor from then onwards on his expeditions into the dangerous quarter round the North Station. In spite of racial enmity a rapid and taciturn friendship sprang up between these two men who had both lost their wives. The result of it was that Yutsing went to America to study medicine in the following autumn. He had hated, feared and fought the West. He had despised the West for its barbarity and yet admired its achievements. The recent fighting had convinced him that China would have to adopt Western methods in a thoroughgoing fashion if it was to survive an age that differed from any other in the four thousand years of its existence. He went to America because the West could give him the knowledge and the weapons he wanted.

He found a people which, though it lived in a capitalistic country, was in possession of all that in Russia was only dreamed of and desired. For a generation it had not known war either within the country or on its frontiers. There was no starvation and there were no beggars. There were droughts and floods, for nature obeys no law, but when want arose help was forthcoming. There were liberty and justice in most cases, and if injustice and corruption came to light there was a great outcry and any man might say what he thought, and no one was executed unless he himself had killed another. There was scarcely a person who could not read and write; there were schools for all, hospitals for the sick and counsel to defend the poor who were accused of any offense. The police did not hit about them with sticks but smilingly conducted children or old women across the street. There were poor, but in China and Russia they would have been called rich. And there were the rich, but they were expected to give away and distribute a great part of their wealth and not keep it all for themselves. Instead of the poor being taxed and the wealthy pocketing the taxes, the poor paid little and it was the rich who were highly taxed. And though there were numbers of very wealthy people, the contrast between the lives of the wealthy and the lives of the poor was constantly diminishing. For even the bellies of the rich cannot hold more than their fill, and their bodies cannot be more than well and warmly clothed. A roof for protection and a bed to sleep in and food for wife and children, these are men's needs; it is only when these needs cannot be met that poverty begins. All the rest is merely luxury and in the last resort unimportant. So at least thought Yutsing, who had seen much.

It was a new experience for him to live in a country which had one law for rich and poor throughout all its provinces. The roads were safe, no soldiers were to be seen; women could mix freely with men without risk, the old were treated with politeness. Although Yutsing had been to a school conducted by white people, he had always imagined that the love of children, politeness in social relationships and consideration for old age were known only to the Chinese. It surprised him and sobered him to find that the barbarians were not in these respects barbarians at all. For a long time he was utterly bewildered by all he saw, and he often thought sadly: Never will my country be able to be as this country is.

He landed on the West coast, and although his father provided him plentifully with money—for he was glad to find that his son, whom he had almost given up for lost, was now coming to his senses—he took his time in traversing the country and getting to know it before going East to New York. He found a city that had many resemblances with Shanghai, and the people of New York were more strident and hurried and less in harmony with the universe than those of the small towns and on the country roads. When all was said, Yutsing came to realize that the Americans, who had more than other peoples dared ever to dream of having, were not so happy as they. High spirits and noise and speed, but not true happiness. They did not know what every coolie in China knew—that it was good to be alive, and that man was only one of the ten thousand things in the universe, and the world one round whole: Yin and Yang, heaven and earth, man and woman, day and night, light and darkness, good and evil, and that it was given to every man to live in harmony with the whole.

Chang Yutsing had already had many names in his life and he was only thrice ten years old. He had been Lao Chang Yutsing, the honored Little Master, John the Christian, Chang Tehum the humble student, Chang the coolie, Tovarich Chang the Communist. Now he was Mister Chang, one of the thousand students of Columbia University. He lived in a small hotel in Chinatown and ate with Chinese students. He went to the Chinese Club and the American theater. He had his share in the white man's neighborliness, his brotherly feeling towards every creature, which he owed to Christianity, but also in his arrogance towards everyone whose skin was not of the same color as his own. And as Mister Chang was a Chinese, most of what he saw and learned seemed funny to him, and he wrote down many ironical and amusing observations in a little book. He worked hard and with a good will, and all the new things he learned crowded much of the old horrors out of his memory.

He did not forget Fong Yung, but she became as the reflection of a willow branch in still water and then as the scent of a freshly mown clover field at sunset, and then as the sound of a flute at night on the lake that recedes and recedes until at last the ear can scarcely detect the moment when it dies away at last. . . .

And so Mister Chang married a girl who also was studying medicine and who was as vigorous and free as an American girl, for she had been born in New York; but she had not lost the delicate skin and the charm and flexibility of her race. She was Pearl Fong, daughter of a merchant in Mott Street, Chinatown. They took their degrees at the same time, and Dr Chang returned to China. He found that his country had made great progress in those brief years, and he joined the New Life Movement and made his peace with the Nanking government.

At the time when this account begins he had an important post in the Municipal Health Office of Greater Shanghai.

PART II

The City

I

WHILE THE BLACK-BEARDED SIKH at the corner of Yates Street held up the traffic to let the stream of cars, rickshas and pedestrians cross Bubbling Well Road, Dr Chang had time to buy an English evening paper.

"Any news?" Taylor asked as he drove on.

Dr Chang glanced at the headlines. His eyeglasses were so thick that his eyes could not be seen behind them.

"Nothing much," he said as he folded up the paper again.

Frank Taylor was disgusted to find that the heat made his hands stick to the steering wheel. Moreover, his white suit had come from the laundry badly ironed and was already creasing again at the hollows of his elbows and knees. He held the wheel with his knee while he took out his handkerchief and wiped his hands. "A horrible place, this," he said. "You're always dirty."

Dr Chang smiled in polite agreement. "It seems to be a law that one never feels happy away from the climate in which one's born," he said platitudinously. "I, for example, am not at all troubled by the heat of Shanghai, whereas the heat of New York drove me almost crazy." He produced the paper once more, unfolded it and after turning the pages finally put it aside. "No," he said, "there's no news."

For some time past there had been fighting between Japanese and Chinese troops in the North, but the North was far away and always unsettled.

"If at least they had something to drink at the airport," Taylor said. His head was still aching from the night before in the Cathay Club. His mouth was parched, and he was thirsty for a long drink of soda with very little Scotch. Yutsing Chang smiled in absent-minded politeness.

They reached the outskirts of the town and drove on for a time between fields and small houses. There was a smell of cabbage and

281

manure, and the air quivered with moist heat. The suburban streets were lined by low Chinese houses and open booths; there was very little traffic. Now and then they met a few rickshas in which sat portly, elderly Chinese, whose houses were out in that district. Then more factories and more cabbage fields.

"How long are you staying in Nanking?" Taylor asked without much interest.

"Two days if I can see all the gentlemen with whom I have to speak," Dr Chang replied. He had his little suitcase between his feet.

"It is about the Jamboree," he added. "It is very important that no mistakes shall be made in the organization. The Boy Scouts go back to their villages and tell what they have seen. It is extremely important that they shall get the impression of order and discipline and spread that impression abroad."

Chang sighed and smiled at the same time, for order and discipline were not native qualities of the Chinese, who preferred to live in a pleasing disorder and liberty. The money designed for the rally of the Boy Scouts trickled away in the usual manner. Nevertheless, walls were placarded with a sturdy Scout waving the Scout banner above a neat array of tents. Intelligence, courage, benevolence were written upon it. Taylor's attention had wandered. Now he began to smile.

"Probably my fiancée will be here by the time the show starts," he said. "I've had a cable from her. Perhaps we'll even be married before your Jamboree."

Dr Chang removed his eyeglasses with an air of respectful astonishment as if he had taken off his hat. "And you only tell me that now?" he exclaimed.

Taylor clapped him on the shoulder. "Who told me it was bad form to blurt out our private affairs as we Americans do?" he said. At this Chang broke into a beaming smile, which still lingered on his face as they crossed a canal on which there were many houseboats and turned down the muddy street leading to the Lunghua Airport. He took his little bag from between his feet while he ceremoniously thanked Taylor for the lift.

"That's all right," Taylor said. "I'm glad to take you along, as long as I had to go to this God-forsaken neighborhood at all." He held out his hand, and Chang took it gingerly as though it were a wet rag or some other unpleasant object. He simply could not get used to the practice of handshaking. A Chinese boy in white uniform took possession of his little suitcase. The airplane was already waiting out on the airfield, gray and silvery in the hazy sunshine.

Frank waved to Chang before turning the car, but the Chinese was too busy with his black case to notice. His lean figure and bent shoulders vanished into the building, which had a derelict and make-shift air. Frank was not quite clear whether he liked Dr Chang or not. A decent fellow but boring, he often thought. Mr and Mrs Chang were the only Chinese with whom he was on friendly terms, and it was chiefly because Chang and his Welfare Center meant better sales to him. Chang had a passion for illustrated health pamphlets and instructive posters, which were very useful to a population that knew nothing of hygiene and could not read. B.S., the head manager, had from the very first impressed on his young assistant that he must pocket his pride and not neglect Chinese customers. The color bar between the white and yellow races was out of date, and only a few die-hard English firms still held to it, to the great damage of their turnovers. The large orders that Frank had got out of Dr Chang by cultivating his acquaintance and co-operating with him in a friendly spirit were one of the chief reasons for his promotion and increased salary. In a way Dr Chang and his posters were responsible for the fact that Frank Taylor was at last in a position to marry Ruth Anderson. He's quite a decent fellow, too—for a Chinese, Frank concluded after reflecting on all this. He stopped and got out on the bridge, in order to inspect the outline of the pagoda which rose up behind dilapidated houses and roofs; immediately he was surrounded by a group of inquisitive Chinese who looked at him in that way of theirs he could never get used to—that drowsy, open-mouthed expression which somehow seemed insolent. Also they had an indescribable stink, so Taylor got quickly into his car again, wiped his hands and drove on.

As in front of every temple there were booths with strings of paper money for the gods, open kitchens with enormous cauldrons emitting a disgusting vaporous steam, booths of letter writers and soothsayers, and crowds of ragged and rickety children.

Although Frank Taylor had been in Shanghai for over two years and had often driven out to the airfield, he had never yet troubled to pay a visit to the neighboring Lunghua pagoda. But today there were reasons of business for doing so, and he got out and looked curiously round about him. Out here there was nothing of Shanghai and much of dirt and China. Taylor clipped his tripod under his arm, hung his camera round his neck by the strap, put a few films in his coat pocket and forged his way through the human wall which had instantly risen around him. A lean youth in the long robe of a student offered in bad English to keep an eye on his car which he left at the temple gate. *"Tshih!"* Taylor shouted at the rabble of youths that closed in round him, and one of them shouted "Scram!" back at him in the best American slang. Taylor suppressed a smile and went on with a frown. Two soldiers were walking two white horses up and down in the outer court of the temple as though they were in a barrack yard. Here too there were booths, and a coughing and spitting mob surged to and fro. Wang Wen, the assistant whom Taylor had told to meet him at the pagoda, had not apparently arrived, and Frank cursed in an undertone at Chinese unpunctuality and muddle. He traversed the first temple which was fairly empty and very dirty and where only a few sticks of incense were smoldering before the goddess of mercy. He observed that some of the praying Chinese looked at him with a furtive but obviously contemptuous smile, and he realized that the sight of a sweating, ill-humored foreigner who carried his own camera and tripod and films was bad for the prestige of the white race. A little old man who read his thoughts with oriental facility instantly appeared at his elbow and in English that sounded like Chinese offered himself as a porter in return for payment. Taylor, with his experience of Shanghai, after a little bargaining brought the price for this service down to one half, namely, ten cents. Then, relieved of his burden, he went on, with the laden Chinese at a respectful distance behind him. An inquisitive crowd had meanwhile attached itself to him. He traversed the courts and halls of the temple; all of them were dirty and hideous, and the incense made his headache worse. He coughed and wanted to spit as the Chinese did in their casual way, but his ingrained reverence for a shrine, of whatever sort it might be, restrained him. At last he came to a place from which the pagoda showed up well against the sky; it was a small, circular, gardenlike space where two priests in their wide-sleeved robes were walking up and down.

"May I sit down here?" he asked one of them, and although the man clearly did not understand English he pointed with a gesture of extreme politeness to a semicircular stone bench which stood in the little garden. Taylor sat down with a sigh, took possession of his camera and his tripod and sent the little old man back to the temple again to keep a lookout for Wang Wen. The priests left the little garden without giving him another glance. There was no shade there, but a small pond in the middle of the circular garden, filled with lotus flowers, cooled the air slightly. Frank bent down over the water, washed his hands and dried them in his handkerchief, which by this time was dirty and crumpled.

Before he had been a month in Shanghai he had caught a disease from a Korean dancing girl. It was nothing serious, and he was cured in four weeks, but ever since he had had the nervous feeling that his hands were always unclean. After washing his hands he relapsed onto the stone bench again and felt better; and with this feeling his thoughts went back to Ruth. He took her crumbled telegram out of his pocket and read it again.

"LEAVING DAY AFTER TOMORROW ON THE KOBE MARU ALL OTHER BOATS FULL STOP ARRIVING AUGUST 9 STOP LOVE YOU MORE THAN EVER RUTH"

High time, Frank thought to himself. You go to the dogs in this place. There was no choice: getting drunk with the other unmarried men at the club. Going night after night to the low-down dance halls in Foochow Road, frequented by prostitutes of all colors. The only alternative was the unutterable boredom of respectable American society: bridge with elderly businessmen, backslappers and handshakers.

As soon as Frank thought of Ruth, everything at once became cool and clear; even his headache felt better. He drew a deep breath.

He tried hard to picture Ruth's face and figure. But all he saw when he shut his eyes was the myriad banners in the streets, Chinese signs and flags hanging limp in the heat. He quickly opened his eyes again and looked up at the pagoda which rose gray against the dense, hazy sky.

As he sat there he became aware of a confused stir. He heard the laughter and chatter of many Chinese voices and saw children and old people running past the low stone walls which separated the little garden from the court. More and more people ran past, laughing and screaming. At last Frank took up his camera and followed them to see what was going on. Perhaps the war has been declared, he thought vaguely. Barley Scott, for short called B.S., his boss and an old experienced Shanghai-hand, had muttered dark forebodings and said that it would not go over so easily as in '32.

When he reached the outer court he soon realized that he was as much in the dark as ever about the workings of the Chinese brain, for the cause of the commotion and the general excitement was not a declaration of war, but a crowd of beggers surging round a white woman, and it was this that drew an ever-increasing throng. Frank's old man was standing near, laughing with toothless gums, and still more and more people ran up to swell the throng. Frank looked round him: there was still no sign of Wang Wen. He suddenly went hot with rage as the stench of the people beat against his nostrils almost as though tangible. *"Tshih!"* he shouted as he tried to force his way into the scrum. But it was only when he hit about him with his fists that the crowd gave way.

The blind, the outcasts and the lepers who formed the nucleus of the crowd had fallen into a sort of trance; they paid no attention either to him or his fists; they danced and screamed round the woman, pushing their stumps and hideous wounds in her face, tearing at her dress, while swarms of flies buzzed round the watering eyes of the blind and the noseless skulls of the syphilitic. Frank Taylor began to feel ill when he saw the empty eye-sockets of a blind man just in front of him, with his eyelids propped open by two little bamboo splinters. He was so nauseated that he could not even hit about him. But the little old man had forced his way in behind him and was putting on great airs as the trusted retainer of so important a gentleman. With a volley of shouts and curses he at last succeeded in releasing the woman from the beggars. They drew back laughing, and an old noseless woman shouted out a joke which was taken up with good-natured laughter by those standing farther off, and then Frank found himself standing alone with the white woman in the middle of the court.

"Are you all right?" he asked, still out of breath.

"Yes, thank you, Sir Galahad," she replied. "It was quite amusing —except the smell."

Frank put his tie straight and shoved his shirt into his belt again. He now had time to look at her. She looked as white and unruffled as a soap advertisement. She wore a large, wide panama hat, white cambric gloves, white sandals and no stockings. The nail of her big toe, varnished dark red as the fashion was, looked peculiarly amused, unashamed and unruffled. She had an astonishingly tight belt round her astonishingly small waist, and her hips were long and slender. What little could be seen of her hair beneath her hat was of an unusual color—dark but very red, and after a while Taylor grasped what it was about her that struck him as so original: although she had red hair, her skin was tanned to a golden brown without freckles.

"How on earth did it happen?" he asked while he noticed all this without knowing that he did so.

"I don't know. I just gave a nice syphilitic old lady a little money, and then they all went crazy," she said, laughing. It was clear that the whole affair had caused her more amusement than alarm.

"How much money?" Taylor asked, irritated by her feminine lack of common sense.

"I don't understand Chinese money," she replied gaily. "One of these dirty bits of paper."

"A dollar!" he cried out in indignation. "No wonder they nearly killed you. It's more money than they've seen in their whole lives."

She now shut the white handbag which so far she had held open in her hand. "Then it must have been a regular holiday for them," she said cheerfully. "My husband gave me twenty-five dollars when I came out, and now it's all gone."

They had been walking slowly towards the first temple hall; the courtyard was now almost deserted, and presumably the beggars had gone straight off with their fabulous booty to buy themselves rice or opium.

"They will smoke themselves sick with opium on a fortune like that," Taylor said.

"That's fine," she replied. "I was afraid they might buy their grandfathers coffins or turn respectable."

"Your husband should not have left you alone here, Mrs Russell," Taylor said. "You never know where you are with the Chinese."

"How do you know my name?" she asked, adding more slowly: "My husband does a lot of things he ought not. That's what's so nice about him."

Frank Taylor knew Helen Russell from the newspapers: they had been full of photographs and interviews on her arrival two days before. "English millionairess visits China." "Lord Inglewood's brother, the Hon. Robert Russell, is staying at the Shanghai Hotel with his beautiful wife." Also he had twice seen her passing through the lounge when he was having a cocktail there. The gossip of Shanghai had already fastened with avidity on this sensational couple, and Mrs Russell's clothes were acclaimed as outdoing in extravagance anything that this extravagant city had seen for many a day. Recollecting this, Taylor gave another somewhat awed look at her faultlessly simple white sports dress and said: "Everybody knows everybody in Shanghai. My name's Frank Taylor, and I'm the fellow from whom you can buy your Eos films under the colonnades and who'll develop them for you."

She looked at him reflectively with eyes that did not go below his forehead.

"I think Sir Galahad suits you better," she said in an absent-minded voice.

At this moment Wang Wen appeared in a crumpled white suit, black boots, eyeglasses and felt hat. Frank waved to him, half enraged, half relieved.

"Here's my assistant at last," he said. "Mrs Russell, may I introduce my assistant, Mr Wang?"

Mr Wang made a low bow. "It is my extraordinary honor," he said, for he knew his English and his manners. The office boy, Petrus, who wore out Frank's cast-off suits, followed in his wake. He was dangling Wang Wen's chattels in a bundle, with two oiled-paper umbrellas gripped in his arm—for Wang also was too great a gentleman to carry his things himself.

"Mr Wang," Taylor said, "you can explain this show to the lady better than I can. I know nothing about these damned temples."

"It is nothing but idols and superstitions," Mr Wang said contemptuously. "There are stupid old people who believe in these things." He spat violently on the temple floor from sheer enlightenment.

"We must make a start at once before the light goes," Frank said with a vain effort not to sound impatient. He would have liked to tell Wang Wen off, but that was impossible, for it would have cost Wang Wen so much face that he would have nothing left. The amount of abuse and irritation a white man had to choke back in this country was bad for the health. Frank secretly wiped his hands on the lining of his trouser pockets while Petrus loaded himself with the camera and tripod and Wang smiled an injured smile. Helen Russell gazed at Frank Taylor as though he were an amusing spectacle. Her gaze made him feel hot and disheveled. His shirt stuck to his shoulders, and he wriggled them uncomfortably.

"Well, I'd better snap a few pictures, anyway," he said nervously in order to distract her attention from himself. "I was thinking—what about the old pagoda and an airplane above it? Or perhaps a view over the airport from here, eh? Old and new China on one picture—that wouldn't be bad. We're bringing out a little folder to be displayed in every room in all the Shanghai hotels as an invitation to visitors to patronize our firm. We want the picture for that. It would be good publicity, don't you think? Thousands of foreigners pass through Shanghai, and if every one of them had our folder in his hands the moment he arrived . . ." Frank had waxed enthusiastic; he now lost himself in optimistic speculations, for he was rather proud of this idea of a little folder which he had evolved himself. Helen was still looking at him.

"Are you an American?" she asked suddenly.

"Why? Sure I'm an American," Frank said.

"You don't look American," Helen said.

"Yes, yes, I'm an American all right. Actually I was born in Hawaii, but that makes no difference. I went to America when I was quite a little kid. My parents were both Americans."

"There, you see—my eyes don't deceive me. Hawaii. That's much better. We went there for three days and stayed two months. Yes, you fit in much better with Hawaii."

Wang Wen, meanwhile, had been conversing in undertones with a bald priest who was busy at an altar with candles and incense. Helen looked up at the image of Buddha.

"Hideous," she said. "We saw much more beautiful Buddhas in Japan. Why do they have this cheap, painted junk fit only for a fair?"

"Probably they've sold or pawned all their good Buddhas," Frank said.

"The priest says that for a dollar he will question the Sticks of Fate," Mr Wang announced.

"Sticks of Fate," Helen said appreciatively. "That's the China I've always imagined to myself from detective stories. We'll certainly question the Sticks of Fate, Sir Galahad, and I'll write a description of it in my diary."

"Fifty cents," Frank said to Mr Wang.

"Shame, Sir Galahad," Helen said. "You can't haggle over fate for half a dollar."

"You've got to bargain in China," Frank answered. "The fellow would lose all pleasure in it if there was no bargaining."

The priest and Mr Wang had in fact embarked at once upon a heated argument; several other people also had come up—two dignified gentlemen in long silk robes, an old lady with a shrewish and managing face, and a young girl in a white cap who was carrying ropes of spirit money on a stick over her shoulders.

Finally the priest and Mr Wang concluded the deal with a fleeting mutual bow. Frank took out a few silver coins which he placed in the ash of an incense vessel. Helen delightedly watched the priest as he gabbled and produced a quiver-like object out of which he shook a few bamboo splinters with an abstracted air. He looked at them, picked them up again, fingered the leaves of a large book with his long dirty nails, ceased gabbling, wiped his nose on the sleeve of his priestly robe, began to gabble again and finally imparted to Mr Wang what he had gathered from the book. For a moment Wang seemed taken aback by what he had heard, but then he turned at once to Frank and announced with a polite smile: "Good augury. The lady will have many sons, and future riches are announced for Mr Taylor."

Helen pulled a face. "My desire for sons is not so extravagant as the two honorable gentlemen seem to think," she said with a laugh. Mr Wang, who did not understand, made a grateful bow. But Frank looked puzzled. "There's something more in this," he said. "It's simply that Wang Wen doesn't want to tell us anything unpleasant."

At this Helen laughed right out. "You're as superstitious as a heathen," she cried.

Frank blushed and then, as he accompanied her into the first court, he began to laugh too.

"Wait a moment," she said suddenly, coming to a stop. "What did you say your name was? Taylor? Frank Taylor from Hawaii? But then I know you. I was to give you a message—from Lester Ingram. He's a relation of yours, isn't he? He promised me you'd take me dancing if British high society here became too boring. And that won't be long, I can tell you. Isn't it nice that we should have met by accident?"

"Very nice," Frank murmured with embarrassment. "Perfectly marvelous. How is my—how is Lester?" He felt hot and disheveled again. His hands were once more moist and dirty. "I and my wretched foxtrot are both at your service," he said, getting up steam. "And in every other capacity at any time. If you would like to employ me as a guide, you couldn't give me greater pleasure. Call me up—here's my card. Any hour of day or night——"

"You are just what I've missed in Shanghai," Helen said with perfect candor. She put the card in her white handbag, from which, as she opened it, there came a swift and fleeting fragrance of lavender. "I'll call you up. Thank you," she said. "And now I must go back to my hotel. How nice that we've got to know each other. We'll meet again soon."

One of the huge hired cars the Shanghai Hotel put at the disposal of its guests at an exorbitant charge was standing outside in the maze of booths. A fairly large crowd of interested spectators watched the departure. Mr Wang made his elegant bows, the office boy, Petrus, with camera, tripod and bundle, waved, and the old man who stood near by held out his hand for a tip. The Chinese chauffeur in white uniform made comments on three generations of the old man's ancestors as he started the car, and the crowd, disappointed but laughing loudly, made way. Frank Taylor stood looking after the car until it had vanished round the corner. The last thing he saw was Mrs Russell's red toenails and white sandals as she stepped into the car. Pretty, he thought. I shall have to buy a new white dinner jacket, he thought also. His headache was gone. Instead of it, there was the feeling of having been rubbed down with cold water and a stiff brush. He moved his shoulders this way and that. No, his shirt did not stick. He took a deep breath.

"Now we'll get to work," he told Mr Wang Wen and Petrus. But when they got to the little garden from which Frank meant to take his photographs, the sun had vanished behind a mass of metallic clouds, the light was yellow and quite unsuitable, and soon afterwards the first large drops of a thunderstorm pattered down.

"Nothing doing for today," Frank Taylor said. "We must put it off till another time." He sounded neither annoyed nor impatient. Mr Wang nodded his appreciation. At first all foreigners were crazy with haste and energy. By degrees they became sensible and behaved not like barbarians but like human beings.

Wang and Petrus opened their umbrellas and waited for the bus. Frank Taylor drove off in his car as a white man should. On the way he did not think once of Ruth. He thought of Helen Russell.

II

IT WAS THREE O'CLOCK in the morning. Yen, the ricksha coolie, had had a brief nap, squatting between the shafts of his ricksha. He had a hard day behind him. Early the morning before he had taken a drunken singsong girl from a hotel to her home in Nantao. It was a heavy load, for the amah, on whose lap the girl sat, was large and fat, and Yen had sweated much before he deposited the two women at their door. There was much bargaining and bickering with the amah, and finally they gave him twenty-five coppers. With these Yen bought himself a dish of rice and tea, which left him twenty coppers, not enough to pay the day's hire of his ricksha. He took his empty ricksha to all the places which seemed to promise a good fare. He hung about in front of the foreigners' hotels and had to give the commissionaire nine cents—the son and grandson of a whore; when evening came he went the round of the large Chinese restaurants in the foreign quarter, but the coolies who regarded this neighborhood as their preserve chased him off. At night he had lain in wait in Foochow Road and loudly sung the praises of the paradises to which he would take the foreigners who strolled by in ones and twos: "Beautiful girls, good in bed, beautiful virgins from Canton, beautiful little boys, good in bed. Beautiful little boys." But every time a ricksha was hailed, other coolies had pushed in front of him, and he knew, too, why he was weak. It was three days since Yen had had his last pipe of the Great Smoke, and his whole being was pining and aching with hunger for opium.

The Peony Club was hidden in such a maze of narrow lanes that no car or taxi, however small, could drive up to its door and its red neon sign. It was a good place to pick up weary dancing girls or their clients, sailors and Chinese clerks. Also not an evening went by without wealthy foreigners visiting the Peony Club, people without sense who paid fares up to half a dollar. Before Yen had sunk into a sleep of exhaustion he had begun to think out what he would do if he could only earn half a dollar. He owed forty cents hire for his ricksha, and he still had eleven cents in hand. He moved his fingers and lips as he calculated his financial situation. A smoke, which at the moment was more urgent than eating and drinking, cost twenty cents. He still owed his friend, Kwe Kuei, seven cents for the last pipe. In the middle of his calculations, which refused to come out right, even if the miracle of the half-dollar came to pass, he fell asleep. The sky grew green above the roofs of the ramshackle houses. Two large rats scuttled over Yen's feet, and a little later a lean and absent-minded cat came along. Three waiting ricksha coolies played the finger game by the light of their lanterns, and three others were asleep. All along the lane the electric signs and red lanterns of the night clubs grew dimmer as the first glimmer of morning dawned over the city. The music within went on, relentless and obstinate.

Yen woke up as he got a kick from a black patent-leather shoe and was between the shafts in a moment. There was the usual shouting and pushing, but Yen's hunger for a smoke was now so vehement that it no longer made him weak but gave his fists strength to beat the other coolies aside.

"Murder and sudden death again," Helen Russell said with a laugh to her husband, who was so drunk that he stood stiffly and yet at an acute angle to the street; it looked like a trick of a cataleptic medium. "Car?" he asked thickly, and even this one word was almost more than he could bring out.

"I sent the car away," Helen said amiably. "A ricksha's more fun. The air will do us good after the fog in there."

"Car?" Bobbie repeated obstinately. He tried, without succeeding, to light a cigarette. Matches and cigarette fell on the moist, slimy pavement. Next moment a shouting group of street boys had flung themselves on the booty. Helen took the cigarette case out of his hand before he could let it drop, and, lighting a cigarette for him, put it between his lips. "Car?" he said peevishly.

"You can take the ricksha to the next corner and we can get a taxi there," Helen said submissively and helped him into a ricksha. The coolies took charge of the drunken foreigner with remarkable gentleness in spite of their shouts and laughter. He smiled benignly and fell asleep even before the wheels began to revolve. Helen got into Yen's ricksha.

He stared at the lady open-mouthed. He was still half asleep. "Shanghai Hotel, Nanking Road, chopchop," said Helen who had hurriedly picked up a little pidgin. English.

"Savvy, savvy," Yen assured her eagerly, although he had not understood. He knew nothing about Nanking Road: for him it was Ta Malu, the street of the Great Horses. But he smiled at the lady reassuringly and set off. His body at once broke out in a sweat, for the air was like steam, even in this last hour of the night, and nothing stirred. He stopped and, taking off his tattered jacket and rolling it up, put it under the lady's feet.

"Very kind," Helen murmured, trying to avoid contact with the dirty object. Her husband's coolie meanwhile had vanished at a steady trot round the corner, and Helen was left behind alone. "Quick, chopchop," she repeated, but Yen could hear that she didn't mean it. He turned his head and smiled at her without altering his pace. Helen leaned back and sighed. The gray light of dawn began to flood the streets, and only a few people were to be seen, all Chinese. One of those ridiculous, gilded Shanghai taxis went past seeming very noisy in the silence. After they had turned several corners without catching sight of Bobbie, Helen asked rather anxiously:

"Shanghai Hotel, savvy?"

"Savvy, savvy," the coolie said with the consoling smile of a patient children's nurse. Nevertheless Helen began to feel uneasy, not on her own account but on Bobbie's. She gave a start as a loud shout in Chinese burst on her ears. But it was only another ricksha coolie padding by on bare feet with two weary, painted night-club girls as passengers. A long-drawn, plaintive cry came from a house. Silence. Then the cry again. Next a sharp report, either a whip or a gun. Here's another fine opportunity for Sir Galahad, Helen thought. The thought of him was so distinct that she was surprised he didn't come round the next corner to take charge of her. She yawned and smiled at herself forgivingly. She had thought of Frank Taylor more than once during the evening before. Sir Henry Kingsdale-Smith, of the British consulate, had given an extremely official and utterly boring reception for her husband and herself: ropes of pearls on old wrinkled bosoms, gossip about people whose names she had never heard, racing tips, polo talk, arrogance and boredom. A tiny, English island, isolated and unapproachable in the middle of China beneath the incessant whir of the electric ventilators. "And how do you like Shanghai, my dear?" . . . "If you go to Hong Kong you must pay Lady Fitz-Scarborough a visit, she's so original! She collects jade rings. Poor dear, what else can she do? Sir Fitz-Scarborough caught malaria in India and one knows what a husband with malaria is like. . . . Count Bodianszky, come here, I want to introduce you to Mrs Russell. Count Bodianszky is our enfant terrible. Don't listen to him if he starts talking about Saigon. . . ." Helen yawned again merely to think of it. She looked quickly round. No, Frank Taylor was not coming behind her. I'm tired out, she thought. It was no light task keeping Bobbie sober throughout a smart English party. He had made up for lost time at the Peony Club. By the time Helen succeeded in getting Frank Taylor's discreet but pleasant shadow out of her thoughts and returned to her husband again, she grew alarmed. They were going on and on; it was becoming more and more confusing, the streets narrower and more foreign. The coolie panted, the sweat ran down his back. Helen saw a vacant taxi at the side of the street. "I want to get out," she said. But the coolie shook his head and trotted on. A little later his panting changed to coughing, and Helen saw with dismay that he was spitting large patches of blood on the street. After they had gone on for an endless time, and always, as it seemed to Helen, come back to the same corner, they arrived finally at a river or canal, and the coolie drew up beside a Chinese policeman. He seemed to be asking the way, and the policeman shouted at him. The coolie shouted back, but this excitement too ended in laughter. Helen was horribly tired by this time, and the ride took on an air of unreality. But after an eternity they did at last arrive at the hotel, without having caught so much as a glimpse of her husband.

The coolie stood panting for breath, dripping with sweat and with an expectant smile on his lips. He was so thin that every rib and every sinew stood out from his body. Thin enough, Helen thought, for a Crucifixion. She took half a dollar from her little pearl bag and put it in the coolie's palm. Her experience with the beggars at the Lunghua pagoda had taught her not to pay too much.

As fifty cents was more than Yen was owed, he began at once to make a great clamor. He shouted that the Tai Tai had given him too little, the Tai Tai was hard, he had come far and run fast; he showed his sweat and pointed to his panting chest from which blood had come; he gesticulated with his arms, he stretched out the half-dollar to Helen as though he wished to return her such miserable payment, and even went so far as to spit on the coin and throw it on the ground. Though the Nanking Road had been empty a moment before, three or four other coolies inexplicably appeared, and all volubly came to his assistance. Helen, somewhat dismayed, was just about to produce some more money from her little bag when the large Irish doorman who was on night duty at the revolving door of the Shanghai Hotel made his appearance. *"Tshih!"* he shouted. *"Gandu!"* And Yen saw his fare vanish into the hotel without his having made the biggest scoop he had ever hoped for since he had been a ricksha coolie.

There were stories current among the ricksha coolies of fabulous and fantastic earnings. Once a drunken foreigner either in error or from stupidity had given a certain Lisan of Haoping twenty dollars. Lisan had retired on it and lived in his native village as the highly respected owner of a carpenter's shop. Another coolie, whose name was not known, had found a pearl earring in his ricksha, and a jeweler in the Chinese town had given him thirty-two dollars and forty cents for it in hard cash. It was not known what became of him, but some maintained that they had seen him leave the Hotel of the Golden Heaven accompanied by a beauteous concubine and drive away in a taxi.

It was these and similar stories which kept the hope alive in Yen's heart that he would one day return to the house of his ancestors with much money, that he would pay the debts of his family, redeem their fields, provide the spirits of his forefathers with much food and incense and bring up his son as a great gentleman. Yen often thought of his son. Particularly when he had smoked the second pipe it seemed to him a perfectly simple and easy matter to see his son again. He had watched his son growing up with the eyes of his spirit, though he was far away. Now his forelock was cut off; now he was going to school; now he was clever enough to drive the buffalo that turned the water wheel; now it would soon be time to betroth him; now he was a man and a better man than his worthless father. Dreaming thus, Yen arrived at his third and fourth pipe before he succumbed to the profound sleep of the opium smoker.

These thoughts, however, were not sheer fantasy: they were nourished by the letters that Lung Seileong's mother wrote to him from time to time. Yen took them to the letter writer who had his stall in the neighborhood of the Old Willow Tree teahouse in the Chinese town. He had the letter read aloud to him for five coppers, and sometimes he had to have it read three times before he had mastered the contents. It cost him ten coppers to have a letter written back; it was a great deal of money in Yen's eyes, but he quite understood that it was more difficult to write a letter than to draw a ricksha and that learning deserved higher pay than common coolie labor. But it was a long time now since he had had a letter, more than twelve moons, and he had gradually forgotten the contents of the last one, often as he used at first to mutter it over to himself while he trotted along with his ricksha.

Yen put the fifty cents away in his belt; he now possessed sixty-one cents. As he took up the shafts of his ricksha again he knew beyond a doubt that he was too tired to go the long distance to Kating Street where he had to pay the hire of his ricksha daily. It did not occur to him that it was even further to Chapei where Kwe Kuei lived. The prospect of the Great Smoke gave him strength and wind enough to hold out until he got there.

Kuei had a little shop which was open to the street and looked harmless enough. It sold soya beans and tobacco and cigarettes, salted cabbage stalks, smoked meat and dried fish—everything, in fact, that could tempt the appetite of the coolies who lived in the neighborhood. The building was small and low and built as a lean-to against the back wall of what had been a factory until in the war of 1932 it had been hit with a shell and burned to the ground. The

Street-of-Blissful-Peace, as it was rather inappropriately named, was unpaved, and in winter it was a morass of mud. But it dried in summer, and every puff of wind raised handfuls of yellow dust and threw it into the faces of passers-by. Kuei's dwelling was behind the shop, and behind his dwelling was a tiny yard with a well and a pump and empty barrels; in the summertime Kuei spread a roof of tattered matting over the yard to keep it cool. Behind the yard there was a room in which Kuei stored his wares and which emitted a strong smell of cabbage and fish and bean curd that had gone sour. At the back of this room there were cupboards so skillfully carpentered that they entirely concealed a ladder leading up into the roof. It was here that the opium smokers lay on old mats in bunks one above the other, with wooden pillows under their heads, and when business was good there were two and three to a mat. Two pale, ragged little orphan girls tended the opium lamps and brought the men hot towels to wipe their exhausted faces. The smell of opium hung everywhere like a cobweb, but the stench of rotting refuse in the yard was even stronger; and that was just as well for Kuei. True, he paid the police of the neighborhood adequate bribes and gave them as much opium as they wanted to keep them quiet. But it had lately become the fashion for students and even young women to poke their noses in everywhere and to take a pride in detecting every ounce of opium in Chapei. As they were stupid, young, inexperienced people, it was easy enough for Kuei to lie to them. But they were a source of annoyance to him, since it was inhuman to deprive poor people of their only pleasure while the rich could smoke as much as they pleased. "How shall a coolie endure life if he has no opium?" Kwe Kuei frequently asked. "Life is too hard without dreams."

Yen put twenty-seven cents down on the counter to pay for what he owed and also to provide for a good deep dream and sleep. He was dizzy, and his hands and knees trembled as he climbed the ladder, for the smell of opium made his hunger for it even more insistent. But with the first pipe calm descended upon him; after the second he became alert and lively and began to philosophize with an old man on the next mat. But the old man soon fell asleep. Yen lay back and shut his eyes. He fanned himself drowsily once or twice with his tattered palm-leaf fan and then saw many flowering peonies stroked by the breeze and heard the ripple of water. It was a sound of great enchantment and penetrating beauty, fresh and cool, a charming sound echoed back from the days of childhood. Yen bathed his tired feet in the stream and then fell asleep.

Some hours later, when Yen was once more between the shafts of his ricksha, he was certainly somewhat rested after his labors, but the drowsiness of opium was still in his limbs. It was midday by that time, but he felt no hunger, and his belly was content and stilled within him. The sky was overcast with black clouds, and thunder could be heard in the distance. Yen trotted rapidly along towards Kating Street, straight through the whole foreign quarter, to the Four Harmonies Ricksha Company to pay the hire for the day before. When he counted up the money in his possession he discovered that he was six coppers short; he must have miscalculated in his dizziness before the smoke. He kept on reckoning, muttering aloud, and as he had not enough fingers they only confused him the more. He had had sixty-one cents. He had paid the seven cents owing and twenty for the smoke. In the openhanded way of the opium smoker he had given five cash to the girl as tea money for lighting the lamp and bringing the hot towel. Again he was short of the forty cents for the hire. The clouds now burst in on his cares, and heavy rain descended from the heavy sky. Just as Yen was taking shelter in a doorway, good fortune smiled. A jaunty-looking young Chinese in foreign clothes with a cigarette in his mouth hailed him. Yen had the hood up in a moment to keep his fare in the dry, and then he trotted off. The rain was not unpleasant on his skin, and soon steam rose from it as though he were being cooked. The young man was going to the Rue Thibet, Sei Young Lu, and this again was fortunate, for it was on the way to Kating Street. When he got out he gave him the right fare, fifteen cents. He was not a foreigner, there was nothing to be said. But the influence of opium made Yen courageous and enterprising, so he stretched out his hand and cried: "A present, sir, a tip for the poor coolie, honored first-born! My son is sick and dying for lack of medicine. Give me ten cents for my sick son." The young man laughed and took some money from his foreign purse, seven round, clean copper coins and four cash. "Liar and son of a liar," he said. "I know what your son is called—Shao Hsingchu!"

Yen laughed gratefully and called blessings after the young man as he went in at the door. The idea that his son was called Shao Hsingchu, Yellow Rice Wine, seemed to him so witty that he was still laughing over it when he had already stopped his ricksha in front of the ramshackle house in Kating Street. There were three other coolies there who were late with their payment as he was, and he lined up behind them, steaming with the rain. The dingy room contained an iron safe which inspired the coolies with great reverence as a sign of immense wealth. The cashier, who sat behind a sort of grid and took the coolies' money, had gold teeth, and this too was very smart and opulent. How wealthy a man must be whose underling could buy himself gold teeth! Yen shrank together and made no reply when the man shouted out in a threatening way that his ricksha would be taken away from him if he did not come punctually every evening to pay for it.

"The town is lighter by night than by day, there is no difference between evening and morning," Yen replied with a great effort at wit and courage. The man wrote something down in a large book. "Is your name Yen, Lung Yen?" he asked just as Yen was turning to go.

"That is right, Lung Yen is my unworthy name," Yen said. He had lost his great name, the name of his family, since he had been in the city, and now it seemed strange to him.

"There's a letter here for Mr Lung Yen," the man said ironically. He flipped the letter through the grating, and it fell on the dirty boarded floor. Yen snatched it up and pretended he could read the address. "Yes, the letter is for me," he said, and his reins moved within him. For even though Yen could not read a single character, he still had eyes and knew what letters from home looked like; they had a face, as people had, by which you could recognize them.

First of all he sat in his ricksha in the street and looked at the letter on both sides and smelt it. There might be larger and thicker letters, but this one was good enough for him. After enjoying the sight and feel of it to the full, he put it in his belt, where he also carried the little linen bag containing his money. He still had sixteen cents, and he also had a letter from home. The commotion in his inwards had caused him a sudden pang of hunger. I can eat later, he thought impatiently, for he wanted to know what was in the letter. "I have got a letter from my son," he called to every coolie he even knew by sight. They all laughed back and shouted, "A virtuous son is better than money," or some such polite remark. He was on the point of crossing the Great Foreign Street in defiance of the raised arm of the policeman. *"Gandu!"* the policeman shouted at him.

"I have a letter from my son," Yen replied, and although the brown, straw-hatted Annamite probably understood little of what he said, he laughed all the same at the coolie's beaming face.

The letter writer to whom Yen took his precious letter was a poor but cultured man. He had held high positions in the days when the Manchus still sat on the Dragon Throne. He was still dressed as a mandarin in a silk robe, jacket and black cap, and he wore a long, thin, venerable beard and eyeglasses with thick horn rims. He was endowed with a capacious and far-reaching memory, and he recognized Yen at once, although it was more than a year since Yen had had his last letter from home and replied to it. The old mandarin took his time, for leisureliness is the mark of education. Yen, too, endeavored not to show any impatience in case of seeming impolite. Several inquisitive people immediately collected round the open booth, for they too wanted to know what was in Yen's letter, and he was proud of the interest they showed. At last the letter was opened, unfolded and held before the lenses of the learned man.

"This letter is written with a newfangled pen, not with a paintbrush," he informed him as he looked at him over his glasses. He inspected the writing once more. "It seems to have been written by a child who has no character as yet and understands nothing of calligraphy," the revered man went on, while Yen felt his ribs vibrating with his excitement.

"The letter was written on the eighteenth day of the seventh month," the old man next observed. "It comes from the village of

Chingsan in the province of Kiangsu. It is astonishing how quickly letters arrive now that the fire wagons run all through the country. When I was young . . ."

He went on to a brief description of the journeys on foot he had undertaken as a young man in the manner of the ancient scholars, who journeyed from village to village with a staff and hollow gourd, as free from care as the birds. Yen folded his hands and listened respectfully until at last his impatience got the better of him. "The letter, revered sir?" he reminded him submissively. And now the old man took up the letter and read it aloud without further interruption:

"Father, exalted person, I hand you this letter on my knees. It is long since I received any instructive words from you. I am full of care. I wish that the body of the exalted person is in peace. For long I have stood on my toes to look to the east in the hoped-for joy of being permitted to give my father the morning and the evening tea.

"On the seventh day of the eighth month I shall come with many other children to Shanghai, where we are holding a festival and rally of all Boy Scouts for several days. We shall be divided into Hsiangs and live partly in tents, partly in barracks. My number is 174, Hsiang Chongshi. If the exalted person will take the trouble to inquire at the town hall in the Civic Center, then my father will receive exact information where his worthless son may be found. I can scarcely wait for the day when we journey to the great city. Confucius tells us: From our fathers we received body, hair and skin; therefore it is our duty to keep them unharmed.

"On my knees I give you this letter and most humbly wish you ten thousand times bliss and golden peace.

"Your son,

"Lung Seileong

"Chinese Republic, in the twenty-sixth year in the seventh month, on the eighteenth day."

Yen listened to this astonishing mixture of modern schooling and Confucian politeness as though fairies had come down from every heaven to make music for him. He did not understand in the slightest degree what it meant. The old mandarin read the letter three times, at a cost of three coppers the first time and one for every other. After the third reading he folded the letter and put it back in the envelope. "Happy news, my elder brother," he said with great friendliness, "and a well-written letter from a son to his father. You must be very happy to be seeing the child again so soon."

Yen still sat with an almost idiotic smile of joy on his emaciated face. His son could write and he wrote to him. His son. His son Lung Seileong. The whole audience murmured congratulations and good wishes.

"What is the meaning of the letter?" Yen asked as though awaking from a dream.

"It means that your son will arrive in this city in ten days from now and that you will be taken to him if you give his name and his number in at the town hall in Kiangwan," the letter writer said patiently.

Yen was completely at sea. "What number?" he asked again and again. "Where is the house where I must say this number? Is there a secret about it? What are Scouts? I do not want my son to be a soldier and a bandit."

It took quite a long time before the old mandarin could explain it all to the coolie. In addition, he made him a present, for he wrote various directions on a piece of paper and charged nothing for it. He wrote them on paper ruled with red lines with his fine brush and put it in a red envelope, because red is the color of good fortune and gifts. Yen put the writing devoutly in his moneybag.

It was only then that he went to the Old Willow Tree teahouse and asked for tea and rice; he told everyone there who would listen to him about the visit of his son. He talked so much and so loudly that the Mahjong players murmured a request for less noise. After this he stood for a time on the zigzag bridge and looked at the turtles in the green, stagnant water. He loitered about the bird market and listened to the song of an oriole. It was a golden bird, called Ying, and his grandfather had had one. He considered deeply whether he should go to the temple and offer some incense to the god of the city, for it was obvious that this god's protection was necessary for the affair that brought his son to Shanghai. As he had plenty of money he did it after all. When it was done and he had impressed on the priest to pray for happiness and a safe journey for Lung Seileong, son of Lung Yen, it occurred to him that he must buy presents for his son. He took his ricksha and left the cramped Chinese town where no money was to be earned and plunged in among the motor traffic of the Avenue Edouard VII. He was now so full of strength and energy that he got two fares one after another and earned thirty cents. But he already owed forty cents for the day's hire, and fatigue slowly overcame him again. He was trotting along the middle of the street and thinking of seeing his son again when a man on a tricycle with a pile of newspapers in the box behind him shouted: "Out of the way, you dirty coolie." Yen jumped out of the way just as he got a good blow on the shinbone. "Son and grandson of a bitch," he shouted after the man on the tricycle.

It was at this moment that Yen realized how dirty and unkempt he looked. A dirty coolie, yes, a dirty coolie was all he was. He drew his ricksha to the curb and squatted down between the shafts to give the matter his full attention. His son, a youth of eleven years, was coming to visit him. Yen had kept count of the years on his fingers and never forgotten the age of his son who was far away—a boy who could write and had the manners of a mandarin. How could his father appear before him as a dirty coolie?

Yen leaned his arms on the shafts and his head on his arms in order to think it out more clearly. He had sent letters home and implored the old letter writer every time to inform his family that he was getting on very well in the City-by-the-Sea. That he was a merchant in a large business, that he was earning much money and that he would soon come home to free his family from debts and all care.

With the eyes of his spirit he saw himself as he appeared in his letters: a well-dressed and well-nourished man in a good situation with money put by: a man in a long gray robe and a hat such as foreigners wore: a man with a round face and hands grown delicate with counting money. And at the same time his eyes looked down at himself as he really was: a coolie in ragged coolie clothes which showed his shameful leanness through many a hole in jacket and trousers; a man without money, who had not even a mat of his own to roll himself up in at night; a man whose flesh had been burned from his face by the Great Smoke; on whom vice had left its mark. It was a miserable quarter of an hour that Yen went through with his head on his arms and his arms on the ricksha at the side of the Avenue Edouard VII. As soon as he had thought it all out, he got up and, without looking for a fare, trotted off with his ricksha all the way back to Chapei. His friend Kwe Kuei was sitting in his shop weighing beans in little bags. It was late in the afternoon. One of the little orphan girls came in and hung a lamp on the wall.

Yen squatted on the ground, and first of all he spat his bitter spittle several times before he brought out what he wanted to say.

"Kwe Kuei, you have always been my best friend," he then said. "And you have not forgotten that we have sworn dry brotherhood and kept to it."

"You have consumed enough smoke for one day, useless one, and I give no credit," Kuei said at once.

"I want no smoke," Yen cried. "Never again, Kwe Kuei. Brother—my son is coming to visit me, my only son. You must help me. I need money. I need clothes. I need a bed and a house and a position. I cannot be a starving coolie when my son comes. You must help me."

He spoke at astonishing length and with amazing eloquence. Kuei heard and marveled; he put aside his scales and then laughed aloud. "So your son is coming, you lucky man?" he cried out. "We will welcome our little guest. We will spare nothing that is necessary. You shall show your son a face bigger than any face he has ever seen."

Yen could feel his breath getting light and his heart large at these cheering and loyal words. Tears suddenly came to his eyes after the manifold excitements of the day, and Kuei's beard dissolved into a black cloud.

"It is true," he said gratefully. "New clothes and old friends are the best."

III

Dr chang came back from Nanking in a state of exhaustion, disappointment and jangled nerves. The airplanes were booked up for days ahead, and he had to take the train. It was nearly two hours late and crowded with refugees from the North as only Chinese trains can be crowded. More refugees were squatting in the stations with children, grandparents and bundles, staring in front of them. Chang knew the drowsy expression of his countrymen. It was as though they effaced themselves as soon as the burden became too heavy. If only they were as strong in fighting as in endurance, he thought for the ten thousandth time. He looked at his wrist watch as he left the North Station. Ten minutes past four. He hailed a taxi. "I can fetch Pearl," he thought and felt a little happier.

The polyclinic, where Pearl was on duty three times a week, was not far from the station in an artisan quarter of Chapei. The small, one-story building, to which a wooden annex was attached, was situated among vacant, dusty lots. Pearl was paid a small sum by the health department for watching over the white doctors who worked there voluntarily, and she took care of the women who could not overcome their shyness at the presence of male doctors. There were three German doctors, Jewish exiles, and they gave their services free. Dr Chang still wondered at the unselfishness of foreigners; it bordered on stupidity, although he often wished with a sigh that his own countrymen understood a little more about their duty to their neighbors. But Pearl, who had been brought up in America, took the help of her German colleagues as a matter of course and was on the best of terms with them.

Chang went quickly through the so-called waiting room, whose wooden walls were covered with illustrated explanations of sexual diseases and advice on the treatment of infants—his work and his pride. One or two half-grown youths, workers from the mills on Soochow Creek, and an old gnarled coolie were sitting along the walls. When Chang entered the room where his wife was working he found her bending over an oilcloth-covered table on which lay a newborn baby. Tiny as he was, he already had a gold-embroidered cap on his head and shoes adorned with tiger heads on his little feet. Pearl was just in the act of taking them off. The child was quiet and contented, but his grandmother was standing there with the anxious face of old people who distrust anything new.

"A beautiful grandson," said the little Chinese nurse who was standing with a roll of cotton ready in her hand. The old lady bowed and murmured something. Pearl looked up and smiled at Chang. She had a smile that extended to every inch of her kind broad oval face and completely altered it. The smile vanished instantly as she turned to the infant. She moved the tiny foot to and fro and bent more closely over it. "Doctor Hain!" she called through to the next room, the door of which was ajar. A confused mumbling followed from the other side, the door was kicked open and Dr Emanuel Hain appeared. He was wearing a doctor's white coat with short sleeves, and he held his hands up in the air. A man could be seen in the next room lying half undressed on the table.

"Yes?" the old doctor asked as he walked up to the table. Pearl turned the sole of the little foot towards him to show him the suppurating blisters and the glassy skin. "Yes," the doctor said once more, this time not as a question but in confirmation. Pearl turned to her husband.

"Thirty-four per cent come to us with congenital syphilis," she said in English.

Yutsing Chang, who was sitting on a chair by the wall with his case on his knee, looked almost guilty, as though he were personally responsible for the high percentage. "One must tackle the evil at its source," he murmured vaguely.

"May I inquire after your honored condition?" Dr Hain asked politely but with a bad accent; it sounded like French rather than Chinese. Yutsing hastened to make an equally polite rejoinder, for the old doctor's efforts in the strange language always touched him. "How does it stand with the ultraviolet rays?" Dr Hain went on, and his English was not much better than his Chinese.

"The petition has been once more urged on by me," Chang answered. "It will be taken further. The health department has had an illustrated brochure on the fighting of tuberculosis printed, and it will be submitted to the government in Nanking."

Pearl meanwhile had finished with the newborn baby boy, and his grandmother was now sitting on the floor, as she was accustomed to do, and bundling him up again in his native dress. His little naked bottom emerged limply from his tiny trousers, which had only a front side to them. "Good fortune and contentment for the man child," Pearl said to the grandmother, who again bowed. "A hundred sons for the Tai Tai," she wished her politely. "Thank you for the good wish," Pearl answered with her face turned away. Dr Chang smiled at his wife consolingly. She could not have any children, but all the same she was very dear and precious to him.

Dr Hain had come to a stop in the doorway of his room after he had digested Chang's answer.

"I can tell you what the worst evil in China is," he said. "You worship letters too much. A petition, a brochure. Anything written or printed. You are not much better than the poor people who burn their prescriptions and drink the ashes in their tea. You are satisfied with a fine brochure; but words are not medicine. I cannot with printed paper cure one of your coolies who get their dose of t.b. at sixteen and spit blood." He waited a moment and then, as neither Pearl nor Yutsing answered, disappeared through the door, closing it after him with his foot.

"Disinfect everything," Pearl told the little nurse. She herself poured antiseptic into a basin and began to scrub her hands with a serious and intent look on her face.

"What good wind brings you here?" she asked as she did so.

"I thought we might go straight out to a meal from here as soon as you were ready," Chang said.

"I am ready," Pearl answered gaily and shook the drops of the reddish liquid from her fingertips. "We'll walk through the park," she said. "I don't think the air here is good."

The air was in fact heavy with carbolic acid and the smell of many sick people who passed hour after hour through the low rooms of the clinic. "Yes, it will be good under the trees," Chang said with a sigh of relief.

Pearl pushed him through the door into the little compartment with a plain wooden writing table, which served her as office. She opened a cupboard and, concealed by its door, took off her white coat. When she emerged again she was wearing a lime-green tight-fitting dress with a high collar, for she had discovered that her patients had more confidence in her when she was dressed in the Chinese fashion. She produced a teapot and two cups out of a padded basket and poured out a cup of hot tea for her husband. "Wonderful," Chang said contentedly. As he drank, his jangled nerves were soothed and a sense of complete well-being took possession of him. Pearl squatted in front of him and watched him while he drank. She waited till he had finished before she poured out a cup for herself. "Do you allow?" she asked politely before drinking. A moment later Number Two, the younger servant, came in beaming with pleasure when he saw that the master was there again. "Good sleep and happy dreams," Pearl called through Dr Hain's door before they left. But the doctor was apparently too much engrossed to answer.

They sent Number Two home with Yutsing's little case and walked to the corner where they could get a taxi. "We ought to have a car of our own," Pearl said for the hundredth time. Chang answered: "Yes, we really ought to." The car would never be procured. Yutsing's position was big, but his salary was small and unpunctually paid. It was considered in private that an official of Dr Chang's rank could squeeze quite enough out of hospital contracts and by the disposal of hospital equipment. But Chang was radically spoiled for the ways of his country. The foreign schools he had passed through had infected him with ideas that were unpractical and inconvenient and endowed him with a sensitive conscience. And beneath all the superimposed layers of education the corner-stone still stood firm: the Confucian ideal according to which the example of the high official ought to be enough to instill virtue in his inferiors. Chang's grandfather on his mother's side, a mandarin of noble birth, had also been unbribable. . . .

As soon as they were sitting in the taxi Chang took his wife's hand in his and began unconsciously to touch the rough spots on her skin.

"Coolie hands," Pearl said with a smile. He took off his glasses and raised her hand to his face to look at it. It was a gesture of great tenderness.

"How did you get on in Nanking?" Pearl asked. Yutsing did not answer at once.

"It was not a great success," he said at last. "Nobody at the moment has any money for the Scouts or takes any interest in them. It was even suggested that the Jamboree should be put off. But we shall carry it through." He sank into reflection for a time while he unconsciously went on rubbing the rough skin of Pearl's hand.

"So far as I've heard, the Twenty-ninth Army is holding its ground magnificently, but all the same it seems to be more serious in the North than we think," he said. "The Generalissimo had come from Kuling. They were telling in the train that the Red Army had killed sixty thousand Japanese," he added. Pearl's narrow eyes blazed.

"Sixty thousand Japanese!" she cried. "Good, splendid, excellent! We must show the Japanese for once that they are not invincible. One pinprick in the blown-up balloon and—piff! They have never yet fought against a united China."

Chang looked at his wife with a kindly but skeptical smile. When she got into a state of patriotic elation, as now, she reminded him sometimes of Fong Yung. Women burned much more brightly than men, probably because they were not so damped by reason. "He who saddles the tiger must be able to ride him," was all he said. They went on for a while in silence and got out at Hongkew Park. It was cooler there, and there were many English nurses taking their incredibly blond and well-cared-for children out walking. Chang and his wife forgot politics as they walked along by the water under the trees. They discussed with great thoroughness and gravity where they should go and what they should eat. They agreed upon Fung Hei's restaurant and upon a Canton menu and at once grew very hungry.

They stood for a few moments near the tennis courts and looked on. A moist, green coolness rose from the short grass.

"We ought to play tennis again, too," Pearl said.

"We ought," Yutsing answered. It was the same as with the car of their own. "We ought to have our own car," they said when they were in the street again and no taxi was to be had. It was the hour when all businesses and offices in the International Settlement were closing and the electric signs began to light up all over the town, although the sky was still bright. At last they found a vacant taxi, and Yutsing at once took hold of his wife's large, rough hand again.

Pearl had shaken off all her fatigue, for the evening stir in the city reminded her of New York and drove away the lost feeling that sometimes came over her. She had come with Chang to China because she had cherished a great love for the unknown home of her family and because she believed she had a mission in China. The tirades of the students in the Chinese Club in New York had filled her with enthusiasm and an ardent longing to play her part in the new birth of a great and ancient nation. But what she found in China had overwhelmed her with burning shame for her countrymen, and she often had to clench her teeth to prevent her disillusionment from getting the upper hand. She tried to persuade herself that what she did was important for China. Treating syphilitic babies. Giving salvarsan. Fighting against opium. Teaching coolie mothers the rudiments of hygiene. Most of them still believed that a priest's magical formula was more potent medicine than cleanliness. Pearl worked on with a desperate sort of optimism, and every little success made her proud and happy. Also she loved her husband with a vehement and possessive love, which she had to disguise because it was so un-Chinese. He seemed to her better, finer, nobler than any other man she knew. Idealism and incorruptibility were rare and precious in China. He never spoke of his past, but she suspected depth after depth beneath the smooth surface of his being. The poet, Liu, who was one of Chang's few friends and had known him for long, sometimes dropped a remark which made Pearl prick up her ears. Sometimes she lay in bed at night with open eyes and listened to him while he slept. My husband, she thought, my husband, mine.

"Shall we pick up Liu?" Yutsing asked, breaking into her smiling thoughts. "With pleasure," Pearl said, although she would rather have spent the evening alone with her husband. Liu lived in the Chinese quarter of Hongkew in one of the little lanes too narrow for the taxi. Pearl waited until Yutsing came back with Liu. In spite of the heat, the poet wore his brown, rather dirty cotton garment. He wore it day in and day out, and it made Pearl sometimes call him an affected poseur. Liu replied to her good-natured mockery with witty poems in the classical form and wording, which he sent to her house accompanied by a few flowers. An alert and resolute head was poised above his shabby brown dress upon a surprisingly white and smooth and slender neck which made Liu look younger than he really was. In actual fact Liu's poverty and solitary way of life were only a whim, for he came of a rich and eminent family and had lands and houses somewhere, as well as wives and children.

"Hello," he said, shaking Pearl's hand.

"Hello," she said, smiling. They always spoke English together, for even though Liu's Oxford and Pearl's New York sounded very different, they could understand each other quite well, while Liu considered Pearl's Chinatown Cantonese unworthy of her.

"Any news?" Pearl asked as she settled herself comfortably between the two men. Now that Liu had joined them she was thoroughly pleased. Liu had become an important ingredient of her marriage with Yutsing. The evening took on a merrier and brighter turn just because Liu was sharing it with them.

"Here's your tea from Luching as promised," Liu said as he produced a small parcel. "And here," and he drew a painted paper fan from his wide sleeve, "is something for the collector of taste."

"Charming," Pearl said, opening and shutting the fan. "For me? I don't deserve it at all." The fan had peonies on one side and a little tender, sentimental landscape of willows on the other.

"Ah," Liu said taking it from her, "it is really a present for a concubine. But as concubines would disturb me in the composition of my philosophical treatise on the psychological value of lewdness, you may have it in token of the expression of my profound veneration."

He flipped the fan open and saw with a smile that Pearl's face flushed under its white powder. For the fan, which a moment ago had been so innocent, now revealed erotic scenes of an extremely unsophisticated shamelessness; ladies, naked but for tiny red shoes, were indulging in varied delights of love with pigtailed, fat and therefore aristocratic gentlemen.

"I know nothing about that sort of thing," Pearl said in embarrassment. Liu laughed to himself, shut and opened the fan, and now the peonies and willows had returned.

"You American prude!" he said, and it sounded almost affectionate. The taxi was now pervaded with the delicate scent of the packet of tea. Yutsing had not looked and probably not heard, either. He was keeping a lookout for a newspaper boy. When they reached the Bund and were held up in the crowd he bought three different evening papers which he held close up to his glasses in order to read them in the quickly fading light.

"War news before the evening rice spoils the appetite," Liu said.

"Is there good news?" Pearl asked her husband. He shrugged his shoulders and read on without answering. "We'll discuss the menu meanwhile," Liu suggested, and two minutes later he and Pearl were quarreling about whether the meal should begin with spiced duck livers or with pigeons' eggs in brown sauce.

Yutsing was rather distracted and silent when they arrived at Fung Hei's restaurant, and Liu tried hard to rouse him with his little digs. He ordered rice wine, forced Yutsing to drink up three of the little porcelain cups one after the other, and as Yutsing had no head for wine he instantly became very much above himself. He had delicate red patches on his cheekbones when they left Fung Hei's crowded restaurant.

They walked off arm in arm like American students, stopped at lighted shop windows, and Liu bought a few twigs of jasmine which smelt of summer and scattered yellow pollen. Again and again they left the smart foreign streets for the seething native alleys, listened to scraps of Chinese phonograph music from the shops and windows and at last came to the Avenue Edouard VII and finished up in a cinema. They saw *Mr Deeds Goes to Town,* and as all three had a great weakness for Gary Cooper they thoroughly enjoyed themselves. On the way home Pearl suddenly stopped and began to laugh.

"Just imagine Shanghai in ten years," she cried out, "when there is no longer any International Settlement. We'll go slumming to Englishtown as the Americans in New York do to Chinatown. We'll laugh over the dirty foreigners and their disgusting habits. Nanking Road will be a street of ill repute just as Mott Street is now, where I was born and where my father lives." Suddenly tears of anger started to her eyes, and the two men looked at her in dismay. She was gesticulating with her hands, in which she held the folded fan and the tea from Luching. And soon there was a small crowd expecting a political oration.

"I am not drunk," Pearl said, abashed, and would say no more. Yutsing drew her on. Immediately afterwards Liu took his leave of them. He held Pearl's hand a moment as though he were going to say something, but instead of saying it he walked quickly away and the night swallowed up his long lean figure. Yutsing hailed two rickshas and they drove home. There were posters everywhere calling for resistance and a boycott against the Japanese and Yutsing's Scout with his flag was quite put in the shade by these large clamorous placards.

The Changs lived in a modern block of flats in the Route de L'Astre. All the flats were furnished in the same style, steel furniture in the sitting room and pink rococo in the bedroom.

"I'm as dirty as a brigand," Chang said as he stood in front of the mirror. Number One was already getting the bath ready. Number Two brought his master the mail which had arrived during his absence. Chang took it with him into the bathroom. Pearl put on an old Japanese kimono and waited for her turn. Chang's bed had no pillows, only a hard little tightly stuffed neck prop, a habit contracted in his youth. He came back with wet hair and nothing on and threw his letters on the table.

"My father has come," he said. B. G. Chang had been spending the hot months in a little hotel which he had built in the neighborhood of the Tienmoshan monastery. Now he was back again and Chang, his son, looked forward to seeing him with an embarrassment he could not explain to Pearl. He put on his pajamas while she sat in front of the glass and oiled and brushed her hair. She was very proud of her smooth helmet of black lacquer, and Chang watched her with half-shut eyes. As he had taken off his glasses he had only a pleasantly blurred impression of her, and he smiled as he heard the electric crackling that the brush drew from her hair. He crossed the room and stood behind her while she went on brushing her hair. "What was that about the fan?" he asked. And Pearl was surprised that he had noticed anything. "Nothing," she said. "Only one of Liu's jokes." The whole room was full of the smell of the jasmine, which Number One had put in a vase; yellow pollen was shed from the white petals onto the table. Yutsing took up the fan and played with it, holding it close to his short-sighted eyes. He laughed softly when he found out the trick of it. "Charming," he said. "Very amusing."

Pearl sighed into the glass and let her brush drop. "Oh, you Chinese!" she said. Yutsing put the fan down.

"I didn't know that Liu was in love with you," he said.

"Nonsense," Pearl answered in English. Yutsing came back to her. He took her hand and tried to lift it up, but she released herself and shook her head with a smile. "I have earned my bath," she said.

Pearl's nightly bath was always a ritual and lasted a very long time. Chang with a drowsy smile heard the padding of her naked feet, the hiss of the shower bath, the gurgling of the water as it ran out of the tub. He was heavy with rice wine. Its warmth ebbed in wave after wave from his body. When Pearl came back into the room he had fallen asleep.

She turned out the light and, holding her breath in order to make as little noise as possible, she lay down, neatly outstretched in her bed. Many noises penetrated the thin walls of the block of flats. Two phonographs were playing on two different floors; Marlene Dietrich was singing on one of them, and on the other Pei Yu-shuan, who was called in Shanghai the Chinese Mae West. Automobiles hooted and braked at the corner in the street, and the distant hum of the great city came through the warm night. Pearl shut her eyes; during the minute before she fell asleep the events of the day flashed past in a medley of rapid pictures as though the lining of her closed eyelids were a screen. "All those warships in the Whangpoo . . . " she thought just before she fell asleep.

Ten minutes after midnight the telephone at the bedside table rang. Yutsing grumblingly took up the receiver, and Pearl turned on the light. "It is so," he said sleepily into the telephone and: "Can it not be early tomorrow morning?" and: "I am tired. Arrived from Nanking today." And finally: "It is good. I will come at once."

Pearl watched him with surprise as he got up with his eyes still shut and went to the bathroom to wash his face in cold water. "Number One!" he shouted. "A fresh suit."

"The servants are asleep," Pearl said and got up to lay out a suit and linen for her husband. "Where are you going?"

"My father wants to speak to me at once," he said, tying his tie. Pearl looked at him and said nothing more.

Yutsing smoothed his hair. When he had gone, Pearl for a few minutes looked vacantly at the scrolls of handwriting hanging on the wall near her bed. It was the only thing in the flat that was her own. Her father, the merchant of Mott Street, Chinatown, New York, had written it for her:

> Little fish
> Swims in the great sea,
> Grows no bigger for that.

Her father's strong and rather stiff characters—he had never quite abandoned calligraphy—soothed her. There was a tender and pleasant irony in the words, something that made her feel small and irresponsible. She smiled, turned out the light and went to sleep.

The Shanghai Hotel, to which Yutsing Chang drove—he took a ricksha so that the open air might wake him up—was in the Nanking Road in the heart of the International Settlement and close to the racecourse. It had been built five years before with great splendor and at vast expense, and it was said in Shanghai that anyone who was anybody sooner or later passed through the lounge of that hotel.

As Dr Chang crossed this lounge, where at that hour every table was occupied by people in evening dress drinking their whiskies or

liqueurs, he was accosted by an enormous lady with white hair:
"Monsieur Chang! Back from Nanking? How do things go there?
Any news? Is the war coming to Shanghai? They say that the rich
Japanese like Furuya and Kikuchi have shut up shop and quietly
vanished. Would it not be a sensation if we had the war here, too?
Never have I been so amused since '32. Do you know, I was standing
close by when Yungho Yunhang mills went up in the air. Will you
sit here with me? I am a lonely old woman, you know, and longing
for a chat."

Madame Tissaud was as much a part of the lounge of the Shanghai
Hotel as one of the black marble pillars on which the glass roof
rested. She was the voice of Shanghai—its rumor, its gossip, its
journal. She had occupied the same post before the new hotel was
built, in the little old red-plush Shanghai Hotel. She had always
been there and would still be there when the last of the hundred
wars, great and small, had razed Shanghai to the ground.

Where she came from, nobody knew. Some maintained that
Madame Tissaud had been living in the swamps where the first
pioneers began to build their town. There were people who took
Madame Tissaud to be the widow of a missionary who had made a
fortune by selling bicycles. Others maintained that she was the owner
of a chain of brothels, the most profitable of which was the famous
house of the Small Boys in the Avenue Edouard VII. However that
may be, she sat there and detained Dr Chang in the middle of the
lounge.

He made an awkward bow and muttered excuses. He was the only
Chinese in the whole crowded lounge, as he could feel rather than
see. And although the hotel belonged to his father, he felt like an
interloper and a despised stranger. Madame opened the sluice gates
and a new flood poured out. "You have to visit your father? He
looks magnificent, he tells me he has caught ten thousand fish in
the river" [she said "ten thousand" in the Chinese manner]. "Do
you know too that he won fourteen hundred dollars tonight at the
Hai Alai? Monsieur Too Fat staked against him—the idiot, to stake
his money against B.G. By the way," and she drew Chang down
by the lapel of his coat, "he has got hold of two of the most beautiful

Korean girls to be seen in Shanghai for a very long time. They say he bought them from a Japanese officer of high rank in the Kwantung army. But I do not believe that. Do you know why he has asked you to come as late as this? And just tell me one thing more: what do the gentlemen of Nanking make of the *Idzumo* lying at anchor so close in front of the Bund?"

Dance music could be heard through every wall of the Shanghai Hotel. There was dancing in the large dining room until two, on the roof garden until three, and the piano played in the bar until the last visitors went home. The clatter of bottles and glasses, the subdued murmur of many conversations, the cigarette smoke, the scent of women, the almost inaudible sound of the felt soles of Chinese waiters and page boys shuffling on the thick sand-colored carpets—all gave an indefinable impression of elegance and the great world. Yutsing Chang clenched his teeth and kissed Madame Tissaud's powdered hand, which she held up to him for that purpose. It was the price he had to pay for getting away from her. He did not take the main elevator, whose glass doors were constantly opening and shutting opposite the reception desk, but traversed a small vestibule, vacant and silent beneath its brightly colored glass cupola, and thus arrived at the rear of the building, where a second elevator went straight to his father's apartments. The hotel had installed this elevator—very discreetly—for the convenience of Chinese, Japanese, Indians, Koreans and all other visitors whose propinquity and contact were not desired by white people. The life of a Chinese in the International Settlement was made up of such pinpricks.

And yet Chang's father possessed such a large majority of the shares that he practically owned the Shanghai Hotel. The famous roof garden on the eighteenth floor was flanked by two turretlike erections, penthouses after the New York pattern, one of which contained the banker's apartments. The other was the bar. Bogum Chang had retreated there when a blackmailing gang had threatened to kidnap him and a political secret society to murder him. Up there, high above the city, surrounded by his servants and bodyguards, he felt safe.

The banker's secretary, Mr Chai, a relation by marriage to a brother-in-law of one of Yutsing's cousins, received him. Chai was a delicately made, rather effeminate-looking young man in a correct white dinner jacket, and his fishlike mouth always wore an air of surprise.

"Your honored father is impatient," he said reproachfully. Yutsing automatically smoothed his hair and went in.

The large reception room was filled with heavy teakwood furniture; there were red, embroidered satin hangings, as though for a wedding, and precious porcelain bowls were displayed on the irregularly fashioned shelves—gifts, as also were the heavy silver platters on the opposite walls. A piece of antique furniture stood in the middle of the room, a so-called kang, something between a bed and a couch, long and wide enough to accommodate two persons with a table for opium or Mahjong between them. There were many telephones, radios and victrolas and all sorts of electrical devices from cigarette lighters to foot warmers, for B. G. Chang was a great admirer of electricity.

He was sitting on the couch, and although he had drunk a lot he was dead sober. It was a sultry night, and he was stripped to his black trousers. His skin was the color of dark copper and his gigantic chest and shoulder muscles reminded his son of the mighty statues he had seen on monuments. A pretty and very much painted Korean girl was sitting on the floor at his feet; she was holding a bottle of whisky in her arms as if it were a baby and balancing a half-empty glass in her fingers, ready to fill it up for her master as soon as he wanted it. The dance music on the roof garden was relayed from a radio in the corner, and at the same time it came more faintly through the walls. The windows, which reached nearly to the ground, were open, and the city lay below in a haze of its myriad-colored electric signs. Two other girls were dancing a slow foxtrot to the music. They were dancing so languorously in mutual surrender that they had a lascivious and provocative air. There was a dim gleam of sweat on their faces.

"Joy, my son has come!" Chang exclaimed making as though to get up, but Yutsing prevented him.

"How is the revered health of my father?" he asked with ceremony, bowing at the same time.

"Good, better than for a long time," Chang cried and drew Yutsing to him on the wide upholstered couch. "I have eaten sun and washed away the dust of the city in the waters of the Tung River." He stretched out his powerful arms and laughed. "What the books say is true: The sky is my father and the earth is my mother," he cried out.

The girl at his feet had quickly filled a glass for Yutsing, and his father took it from her and gave it to his son. "Contentment," he said and emptied his own glass to the bottom. Since boyhood Yutsing had never got over the fear that his father would take him for a weakling. He bravely drank the whisky down and instantly discovered untapped sources within him.

"How is the revered health of my mother?" he asked.

"She still walks with a stick, and your aunt has to support her, so great is the weakness she feels. But she lives," Chang replied. He laughed loudly. "She is planning soon to visit the Temple-of-the-Purple-Cloud. That shows that she is well," he said cheerfully.

His mother had had a gastric fever earlier in the year, which lasted a long time and wasted her strength. Yutsing had paid her many visits and been very anxious about her, for he loved his mother; she was as refined and as untouched by the upsets of modern days as an old ivory statue of the goddess of mercy. With his mother he himself was no good as a doctor; he was more suited to his office as son. But he had at last persuaded her to be treated by Pearl, and she had got better. In spite of this his parents continued to regard his wife with mistrust and coolness.

"I will write to her and tell her not to fatigue herself too much," he murmured anxiously. His father had been watching the two girls with absent-minded satisfaction as they danced; now the dance was over and they relapsed laughing and breathless onto the silk cushions of a low window seat. B. G. Chang nodded to the girl who held the bottle, and she quickly crossed the room and turned off the radio. It was now quieter, but the music still came seeping faintly through the walls from the roof garden. Chang noticed several empty bottles and glasses on a table. "I brought in a few friends from the Hai Alai," his father said in reply. "I sent them away early, for I was impatient to talk with you."

He took up the telephone from a little table on the couch and said: "Chai, you can go to sleep. I want no one more tonight."

At this signal the three girls slipped from the room without waiting to be told. When they had gone the room seemed suddenly very large and empty.

His father had not inquired after Pearl, and this intentional impoliteness made his son look forward to the late and urgent talk with grave discomfort. His father smiled at him for a moment in silence; just as in his childhood, Yutsing had no idea whether this smile betokened kindliness or ironical criticism.

"It was unreasonable of you to go to Nanking if you wanted money for your little games," Chang said at last.

"The athletic displays in the stadium are not games," Yutsing replied quickly; he was full of whisky and courage. "The gentlemen in the education department in Nanking know very well that the Scouts are of great importance in spreading the principles of the New Life."

"But they gave you no money for them," his father said, and now his mockery was unconcealed—a good-natured, matured and almost wise mockery.

"It is not a favorable moment——" Dr Chang began.

"Very unfavorable, extremely unfavorable," his father answered. "Airplanes are at present more important than—what do you call them?—spreaders of ideas. Airplanes and fly-fly eggs," he said reflectively, and Dr Chang could not help smiling when his father used the coolie expression for airbombs.

"Nevertheless the Jamboree will take place," he said obstinately. "Now particularly it is absolutely necessary that the children return to their villages and strengthen the national feeling against the Japanese. The gentlemen in Nanking who want to cancel these athletic games are political dilettantes. Cousins are mostly blockheads."

The elder Chang smiled at his son's outburst against the law of relationship on which China was built up. It was a favorite idea of his unreasonable son's, who would not see that it was better and more advantageous to have to do with relations rather than with strangers. But he had no desire at the moment to embark on a discussion of this point. He merely said: "The blockheads are right for once. There is no sense in bringing five thousand children to Shanghai just when war is breaking out. It would surprise me if the villagers thought much of the New Life if Japanese bombs destroyed their five thousand children."

"Why should the war spread to Shanghai? It is, after all, highly improbable," Dr Chang said quickly. His father laid his large copper hand on his knee as though to calm him down.

"I am no war lord," he said. "I understand nothing about it. But clever people have explained to me that it would be more favorable to us to split up the Japanese front and to fight in many different places."

Dr Chang was silent from dismay. He knew from experience that his father was well informed and generally in the right.

"How much money did you hope to raise in Nanking?" the banker asked while his son was lost in reflection.

"We still need about four hundred dollars for transport and food."

Bogum Chang waited. He hoped his son would ask him for the money. But his son did nothing of the kind. He is obstinate and sour with virtue, Chang thought bitterly.

"Where do you think of getting the money from?" he asked.

"I don't know. Perhaps from the Jews," his son said. Chang laughed aloud at this idea. Dr Chang too knew that it was foolish. For a year past Pearl had been trying in vain to get her three ultra-violet-ray lamps from the Jews who had founded the Chapei clinic. As he was without the wide Chinese sleeves, he put his hands in his pockets to give himself confidence.

"Listen, my son," B.G. said after drinking another glass of whisky. "I will give you the money because I won tonight at the Hai Alai. Perhaps it will bring me luck at play. Chai will see that you have it tomorrow. But do not forget that I am against bringing the children to Shanghai."

While Dr Chang returned thanks for the unexpected gift, which took a heavy weight off his mind, he wondered what his father's motive was. Did he want something from the government? Was he doing it to annoy some enemy? Did he want to be praised in the newspapers? Or was it simply to gain face? It did not occur to the son that his father might have no other reason for giving him the money than wanting to give him pleasure.

"You called me in order to discuss something of importance with me?" he asked, and it occurred to him that he had sold himself to his father at the cost of what must now be coming.

"You remember what you promised your mother when she lay gravely sick?" Chang Bogum asked without further beating about the bush.

"I do remember," Yutsing said. In fact he had scarcely been able to forget it for an hour, and the word memory was in no proportion to the agony of mind it had caused him.

"Well? And how is it? Is your wife with child?"

Chang swallowed twice. "No," he said.

"Your mother is still too weak to pick out a concubine for you. She has left it to me to make the choice," Chang said. From his pleased expression it was clear that the office put him in no great difficulty. "The girl is eighteen years old, experienced enough to give you pleasure and innocent enough to make a good mother. She has four brothers and comes of a poor family but one that has always been rich in sons. She is called Meilan."

"I do not want to take a concubine. I shall ask my mother to release me from my word," Yutsing said. His father looked at him and shook his head.

"We are not putting a poisonous toad in your bed, but a beautiful girl," he said irritably. "You behave as if you were no man."

"My wife is young. She may still have many sons if my parents give her time," Yutsing said. He knew that he was lying. Pearl had had three miscarriages. She had been examined by several doctors. She had wept bitterly and at last become reconciled to the fact that she could have no children.

Chang stood up, and his forehead, copper-colored in any case, turned still darker. But he controlled himself again and said with great gentleness: "You have never bothered yourself much about your parents' wishes, and whenever you have opposed us sorrow has come of it for you. It cannot be otherwise when a man mars the harmony laid down for us. But you cannot neglect the most important duty of life, namely, to insure that you have issue. I do not ask, as I might, that you send back the fruitless woman whom, without asking me, you brought with you from a foreign country. But you promised your mother to give her grandsons, and you will keep your word."

"I cannot allow you to insult my wife," Yutsing exclaimed, now losing his patience, too. "You do not understand my marriage. Pearl is very dear to me. She is the dearest companion, the truest and best of wives, and not even my parents have the right to give her pain."

His father smiled at this. "What has that to do with your taking a concubine and seeing that you have issue?" he said with amusement. "Your mother is in my opinion the best wife in the whole world, and I honor her above anything on this earth. What has that to do with my fairly numerous concubines? You young people always think that you have discovered heaven and earth and everything in and upon them, afresh," he added more seriously. "There have always been good wives who were good companions to their husbands. Look round about in the country. Everywhere wives work at their husbands' sides—in the fields, in the houses and on the boats. Wives have always disposed of what the huband earns. How old is the saying: The husband labors the earth, the wife sits at the spinning wheel."

Yutsing Chang did not listen. He jumped up and went to the window to snatch a breath of the night air. "I shall not take a concubine," he said. He heard his father's voice behind him in the room: "A son without education is worth no more than a pig!" He heard the bottle clink against the edge of the glass, as though his father's hands were trembling, and all the time he heard the dance music from the roof garden; he even knew the tune: "Night and Day."

"We are Christians, Pearl and I," he said without turning round and speaking as though to the electric signs down in the city. "Ours is a Christian marriage. We are happy and contented. It would be a sin to bring a second wife into it."

He waited, but his father made no answer. Yutsing Chang brought out a last argument. "For many years we have been working and preaching against the practice of keeping concubines. How then can I go and take a concubine? I should lose face," he said loudly. *"Night and day you are the one,"* came from outside on three saxophones.

"Come, my son, and sit down here beside me," his father said from behind him with unexpected gentleness. Yutsing Chang turned round and pulled a chair up to the couch, on which Chang settled himself with crossed legs.

"I climbed several times up the mountain-that-looks-at-heaven," the elder Chang said reflectively. "I spent several nights in the eastern monastery and made friends with the abbot. He is a simple man and a very holy man. He eats no flesh and spends many hours in meditation. He consulted the Book of Transmigrations."

Yutsing's tension gave way, and he began to smile. Calm welled from his father's words as though from an old book.

"The sticks say that I shall die this year," Chang went on, "and for that reason I cannot allow you further delay. I must insist that you beget me a grandson and do not break the line out of lack of understanding and obstinacy and selfishness. You too will want to have sons when you are older and think of returning to your fathers."

When Chang had said this he poured himself out another glass of whisky, this time a tumblerful, and drank it slowly as though to quench a great thirst. It is incredible what he can drink without getting drunk, Dr Chang thought.

"You cannot ask me to take such superstitions seriously," he said as he surveyed his father's gigantic frame. "You will live many years yet and be as old as a cliff or a mountain."

"The abbot consulted the book twenty-three times, and twenty-three times he cast the sticks. The book always gave the same answer," Chang said. "Before I returned to Shanghai I went as well to the temple of Lingyin, merely from curiosity. There too the book had nothing else to say. I am an uneducated man of the old days

and believe in what is decreed," he added with a smile full of irony.
"I have given you money so that you can fulfill your wishes. You
ought on your side to have regard for the wishes of your father who
will soon leave this vale."

Yutsing did not know what to reply. For two years he had striven
against his parents, and suddenly he did not know why. The wish
for a son was enclosed in the innermost kernel of his being, deep
within all the wrappings of education. A little son, resplendent in
his golden skin, a son who would carry on his work and his ideas.
A better man in a better China.

"Now it has stopped," he said.

"What has stopped?"

"The music," Dr Chang said. A church clock struck three in the
distant French quarter. He looked at his father and saw that sweat
stood in large drops on his face. Gentle persuasion was hard work
for the man of violence. White scars stood on the copper skin of his
shoulders—marks of his coolie days, of the loads he had carried, of
the ropes he had pulled. Suddenly he felt sorry for his giant of a
father. "I am too tired to come to a decision tonight," he said formally. "I beg a few days to think it over. May I now take my leave?"

When he left the hotel he found the streets wet and shining after
a brief rain. The air steamed. There were no stars left in the brighten-
ing sky. Lost in thought and with knitted brow, Yutsing Chang set
off on foot along the streets. Small boys on the edge of the racecourse were shouting an extra edition. He read it in the failing light
of a street lamp.

Peking had fallen. The Japanese were besieging Tientsin, and it
could not hold out much longer.

IV

KURT PLANKE LAY ON THE BED and gazed through the mosquito net
at Meilan, who was packing her clothes in a little case. She was small
and amazingly slender and well made, and her hands were so delicate and aristocratic that all other hands he had ever seen were like

the paws of animals in comparison. Meilan was clothed in white silk trousers and a tight embroidered jacket; it was unbuttoned, and her soft breast and the delicate hollow of her belly was visible from time to time. Kurt clasped his hands behind his head and let his cigarette hang limply from his underlip.

"There is a beautiful German song that suits you perfectly, Gretchen," he said in German, for he knew no Chinese, and it was all the same to Meilan which of the incomprehensible foreign languages he spoke. "It goes like this: 'You are made for love from head to foot.' I'll bring the record next time and play it for you. Look at me just once more, Gretchen."

Meilan turned round, smiled at him and went up to the bed, for she understood his tone even if not the words. Kurt took his hands from behind his head and, pushing the netting aside, carefully stroked the delicate skin beneath her open jacket. "It just occurs to me that there won't be any next time, Gretchen," he said, "as far as I can see from your movements. Does that packed box mean *adieu pour jamais?*"

"My little prince must get up and dress," Meilan said in Chinese and bent down over Kurt. She pulled him by the fair hairs on his chest and began to laugh. Immediately afterwards she knelt beside the bed and buried her face in his shoulder.

"I know, I know," Kurt said. "It is to my hairy chest that I owe my success with you. And now you are going away with your little box to another master. What a pity, Gretchen, what a pity!"

He clasped his hands behind her slender back and looked up thoughtfully at the cracked and patchy ceiling. He had made up his mind not to involve his feelings in this brief affair with a little Chinese girl, but now it was not so easy to part from her and her playful caresses. He raised her face from his shoulder and looked earnestly at her. She laughingly shook her head. "The undersigned would be extremely obliged by an explanation," he said. She pressed her lips to his throat.

"No, my child, not now," he said severely, sitting up. She sat primly beside him under the much-darned mosquito net, with her hands loosely folded in her white silk lap.

"Can you not at least give me your new address, Gretchen?" he asked.

She said slowly: "Ku—my—dar-ling."

"Beautiful, beautiful Meilan, my darling," Kurt said. "What I want is your address. Now listen, Gretchen. I live—Ku lives—Shanghai Hotel. Where Meilan live? Where? Do you understand? Where? Suppose I want to send you an invitation to the dance at the Y.M.C.A. Where?"

Meilan dropped her head and began with lowered eyelids to repeat her story.

"Meilan is the property and the slave girl of the great lord, of the Lord Chang Bogum. The great lord bought me and my sister as little children. He gave us clothes and rice and had us brought up by a lady who understands the arts that serve to entertain the gentlemen. The Lord Chang Bogum has done my sister the honor to take her as his concubine. But he has spared me for the great lord, his son, Chang Yutsing. His son is pleased with me, and I shall live in a large house and wear bracelets and earrings of jade, and I shall see the foreign shadow plays and have as many silk dresses as I want. And if I give him a son he will put away his wife, the fruitless one, and set me over his house. Nevertheless I am sad to part with you, my little prince."

"That is all very interesting, Gretchen," Kurt said when the flood of Chinese ceased. "I quite understand, blast it, that you are onto something good. And that is all the same to me—who cares? We can go back to the pipe again, you are not ever to be compared with the joy of opium. Sublime, if you understand me, Gretchen? Adieu, my treasure. It's been charming to know you." And with that he got up and began silently to dress. Meilan sat on the bed and watched him. The amah made ostentatious noises in the outer room to imply it was time for the lover to leave.

Kurt whistled while he put on his clothes. Meilan got up and handed him his clothes bit by bit, but he picked her up and put her down on the bed again like a doll. He was in a rather desperate mood, and he whistled more loudly and tied his tie so violently that he might have been wishing to strangle himself. The tie, a yellow one with green spots, was a present from Meilan. She had also bought him the frightful cuff links from some Japanese bazaar. It was a remarkable and shocking state of affairs that Kurt never paid a woman or gave any woman a present. It was always the other way round.

He looked for a hairbrush and dipped it in the cracked basin which stood in one corner on a dilapidated stand. He applied himself with earnest attention to his hair. When he looked round at Meilan she had small, clear tears in her eyes.

"That's all we need," he said and put his hands in his trouser pockets to have them safe somewhere. "Chinese girls never make a scene. It says so in every guidebook. Done is done and finished is finished. Who cares?"

It was more than a year since Kurt had come to Shanghai. The murderous town had carried on the havoc which Paris had begun. The terrible first weeks, during which Dr Hain received a pittance from a committee that helped German Jewish exiles and shared it with Kurt—for he was an Aryan and had no claim to assistance; the stench of bedbugs in the miserable hotel where they lived; the fear of sinking down below the level of the white man into the dirt of the colored races; the hopeless outlook in a society where a white man might not undertake menial work and could find no other. At last he was employed to play the piano in the Dragon Club, which in fact was nothing but a brothel. He had a room in the attic among a crowd of girls of all colors who, owing to disease, drunkenness and conflicts with the police, had been ejected from the night clubs in the International Settlement and now tried to get a living on their own. There was bitter rivalry between the slender and youthful Asiatic girls and the overblown, worn-out and yet arrogant White Russians, who all claimed to be descended from the czars. He had an affair out of pity with one of them, Natasha, when he once brought her back to her room after an attack of hysterics. Natasha had too much soul. At it was always overflowing, Kurt hardened his heart. The emotion which was second nature to him as a German and a musician dried up. He became cynical and insolent with the peculiar grim humor which thrives in Shanghai as nowhere else. Natasha came to blows with a Korean girl called Betsy. He was the bone of contention. It was in Betsy's room, which she shared with another girl, that he first became acquainted with the unforgettable smell of opium. Betsy had become a complete addict, and with the passionate proselytizing of the chronic victim she introduced him to the pipe. As soon as he had got over the discomforts of the beginner he reached the state the Chinese mean when they speak of harmony with the universe.

The craving for women had tortured Kurt vehemently from early years. Now he was filled with a wonderful peace and contentment and needed women no longer.

Suddenly Betsy vanished. It was not the girl he missed, but he became sick with longing for the pipe he was accustomed to. As he had no money to buy the costly poison, which could be obtained in the town from a hundred secret sources, he soon sank to the depths where the poor men, the coolies, porters and workers in the cotton factories, obtained their little bit of smoke. The cheap opium they smoked was bitter and strong. It was concocted from leavings and produced deep intoxication. Life is so full of hardship that only the Great Smoke makes it bearable, they said, and Kurt agreed with them. Nothing matters, he thought. Who cares?

Chance rescued him and Dr Hain from starvation. The sumptuous automobile of the banker B. G. Chang ran over the young wife of a Chinese railwayman and her little son in the narrow Yueng Min Yueng. Dr Hain, who saw the accident, gave first aid to the mother and the child, took them to the hospital, got a blood transfusion for the child and did all that was necessary to save the lives of them both.

Although the occasional running down of pedestrians was part of life and attracted little attention—for B. G. Chang's chauffeur could only show how great his master's face was by disregarding all traffic rules—this case was an exception. For once the victimized party had face, too. The railwayman had connections that extended as far as the Ministry of Transport. He belonged to the honorable and influential clan of the Wu, and although he only clung to the extreme fringes of the family, it was enough to put him in a position to extract an enormous sum in compensation should his wife and child die. Thanks to Dr Hain's interposition it did not come to that, and the banker showed his gratitude.

Dr Hain was allotted a back room in the Shanghai Hotel and was regarded from then on as the hotel doctor. Now and then he even had a patient: somebody who got diarrhea and was afraid he had cholera; or one of the itching dust infections rife in Shanghai; simple and complicated hangovers. And occasionally there was a woman who took too much veronal to give her lover a fright. For Kurt he wangled the job of pianist in the bar in the roof garden. He now took turns there with a colored boy who was engaged for syncopated jazz, while he himself played French tangos and Viennese waltzes whenever sentimental, tipsy, love-ridden cosmopolitans had a craving for them. He occupied a wretched little room without windows and was given his dinner at night and fifteen Shanghai dollars each week. He played by night and slept by day. Whenever it happened that the last patrons went home early, he was off to Chapei to smoke opium. Who cares? he thought.

Ten weeks before this, B.G., the great man of Shanghai, had brought two little Chinese girls into the bar, Meilan and her sister. Kurt came to life and fell in love with Meilan on the spot—if the faint excitement he felt at the sight of her slender gazellelike figure can be called falling in love. The Eurasian headwaiter was able to give him Meilan's address and tell him something about her. She lived with her amah in a derelict lodging house in Yangtze Po. By the time the banker went into the country they had already come to an understanding, although their conversation consisted of monologues in different languages. Kurt succeeded after a great effort in giving up opium. He who can be without opium for four days is cured, is a Shanghai saying. The four days were ghastly. "Gretchen," Kurt said on the sixth day—he spoke nothing but German to the Chinese on principle—"Gretchen, you don't know what a heaven I have given up for you. You will have to exert yourself to compensate me." Meilan snuggled up to him laughing, and for six weeks everything went better, even if not well, in Kurt's wasted life. And now it was over. Meilan put her beautiful peach-colored silk dress in her box, smoothed it down with her incredibly lovely hands and snapped the lock.

"So that's that," Kurt said and went rapidly out of the room. The amah in the gloomy passage held out her hand for a tip. "My last dollar, revered lady," Kurt said and went on his way. The house had narrow little galleries running round a tiny yard, and the four stories looked like the cells in a beehive. It smelt Chinese, of dishwater, of burnt oil, of incense, of garlic and old clothes. The stairs were narrow and steep and dark. The coolie who had brought Kurt two hours before was sleeping below in the narrow street. "Wake up, Franz," Kurt shouted as he gave the ricksha a shake. Yen woke up at once and greeted him with a broad smile which stretched the skin over his cheekbones. "Man, what a sight you are again," Kurt remarked, surveying the wasted figure in its rags and tatters. "Master catchee hotel?" Yen asked. "You've guessed, Franz," Kurt said and got into the ricksha. "Catchee hotel velly muchee quick."

Yen took up the shafts, but then put them down again and produced a little bundle out of which he drew a dirty and thumbed letter in a crumbled envelope. He held the document up to Kurt's face and watched him expectantly. Kurt looked at the Chinese characters and nodded his head. "You've shown me that three times, Franz, and I still can't read it," he said. "Now off with you and quick, chop-chop."

Yen put up the letter again, harnessed his arms to the shafts and trotted off. It was hot and early in the afternoon. When they reached the hotel Kurt found twenty cents in his pocket and gave them to the coolie. Yen took them without protest, for Kurt was a regular client. "Master," he said in an undertone as Kurt was entering the cool colonnade which surrounded the Shanghai Hotel. "Nothing doing, Franz," he said. But Yen came up behind him and barred his way. "Master," he said, "like catchee Apenyon? Velly muchee good Apenyon."

Kurt pushed him aside and then went on as though he had not heard. It was this coolie who had first introduced him to the opium den in Chapei.

Madame Tissaud was sitting in the lounge with the wealthy English couple whom Kurt had seen several times in the bar. "She's a beautiful woman, but she dances too well for a lady," Kurt said to the Eurasian headwaiter after observing her for the first time. "That is not our affair," Eugen had replied.

"Monsieur Kurt, come here one moment," Madame Tissaud cried, just as he was hoping to slip past her, for he hated her from the bottom of his heart.

"Mrs Russell, may I introduce our young genius to you? Make your bow, Monsieur Kurt, Mrs Russell is a connoisseur." She held her hand close up to his face, but instead of kissing it he shook it. Russell, her husband, the Honourable Robert Russell, looked sleepily at him while he waved his glass to and fro to stir the ice. "You French, too?" he asked without the slightest interest. "A little of everything," Kurt replied; he was weary of narrating his entire life story, including his escape from Germany, to everyone who had a whisky in the bar. Mrs Russell looked him up and down not too politely. "If we come up tonight you must play Mr Russell's favorite tune," she said. "With pleasure," he answered with a professional bow. "What is it?"

" 'The More We Are Together,' " Mrs Russell said. "It brings tears to his eyes, but only after three o'clock in the morning. His sensibilities do not function very well before that."

"Monsieur Kurt must tell you sometime how he and the charming Dr Hain fled from Germany. It is better than a novel," Madame Tissaud said. "You take an interest in politics, I know, Mr Russell?"

"That's my brother," Russell said and buried his face in his glass.

A silence followed. "Well, I think I'd better go," Kurt said uncomfortably. No one had asked him to sit down.

"Au revoir in the bar," Mrs Russell said vaguely.

"Did you see?" Madame Tissaud asked the moment his back was turned. "His eyes? The expression?"

"No. What about it?" Mr Russell asked.

"Opium," Madame answered and leaned back. The chair creaked under the weight of her body.

"Oh!" Helen said.

"I don't know how it goes with the profession of a gigolo," Madame went on with zest. "Every child knows that opium causes impotence. But he is a handsome young fellow all the same. Oh, here comes B.G. himself! Monsieur Chang! Do come and sit down with us, Monsieur Chang!" she cried, waving both hands. But the banker, who was clothed in a Chinese robe of bright green silk, merely made a bow in passing, shook his own hands and went on. He had given Helen the glance of a man who appreciates feminine beauty. Helen caught his look as a woman who knew men. She smiled to herself. Madame had perceived and enjoyed the faint vibration.

"That is B. G. Chang, the most powerful man in Shanghai, they say," she explained as he went on. "In the war between Chang Tso-lin and General Fong Yuhsiang he financed both sides. Fong has sworn to have him murdered. That's why Chang lives in the hotel. Once he just annihilated three men who tried to kidnap him. It is said he is so strong that he can stretch out a buffalo; and a little Kunyang, whom he bought for himself, bled to death the first night. But the most charming of all is the story of how he disentangled himself the second time. Imagine it: he was leaving his bank, and before he could get into the automobile there were two men there with their revolvers in his ribs. A Sikh was standing ten yards away, but naturally B.G. could not call to him. What do you think he did? He quickly undid his belt—you know that the Chinese keep up their trousers only with a belt—and his trousers fell down, plop. Of course the Sikh came running up in a rage when he saw the indecency— an enormous Chinese with bare behind in the middle of the Inter-national Settlement—thus Chang was saved. Presence of mind, eh? And a sense of humor."

It seemed that Russell had not been listening, for he took up an earlier remark of Madame's.

"You mentioned opium," he remarked sleepily. "Everybody talks about opium. Is it so easy to get hold of it as all that?"

"As simple as anything, my dear Monsieur Russell. Every second person here has opium. I've been told that it is the same as with gin during Prohibition in America. There is nothing simpler than to buy opium in Shanghai."

"How, for example?" Russell asked. Helen gave him a quick searching look.

"You only need to ask anyone who smokes opium," Madame said gaily. "I do not need any artificial stimulants for the present myself. There are Japanese hotels—with girls, I believe. Since the Japanese have opened the gap in the North they have flooded the country with their Korean stuff, so at least everyone says—morphine too and heroin and I don't know what——"

"I'm very keen to go to Peking, if possible," Helen said to change the subject. "It is the next item on our program. Rotten luck to come here just when a war is breaking out."

"There is always war somewhere in China," Madame Tissaud said. "It is not to be taken so seriously. There is a lot of look-see about it. Here comes Dr Chang. Here we are, Monsieur Chang—here."

Dr Chang was wearing a freshly ironed white suit of Shantung silk, and he had a new panama hat in his hand. He wore white shoes, bright green silk socks and a tie of the same color. He smelt of hair oil and eau de cologne.

"I must beg a thousand times for pardon if I am late," he said in polite embarrassment.

"Not at all. I bet we'll see quite enough as it is," Russell murmured. From the beginning he had been averse to accepting the invitation of the Chinese, but Helen had the sight-seer's disease and wanted to see everything wherever they went. And Bobbie had not enough energy not to do what his wife wanted him to do.

"I mean we don't want to give you too much trouble," he added, for Helen had impressed upon him how necessary it was to be polite to the Chinese.

Now it was for Dr Chang to protest. His offer to show the Russells something of Shanghai was in a sense caused by an official hint. The Chinese ambassador in Tokyo was a friend of his and had written to him to say that the Russells had been very much fêted in Japan and that Robert Russell belonged to a family of political importance in England. It was highly necessary to give him a good impression of the New China in order to counterbalance Japanese influence. It was with this aim that Yutsing Chang, clad in new clothes from head to foot, fragrant and grinning, hot and uncomfortable, did his utmost in the way of bows and politeness, although the English language was not suited to politeness at all.

A gigantic limousine with a chauffeur in white uniform was drawn up in front of the hotel; Chang had borrowed it from his father in order to impress these English people. Look-see, Helen thought as she got in. "I'm told there's some good polo in Shanghai," her husband remarked. Dr Chang confessed with a smile that he knew very little about it.

"I'm told there's good polo in Hong Kong too," Russell said.

"My father has a set of figures of the Tang dynasty," Dr Chang said, "which might interest you. It is a polo team of women on horseback in their long dresses and wide sleeves. It shows that polo has been played in China for more than a thousand years. It must have been very popular, since not only the men but the women as well played it."

"Indeed," said Russell, who was too drowsy to have patience with the long-winded explanation.

Dr Chang took up the speaking tube and directed the chauffeur in Chinese. He was just in time to prevent the man from going through the squalid and dirty quarter along Soochow Creek.

He was in a flurry as usual when it came to showing that China had made great strides. There was a peculiar mixture of feelings in him: contempt for the ignorant and barbaric inhabitants of other continents, hatred of the interlopers who squeezed money and sweat out of the country, bitter shame for the racial weaknesses of his own countrymen and admiration of the arrogant. An odd mixture which everywhere marked the relations between East and West.

"We will stop for a few moments at a school," he proposed to his companions. "The children are giving a little play, and I think it will interest you to see what is being done in China in the sphere of education."

Helen saw the horrified expression on her husband's face and hurriedly intervened. "Certainly," she said. "Schools are quite a hobby of mine."

Yutsing revived at these encouraging words. "Next week I can show you something really astonishing: a Jamboree of about five thousand Scouts from the whole province of Kiangsi. That is my hobby, Mrs Russell. Youth, the next generation! It is difficult for our older people to alter their ways, but the next generation will be quite different, we can promise you that. Even Moses had to stay for forty years in the desert with the chosen people until a new generation had grown up. What are forty years? What are a hundred years in the regeneration of a people?"

Helen looked at the ardent face of the little Chinese. "You know your Bible?" she asked politely.

"I am a Christian," he replied modestly. Bobbie took no part in the conversation.

The school was a dreary cement building with enormous windows and playgrounds near by. There was a smell inside of cleanliness and soapsuds. The schoolgirls in stiff, bright blue tight Chinese dresses crowded the steps and passages, and little mistresses with spectacles and virtuous faces bade them keep quiet. Even in the automobile Bobbie Russell had held his breath in dread of the smell of their Chinese guide. Now he took out his handkerchief and held it to his nose, unobtrusively, as he thought, but obviously enough for the sensitive Dr Chang to notice it.

"We are very proud of the ventilation system in this school," he said. "The air is continuously circulated by an electric installation, cleansed and cooled, or warmed as required. An American invention."

"You know, in England such modern equipment is openly condemned as bad style," Helen said, who was thoroughly enjoying the exertions of their Chinese guide as well as the disgust her husband could not conceal. "Our schools, if they are of any standing, are dark and stuffy and come down from the fifteenth century."

Dr Chang made a bow at the mention of the century. They had now reached the auditorium, which was full of Chinese children. All the shining black heads looked straight in front of them; probably their mistresses had forbidden them to show any curiosity over the foreign visitors. Dr Chang introduced some of the virtuous, spinsterly creatures, and they expressed their pleasure at the visit they were honored with in the best and purest English. A curtain on which there were large Chinese characters went up, and the performance began.

The girls on the stage sang and declaimed in squeaking and quite unnatural voices, and the visitors were left in complete darkness as to what was going on. Three little children knelt at one side of the stage and beat small drums and instruments of wood. Dr Chang meanwhile murmured explanations and statistics of modern Chinese education in Helen's ear. The noise was exasperating and Bobbie looked as if he were sitting in a dentist's chair. Dr Chang noticed it.

"I can still clearly remember the night when I first went to the Metropolitan Opera House in New York," he said with an irony too delicate for the Europeans to notice. "It was terrible. Your opera is stylized in the same way as our plays. The voices are disguised and forced, and the action is incomprehensible unless one knows what is going on."

Helen took out her powder box and began carefully to renew her make-up. It was hot in the crowded hall and was getting hotter every moment.

"How long is it going to go on?" Russell asked, feeling that he could not bear it a minute longer. Dr Chang bent down to one of the little teachers and whispered to her.

"About four hours," he said with an agonized face. "You know, of course, that we Chinese have a different notion of time than you have in the West?"

He knew already what was coming. The visitors would leave in the middle, and he himself, the teachers, the school, the children, the whole New Life would lose an enormous amount of face. He whispered once more with some of the teachers, looking pale and beseeching, but he had not got through his apologetic explanations before Russell and his wife were squeezing their way along the row and making for the door with insulting haste.

"We hope you have a lot to show us, and so it is better not to spend too much time on one thing," Helen said when she saw the blanched and despairing, though politely smiling, face of the Chinese. Her husband screwed himself up to a rare intellectual effort.

"I suffer from something the doctors describe as a phobia," he said. "I cannot see a school without getting into a state of panic. I was a very bad scholar, and I still have nightmares of all the examinations I was put through."

Dr Chang laughed gratefully and too loudly. "I understand that. I understand that perfectly," he assured him, feeling slightly relieved. They climbed into the automobile again and went on.

"Rather hot, isn't it? A little drink wouldn't do any harm," Russell said, for his morning whisky had left a parching thirst behind it which only more whisky could assuage.

"I am sure my friends in Civic Center will have a little refreshment ready for us."

They said nothing more all the way to Kiangwan, for each of them was lulled by the rhythm of the car and lost in his own thoughts. Bobbie thought urgently of a drink; he conjured up every sort of iced and invigorating combination of alcoholic liquids, while at the same time he got drier and more exhausted and parched. Helen thought of Frank Taylor, of Sir Galahad, whom she was going to meet again at the Chinese dinner to which Dr Chang had invited them. True, Frank wasn't important enough to make her visit his store (unless it were that she did not wish to see him as a clerk in a stupid store), yet he was not so unimportant as to let her forget him altogether. He looks marvelous, she had thought frequently during the past few days. Why doesn't he call me up? I should like to dance with him, she thought with a twinge of impatience.

Yutsing Chang was more deeply lost in his thoughts than any of them. He had had his first meeting with Meilan two days before. The unexpected, the entirely unforeseen had happened: he had fallen in love with her. His whole being was steeped in her sweetness, and he was restless with longing for her artful and experienced caresses. It turned his whole life upside down. It made his beautiful, calm companionship with Pearl colorless and unmeaning. His profession, his mission in New China, the fighting in the North, the uncertain and precarious future of his country: all suddenly seemed of no importance compared with the emotions raised by Meilan's husky voice in his darkened room and the tender shape of her breasts.

The refreshment offered them in a reception room of the Town Hall out in the new imposing quarter of the new Civic Center consisted of hot, green tea without sugar, on which flowers were floating, and of colored rice cakes. The sight was a nightmare to Russell, and Dr Chang's proud disquisitions could not enter a brain paralyzed by the craving for whisky.

Immense concrete construction in Chinese style, upswept roofs, old ornamentation painted in new aniline colors, lifts, staircases, chambers, halls, offices, fountains, marble horses, walls that seemed about to fall on him. Chinese who spoke English, and Chinese who could merely smile; and everywhere the same penetrating smell of cleanliness and soapsuds. Street after street of suburban houses; the stadium, the swimming pool, the endless vistas of pleasure grounds. An imposing conglomeration of costly progress, to the accompaniment of lectures and comments by their guide, interrupted only by endless introductions and politenesses the exchange of which meant nothing.

Bobbie Russell, utterly worn out, drew his wife to one side.

"If we don't get out of this at once I shall drop in a.faint," he said threateningly. "I've had enough. I can't go on. I shall shriek if we don't push off right away."

Helen saw that his face was suddenly covered with large freckles. It was a sign that he had gone pale.

"We're going at once, Bobbie," she said hurriedly. "Pull yourself together for five minutes." Another retreat, too hurried and very insulting. Dusk was descending as the automobile bore them away and soon deposited them at an airport. Dr Chang crammed them into a little airplane which was already waiting for them. Bobbie was so paralyzed that there was no more kick left in him. They hovered over the immense city while the lights crept out below in the reddish haze. Bobbie flopped in his seat like a man shot dead. Helen had the sights pointed out to her.

The banks and skyscrapers along the Bund looked very small; Soochow Creek was only a thin, brown band between China and England. The French quarter nestled up to the International Settlement, and more and more lights twinkled out below. On the other

side of the Creek lay Hongkew, a large expanse with its green
patches of parks; Chapei, a maze of small streets in which the quad-
rangle of factories with their tall chimneys stood out. More factories
on the other side of the Whangpoo in Pootung. Yangtze Po, following the bend of the Great River, with piers gripping the water like
narrow clasps. A gray patch forming an irregular circle, ribbed with
innumerable roofs, was the old Chinese town in the center, bounded
by the dotted lights of a main street on the side of the International
Settlement. Another watercourse separated Nantao in the southwest
from the French quarter; new suburbs stood out vividly and with
green garden plots and unbuilt sites. Far away to the southwest the
city was lost in haze beyond the arsenal and airdrome. The innumerable junks on the river looked like sluggish brown beetles, between
them the warships of all nations lay motionless, hung with delicate
chains of light. By degrees the dusk sucked up every outline and left
only the lights suspended in the haze.

  Helen asked questions, and Dr Chang answered them assiduously.
As at any other stage of her journey, Helen did not know now
whether any of her information was worth communicating to the
intelligence service in London. She felt amateurish and no good at
the job. Her whole life was a striving for perfection, and it always
took her in the wrong direction. She had been an excellent pupil at
school, a pattern dressmaker in the Maison Leibel, the best of mannequins, the most beautiful show girl, the most French of the Parisians. She had made a faultless English lady of herself during her
unfortunate marriage with Alden, and she played the part of the
Honourable Mrs Russell to the best of her ability. It annoyed her
that she should fail as the elegant spy. She was in a country where
war was being waged and where England had important interests.
There must be important information to pick up, but it seemed to
elude her. She had let herself in for this boring expedition with the
Chinaman only because Madame Tissaud, the Lexicon of Shanghai,
had told her that Dr Chang was always on the spot when anything
was going on in China. She made a mental note of the numbers and
nationalities of the warships in the river and knew that this was
idiotic. She tried to find out what lay behind the unbending polite-

ness of this Chinese, but she did not succeed. Bobbie took out his cigarette case, but his hand again trembled so violently that his match went out. He looked at her piteously. She put the cigarette in her mouth, lit it for him and stuck it between his lips, which were now quite colorless. Dr Chang turned his head away from the shameful sight. At last the little plane landed and Bobbie reeled into the waiting automobile.

"Now for the Imperial and a cocktail," he said with a pale smile. Dr Chang coughed. The Imperial Club did not admit Chinese.

"May I advise earnestly against drinking cocktails before a Chinese dinner, they do not go well together," he said quickly. "We are just at the restaurant where my wife and the other guests are awaiting us. The hot rice wine will please you, Mr Russell, I pledge my word."

Let's hope so, Helen thought. She spent her marriage mostly walking on hot bricks. The car stopped in a narrow alley, hung with banners and lanterns and crowded with Chinese who went along with the soft shuffle of their felt soles.

"I'm afraid Mrs Russell is too tired," Bobbie said in desperation. Helen was on the point of throwing politeness overboard and agreeing with her husband, when Frank Taylor emerged from a narrow doorway behind which a steep staircase ascended. He stood between two gigantic lanterns with large red Chinese characters on them and smiled uncertainly. It occurred to Helen at this moment that he looked like an islander of the South Seas, primitive and childlike, with his open mouth and the bright gleam of his large broad teeth.

He hurried to open the door of the car. "I can't tell you how I have been looking forward to this evening," he said while Dr Chang dragged rather than pushed her husband out. Some sort of crazy Chinese music surged from the red ill-lit shaft of the stairway at Frank's back.

A moment before, Helen was still feeling disgusted by the whole affair. Now suddenly it all seemed gay and full of color: the Chinese street, the lanterns, the disreputable entrance and the indefinable smell of alien land.

"How are you, Sir Galahad?" she asked, holding out her hand. He held it for a moment as though he did not know what to do with it. Then he suddenly bent over it and kissed it. "Like a French-man," Helen said mockingly and looked down at his neck.

"In so far we resemble the Parisians in that our best restaurants and shops set store by being as concealed and invisible as possible," Dr Chang said laboriously, and Helen came back quickly to the others. For a second she had been quite alone with Frank. She smiled at herself. "I am still dazed with all we have seen. Come along, Bobbie, it will do you good to have something to eat." She ascended the narrow staircase close behind Frank without giving her husband the opportunity to protest. The fat proprietor in a white jacket welcomed her on the landing, backed up by two zealous youths. They passed several rooms, whose doors were half open, where there were parties of Chinese, and with many a "This way, if you please" and "May I ask you to step in?" Dr Chang ushered the Russells into the room that he had reserved for the banquet.

By this time a storm cloud of rage and exasperation had gathered in Bobbie Russell, and he took no notice of the other guests. His face, which had the handsome regular features of the young English-man of good family, wore an arrogant expression, and though not intentional, it gave him the look of an ill-tempered camel. So at least, Liu, the poet, remarked in Chinese to Pearl, who was dressed foreign style for the occasion. She suppressed her mirth and in-troduced her guests to each other, feeling rather proud that she had two white friends.

"Dr Hain, my celebrated colleague," she said. And Dr Hain in a gray alpaca suit bowed abstractedly to Helen. "Mr Liu, our best friend and a great writer. Miss Lin Ying, our Chinese Greta Garbo. Mr Taylor you know already."

The room was vacant but for a round table with chairs in white linen covers and a second table on which a few mangoes were piled up. This room too was of an almost oppressive cleanliness and smelt of soap. A boy came in with a basket containing moist towels twisted sausage shape. Bobbie looked at them distrustfully, but when all the others wiped their faces he tried it, too. The towel was steaming hot and very comforting. Liu, after taking a look at him, came up to him. "I know your brother fairly well," he said. "We were at Lincoln College together. He was better at international law than cricket—eh?"

"My brother's no good at games," Bobbie said, completely flabbergasted.

"Mr Liu's father was our ambassador in London," Pearl said across the table. A Chinese boy was suddenly at Bobbie's elbow with a sort of teapot out of which he poured something into a tiny porcelain cup.

"Don't be afraid," Liu said. "It tastes like sherry."

Bobbie was put out because his hand shook so that he spilled half the contents of the little cup before he got it to his mouth. Liu looked away tactfully. The drink coursed warmly and pleasantly down Bobbie's throat, and he wanted some more.

"Were you at Oxford, too?" Liu asked. "Sandhurst," Bobbie replied, slightly cheered up. Liu saluted nonchalantly. Dr Chang stood beside them.

"You must have a look at the military academy in Nanking, Mr Russell," he said. "It is worth the trouble."

"Definitely. Officers are bred there as silkworms are in other parts of the country. The Japanese are opposed to this new Chinese industry," Liu said. He nodded to the boy to fill Bobbie's cup again. *"Kanpei!"* he said. "That is the Chinese for 'Bottoms up!'" Bobbie drank with avidity and immediately held out his cup again.

Helen was distractedly talking to the old doctor in German. "How long have you been in Shanghai? . . . Do you like it? . . . No? Why not? It is much more modern than Paris, don't you think?"

Dr Hain got ready to reply. He had lost the habit of speaking. He had the rusty voice of people who live quite alone. "Shanghai is not a town at all," he said. "Shanghai is a poison. Man eaters live here, naked cannibalism rules here. This town is the world's refuse heap. Whoever comes here, white or Chinese, has cracked up somewhere before and Shanghai does the rest."

"And are there no exceptions?" Helen asked, looking across the room at Frank, who was handing melon seeds to Dr Chang's wife.

He seemed to her extraordinarily young and undamaged. He felt her eyes on him at once and came across to her.

"Got any new patients, Doctor?" he asked.

Dr Hain smiled sadly. "My Chinese colleagues always call me in when it is too late, and so all my patients die. It does not give me a particularly good reputation," he said.

Pearl led Helen to the table, and the two waiters put a few dishes in the middle of it. "It was not at all easy to entice the doctor here. He is a hermit," she said with a smile. Helen mechanically took up her chopsticks. She had learned to handle them in Paris when she used to go about with Japanese students.

"I shall in any case have to withdraw myself soon," Dr Hain said in his halting English. "It is Wednesday, and we play chamber music. It is a funny habit to which I have held fast all my life."

"If it is more convenient to you, Mr Russell, please be so good as to use knife and fork," Dr Chang said to Bobbie. "This is a specialty of which you will surely have heard: preserved eggs."

Bobbie looked down miserably at the eggs, which were blackish green inside, and laid down his knife and fork again. He emptied his cup of rice wine and held it out to the boy. Liu, who had also drunk a few cups of rice wine and whose cheeks were flushed, began to feel annoyed at the expression of nausea with which the Englishman regarded these delicacies.

"You don't think much of this invention of our cooks?" he asked. "A pity. We Chinese are, all told, a fairly inventive people, only we never know what to do with our inventions. For example, as you know of course, we invented gunpowder—and what did we do with it? We made rockets and shot off fireworks for thousands of years. It simply did not occur to us how useful it was for murdering people. Or take the invention of printing. We printed nothing but poems, sentimental discourses, history, philosophy, poetry. We are a ridiculous race, Mr Russell. We fail to employ our letters for the only thing which is useful: propaganda. Nationalist propaganda. Party propaganda. War propaganda. But we are in process of learning."

Russell listened in perplexity and without understanding a single

word. He was as afraid of the dark green eggs as of some unknown
and evil-smelling vermin.

"Are you interested in literature?" asked Liu, whose affability increased with his annoyance. "No? What a pity! I, as a writer, have
always envied the English their language. Only the English language
possesses so lapidary a prose; take for example the sentence which
until lately was to be read in Hongkew Park. A masterpiece of terse
and forcible expression."

"What is that?" asked Frank Taylor who had only been half
listening.

"Dogs and Chinese not allowed. *Kanpei,* Mr Russell," Liu said as
he emptied his cup.

"If chamber music is played every Wednesday in Shanghai, the
town cannot be so bad as you say," Helen exclaimed quickly and
loudly before another silence could intervene.

"Yes, we are a strange quartet," the doctor said. "Three German
Jews and one Nazi. Music is more important than politics, it appears."

"That is almost Chinese," Dr Chang said amiably. "In the Analects
of Confucius it is said already that manners and morals form the
character but only music can give the last perfection:

> "Man shares
> The brief existence of every creature,
> And only his song endures
> With hundredfold echoes through time.
> But you, cicada,
> Make music for yourself alone . . ."

Liu quoted voluptuously. Pearl looked at him with a smile. "On-
yang Hsui," he said with a little bow. "Eleventh century, according to
the Christian reckoning."

The hors d'oeuvres were left on the table and a dish of crabs in
hot sauce was added to them. Pearl took the choicest pieces out with
her own chopsticks and put them on Helen's small, deep plate.

"You manage your chopsticks like an old Shanghai-hand," Frank
Taylor said enthusiastically to Helen. She smiled at him and forced

herself to eat. "But it's simply delicious," she said in astonishment. The beautiful film actress with face powdered snow white, who up to then had not opened her mouth but sat with downcast eyes, now said unexpectedly in French: "Our cooks know how to cook the meal differently for the old and for the young and differently for him who will sleep and for him who will spend the night in bed with his mistress."

Liu laughed aloud and added in French: "Our honored guests can safely eat the chicken mousse; it contains no kind of erotic charm."

The new dish was heaped with a light-colored flaky mass and served with porcelain spoons.

"Why do you stay in Shanghai if you hate the town so much?" Helen asked the doctor. He looked up at her with the eyes of a sick dog and replied after pondering his words: "It is the only town that admits the poor exiles. Here come the Jewish emigrants who in London and Paris and New York have in vain tried it. Many were first in Spain and Palestine, and also from there must they fly—before bombs and Arabs."

"Don't you believe a word the doctor says when he rails at Shanghai," Pearl said. "He sacrifices himself for our poor coolies, and he is the only European I know who has tried to learn our language. How many characters d'you know by now?"

"Not yet six hundred," he said downheartedly. "That is to say that I possess perhaps the education of a porter, Mrs Russell. But I shall it still learn. Thank God, the German brain has a quite decided ability to acquire knowledge. I have made up my mind to master Chinese before my wife comes here."

"We shall have to make great celebrations," Liu said. "Mr Tai Lo's bride is expected next week, and Dr Hain's wife will also be with us soon. Pearl, you must begin dyeing eggs red."

Dr Hain looked down at the white tablecloth. God knows what he saw there. He shook his head and relapsed into silence. Meanwhile a dish of fried fish had been put on the table, followed by something indescribable that swam in a brown sauce. The Chinese at the table sat in awed silence, for this was *hung shao yü ch'ih,* the costly and delicious sharks' fins, a special honor for the distinguished guests. Dr Chang fished about with his own chopsticks in the smooth mess and put some on Bobbie Russell's plate. "As a polite Chinese I have got to say that our poor meal is badly cooked and unworthy of our guests, but nevertheless I should like to draw your attention to this—it is sharks' fins. You must have heard of it before."

Liu spoke up and thanked their host for the excellent meal. The room was now filled with the odors of the various foods, and beads of sweat stood on every brow. The waiters brought fresh hot towels and fresh jugs of rice wine. After that there was asparagus in white sauce, and the proprietor came in and whispered in Dr Chang's ear that the cook was about to serve the *pièce de résistance*. Chang nodded his assent. He was so filled with joy and contentment by the excellence of the meal that he tried to overlook the rudeness of his guest who played about with his food without eating it. He remembered a frightful evening in America when out of politeness he had tried to eat cheese, and it made him indulgent towards Mr Russell.

Now the chef d'oeuvre appeared, borne in by the proprietor himself. It was a large fowl whose form was preserved intact, although every single bone had been withdrawn from it. Only a few old cooks who had been employed in other days at the Imperial Court in Peking knew the secret of this confection. The fowl was stuffed with lotus kernels, and Dr Chang carved it with care and gave his guests the best pieces with his chopsticks. As politeness required, he sent for the cook, a fat, flabby old man, who stood in the doorway and bowed to the floor. Chang thanked the cook for the display of his art, and the cook bowed perilously low again and retired. Now all began to talk at once. Liu improvised a Chinese poem, for he had drunk himself into that fine, creative elation which rice wine inspires in poets, the elation of Li Tai Po, as he called it. A modest dish of mushrooms with trimmings was soon disposed of, and the second glory of the menu appeared, the mandarin fish.

For the second time that night the film star opened her mouth at the very moment when a sudden silence arose: "Is it right for the two gentlemen to let their bride and wife come here at a moment when Shanghai is going to be shelled?"

"It is not certain we shall have war in Shanghai," Liu said quickly, for political discussions were not conducive to the festive mood which ought to prevail at a banquet. But by this time Yutsing Chang was too elated with wine to understand such scruples.

"We shall have war, and it will be a long and great war," he said, and his face glowed. "China is prepared for this war and will carry it through to the end. The invincible Nineteenth Route Army, which gave the Japanese so much trouble in 1932, is on the march. Also the picked troops of the Generalissimo are reputed to be invincible. We have tremendous reserves of men, and there are many among them who are ready to fight to the death. The more numerous the fronts on which we fight and the longer the war lasts, the better for China and the worse for Japan. For the first time China is united; for the first time the Red Army fights side by side with the Nationalist troops and not against them. The days when the brown dwarfs could insult us are gone. China has found itself; it is a giant who has slept for a thousand years but now rises to his feet and is ready to strike home. Our country has borne too long the disgrace of foreign dominion. Foreign warships in our rivers, foreign jurisdiction, foreign railways. Foreigners levy our customs, and everything of value in our country is in foreign hands. Not much longer. Not much longer, I say. *Kanpei!*"

Bobbie Russell had listened to his host with growing astonishment. He felt quite clearly that something had to be done about it. He had to get up and knock out this Chinaman or something of the sort. But as he rose to his feet he noticed that the room went round, and he quickly sat down again. Frank Taylor raised his wine cup and said with a laugh: "*Kanpei,* Dr Chang! You make good jokes when you've got some wine in you. How do you think it would be with Chinese judges and Chinese customs officials in authority over foreigners? You know yourself that Chinese justice is nothing but graft and squeeze. It is only the foreign customs officials that protect the country from wholesale smuggling. Make your war against the gang of Japanese, but leave us foreigners in peace. Without us this country would go to pieces. We know it and you know it, too."

Pearl looked in alarm from Frank Taylor to her husband. There was a perilous moment when it seemed that a quarrel would break out round the loaded table. But Yutsing had already recovered his self-control. He smiled, and his smile covered his face tangibly and compactly, like a well-fitting mask.

Dr Hain had sat there as though he did not understand a word of the heated discussion. He raised his head and said: "Shall you then fight if it should come to it, Mr Liu?"

"I? No, certainly not," the poet said. "One does not make nails out of good iron," he quoted in Chinese. "If the war comes to Shanghai, I shall retire to one of the many monasteries and live in harmony with the ten thousand things of the universe. There would be no object in killing off the few people who are still real calligraphists and can compose poems in the classical style."

The beautiful Lin Ying looked at him admiringly. Suddenly Bobbie Russell reeled to his feet, propping himself with both hands on the table. "Yellow," he said, "yellow coward! Dirty Chinese coward!" He looked at everyone in turn and sat down again as though he had made an adequate and satisfying speech. Liu broke the silence in a casual voice:

"The exaggerated esteem of martial prowess has made the world the slaughterhouse it is. Idiots have courage. Cowardice is the greatest virtue of the philosophers." A smoking dish filled with a thick brown liquid was placed on the table and Liu broke off abruptly and said amiably: "Eat this with care, Mr Russell. A guest of mine once died of it. Internal burns. More dangerous than dynamite." The little actress exploded with a birdlike laugh, and everyone joined in with relief.

Bobbie Russell's glazed eyes stared round the table. He felt ill, very ill indeed, and at the most inappropriate moment. The whole day had been a chain of unbearable suffering, and he felt that a great wrong had been done to him. He was drunk, and it had needed large quantities of rice wine to make him drunk. The food nauseated him, and it dawned upon him ever more clearly that the company in which he found himself smelt like rancid oil.

The calm way in which these Chinese took their chopsticks out of their mouths in order to pinch hold of bits of food and dump them on his plate had brought cold sweat to his forehead. As the mandarin fish slowly vanished down their throats he saw with horror that they took the bones out of their mouths and deposited them in little packets on the white tablecloth—not on their plates, but on the tablecloth, which in any case was smeared with grease and sauce. He felt sick. He knew what he wanted to do. He wanted to get up and give the most impertinent of these Chinamen one in the jaw, but he felt too ill.

"Damn it," he said. "Damn it, damn it." He was dizzy. Everything went round. He put his hand to his mouth and, dizzy or not, got up and staggered from the room.

Helen put down her chopsticks. Frank Taylor jumped up and ran out after her husband. The faces of the four Chinese were turned towards her with fixed smiles, as though they awaited an explanation from her.

"My husband has not been very well for some days past," she said. She saw the two waiters grinning as they came in with the next dishes.

"Ducks' tongues with bamboo shoots. Madame will love this course," Liu said, suddenly speaking French again with great fluency. "There are only two towns in Europe who know enough of eating to deserve the name of culture, Paris and Vienna. You, madame, combine the charm of both these cities, if you will allow my unworthy self to say so."

His bombast was of no avail. Mr and Mrs Chang had ceased to pay the least attention to the dishes; husband and wife sat opposite one another with a pathetic expression of despair in every line of their faces, in spite of the fixed smile superimposed upon them. Frank Taylor came back into the room, without Bobbie.

"Your husband wants to be excused. He is not well. He is waiting for you down below in the fresh air," he said. "I'll take you to a taxi if it's all right with you."

Helen did her best to depart gracefully. "A charming evening, such a pity that I have to break up the party, a thousand thanks, Dr Chang. I hope we shall soon meet again, Mrs Chang. You must forgive my husband, he has such a wretchedly poor digestion. I only hope he is not seriously ill. I'll ring you up soon. You must give us the pleasure—good night."

"Did you notice how white this Dr Chang turned?" she asked Frank as they went downstairs. "Has he never seen a drunken man before?"

"He has lost face," Frank said tersely, taking her arm. "There were at the very least six courses to come. It is a deadly insult. We shall have to think out some way of making up for it."

Helen stopped and looked at his deeply worried face. "Tragedy in Shanghai," she said mockingly. "What really brings you among these Chinese?"

"Business," Frank Taylor said with a shrug. "After all, I am only a salesman who wants to come up in the world," he added with a cramped little smile.

"What a pity we didn't meet in Hawaii," Helen said, going before him down the narrow stairs. It had no relation whatever to what he had said.

Bobbie was sitting in a fuddled heap on the lowest step. Helen surveyed him with a strange expression.

"Shall I take you to a taxi?" Frank asked. His face was illumined by a large lantern. Helen continued to scrutinize her husband in silence. The road was narrow and crowded with Chinese who made jokes as they went by.

"Please, Frank, don't go back to them. Come with me. Help me," Helen said suddenly. He looked from the wife to the husband.

"With pleasure," he said uncomfortably.

Strange are the things that happen to the people of our times, these chaotic, convulsive and shaking times, that leave nothing in its old place. A bloody network of wars and revolutions spreads all over the world and millions of people are caught in it to die horrible deaths—millions in the World War, hundreds of thousands in the Russian Revolution, millions more in the conflict between Chiang Kai-shek's government and the Chinese Reds, millions again in the floods, famines and plagues of that stricken country. How many men have paid with their lives in Abyssinia, Manchuria, Spain, how many have died or been killed in German, Italian, Russian and Japanese prisons? How many unwanted people have simply disappeared, how many have committed suicide from fear or worse, not to speak of those who starve every day, starve in the very streets of civilized and humane countries? It is an age of catastrophes and perhaps of new birth. There is scarcely anybody left who has not been through great and frightful events. But just look at these very people who at some moment of their lives have been heroes or victims, who have been through hells beyond description: they live, they eat, they sleep, they telephone and pay their laundry bills, they are absorbed in the thousand and one trivialities of everyday life, they miss the bus, they offer their superiors a cigarette, they have frightened little savings in the bank, they catch cold and are annoyed about it. They dance foxtrots and hum the latest hit, they make acquaintances and talk nonsense, they read newspapers and forget their handkerchiefs, they get a raise of salary and pay their insurance premiums, they buy raincoats and join clubs, they sleep with their wives and beget children—in short, they are human beings, and nothing is tremendous or frightful enough to make them forget to return again to the simple unimportant joys and pains of their lives, which in the long run are so much more important than the murderous conflicts of a world in disintegration. For though humanity has invented the microscope with which the smallest objects can be seen and recognized, it lacks the faculty of grasping and of retaining in their minds the events which are too big for them.

Often when we meet again a man whose past we know and find him utterly lost and absorbed in his exiguous and commonplace present, we ask ourselves in astonishment: How is it possible?

How is it possible that the people we have followed from their birth all the way into Shanghai can live there as they do? Don't be surprised. Millions live as they do, on the graves of the millions who have perished. For the power to forget is the greatest blessing given to us, and the simple and common has been assigned to us as our element and as the dwelling place of our souls.

V

As soon as he got to the club, Bobbie Russell recovered with astounding speed, and for about an hour he blossomed in all his glory. He told stories of Sandhurst, paid his wife compliments, struck up a friendship with Frank Taylor, and spoke with indulgence of the Chinese who had given him such a fearful day of it. On the crest of the wave he was borne on to the conclusion that they must make a night of it after all they had been through. They drove to the Shanghai Hotel to change their clothes, for they were hot and disheveled. They were fortunate in getting through the lounge without being caught in Madame Tissaud's net. They were calling each other by their first names even before they left the club, and now Bobbie took Frank with him into his dressing room and offered him the shower. Potter, Bobbie's man, who had a long Sunday-school face and a colorless manner, ordered black coffee and administered it to his master while he put out a clean shirt. Frank sang loudly and lustily under the shower, for he too had drunk three whiskies and sodas on top of the rice wine and was in fine form.

"We'll make a night of it," Bobbie shouted in the bathroom.

"And how!" Frank shouted back.

"We'll go to some low-down haunts," Bobbie shouted with glee while he stuck his feet out for Potter to put fresh shoes on for him.

"We'll go to the dirtiest joints in Foochow Road," Frank replied, full of enthusiasm.

"It's a regular lark taking Helen to places like that," Bobbie shouted. Frank went dumb and began to dry himself. He didn't feel sure it would please Helen if he dragged her husband through all these dirty joints.

"The maize-yellow," Helen was saying to Clarkson, her lady's maid, in her bedroom. The maize-yellow was one of those simple dresses that cost a fortune. Helen searched seriously among her perfume bottles as though a great deal depended on the right selection. She sang softly to herself as she powdered her brown arms with a dark powder and put on a little hat consisting merely of a wreath of silk, as the fashion of that summer enjoined.

"Are you wearing any jewelry, madam?" Clarkson asked.

"No, Clarkson, we're going into the slums," Helen said, examining herself in the glass.

"At what hour shall I call you, madam?" Clarkson asked at the door.

"I don't expect I'll go to bed at all," Helen replied. And Clarkson remarked earnestly: "You look so happy, madam, if I may be allowed to say so."

Helen tapped her maid on the cheek; it felt like crumpled tissue paper. All her inferiors adored Helen. She had the faculty of bewitching waiters, taxi drivers and hotel servants by inquiring after their families, sweethearts and financial conditions and never forgetting the names of their children. Consideration oils the wheels of life, she used to say.

When she entered the large sitting room which separated her bedroom from her husband's, she found the very expression on Frank's face she had expected and wished to see there. Her maize-yellow dress was the one in which she always made conquests.

"Coffee?" Bobbie asked.

"I don't need any," she sang out, gave him a pat on his wet hair in passing and went up to Frank.

"We're going to have a heavenly time, Frank," she said softly.

"Just when I've got used to Madame's looks, they've changed again," he said almost complainingly. She smiled because he was afraid to use her Christian name. She took a cigarette from the table, tapped it once or twice against the back of her hand and lit it from a match Frank held out to her.

"I've read somewhere that when a woman taps her cigarette like that you can tell she's of doubtful reputation," Bobbie said from his chair behind them; it was a great effort for him and quite unexpected. Helen gave him a look that might have been either injured or amused. Coffee had counteracted the alcohol and Bobbie had reached a new stage. Melancholy mistrust was written all over his face.

"Let's go to the bar first," she said, disregarding his remark.

It was not yet ten o'clock, and the bar was filling up slowly. It made a vaguely Chinese impression, with little gilded Buddhas in niches, concealed lighting and silk cushions on the seats along the wall. Kurt Planke sat at the piano in his white dinner jacket, playing as though to himself. Bobbie ordered absinthe, Helen drank sherry, and Frank wanted a big soda with a little splash of whisky. He was resolved to keep sober.

"Shall we dance?" asked Frank when Helen drummed on the bar in time to the music. There were only two other couples dancing on the small floor space.

The moment they touched each other something happened. It was like a short circuit and so vehement that Frank stopped in the middle of a word. They danced on in silence. The pianist smiled almost confidingly at them and played on and on.

"Yes?" Helen asked after a long time.

"Yes," Frank said.

Bobbie sat at the bar hunched up and drinking. He pushed his glass over to the barman. "Another one," he said.

"Right, sir," the barman said, bringing the bottle. Bobbie looked at him in a daze.

"You English?" he asked.

"From Shropshire, sir," the man said. It was a lie. He came from the Bukovina.

"Been long in Shanghai?" Bobbie asked.

"Too long," the man sighed. "Much too long, sir. Six years."

"Funny sort of a place, Shanghai," Bobbie went on, getting nearer his goal.

"You're right, sir," the man agreed. "There's nothing in the world you won't find in Shanghai. A very funny city, sir."

"How d'you mean?" Bobbie asked. His glass was empty again, and he shoved it across the counter.

"You could write a book about all we see just in this bar, sir," said the barman. "The other week a man shot himself in the gentlemen's lavatory. And last year a drunken couple fell from the roof garden, eighteen floors down. And the women! And the men! And the mixtures of both! And the money there is here. And the destitution. The way people get rich and the way they get poor. It's a godless town, sir. It doesn't even believe in the devil."

"Lot of opium, eh?" Bobbie asked.

He gave a glance round to see where his wife was; she was standing with Frank near the piano. "Lot of opium?" he repeated. The barman was busy mixing a Planter's Punch.

"Stacks of it, sir," he said.

"I say—where do the people get it?" Bobbie asked. It exasperated him to hear everyone talking of opium, to smell it wherever you went, to meet people at every turn who appeared to smoke the stuff, and yet no one would tell him where to get it. The barman gave him a passing glance. "I don't worry about the muck," he said. "But the pianist over there could give you a tip, sir, if you are interested."

Bobbie drank up his absinthe, and after loitering a moment or two in front of the bar he finally lounged across to the dancers. He clapped Frank on the shoulder. "My turn now, old man," he said. Frank let go of Helen, and Bobbie took her round the waist. The absinthe had put heart into him again, and he was a good dancer. He was a good horseman, a good tennis player, and he was a tall lean handsome fellow, as he could see for himself in the mirrors along the walls. He was of good family, he had a beautiful wife, he had a lot of money. All told he felt at the moment very pleased with himself.

"Damned nice being married to you," he said as he pressed Helen against him. She smiled vaguely. Frank was standing by the wall with his hands in his pockets in a shaft of light that fell on him from the incense bowl in front of a Buddha; he followed her with his eyes wherever she danced.

Her husband restored her to Frank after one dance; at once she felt herself vibrating again like the strings of an instrument too sharply tuned, too tightly stretched.

"How about some fresh air?" he asked, opening the door leading to a small balcony. The town lay below, fantastically seamed with streets and lighted up with white, red, green and blue lights, and the endless beams of the searchlights swept the river and stabbed the sky and quivered again over the junks and the distant shore.

Helen put her hands on the stone balustrade and looked down. Frank's hand was some distance from hers, but the current was not cut off.

"You're engaged, aren't you, Frank?" she asked after a moment.

"Yes," he said. "I've been engaged for a long time. She is coming three days from now."

"Would you like to tell me anything about her?"

"Ruth's a darling. I hope you'll get to know her. She has brown eyes. She's a nurse."

"She sounds charming."

"If I'd known what was going to happen, I shouldn't have let her come just now. It's the wrong moment."

"Yes?" Helen asked.

"Yes," Frank replied. "The shelling may start any day now. We're being drilled already for the volunteer guard. And besides——"

He moved his hand along the balustrade and, summoning up all his courage, put it over hers.

"It's nice we've met," she said.

Bobbie meanwhile had edged his way up to the piano and was patiently waiting. "Will you have a drink with me?" he asked when Kurt was at last relieved by a colored boy who began hammering frantic syncopations out of the piano.

"Thanks, but I never drink before midnight," Kurt said.

Bobbie did not quite know how to go on. "You play very well," he said hurriedly. "Shall we sit down somewhere?"

Kurt sized him up: the faultless clothes, the watery eyes, the pale, handsome face, the thoughtless, arrogant mouth.

"I play like a swine," he said, unfriendly.

Bobbie was depressed by this cynical self-depreciation. He took Kurt by the arm and led him to a table in a corner. "It 'll do here," he said hastily. "What 'll you drink? Oh, of course, you don't drink before midnight. Very right, too. To come down to brass tacks, I wanted to ask you something."

Eugen, the headwaiter, powdered and groomed, came sliding along as if the dance floor were an ice rink. He winked when he saw Kurt in the company of the wealthy Englishman.

"Before we say any more I want to make three things quite clear," Kurt said in a rage. "I'm not a homosexual. I cannot procure you any girls of tender age, and I don't sell dope."

He was upset and unhappy, and he was spoiling for a fight at the first opportunity. Bobbie gasped at the stinging rejoinder. "Wonder what I'd better drink now?" he asked the waiter.

"Old cognac goes with anything," Eugen suggested. "We have an '89 Courvoisier I can recommend with a good conscience."

"A lemonade," Kurt said. Eugen flitted off with the grace of a skater.

"I don't drink, but I get a percentage of all you drink yourself," Kurt went on doggedly. "I shall have at least seven cents from your '89 Courvoisier."

"Oh?" Bobbie said, taken aback.

"You're right there," Kurt proceeded. "I'm a sort of male dance hostess. When there are not enough men here, and ladies who are traveling alone are in the mood for it, I am put at their disposal as a dancing partner. Specialty, tango, plain or erotic. But I take no money for it. You wanted to ask me something, honored, honorable——"

"It's about opium," Bobbie brought out.

Kurt's pupils contracted. "Opium?" he said. "And may I ask why you come to me? Why don't you ask your friend Sir Henry Kingsdale-Smith or Count Bodianszky? Or any other gentleman in your smart circles? They all know a lot more about opium than I do. They can offer you opium orgies with girls and all the rest of it. I'll have nothing to do with opium."

As he spoke his face broke out in a sweat. Bobbie took out his handkerchief and wiped his own face, for it too was moist. He drank his cognac in one gulp. The wide glass gave out a musical ring as he put it down unsteadily. "You don't understand—I must get hold of some opium. I need it," he said. "I'm miserable," he added sadly.

"Here comes your wife," Kurt said, getting up. He bowed, but

Helen simply didn't see him. She still saw and felt nothing but the moment on the balcony.

Outside, in the gentlemen's cloakroom, Kurt was inspecting himself carefully in the glass. His white dinner jacket was once more dirty at the lapels, and he had not yet paid his last bill at the cleaner's. It was nothing to women if they left lipstick on their dance partner's coat. Kurt shuddered. He had got into that dangerous condition when women nauseated him, and he wanted nothing but the peace that opium gave. He went into the kitchen behind the bar and, taking the chalk that hung from the black service board, he chalked his stained lapels white.

"What time is it, Auguste?" he asked the cook who had charge of the cold buffet.

"Ten minutes past eleven," Auguste said, brandishing his large carving knife in the air.

"Have you heard that a hundred thousand Japanese are said to have landed?" he whispered, rolling the whites of his eyes. "Who knows whether we shall still be alive tomorrow morning, Santa Madonna Maria, Mother of God?" Auguste was the only man in the whole Shanghai Hotel who was alarmed about the war.

"*Auf Wiedersehen in Massengrab*, Franz," Kurt said and went back to the bar. The Englishman had gone.

At about midnight they were in Wing On's establishment. A house of Chinese entertainment, with jugglers, conjurers and dancing girls, and many little stages on which coarse farces were played with much chirping and screaming to the accompaniment of wooden instruments and varied and powerful stenches. The Chinese stood crowded in front of it, bursting with laughter. Paper flowers, lanterns, banners, letters of red and gold and an air so thick it exceeded anything the Russells had hitherto endured. They recovered in a smart little night club in the Settlement where the Chinese, Korean and Japanese girls twirled their partners on a lighted floor of glass. At one o'clock they were in a shabby place not far from the Bund, where French sailors danced with Russian girls and Japanese imitations of American drinks were gulped down. At two they were leaving a Chinese hotel where the native crooks took their pleasure, where yellow-skinned gangsters, blackmailers and leaders of thieving gangs with their exceedingly beautiful girls danced the rumba to a Philippine orchestra. Somewhat later they were walking down Foochow Road, Bobbie maintaining himself in a perpendicular position between them with extraordinary ingenuity. Bobbie's condition had its well-marked ups and downs, mountains and valleys of exhilaration and melancholy. Now he had become obstinate and refused to go home. Inebriation produced an urge to self-annihilation in him: he wanted to press on deeper and deeper into the dirt and corruption to which whole quarters of this city were given up.

"Your wife's tired, Bobbie," Frank said at intervals.

"She can go to the devil," Bobbie replied each time.

Frank looked at Helen; she smiled gaily at him, unapproachable and unmoved. Her hair was smooth and shining under the silk of her hat, the maize-yellow dress was without a crease, and her skin looked perfectly fresh. Like fruit, Frank Taylor thought thirstily.

On they went—to the White Chrysanthemums, a Japanese place far out in Chapei, to the Dragon's Cave, where there was only an electrical piano, and to the Flower Boat, a Chinese brothel, where landscapes of the Bavarian Alps hung on the walls, where children turned cartwheels, where there was not a girl over sixteen and not a man was sober.

Towards three o'clock in the morning they rose again from the depths and arrived at Delmonico's, where at this time of day the whole of Shanghai went for scrambled eggs or onion soup. Every shade of race, elegance and intoxication was to be met there.

It was at Delmonico's that Bobbie began to storm. At first he sat mute for some time, staring into vacancy over his soup with a fixed smile. "Bobbie——" Helen said, touching his sleeve. Suddenly he got up and walked stiffly and in a beeline to a distant table and said to a lean, gray-haired Chinese in a dress coat: "I forbid you to stare at my wife, you Chinese swine."

The Chinese pretended not to have heard and went on talking with the Frenchman at his table. Everybody in the place knew the gentleman in evening dress: he was a man of great importance in the government.

"You swine of a Chinaman!" Bobbie roared so loudly that his voice broke. People turned to look at him. Their faces showed neither astonishment nor annoyance, only that toleration of eccentricities which is second nature in Shanghai.

"Conduct the gentleman into the fresh air, he seems to be suffering," the Chinese in the dress coat said to a waiter, also in dress clothes. The maître d'hôtel, a pale, swarthy, handsome Portuguese, took hold of Bobbie with a jujitsu grip and lugged him outside. The Chinese turned back with a smile to his friends. "How ashamed he will be when he is sober and remembers his behavior," he said with a tolerance that was contempt. "The climate of Shanghai does not always suit the English race very well."

Bobbie was not going very willingly. He raged about, he pulled a tablecloth to the floor with everything on it, he trod women's trains and tore them, and above the clatter and commotion and laughter he could still be heard raucously and idiotically shouting: "Swine of a Chinaman, damned swine, the whole lot of you . . ."

When the door had shut behind Bobbie, Frank sat for some while beside Helen, frozen, miserable and smiling idiotically, while she took out her powder puff and started making up.

"What now?" he asked helplessly.

"Pay and go," she said. She drank a glass of water and smiled at him consolingly. "I shall make my husband's apologies to the Chinese," she said, and got up.

"You're marvelous," Frank said honestly.

"No," she replied. "Used to it, that's all."

He watched her as she walked gracefully to the great man's table and said something to him with a smile. Frank paid the bill. When he looked up again he saw that the Chinese was on his feet, making a low bow as he kissed Helen's hand. She came back. "Now we can go," she said. Suddenly she looked tired. The fine skin under her eyes shone like bluish mother-of-pearl. Frank followed her across the room, feeling that the sky had fallen in.

I'll give this Bobbie a kick in the stomach, he thought bitterly. It was the second time that night the Englishman had involved him in a scandal, and he cursed the whole foolish and damaging acquaintanceship. With his shoulders hunched up to his ears, he searched the room for anyone who knew him. If only B.S. doesn't hear of it, he thought in a panic. It was improbable that B.S. would not hear of it, for the speed with which rumor spread in Shanghai bordered on telepathy. Over two years, Frank thought bitterly, over two years, over two years. For over two years he had lived like a member of the Y.M.C.A., correct and bored, because he wanted to marry Ruth, and for that he had to extort B.S.'s approval and the esteem of his clients. B.S. himself—Barley Scott, the head of the branch—was a model of uprightness and respectability. Industrious, sober, intelligent and a pious Methodist, he led the life of a decent American businessman quite unaffected by Shanghai— a wholesome plant in the bog, an example often held up to the young clerks and salesmen, a cautious bridge player, a friend of the missionaries, furnished with mother-in-law, wife and children, a dog and a canary, a bank balance and an insurance policy, a man whom the Chinese respected, although the only use he had for them was as clients of the Eos Film and Foto Co., Shanghai Branch.

Frank had a cold feeling between the shoulder blades when he thought of B.S. He cursed the alacrity with which he had drifted into the society of the Russells. He cursed himself for having been a snob. The English aristocracy, he thought scornfully. My eye! My friend, the Hon. Robert Russell, he thought in a fury. I've had enough of it, he told himself as he crossed the entrance hall and took his hat. Enough of those Russells and all the rest of them.

At the back of his mind he had been hoping not to have to see Bobbie again; but there he was. Three men, two coolies and a chauffeur, were trying to hoist him into the large automobile which the Russells had hired for the duration of their stay. But Bobbie either refused to get in or fell out again, raging and shaking his fists. All the beggars, children and ricksha coolies in the neighborhood of Delmonico's were there enjoying the fun. Helen was standing under a lantern with a strangely thoughtful and detached expression as though all this had nothing to do with her. As Frank came down the steps, on which he had paused for a moment to take stock of the

situation, she raised her hands to him in a quick gesture and said:
"I'm so sorry, Frank—really——"

Something in him clicked like an electric switch, and his rage
turned to a torrent of pity. Just as he came down the steps to tell
Helen it was all right, Bobbie tore himself from the Chinese. They
laughed good-naturedly, for a drunken foreigner, even if no rare
sight in Shanghai, was all the same a good joke. "Frank!" Helen
cried. "I'm afraid——"

He was one second too late, for Bobbie had already seized her
by the shoulders and was shaking her to and fro. He said nothing;
he simply shook her more and more violently. She clenched her
teeth and shut her eyes. Suddenly he let her go, took a step backwards and struck her in the face with the palm of his hand. There
was the ridiculous sound of a faint slap. The Chinese had stopped
laughing.

The whole thing was senseless and incredible. Frank Taylor had
never in his life seen a woman struck by a man—not even in China.
His fists clenched of themselves. One, two—first the left, then the
right—went of their own accord in the most elementary boxing style
to Bobbie's diaphragm and chin. Bobbie collapsed to the street,
dumb and smiling and as limp as an old stocking. Frank lifted him
up, and the chauffeur helped him, overcome with admiration, to
shove him into the automobile. Russell smelled of alcohol, and Frank
swallowed, for he himself had a bad taste in his mouth. He rubbed
his knuckles. Right on the button, he thought with satisfaction. To
judge from Bobbie's freckled and smiling face, it would be some
time before he came to himself. Frank slammed the door. "Put him
down at the Shanghai Hotel," he told the chauffeur. The automobile
drove off, and the crowd unwillingly but laughingly made way and
then collected at once round Frank and Helen, for they wanted to
see what would happen next.

Frank rubbed his hands together as if they were dusty; his
knuckles began to ache more distinctly. "I'm sorry," he said awkwardly.

"I mustn't leave him alone," Helen said. Her face was white in the light of the lantern. "He'll jump out on the way and break his neck."

"All the better," Frank replied grimly. The sky was getting lighter and the lanterns going dim in the gray of dawn. "Where shall I take you?" he asked gently.

"To the hotel, at once," Helen said.

"To another hotel?" he asked. "You can't stay with him alone. He's crazy. He'll kill you."

Helen answered only with a smile which hovered and spread over her face until it illumined every pore. Frank watched the phenomenon with awe. He had never seen anything so beautiful. He had never seen a woman so beautiful and wonderful as Helen Russell, a woman so wonderful through and through, plucky, unhappy, helpless and at the same time strong. He hadn't even known that such a woman could exist. Ruth Anderson, on a Japanese boat, was drawing nearer and nearer hour by hour. And yet he was farther from her than he had ever been before.

"Taxi," Helen said, and the gigantic Russian commissionaire, who had so far held aloof from the distressing occurrence which was not within his province, took out his whistle and blew it.

"I'll take you home," Frank said. "I shall not leave you alone. I shall stay with you."

She went on looking at him with a wondering smile while she gently shook her head. The taxi drew up and Frank helped her in. There was the usual incident at the last moment when all the Chinese onlookers shouted and held out their hands for money—for bounty and tea money in return for their services as onlookers. Frank shut the window, but the driver did not drive off. Frank cursed and threatened him. "Oh, give them something," Helen said. "He wants to help them, and that's why he won't start. They're poor."

"Or else he gets a squeeze," Frank grumbled. He shouted all the abuse his pidgin English ran to, and with an unexpected jerk the taxi at last got under way. There was a silence as soon as they had left the shouting crowd behind them. They said nothing for some minutes, sitting close together so that their shoulders, arms and thighs touched. They were unconscious of it; it was instinct that drove them to each other.

"Is that—— I mean, has anything of the sort ever happened before?" Frank asked after a while. She smiled as she had before and made no reply. He now saw in the light of the lamp that tears were running down her cheeks, although the smile did not leave her face.

"Yes, Sir Galahad," she said finally. "That's what my life is now."

She tried to wipe away her tears with the back of her hand; it looked clumsy and childish, and her cheeks were just as wet a moment later. Her tears poured down with the quiet persistence of summer rain. Mamo, Frank thought. It was an utterly unexpected thought, he had not thought of Mamo for a long, long time. The rain from Wai Alealea, said a long-vanished voice deep within him. "The rain from Wai Alealea," he heard himself saying as he bent over Helen's face.

"Sorry," she whispered. "I haven't had any practice at crying."

It's this town, she thought. One gets soft here. She hadn't cried for many years. Now the tears poured out of her eyes as if she had to weep all the tears she had kept back for ten years.

"Don't cry any more," Frank begged and drew her to him. She dried her eyes on the hem of her maize-yellow dress, for she had left her handbag behind on the table at Delmonico's.

"When I was a child," she said, still sobbing, "in my room—there was a crystal——"

"Yes?" Frank asked when she said no more.

"That's all," she said.

"How long have you been living like this?" Frank asked angrily, with his face so close that his hair was stroked by her breath.

"Three years."

"Why did you marry him?" he asked. She heard rage and jealousy in his voice, and she carefully considered her reply.

"Out of pity," she said. "I wanted to help him—but I can't. I don't love him enough—that is why."

Before Frank knew what he was doing he was holding her in his arms; her cheeks were still wet, her mouth was fragrant, her hands were clasped behind his neck. They knew no more of themselves as they drove on like that; it was light, it was dark, light and dark, in time with the street lanterns gliding by.

Somewhere, far out in the river a ship's siren sounded three times its long-drawn hollow call.

VI

YEN WAS A POOR COOLIE, but in the hour of need it came out that he had friends who were willing to help him. Friendship makes even water sweet, the proverb says. They got together and formed themselves into a sort of society, which subscribed the eight dollars it would cost to turn Yen, the starving coolie, into a prosperous and presentable Mister Lung Yen who could meet his son unashamed. Twelve men each lent fifty cents. Kwe Kuei put up two dollars off his own bat. Yen was to pay back the whole sum at the rate of fifty cents a month. As the loan was a friendly one, there was no interest to be paid. If he gave up the Great Smoke he could manage this without too great difficulty. But if he had the good fortune to introduce foreigners to Kwe Kuei he would be very soon quit of his debt, for foreigners paid for the Great Smoke with silver money, and Yen got a large commission. Naturally it took some days before Kuei got this friendly loan together, and then there were only three days left in which to complete Yen's transformation. He began at once choosing the articles of clothing he wanted to buy.

He trotted off to Fooking Road, where the open stalls with second-hand coats and trousers and robes were so close together that the chorus of salesmen besieged the ear of the passer-by without ceasing. They picked up one article after another and sang its praises as well as the ridiculously low price for which it could be acquired:

"A long robe of heavy silk, all strength and virtue, worthy of a mandarin, four dollars, you will never come across such a bargain again. . . . A jacket of strong black cloth, only worn once, a jacket good enough for a bridegroom, half a dollar; half a dollar less five cents. . . . These trousers that a banker wore on a feast day, shining like the water of the silver sea, the finest silk of Chekiang, untearable, thirty cents for the lucky man who can make use of them. . . . A long robe of heavy silk . . ." and on again from the beginning. Yen did not stop at the first shop to buy what the salesman vaunted, for the occasion was too serious. He sauntered up and down the street, stood and listened, looked at each article as it was lifted up for inspection, felt the material, examined its color, stoutness and cleanliness, and held each one against the light to look for weak spots; then he put it down again, hesitated, went on, came back, bargained, and finally went away without having bought. He did this in every booth; he dived into its recesses where old clothes lay in heaps as a clear sign that business prospered and that the choice was ample. He pulled out a long coat that peeped from the very bottom of a pile, because it seemed better than the ones that were openly exposed for sale. The chant of the salesman put him on his guard instead of enticing him. How can a thing be any good if they have to cry it out at the top of their lungs? he argued to himself. The salesmen all employed different methods in their efforts to win him over. Some were highhanded and tried to frighten him by snatching away the jacket he was feeling for the tenth time and said: "If this fine jacket is too dear for you, you need not wear it out with your dirty fingers. We have coolie clothes at forty cents and not a hole in them." Others again treated him as a buyer of means, they called him sir and even old sir and first-born, so far did they go in politeness, and said: "These fine trousers are not good enough for the great old lord, cotton is not worthy of you, but here are some black silk trousers which will be as good in ten years as they are today."

At first all these tirades only confused him, but when he had spent some hours in Fooking Road and knew almost every article exposed for sale there, he had got used to the pressure of the younger traders and paid no more attention to them. He had such a clear picture of the impression he wanted to make when he met his son that he had no doubt what to buy: black trousers tied at the ankles, clean white stockings and black shoes, a long gray coat and a hat such as the foreigners wore.

But it was afternoon before he had made his first purchases—stockings and shoes for forty-three cents in small cash. Then, when a man with an ambulant kitchen trotted by, Yen gave a start, for in the heat of choosing his purchases he had forgotten his morning rice. He was not hungry, it was rather that his belly ached in a vague uncomfortable way. But this was due to Yen's resolution to forego the smoke. Kuei had wisely advised him to eat a lot in the few days that remained.

"The finest clothes will not conceal from your son that you are as lean as a beggar or a stray dog. Even if you cannot get so fat in three days that people would give you the place of honor at table, you can at least attain to a respectable plumpness," Kwe Kuei advised him, and his good sense was well known. The sum of eight dollars, which Kuei had collected to finance his friend, made ample provision for this course of fattening. The men who had contributed to the loan were not relatives of Yen, for Yen had no family in Shanghai, and this gave his poverty a tinge of dereliction that bordered on dishonor; but Kuei knew three men who likewise had the Dragon-name Lung, and this suggested that they might at least belong to the same clan as the coolie Lung Yen. Kuei himself, as well as four other men, came from the same district as Lung Yen—for he had already begun to resume his Great Name of Lung Yen. They came from Hsieng Chanshi and they acknowledged the duty of standing by a fellow countryman in straits. His eight friends, including Kuei, had induced relations of their own to take a benevolent share in the loan. For this reason Lung Yen on his side felt bound to increase his girth in order to show these good and loyal friends that their help was not given for nothing. So he stopped the itinerant kitchen and squatted down at the side of the street to have a good meal. Here too choosing was no easy matter, for the cook had pork as well as vegetables to be eaten with the rice, and it was months, even if not years, since Lung Yen had tasted meat, and he pondered for a long time whether it was proper for him to eat it.

"You can give me a bowl of vegetables and a bowl of meat, too," he said at last, and the cook replied politely, "If you eat meat you get the tea free and as much as you like."

Yen ate three bowls of rice with vegetables and pork, although his belly even at the second bowl announced that it was full. The cook put a few tea leaves in the teacup and poured hot water on them, and Lung Yen eagerly sipped the drink. He smacked his lips appreciatively as befitted a rich and well-fed person and said, "Your rice is almost as good as they sell in Hongkew market." He said this, however, merely from amiability, for though he imagined that one fed very well in the cookshops of Hongkew market, he had never been there himself.

"More tea?" the cook asked and poured more hot water on the old leaves. Lung Yen drank eagerly, for it seemed to him that the hot tea would surely give him contentment and still the strange gnawing in his vitals. This was not the case, and when the cook hung his kitchen on his bamboo pole and went his way, crying his wares in a chant, Lung Yen made up his mind to a great enterprise. He went and bought himself a packet of cigarettes for six coppers, with a picture of a beautiful girl on the wrapper. He was sometimes lucky enough to pick up thrown-away cigarette ends in the foreign quarter, but there was little hope of this in Fooking Road. Yen's countrymen smoked every cigarette to the last end, and what they threw away was pounced upon the next moment by an old man whose trade it was to make new cigarettes out of old butts.

With a cigarette in his mouth and a loaded belly, Lung Yen went back to the task of buying the long coat which was to give him dignity and show that he was a man of some position. At last he had picked out three possible ones, and the afternoon was far advanced before he could make his final choice. The trouble was that his eyes and his desires fixed themselves upon a silk robe which was in no way suitable for him. Its price was four dollars, but Yen was convinced that a little haggling would bring it down to half. It was made of a heavy, but not too heavy, dark gray silk with an elegant pattern woven in it in the same color, and this pattern particularly claimed his eyes by its dignified lines. Three days before, huddled in his coolie rags, he had never dreamt of possessing even the cheapest of long robes. Now of a sudden cotton garments seemed mean-looking compared with this wonderful, dark gray silk coat.

He could not explain it to himself, but he felt that, once dressed in it, he would win the love and respect of his son at one blow. He took it up again and again and laid it back on the pile, he let the silk slip between his fingers and put his eyes close to the pattern to examine it minutely. "The gentleman is a connoisseur, it is clear," the salesman said. "It is the pattern of blessing. A great and old teacher used to wear this robe. It is so costly that his heirs could not bring themselves to let him take it into the other life."

Meanwhile dusk had fallen and the shops were lighted up. Some of the merchants were beginning to shut up and lock their stalls. Lung Yen tore himself away from the silk coat and bought a light gray cotton one which was a little too short for him. He paid eighty cents for it. As he was now utterly exhausted and his eyes dazed with all he had been through, he put off his other purchases until next day and walked slowly back to Chapei, where the tailor Lung Wang had given him shelter.

For his syndicate of helpers had decided that Lung Yen in the three—now only two—days that were left to him should not think of pulling a ricksha, for they said: "A buffalo does not get fat in the plow, and much rubbing makes even iron thin."

Yen agreed that there was no sense in buying food with good money and then wasting it away in sweat and blood instead of collecting it on his body in respectable fat. Also he had come to an arrangement with the tailor Lung Wang. He was to be given a room and a bed free of charge until his son came and for as long as he remained in the city. The tailor Lung Wang, an elderly man with three moles on the right cheek from which grew three long and venerable hairs, was content to do without payment because it could not be said with certainty that Lung Yen might not be a member of his family, and besides, Lung Wang was a religious man who wished to acquire merit.

Yen was glad to spend the nights far from Kwe Kuei's house, for he was afraid of the smell and the propinquity of the Great Smoke. But as he was not used to sleeping in a bed and under a roof, he spent a weary and restless night. The discomfort in his inwards increased in the darkness and became almost intolerable when the last of the expensive cigarettes had been smoked and the last spark of them was extinct. He eagerly breathed in the acrid smoke that hovered within his mosquito net, but it made him cough. He made great efforts to restrain his coughing, for he did not want to disturb his kindly host in the next room. After a time he became aware that his mouth filled up with the sweet and hatefully familiar taste of the blood he had not coughed away, and he felt for his towel and spat the blood into it as a well-brought-up person should.

As he lay there, unable to sleep, the silk robe appeared again and again before his closed eyes, and he was sorry he had not bought it. I shall go and have another look at it tomorrow, he thought, feeling dissatisfied with himself. He had almost lost sight, in the midst of his picking and choosing and buying, of the joyful occasion for it all. But suddenly the thought of his son overwhelmed him with a great and hot and immeasurable joy and, clasping this joy tightly to him, he fell asleep at last.

The first thing he did in the morning was to look at the coat he had bought, and it did not please him half as well as the day before. He showed it to the old tailor, who unfolded it and examined it, muttering the while as he pulled the hairs on his moles as though they were a beard. "How much did you pay for it?" he asked, and when Yen told him eighty cents, he cried, "Too much, too much. . . . Eighty cents for a robe with wine stains which will never wash out," the old tailor said, pointing to a discolored patch in the cloth.

"Your spectacles see defects where my naked eyes detect nothing," Lung Yen said, much cast down. Truly he did not wish to appear before his son in a wine-stained garment as a drunkard might. He rolled the coat up and took it back to Fooking Road. His first anxious glance told him that the silk robe was still there. Even now he did not let it be seen that he was determined to buy it but made a great outcry over the wine stains and rated the salesman as though he himself were a great gentleman. By this means he abashed the young salesman, and at last the silk coat was his for half its original price. That is to say, he returned the gray cotton one with its wine stains, and after paying a dollar and twenty cents in addition he clasped the costly dress under his arm and went away.

As he had not got much stouter in spite of the sumptuous meal and the idleness of the previous day, he went out this time to Hong-kew, where near the market there was an eating house famed among the coolies on account of the excellence of its cook. He had two objects in view in making this expedition; first of all he wanted to eat a lot that day without incurring the discomfort in his belly he had suffered from the day before, and secondly he had this place in mind for the entertainment of his son. So it was only natural that he should taste and prove with his own tongue whether the food was up to his expectation and good enough for the forthcoming feast.

"My son is coming to Shanghai on important business," he told the waiter. "If I am satisfied with your food I will entertain him here. He is a great scholar who knows all the fifty thousand charac-ters and has read all the ten thousand books, so tell the cook to be-stir himself."

"Rice, five cents the bowl, vegetables one cent more, pork seven cents, tea thrown in," the waiter said, unmoved. He did not see inside Lung Yen, but only the tattered and lousy coolie clothes he still wore. His jacket was open so that the air might cool his lean chest, and his frayed trousers were turned up as they were when he was running with his ricksha, and his hair was coated with dust.

"I did not ask you for a coolie meal but for something superior and out of the common. Duck from Szechuan, such as rich people eat, a fish in a sour-sweet sauce," Yen said loftily. He had heard of these dishes when the doorkeepers of restaurants paid him his com-mission for taking his fares there. He did not for one moment let go of his silk robe, for he was afraid it might be stolen or get dirty. And the warm soft touch of the costly garment under his arm inspired him with a feeling of grandeur and pride.

"A meal with these dishes must be ordered in advance and also include four other courses. It costs a dollar without any bargaining," the waiter said loftily. Yen contented himself for the time with ordering rice with stewed mushrooms.

"If I am satisfied with the cook, it is not impossible that I may order such a dinner with the four other courses," he said. He ate three bowls of fried rice and drank a lot of tea, but he did not smack his lips in case the price might be raised if he showed too much appreciation.

Before leaving the eating house he ordered the meal with duck and fish for the day of his son's arrival. The waiter distrustfully demanded a deposit of thirty cents, but when Yen put down the money he bowed and wished him ten thousand years of happiness and contentment.

Lung Yen next went to the house of his friend Kwe Kuei to get him to give him an account of his capital, for he himself was at a loss when it came to such large sums. Also he wanted to bring Kuei's counsel and understanding to bear on another highly important matter. "Kuei, my elder brother," he said, "it is indispensable that I give my son a present. You know more about the young men of today than I do, so give me your advice."

Kwe Kuei nodded and after consideration gave an account of Yen's resources. Of the eight dollars there were still four dollars and ten cents left. Of this, seventy cents had to be earmarked for the meal he had ordered. A hat and a sleeveless waistcoat had still to be bought, and it must be a silk waistcoat, for Lung Yen could not possibly wear a cotton waistcoat over the silk robe. He had not thought of that in the exhilaration of making his purchase. Also he had still to eat a lot, and he felt the need of more cigarettes. In any case his hands trembled and his heart fluttered as a bird in a cage all the time he was in Kuei's shop; he could smell nothing but the smoke, even though the inspectors of the anti-opium office had no noses for it.

Kuei reckoned that Yen could well afford fifty cents for a present and then he would still have money left for unforeseen expenses in connection with his son's visit. They discussed at length what would give his son pleasure. Yen thought of a hat such as the foreigners wore, for a hat of this kind had been his own most vehement desire when he was of his son's age. But Kuei observed that the boy soldiers had hats and uniforms and were not allowed to dress in any other way. Yen grumbled a little over this restriction of his son's liberty, but Kuei explained to him that the young people regarded their uniform as a dress of honor and were proud of it.

While they were talking, Yen went green; even the skin beneath his open jacket went green, and he hurriedly got up and went out. He felt his eyes sinking into his head, and everything went black, so vehement was this excess of craving for the Great Smoke. Thus for that day he came to no conclusion, and he had only one day left in which to buy a hat and waistcoat for himself and a present for his son.

That night Lung Yen suffered from acute wandering pains in his inside; they were first here and then there and finally everywhere. But at last they wearied him out and he fell asleep. Yet in his dreams he suffered the same fate as the wretched coolie of whom story-tellers in the market often told, to pass the time of their poorest audiences. This coolie, who ran about all day and dragged his load and poured with sweat, dreamt every night that he was a rich man who ate his fill of delicious foods, drank rice wine, had beautiful concubines and did nothing but take his ease on the silk cushions of his couch, smoking his water pipe and taking his pleasure; while the rich man for whom the poor coolie had to work was tortured every night by horrible dreams in which he was a coolie, had nothing to eat, was beaten with bamboo rods and had to work so hard that he collapsed. For, thus the storyteller concluded, he who sits in the chair is a man, and he who carries the chair is a man also.

In his dream, then, Lung Yen was happy beyond measure, even though in the morning he had only a hazy memory of it. He had clasped his son to his breast, as he had when he was a newborn baby, he had talked with him and eaten with him, and at last his son had knelt before him and offered him incense and bowls of food, just as though he himself, Lung Yen, the father, were already dead and no more than a revered name on the tablet of his ancestors and a spirit at peace in the shade of the cypresses.

On the third day Yen bought his hat and the black sleeveless silk waistcoat. He tried to eat again, for the old tailor had grumbled at him that morning and said that he still had no flesh on his bones.

But after the very first mouthful of rice which he put into his mouth with his chopsticks he felt so ill that he had to give up. He was sitting in an open cookshop in the old town, where he had gone to look for a present for his son. He sat on there for a time, buying one cup of tea after another, swallowing down the soothing liquid and trying to retain what little he had in his stomach; but after the fourth cup of tea a cheering thought came to him, and as soon as he could place some reliance on his refractory and incomprehensible belly he got up and made for the town of the foreigners. It had suddenly occurred to him that his son, who had had a modern up-bringing and had perhaps partaken of the learning of the foreigners, would have most pleasure in a present from the foreigners' stores.

The confusion of things in the foreign town at first completely bewildered him. Up to now he had merely trotted by the stores without looking at them. It was another matter when it came to choosing and buying. But when he had spent several hours and had handled things by the hundred he came at last on the perfect gift. It was a little stink-cart, new and shining and an exact imitation in every detail of the large stink-carts of which the streets were full. The marvelous thing about it was that the little cart contained a machine like the big ones. You wound it up, and the cart ran quickly all by itself, rattling and living, like its elder brothers. Yen was completely won. He had the cart wound up again and again, and while it ran about the floor of the shop he stood with a dull smile of wonder and delight on his face. "It is for my son," he said again and again. "My son has a bellyful of learning, and he loves newfangled things."

The shopman asked sixty cents for the cart and very rudely declined to indulge in the joys of bargaining.

The happy excitement caused by his find gave Yen an appetite. He squatted on the bank of Soochow Creek and bought some rice from an itinerant cook, who was trying to entice people from the boats with his cry. A few young fellows came up the ramp and squatted down beside Yen. Their manners were rough, but they were cheerful fellows, and Yen held his chopsticks in the air while he listened to the jokes they made. He pulled a face in the middle of his laughter; his pains had returned, and with such violence that he doubled up, helpless with the spasms.

"Sick, brother?" one of the youths asked, and another said with a laugh, "Filled his stomach too full."

Yen wiped away the cold sweat that streamed down his face. If the river folk had not been there he would have groaned aloud. But during the last few days he had got beyond the uncouthness of his coolie existence and taken great pains to remember those principles of proper behavior which his revered grandfather had impressed upon him long, long years ago. He reeled as he got up to go. In his extremity he bethought himself of what he could do to drive away the pains. He must not smoke. Never smoke again. But yet he could not confront his son with a father who was doubled up with pain and whose stomach revolted and emptied itself at the most awkward moments. He dragged himself to the streetcar and took a tram to the clinic in Chapei where he had sometimes been treated before without payment.

Yen had always hated the trams; they came swiftly along with noise and glitter and stowed away enough people to fill thirty rick-shas. And now that he rode in one for the first time he liked it no better; for though the inside of the car was bright and glittering and almost too smart, the speed made his sick stomach feel worse, and he sat hunched up and let himself fall this way and that as the car took the bends. But at last this agony too was overcome and he stood on his own feet again as a man should.

Yen was not wearing his straw sandals that day but his new black shoes, for it would not do if his honored son should notice that his father was unaccustomed to them. It saddened him to see the yellow dust of the outskirts of the town dim their black radiance, but he consoled himself with the thought that it was only surface dirt that could easily be brushed away again. He dusted them with his frayed palm fan before entering the house of the sick. A young lady was sitting inside, dressed in white as though for a funeral. She asked him his name and whence he came and whither he went, but she did not do it out of politeness and in the manner prescribed —What is the name of the honored gentleman? Whence has the gentleman the goodness to come? What may be the wish of the honored gentleman? On the contrary she barked out like a young she-dog:

"Name? . . . Address? . . . Where do you live? . . . What's your work? . . . What is the matter with you?"

Yen dropped his eyes and announced that he was a coolie and that in his unworthy belly a pain chose to wander. The rude young woman wrote this on a card which she thrust into his hand. She also compared his answers with what was written in a thick book and said: "You've been here twice before?" Yen said "Yes," and she barked: "Wait here." He sat down on the bench against the wall. As his belly seemed to be just as afraid of the doctor as he was himself, his pains vanished at that very moment as though by magic. But it was too late to make his escape now. He felt a great desire to take out the little automobile and set it going. It would made his face much bigger and put the young she-dog to shame when she saw what a thing he possessed. But before he could do so, another lady came in at the door, looked at him, smiled, took the card from his hand and said quite amiably: "Come in, old Lung Yen, if you please."

Although the young she-dog spoke as he himself did and this lady spoke in a foreign manner, he felt an immediate confidence in her all the same.

"I have the wish to bring my low presence before the high person of the Old Doctor," he said with all the politeness at his command.

"I am the doctor," the lady said with a smile. "You can tell me what is the matter with you."

"Great Old Lady," Yen began in dismay, making a bow, "it is a pain in my belly which turns round and bites like an animal."

The lady doctor took his hand as no one ever had taken it since the days when Jasmin used to go with him outside the city gate. At the same time she went on smiling and looking at him so that he began to sweat in his embarrassment. The young she-dog came in and read something out of a book which he did not understand. Whereupon the lady doctor gave up smiling. It did not please him to see them both dressed in white; it looked as if they were always ready to let their sick die at any moment and bury them.

"Now, Lung Yen," the lady doctor said severely, "two years and thirty-four days ago your name was written in the books of the anti-opium office and you were warned. Do you remember that?"

Lung Yen let his head fall and passed his tongue twice over his dusty lips.

"I remember, Great Old Lady," he said submissively. All the time he kept the parcel containing the little stink-cart clasped to his breast.

"You know too that you will have to be beheaded if you are caught smoking again," the lady doctor went on. Yen could think of no reply. She went on looking at him, and he felt that her eyes bored into him like long sharp nails. He felt every bone in his emaciated body and every hollow in his face betraying the fact that he had succumbed to the Great Smoke.

"Dr Hain!" Pearl Chang called through to the next room. She attempted in an almost absent-minded manner to unclasp the packet from Yen's fingers.

"You will have to undress so that the Old Doctor can examine you," she said. But Yen gripped his treasure tightly. "What have you got there?" she asked. "We shall not steal it, we'll keep it safely for you."

Yen was thankful that she did not ask any more about opium. A pleasing weakness overcame him, and he felt a desire to reveal all that was in his heart.

"It is a present for my son, Great Lady," he said. "He is coming to visit me tomorrow. I have not seen him for a long time."

"It is a great occasion, Lung Yen, and I wish you happiness," the lady doctor said. "I can understand that you want to be strong and well for the occasion."

She turned to Dr Hain, who came out of his room drying his hands.

"What have we here?" he asked in English, going up to Lung Yen. "Opium," Pearl said. "Obviously. It's a bad business altogether. He is registered and ought, properly speaking, to be run in."

"I find our principle better—not to have the heads hacked off the people on a diagnosis. We are doctors, not judges. If one only knew how to help the poor devils."

"He is expecting his son. He has probably stopped suddenly, and now he's crazed with pain and doesn't know what to do."

Lung Yen listened with open mouth to the incomprehensible talk. He began to feel apprehensive again.

"The pains are from work and hunger, Great Lady," he said in exasperation. "I cough blood, because I suffer from the sickness called the Dark Weakness. I have not consumed the Great Smoke since I had the warning."

"Of course he's trying to lie," Pearl said with a shrug. She broke into a laugh. "I can't even tell him he's lying. He would lose what little face he has and go to the dogs."

"Come in," Dr Hain said, beckoning to the coolie. In spite of his dread Lung Yen could not help laughing, for the doctor spoke a very funny speech and nodded in the wrong way.

Dr Hain shut the door. He tapped him and listened to him, shook his head when he detected the rattle of the affected lung and finally said, "I would recommend a bath."

Yen began to grow accustomed to the doctor's funny Chinese. "I have the intention of bathing tomorrow morning," he assured him. He was in great fear of the instruments in the glass cases along the wall. He had heard that many of the foreign doctors cut up and mutilated the sick so that they were incomplete when they entered the realm of the dead.

"I will not have anything cut away from me," he said resolutely when the doctor approached him with a shining object hidden in his hand.

"We do not cut anything from people here," the doctor muttered and pricked Yen's arm with a sort of needle. Lung Yen looked on with satisfaction. The prickling with needles was an old and well-attested proceeding of the doctors. He hoped for many needles, but there were no more.

"The pains will cease and you will be happy," the doctor said. "You can come to me every day. I will try to help you."

He held Yen's jacket out for him, for the coolie was trembling so much that he could not find the sleeves. Then he pushed him into the other room again. "Talk you with the man, Pearl," he said in English. "I shall need ten more years before I will know some Chinese."

Pearl had a little girl sitting on the table in front of her whose red scalded hands she was rubbing with ointment. The nurse was standing by with a roll of lint. The child was smiling bravely, her teeth pressed on her underlip, while her little black eyes followed every movement of the lady doctor.

"Wait," Pearl said to the coolie. "Sit down again and rest a little. I have something more to say to you." Yen sat down obediently. He felt a pleasant calm spreading through his inside like the calm after the first pipe.

"Always these scalds," Pearl said to Dr Hain. "Did you ever go to the Japanese silk factories at Pootung? All the mothers bring their children with them so that they can earn a few coppers, too. They pull the cocoons out of the pans of boiling water. That's what does it. If we could only get better factory legislation pushed through!" She bandaged the little hands and smiled cheeringly at the child.

"And the new labor regulations?" Dr Hain said.

"Only in the International Settlement," Pearl said. "We have no control yet over what goes on outside. It will need a lot of hard work yet, Dr Hain, before we have humane conditions."

She lifted the little girl from the table and held her clumsy bandaged little hand in hers.

"Tell your mother that you are not to go to work for several days," she said. The child dropped her head and bit her lips. "How much money do you earn in a day?" Pearl asked.

"Thirty cents," the little thing muttered. Pearl sighed, took her handbag from the writing table in the office and put a few coins in the pocket of the little girl's dirty white, worn jacket. "I have given you your pay for four days," she said seriously. "For those days you must work for me. Do you understand? You must come here every morning and wait for my orders. Will you do that?"

The little girl nodded and ran away. "There are too many things the universities do not teach, Doctor," Pearl said, turning to Yen again. "Do you feel better?" she asked him. Yen had seen with astonishment that here you were paid for sickness. He was not disposed to admit that he felt better. He too hoped to earn a few cents. Pearl gave the nurse a nod, and she and Yen were left alone. She sat at the table and looked at him.

"Tell me why you have not seen your son for so long," she began. There was always the same difficulty for her in winning the confidence of the people who came to the clinic. After some consideration Yen began on a stumbling explanation, but he soon grew confused and forgot a great deal of it.

"I have a letter from my son," he said with a flush of pride and, unwrapping the document from his handkerchief, he handed it to the lady doctor. She read it with great attention.

"It is a good, clever and polite letter," she said, giving it back with the indication of a bow. "And now you do not want your son to find a sick father. That is natural."

"That is it, that is it, Great Lady," Yen said eagerly.

"You look as if you might have ruined your health with opium," Pearl began, looking in his dazed coolie face. "I do not say that you have done it, for how could I, an unworthy young person, impute a lie to you? I only say that you look as a man would look who had given way to the vice. What will your son think when he sees you again? Now if—I only say if—the Great Smoke was the cause of your sickness, then the Old Doctor and I could perhaps help you. It is difficult to break the habit of opium, but thousands have done it. It is pleasanter to give up smoking than to have your head cut off. Do you not think so, too? If opium had made you sick, then you could come here every second day and we could make a strong man of you, so that your son could be proud of his father. But as you say that your condition has nothing to do with the Great Smoke, we do not know from what sickness you suffer and what medicine would help you."

Yen hung his head, for the stern kindliness of the woman made him weak, and he would have liked best to tell her the truth. He just had enough sense left to reflect: She will catch me in a trap and hand me over and have me executed.

"I understand nothing, I have not smoked," he muttered obstinately. Pearl shrugged her shoulders. She gave him back the parcel he had so unwillingly confided to her. Yen's face brightened as he pressed the precious object to his breast once more. The little cart was wrapped in newspaper, so reckless were the salesmen in the foreign shops with expensive things like paper.

"Perhaps it would give the Great Lady pleasure to see the unworthy present I have bought for my son," he asked eagerly, already unwrapping the paper from the resplendent object. He squatted on the floor and set the automobile going. The miracle was repeated. The little vehicle rattled swiftly round in a circle. Yen looked up to see the lady doctor's admiration.

Again and again Pearl was reduced to helplessness by the poverty and simplicity of these people. In America she had been a Chinese, in China she felt she was an American. "I wish you a happy meeting with your son," she said to Yen. She looked after him as he withdrew with many bows. If Chang leaves me I shall still have my work, Pearl thought as she stood there seeing nothing. She went to the basin and washed her hands.

Yen went his way and felt better every minute. He felt strong again. He would have liked best to get his ricksha from Kating Street and work all night. It occurred to him that it was perhaps his unwonted laziness that made him sick. Involuntarily he broke into his customary trot; dust and dirt rose in clouds from beneath his shoes. As Yen passed the North Station he saw many people stretching their necks; flags were being carried past, and there was music of drums and trumpets. This just suited him, for he did not know how he was to spend the hours until he should see his son.

"What is it? Soldiers?" he asked another coolie and tried to look over his shoulder.

"Child soldiers," the coolie said without paying him much attention. "Fine little devils."

The words did not at once enter Yen's thick head, and he

squeezed his way through the people only from aimless curiosity. It was only a few minutes later that the meaning of what he had heard came to him.

"Child soldiers?" he shouted. "Are they the Scouts who are coming to the town for a festival?"

A few people laughed at him, and a boy shouted: "There's a prize offered for the dumbest coolie in Shanghai; are you going in for it?"

"Son and grandson of a tortoise!" Yen cursed. "Your mother slept with a dog!" He fought his way into the front row and watched the show with gaping mouth.

From the gates of the station there poured an endless stream of boys, children of all sizes, wearing uniforms like soldiers and marching by in rank and file like soldiers: The tramp of their boots was loud and rhythmical, the brass instruments of the band shone, flags and banners streamed above and beside them. But what excited and amazed Yen most of all was the cleanliness and the healthiness of all those boyish faces under their wide-brimmed hats. "What's on the flags?" he asked an old man beside whom he was standing. "'Intelligence, Courage, Benevolence,'" the old man read out without hesitation. Yen thanked him in a daze. A thought had swept through him, taking his breath away and nearly bursting him. "One of those children is my son," he said to the old man, but the noise of the drums drowned his voice.

He stayed outside the station until the last lot had come out, formed in line and marched away. There were hundreds and thousands of children, and it took more than an hour before the last of them had moved off. Yen stood there patiently gazing at each of the ten thousand young faces. One of them is my son, he thought. One of them is my son. When there were no more to come and the last of them had joined the column, he sighed deeply as though asleep and looked distractedly round him. The spectators were leaving the square, and Yen too went away. With many others he followed the retreating sound of the bugles. His stout coolie's legs carried him of their own accord behind the marching children. One of them is my son, Lung Yen told himself.

VII

ALL HER LIFE long Helen had lived by calculation, not by instinct. Men were the material out of which she had raised the structure of her life, a material that was sometimes weak, sometimes intractable, sometimes repulsive and sometimes pleasant, but always abjectly within her grasp. But it is a law of human nature that it cannot quite escape from feeling; for feeling grows subterraneously, seething up and the more likely to erupt the more it is suppressed. Feeling took its revenge on Helen by overwhelming her with love at an inappropriate moment for an inappropriate object. An insignificant American salesman, an average person with an average heart, Frank Taylor, assistant manager of the Shanghai Branch of the Eos Film and Foto Company, the fiancé of a middle-class nurse, who had reached a weekly salary of sixty-five dollars. Helen could see all this perfectly clearly as long as she thought soberly about it. But she did not want to see clearly or to think soberly. She wanted to be carried away and to let herself be carried away. In each beginning love there is a moment when there is still time to draw back, to quench the spark and to forget. Once this moment has been allowed to pass, either from carelessness or deliberately, love becomes something irrevocable. Helen's senseless love was irrevocable.

Since she had never loved before, she behaved as girls of sixteen behave when they experience their first love. She often stood in front of the glass and long and critically scrutinized herself to see whether she was beautiful enough for the man she loved. She had her hair done in a different way. She drove to the French quarter and bought dresses, hats and perfumes. Her heart beat violently whenever the telephone rang, and she was overcome with sadness when it was not Frank. She questioned Clarkson, her lady's maid, about her faded and forgotten loves. She sat for hours in the lounge with her eyes fixed on the revolving door lest she miss the very moment when Frank might come in. She sang softly to herself over the many letters she wrote him and never sent. She cried often and without reason, and she was happy, she was really happy for the first time in her life.

Nothing was the same as before, not even her sleep. It used to be deep and dreamless. Now she began to dream, and it was odd that all her dreams went back to her childhood as though all her later life had never been lived. Frank was always there in these vivid dreams, not as a person but only as a vague delight.

It so happened that during the three days between their first kiss and the arrival of Frank's fiancée, Bobbie made only fleeting appearances and vanished altogether at night. Potter, who kept a conscientious diary in which he noted the condition and whereabouts of his master, made distracted entries: "Absent from 7.34 P.M. to 9.10 A.M. Not drunk." "Slept from morning till afternoon. Ate nothing. Good-tempered and sober. Don't know where he goes."

Helen went to Bobbie in his room and looked at him. Even in his sleep he had a look of exhaustion, and his face was shining with sweat. His pocketbook and his wrist watch were on the bedside table. Helen casually inspected the contents of the pocketbook. It was bulging with the paper money of Shanghai. She put it down again and called Potter.

"When my husband wakes tell him that I am going to a lecture on Chinese art and afterwards to the Changs," she lied. She knew that Bobbie would rather plunge into a blazing house than venture again into the society of the educated Chinese. She telephoned to Frank, not from her room but from the public telephone box on the mezzanine floor of the hotel. They rode in taxis, they sat on park seats, they ate in hidden French, Russian and Chinese restaurants. They danced all three nights. They rode along the silent empty streets at night in two rickshas close together and without letting go of each other's hands. The ricksha coolies laughed and ran with care, so as not to disturb the foreigners and to earn a large tip. They stood at a corner saying endless good-bys; they could not bear to part. Three days and three nights.

One night she paid Frank a visit in the little flat he shared with Morris, the newspaperman. Frank had threatened Morris with slow torture if he put his nose into the flat that night, he had made delirious preparations, he had reduced his servant, Ah Sinfu, to resigned, speechless Chinese despair, and he had had his hair cut. He had borrowed silk coverings, bought flowers, put champagne on ice, for he had a vague notion that champagne rightly belonged to an adventure with a woman of Helen's standard. He himself detested champagne and slipped out and drank whisky. He took Helen in his arms and kissed her as if he were crazy. The drop of the South Seas in his blood came to life for the first time. It touched Helen to find him such an awkward lover. He had no vocabulary to match his plight. "I love you," he said. "Today more than yesterday, tomorrow more than today."

"And the day after tomorrow we shall be executed," Helen said. He pressed his hand to her mouth till she could not breathe. While they were still in each other's arms tears began to stream down her face again. "What's the matter?" he asked in dismay. He looked like a young savage with the dank hair over his forehead and his strong brown bare neck. "I can't give you up any more," Helen muttered.

This is a fine mess I have got myself into, he thought as soon as he was alone. I love Ruth, he thought with exasperated obstinacy. He knew it was no longer true. Nevertheless, he imagined that when Ruth came all these confusing problems would clear themselves up. Once before she had intervened at a moment of confusion and reduced everything to order. Her eyes, her voice, her calm healthy being, her firm little nurse's hands. At breakfast he surprised redhaired Morris with a piece of philosophy. "There's love and love," he remarked. "There's a sort of rocket love, red, green and blue, lots of noise and dazzle. Soaring up, you know—right up to heaven —and then all over. And nothing left but an ugly charred stick. And then there's the other sort, the fireside love, nothing sensational but warm and steady, and you can sit by your own fireside every day of your life and be glad that you are at home."

Morris was so astonished that he stopped eating his scrambled eggs. "Ovid with his 'Ars Amandi' is nothing compared with you," was all he said.

It was the last night before Ruth's arrival. They danced under the wheel of light in the Peony Club. "If we were both free, Frank," Helen said. Little bright reflections leaped up and flitted over her face. He squeezed her so tightly against him that it hurt. "We are not free. Don't let's torture ourselves," he said roughly. They danced on and on. Thick blue smoke lay in layers above them, and the room was dark but for the revolving colored lights of the wheel. "I should like to kiss you in front of everybody," Frank muttered. "Then do," she said hungrily. He kissed her behind the paper flowers of the peony shrub. The saxophonist saw it and winked an eye in masculine sympathy. He had been an ensign in a Russian guards regiment, the saxophonist of the Peony Club.

At three o'clock the musicians packed up their instruments. It was over.

"That was our last dance together," Helen said as Frank put her long cape of white chiffon round her shoulders.

"Why shouldn't we dance together when Ruth is here?" he asked lightly. She shook her head with a weary smile. It was neither night nor daylight out in the little tumble-down square in front of the club.

"Ricksha or taxi?" Frank asked.

"Ricksha," Helen said. "It lasts longer."

"Are you never tired?" he asked as he helped her into the ricksha.

"We have still half an hour," she said. She looked very white in the light of the little ricksha lantern.

"Sang Hai Ler Kwang," he told his coolie.

During the few moments they had to wait until the fighting, shouting and laughing throng of coolies had sorted themselves out and could trot one after another with their loads along the narrow street that led to North Szechuan Road, there was a little scene to which Frank attributed no importance. At this time of night there were always a lot of beggars collected in front of the Peony Club, lying in wait for the rich people who came out of the club. Small, alert boys turned cartwheels, and old women with maimed hands held out their begging bowls. "No chow," they cried out, "no chow, nothing to eat." Suddenly a white man stepped out from this knot of Chinese destitutes and approached Helen. He held out his palm and said: "No chow." Helen did not understand at first. "What is it?" she asked.

"No chow," the man repeated almost threateningly. He had fair hair and a fair Christ-like beard. He was clothed in dirty rags like a Chinese beggar and stank like one. Helen shuddered to think that a white man should sink to these depths of destitution and be in the company of these Chinese. The man had deep-set blue eyes, and his face had a look of nobility under the crust of dirt and poverty. Helen's coolie shouted at him and pushed him roughly aside as he picked up the ricksha and started to run. "Wait, wait!" Helen cried, and turning to Frank whose ricksha was coming on behind, she cried out again, "Tell him to stop."

"Stop," Frank said, and the two rickshas came to an abrupt stop. The coolies put on an injured look, for the double start and the labor of pulling up took much of their strength. The beggar was once more close to Helen. "No chow," he said.

"Are you a Russian?" she asked in Russian.

"Yes, lady, Russian. Hungry, nothing to eat. Alms," he said.

Helen opened her handbag. She looked keenly at the man. "What is your name?" she asked.

"Grischa," the man replied.

"Grischa what?" she persisted. The beggar only shrugged his shoulders.

"Have you no father's name?" she asked impatiently.

"No little father, no little mother, and my belly is empty," he said plaintively. She crumpled a dollar bill together and tossed it into the beggar's hand without touching it.

"Go on," she said urgently, and the coolies started running again. Frank was surprised to hear her talking Russian.

"How come you know Russian?" he asked her when they reached the wide street and their rickshas bowled along side by side. Helen put out her hand as she had got accustomed to doing in these brief days of love.

"I know a lot of things you don't know, darling," she said.

The town was full of outcast Russians, prostitutes, bawds and swindlers of every description. Respectable people avoided being seen in Russian company. Helen knew that Frank's puritan heart had a wholesale contempt for every Russian. She could not possibly tell him that she too belonged to these Russian exiles. Still less could she say why the brief encounter had shaken her to the depths. This Grischa might be my brother, she thought. Perhaps he is my brother. My little brother Grischa in his cadet's uniform. The chandelier trembling above her bed with all its crystal lusters. The station, shots, shouts, corpses. "Is Grischa dead, too?" she had asked when the Tschirikows picked her up. . . .

"What are you thinking about?" Frank asked.

"Nothing. That I must have my hair shampooed at last tomorrow morning," she answered, laughing. The sky above them was brighter already. Suddenly all the lamps went out. The first streetcars came along with a distant rumble.

Usually there were coolies waiting at the bridge over Soochow Creek to lend the ricksha boys a hand up the slope and down again, for the bridge was steeply arched. But at this late hour there was no one, and Helen heard her coolie panting like a wind-broken horse.

"Let's get out," she said to Frank. It was a last excuse for delay. Across the bridge there loomed the Bund and the tall buildings of the Settlement. The night was coming to an end. Helen would have gladly taken the sun in her hands and pushed it down below the horizon to put off the dawn. A morning breeze stirred the still and heavy air, lifted a corner of Helen's cape and let it fall again. She leaned over the railing and looked down. Frank put his arm round her and drew her towards him. Houseboats were moored below, close and crowded, gray and motionless in the water, with their arched matted roofs and the little lanterns inscribed with foreign characters along their sides.

Duckboards led from one boat to another. A great stillness hung over these boats in which people were sleeping closely packed. Something stirred in one of the boats. A slender naked man went to the stern, looking gray in the gray light. He took up a bucket and let it down into the water by a rope. It struck the water with a dull splash. The man stood quietly, waiting until it had filled with water,

and then drew it up again. He raised it above his head and poured
the water over himself. The splashing and trickling had a sound
of coolness. The man sat on the side of the boat and looked into
the water. His body became one with the boat again as he sat there
in motionless repose. The wind sprang up again and passed by.
The two coolies were squatting at the end of the bridge, waiting
to take up their loads. A rudder creaked below, an infant wailed
plaintively and then was still again. A cock crowed.

Helen let go of the railing and smiled at Frank.

"How important everything seems when one is in love!" she said.
She let her head droop and held out both her hands to him. He
did not take them, for once more he had that nervous feeling of
being dirty. After a moment Helen withdrew her hands and put
them under her thin cape.

"Please, will you send the rickshas away and we'll walk," she
begged. Frank wanted to protest, but he didn't. He paid off the
coolies, put his arm through Helen's, and they walked slowly on.
A Sikh policeman met them and looked them up and down severely.
A morning bird was awake in the small Wei Tang park, timidly
practising his scales. When they got to the beginning of Nanking
Road Helen stopped.

"Look at the sails," she said. The cumbersome junks were moving
slowly on the Whangpoo, and their bat's-wing sails had a thin edging
of light. There was not a sound. An old Chinese who passed them
made no noise with his felt soles.

"Aren't there any sea gulls?" Helen asked absently.

"No, not in Shanghai," Frank said.

"Don't take me as far as the hotel," she said. "I'd like a taxi now."
They waited until one of the gilded taxis came along, and Helen
got in.

"I'm glad to have met you," she said. It sounded ridiculously conventional. Frank put his head in to kiss her, but she smilingly shook
her head. He stood on the curb as the taxi started off. She put her
palms to the window, and he pressed his against the outside of it.
That was their good-by.

The hotel was loud with the hum of early vacuum cleaners. Potter had put two chairs together in front of the empty fireplace in the sitting room of their suite and was lying asleep on them. The ventilator droned above his head. He woke up when Helen came in but remained where he was.

"Has Mr Russell not come in yet, Potter?" she said.

"No, madam, I am waiting for Mr Russell," Potter said.

"Very good, Potter. Thank you, Potter. Good night," Helen said. She stopped in the door of her bedroom. "Tell Clarkson not to wake me," she said. She was as exhausted as after a childbirth.

The town emerged slowly out of the white morning mist, the gigantic town, the vicious town, the industrious, dangerous and endangered town of Shanghai, the City-by-the-Sea. Foreigners had raised it from the marsh and mud, they had made their pile with opium and smuggling, foreign fortunes had been squeezed out of the sweat and blood of the Chinese coolies. Now it had the wild years of its first youth behind it and was beginning to reflect, to learn refinement and to be a little ashamed of its past. Three and a half millions slept under its roofs, in skyscrapers, in mansions, in luxury hotels and on tattered mats, in boats, in good beds and in dirty, slimy corners. They slept, they dreamt and woke up, missionaries and millionaires, victors and victims, the blackmailers and the blackmailed. Factory sirens summoned the hands to labor, women, children and coolies streamed like beetles into the mills to spin silk and weave cotton. The early airplanes took the air and vanished into the sky. Soldiers drilled, porters carried goods to the quays, automobiles were washed, gamblers reeled from the clubs, losers and winners. Indian, French, Russian, Annamite and Chinese police kept order. Bands of thieves and burglars shared the booty of the night. Banks rolled up their shutters, night clubs closed. Sailors trooped back to their ships, and the brown sails of a thousand junks were spread. Craftsmen of every color and trade bent to their work. Tea was sipped from innumerable blue-and-white cups, and those who were too poor for tea drank hot water. The merchandise of the whole world was unloaded in the port; Chinese compradors did business for foreigners, and foreign money stuck to their hands. At the gateway of that seething world called China, competitors thronged with their wares. Underground conflicts and briberies were carried on between smugglers and customs officials. Students poured into the universities to fill their bellies with foreign knowledge for the benefit of their country and their nation or to their own advantage and that of their clan and family. Muttering priests lit candles and incense, and people of all religions prayed before the altars of every faith. Buddhists, Taoists, Lamas, Catholics, Protestants, Mormons: Christians of every shade and sect scuffled for the souls of the Chinese; and salesmen of all nations scuffled for their money. Like foam on the city's turgid current swam the philosophers and poets, the journalists and learned men, the writers, actors and artists. Ten thousand busybodies ran to and fro between the cultures of West and East, trying to act as go-betweens and explain the one to the other. Ten thousand castaways clung to the edge of society before they went under. Ten thousand who had made good gave them the last murderous push. Ten thousand others fought their way up step by step by infinitesimal degrees and imperceptible successes, with the tenacity of ants and their callousness. Many had come and vanished again. Many had struck root in the foreign soil, founded families and built homes and could no longer breathe any other air than the hot, moist, heavy air of Shanghai. The town gave out a mighty hum, the hum of ceaseless labor. It relied on the industry and sweat of the middle classes, whether white or yellow, those who were neither very rich nor very poor and whose part it was to live through the unceasing toil of the daily round. Their pleasures were simple and cheap: a visit to a cinema, a game of mahjong, a modest meal with friends. New China rioted with gigantic building schemes, with barracks, schools, sports grounds and airports. The old China lived in narrow alleys, echoing with the chanted cries of the coolies and peddlers; it hung birds before its doors, smoked water pipes, bargained and haggled, ate and slept, played and smiled, and was happy.

Much blood has flowed in its streets, for every war in the country must come to Shanghai. The city treated man as a stage play and shook bombs and destruction off as though they were all in the day's work.

The foreigners had sown benefits and crimes in equal quantities over the city, and they had reaped much hate and very little gratitude. The foreigners despised and marveled at the Chinese. The Chinese despised and marveled at the foreigners. The foundations of the city were riddled with rats, conspiracies and secret societies. The warships of many nations lay at anchor in the river; their guns were not concealed but always ready and visible in warning or in threat.

Would the war come to Shanghai? And if the war came to Shanghai, would the town be able once more to shake it off like a noxious or insignificant insect?

From the West and South, Chinese soldiers by the hundred thousand were on the march. In the river six Japanese ships lay at anchor, in which thousands of soldiers had been transported through storm and typhoon to the mouth of the Yangtze Po. The stage was set. The play could begin. Newspaper boys roared the latest headlines in the streets. A little old Chinese sat smiling on the steps that led down to the water near the Bund with a tiny cage on his knees. In the uproar that shook the world he heard nothing but the fine clear summer voice of his cricket.

VIII

RUTH ANDERSON WAS WAKENED very early in the morning by the sound of the foghorn. A drifting white wall of fog lay in front of the porthole. The ship scarcely moved. Ruth lay for a time with wide-open eyes. Today, today, today, went her heart.

After some time the foghorn ceased. The white wall became thinner and grew luminous as the sun rose behind it; it became a veil, a haze, and at last vanished into nothing. Ruth jumped out of bed and looked out the porthole. Chinese boats were drifting past

looking like the photographs Frank had sent her. The sky was not
blue, but white with heat, the river was yellow, the banks flat and
yellow and far away. Ruth put her head through the porthole and
sniffed the strange air inquisitively. More boats came by with blue
people in them. Ruth waved to them when they came close, but
they did not wave back. She withdrew her head again and looked
at the time. Not six yet. She sat on the edge of her bunk and looked
at her bare feet on the carpet. They looked hopelessly innocent and
childish, as if they still belonged to a little child in Fourteenth Street,
Flathill, Iowa. She sighed and picked up a little bottle of red nail
varnish she had bought in a ten-cent store. She took out the little
sticky brush and, with her tongue between her teeth, began very
seriously to paint her toe nails. She spread out her toes to let the
varnish dry and looked out of the porthole again. Nothing had
altered. Sometimes there was the gray or white patch of a house
on the shore, a green blob of a tree, a strip of grass. More sails.
Yellow river, yellow banks, yellow day of a foreign land. She looked
at the time. One minute past six.

She cautiously felt her nails. The varnish was dry and looked smart
and gay, and her feet were not quite so childishly innocent as before.
She put on her dressing gown, collected her washing things and
went in old tennis shoes to the bathroom. She had bought some
luxurious tablets of bath salts, likewise at a ten-cent store, and she
threw the whole lot into the water. In spite of this the bath smelt
of boiled fish as it had throughout the voyage. The pounding of
the engines could be heard distinctly in there. Today, today, today,
it went. Ruth spent ages in the bath, renewing the vain fight with
the soap, which would not lather, rubbing herself down with her
sponge, massaging her arms and ending up under the cold shower,
by which time there was a knock on the door: the next comer was
impatient and had sent the bath boy to protest. Ruth returned to
her cabin. She looked at the time. Eleven minutes past six. She sat
in front of the glass and brushed her hair—a hundred strokes of
the brush, as her mother had taught her. She had had a new permanent before she set out and was pleased with it. She twisted little
curls round her forefinger and distributed them all over her head.

The banks had drawn a bit nearer. It was a quarter past six. She shut her trunk. She had packed it the night before. Then at last she put on her coral-red dress which she had saved for this day. "Suits you," Frank had once said when she was wearing a coral-red dress. She gave a last look into cupboards and drawers. "Ready," she said aloud and rang for the steward.

"Do we arrive soon?" Ruth asked.

"Yes-yes," the steward said.

"Is breakfast ready?"

"Yes-yes."

She went up onto the promenade deck and leaned on the taffrail. She went into the dining saloon and had breakfast. She went back on deck. She played hide-and-seek with the two little Chinese girls who looked like dolls and who had been her great delight from the first day of the voyage. She had a brief talk with the noisy American who had been imprisoned in Japan because he had photographed the Daibutsu of Kamakura from the forbidden side. She said good morning to the lady from Cleveland whom her son-in-law had sent on a world tour and who spent her time sitting with her back to the sea sewing at a vast patchwork quilt. She said good-by to the Australian millionaire, whom for a long time she had mistaken for a stoker. She distributed her tips with great embarrassment according to the scale advised by Mr Murata, a Japanese. She returned to her cabin, quite out of breath with excitement. Ten minutes past seven. Ruth sighed with relief to find that she had succeeded in killing so much time. She put on her hat. The steward knocked at the door and pointed aloft with his thumbs when she opened the door. "What is it?" Ruth asked. "Yes-yes," the steward said. "Disembark?" she asked, with an inquiring look at his thumbs. "Yes-yes," the steward said. Ruth's heart had missed a beat and now picked it up in a great hurry. But it was only the passport officials who had come on board to inspect passports.

When she arrived on the promenade deck once more, the river looked much narrower, and it was crowded with shipping of all sorts. Warships, a schooner with its sail spread, little fussy junks on which small women in blue trousers and jackets did the hard work of men.

White factories rose up, the hazy outlines of skyscrapers shut out the distant horizon.

"The Bund," Mr Murata said beside her at the taffrail. He had joined the ship at Kobe and had sat at her table. The young Mormon missionary who had been her neighbor up to then had left the boat at Yokohama.

"How do you do today? A beautiful day," Murata said. It sounded like the first exercise in a conversation primer.

"Fine, thanks," Ruth said. "And how are you?"

"Thank you," Murata replied. "Okay." Ruth searched the horizon with her eyes. The river must have made a bend, for she could no longer see the distant skyscrapers. "Aren't we going very slowly?" she asked plaintively.

"Always on the Whangpoo," Murata said. "Will you play one more game of ping-pong?" he added politely.

"Thanks, but I'm too fidgety," Ruth said.

"Okay," Murata said. He went to his deck chair and brought back a parcel he had left there. "The books," he said.

"What books?" Ruth asked. She flushed slightly, for she was afraid the Japanese wished to make her a parting present which it would be equally difficult to accept or refuse.

"The books you were so kind to lend me," Murata said with ceremony.

"Oh—those!" Ruth said.

She cared nothing about the books. They were a parting gift from the girls of the Nightingale Club. She had lent them to the Japanese because he seemed to be positively starving for American literature.

"The steward has taken my trunks below, and I can't put them in now," she said.

Murata heard this with dismay and even with a sort of despair. "That is my mistake, my mistake," he said repeatedly, bowing each time. "My mistake, Miss Anderson. I ought to have brought the books back sooner. What shall we do now?"

Ruth had no more time for the Japanese. Shanghai was there. China was there. The shore was there, where Frank was awaiting her. The boat was pervaded by the nervous excitement that immediately precedes the moment of putting into harbor. The engines stopped and went on again. The pier was close with its throng of blue Chinese and white Europeans. Ruth's heart fluttered as though with the wing beats of a bird. There was a pain in her chest.

" . . . Miss Anderson?" Murata said beside her.

She had not heard what else he had said, her ears were buzzing, chains rattled, the passengers all streamed in one direction from the promenade deck. The sun appeared. It was hot, and Ruth caught at what little breath she had left in her body.

" . . . where shall I send the books to you?" the Japanese asked.

"We shall meet again," Ruth said. "I will give you my address. We're there—I think we're there."

She held fast to the rail and gazed at the people on the pier. There were thousands and thousands of them, all shouting and waving bunches of flowers and panama hats—white men, and women with gay Japanese kimonos among them, and Chinese coolies who stippled the whole shore with blue. Ruth could not discern Frank. A crazed idea suddenly came to her: Suppose I can't recognize him? she thought. Suppose he can't recognize me? For a second or two it seemed to her quite likely that she and Frank might have entirely altered in these endless three years. Mr Murata was making one of his ceremonious orations at her elbow.

"May I repeat, Miss Anderson, how great a pleasure the acquaintance with you has been? Please give my respects to your honored bridegroom. I hope to have the honor to meet you again in Shanghai and to be able to restore the books to you. Thank you. My best thanks to you and my best wishes, Miss Anderson."

Ruth had long since ceased to listen. She was gazing at the tumultuous excitement that every arrival and departure occasions at Shanghai. "Can we land?" she asked one of the ship's officers who was hurrying by. "Yes-yes," he said.

Ruth stood on the pier. Everyone surged and shouted all around her; the white people embraced, the yellow made repeated low and ceremonious bows. She was pushed this way and that as she searched the crowd for the hundredth time with bewildered eyes. Coolies surrounded her, pulled at her, shouted incomprehensible offers of service in her ears, while orderly Japanese walked back and forth trying to organize the unorganizable. A million people had come to the pier, but Frank was not among them. Frank was not there. He was not there. "Taxi, lady?" a Japanese in white uniform asked her. "I don't know," Ruth replied helplessly.

"Hello, Tiny," Frank said behind her.

"Hello, Frank," she said breathlessly.

"How are you?" Frank asked.

"Fine, and you?"

"Let's get out of this first," Frank said, taking her arm.

"My luggage——" Ruth said.

"Come along," Frank said, leading her off. His hand was warm and a little moist on her bare arm.

"Is it always as hot as this here?" Ruth asked.

"In summer, as a rule—and a lot hotter," Frank said.

"And it's still early in the day," Ruth said.

"Come on," Frank said. "Your luggage—customs examination first."

"Let me look at you," Ruth said when they were out of the worst of the crowd. She looked. His face was pale and moist, and his eyes looked different. "Have you been working too hard? You look a bit run down," she said.

"It's the climate," he said uncomfortably. "And you? Fresh as a spring morning—of course." He looked her full in the face for the first time and then took out his handkerchief and wiped his hands. "One's always dirty here," he said in excuse.

After the parting from Helen he had driven home, had a very hot bath and shaved. Ah Sinfu was told to make some strong coffee in the hope that it would drive the fatigue and the alcohol from his system. Morris had not come home at all that night, and finally Frank sat down alone with the newspaper until the arrival of the boat. He fell asleep over the news of the war in the North and woke too late with a frightful headache. He shouted at Ah Sinfu, knocked his elbow against the door, rushed in a taxi to his garage, where some minutes were lost in inducing the Chinese garage man to surrender his automobile, for it ought to have been washed and this was only half done. Nevertheless Frank was proud of it when he showed it off to Ruth. They had often talked in New York of an automobile of their own . . .

"Ruth, here's Lizzie," he said. "I hope you two will get on well together. Lizzie has not quite finished her make-up, but she's not accustomed to getting up in the middle of the night."

Ruth surveyed Lizzie with awe. "So that's your car!" she said, stroking Lizzie's radiator.

"She is not exactly a Duesenberg," Frank said, feeling flattered, "but she is not bad at all. You'll see how she pulls. And she has one or two little tricks, clock and so on. Lots of people here are afraid of the sun, but I keep her open in the summer. We have a radio, too."

"What is it? A '36?"

"No, '35—I bought it cheap."

"They say the '35 is a better car than the '36," Ruth said comfortingly. And now that Lizzie had helped them through the first awkward moments, they got in at last and Frank started the car.

"So here you are, Ruth," he said without looking at her, and Ruth replied joyfully, "Yes, here I am."

The streets were in an indescribable turmoil. They went through a sort of market with mountains of melons and onions. Ricksha coolies squeezed their way through the automobiles, and more coolies carried loaded poles to the pier, singing a chant as they went that sounded more like a groan or a wail.

"Look!" Ruth cried, grasping Frank's arm. He gave a passing glance. A beggar was sitting at the side of the street, an old woman in a tattered jacket with a black band round her forehead and the tiny deformed feet of the old days. In front of her was a blind ragged child holding out a bowl for alms.

"Yes, you don't see bound feet very often nowadays," Frank said carelessly.

"It's the child," Ruth said. "It had flies settling in its eyes."

"You'll have to get used to that," he said. "It's not quite so clean in Shanghai as in your hospital consultation room."

Ruth obediently took her eyes from the street and looked at Frank.

"There's nothing wrong with you, is there?" she asked after looking at him for a moment or two.

"Wrong? No. Bit of a headache," he said. "I couldn't sleep," he added.

Ruth smiled happily. "Neither could I, Frank," she said softly.

He gave her a fleeting smile. "You—tiny midget!" he said.

"I have some aspirin in my suitcase," she said. "We'll soon get rid of your headache."

He was irritated by her bright and cheery tones of a nurse. "You won't cure a headache like mine with aspirin," he said. "It's the size of a whale's. Gunpowder might help."

"Suicide?" Ruth asked.

"Not exactly. You take a plum, remove the stone and put gunpowder in instead. It's Morris's patent, and the fellows in the club swear by it. Here we are in the Settlement."

"What a lot of Chinese there are here!" Ruth said.

"We're in China, after all," Frank answered. She had laughed when he confided his prescription. "Do the people in Shanghai buy gunpowder at the drugstores?" she asked in delight.

Frank glanced at her as she chattered on. At first he was annoyed at her amusement over his headache, and then he joined in her laughter. He held the wheel with one hand and groped for Ruth's hand on the seat with the other. When he found it he closed his own round it and put it in his coat pocket as in a nest. Ruth sighed deeply, as people sigh when they dream. It was the old, familiar, tender caress, the old closeness and communion. She made her hand quite soft and pliable, suiting it to every joint of his. "It's a long time since we saw each other, isn't it, Frank?" she said shyly.

"But you're here now," he said again.

"Are you glad?" she asked.

"Am I glad?" he repeated. "Yes, Tiny, I am glad."

But after a few minutes his hand grew restless and he released it from hers. He removed her hand from his pocket and put it back on the seat like an unwanted object. He took out his handkerchief and, steering with his knees, wiped his hands. "Filthy hole, this," he said as he took hold of the wheel again in renewed spirits and turned into Nanking Road. Ruth looked about her with curiosity, but her eyes came quickly back to Frank again. He shifted his head in discomfort, put his tie straight and smoothed his hair.

"Shanghai Hotel, madam," he said and brought the car to a stop. Ruth put her head back to survey it right up to its eighteenth floor. "Looks smart," she said appreciatively. Frank gave her suitcase to the Chinese page boy who had risen from the ground at their feet and said uncomfortably: "Hope you'll like your room. Anyway, it's only till Saturday."

Complex reasons had decided Frank to take a room for Ruth in the Shanghai Hotel of all places, and his decision was the outcome of strenuous mental exertion. It was a precaution, a padlock and a safety device, an unscalable barrier between Helen and himself. With Ruth and Helen in the same hotel he was fortified against temptation, and even though he might wish to see Helen he would be prevented from doing so by the mere fact that Ruth was close at hand.

Just as he put his hand on her elbow to conduct her into the hotel a child plucked at her skirt. Ruth looked round in surprise and saw an impossibly dirty little boy, whose grubby face was lit up by a winning smile that revealed two rows of large gleaming teeth. He said something that Ruth could not understand and pointed to a small rush basket held up for her inspection. It was full of yellow down that made a peeping noise.

"What does he want?" Ruth asked. The commissionaire was already on the spot to drive the child away, but Ruth held onto the thin little hand which had pulled at her skirt. "He wants to sell you a dozen ducklings," Frank explained. "Ducklings!" Ruth said in bewilderment. She looked into the basket. From under the downy wings several little heads with oddly large ducks' bills emerged with a chorus of peeping. Ruth was enchanted as she gazed at the brood of tender, newly born life. The boy quickly took one of the ducklings out and put it in the palm of Ruth's hand. It snuggled down into the warmth and decided to take up its abode there. Frank shouted at the boy, but he only laughed and rapped out a smart reply. Some ricksha coolies, of whom there were always several waiting about

outside the hotel, gathered round and laughed; Ruth had not heard
such loud and hearty laughter for years. She stood with the duckling
in her hand looking from Frank to the boy and then at the row of
foreign dirty laughing faces.

"Why do you shout at him?" she asked.

"Chinese don't understand anything else," he said. He wanted to
pick the duckling up and put it back into the basket, but it said
a few words in its own language, rapidly and indignantly, and Frank
involuntarily drew back his hand. There was a fresh outburst of
laughter.

"What are we supposed to do with it?" asked Ruth, who was
aware of the tiny creature in every vein of her body.

"Rear it, I suppose and eat it. You can buy hundreds of them any
day you like. They peddle them around everywhere. Who buys them
all?" he asked the commissionaire.

"The rich Chinese," the commissionaire said; "for their children
to play with. They torture them to death, sir."

Ruth held the little duckling to her breast, as when a little girl she
had held dogs, blind cats and frogs who felt chilly.

"Would you like the basketful?" Frank asked. Dear Ruth, he
thought, dear, darling Ruth.

"Only this one," Ruth said. "It'll bring good luck for sure. It knows
me already. Do you see? What a pity it only talks Chinese!"

The bargaining proceeded with the usual commotion and so much
advice and curiosity on the part of the public that there was a traffic
block in Nanking Road. Ruth became the possessor of the duckling
and the basket. The boy acquired some small change and stowed
away the remaining ducklings in the sleeves of his ragged jacket.
And Ruth, clasping the downy morsel of living warmth in her hands,
entered the black marble splendors of the Shanghai Hotel with a
beaming face.

"Monsieur Taylor, Monsieur Taylor," screamed Madame Tissaud
who was occupying her usual seat, surrounded by the French morning papers. "Do not speak a word—here is our little bride, I know
all. And you have nearly overslept the boat, bad young man! She
is charming. You are charming, mademoiselle. I hope the climate

will suit you. It is not for everyone, Monsieur Taylor, eh? So now
you will be tied to the bedpost. That is the best for you, much the
best. He is too good-looking to be left free. Welcome, mademoiselle,
welcome to Shanghai," she ended, inspecting Ruth as though she
had to take her measure for clothes, shoes and a brassière. "But what
have you there?" she asked when she spied the duckling between
Ruth's embarrassed fingers. "A *ya,* a little *ya*—how droll! Unfortunately it will die, but there are plenty more. You have come just
at the right moment, mademoiselle—how is it? . . . Anderson? It
is going to be interesting, I tell you. Have you heard, Monsieur
Frank, what has passed at Hungjao Airdrome? . . . No? On what
planet do you live, Monsieur Taylor? A Chinese guard has shot two
Japanese, a lieutenant and a sailor, in the middle of Monument Road.
There you have the spark in our nice little powder cask. You have
not yet assisted at a war in Shanghai? Well, you will now! How
long is it you are here? Over three years? And no war? *Mon Dieu,*
how this town has changed itself! But now it must soon commence.
And when is the wedding? . . . Saturday? My felicitations! And
have you heard the rest? They say cholera has broken out among
the refugees. That is nothing. No summer without cholera, believe
me, and I know my Shanghai. *Au revoir, à bientôt, ma chère.* We
must have a good talk together before long."

Frank made a colossal effort, as though it were a question of rescuing Ruth from Niagara Falls, and got her away. "The hyena,"
was all he said. There was another delay at the reception desk, where
Ruth entered her name and Frank took charge of the key of her
room.

"Miss Anderson," Mr Murata said, joyfully confronting her. He
looked much smaller than he had among the other Japanese on the
boat, and he was heavily laden with two suitcases and a parcel, which
he gripped under his arm.

"Frank," Ruth said, "this is Mr Murata. My fiancé, Frank Taylor—
Mr Murata."

Murata put one suitcase down in order to be able to take off his
hat. He smiled his Japanese smile. "I am enchanted, delighted," he
said with a bow.

"Pleased to meet you," Frank said, holding out two fingers.

"May I ask—do you also stay here, Miss Anderson?" Murata asked. "That is extremely fortunate. Then I shall permit myself to send the books up to your room. Number 615?" he said with a glance at the brass label hanging from the imposing key. Frank instinctively dropped it into his pocket.

"Just look what I've got," Ruth said, opening her hands to show the duckling. She had gone every day onto the boat deck with the Japanese to visit the dogs in their kennels. There were two young Australian cocker spaniel puppies who had particularly fascinated them. This time too Murata bent enthusiastically over the little peeping duckling.

"Enchanting," he said. "We Japanese would say *'omoshiroi.'*"

Frank stood by impatiently. He took Ruth by the elbow.

"I'll see you later," Ruth said as she was hurried off to the elevator.

"Okay," Murata murmured behind her.

"Sixth floor," Frank told the Chinese elevator boy. The more expensive rooms were all much higher up. Helen's were on the sixteenth floor.

"Yes?" he asked as Ruth clutched his arm.

"A little dizzy, that's all—with everything," she said in excuse.

The elevator stopped. The boy with her suitcase was waiting, and they went on past bamboo furniture and carpets that tried to look Chinese.

"What have you had to do with that Jap?" Frank asked as they went.

"Nothing. We played ping-pong together. The Japanese don't play it as we do—they slash about as if they were on tennis courts."

"It's hardly necessary to get mixed up with these Japanese swine at this moment of all others," Frank said. "You shouldn't have done it."

"What's wrong with the Japanese?" Ruth asked.

"What's wrong? Don't you read any newspapers over there? Good Lord, didn't you see all those warships in the Whangpoo? We shall very soon know what's wrong, I'm afraid."

Ruth looked at him in perplexity. "I'm sorry," she said shyly. "Of course there was not a word about it in the news on the Japanese ship. Is it serious? I mean does it matter to you whether the Japanese quarrel with the Chinese?"

"It matters a whole damned lot," Frank said heatedly. "In the first place it's bad for business. Just when one's begun to get on one's feet. And then naturally I'm in the volunteer guard. But we won't think of that now."

The boy opened the door, followed them in with the suitcase, threw a glance into the bathroom and another at the screens in front of the open window, turned on the ventilator which at once began to hum, and waited submissively but expectantly for his tip. As soon as he had gone, Frank locked the door and stood still. "What a lovely room," Ruth said awkwardly. She had dreamt too often of the first minute alone with Frank. He cleared his throat. "It's not exactly the Taj Mahal," he said with a twisted smile and remained standing where he was, near the door. Ruth went to the window and looked out. The room gave onto the courtyard. There was a glass cupola below and the din from the hotel kitchens. Above was the white haze of the sky in which, as Ruth looked up, there were three black planes.

"Now's the time for your aspirin," Ruth said after a searching look at Frank's face. She went to her suitcase and unlocked it after putting the duckling carefully down.

"Do you mind if I go and wash my hands?" Frank asked. She nodded in reply. They had not yet kissed each other.

Ruth found the aspirin tablets and put out two. She filled a glass with water from the thermos flask on the chest of drawers and dropped the tablets into it. She looked round the room for a good place for the duckling and decided on the corner next the chest of drawers; so she put the basket there, gave the little creature a kiss on its yellow beak and put it in its basket. Then she walked slowly to the looking glass and looked at herself. Frank was whistling in the bathroom and turning the taps full on over his hands.

The stress of this first hour had been too much for her. She could see that the arteries in her neck were throbbing like mad. That's a pity, she thought. Being with Frank was like swimming in the sea at high tide, when you were caught in one wave after another before you could get your breath. He came back from the bathroom with wet hair. "Here's your aspirin," Ruth said. "Sorry I haven't any gunpowder." She watched him while he drank the water with the tablets dissolved in it. He shuddered. "Tastes bitter," he said. The room was small and had only one chair. Frank sat down on the bed and looked down at his white shoes. "We must think of a name," Ruth said, returning to the window. "What for?" he asked puzzled. "For the duckling. He must have a name, and then he must have hard-boiled egg chopped up. That's what chicks like," Ruth said. Frank took up the telephone and ordered a hard-boiled egg.

"Have you had breakfast?" Ruth asked. He was sitting on the bed again.

"Best thing would be to call him Confucius," he suggested. Ruth wrinkled her forehead.

"Perhaps it's a girl," she said.

Frank was not listening. Confucius was peeping softly in the corner. Ruth knelt down and looked at him.

"He's asleep," she said in a whisper. "He's talking in his sleep."

When she got up again and smoothed her dress, she felt Frank's eyes on her.

"What a little mite you are, Tiny," he said from the bed. "What a midget to come traveling all alone to China. Such a midget *sans peur et sans reproche.*"

The bed was large; it occupied most of the room. Frank stretched himself out and shut his eyes.

"Have you still got a headache or has the aspirin done any good?" Ruth asked.

"It's gone. I feel fine," Frank murmured, without opening his eyes. "Now you're here, Ruth, nothing hurts any more."

She went over to him and put her hand on his forehead. She could feel the blood pulsing in his temples. He took her hand and stroked his face with it. "That's good," he murmured. "Cool and so—clean."

He put his arm round her waist and drew her down. Ruth dropped through a dizzy, whirling, bright red, long-lost happiness until her mouth lay on his.

But Frank in the moment of kissing her felt nothing but a hope-less strangeness and the burning, poisoned, hungry, unappeased yearning for another woman.

IX

THE ROOF GARDEN of the Shanghai Hotel was always crowded at tea-time. Half of it was covered by an awning of the rust-brown color of Chinese sails, and a large number of tables were under gaily-colored umbrellas outside the shade of it in a rectangle round a fountain which somewhat cooled the air. The trees and vines in large Chinese oil vessels looked faded, although they were regularly sprinkled with water. Even the floor, tiled with large flat tiles, was wet and gleam-ing, for it too was sprinkled with water hourly during the summer to temper the heat. Attentive little Chinese waiters hung about the tables with iced drinks and fragrant hot tea for the residents of the British concession. A string quartet was playing from somewhere unseen in a thin pizzicato which was entirely drowned by the con-fused burble of talk.

Four American businessmen, shrewd, gray-haired and alert, with their tall highballs in front of them:

"If we get it now it will be more serious than in '32. America can't just fold her arms and look on."

"What the Japanese want is the Monroe Doctrine for Asia. Asia for the Asiatics. Even this they have to copy from us."

"And we'll have the world market flooded with Japanese-dumped goods. And what about all the American capital that's been sunk in China? And what about the oil? If Japan puts China in her pocket who's going to buy our cotton?"

"America's bound to protect her citizens on land and sea, and the Chamber of Commerce will look to it."

"Yes, but we're told that those who do business in foreign coun-tries do so at their own risk."

"The neutrality act——"

"The democratic countries have got to stand together against Japanese Fascism or else go under."

"There's only one thing to do—to make as much money as you can as fast as you can and then beat it for the States."

"That's what we all say, and yet we've been in this infernal hole for thirty years."

"My wife couldn't exist now without six servants."

Two Chinese compradors, one in European dress, the other with an unusually well-cut sleeveless jacket over his long silk robe:

"I always say, better a dog in peace than a man in war."

"The mayor of Peking was bought. He let the Japanese march in without defending the town. He simply opened the city gates."

"It makes no difference. The North was Japanese long ago. It only means the legalization of smuggling through the gap in the North."

"The only question is: can we do better business with the Japanese or against them? Whoever gives me milk is my mother."

"Let us forget these little unpleasantnesses. A man for whom I was able to do an insignificant service has sent me a mandarin fish, and my cook is an artist in cooking it with brown sauce. May I have the pleasure of your company tonight . . . "

Another group, intellectuals, white people, Chinese, a young Siamese, a Norwegian woman with red dyed hair:

"Unless opium is suppressed, China cannot be saved. It is a terrible, ineradicable national vice."

"Like booze in America. Don't forget Prohibition. It only means driving up the price and the consumption."

"Alcohol makes people stupid, and drunkards go home and slaughter their wives. Opium makes you wise and benevolent."

"They say it has an erotic influence."

"Nonsense. It makes you impotent."

"I smoke eight pipes a night, and my hands are steady. You smoke forty cigarettes and your hands shake."

"The anti-opium office does a lot of good. So one hears at least."

"Certainly. They chop the heads off fifty incurables now and again. They give them opium before they do it—to make their death pleasanter."

Four slender and elegant Chinese women under the awning, eating iced fruit:

"Sleeves are now going to be worn shorter, my tailor has copied Anna May Wong's."

"Green silk with a bamboo spray of clipped velvet all the way down, at Sincere's sale, a real bargain."

"If my husband brought a concubine into the house I would shoot him."

"The American method. Did you hear Professor Cheifong lecture? It appears that free love is the only system possible for modern people."

"What we need is missionaries for birth-control propaganda."

Two Chinese fanatics sitting over their fine porcelain cups of jasmine tea:

"China is united for the first time. A united China is unconquerable."

"Four hundred million people. We will build walls of our bodies against the Japanese. A beginning has been made."

"We have the people and the patience. In five hundred years China will be the best country in the world. And how short a time is five hundred years!"

"That is so. Ten thousand years of life, my friend!"

"Thank you, honored first-born. Ten thousand years of blessings and contentment!"

The burble of voices, noise and scraps of conversations: they say that Mei Lan Fang has grown old. The New York Stock Exchange has weakened. Whoever wins this war, one thing is certain—we whites can only lose. Better the Japanese than Communists. It is the end of extraterritoriality. What's India going to live on if we cannot export any more opium? Never again shall China be treated as if it were a colony. China—what a hopeless mess! China—what a marvelous country! . . .

Optimists, pessimists, Westerns, Easterns, men, women. Europeans, Americans, Orientals. Courage and cowardice. Idealism and greed. Enmity and love. People of every sort and color and tendency. Voices, noise, laughter, *tristesse,* tea, whisky. The full orchestra of every description of humanity: that was teatime on the roof garden of the Shanghai Hotel.

Just before half past four Ruth Anderson entered the roof garden and rather embarrassedly followed the smart headwaiter who flitted in front of her.

"I'm looking for Mr Taylor," she said, after she had searched every table without finding Frank. She had put on her best dress, white silk printed all over with flowers, sixteen dollars ninety-five. Madame Tissaud, who emigrated every afternoon from the lounge to the more fertile fields of the roof garden, waved and signaled. "Come here, my child, come here. If you do not mind the company of a lonely old woman."

"It's a pleasure," Ruth said irresolutely. She was not really sorry to have the white-haired old lady as a bulwark.

"All alone? And on the first day?" Madame asked, with her nose to the scent.

"Frank will soon be here. He's still at the office. I don't want him to neglect his work for my sake."

"But how you are reasonable! Magnificent!" Madame said.

"Iced coffee," Ruth told the waiter. She looked round and breathed more easily. "It's cooler here," she said. "I should have brought Confucius with me."

"Ah, you study Confucius?" Madame asked approvingly. "He is quite out of fashion. Only we Europeans still read him sometimes."

Ruth did not disillusion her. The waiter brought her coffee, and she began to sip it contentedly through the straw.

"How do you like Shanghai?" Madame asked.

"Very much—that is, I have not seen much of it yet. Frank took me to his office and introduced B.S. to me. I mean Mr Scott, he is going to give me away. He was very kind. His wife is helping me to find a little apartment. I liked him very much."

"Babbits are an affair of taste," Madame said. "And for when is the wedding?"

"Saturday," Ruth said. "Frank is getting a week's leave, and B.S. is lending us his houseboat for our honeymoon. Isn't that romantic?"

"Saturday—*alors*. And until then we live *en célibataire?*" Madame asked. Ruth made no reply: she returned to her iced coffee, which was not as cold as it ought to have been. The ice had already melted.

"How is it that they all sit together, Chinese and Europeans?" she asked. "I thought that wasn't done."

"It is only so since a few years, my dear child. When I came here it was quite another affair. But race prejudices do not advance one, and it is better for business to be large."

"I haven't any race prejudices," Ruth said quickly. "At my hospital we had people of all colors side by side. When they suffer they are all alike."

"Yes—or when they have money," Madame observed. "You were a hospital nurse, mademoiselle? A very romantic profession."

Ruth thought of all the bedpans she had emptied in the course of her career and could not help laughing. "Here comes Frank," she said, half rising from her chair in her delight. He looked a little less jaded than in the morning and was resplendent too in a fresh white suit without a crease. He saw Ruth at once and came quickly to her table, smoothing back his nice dark hair as he came, although it was smooth enough in any case.

"Here you are," he said. "Good afternoon, Madame Tissaud. How did you like our store, Tiny? Perhaps it doesn't seem anything very great at first sight, but we've made great strides in the last twelve months. You completely conquered the old man, by the way. I only hope that Mrs B.S. will not be jealous."

Frank talked a lot and very fast and with the same twisted smile which had chilled Ruth in the morning. "Scotch—straight," he ordered. As soon as the waiter brought it he gulped it down, shuddered a little and ordered another. Ruth looked surprised without knowing it. "You'll soon find the same thing," he said. "At this time of day in Shanghai you need something to pick you up." He drank his second whisky and went on making nervous, trivial remarks one after another.

He had seen Helen at the very moment of his arrival in the roof garden—or rather, he had seen nothing but Helen. She was standing with a group of Englishmen and ladies at the railing surrounding the roof and listening to the observations of a lean, gray-haired man, Sir Henry Kingsdale-Smith, who was sweeping the river and the panorama below with a pair of field glasses and discoursing with outstretched palms. Then he took the strap from his neck and gave the glasses to Helen. She adjusted them with a smile and obediently looked at the warships in the river.

Frank had instinctively sat down with his back to this group, which in any case was separated from him by many tables, umbrellas and people. Nevertheless the delicate edges of his shapely ears began to burn, and he talked without ceasing in order to drown something that no one heard but himself.

"What is extraterritoriality?" Ruth asked. "Everyone is talking about it, and I feel so stupid."

"Extraterritoriality—as long as it lasts—is the contracted right of foreign nations to settle in certain districts or cities and to submit only to the laws and judiciary of their own country. If you had any notion what happens in Chinese courts and prisons, you would understand that nothing else is possible. But the Chinese behave as if our privileges were nothing but boils on their bodies. Is that right, Madame?" Frank explained, much too long-windedly. It's like a stinging nettle, he thought as he felt Helen's eyes on the back of his neck.

"The affair is quite otherwise," Madame said. "Originally extra-territoriality was not a privilege but a humiliation for the foreigners. The Chinese were too proud to permit the barbarians to live in their towns. Foreigners had to settle outside in marshy, disgusting places which were rigidly demarked, and the Chinese officials would have nothing to do with them and their legal disputes. That is how Shanghai commenced. Naturally now they are sorry, and they complain loudly and bitterly."

"How interesting," Ruth said, looking at a woman who was standing behind Frank's chair.

"I always thought that——" Frank said and then stopped speaking. Helen's perfume had struck him like a blow on the head.

"Good afternoon, Frank. Good afternoon, Madame Tissaud."

She was wearing a short white dress and holding her hat in her hand. Her hair was rather disheveled, as though she had run her hands through it, as though she had come through a storm, as though she had just left a lover. Frank cursed his heart that had begun to beat so loudly that Ruth must surely hear it. "Good afternoon, Frank," Helen said. "Good afternoon," Frank said. Madame Tissaud thoroughly enjoyed the situation. She joyfully took it on herself to introduce the women to one another.

"Mrs Russell, may I introduce Mademoiselle Ruth to you—the little fiancée of our friend? We marry on Saturday—we drive to Soochow, we pass a honeymoon in a houseboat—I cannot help myself, I find marriage something enchanting. Will you not sit down with us, Mrs Russell?"

"For one moment," Helen said. "I must go back to my party. Sir Henry is a tyrant, and he is going to drag us off to a frightful cocktail party. There's something cannibalistic about the English colony here, don't you think? At least I feel as if I were being devoured alive."

Thereupon Helen sat down beside Ruth and looked at her with desperate amiability.

"I am so glad to make your acquaintance," she said. "Frank has told me a lot about you."

"Mrs Russell and Monsieur Frank are great friends," Madame put in, kindling with joy over the situation. Frank put his empty glass to his lips with a hand which he could only with the greatest effort restrain from trembling. It escaped Ruth's notice, but it did not escape Helen's.

"Frank has been very kind and acted as guide for my husband and me once or twice," she told Ruth. "It is true that Bobbie has taken a great fancy to Frank. It's odd because as a rule he can't stand Americans."

"Mr Russell is the brother of Lord Inglewood," Madame said in explanation. Ruth made a little respectful bow to Helen, she was deeply impressed that Frank had such smart friends.

"How did you enjoy the voyage?" Helen asked.

"Very much," Ruth answered.

"And how do you like Shanghai?" Helen went on merely for the sake of saying something.

"I haven't seen very much of it yet," Ruth said. She thought hard, for she would have liked to say something intelligent. "Frank has given me a little duckling, it's sweet. It's called Confucius," she announced.

"How charming," Helen said in a brittle voice. And now she looked Frank straight in the face, and her pupils suddenly went so large that her eyes grew quite dark. "On Saturday then——" she said. It sounded as if she were alone with him. As Frank made no reply, there was a brief silence.

"Waiter!" Frank called. "Another whisky. What will you have?" he asked Helen.

"A bathful of ice," she said instantly. Ruth laughed politely.

"What a wonderful perfume you have, Mrs Russell," she said with a clumsy effort to avoid a second silence.

"Do you think so?" Helen asked casually. "I have it made for me in Paris. There's a chemist there who has invented individual scents; perfume with a monogram, he calls it. At first he looks at you, then he pays you a few visits and talks to you, and when he feels he has grasped your personality, he concocts your perfume for you. Very snob, don't you think?"

"The things they do nowadays——" Ruth said.

Helen looked at Frank even while she talked to Ruth. "If you like I'll gladly give you some of mine," she said. "Though I don't really think we're a bit alike. But contrast lends enchantment, doesn't it, Frank?"

"Men understand nothing of these subtleties," Madame Tissaud said in reply. Frank shuddered when he thought that Helen's scent would rise between him and Ruth like an invisible, exciting and heartbreaking ghost.

As though in answer to his thoughts Helen said: "How is it there is nothing so sad as a perfume or an old gramophone record which reminds one of some scene or some person!"

Ruth asked politely: "Do you live in Shanghai or are you on a visit here, Mrs Russell?"

"We are passengers," Helen said. "We are vagabonds and gypsies. We don't stay long anywhere. Instead of making friendships we collect addresses of people to whom we send picture postcards. We know the best hotel in every town, the English colony and the streets where the brothels are, for they are always considered one of the sights. You're always left with a little foreign change that you can't get rid of, and Clarkson collects it to take home. Clarkson is my lady's maid. My head is just like her purse, nothing but rubbish. A little rubbish from every country that I can't get rid of. No, we're not staying long. If you'll give me your address, Frank, I'll send you a postcard too, for Christmas perhaps. I mean your new address. I have the old one somewhere. Yes, I really ought to wear the sort of ribbon you see on funeral wreaths. Good-by until we meet again —isn't that what it always says?"

She broke off, for as she spoke she felt a flood of tears rising in her.

"I think I'd like some vodka," she said softly to Frank.

"Waiter, a vodka," he called, "and another whisky."

Ruth had listened with astonishment and awe. I'd give my little finger to be able to say such interesting things, she thought, overcome with modesty.

"We're going to have a very quiet wedding," she said. "Mrs Scott is going to arrange it in her garden, the ceremony, lunch and everything—only a few friends. If you are still here on Saturday and if it wouldn't bore you, will you please give us the pleasure?"

"Thank you. I know how to value such a mark of friendship," Helen replied with an irony that wounded only herself. Madame Tissaud relished all this from the bottom of her heart. Frank pulled out his handkerchief, first rubbed his hands and then wiped his forehead.

"Where is Mr Russell?" Madame asked to change the subject.

"He's writing a letter to his mother, and that is always a very grave ceremony," Helen said. "But he can't be long now. He gets a telepathic shock the moment the bar opens."

"He likes to gad about with the little pianist, is it not?" Madame asked. Helen looked at her with raised eyebrows as though to ask: Do you know that already? Frank felt about under the table for

Ruth's hand, for he needed it to hold onto something. Ruth didn't notice.

He wanted her hand because he was sorry for her, because she was so diminutive and unsuspecting, because she sat there like a child who wanted to play and did not know the rules of the game. Ruth beside Helen was like a glass of water beside an ocean, a little flower beside a jungle. So at least it seemed to Frank as he put out his hand to her. Everything about Helen was untamed and untamable and ravishing. Ruth can administer aspirin, and that's about all, he thought with the unjust bitterness of a man for the woman who belongs to him, while he has admiration only for the woman he can't have. At the moment when Madame Tissaud took pity on him and switched Helen off him, he felt like a drowning man who had come once more to the surface and taken a gulp of air, the last breath, before he perished. I cannot, cannot marry Ruth, he thought. I cannot give up Helen. It is not possible. I cannot do it. Already Helen's eyes rested on him again, appealing, tender and pathetic. Across the table with all its glasses, cigarettes and plates, among all these people in the roof garden, beneath Ruth's very eyes, their eyes embraced each other, shamelessly, insatiably and despairingly.

"Here is Mr Murata," Ruth said, and in the goodness of her heart and with an instinct she could not repress she waved her hand to the little figure in white linen, although she remembered—too late— that Frank could not stand him.

Murata was hesitating at the door which opened from the staircase onto the roof garden, and he was looking all round in bewilderment through his thick spectacles.

"Every table is taken," a waiter said as he flitted by. Murata smiled his best Japanese smile. It was just at this moment that Ruth beckoned him, and he gratefully made his way towards them. Another waiter, running past, splashed his white suit with strawberry ice without apology. Murata looked pitifully small and embarrassed as he zealously approached the table on his short bandy legs. And although Ruth was sorry she had beckoned him, she could not help having come into the world with an ineradicable instinct for all that was sick, weak and helpless.

"This is Mr Murata. Hello, Mr Murata!"

"Hello, Miss Anderson. Hello, Mr Taylor," Murata said. "I hope I cause no inconvenience," he said as he pulled a chair forward and sat down. No one had invited him to do so. Ruth looked beseechingly at Frank and distractedly at Mrs Russell. It occurred to her too late that the English were possessed by a devouring racial pride.

Mr Murata looked at them all one after another. He had many Japanese, smiling teeth and no eyes whatever—only a reflection of the late-afternoon sun in his rounded lenses.

"Hullo, Jelena," he said.

Helen Russell inspected him coldly. He put a black attaché case on the table in front of him. "Where have we met before?" she asked the Japanese. "In Paris," Mr Murata said. "Don't you remember Yoshio, Jelena?"

"It is very difficult for Europeans to distinguish one Japanese face from another," Helen said almost insultingly. "Probably the difficulty is mutual. And I think you have made some mistake, Mr Murata."

"There are faces which one cannot ever forget, Jelena," Murata said in discouragement. "I am Yoshio. We have read Rimbaud together. 'Le Dormeur du val.' Do you not remember? My God, Paris —Rimbaud! *Les parfums ne font pas frissonner sa narine; il dort dans le soleil, la main sur sa poitrine tranquille. Il a deux trous rouges au côté droit.'* That you cannot have forgotten, Jelena. Even if my insignificant person has vanished from your recollection."

He folded his hands on his black case. They all looked at him in astonishment. In the sudden stillness at their table the music was suddenly audible again, playing the great waltz from *The Merry Widow;* and from the street far below, eighteen stories down but shrilly and loudly all the same, came the cries of Chinese children selling the English evening papers.

X

YOSHIO MURATA HAD A BAD DAY behind him and arrived at the roof garden of the Shanghai Hotel in a state of perplexity and perspiration, for by birth and breeding he was retiring, modest and reserved. Yet it was on him, the weak and colorless survivor of a brother whose death made him all the more a shining light, that the events of the day had laid a task that compelled him to behave badly and to say impossible and tactless things. He concealed his shame and helplessness behind his spectacles, his smile and the lines of a French poem. Yoshio Murata had come to Shanghai with instructions to go to the Shanghai Hotel where a room had been reserved for him and then to repair to a certain Noboru Endo in Pinghi Street in Yangtze Po, from whom he would receive further orders; but everything had started badly and got worse and worse as the day went on and evening descended.

He had arrived at the Shanghai Hotel that morning with his suitcases, but nobody seemed to want to be bothered with him, and the Chinese page boys hurried past him as though busied over more important guests. So at last he carried his luggage himself through the lounge and put it down on the stone floor in front of the reception clerk's long counter. He took out his fountain pen in order to enter his name, but the reception clerk, an oily Greek, said at once, "Sorry, sir, we have no rooms free."

"My editorial office has engaged a room for me by telegram," Yoshio said with irritation even though smilingly. "My name is Yoshio Murata, of the *Morning Sun* of Tokyo. Please consult your reservations."

"Sorry," the Greek said. "We cannot make any reservations. The whole hotel is full. Perhaps you might try the Myako." He left Yoshio where he was and turned to a small stout woman who seemed to consist entirely of silk bows and spoke Spanish. He gave her a room.

Yoshio swallowed the insult outwardly smiling but boiling inside. The Myako was a second-class hotel near the North Station, patronized by insignificant Japanese commercial travelers. "Where is the telephone?" he asked a junior clerk who was lounging behind the counter and examining his nails. "Beside the elevator," he said without paying him any attention. Yoshio waited outside the telephone booth until a young and very smart Chinese woman had concluded her conversation; the booth was pervaded by her scent when at last he was able to get into it. He put his notebook with Mr Noboru Endo's address in it in front of him, and after some searching he found Mr Endo's telephone number also. There were an astounding number of Endos in Shanghai. He said the number over to himself with the coin in his hand and first leaned against the wall and sighed deeply. He was one of those ill-fitted people who are afraid of the telephone. As he always expected complications whenever he made a call, complications always arose. He shouted the number desperately into the mouthpiece, could not understand the instructions given him in a high-pitched Chinese voice, and put the money in at the wrong moment. Nothing happened. He had to begin all over again and endure the same torture a second time. He was not surprised that it did not go right, for even in Tokyo telephoning was no simple matter. It seemed to him that he had been in the booth for hours and still nothing happened, while outside more and more people collected in front of the glazed door waiting to telephone. A bearded elderly gentleman of French appearance lost his temper and drummed on the glass. Yoshio conducted his conversation to this accompaniment and could scarcely understand the replies he received.

"My unworthy name is Murata, Yoshio Murata, of the *Morning Sun,* Tokyo. I have been directed to you, honored Mr Endo. I am to receive further instructions from you. I was to stay at the Shanghai Hotel, but they will not give me a room. What shall I do now? . . . What? What was your honored reply? I cannot understand your honored voice . . . The Myako? Good. I will take a room in the Myako Hotel and then give myself the honor of calling upon you in your honored office. Thank you, thank you."

He was hot and flushed when he emerged. I look like a drunkard, he thought with annoyance, as he caught sight of his face in a mirror. It looked bloated. His suitcases were still in front of the reception desk. Nobody seemed to want to carry them for him. He picked them up himself and beat a retreat.

He stood outside the revolving door of the hotel with his suitcases beside him on the sidewalk; several taxis drove by without stopping. A little Chinese newspaper boy of extraordinarily filthy appearance spat so skillfully that he hit Yoshio's white trousers. He felt ill with nausea, his stomach rose into his throat, and he choked it back with great effort of self-control. China was a country that physically nauseated him; the dirt, the stench, the seething disorder of the streets. At last a taxi drew up and consented to take him on his way. "Myako Hotel," he said. He was not very well up in pidgin English, although he knew whole pages of Byron as well as Lao-tse by heart. It took a long time before the taxi driver understood him, and finally the hotel porter had to intervene before he could get off. They left the International Settlement and went through crowded streets of small dirty shops to the North Station. There in a side street was the Myako Hotel.

They consented to give him a room but with ill-humor, and not a trace of Japanese politeness showed itself in the behavior of the manager or even of the servants who at last relieved him of his suitcases.

"As ill-mannered as Americans," he thought irritably. It always struck him on his voyages how quickly his fellow countrymen lost the refinement of manner which distinguished them in their own country.

The air in his room was suffocating and the furniture shoddy. He turned on the electric fan, but after a few reluctant revolutions it stopped again. He opened the door onto the wooden veranda that ran round the building. Two Japanese businessmen were sitting there, fanning themselves and conversing pessimistically.

"The war party ought to be isolated," one of them was saying. "They are hotheads, an unbalanced lot of fellows, who plunge the country into war so that they can distinguish themselves and get promotion. The navy at least used to keep their heads. Now it has come to this, that the army and navy compete with each other which can shoot off most guns——"

"All the same, all the same, my honored friend, you must admit that Japan cannot look on while our goods are boycotted. This persecution of us by the Chinese must be broken, if necessary by punitive measures."

"The boycott exists only on paper; that's why we're in China. They write and make speeches and summon assemblies and hang out placards and then they are satisfied. It never gets as far as action. Do you happen to be acquainted with the honored figures of Japanese exports to China during the past year?"

"You are right in many respects, honored sir. Yet it remains to be seen whether flyfly-eggs are good propaganda for our trade."

"For a third of the money which a campaign costs one could buy up all the northern provinces. But the young officers want glory, not profit."

Yoshio shut the door again. The air outside was no better. The pidgin name for bombs had told him that the two were long acquainted with Shanghai. He was not inquisitive about their opinions. They said what everyone in Japan thought in silence. As a journalist he could make no use of such stuff on account of the censorship; it was also too obvious to be interesting.

The Myako was not sufficiently up to date to provide a private bathroom, so he went along the dark passage in his kimono to find the public bathroom. The shower at first refused to work and then came down with a sudden rush on top of him before he had time to undress. This was his second bath that morning, for though he had only just arrived he felt as dirty as a Chinese; and after this he went back shivering in his wet kimono to his room. When he had dressed again he inspected himself in the looking glass and felt a little more cheerful. He was eager to know what the mission was he was to be entrusted with. He had learned a lot in the Manchurian war. He hoped he was going to be sent to the North again to report for his paper.

This time he got a taxi right away, for the hotel was connected with a Japanese garage. "Does the honored fare choose to be in Shanghai for the first time?" the driver asked with the impetuous curiosity of the common people. "No? Arrived with ship today? What do they think in honored Tokyo about honored war?" He politely drew his breath between his teeth in order not to annoy his honored fare with his unworthy breath. With his head turned round to converse inquisitively, he drove his vehicle through the crowded, hurrying traffic of the midday streets. Yoshio would have preferred it if he had kept his attention on the streets instead of on his fare, but the man seemed to suffer from homesickness and wanted to savor all the news from home at first hand. He came from the village of Okami, near Kyoto, and his stupid parents were still living, as he said. His stupid wife and two stupid daughters lived and worked in Pootung on the other bank. Every night he had to cross by the ferryboat. But what could he do?

Noboru Endo was a small, quick-witted, alert gentleman with gray hair and mustache. The name of a large Japanese insurance company stood in gilt letters on his door. Inside there were shelves of cardboard boxes which presumably contained trade samples. Mr Endo made the merest suggestion of three bows and with that the ceremonies were over. Yoshio, who was expecting to find himself in some sort of editorial office, looked round in surprise.

"Have you already dined? . . . No? I recommend Fuji for fish and Shigoyama for chicken, or perhaps you prefer Western cooking? I myself worship the French cuisine," Mr Endo said rapidly. He clapped his hands, and a good-looking boy of about thirteen brought English tea. From Mr Endo's speech and movements Yoshio could tell that he was a man of education, but he appeared to have jettisoned all wearisome, ceremonious locutions and came very straight to the point.

"The commission I have for you is not journalistic but rather—how shall I express it?—of a personal nature," he said, rubbing his quick little hands. "I am of course vaguely connected with your honored newspaper, but that is only in the way of business; it has to do with trade in China, not with the literary side. It is true in my youth I could compose a poem now and again, but the prose of life has taken this gift from me. Well now, to come to the point, my honored Mr Murata——"

Without concluding his remark Mr Endo went to a large iron safe in a corner which he opened with many turns of the secret lock. "Do your honored activities concern themselves with insurances?" Yoshio asked in order to bridge the pause.

"Among other things," Mr Endo replied. "I am concerned with insurances among other things. But I have more important tasks as well." He took a black leather case out of the safe and, putting it down in front of him on his desk, he looked Yoshio Murata straight in the eye. "I do my best as far as my inadequate and modest resources permit to be of use to our country," he said.

Yoshio drank his tea. "Do you smoke?" Mr Endo asked. "Of course you smoke. I must beg you to excuse me. As I do not smoke myself I always forget in this idiotic way to offer my friends cigarettes."

He pushed a packet of Japanese Cherry cigarettes across to Yoshio and lit a match for him.

"I understand that after the death of your very highly honored brother you put yourself at the service of the cause?" Mr Endo next said. And at the mention of the deceased Kitaro, he rose from his chair in order to make a bow.

"It was his wish," Yoshio said. He could never think of Kitaro without feeling an odd tinge of bitterness. Senseless as Kitaro's death had been, it had all the same shed great and romantic glory on him. While Kitaro lived, he had been the handsomer and the more brilliant of the two—the younger brother but the son of the more dearly loved wife. Yoshio had loved his brother, and so it had been easy for him to be overshadowed by him. Now that Kitaro was no longer there to blunt the edge of jealousy by the charm of his presence, Yoshio sometimes felt this tinge of bitterness. The dead lived much more vigorously and vehemently and exactingly than the living. Yoshio had had to take on responsibilities in which he himself did not believe. The holy suicide with the ancestral sword had turned a childish, ill-considered affair that was injurious to his country into something for which the survivors had to stand up. It was as though Yoshio since Kitaro's death had lost the right to live his own life and had to carry on his brother's which had been left uncompleted.

Nothing of this could be put into words. It was something of which he could never speak.

"May I know what the commission is?" he asked.

Mr Endo sat opposite him and looked keenly at him. There was a pause. The electric fans hummed in the hot air.

"You are fairly well acquainted with the honorable Mrs Russell?" he asked finally; it sounded casual and conversational.

"No, that must be a mistake," Yoshio answered in amazement. Again the elder man looked hard at him, and his eyes seemed to point between Yoshio's brows like a finger. "We have had a report from Tokyo that you met and spoke to Mrs Russell at a flower show and that you were later seen with her again in the bar of the Hotel Imperial. The conversations you had with her gave the impression that you knew the lady well."

"Oh—that was Jelena," Yoshio said with an obliging smile. "I did not think of asking the name of her husband. What is she called now? Russell?"

"Jelena, that's right," Mr Endo said. "Jelena Trubova before her various marriages. Now Helen Russell. It is correct, then, that you have known this Jelena Trubova for some years and known her well? Was it in Paris?"

"Has this anything to do with the orders I am to receive?" Yoshio asked politely and smilingly but with discomfort. His two encounters with Jelena in Tokyo had been not only accidental but somewhat humiliating. She had greeted him politely and graciously, although she had obviously not recognized him. She was the only European woman he had ever known intimately, and she meant a lot in his life. Sometimes he blamed her for the fact that his own wife seemed boring and uninteresting to him. Sometimes he suspected that the strange emptiness of his life might have something to do with her, even though he could not say exactly why. He had given her a stiff silver green robe which had once belonged to a princess of the old Imperial Court. But she, it was clear, had no recollection of him, and he meant nothing to her. He sat up erect and put his hands flat on the table. Involuntarily they took the position he had learned as a child from his grandfather.

"In one word, the point is that this Mrs Russell is an English agent," Mr Endo said.

"Oh——" Yoshio said.

"We were convinced that you knew nothing about it. On the other hand your previous acquaintance with the lady makes you particularly fitted for the simple task we entrust to you and which, though entirely without danger, will bring you great credit. No doubt the personal pleasure you will have in carrying it out will be sufficient reward."

Mr Endo looked at Yoshio with a knowing smile. Yoshio took a second cigarette immediately after stubbing out the first in the ash tray.

"This Mrs Russell or Jelena Trubova, whichever you choose to call her, sends written reports to the military secret service in Whitehall. She does it in a dilettante manner as a sport. For the English, you know, sport is everything. Mrs Russell is immensely rich and has married into a family of political importance. It is creditable to her that she does not send these reports for money. Now, we think it advisable that her reports should be in our favor."

"I understand," Yoshio said. In fact he understood nothing whatever.

Mr Endo snapped the lock of the attaché case open and shut again and pushed it over to Yoshio.

"In this attaché case there are drawings and plans we have made, and we want Mrs Russell to send them to London," he said, stroking and patting the case as though it were a living thing. Mr Endo had a flexible and elastic apelike mouth which he pursed when he was particularly pleased. Yoshio tried to get used to this new and unexpected situation in which he found himself.

"And what have I to do about it?" he asked.

"It is the simplest thing in the world. You meet Mrs Russell in a friendly way by chance as in Tokyo. The Russells are staying at the Shanghai Hotel, as you may suppose. It is a pity that they could not give you a room; at the moment there are so many curious undercurrents in this town. But all the same there will be plenty of opportunities of meeting the lady by accident. It would, in fact, be a matter of difficulty to avoid an encounter at tea or in the bar or in the lounge. Well then, you meet Mrs Russell, you are astonished and enchanted. You resume the old friendly relations. You hint that you are in Shanghai on an important secret mission. Mrs Russell will then do the rest; we can rely on that. She will see a lot of you. She will try to wheedle things out of you; you will not require much dramatic talent to convince her that you have no secrets from her. You will let her see that this attaché case contains documents of great importance. Mrs Russell will then steal it from you. She will copy the sketches and plans and send the copies to London and restore the attaché case to you on some innocent pretext. You will pretend to have noticed nothing. She will seal your old friendship with a few cocktails in the bar of the Shanghai Hotel. That will be the end. Then you can return to Tokyo or you may remain here in case anything of journalistic interest may turn up. I hope this mission will give you pleasure."

Yoshio had followed these glib instructions with a puzzled frown. "I am a clumsy, awkward person, and I don't know whether I shall be able to carry it out to your satisfaction, but on the whole it does not sound as if it would be difficult," he said uncertainly.

"There is one difficulty about it, a little difficulty which I cannot conceal from you," Mr Endo said. "You have not much time left. We have reason to believe that Mr and Mrs Russell will leave Shanghai the moment a gun is fired. So you have only—shall we say?—a week. Probably not even a week. Take the attaché case with you. I would recommend that you take steps this very day to renew your relations with Mrs Russell. How far you choose to let them go is entirely your own affair."

Endo laughed cynically as a man of the world, and Yoshio politely joined in. "I don't know whether my modest understanding is sufficient," he murmured irresolutely. "I am only a stupid person and quite without talent."

Mr Endo took this as the usual polite formula and put the attaché case in Yoshio's hands. "You will see," he said. "It is more amusing than poker. Do they still play as much poker as ever in the newspaper offices? Another cigarette? . . . No? Some more tea? You must be hungry. Remember Fuji for fish and Shigoyama for chicken. My sincere wishes for the happy outcome of the enterprise. You will telephone me about your progress? No names, of course. We might say, for example: the chrysanthemum blooms. Good, good. Come again soon and be cautious. *Arigato goseimas.*"

Smiles and bows, and Yoshio stood once more in the street with an attaché case full of forged plans under his arm and in a state of complete bewilderment. If only I had been sent to the front, he thought unhappily. The more he thought of his task, the less capable he felt of carrying it out.

The taxi drivers in this district were not so hostile to the Japanese as they were in Nanking Road. "The Shanghai Hotel," he said despondently. On the way he bought every newspaper that was on sale. The foreign papers were cautious and marked time. The Chinese ones burst out in manifestoes and bombastic threats. We have put the enemy to flight, sword in hand. It is a fight to the last drop of our blood. China for the Chinese. No peace so long as a soldier remains alive. Our mighty air force. The unconquerable Nineteenth Route Army. . . . Just the same as at home, Yoshio thought. He put the papers on the seat beside him and shut his eyes in order to think better. He must have some plan before he met Jelena. Did she, he wondered, still wear the green-and-silver kimono he had given her in Paris? The tender green of the stiff old silk of the court dress from Kyoto on the white-skinned, red-haired woman. He quickly opened his eyes to obliterate the picture and unlocked the case to look inside. He understood nothing of the plans in red and blue Indian ink and still less of the notes, which consisted of figures. He read some of the vertical Japanese lines along the edge, but they had no meaning for him. Code ciphers, he thought with passing interest. He toyed with the idea of finding the key and gave it up. The taxi had arrived at the Shanghai Hotel. He left the newspapers where they were and got out, and for the second time that day he confronted the ironical Greek across the reception desk. This time

he was informed that Mrs Russell was out. He insisted on speaking
to her maid. "You can ask Miss Clarkson," the reception clerk said.
"Her number is 1852."

Once more Yoshio went to the telephone booth, and once more
people gathered impatiently outside. A duel took place between
his and Clarkson's English accent in which his was victorious. He
left the hotel again and now had a meal in some little café with a
French name and uninteresting food. He wrote a picture postcard
to his wife on the marble top of the table and forgot to post it.
Somehow he managed to spend the hours until the time which
Clarkson had vaguely indicated for her mistress' return. For the
third time Yoshio Murata presented himself in the Shanghai Hotel.
This time it seemed possible that Mrs Russell might be with Sir
Henry Kingsdale-Smith's party on the roof garden. He sighed deeply
as he entered the lift.

He was a pacifist on the war path. All alone, without guns, warships or bombs, he fought his way into the hostile and worldly roof
garden on the heights of the fortress whose name was the Shanghai
Hotel.

XI

LUNG YEN GOT HOME TIRED, wet and happy after marching for hours
with the Scouts who were being shown the town. It was only when
a cloudburst descended and they ran hurriedly in little groups to the
station and got into the train from Hongkew to Kiangwan that
he decided to make his way home. The wet streets suddenly seemed
to him very empty in the pelting rain. Three lorry loads of soldiers
drove noisily past him. Perhaps the war has already begun. Yen
reflected, with his fragmentary knowledge of the world. The soldiers
were dirty as soldiers always were. The child soldiers on the other
hand, one of whom was Yen's son, had looked so clean that it almost
frightened him. It was a pity that Lung the tailor and his family
were already asleep when he reached the house, for he would have
liked to tell them that his son had already arrived. He made his way

cautiously between their beds and reached his room without waking anybody up.

Before lying down to sleep he once more examined the little automobile and set it going. It seemed to him that it ran rather more slowly than before. Perhaps, he thought with a smile, it is tired at night, as a coolie who has had to run all day. He wiped his face with his handkerchief and took off his wet shoes. He looked with dissatisfaction at the mosquito net round the bed. It was unwashed and gray, almost black in many places, and the holes were not mended. The air within it smelled old and stale. Since Yen had seen these alarmingly clean child soldiers he had new eyes for dirt. But when he cautiously removed the net, he discovered with joy that the tailor's wife had spread a clean linen coverlet on the bed, and he decided to sleep on the floor so that the bed might remain clean for his son. Besides, he was not used to sleeping in a bed, and it had occurred to him that his sleeplessness during the last few nights might be due to that. But although he crouched in his usual manner with knees drawn up, as he did between the shafts of his ricksha, long hours went by before he could fall asleep. He heard the drums, he saw the young faces under their wide hats, and he thought about the meeting with his son. It was not until dawn seeped in gray streaks through the shutters that sleep overcame him.

When he woke up it took some time before he knew where he was. He felt for the shafts before his eyes were even open and jumped to his feet as usual. The polite cough of the tailor's wife outside the door brought him back to the room which he was to share with his son. He was bathed in sweat, as though sleep had been severe toil, and he quickly wiped himself with his towel. Then he opened the door. The kindly old lady stood outside with a cup of tea in her hand.

"Ten thousand happy years," she said benignly. "I have brought you some tea to make a good beginning to a good day."

Yen thanked her and, taking the cup in both hands, drank down its welcome warmth. He rolled up his new clothes in a bundle, for he did not want to dress until he had had a bath. He stowed his son s present away in the middle of the bundle. He carried his money, the letter and the precious directions in the red envelope in his belt. "This evening I shall come back with my stupid young son so that he can greet my friends," he said before he went. Although it had not been said in words, it was an understood thing that the tailor's family would make no allusion to Yen's lowly position and undignified circumstances.

Yen walked quickly; it was a beautiful morning with freshness in the air, and the streets were washed by the rain of the previous night. He breathed the coolness deeply and did not have to cough. At first he went to the baths, which were not far away. The building was cleaner and wider inside than a temple, and Yen was somewhat embarrassed. "A big hot bath for myself alone," he demanded nevertheless. A man with a red face and stripped to the waist showed him into a room where there was a long, large modern bath of porcelain and filled it with steaming water that came out of the wall.

"Soap also?"

"Do you think I am a pig that I can bathe without soap?" Yen asked grandly; and the man put a towel and a small piece of green soap on the wooden stool by the wall. Yen was left alone with his princely bath. The soap had a sweet and pleasant smell, and he washed himself all over with it, hoping that the smell would stick to him. He played with the lather on his body and looked down at himself to see whether his three days of idleness and good feeding had made him any fatter. It seemed to him that he was a little fatter, fat enough at least to make a favorable impression on his son. He dipped the towel in the hot water and wrung it out and rubbed himself down with it until his blood began to tingle. Then he unrolled his bundle of clothes and dressed slowly and luxuriously.

It was the first time in his life he had known the feel of silk against his skin—for of course he could not remember the red silk frock which he had worn at the feast of his third month. He tied his trousers securely at the ankles, put the waistcoat on over his robe, put on his hat and took the present under his arm. He had not even forgotten a new paper fan, a red one in token of joy. And now, when he was about to roll up his old dirty rags with his freshly washed hands, he felt sickened. They were dirty and full of lice, and with a sudden impulse of megalomania Yen kicked them into a corner.

"You can keep my clothes," he called out to the half-naked man when he came across him in the passage. In the elation of that morning it occurred to Yen that this crazy deed had been an economy, for there was no necessity now to give the man a tip.

As soon as he was in the street he found that he was unaccustomed to walking in a long robe, but he soon observed that the enforced gravity of his progress lent him dignity. He made his way to a barber's shop where two small Korean women acted as barbers. He had his hair washed and cut in a becoming manner, and he also had his ears and nostrils cleaned. The women were adroit and also extremely polite, which showed him that his clothes made the right impression. He held his present in its paper wrapping clasped to him the whole time. Two other men were sitting on chairs—one of them a coolie, as he had still been yesterday, the other an old man with spectacles, who was reading a paper while he waited.

"It says here that Japanese warships are on the way to bombard Shanghai," the old man said. "Now I do not believe that. Why should the people from the North flee here, if there is going to be war here, too? The newspapers always want to have something new to tell."

"War is good for trade," the coolie said from beneath the hot towel which the younger of the two Korean girls was holding to his face. Yen wondered why business should be better in war and what sort of business a coolie like that carried on. "I hope," he said, "there will be no war this week, for my son has come to the town with many child soldiers. The government would not send children here if they were going to start a war."

The old man looked up at him without making any reply; Yen paid, gave the Korean girl a tip that corresponded to his fine clothes and went. He had made up his mind to have his morning rice in the restaurant near the markets and to take the opportunity of reminding the proprietor once more of the dinner he had ordered and paid a deposit for. As he walked along the streets it occurred to him that new posters and regulations were posted up in many places. Also men were standing at corners and in doorways engaging in conversation with anyone who had the time to stop. Yen had neither the time nor the wish that day.

Lung Yen was very hungry that morning, and he told himself that the foreign Old Doctor had done his inside good with his needle. I shall go to him every second day as the lady told me to do, he thought. It costs nothing and is almost as comforting as the Great Smoke. He ate three bowls of rice and drank three cups of tea; then he rinsed his mouth at a public fountain and was ready to go and find his son. He had still five small and two large silver coins in the little linen bag in his belt, and he didn't quite know what had happened to all the rest of the money.

He got onto the suburban tram from Hongkew, and this time it did not make him sick; on the contrary, the swiftness and ease with which the vehicle shot along amused him. It was really as if the expensive silk clothes possessed a charm and the hostile spirits concealed in the air were afraid of him. I cannot understand how it happens that rich people in silk clothing are unkind and even rude, Lung Yen thought to himself. In clothes like these I would always smile and be kind to everybody.

Lost in these benevolent thoughts, he arrived at Kiangwan and the Civic Center. Fortunately he knew the neighborhood, for he had often taken foreigners out there, groaning and panting with the long run. There were many people about, and banners were waving everywhere from poles, which looked gay and festive. Street vendors were selling all kinds of wares, sweet, colored ice, candies, melon seeds and sugar cane, mangoes and colored rice cakes. Lung Yen bought himself a bag of melon seeds and took the note in its red envelope out of his purse and began politely asking the crowd to make way for him.

It was a good thing he was wearing his costly clothes; otherwise he would never have arrived at his goal, and when he at last reached the main building that looked to him like an emperor's palace he was directed from one man to another, from floor to floor and from door to door. The silk began to make him sweat, and he was sorry that he had left his towel at home from sheer pride. He went up aloft in an elevator while his stomach remained below. And then he came down again and his stomach hovered above him in the air. In spite of this he did not feel really bad and he did not have to cough. At last a very fine and jolly young man took charge of him and conducted him along a wide echoing passage into which the sun streamed through immense windows.

"You want to know in which barrack your son is accommodated, old gentleman?" the young man asked politely. "Nothing is simpler. The committee has everything arranged. Step in here, if you please." He opened a door and showed Lung Yen in. He made Lung Yen go first. He was a young and fine gentleman, an official, a man of the highest position, and he addressed Lung Yen as a gentleman, bowed to him and made him precede him through the door. Lung Yen sighed deeply for joy in his silks.

The sun was at its zenith and the stone horses of Kiangwan cast short shadows as Lung Yen finally arrived at the large swimming pool where he had been directed and where a swimming contest was just going on.

He had to pay ten cents to get in, and in spite of this large expenditure he found himself quite at the back and high up on the terraced benches which were nearly all occupied by shouting, gesticulating and extraordinarily happy people. As soon as Lung Yen had settled down in his seat and looked about him, he found out what was the reason of all the shouting. Far below him there was a large greenish patch of water into which group after group of boys were diving and swimming away faster than fishes. Lung Yen opened his mouth wide with astonishment; and he too shouted when he had to look on while their bodies shot from great heights into the water. But he went dumb and became cold inside with fear when it occurred to him that one of these madly reckless swimmers might be his son. In his agitation he began to nibble his melon seeds and to spit out the black husks. This was only doing as his neighbors did, who for the most part were young and noisy. All the time a great voice out of great loud-speakers announced things which Lung Yen did not understand in the least. After a considerable time a bugle signal was given and the people on the benches got up and streamed out. "What happens now? Are the games ended? Do the young men go back to their dwellings?" Lung Yen asked his neighbor, who looked at him contemptuously. "Never been here before?" he asked roughly, but when Lung Yen told him very loftily that his son was taking part in the performances, his neighbor looked rather small. "Come with me, old sir, it's in the arena next," he said and pushed his way between the rows of benches. Lung Yen followed him. Once more he sat high up, far from the sand of the arena, and once more he understood nothing. Banners waved from lofty poles with inscriptions which he unfortunately could not read. Boys marched in troops far below, then they extended all over the arena, and it looked like a pattern on silk, white and black on a grayish-yellow ground. The pattern changed as all the thousand children carried out the same movements. There was a roaring above the arena and a topside ricksha appeared in the sky that wanted to look on, too. Lung Yen had finished his melon seeds and began to long for a cigarette. Again, as on the evening before, he kept thinking: One of them is my son. He is one of those boys. One of those is my son. But the children were so far away that he could not have discerned his son even if he had known what he looked like.

Hours passed and the sun got lower. Two beautiful small clouds came sailing over the blue of the sky and veiled the sun for a time while their edges grew radiant, and then they let it free again. Lung Yen was feeling thirsty and bought a piece of colored ice on a stick and held it with relief against his parched tongue. He paid five coppers for it. One of those boys down below is my son, he thought without ceasing.

As the afternoon wore on and got cooler, Lung Yen began to feel worried, as he had before over the swimmers. The boys were insufficiently clothed; he could see it even at that distance. They wore black shorts and white sleeveless jackets or shirts, things in any case that Lung Yen did not know the right name for, and which gave very little protection to their heated bodies. Labor and sweat were things Yen understood. I do not want my son to get the coughing of blood, he thought in distress. It got cooler and cooler, more clouds drifted up and then a light shower of sun-lit rain came down. The onlookers laughed and opened their umbrellas, the Chinese oiled-paper umbrellas as well as the silk ones of the foreign devils. Yen was bitterly grieved that he had not thought of bringing an umbrella to protect his costly raiment. But his neighbor, who had been eagerly talking to him and giving him many confusing explanations, now added to his kindnesses by making room for Yen under his umbrella. After a few minutes during which everybody laughed and moved closer together, the rain stopped and the games went on again below.

When the wrestling started, Lung Yen began to understand what was going on, for he had seen wrestlers before in the markets and in the New World, the Roof Theater in the Street-of-the-Great-Horses. But it was only when the running began that he was quite at home; running—that was his calling and his life.

"They start too fast," he said, and: "That lanky thin one will get in first, he carries no useless weight and he has a long stride."

He cheered with the crowd when the lanky thin one won. Yen's neighbor became attentive when he realized that he had a knowing fellow beside him. As soon as the next runners lined up for the start, he rattled the money in his pocket and asked: "Which one will you bet on?" Lung Yen studied the six boys. "I cannot decide before they start running," he answered warily, though he itched to bet and win some money. His cash in hand had vanished as though the sun had melted it. He had still to pay the seventy cents and a tip at the eating house and there were only seventy-four cents in his little linen bag. "It's too late by the time they start," his neighbor said. Lung Yen took stock of the runners once more. It was difficult to size them up at that distance.

"The third one," he said.

"How much?" the other man asked, and to his astonishment Lung Yen heard himself say:

"Two small silver pieces."

Meanwhile the race had started, and Lung Yen drew in his breath when he saw that the third one had taken the lead. He was running at a regular easy pace and seemed to have plenty of wind. Lung Yen would have liked to think that this was his son, but he was an older boy than Seileong could be. Lung Yen got more and more excited as the runners got further round the circular track. He jumped up, waved his arms and shouted encouragement. If he lost his twenty cents he would not be able to invite his son to eat duck and fish in sour-sweet sauce; he would have to sacrifice his deposit and take him to a street kitchen where there was only rice and pork. But in the fever of gambling he did not think of this. It must have been the magic residing in his clothes that made a great man of him, a great man for one day.

The third boy won. His neighbor grumbled but took twenty cents out of his jingling purse and gave them to Yen.

"You seem to understand the business, sir," he said, and it did not sound like a compliment. But Lung Yen was now very intent, for the boys who came forward and lined up for the next race, bent their knees and touched the earth lightly with their fingers were young, and one of them, Lung Yen was certain, must be his son. He could scarcely breathe as he looked down the arena and searched the row for his son. No voice told him and no sign showed him which of the boys was of his blood and begotten to carry on the unbroken line of his family. The one on the outside was strong and well built, but he had a brown skin of the common people; the fourth was lighter built and his body was the color of a peach when the sun shines on it. Lung Yen sighed deeply, for he could not decide which of the two he would like to be his son. Then the pistol shot that started each race rang out and the boys shot forward.

"Too fast, too fast," Lung Yen cried out anxiously and let his hands fall. Used as he was to running long distances with his ricksha, he could not imagine that the boys had only a short distance to run. Neither the brown one nor the peach-colored one won; it was the smallest of them all, who with his head thrown back outdistanced the rest. Lung Yen instantly wished that this might be his son; but when the boy breasted the tape amid thunderous applause and immediately afterwards fell down exhausted, Lung Yen then hoped it was not his son. For he felt a pitying contempt for the boy who lay there on the sand with no breath left in his body.

The races went on and on, and Lung Yen was bathed in sweat by the time the loud-speakers announced that they were over, for he had taken too many of the competitors for his son. He had lived in each one and longed with clenched fists for him to win, and at last he was as tired as if he himself had run every race.

"It is over," his neighbor said and got up. Lung Yen stretched himself and pounded his legs, which were stiff from long sitting. "Your parcel, old sir," a woman called out after him, holding out his present. He had been so eager to identify his son that he had forgotten the precious and irreplaceable automobile in its paper wrapping. He clasped it to him once more, thanked the woman and went down the steps with the crowd. The paper was torn by now and did not look by any means so smart as at first, but the feel of the precious object, as he clasped it to his breast, filled Lung Yen with pride and joy all the same. He stood irresolutely in the crowd for a time and then hesitatingly set off again, for the moment had come to seek out his son among the other boys. The crowd was thinning, it was getting dusk, and bugle signals could be heard from many different directions at once. Lung Yen once more pulled out the precious piece of paper on which the letter writer had written down his son's number and location. His silk garment gave him courage to make inquiries of a soldier. The soldier was not rough as soldiers usually were, but smiled at Lung Yen agreeably and himself conducted him to the entrance of one of the many roads which ranged out from a circular open space. Lung Yen thanked him in a manner becoming his fine clothes and went on between two rows of clean white buildings. He could hear drums in the distance, but he heard his own heart, too.

After a time he was overtaken by a column of marching boys; their feet raised the dust, and they looked rather tired but happy, too, Lung Yen thought as he searched the ranks of these unknown boys for the unknown face of his son. He marched beside them until he grew impatient and started running as though he were pulling his ricksha, in order to come more quickly to the place to which the friendly soldier had directed him. Drums and bugles were far behind as he hitched up his long robe in order to run unhindered

He still had to ask his way several times with the help of his paper, but at last, after losing his way more than once, he reached his son's barrack. It was a one-storied building of wood, not so white and beautiful as the houses he had recently passed. The door stood open, and Lung Yen, after hesitating with a modest cough, went in. But there was nobody inside, and he came out again, irresolute and hot with the haste he had made. Now he heard the sound of trumpets and bugles drawing nearer, a cloud of dust appeared at the bottom of the road, and through the dust he soon saw the marching boys. They tumbled into the house with a clamor of shouting and laughing and young voices. Their two orderly ranks broke into a turmoil of children who streamed past Lung Yen and into the building. He involuntarily put out his hands, but it would have been as easy to hold up flowing water. Yen smiled shyly to every boy whose face he could focus for one second, but not one of them stopped to say "Father." His knees felt like broken wood, stiff and undependable. He took the red envelope from his belt and held it up in the air, then took a deep breath and decided to shout his son's name. "Lung Seileong from Fukang," he shouted, or thought he shouted. Actually only a thin sound came, and this was lost in the laughing tumult, and not one of the boys stopped. "Lung Seileong! Lung Seileong!" he shouted time after time. A thin boy with a sensible face but unfortunately a slight squint asked: "Is it Lung Seileong from Fukang whom the gentleman is seeking?"

"That is the name of my sought-for son."

"I will call him," the boy said and ran into the house. Lung Yen breathed again, for though this boy seemed intelligent and civil, he squinted, and Lung Yen did not want a son who squinted. The air was full of dust the children had kicked up with their feet. The bugles were silent. The last stragglers ran past Yen down the road.

"I am Seileong," Yen heard behind him. He turned quickly round, and close in front of him was a boy whose head reached up to his mouth.

"I am Seileong," he repeated.

"Seileong, Lao Seileong," Lung said, addressing his son with the polite term that means Old. "Lao Seileong, I am your father."

But as excitement had so parched his throat that his voice was like a dried stream in the desert, the boy did not understand him. He looked at Yen in earnest inquiry, while he began the conversation in the ceremonious way that was fitting.

"What is the name of the honored gentleman? Whence does the gentleman choose to come? What may be the honored gentleman's wish? Has my father sent the honored gentleman to me?"

As Lung Yen looked at his son and heard him speak in this manner, he swelled with pride and joy. His son was a finely built boy, and he had a round face with beautiful black eyes that shone with intelligence and life. His skin and hair were smooth and showed that he had a good mother who took great care of him. But Lung Yen saw at the same time that his son was panting and that his chest beneath his thin sleeveless white shirt quickly rose and fell. He cleared his throat, and as soon as he could find his voice he said: "Nobody sent me, son, nobody sent me. I am your father."

Thereupon his son looked at him for a moment more earnestly. Then his face lit up with laughter and he cried out: "Did my father see how I won the 220?"

Meanwhile some of the other boys had gathered round in a half-circle to listen.

"Go and get changed," Seileong said, and Lung Yen saw with pride that they obeyed him. And now Lung Yen was left alone with his child outside the door, and there was only the yellow dust between them, which the boys had kicked up with their feet.

"I saw. I was watching," he quickly assured him. It was wrong that he should be afraid of his son instead of the other way round, but the boy's eyes looked him over so keenly that he could feel every one of his lean ribs beneath his silk clothing.

"You do not look as you do in the picture," Seileong said slowly, and it seemed that it cost him some trouble to keep the smile on his round face.

"In what picture?" Lung Yen asked in surprise.

"My mother has often shown me a picture of my father. It is in the book in which the names of our ancestors are written," Seileong said.

Lung Yen remembered the picture now. It was a photograph he had had taken at the request of Seileong's mother on the day after their wedding.

"People alter in large cities," he said gently. And it was only after he had said it that he realized how truly he had spoken. Indeed people did alter, and the city had altered him greatly. But as he felt safe in the protection of his silk garment he put out a finger and touched his son's warm young body.

"Are you not cold? You must put on warmer clothes after running," he said anxiously. His son laughed.

"We are hardened, Father," was all he said.

Resting the weight of his light frame on one leg, he continued to search his father's face as though waiting for something that did not come.

"My mother told me to give my father many greetings of devotion," he said when this occurred to him.

"How is the health of your honored mother?" Lung Yen asked, for the fine courtesy he had learned in his own childhood, when his grandfather was still alive, was slowly coming back to him.

"She is well," Seileong said as casually as though he were speaking of his younger sister. He reflected for a moment as though trying to remember something he had learned by heart and then added:

"My mother told me to say that nothing was lacking to her complete contentment but the homecoming of my father."

After he had succeeded in delivering this message he began to smile again, and his smile made a deep dimple in his cheek. "We won the 220 and the free-style swimming race, and we were third in the high jump and wrestling. We are points ahead of the Mutuh District."

"I am glad and proud to hear it," Lung Yen said rather uncertainly. He was wondering whether the moment had come to give his son his present. He was more pleased than ever that he had bought something modern and foreign, for he could easily see that his son would have thought little of anything else. But no, not now, he thought to himself. The other children would break the little stink-cart, and this is not a good place to set it going. So he said:

Put on some warmer clothes and come with me. We are going to have a good meal to celebrate our reunion."

"Good, good," Seileong said, obviously relieved. "I will ask leave of the troop leader. If my father will be so good as to wait here——"

He ran into the house, and Lung Yen smiled to himself over the boy's efforts to keep up the old-fashioned courtesies which seemed to be strange to him. His heart now beat as fully and regularly and evenly as the strokes of a gong or a temple bell. Seileong was soon back again. "I have leave till midnight," he said joyfully. Lung Yen again felt the boy's clothing and thought it much too thin. He would have liked to show his love for his son by putting five coats on him, one on top of the other, and filling him up with all the food he could hold.

"We will go by the streetcar," he said after they had started. Seileong still wore his shorts, but he had put on a linen jacket over his white shirt.

"Are you not cold?" Lung Yen asked again. And his son said, "We are a hardy generation." Lung Yen at a steady pace set off for the place where the streetcars left.

"You need not be afraid of the speed, it is quite safe," he said.

"We have a streetcar in Fukang, too," the boy replied, to Lung Yen's great astonishment. The town must have greatly altered since he was a child. They got in, and Lung Yen quelled his rebellious stomach. He smiled rather a forced smile as they rounded the curves, trying at the same time to answer the ten thousand questions that Seileong shot off at him. What is this street called? Is it true there is going to be a war? What is the latest news from the North? How much does it cost to travel from one end of the city to the other? How many soldiers are there in Shanghai? Has the Nineteenth Route Army arrived yet? How many refugees can Shanghai take in? Lung Yen was helpless under this bombardment, and he had no answers to give.

"I know little about these things, as they do not concern me," he said rather reproachfully. "I look after my business, and that is sufficient."

"What is your business?" his son asked.

Lung Yen had prepared his answer long in advance, and it came out of itself:

"I am a partner in a shop in Chapei."

"What sort of shop? What do you sell?" his son asked.

"All kinds of things," Lung Yen said. "Silk, cotton, and also ready-made clothing."

Seileong did not appear to be quite satisfied with this. "How much do you earn by it? he asked.

Lung Yen took a flying leap at a very tall lie.

"You will understand that the profits vary from month to month and at different seasons. But I can say that in the year I do not make less than two hundred dollars of Big Money, and some years even more."

Seileong kept still for a moment, moving his lips and reckoning on his fingers. "My mother earns twenty-seven dollars every month. That makes three hundred and twenty-four dollars in the year," he said calmly.

Lung Yen did not believe a word of it, but smiled indulgently. He realized that his son wished to give his mother much face.

"By what manner of means does your mother earn so much?" he asked good-humoredly.

"She works in the telephone exchange," Seileong said. After that there was a silence. A foreigner who was sitting near them, and who had been following their conversation, now addressed the boy in English, and with awe and pride and joy Lung Yen realized that his son replied in the language of the foreign devils. Seileong's mother too had understood this language, the coolie reflected. It appeared that his son had a ready wit, for the foreigner broke into a laugh and touched Seileong's cheek. "The gentleman has an intelligent son," he remarked politely to the father before getting out.

They were received with every mark of honor at the restaurant, and their host himself came up to announce that preparations for their dinner had been made and it should be cooked at once. There were no separate rooms here as in the smart restaurants in the large streets, but all the same the room was divided into little compart-

ments, in one of which Lung Yen sat down with his son. To make
the right impression he fanned himself with his new red paper fan,
although a strange hint of chilliness had begun to creep up his spine.

"How many characters can you read by now?" he asked while
they were eating the hors d'oeuvres and steaming dumplings, for
he wanted to talk like an educated man.

"I don't really know," Seileong said casually, and it did not seem
that he spoke in that way from modesty. "More in any case than
are necessary nowadays."

"Eat some more, eat some more, you must be hungry after your
victory," Lung Yen urged him. The sharp appetite he had felt only
a few minutes before had left him. It seemed that the mere sight
of food pressed on his stomach, just as the sight of the soft bed in
the tailor's house drove sleep from his eyes. At the same time he
was overwhelmed with happiness and contentment as he watched
his child eating with a good appetite. "Eat all you can, but keep
some room in your belly for the duck and the fish," he said, almost
bursting with pride over the fine meal he was giving his son.

"Duck?" Seileong asked with round eyes.

"Duck. A fat Szechuan duck crisply roasted," Lung Yen said.
It was not necessary for him to decry the costly meal to his son.

"I shall tell my mother what a fine meal I have had," Seileong
said with his mouth full. His cheeks were hot and flushed, although
he had not drunk any rice wine. When the waiter brought the hot
towels Lung Yen seized them with relief. He had a strange sinking
feeling which got worse every minute. "Cigarettes," he said to the
boy who was pouring out their tea. He smoked eagerly and was
annoyed to see how his fingers trembled.

Dr Hain's injection, that ampoule of Eucodal, had held out till
then, but now its influence was exhausted. But Lung Yen did not
know that. He just fought on heroically in order to show up in
his son's eyes as a well-mannered and even easygoing father who
was prosperous and benevolent. For this reason he even ate some
duck, although each mouthful felt ten times as large as his throat.
He also criticized the side dishes and behaved as though duck were
his daily fare. Seileong made the proper remarks.

"I shall burst," he said and: "Thus I imagine to myself the meals which Kung Ming and Chou Lang used to eat."

"Kung Ming and Chou Lang, the heroes," Lung Yen said quickly to show his education. He too had heard the story of the Three Kingdoms from the storytellers in the markets sometimes.

"Where are we going after dinner?" Seileong asked.

Lung Yen gave a start. He had only ninety-four cents, including the twenty cents he had won by his bet. "Where would you like to go?" he asked in a weak voice.

"To the cinema," Seileong said without hesitation.

I shall have to borrow another dollar from Kwe Kuei, Lung Yen thought in a panic. With money you are a dragon, without money a worm, he thought. In all the ten years he had lived in the great city he had only twice been to the foreign shadow plays. If he had twenty cents to spend he preferred to spend it on the Great Smoke. That was now over forever. He exerted all his strength to put the thought of Kuei's opium den out of his head. Yet when it came to the fish he gave out. He knew that he would be ill if he tried to swallow even one mouthful of this luxury in its sour-sweet sauce. He smoked and fanned himself and did his best to smile. As through a mist he saw his son looking at him with grave and anxious eyes.

"Are you sick, Father?" he asked, subduing his clear boyish voice in his concern.

"Sick? I? No, I have never been sick in my life," Lung Yen boasted and struck the table.

He had to cough; for the last hour he had felt he must cough and had held it back. Now he coughed. A few drops of blood came into his mouth, and he turned round and spat into the large round spittoon which happened to be near. Seileong had jumped up. "You are sick, Father," he said in agitation. "What is the matter with you? What shall I do?"

Lung Yen wiped his forehead with the hot towel. "Sit down and go on eating, son," he said with a contorted smile. "I am not sick. If you are quick we can still go to the shadow play. Afterwards you shall sleep in my house. The bed is ready." Many of his dreams and joyful anticipations had in fact revolved round the thought of having his son beside him in bed, his child, his flesh and blood, begotten by him, of having him beside him in warmth and peace and contentment. He longed for it more eagerly than he had ever longed to sleep with a woman.

"I have not leave for the night," Seileong said. "It is sad, but discipline is the most important thing in life."

Lung Yen listened as the word came as a matter of course from his child's mouth, the great word he had never heard before.

"What do you say? Discipline?" he asked. "There was no such thing in my day. Is it a discovery of the foreign devils?"

"It is what makes the foreigners strong, it is the lack of it that is the ruin of China," Seileong said precociously. This was a lesson he had learned by heart.

"If this dis—this thing is something that forbids a son to serve his father, then it cannot be anything very good," Lung Yen said indignantly. His son had written: "I cannot wait to hand you the evening and the morning tea," now he sat there and talked of unfriendly, foreign inventions. Since he had spat out the rebellious blood, Lung Yen felt a little relieved. The meal too came to an end, and the waiter put the rice on the table. This was the great moment for which Lung Yen had been eagerly waiting. He watched the child eating and forgot all Seileong might have said. He was a handsome, blooming, well-principled, sensible son. He did not stuff in his rice as a buffalo did grass, but ate daintily and manipulated his chopsticks with delicacy and propriety. Lung Yen had often thought of his own son but very seldom of his wife. He thought of her now.

"Your mother is a good woman and better than most," he said. His son looked him full in the eyes and said earnestly, "My mother is dearer to me than anything in the world."

Lung Yen now produced the parcel which he had put safely between his feet under the table so that he could feel it with his toes and be sure it was still there. "I have got a present for you, son," he said rather breathlessly. He slowly unwrapped the paper, folded it up and put it in the pocket of his smart waistcoat, for it was still good enough to make shoe soles out of. Then he set the automobile on the floor and wished there were ten lamps instead of one, to make it shine out better.

"An auto?" Seileong asked in astonishment.

"Yes, an auto," Lung Yen replied, beaming with pleasure. The chill he had felt up his spine before gave way now to a wave of warmth. "An auto, yes, an auto," he said, repeating the foreign word, "and it can go like the big ones."

He wound it up, and Seileong got off his chair and knelt down, leaning his young confiding warmth against his father, and his hair stroked Lung Yen's cheek. "Let me see, let me have it," he said impatiently. But Lung Yen wound it up tight and then put the auto down again on the floor. It ran. It did not run quite so fast as at first, but it ran. He knelt down to get closer to it, and even the boy who was pouring out the tea stopped to look at the little vehicle. It ran in a circle, got slower and stopped.

"It has stopped," Seileong said.

"You only need to wind it up again and it will go on," Lung Yen said. "It is nothing particular, only a little present for my son."

Seileong, in his surprise, had forgotten to thank his father. But it was enough for Lung Yen to see him kneeling on the floor and gazing at his present with obvious delight. The boy wound it up, and the little auto did in fact obediently run on again, even though slowly and only for a short time.

"I have carried it about with me all day, and perhaps it is tired," Lung Yen suggested, but Seileong said eagerly, "It is only the spring; I can twist it tighter." He turned the toy over and, bending over it, he began to busy himself with its strange mechanism as if he had played with such things all his life.

Lung Yen smiled and watched him with great astonishment, but suddenly his child's face darkened. He stood up and put the auto down on the table. "I might have known it," he said. "Japanese trash."

Lung Yen did not understand the sudden anger and contempt in his child's face. He picked up the little auto, rubbed it with his costly silk sleeve, breathed on it and rubbed again. He handed the shining toy back to his son, but Seileong would not take it.

"Why did you buy it, Father?" he asked, digging his hands into the pockets of his Scouts' shorts, to ward off any contact with the auto. He did not look like a child any longer; he looked like a grown-up man in a furious rage. Lung Yen wondered what to reply. Why did you buy it, Father? Because I wanted to give you a great pleasure, he might have said. Because it was the most beautiful thing I could find in this great city. Because you, my unknown son, are as dear to me as the light of my eyes. But he said nothing of this and could not have found words in which to say any of it. Instead, he said sternly, "It is impolite to behave badly over a present, my son."

"You talk as if you did not know we are at war with Japan," Seileong exclaimed. "You can read it on any wall, it is printed in every newspaper. For years we've fought for it: Boycott Japan! Buy no Japanese goods! Where were your eyes, your understanding, your principles when you bought this thing? It is people like you who in their indifference are the ruin of China."

Lung Yen was speechless as he heard his son's fury. He understood only half what he said. Just enough to make him wretched and confused. He might have confessed that he could not read and understood nothing of all these things, but he was ashamed. He took hold of the little auto in his trembling hands and tried to wind it up, but the key stuck fast.

"Will you not have the little auto?" he asked almost humbly. Seileong's eyes filled with tears of rage.

"No, I will not have it, Father," he said. "I will not have it. I will not have anything Japanese."

Lung Yen raised his hand, and Seileong drew back as though he expected a blow. But Yen did not strike him. How could he have struck his son? But it was this uncontrolled and threatening movement that put the boy beside himself. "You can strike me, but I will not have the auto," he shouted in blazing anger. He took his little brown scratched boy's fists out of his pockets, and they quivered with the constraint he had put on himself. He seized the toy, he dashed it to the ground, he spat on it, he trod on it with one of his heavy, hard foreign shoes. The auto crunched under his heel and then lay dead, as Lung Yen had sometimes seen real autos lie in the streets after a bad crash. It was all a bad dream, and he struggled for breath as he did when dreaming.

"What have you done?" he muttered, clutching his breast with his hands, for there was a great tumult of anguish and pain within it.

Seileong tried to regain control over himself. "With the money you paid for this trash, guns will be made to shoot our soldiers with," he said more calmly but not less cruelly. "You are an enemy of China. My father is an enemy of China." At this his distress came over him afresh, and he spat once more on the murdered toy and rubbed the tears from his cheeks with his fists. He gave one sob and wiped his nose with his hand and then, remembering his up-bringing, he produced a red handkerchief and dried his eyes and nose and his whole face; it was flushed with insult and indignation.

Lung Yen looked on helplessly. He had no words; he could not explain anything. He bent down to pick up the ruined object from the floor. But he did not get as far. Something happened inside him. The agitation and the pang of disappointment broke something within him. He reeled and stood upright; he gave a low groan and fell against the table. His mouth was filled to overflowing with molten metal, and he would have suffocated if he had not opened it. A torrent of blood welled out over the tablecloth. "Father!" Seileong shrieked with horror. A moment before he had nearly killed his father with his big words and his contempt. Now when Lung Yen in shame and dismay gazed at the filth which had poured from his sick inside, Seileong was not nauseated; he put his arms round him, he stroked his cheeks, he put his face to his temples and tried to comfort him as though he, Lung Yen, were the child, and Seileong the father.

The two waiters brought wet cloths and grumblingly wiped up the blood on the table. The proprietor stood by, waiting for his payment now that the meal was over. Lung Yen tried to speak, but he could get nothing out except a long-drawn groan.

"Father, Exalted Person, forgive me. Father, listen, forgive me," Seileong murmured in Lung Yen's ear. At last the spasm passed and he emerged again out of the access of the Dark Weakness which had come upon him at such an unfortunate moment.

"It is all right, do not be afraid," he whispered to the child and made an effort to smile. Seileong's hands were now trembling too, for the idea that what he had said about the boycott of Japanese goods had something to do with his father's sickness frightened him greatly. On the banners that waved all day above the arena were the words: "The best weapon against the enemy is the boycott." But there were these words also: "Remember age. Do not forget love and respect for your parents." He would gladly have wept with his head hidden in his mother's skirt, although he was now a man. He forced back his tears and supported his father with his arm.

"Can you walk?" he asked in keen anxiety. Lung Yen smiled bravely. He tried by a show of education to obliterate the miserable impression his sickness must have made on his son. So he said in pidgin English: "Can do."

He felt rather unsteady on his feet, which were cold and cramped in his unaccustomed shoes; but he took out his little moneybag and paid the proprietor and gave the two waiters their tea money. He gave them more than he had meant, for they had had more bother with him than they would have had with a healthy man. In spite of this they grumbled behind his back. Seileong put his shoulder under his father's arm to support him. "Do not feel worried. It is good when the unclean blood flows out of the body," Lung Yen said to console him.

"That is so. That is so," Seileong eagerly agreed.

The air did Lung Yen good, although he began to shiver. He did not dare look down for fear he might find his silk robe was stained.

"Where do you live?" Seileong asked, for he had now taken charge.

"In Chapei, Lane-of-the-Four-Virtues," Lung Yen said. Seileong whistled to a taxi which was passing by, empty. It stopped with a screech of brakes.

"No, it is too dear," Lung Yen said in great agitation. He knew that he had only eight cents left in his purse.

"Get in and be my guest," Seileong said rather too grandly. "My mother gave me plenty of money." When they were in the taxi he instantly seized his father's cold hand and held it tightly to his breast to warm it. Also he put it twice to his mouth and breathed on it. In spite of his misery Lung Yen could not help smiling. Just so he himself as a child used to breathe on butterflies when they were numb with the cold. In a few minutes they were in the Lane-of-the-Four-Virtues and Seileong paid the driver. Lung Yen did not look, for he did not want to know how much money had gone on this brief journey. Then his son helped him out of the taxi and into the house.

The tailor's family had not gone to bed. They were waiting up to see and to greet their guest. Lung Yen had pictured his entry very differently, very differently indeed; yet it was good to feel the boy's care for him and to see the gentleness with which he helped him to undress. Lung Yen was glad that he had had a bath that morning and had a clean body to show to his son. A chill had come over him while they were still in the taxi, and now it got worse. He was so cold that he could not keep his limbs still, and his teeth chattered. He was chilled to the marrow with a coldness that did not come from outside but came from his inwards and was all through him. Seileong covered him up. He shut the shutters more tightly to keep out the air and unfolded his father's clothes again and spread the silk robe over the bedcovering to give more warmth. The tailor's wife shuffled up to the door on her felt soles, coughing politely, and brought some tea. Seileong whispered to her, and she went away after giving an anxious look at Lung Yen with her old eyes. Seileong sat on the edge of the bed and put both hands flat on his father's chest. The warmth penetrated the silk garment and the bedcovering and comforted Lung Yen. He stopped shivering, and only the dryness of his lips troubled him a little. He moistened them with his tongue and smiled at his son.

"We've missed the cinema now," he said jokingly.

"There is still time; I am staying two more days in Shanghai," Seileong said. Lung Yen considered this closely and at length. He shut his eyes. Eight cents. If I sell my robe and buy clean coolie clothing

I can make seventy-five cents on the deal, even eighty perhaps. If I can introduce a foreigner to Kwe Kuei I shall have twenty cents commission. Two foreigners, forty cents. Five foreigners for Kuei, two dollars for Yen. There are many ships in the harbor and many sailors. Sailors don't want smoke, they want women. I shall get the ricksha tomorrow and lie in wait for inquisitive foreign devils at Sang Hai Ler Kwang. Perhaps young Mr Ku will come with me to Kwe Kuei. Young Mr Ku likes the Greak Smoke. It is a long time since he came to Kwe Kuei. I will wait for him. Ten cents for the doorkeeper. Ten cents for the policeman at the corner. Forty cents for the ricksha. Thirty cents' contribution to the Guild. Eight cents. Eight dollars owing. My son is here. My son wants to be taken to the cinema. If only a lady would leave her handbag in the ricksha, sometimes there are twenty dollars in a foreign lady's handbag, that's what Kuei says, and he ought to know, he was a good thief in his youth. Twenty dollars in one bag. What do twenty dollars look like?

He opened his eyes and encountered his son's attentive gaze. "Must you not go away? You have no leave. Will this dis—this new thing you have to have not punish you?" he asked anxiously.

"I shall stay with you," Seileong said. "You are sick. My troop leader will surely understand that."

"I am not sick," Lung Yen said. He was glad they had taken away the dirty mosquito net. True, the small room hummed with mosquitoes, but the bed was clean, and mosquitoes never stung him, for his blood was not sweet enough for them. He stretched himself and put his hands on the silk of his gray robe.

"I am content, son," he said, blinking his eyes. Seileong sat up and began to talk.

"The city is bad for your health," he said. "Why do you live here and leave your family alone? Are you fonder of your business than of us? Can you not sell it? Money is not everything, even though they say it makes the blind see and the deaf hear. Come back to us, and my mother will make you well again. She made me well three times when all other children died and the plague was so bad that there were no more coffins to be bought in the whole town."

He thought hard and brought out a scrap of wisdom he had picked up somewhere. "Better a living beggar than a dead king," he said solemnly. "This town is not good for you, Father, not good. Will you not come with me when we leave Shanghai?"

His words sounded to Lung Yen like an old cradle song. He did not know whether his clever son had seen through his piteous life. Seen through his silk clothes, his borrowed wealth, to the shameful fact that not even the bed on which he lay belonged to him. Seen through all his pretenses to his starved and wasted sick body. He breathed deeply and regularly. He felt no pain now, no pain at all. No, he thought, this city is not good for me, this city has been bad from the very start. He thought of the war which had swept him into it, of the burning and killing, the fighting and dying with which it had first greeted him. They say there is going to be another war and a worse one than ever, he thought. He thought of the loads he had carried and the factories in which he had had to slave as no buffalo ever toiled at the wheel. Unite, unite, it had been said. Twenty cents' deduction from his earnings. What for? For the strike fund. The factories closed, his belly empty. Unite, unite. Thirty cents for the ricksha coolies' guild, and again thirty cents, and again thirty cents. Union filled no empty bowl with rice. No, the city is not good.

I am a poor coolie, my son; a miserable, destitute coolie, who owns nothing, not even the ricksha he pulls and not the mat on which he sleeps. Not even the head which is on my shoulders belongs to me, he thought with horror. Without the Great Smoke I am too weak to work and my sufferings are unendurable. But if I smoke they will catch me and execute me and I shall never return home.

"Son—" he said, "I must tell you something——"

"Yes, Father?" Seileong asked expectantly. Lung Yen wanted to tell the whole truth, because he felt that then the heavy load would leave his breast. I am a poor coolie, he began again from the beginning, a miserable, destitute coolie, who owns nothing . . .

"Yes?" Seileong asked again, and Lung Yen noticed that he had only been thinking and that not a word had left his lips. It is too difficult, he thought sadly.

"The pear tree," he said instead. "Does it bear many pears? It must have grown tall by now."

"What pear tree?" Seileong asked.

"The pear tree beside the house of our ancestors," Lung Yen said wearily.

"There is no pear tree," the son said.

"No pear tree!" Lung Yen exclaimed. "That is impossible. You must have overlooked it. You are a child of the town and have no eyes for trees and fields. It must have grown higher than the roof by now, the pear tree beside our house in the Village-of-the-Clear-Mountains. No pear tree!"

"Come with me and look for yourself," Seileong said very slyly. "I should like you to teach me about trees and fields."

"I shall think it over," Yen said. I owe eight dollars, he thought. I shall have to work for a year and pay my debts. Then I can go back home. A year is not long, he thought again. I shall go back and get strong. The air of my village will cure me. The sight of my son is better than all the dreams the Great Smoke can give.

Seileong went on stroking the bedcovering with his hands, but he got slower and slower.

"Son," Lung Yen said, "your father is not rich. Your father is a coolie and very poor. But your father will come home, he will come soon. It cannot take long . . . "

He opened his eyes, for Seileong's hands had slid from the covering. The child had fallen asleep and had heard nothing. His head had fallen forward, and only his hair and the childlike round of his cheek was touched by the light of the electric lamp which hung from the ceiling. A mosquito buzzed above his cheek, and Yen carefully flicked it away. He moved to the extreme edge of the bed to make room for Seileong and drew the child to him. He would have liked to clasp him to his breast as he had long ago, but he was afraid his breath might give the child his sickness, and so he turned away from him. "Sleep, son, sleep in peace," he said when Seileong muttered something. He sat up and took off Seileong's heavy shoes so that his feet too could breathe. He switched off the light and covered the child over. The mosquitoes whined in the darkness. The warmth of the young body entered into him, and its regular breathing composed his own. And as unconsciousness descended in cloud after cloud, he thought happily: son, son, son.

In the morning when Lung Yen woke, Seileong had gone. On the bed lay a letter and a silver half-dollar.

XII

IT WAS ONLY FROM HABIT that Dr Hain looked in his little pigeonhole for letters as he passed the reception desk. There had been no letters for him when he left the hotel to buy his supper, and it was too late for another delivery. He did not confess to himself that he was vaguely hoping for a miracle, a telegram perhaps. . . .

"Good evening, Doctor," the chief clerk said.

"Good evening," Dr Hain replied and went to the elevator.

"How are things looking outside?" the clerk called after him. He only shrugged his shoulders. The lounge was emptier than usual. "All lines engaged, quite impossible to get through to anywhere," the Greek observed to his assistant. Dr Hain went up to the sixth floor where his room was. He had a long way to go from the elevator to his door, round corners and up two steps to the farthest end of the passage. Here was the service elevator from which, with discreet rattle, the tables were trundled along with breakfast or tiffin to the rooms of permanent or indolent residents.

Opposite the service elevator was the service closet for that floor, where little Chinese boys rummaged about with buckets and talked in voices that always reminded the doctor of the sound of xylophones. He was often devoured with envy as he listened to them, for the four distinct tone pitches of the Chinese language caused him insuperable difficulties, although his ear was capable of grasping and enjoying the complicated texture of Beethoven's late string quartets.

His room was long and narrow and separated from that closet

only by a wooden partition. His bed was next the door, and then came a chest of drawers on which his violin case lay beside his water bottle. The lamp with the green shade was his own property, and so was the electric coffee machine. The screen in the window and the electric fan in the corner were his share in the luxury of the Shanghai Hotel. It was not yet six o'clock, and his room would have been light but that the window opened onto a narrow airshaft. Dr Hain turned on the light and put down his small parcel. He took off his coat and waistcoat and hung them methodically on a clothes hanger, for he had to take great care of his clothes. He washed his hands in the small basin fixed to the wall, set his coffee machine in motion and unwrapped his supper. Sometimes, as he had done that evening, he took the trouble to go as far as the little German delicatessen shop in Peking Street, for it is a characteristic of the uprooted and exiled to cling to the books and the food of their native land when they have long since become estranged to all else. He cut slices of the black bread, spread them with a thin scraping of butter which the heat had melted, and put the slices of wurst he had bought on top. The coffee machine began to hum. Dr Hain sighed contentedly as he sat down at his table. He had become attached to his room, to his penury and his peace. It reminded him in a way of the rooms of his student years. "Just ready," he said to the coffee machine, for during his years of solitude he had got into the habit of talking to himself and also to the objects around him. There were two photographs on his table. One was of his wife, Irene, in an evening dress of a past fashion, smiling rather stiffly at the onlooker. The other was a snapshot of his son Roland that Irene had taken in the garden when he was fourteen years old. He was naked but for a pair of shorts and was running in front of his dog and looking round at it and laughing. Even this old snapshot gave an idea of Roland's beauty. Irene had sent it to her husband in his exile, and along the edge in a thin sloping hand was written: "Whom the gods love die young."

Emanuel Hain drank his coffee and ate his bread standing up. He washed the coffee pot in the basin and put everything back in its proper place. The last few years had taught him that only great tidiness makes poverty tolerable. "Now we'll write a letter," he said to the writing table. He took some sheets of the hotel stationery out of the drawer, put them under the light of the lamp, took out his fountain pen and began writing.

MY DEAREST WIFE [Dr Hain wrote]:

The day has gone by without a word from you. Probably it is childish that I so firmly hoped for a letter from you. But it is the first time you have forgotten my birthday, and it makes me anxious. Are you sick? Or has something even more serious happened to you? You know how anxious I am if I do not hear from you for some time. Perhaps it is only a delay of mail here, although it is as a rule so reliable. In a country where everything else is in a chaos of disorder, letters arrive with great certainty and speed. They say that this goes back to the time when the delicatessen of the South had to be sent in furious haste to the Imperial Court in Peking. But that is only by the way. They say here that from today the airlines and railways are barred to civilian traffic so that Chinese troops can be hurriedly transported to Shanghai. Nobody believes any more that war can be averted here, for the Japanese have landed too many troops, and the river is full of their destroyers. I cannot at present imagine what a war in Shanghai can be, for the International Zone is sacred and old Shanghai residents talk of the affair of '32 as if they had sat in the stalls and looked on while the Chinese quarters lying all around went up in the air. However that may be, it is possible that a letter from you is lying somewhere and has only not reached me in these disturbed days. If war should start here, I should at least have an aim in life, for they will organize ambulance work and my old war experience will stand me in good stead.

Dear, dear Irene, my dearest heart, you ask about my life. My life is in your letters, that is all the answer I can give you. The longer I am in this country the less I understand it and the more I wish myself away from it. You know, Irene, that my life has only one aim and one motive: to be with you again. Here in Shanghai I see that this can never be. But I have one little hope of which I must tell you. You remember Dr Weininger, my pupil who for a time was house surgeon in the Mannheim Clinic Hospital? Through the help of relations he was able to settle three years ago in San Francisco, and it appears he has a good practice. This true friend has now suggested that I should go to San Francisco and settle there as a surgeon. He offers to give me a share of his practice, in so far that he would hand over to me some of the operations that came his way.

You can imagine, my dear, how this proposal excites me. It would be paradise. To have real work again, to be with you again, to belong once more to the living! I should have to work for a year in San Francisco as a student and then take my medical examination in English. It is a comical situation, I grant, for Professor Emanuel Hain to join young American students at the age of fifty-five. But others have done it before me, and why should I not be able to do it, too? I have learned English here, and to pass an examination in English cannot be more difficult than getting on with Chinese coolies. There is only one difficulty, the same old, miserable, unworthy and ridiculous difficulty: money. Enough money to live for a year in San Francisco and then a few hundred dollars so that I can wait until the practice begins to bear fruit. I rack my brains to know where this money shall come from and find no answer. We cannot live on the ten marks a month which would perhaps be allowed you. Nevertheless I feel it is high time at last for us——

Someone knocked at Dr Hain's door—once, twice, thrice before he heard. He was far away with Irene. Now he put a newspaper over his unfinished letter with an odd, shamefaced movement and opened the door. A Chinese boy stood outside.

"Doctor go catch room number sixteen seven eight chopchop, boy say master velly much sick," he announced with wrinkled brow. Dr Hain took in this message in pidgin English. "All right," he said, and shut his door again. He always had his bag ready to his hand. "Too much to drink, probably," he confided to it as he picked it up. He had some experience of hotel practice.

Helen Russell had been all round the town that afternoon to buy a wedding present for Frank Taylor. As he appeared to be resolved to carry through his infernal marriage with his little American, Helen took a grim pleasure in giving the pair too large and costly a present. She had almost decided on a beautiful celadon plate of the Ming period; but she concluded, in the same spirit of somber irony which inspired her enterprise, that Ruth Anderson, the future Mrs Taylor, would have no notion of the value of such a present. Probably she would take the plate into the kitchen to serve a pudding on it. As Helen, up to her arrival in Shanghai, had been unacquainted with love and consequently with the tortures of jealousy, her sufferings were now unendurable, and it gave her an agonizing joy to keep on hurting herself afresh. A second, cool-headed Helen stood by, scornfully regarding this lost, jealous and tortured woman. It's like toothache, only worse, this detached Helen thought. One always bites on the place that hurts. Celadon for Ruth Anderson, indeed!

At last she found the atrocity she was looking for—an enormous silver cocktail shaker with twelve silver goblets, all on a silver salver, and so heavy that only a prize fighter could have carried it round. "I want the date engraved on it," she told the salesman. "Shanghai, August 14, 1937."

Helen's automobile was waiting outside. Shanghai, fourteenth of August, nineteen hundred and thirty seven, she thought. The day of my execution. She took out her powder box and earnestly studied her face in the mirror.

When she entered the sitting room in her suite she found Potter looking through the keyhole of Bobbie's bedroom. He paid no attention to her when she came in except to raise his hand as a warning to be quiet.

"The doctor is in with Mr Russell," he whispered.

"Anything wrong?" Helen asked, taking off her hat.

"A slight attack," Potter said, still with his eye to the keyhole. Helen looked round the room for signs of destruction. But there was only one chair overturned, and the glass inkpot on the writing table had been upset.

"Would you mind tidying the room, Potter," she said. Potter left his post and casually picked up the chair. Potter as well as Helen was accustomed to take Bobbie's attacks, which usually began violently, with comparative calm.

"What doctor have you called in?" Helen asked as he wiped up the ink with his handkerchief, held daintily in the tips of his fingers.

"The hotel doctor—a sort of an old German," Potter replied with deep distrust. "I couldn't get onto an English doctor. It's impossible to get a phone call through. I did not think delay advisable."

Helen laughed to herself. "How do you like Shanghai, Potter?"

she asked, openly making fun of him. Potter raised his hands in resignation. "A rotten hole," he said. "Rotten through and through, madam."

"You must have patience with the telephone," Helen went on with amusement. "Remember there's a war on."

Potter looked at her thoughtfully for a moment. "Madam is too young, if I may say so, to know what war is," he said after reflection.

Helen sat down by the radio and fingered the switch. A high-pitched Chinese woman's voice that sounded like an unoiled cart wheel. An asthmatically whining electric organ trying to play jazz. Potter, who had returned to the keyhole, opened the door just in time as Dr Hain came out. Helen gave a passing glance through the crack of the door and saw Bobbie lying on his bed in his shirt sleeves with his shirt open at the neck, but smoking and apparently quite calm. Potter instantly shut the door again.

"Very good of you, Doctor, to take care of my baby," she said casually. "Is he better now?"

Dr Hain looked at her with surprise. He could never get used to the way the English kept everything to themselves and never showed their feelings. In Germany they liked expansiveness and tears.

"Yes, I think it's over for this time," he said, waiting irresolutely before he went.

"Will you sit down a moment, Doctor? Just in case there's a relapse. What will you drink?" Helen said, taking up the telephone to give the order.

"Thank you, thank you very much," Hain said, sitting down after a slight hesitation. "I drink nothing at this time."

"A vodka," Helen said into the telephone. She had got used to vodka in Paris in token of her Russian grand-ducal past, as part of her make-up, so to say. She went back without thinking to the clean strong transparent drink at moments when she felt limp or unhappy. "Well," she asked as she took a chair opposite the doctor in front of the sham fireplace, from the shelf of which an idiotic Buddha smiled down, "had you something to tell me?"

Potter had left the room, silent as a rainworm. Dr Hain cleared his throat. He spoke so little and was so much alone that he always had to dig out his voice before speaking.

"Your own doctor has probably told you already that your husband has not a very sound heart," he then said. Helen looked at him with attention.

"There has been some talk about nervous disorders of the heart," she said lightly.

"Nervous—now, yes, nervous disorders of the heart is a somewhat —how shall I say?—euphemistic expression. Mr Russell appears to have worked his heart pretty hard," Dr Hain said without beating about the bush. Helen smiled encouragingly.

"Never mind, Doctor. I am quite used to these consultations," she said.

"I could not take the responsibility of passing it off with a few pleasant phrases," the doctor went on. "Your husband is in a state in which anything might happen. I consider it necessary that you know how you stand."

"And how do I stand?" Helen asked. The discussion amused rather than worried her. There was a knock, and a French bedroom waiter floated in with the vodka. He had the profile of an Apollo and a squint. He poured out two glasses and left the bottle on the tray. Then he poised himself behind Helen's chair, bending obsequiously forward.

"All right, Gaston. Thank you, Gaston, I shall want nothing more," Helen said. Gaston floated off.

"He once slept with an American millionairess who was staying here," Helen said when he had left the room. "Ever since then he feels it is his duty to be gallant to all female visitors." She handed Dr Hain his glass. *"Prosit,* Doctor," she said.

"Prosit," Dr Hain said and took a drink from politeness.

"What must I be ready for? How do matters stand?" Helen asked amiably.

"Mr Russell seems to have indulged in excesses of some kind lately which are too much for his heart. You must restrain him from them," the doctor said. Helen laughed, and it looked as though she were laughing at him.

"Excesses! I should think so, and not only lately," she said, relapsing into English. "It is no light matter to keep Mr Russell from excesses, particularly in Shanghai. This town was invented for people who run to excesses, don't you think so, Doctor?"

"Why do you not leave? You would have more control over your husband on board ship. Besides, it is not exactly inviting here at present," Dr Hain said.

"We are leaving—soon," Helen said thoughtfully. Up to now she had not been able to face leaving the town in which Frank lived. She might have been hoping to be able to hold him back from his marriage at the last moment and to run away with him, away from everything, to some secret paradise of love where there would be nothing but him and her. Helen, the adventuress, had no idea how simple and ingenuous her wishes were. Everyman's wishes, the banal wishes of all lovers.

"There's that little pianist in the bar," she said meanwhile. "My husband's always going about with him. I have no idea what they do night after night."

Dr Hain pricked up his ears at this mention of Kurt. "Do you know Kurt Planke?" he asked uneasily.

"I have been into too many bars—for me everyone in a bar is called Jack. It makes life simpler," Helen said. "It's that good-looking rascal who plays tangos so nicely. Is he German? I took him for something exotic."

Dr Hain held his glass of vodka up to the light. He was not listening to what Helen said; he was occupied with his own thoughts. It's true, he thought, I've been neglecting Kurt. He would have to talk to him. Helen too lifted up her glass and with a lost smile looked through the transparent liquid which refracted the light into rainbow colors. "That's why I like drinking vodka," she said inconsequently.

"If you please?" Dr Hain asked, for he had not been listening.

"Nothing—just a memory of childhood," Helen said, emptying her glass. The disjointed conversation petered out.

"I must take my leave," Hain said, getting up. I must speak to Kurt at once, he thought. He must not relapse into opium again.

"I will speak to the pianist; I know him well," he said. "I will tell him not to get opium for your husband—or whatever it may be," he added hastily. Helen accompanied him politely to the door.

"And what about his heart?" she asked at the last moment. "Did you mean to suggest that it might be dangerous? I mean—is it possible that something might happen suddenly?"

"Mrs Russell," Dr Hain said, feeling unpleasantly disconcerted as all doctors are by too direct a question, "Mrs Russell, I cannot answer that question. When a heart that is not quite sound means to go on strike, there is never any warning. I have known people die of a heart attack who had much sounder hearts than your husband. And I have known very feeble hearts which were like old automobiles: if you know how to look after them they go for years. My only advice is caution. Good care and quiet. A deck chair or a boat where the bar is shut at nine o'clock. Good evening, Mrs Russell—it was an honor . . . "

As soon as she was alone Helen stood in front of the fireplace lost in thought and gazing at the paltry little gilded Buddha of wood. Idiotic, she thought, how idiotic these hotels are. They have to be Chinese at any cost. But her thoughts were very far away from the Buddha whose round face looked down at her indifferently.

"It's out of the question," she said aloud, and walked from the fireplace to the window. If excesses might put Bobbie's heart out of action, she was the last person in the world to keep him from them. She stood for some time by the window looking down into the street, a narrow slit far below in which there was a continual procession of automobiles, people and rickshas. She poured out another glass of vodka and drank it slowly, after looking again at the light sparkling through it; then she got up with a decisive movement and went into her husband's bedroom. He lay on the bed as before and appeared to be asleep. She sat down beside him and looked at him. It had got dark meanwhile, and she reached out and switched on the bedside lamp—an idiotic lamp, as was everything else in the Shanghai Hotel, with a shade of pleated baby-pink silk. She saw now that Bobbie's eyes were not quite closed but were looking at her through a slit between his eyelids. His attack had left him pale, and the freckles once more showed up on his handsome, slackened face.

"Are you pretending to be asleep?" she asked and shook him by the shoulder. He started to laugh without opening his eyes any wider and put his arms round her.

"Let me look at you," he said lazily. "It looks as if you had an aureole around your head like a madonna." He spoke slowly and with difficulty, as always after he had had a sedative, and he slurred his consonants because he was too indolent to close his lips.

"Wake up, idiot," Helen said not unkindly. "Wake up, drunkard, and pull yourself together." She tried to free herself from his arms, but he held her with unexpected strength.

"Stay with us, we are getting on fine now," he muttered, going so far as to open his eyes. He gave a deep sigh and stretched himself. "Oh, Helen," he said. "Oh, Helen——"

I wonder if I could strangle him, Helen thought while she went on smiling at him. No, she thought, I couldn't do it. Bobbie let go of her, sat up and buttoned his shirt and stroked the hair off his forehead.

"Forgive me," he said politely. He suddenly looked quite awake and sensible. "I'm sorry I lost control of myself. It shan't happen again, Helen, I promise you."

She watched him as he got up and put on his white linen coat in front of the glass. He pulled out the correct triangle of handkerchief from his pocket and came back to her.

"This place is too much for me," he said. "Better men than I—as Shakespeare said, or was it Byron, eh?"

Helen did not reply, and he went on with his fooling. "I have eaten too many sweets and upset my stomach, that's all. Let's clear out of it."

He sat down beside Helen on the bed and went on more urgently. "Helen, let's clear out of it. What are we doing in this hole? If we stay here any longer I shall not only poison myself but we'll both of us get ourselves shot, eh? Let's clear out of it."

"It's no fault of mine if we're here still," Helen replied most unjustly. "When d'you want to go and where? There are no trains now. There's no chance of getting to Peking."

"To the devil with Peking. There are boats. We can get to Hong Kong, for instance. A decent clean British town. British—not like this filthy Shanghai."

"I'll tell Potter to find out when there's a boat sailing," Helen said. It was all stupid nonsense. What was she to do in Hong Kong tied to this corpse? And Frank in bed with that American. I hope she's hit by a bomb, she wished with all her heart. Suddenly Bobbie put his head in her lap.

"Helen," he said, "Helen, do help me, Helen."

She looked down at him without a trace of pity. She had pity only for herself. "How can I help you?" she asked coldly.

"What did you marry me for?" he asked, pressing his face against her diaphragm. She held her breath from disgust.

"You are not crying, are you?" she said.

Bobbie made no reply. His breath came spasmodically, and she felt it hot and moist against her skin. She shook him off and, putting his head on the cushion as if it were an inanimate object, got to her feet.

"I'm hungry," she said, going to the glass. "It is time to change." She went out of the room without giving her husband another glance. She met Potter in the doorway.

"Potter," she said without stopping, "ask for a list of sailings to Hong Kong and Singapore. A British boat if possible, and not before Saturday."

"I'll do so at once," Potter said, his relief written all over his face. Before Helen reached her room he had already taken up the receiver.

XIII

WHEN DR HAIN LEFT the Russells' luxury suite, he went straight to Kurt's room, if the room the hotel allotted him deserved that name. It was a hole on the tenth floor which had formerly served as a linen closet but was found to be too small for the purpose. Kurt could only open his door if he sat on the bed to make room. The room had no window, either, only an airshaft such as inside cabins have on a steamer. But as Kurt was on duty all night in the bar and slept by day, a window would have been—as he expressed it—casting pearls before swine.

If Kurt wanted a bath he had to get hot water from a Chinese hot-water shop and borrow a wooden tub from one of the boys to serve as bath. There was no elevator to the bar from Kurt's corner of the hotel, so he had to climb the eight stories by a narrow stair with exits marked by red lights, for it was only a fire exit. As Kurt had no secrets and no possessions, Dr Hain found the door unlocked, and in any case there was no lock on it. But the room was empty.

"Where master go?" the doctor asked a boy who came along.

"Master go topside," was the answer, emphasized by a thin forefinger pointing upwards. Dr Hain, who did not know the secret of the fire stair, went all the way back to the elevator. He went down to the ground floor, emerged opposite the reception desk, glanced automatically and without even admitting it to himself at his empty pigeonhole, strolled through the domed lounge, reached the second elevator and was now at last conveyed right up to the bar.

He could already hear music in the anteroom; he listened in surprise and smiled involuntarily when he recognized the second movement of the C Minor Sonata by Beethoven. He went in on tiptoe.

The bar was empty, for it was still early, and its vacancy made the place seem of an exaggerated size. There was still a hint of dusk over the town outside, but the windows of the bar were heavily curtained and allowed no light to penetrate either from without or from within. It was as though a blind man played there in the darkness. It was second nature with the doctor never to interrupt music, so he felt his way to one of the silk-cushioned seats by the wall and sat down patiently to hear the movement to an end. From far below came the hooting of automobiles, the screeching of brakes and the whole thunderous murmur of Shanghai. Up there in the bar was Beethoven, the C Minor, the last sonata.

Kurt held the pedal down at the last note until it had completely died away, then to his amazement the doctor heard someone clapping. Immediately afterwards Kurt switched on the piano lamp, which threw a circle of light over the keys and the immediate neighborhood. He now saw that a girl was sitting beside Kurt on the piano stool. Before he had time to feel embarrassed at disturbing them, Kurt said, "This is Ruth, Doctor. One of those poor Chinese orphan children who earn their living by copying Venetian lace."

Ruth was rather disconcerted and said with a laugh: "Doesn't he say the craziest things?"

"Dr Hain specializes in grafting glands," Kurt said, continuing his introduction. "He has just succeeded in making an English naval lieutenant out of a baboon. It's all glands with him, nothing but glands."

"Are you fond of music?" the doctor asked for something to say.

"Crazy about it," Ruth said enthusiastically. "I could sit here and listen all night."

"She thinks Stravinsky is the name of a dessert and that Beethoven is conductor at the Metropolitan in New York," Kurt said in German. Ruth watched his lips as though this would help her to understand the foreign language. "Miss Anderson does me too much honor," Kurt went on in an abruptly formal English. "She is the young lady who is going to marry Frank Taylor on Saturday, and whom we have all been looking forward to seeing for so long." At this the doctor bowed several times and shook Ruth's hand.

"I was to wait for Frank in the roof garden," she said, "but there's no roof garden. Then I heard Kurt playing the piano and crept in. It must be getting late."

The doctor went to the door that led from the bar to the roof. "No roof garden?" he asked in bewilderment when he saw that the whole wide space was empty and that tables and umbrellas and flower pots had been cleared away.

"In case of air raids," Kurt said from the piano. "No roof garden for the present."

"Then the bar is not any safer," Dr Hain said, stepping back quickly, as people do from a flash of lightning at a window.

"Oh, the bar? That's quite another matter, isn't it, Ruth?" Kurt said with a smile at the girl.

"I'm not afraid," Ruth said.

"No, we're not afraid," Kurt repeated. "We'll crawl under the piano when it starts. That's bombproof." He put his fingers on the keys and began the last movement of the sonata. Ruth was still sitting close beside him and listened.

Dr Hain resumed his place by the wall and gave himself up to the music. He had not heard Kurt play for a long time. It was really surprising that the boy had not forgotten his Beethoven. He played beautifully, with restraint and yet with feeling; there was nothing weak or sentimental in his playing. There was strength and expression, almost greatness. What a pianist he might have been! Hain thought sadly. The greatest of German pianists, if he had been allowed to mature. The shadow of his dead friend Max Lilien flitted as a ghost through the dance bar of the Shanghai Hotel: the doors onto the terrace were wide open, outside lay the garden in Grunewald; Irene, Roland, Beethoven, the last sonata, the long trill—and then cataclysm. . . .

"You are not afraid either, Doctor, it seems to me," Ruth said when this movement too was over.

"Child," he said, "you get to a point in life that lies beyond all fear."

Kurt gave him a quick, searching glance. During all the years of their common exile the doctor had never breathed a word about the past. "How does the old German doctor really live?" someone had asked Kurt. "He waits for letters that do not come," he had replied.

"But would it not be better if you waited for your fiancé somewhere else? In the lounge, for example? Shall I bring you down there?" Dr Hain asked, going to the piano.

Ruth shook her head. "I've had enough of the lounge," she said. "If I only knew where Frank was! You can't telephone. I went to his office, but he isn't there, either. There's that fat French lady sitting in the lounge, and she wants to sell me to a very, very rich Chinese. It's much nicer for me up here."

"Ruth was born to be a heroine," Kurt explained. "First of all she's a hospital nurse, and secondly she's been through the wildest things as an airplane hostess, and thirdly she's come on her own to Shang-

hai to take part in the war, and fourthly she's not afraid to sit in the
dark with a down-and-out like me. Is that all, Ruth?"

The doctor listened with slight uneasiness to the young man's ran-
dom chatter. Either he's very unhappy or else it's the opium, he
thought, weighing it all up.

"A nurse?" he said to Ruth. "Then we're almost colleagues. Will
you help us if we organize a voluntary ambulance service?"

"Sure," Ruth said as if to say: Why ask?

Suddenly all the lights in the bar flared up. Somebody must have
switched them on somewhere. Kurt struck a harsh chord on the
piano and got up. "Excuse me, Miss Anderson," he said, with much
too low a bow, "I must put on my livery."

She looked after him with astonishment as he went to the door.
"Is he angry?" she asked the doctor. The doctor shook his head.
The bar mixer came in and began putting his bottles and glasses in
order. Behind him Eugen, the headwaiter, came in a sweeping glide
over the polished floor. He gave a fleeting and anxious glance
through the door to the roof garden and then shut it. "We shan't do
much business tonight," he said to the bar attendant. The Negro
who shared the piano with Kurt crept in with his head down, black
face above a white dinner jacket. He stretched his long, thin, double-
jointed fingers until they cracked and then put them on the keys
without looking.

"There's Frank," Ruth said, long before Frank was actually there.
Kurt Planke had stopped in the doorway and never taken his eyes
off Ruth. When he saw the radiant and beaming and unmistakable
transformation in her face as she gave Frank her hand, he screwed
up his face as if he had bitten a peppercorn. He put his hands in his
pockets and came back into the bar.

"Sorry I'm so late, Tiny," Frank said. "Fact is, it's getting serious
with the volunteers. They turned us out for a little drill, and it went
on for hours. This is Morris," he said, pointing to a young man who
had come in with him. "Morris is going to be my best man; a decent
fellow, Morris. You mightn't think it, the way he's looking now."

Morris, as well as Frank, looked tired out, and their white suits
were crumpled. Morris' hair was too red and his eyes too blue; a

cigarette hung from his underlip whether he laughed, talked or drank. Ruth shook his enormous hand. "Frank has told me a lot about you," she said. Morris pulled a face.

"Time the boy was tied up," he said. Why do they all tell me that? Ruth thought in passing.

"Morris is a newshawk. He knows the East upside down. He says we're in for it in a day or two," Frank said.

"It's begun already," Morris said dryly. "There's been a little scrap already, and I shall find out where, too. The Chinese mean to force the Japanese to fight."

"The Chinese? I always thought the Chinese were cowards," said Ruth.

"That's why," Morris said. "Less than four thousand Japanese have disembarked so far, and there are enough Chinese soldiers in Shanghai—I'll eat my hat if there are less than a hundred thousand."

"You have no hat," Frank said, and he wiped his hands.

"Midget," he said, "I'm afraid the houseboat's off. I'd have loved to give you a romantic trip, but the trains are not to be relied on—now."

"Never mind, Chippy," Ruth said. "I'm here for good. Later on perhaps."

"That's right—later," Frank said. They were talking about B.S.'s houseboat, which was in Soochow Creek and on which they had been planning to have a honeymoon trip over the week end. Frank looked round. "Not very cheerful—with no one about," he said, moving his shoulders in his white suit. Eugen came up. "Probably we shall soon have to close the bar for tonight," he said officiously. Dr Hain joined them under the influence of a vague and anxious curiosity.

"Is there going to be shooting already?" he asked.

"Nothing serious so far, but we shall get it all right," Morris assured him. For a moment Dr Hain could distinctly smell powder, that unforgettable burning smell in the nostrils that hung over the trenches after a raid. Powder, blood, dirt, death and the fear of death. Frank took him by the arm and led him up to the bar.

"What will you have, Tiny? What's it to be, Doctor?"

Ruth held tightly to Frank's hand and looked at him seriously. "I'm thirsty," she said. "What shall I drink?"

Frank considered the matter. "White Lady or gin fizz," he said. "I suggest a White Lady."

"All right—a White Lady," Ruth said obediently. Two other men had strolled in, but the bar looked deserted.

"Thank you, but I will drink nothing now," Dr Hain said, too awkward to find an exit.

"Scotch and soda," Frank ordered. "What's yours, Morris?"

"Double Scotch for me," Morris said. Both men had been drinking already; Ruth could see that. Frank smiled at her over the edge of his glass and winked. "I'll be glad when it gets started," he said cheerfully. "It's a strain on the nerves waiting for the first bomb."

"All the best," Morris said, and emptied his glass.

"The same to you," Ruth said, thirstily drinking her cocktail. Kurt stood by and watched them. The Negro was whipping syncopations out of the piano. Beethoven vanished like a ghost from the bar.

"It's a pity Miss Anderson is so conventional," Kurt said unexpectedly in a loud voice. Frank looked round in astonishment.

"What do you mean?" he asked. "Another Scotch," he told the barman.

"If Miss Anderson were not so conventional she would fall in love with me instead of marrying a nice successful American businessman like you," Kurt said, loud and quarrelsome. "She would try to pull me out of the mud on which, as everyone knows, Shanghai was built, instead of living on American exports at two hundred dollars the month. Or is it three hundred?"

"What will you drink?" Frank asked good-naturedly. He was obviously a little exhilarated, and he pushed Kurt down onto the stool beside him.

"Gin and nothing," Kurt said, settling his foot on the brass rail. He waved his glass with an exaggerated air. "To Miss Anderson," he said. "Beautiful as the dawn and virtuous as the missionary's widow."

"A double Scotch," Morris said.

The bar was no longer empty, though it was far from crowded.

The few who came in were noisier than usual, as though they wanted to drown some other menacing sound in the air.

Dr Hain waited. Kurt had forgotten he was there. "Another gin," he said loudly. Eugen, the headwaiter, whispered in his ear that it was time he changed. "We want atmosphere," he insisted in a whisper, and Kurt burst out laughing. "Atmosphere is right," he shouted, laughing. "The atmosphere here is like a mass burial. A few shovelfuls of earth and done with it." He drank up his gin and pushed his glass across again.

"You shouldn't drink so much, Kurt," Ruth said anxiously.

"Why not? Why not me in particular, beautiful damsel? Why am I in particular not to drink?" he asked irritably. Suddenly he became serious; he put down his glass and looked in Ruth's face.

"It's really a pity with me," he said in a low voice. "You must admit it's a pity, Ruth." He put up his arm in mock salute: "Heil," he shouted, "Heil! If I had not got among Jews and intellectuals I should have been all right. I should have stayed at home and become a chauffeur like my father or an engineer like my uncle; I should have worn a brown shirt and shouted 'Heil' and been happy. I am an Aryan; you see, Ruth, a pure Aryan. It does not do us Aryans any good to be intellectual. We cannot stand it. The Baltic Sea," he went on, "I often feel homesick for the Baltic." He encountered Ruth's anxious look. "But there!" he said contemptuously. "To you it's all —Stravinsky. Good evening, gentlemen."

Dr Hain's gray face had gone rather pale as he listened to what Kurt had been saying. "Why do you never come to our chamber-music evenings, my boy?" he asked as though that might help him. "We play every Wednesday night——"

Kurt did not even hear him, he did not even see him. The doctor stood there in his old shoes, awkwardly, for a moment longer, shifting from one foot to the other; then he turned round and crept slowly out of the bar. At the door he met Mr Russell, coming in; he looked clean and well turned out as usual.

"How are you feeling now, Mr Russell?" the doctor asked. Russell did not recognize him and looked at him in surprise. "Thanks, thanks, fine. How are you?" he asked as he went on. He sat down next to Kurt and ordered a Pernod. "Potter tells me the bar is going to be closed," he said, looking sleepily and yet intently at Kurt.

"You all know each other? Miss Anderson, the Honourable Bobbie Russell," Kurt said, introducing them.

"How are you, Frank?" Bobbie asked.

"Fine, thanks. How's yourself, Bobbie?" Frank replied.

"Telephone call for Mr Taylor," Eugen said, gliding up to Frank.

"For me?" Frank said in astonishment. Eugen waited at his elbow. "Who is it?" Frank asked.

Eugen shrugged his shoulder. "Must be B.S.," Frank said. "It's *our* wedding, and *he* gets the stage fright. Won't be a moment," he said to Ruth. He emptied his glass and went out.

Morris meanwhile had been getting obstinately and quietly drunk. "Best of luck," he kept on saying to Ruth every time he had a fresh whisky. "Best of luck. Time he was tied up. Well, best of luck."

The Negro had stopped playing. "Music," Eugen told Kurt. Kurt pretended not to hear. "Music," Eugen said in a rougher tone.

"What's the use?" Bobbie asked. "There's not a living soul in the bar. Much better shut up. Dreary hole. And dangerous into the bargain." He gripped Kurt by the arm as he got up. Kurt shook him off, and the stool overturned.

"Come to the piano with me, Ruth," Kurt begged her with sudden gentleness. "I'll play for you."

Ruth was glad to leave the bar. She followed Kurt across the smooth, vacant floor. He walked stiffly in front of her and pulled up a chair for her beside him at the piano. "Schubert," he said. "No one's listening."

Ruth sat erect with her hands in her lap like a well-behaved child. Kurt observed it with tender amusement. "I've got to talk to you, Ruth," he said. "It's very important. You don't know how important it is. It is a matter of life and death, Ruth."

He had begun to play while he spoke, and he went on playing without looking either at the keys or at Ruth. His eyes were riveted on Bobbie Russell's back. "Lifesaving is your speciality, isn't it? Nursing, love of humanity and so on. Well then, listen, Ruth: spend this evening with me. Leave your Frank Taylor to his own devices. He doesn't need you. I do. I'm—in danger. I am sick. I must be looked after and protected. I cannot be left alone. Listen, Ruth, I want nothing from you, you understand that, but I need you this evening. I'll play the piano for you. Or you can tell me something, or I'll tell you something, I'll be quiet and sensible, I promise. Yes, Ruth? You will? Tell Frank you'd promised me. He and that Morris are just ripe for a night at the club. You can't refuse to save my life. It's against your oath as a nurse."

Ruth listened to this fevered nonsense in growing astonishment. "You're drunk," she said not unkindly.

Kurt banged the keys. "There—you're drunk. I might have known that was coming. No, beauteous damsel, you don't know what I am like when I'm drunk. Just help me, stay with me. Quick, say yes before Frank comes back from the telephone."

Ruth laughed embarrassedly. "You must be crazy," she said, worriedly. The dread, the despair and the candor of Kurt's words touched her, even though what he said made no sense. "You must be crazy, Kurt," she said. "Frank and I have been invited to a party, and it's practically the eve of our wedding, and so how can I possibly stay with you? Do be a good boy and not so unreasonable," she begged him. His hands raced faster and faster over the keys like scared animals, and each separate finger had a mind and a fear of its own.

"Now listen to me, Ruth," Kurt said. "If you were crossing Nanking Road down below and I had the luck to jump down from the roof garden at that very moment to land at your feet with a cracked skull and in no end of a mess but with a flicker of life left in my carcass—would you go to your party or would you pick me up and take me to a hospital and try to save me?"

Ruth laughed. "What a silly question!" she said. She looked towards the door, but Frank did not return.

"You would come to my rescue, wouldn't you? Answer me! Yes, of course you would. Well then, Ruth: I have actually jumped down and there *is* only a flicker of life in me. Only instant help can rescue me. You cannot possibly go to your wedding-eve party. You must see that. You've got to lift me up and look after me. If you leave me alone tonight——"

"I am sorry—there's Frank," Ruth said. She hurried to the door as Frank came in. He looked pale and not at all well. He was wiping his hands on his handkerchief, and there were drops of water on his face, as if he had only just washed. Bobbie Russell got up from the bar and sauntered over to the piano. Kurt went on playing like mad, no longer the Schubert impromptu but one of Brahms's Hungarian dances.

"Well?" Bobbie Russell said.

"Right," Kurt replied as he shut the piano.

"What was the matter with the phone?" Ruth asked in the doorway. Frank looked at her as if she were a ghost.

"With the phone? Nothing," he said.

XIV

HELEN SAT ON HER BED with the receiver still in her hand, long after Frank had rung off. The words they had spoken still hung in the air as clearly as if written there.

Frank, I can't bear it any longer, I must see you, just once more, just tonight. You must get free. I must talk to you.

Madness, Helen. Can't be done. I can't leave Ruth alone. We're invited to B.S.'s, a party in our honor. I'm sorry, Helen.

I am afraid I'm behaving clumsily, Frank. It sounds ridiculous, but it is the first time in my life I have ever loved anybody. I'm only a beginner, so forgive me. What are we to do, Frank?

It's just our luck, darling. Nothing to be done.

Do you love me, Frank?

You know I do.

And you're going to be married the day after tomorrow? You stick to it?

I must stick to it, Helen. I love you, but that doesn't mean I'm a cad. Can't you understand that?

What did you say?

Nothing.

Please come to me for one moment. I'm in my room. I can't talk to you on the telephone. Only for five minutes, Frank. Come, now —at once. . . . Did you say something, Frank? Why don't you answer, Frank?

Silence.

I'm sorry, Helen darling. You know yourself what would happen if I came to you now.

Frank? Frank? Frank?

The room was much too silent now that the telephone gave no sound. Helen had turned off the electric fan in order to hear Frank's voice more clearly. She still held the receiver helplessly in her hand. Clarkson came in, the white dress with the green bamboo pattern over her arm.

"Did you call me, madam?"

"No, Clarkson, thank you. Put the dress down. I don't know whether I shall go out."

What am I to do now? I thought I could bear it. I can't bear it, Frank. I can't. She switched the fan on again and the radio, too. Dance music from the Peony Club. Intolerable. She turned it off. I shall go to the bar and make a scene. I'll write that Anderson girl a letter and tell her the truth. It's impossible that Frank should give me up for her. Her curls and her voice and her dress. I wouldn't take her as a servant, and he wants to marry her. Idiotic, ridiculous, impossible. Frank, listen, it's all impossible. If I could only speak to him; if he wouldn't avoid me—it's enough to drive one mad, it's paralyzing.

Hello, hello, please put me on to the bar again. . . . Hello, hello, will you ask Mr Frank Taylor to come to the telephone. . . . Frank Taylor, yes, yes. Mr Taylor. . . . What? He's not there any more? Do you know where he's gone? . . . No? Thank you.

Helen stared at the telephone, that evil invention from which issued nothing but disappointment and denial. She banged the receiver back and began raging up and down the room. There was not enough room, as in all hotel bedrooms in the world. She pushed some chairs aside to clear a little space.

I shan't put up with it. I refuse to be treated like this. Who does that little clerk think he is? Does he think because he's good-looking, a good-looking, uncontrolled young animal without a sensitive nerve in his body, does he think he can behave as he likes? A good-looking young animal—oh, Frank, the back of your neck. Your hair, your mouth. Oh, Frank, oh, Frank, oh, Frank, what on earth are we to do?

She encountered herself in the mirror, a tall, pale, utterly strange woman with wide-open mouth; the mouth was fixed like a cry of pain, like a Greek tragic mask. She passed her hands over her face as though to wipe it out, and then she began to caress her cheeks with her fingertips. She tried to console herself, but she was inconsolable. She knelt down in front of a chair and, putting her head in her arms, tried to cry. It was no good. She could not cry. I can't even cry, she thought in despair. You're all alone, she said in self-pity, all alone with no one to help you. Jelena, poor Ljenotschka, all alone. No little father, no little mother—the words came to her of themselves; where had she heard them? Did they come from an old song? No little father, no little mother. Grischa, the beggar outside the Peony Club—that was after our last dance. . . .

She turned the radio on again, and instantly the dance music was there. Most people can cry when they hear music, but I can't. Nonsense. Why should you cry, Jelena? You ought to think, coldly and clearly. Sentimentality is only harmful. I've always got what I wanted. I shall not allow this marriage to take place. Do I want Frank? Yes, with every drop of my blood, with every pore of my body, with every hair on my head, I want him. Good, then I shall have him. Keep calm, Ljenotschka, little dove, we shan't allow this absurdity to happen. Frank loves me and I love him. How many hours are left in which to put a stop to this marriage? Let me see, let me just see——

She picked up her small traveling clock from the table by the bed, gave it a shake, held it to her ear and scrutinized its little hands. Ten minutes past twelve. How the time goes on. I must have lost consciousness. I must have been beside myself. Yes, beside myself.

It's funny how that phrase hits the nail on the head. What nail? Nonsense. I was beside myself, and now I have come back to myself. There are still thirty-six hours left. That's a long time. This whole affair with Frank has only lasted seventy-two hours from beginning to end. Be quiet, it is not the end. There is no end. Much can happen in thirty-six hours. Concentrate. Think. Strategy, that's the thing.

She rang, and Clarkson came in with the faint reproach on her puckered face that servants wear who have not got to bed in good time.

"I am sorry, Clarkson," Helen said at once. "I want a white linen suit, a blouse and my panama hat with the green ribbon. Then you can go to bed."

"Are you going out now, madam? Will you want the car?"

"No, I shall take a taxi if I do go out. Is Potter still up? Mr Russell has not come home, has he?"

"I don't think so," Clarkson said, pursing her lips. "Shall I call Potter?"

"Yes, call him, if you don't mind, Clarkson. Good night, Clarkson."

After a while there was a knock, and Potter came in. "You wanted me, madam?" he asked, with an alert look on his face.

"Have you any idea where Mr Russell has gone?" Helen asked. Potter merely smiled at the notion. "And you don't know when he may be back?" she went on. Potter raised his shoulders to his ears and let them fall again very expressively.

"Well, it doesn't matter," Helen said. "When he does come home let him sleep: you understand me, Potter, let him sleep on, even if he sleeps all day. I shall be very busy tomorrow. Kindly tell Mr Russell he need not worry about me." She thought hard and then added as an inspiration: "I have to buy farewell presents, tell him that."

"Very good, madam," Potter said. "And as regards the boat——"

"Yes?" Helen asked, distraught and impatient. She was already turning over the leaves of the telephone directory.

"There is only one boat for Hong Kong. That is, there is not a berth left on any of the others. It is a Dutch boat, very small and second-rate, called the *Soerabaya*. It goes between Japan and Java, and it sails on Saturday, the 14th of August, at one o'clock in the afternoon. It takes three days to Hong Kong with a short stay at Amoy."

"Doesn't sound too good, Potter," Helen said, putting the directory aside.

"No, indeed, madam," Potter replied. "I have taken four cabins. There is only one class. In their steerage they transport Chinese coolies for the rubbber plantations in Sumatra. Unfortunately they have no cabins with private bathrooms. Not like an English boat. All berths on the good boats have been reserved for a long time. Everyone who can is pushing off from here."

"Yes, that's certainly the most sensible thing to do," Helen said in order to reassure Potter. "Well then, we can leave the day after tomorrow. You have done very well, Potter. You have done very well. You look tired, you had better go to bed, Potter."

"Madam's had nothing to eat tonight," Potter said in a slightly worried tone.

"It's too hot," Helen said. "Listen, Potter," she added quickly, "have your sleep out, don't wait up for my husband. Go to your room. I shall be up for a long time."

"Very good, madam," Potter said with a meaning look, and withdrew in his casual manner. Helen listened until his step had retreated from the sitting room and then took up the telephone receiver once more. She had made up her mind to see Frank that night whatever happened. She knew the number of his flat by heart, but it took almost ten minutes before she got through.

"What on earth is the matter with the telephone?" she asked, raging with impatience. The telephone girl murmured excuses which conveyed nothing to Helen. "The lines are always engaged," she said. "It's due to the troop movements."

Helen was annoyed to feel her knees trembling while she sat there waiting for the connection. The burning, smarting and writhing thought had come to her that a call at this time might interrupt Frank in the arms of that Anderson girl.

"No reply," the operator said.

"Ring again," Helen said obstinately. Finally there was a click. "Hello," came a drowsy voice. "Frank," Helen said in a parched voice.

"Ah Sinfu speak. Master Tai-lo boy. Master Tai-lo no home," the telephone said drowsily but dutifully.

"Where is Master Tai-lo?" Helen asked.

"Big party," the telephone said.

"Where?" Helen asked. "Where? Savvy? Where?"

"Master Tai-lo go Master B.S. big party," Ah Sinfu said with composure.

"What telephone number?" Helen shouted into the mouthpiece; but Ah Sinfu had already rung off and was creeping back under his mosquito net. Helen put down the telephone and thought hard. The clock ticked on and on. Time was passing. She forced her brain to function. B.S.—B.S.—B.S.—"Scott," she said aloud and applied herself once more to the directory. She could not tell in what pigeonhole of her subconscious self the name which Frank had once mentioned in conversation had taken up its abode. There were three pages of Scotts in the directory. There were five Scotts with B in their first names. Helen chose one of the five and began her fight with the telephone afresh. She was now as desperately clear and decided as when Lord Inglewood died just before her wedding and she had to make up her mind to marry his money—and his nephew. The clock ticked, time passed. The half-hours struck from the church in the French quarter with that pleasant homelike sound of all church clocks. The little Chinese telephone operator with the weary and obliging voice worked away diligently with her plugs. The telephone was full of confused voices and noise.

"We must give it up. I am extremely sorry, the circumstances today are quite exceptional," the operator said.

"Never mind, never mind. Thank you," Helen said. She had kept her forefinger in the place in the directory. She looked at the address of this Barley Scott: 367 Squarefield Road. She took a sheet of notepaper out of the drawer and wrote down the address. Next she put on the white linen suit Clarkson had laid out for her, washed her hands, fleetingly powdered her pale face with her sun-tan powder, which clung darkly to her blanched skin. She took the glass stopper form her perfume bottle and dabbed the lobes of her ears. Then she put the address in her purse and left the hotel.

It was an endless taxi drive to 367 Squarefield Road, and Helen had no idea what to do when she got there. She was driven on and on, and the night air restored her slightly. She was taken all along Bubbling Well Road and beyond; the houses were detached and stood among vacant building sites; now and then large lorries rattled by, loaded with soldiers. The journey ceased to have any reality; it traversed sparse and dreary realms of dreamland. At last the taxi stopped at a garden gate. It was dark, for there was a lamp only at the corner of the street, and the house stood between two vacant lots. Helen got out and looked through the bars. There was a small lawn on the other side, as far as she could see, and perhaps a little pond, for frogs croaked from the darkness. The house was in darkness too and scarcely visible; the garden gate was locked. Helen tried the handle once or twice and then gave it up. Suddenly she felt tired, so suddenly that it came on her like a fainting fit. But Helen did not faint. The taxi was still there, and the Chinese driver was smiling inquisitively and happily with his large mouth open. Two soldiers came by. They were Europeans—English.

"Can I help you, madam?" the taller of the two asked, looking rather dubiously at her.

"I was invited to a party, but I got here rather late," Helen said.

"There were a lot of lights and cars here only a quarter of an hour ago," the soldier said. "A wedding or engagement party or something of the kind. The fun is over now, lady."

"Thank you," Helen said. She got into the taxi. "Back to the hotel," she said.

It was just before two by the time she reached the hotel. The musicians from the large ballroom were just leaving with their instruments in their hands. The sky above the roof garden was low and overcast. The searchlights by the river pierced unceasingly into it for signs of danger. The night doorman held the door open for Helen.

He sniffed the night air. Smells like damp gunpowder, he thought to himself. Madame Tissaud was sitting in the empty lounge, lonely as a monument, surrounded by magazines in every language which she had read to the last word.

"Madame Russell, so late? And all alone? What news is there? Stay a moment for a nightcap," she implored.

"I'm tired," Helen said. She had become dizzy as soon as she entered the brightly lighted lounge. She had come back as though from a distant and dangerous expedition. She leaned for support on the black marble top of the nearest table.

"Our little Japanese has been looking for you," Madame Tissaud said, and her nostrils quivered like a rabbit's. Helen smiled vacantly. What am I to do now? she thought. Where can I find Frank now?

Outside in Nanking Road Frank brought his little car to a stop and took his right arm from Ruth's shoulder, where he had put it from habit. "It's late, Tiny," he said. "We've been around enough. Now back to the stable. I have to shave tomorrow morning and you haven't."

Ruth rubbed her cheek drowsily against his sleeve. "Are we happy?" she asked.

"Happy as bullfrogs," he replied.

She considered this earnestly. "Are bullfrogs very happy?" she asked.

"You only have to hear them in a rice field, in June, say at full moon," Frank said.

He got out and walked round the automobile to open the door. She was stalling. "Good night," she said without moving. When Frank realized that she was waiting for a kiss he looked round on all sides; but he had just had enough drink not to bother very much about Nanking Road at night. Ruth's lips were fresh and cool; dawning mouth, he thought as he bent over her. The fever is giving way, he thought. It will soon pass, he thought. It must pass, he thought.

"Now I'm in Shanghai," Ruth said.

"Yes, now you are in Shanghai," Frank agreed. He now helped

her out of the car and gave the revolving door a push to let her in. They walked across the lounge without noticing Helen.

"There's our couple," Madame Tissaud said.

Helen yawned quickly. "I am so tired. Good night," she said hurriedly. Madame's hand, smelling of powder and vanilla, still lay on her arm; she breathlessly shook it off.

"I always say the lounge of the Shanghai Hotel is more to me than any theater," Madame said to her retreating back. Helen crossed the lounge with a roaring in her ears as though she were swimming up through a great, high waterfall.

Frank had the key of Ruth's room in his hand. She was already at the elevator and pressing the bell. There was a rumbling in the closed shaft, and then it opened.

"Shall I take you up?" Frank asked politely. Ruth scrutinized his face for an instant. "No, thanks, Frank," she said as politely.

"Good evening," Helen said. Her perfume had preceded her by half a second, and Frank had had time to get himself under control.

"Good evening," he said.

"Good evening, Mrs Russell," said Ruth. "Isn't it a wonderful night!"

"Is it?" Helen asked. All three stood waiting for a moment. "I am glad to see you once more," Helen said. "It'll do for good-by as well. We are leaving the day after tomorrow."

"Are you?" Frank said. "I hope you'll have a good voyage," he said as an afterthought.

"Thank you. Thank you very much," Helen said. "Perhaps we'll come across each other again, someday, somewhere."

"I hope so. I hope so," Frank said, rather too impulsively. "You're sure to come back to Shanghai. Everyone who's been here comes back again."

"Good night, Chippy," Ruth said to Frank. "It's time I got home. Confucius will be impatient. Are you going up, Mrs Russell?" she asked, stepping to one side to let her enter the elevator first. Helen's white lips, on which there was only a little cracked rouge left, laughed. "What a nice nickname and so suitable——" she said with a break in her voice. Frank had his hands in his pockets—the helpless, ridiculous male. Ruth was waiting, and Helen got in the elevator. There was nothing else for her to do. I must just speak to Frank for a moment. I have to post a letter. I haven't drunk up my coffee. I am going to play a game of draughts with Madame Tissaud. The elevator was already going up with her by the time these pretexts occurred to her. I shall tell this Anderson woman the truth, and right now, she thought savagely. She took out her powder box and powdered her nose, pointlessly.

"I am glad to see you alone for a moment, Miss Anderson," she said.

"Me?" Ruth asked in astonishment.

"It's about Frank and you," Helen said.

"I know," Ruth said. "He's nervous and he doesn't look well. But I shall soon put him right."

"I did not mean that," Helen said.

"Please don't speak about it," Ruth said quickly. "It's so kind of you to worry about him. I think all the men in Shanghai drink a bit more than they ought to. But it will all be different as soon as we are married."

The lift stopped. "Sixth floor," the elevator boy said as he opened the gate.

"Good night," Ruth said. "And thank you again—thank you. It's been so kind of you, Mrs Russell."

"Good night," Helen heard herself say. The gate clanged to. She discovered the politely expectant Chinese smile of the elevator boy directed upon her.

"Sixteenth?" he asked.

"No. Down again—to the lounge, quickly," Helen said.

But Frank had gone. Madame Tissaud sat alone. Helen clenched her teeth and simply walked past her, through the revolving door, out of the hotel and into the street. The night sky was already going lighter.

"Taxi," she called out.

The door of the house where Frank Taylor lived was locked. There was no bell. I shall wait here till morning, Helen thought as she leaned against the wall. She let the taxi go. This is hell itself, she thought, dizzy with fatigue. The first factory sirens were sounding far across the river. A few men accosted her as she stood leaning against the wall of the house; sailors, Jews, and Eurasian, a Frenchman. A funny town, Shanghai. Two more lorry loads of soldiers. A ricksha went by. A fat old Chinese woman was sitting in it with a slender Chinese girl on her lap. The young one was drunk and the old one worried. The ricksha had Chinese characters in neon lights at the back. Noiselessly as a boat the apparition vanished round the corner. Next the surface of the street stirred beneath Helen's eyes. A heap of humanity had been asleep there, and now their gray forms crept apart in the gray light. One groaned, another shouted a curse, the others laughed. They settled down afresh and grew again into the street in their protective coloring of destitution. Rats scurried close to Helen's feet. Strange air of a strange night in a strange and utterly alien town.

A patrol of four Irishmen took Helen for a whore and chased her roughly away. She could not find a taxi and went back to the hotel on foot; it was not far. I can do no more, she thought in exhaustion. Her will had driven her to a standstill, emptied her. When she got upstairs she opened the door of her husband's bedroom. He had not come in. His bed was untouched, the electric fan hummed all by itself, all the lights were on. Helen looked in Bobbie's bathroom for a sleeping powder, but to her surprise she could find nothing of the sort. His dressing gown hung on the door; it was of white Shantung silk with black facings and a large black monogram on the breast pocket. Very elegant, Helen thought with dreary scorn. She was as nauseated by the garment as if it were Bobbie himself. She took care not to collide with it as she went out of the door. She went to her bedroom and began to undress.

"It's tomorrow already," she thought. "I can sleep all today and the boat leaves tomorrow."

She lay down and pulled the clothes over her. They say Hong Kong is a beautiful town. Not so amusing as Shanghai. Amusing town, Shanghai. Why do they give anesthetics for operations only? There are things that are much more painful. An anesthetic, please— I want to go to sleep. I must go to sleep. Jelena must have sleep.

I shall ask the German doctor for a narcotic of some kind. Narcotic. Narcoticum. Perhaps Bobbie is right with his opium. Frank. Not Frank any longer. Don't will anything any more. Tired. Good. Frank. Sleep.

XV

FOR TWO DAYS Yoshio Murata had been sitting despondently on the wooden balcony that ran all round the first floor of the hotel, watching the Chinese troops pouring out of the North Station. At night windows and doors rattled as the heavy lorries went by with soldiers clinging to them in clusters. He could not sleep for the noise. It occurred to him that the troops were not half so badly equipped as people liked to believe in Japan. Things had altered a lot since the war in Manchuria, where it had been difficult to distinguish between Chinese bandits and Chinese soldiers. If Yoshio had been a real reporter he would have been out in the streets and telegraphing a thousand interesting items to his newspaper. But as he had only the thin blood of the literary person who found himself on the staff of a newspaper merely because modern times had little use for the composer of thirty-one syllable poems, and as he was one of those people who are slightly nauseated by the stench of reality, he sat planted on his balcony with his hands before him as though paralyzed.

The telephone was not working. The manager of the hotel, distrustful, apprehensive and annoyed by the loss his business suffered because the Japanese generals and admirals were so clumsy as to allow the war to spread to Shanghai, had given up saying more than good morning and good evening. As for Mr Endo, Yoshio was afraid of him. Mr Endo had too facile and optimistic a character. In his mouth Yoshio's mission had sounded perfectly simple and obvious; but Jelena had done nothing, had not done one of the things that Mr Endo had prophesied. Every effort to arouse her interest in the mysterious portfolio containing the plans had come to nothing. Yoshio was not sure whether this was due to her indifference or to his own clumsiness. Jelena has very greatly altered, he thought in distress. She had transformed herself from a charming little French woman into a tall, cold, unapproachable English lady. It was quite impossible to remind this new Jelena of their common past in Paris. He dressed, drove to the Shanghai Hotel, loitered about in the lounge, got caught in Madame Tissaud's toils, waited, lay in ambush, laid plans, drank tea, drank whisky to give himself courage, and waited again: Jelena remained invisible. With much anguish he telephoned up to her room from the telephone booth in the lounge, and she sent her lady's maid to the phone instead of coming herself. In despair Yoshio Murata went and bought flowers, an ostentatious Japanese arrangement in a flat, square tray: red dwarf maple, moss and three white, wild orchids on clammy, stiff stalks. Jelena made no acknowledgment. Yoshio drove back to his hotel, through the excited crowds to the North Station. He tried to write a poem in English, but keeping the Japanese syllable form —a tender and also allusive poem which was intended to lead up to a new encounter with Jelena. It was a difficult and ticklish task he had set himself, for the English language was not well adapted to it, and thirty-one English syllables scarcely enabled him to open the subject—not to speak of the impossibility of expressing anything that was not pure nonsense in the more elegant form of seventeen syllables. The greater part of the following day was spent in this way, and the only result was that numerous rolls of thin, long, Japanese writing paper littered the floor of Yoshio's uninviting room.

In the evening he sat on the balcony and waited—for nothing. The square below was seething with soldiers, lorries, bayonets, shouts, commands and laughter. I have failed, Yoshio thought. When he had thought this a thousand times over, he was ready to commit suicide. Suicide is the proper punishment for a man who has been given a mission of importance and failed. Besides, it was much easier and simpler to commit suicide than to present himself before Mr Endo. So at least his Japanese soul whispered to him in the course of many mute colloquies.

The fear to live and the courage to die dwell close together in the Japanese soul—so near that they are almost one and the same. Yoshio

Murata was in any case so afraid of confessing his failure to Mr Endo, and thereafter returning to his empty and tedious married life without having earned the little scraps of merit and glory this mission offered, that he thought of his death with joyful anticipation. After some reflection he had decided to cut his arteries in the bath; it was not a very heroic, but it was at the same time a fairly painless, form of suicide. For the moment he was prevented because at this hour before the Japanese dinnertime the common bathroom at the Myako Hotel was occupied without intermission. But a letter to his parents was already written, and he had put on his thin blue-and-white kimono and got a new razor blade ready.

There was a knock at his door, and the surly servant gave him a letter. The letter was from Mr Endo. Yoshio read it with a wan smile while he felt a little chill shiver creeping about the roots of his hair.

HONORABLE FRIEND [the letter said]:

Permit me to express the great disappointment it has caused me to have heard nothing as yet concerning the chrysanthemum blooms over which we had such a delightful and hopeful conversation together. Our friends rely with the greatest confidence on the adroitness of your esteemed hands and are convinced that you will overcome every difficulty that the climate of Shanghai may place in the way of the unfolding of the noble blooms. I beseech you to assuage my impatience and curiosity over your horticultural experiment by a speedy answer. As there are regrettable and unexpected little difficulties of late with the telephone, I suggest that you honor my unworthy house with a visit tomorrow morning, when I am sure you will only have good news to give me. With the hope that your honorable health . . .

"The lady is waiting for an answer," the servant said. It was only now that Yoshio Murata noticed that a Japanese girl in modern dress was standing in the passage outside his door and watching him through the chink while he read the letter. "Hello," she said with a smile as soon as he looked up at her.

"Hello," he replied absent-mindedly. He read the letter a second time. "Perhaps you would be so good as to wait in the hall while I answer the letter," he said with embarrassment. But the young lady came in and shut the door, leaving the servant outside. Yoshio pulled his kimono more closely about him.

"Have you been out today?" she asked without more ado.

"No," Yoshio said with hesitation.

"But you're going out? You'll have a surprise. You can hardly get along, patrols everywhere, town's lousy with soldiers." She had been speaking in English all the time, that commonplace, ordinary English of the American West, mixed with slang.

"Really!" Yoshio said.

"Sure. You want a pass and then you're okay. Here you are. Our friend has seen to that."

Yoshio took the small stamped document with a bow. "Has Mr Endo——"

"No names," the girl said. "This pass enables you to go where you like. And you're expected to get about a bit. It's going to be hot stuff here now. You know what happened in East Paoshan Road?"

Yoshio conveyed in a mutter that he did not. The girl, though young, was far from pretty. She was loud and pushing. It sounded as if she had come to give him orders. She was to the last degree what in Japan would be called *moga,* a modern girl, but of the most unpleasant sort.

"There's been a scrap in Hongkew Park already. Our troops were attacked as they disembarked. They say they've killed two thousand Chinese. Fine, eh?"

"Two thousand?" Yoshio asked in a matter-of-fact tone.

"About. Well, I've no time to waste. Any answer?"

"I will write a few words if you'll be so kind as to wait," Yoshio said, offering her a chair.

"Okay," the girl said. She whistled while he wrote. Without any doubt the most exasperating creature he had ever come across. He sat down at his table and got out some paper. He adjusted his spectacles, took out his fountain pen and with a sigh began to write. There was no question now of suicide, although, or perhaps because, Mr Endo's letter sounded more like a reproach than an encouragement.

HONORABLE MR ENDO [Yoshio wrote]:

Your revered writing has reached me at the very moment I am going out to have dinner with J.R. This night will decide much, and I am full of confidence. Be so kind as to give me a little of your honorable patience, and I am convinced I shall be able to bring you tomorrow morning a chrysanthemum in bloom. Meanwhile I hope that your honorable health . . .

Yoshio wrote his signature beneath the flourishes of politeness with which he ended his letter and, folding it up, gave it to the unattractive young Japanese, who put it in her pocket, said "Bye-bye" and departed.

He began at once to dress in great haste. The air of mystery about the chrysanthemum struck him as childish, but it also cheered him up. As he had so little practice in deception he soon began to believe what he had told Mr Endo. Suddenly it seemed a much simpler matter to encounter Jelena and to interest her in the forged plans than to repair to the unalluring bathroom of the Myako Hotel and to cut into his own veins with a razor blade. He held the blade in his hand for a moment before he put it away. There is still plenty of time for that if I fail this evening, he thought. On the stairs he solemnly promised himself either to succeed or to die. And so with only these alternatives before him, he valiantly paced his way through the surging, spitting, cursing Chinese soldiers who crowded the sidewalk outside the hotel. This time he had left the leather case behind, but he had put the plans in his breast pocket. The weather looked uncertain, and so he took his black umbrella with him, although it did not fit his exuberance.

The streets round the North Station were crowded with Chinese troops, but all the same nobody stopped him and nothing impeded his way. The soldiers looked through him as though he were a transparent or invisible ghost. It was an uncomfortable feeling. After a time he stopped an empty taxi and was driven to the Shanghai Hotel. The nearer he got to the International Settlement the more normal the traffic on the streets became. The Russian shops were shut, but all the open stalls of the Chinese were still doing business; phonographs could be heard from every window, women strolled about, the men had their jackets unbuttoned to expose their lean chests to the cool evening air. Yoshio bought two evening papers, but there was not a word in them about any battle. As he had been a war correspondent he started with a distrust of all sensational news. In any case, at the moment he himself was more important to him than two thousand slaughtered Chinese, and so he resolutely put all war news out of his mind. He had his own battle to fight. He had to suppress all the better and finer and more sensitive instincts of one who had been born for beauty before he could induce himself to enter once more the hostile precincts of the Shanghai Hotel. But as he was bound by oath to open his arteries if he failed to find Jelena, it was with considerable energy and dash that he hurled his weight against the revolving door.

At the very moment that the door shoveled him in, it was giving Jelena access to the street. Yoshio saw her flit by merely as a hallucination, a flash of white through the two plate-glass panels of the door. He took a deep breath and, making a complete revolution as in a merry-go-round, emerged again outside the hotel. Jelena was still there; she stood looking to right and left, up and down the seething Nanking Road.

"*Bonsoir,* Jelena-san," Yoshio said.

"*Bonsoir,*" she replied. She then looked round to see who it was that had greeted her. "*Bonsoir,*" she repeated absent-mindedly. She looked through him in the same way the Chinese soldiers had done, making of Yoshio an invisible specter.

"How do you do? I have been hoping so very much to see you again," he went on quickly, eagerly and imploringly in order to arrest her attention. These commonplaces did in fact sound so urgent that Helen woke up, as it were, and saw with surprise the little Japanese standing beside her. "How do you do?" he asked once more.

"How do I do? Very well. Excellently—dazzlingly. In fact I do exceedingly well," Helen said with irritation; her laugh was as brittle as heated glass.

"Why are you nervous, Jelena?" Yoshio asked. "Has something unpleasant happened to you? Can I do anything for you?"

"What day is it today?" she asked, instead of answering his question. She has very much changed, quite changed, Jelena-san, Yoshio thought as he saw her abrupt movements and her nervous smile.

"It is Friday," he said. "Friday the thirteenth."

"Friday," Helen said. "Then tomorrow is Saturday, isn't it?"

"Presumably," Yoshio said with a faint attempt at humor.

"Friday the thirteenth. Superstitious people would call that an unlucky day, wouldn't they?" she said, looking up and down the street again.

"Are you waiting for somebody?" Yoshio asked. "Or would you like a taxi, Jelena?"

"I am waiting for my husband," Jelena said after a short pause. "He has not come home."

"He might be staying late at the club; that is the fashion in Shanghai," Yoshio said with the air of a man of the world. Helen again looked straight through him. "You're right," she said with a laugh. She snatched her hat from her head and stroked back her hair. "I have a headache," she said. "I haven't had any breakfast."

At these words Yoshio's cramped sensations were suddenly relieved and released, for now at last he recognized Jelena. The woman who stood with bare head and ruffled hair at nine o'clock at night in Nanking Road and announced that she wanted breakfast was not the Honourable Mrs Robert Russell. She was the crazy girl of Paris, who was ready at all hours to eat, to cook, to play, or to be made love to. A surge of happy memories rose in him like silver bubbles to the surface of stagnant water: onion soup at five in the morning near the stalls; sunrise on the Butte: two whole intoxicating days of love behind closed shutters in a village on the shores of the Lake of Geneva: you must learn to live without your Japanese armor, Yo, then you will be happy: tonight we will go on the spree, and tomorrow I will make my famous omelette for breakfast. Jelena, pleasant companion in the green-and-silver kimono from Kyoto . . .

"Then it's high time you went and had breakfast," Yoshio heard himself say, moved and with the courage of despair. An unexampled and intoxicated recklessness took possession of him. "It is nine o'clock at night, Jelena, an extremely favorable hour for your neglected breakfast. It is so long since we had breakfast together—and we did so well at it in the olden times. Are you so kind as still to remember Chez Marguerite—the little bistro with the good brioches? What shall we have for breakfast? Chocolate? Tea? Coffee? Jelena," he said with a fresh inspiration, "shall Yoshio take you to a charming sukiyaki restaurant? I promise you it will please you. You can leave a message for your husband in the hotel."

He had got all his languages mixed up in his excitement. His studied English of which he was secretly so proud was mixed with the faulty but fluent French that Jelena had taught him, and Japanese words popped up when he was in danger of sticking fast. Jelena now took notice of him for the first time and asked: "Who are you?"

"Did you not receive Yoshio's flowers, Jelena? Unworthy wretched flowers which all the same tried to recall a friendship which is precious to Yoshio—the most precious thing in Yoshio's life," Yoshio said rhetorically and with emotion. He was up in the air, swinging on a high trapeze; it was dangerous, and he was a little dazed, but it was magnificent—marvelous.

"Who is Yoshio?" Helen asked soberly.

"Yoshio? I, Yoshio Murata. Yo," he said insistently.

Helen smiled fleetingly. She remembered the Japanese habit of speaking of oneself in the third person, she did not know whether from modesty or pride. "You are Yo," she said, pleased with the sudden functioning of her memory. "Of course you are Yo—we met in Tokyo, didn't we, at the flower show?" She considered him thoughtfully. Another memory came to light. "I still have the beautiful kimono you gave me once," she said kindly. So this was Yo, a shy ghost of the days when she valued and distinguished men according to the presents they gave her. At this unexpected allusion to their past intimacy, Yoshio felt himself tremble with hope and joy. At last she was beginning to take the cue and play her part. They were still standing outside the revolving door of the hotel; Nanking Road flowed past them—people, automobiles, rickshas, beggars and street vendors, policemen and pickpockets, prostitutes and missionaries.

"Good, let's go to the sukiyaki restaurant," Helen said. "You've just appeared at the right psychological moment, my good Yo."

She had waked at six o'clock that evening with a violent headache. Potter and Clarkson were busy packing the trunks in the sitting room, an operation which for some reason always began with a great expenditure of pungent moth balls and always ended with a nervous breakdown on the part of Clarkson. Bobbie had not yet returned from his expedition of the previous night. Helen received Potter's reproachful announcement almost with relief. Shortly after seven all the trunks were packed and Clarkson had regaled herself and recovered. Helen, whose nerves were racked by the flurry and fluster of the two servants, told them to take the luggage to the boat at once, to make the cabins habitable and to spend the night on board. The state of resignation in which she had gone to sleep that morning had survived her waking, and the vestiges of it still remained with her. She was determined to leave next day. Clarkson took her leave; she was thankful to be going away from Shanghai, for war was prophesied by everybody. Potter was stalling; he moved pieces of furniture from one place to another and kept opening and shutting Bobbie's trunks.

"Yes?" Helen asked.

"I was just thinking perhaps Mr Russell will want me when he comes back," Potter said.

"Thank you, Potter, but I shall be quite able to look after him myself," Helen said. Potter sighed and retired. He wore large, serviceable, well-blacked shoes that looked like shovels. Helen had a vague hope that her headache would go as soon as she was alone. But as soon as she was alone in the empty rooms she found that solitude was unendurable. I shall go mad, she told herself. I shall go mad. She took up the telephone receiver and put it down. Took it up and put it down—how often she did it, she didn't know. As she called Frank up, first in his flat, then at his office and finally at the club, it dawned on her that she was expending her energies in vain, for she did not once get through. Perhaps a brief talk with Frank might have calmed and appeased her. I only want to say good-by, she thought, only a few words, only to part like civilized people. Good-by, Frank. Best of luck and success. Take care of your-self if things get bad here. Don't forget me altogether; perhaps we shall meet again somewhere. Kindest regards to your wife-to-be. Adieu.

But as she could not have this ordinary little conversation, a rest-less craving took possession of her. Soon she was nothing but one furious longing to be alone with Frank in these empty rooms, for a last time, all alone. For Jelena was so made that she could not brook opposition, that she had to have what was denied her, and that it was her fate always to wish for the wrong thing.

She filled the bath with cold water and lay in it for half an hour. Insane people too are given prolonged baths, she thought in self-contempt. It did her no good. She got out shivering, rubbed herself warm again and dressed with care. I've still to buy some colored film before we leave, she thought.

When she encountered Yoshio in the revolving door she had just come from the closed store of the Eos Film and Foto Company under the colonnades. For ten exasperating and despairing minutes she had stood rattling obstinately at the unyielding handle. She was as unhappy as a beaten child, as lonely and forlorn as a lost dog, as helpless, hungry and exhausted as a wounded soldier whom victorious regiments leave to die as they march past.

"You have just appeared at the right psychological moment, my good Yo," she said. . . .

As Yoshio Murata took her in a taxi to the Japanese restaurant in the neighborhood of the Rue Thibet, the only thought in his head was that clever Mr Endo had been right. Jelena had accepted his reckless invitation and therefore shown that she meant to encourage him, as Mr Endo had foreseen. He, Yoshio, had been adroit enough to let her know at their first encounter that he had papers of im-portance in his possession. Now she was doing the rest and every-thing was happening as it should happen. His triumph and his new confidence in life nearly sent Yoshio rocketing. He inhaled great deep breaths of air that smelt of petrol and stagnant water. He involun-tarily clutched the breast pocket of his linen suit which contained the forged documents. He laughed in self-glory and talked incessantly to disguise his uncontrollable laughter. She was only keeping me at a distance, he thought, she is not so clumsy and naïve as to betray herself at the first opportunity, not a woman like Jelena-san. He felt that he was now involved in the fine mesh of international espionage and plumed himself on playing a superior and distinguished part with this beautiful, adventurous spy as vis-à-vis. He tasted success; for the first time in his life he tasted success. His French began to thaw, and phrases which must have been in his Japanese schoolbooks drew together in wayward counterpoint. "If you only know what it is to conquer and not what it is to be conquered, then woe to you: it will go wrong with you." He talked and talked, he gesticulated with his short arms and his little Japanese hands; many a closed door within him was thrown open, and he realized with a sudden shock that he had never really been happy before. He was happy now. Helen, for her part, listened with head turned away and vague surprise to what he had to say. She was thankful in a feeble, exhausted way that she was not left to her thoughts, that she would not be alone during this infernal evening, that she had found someone whose mere presence forced her to control herself, to make conversation and to behave in a halfway civilized manner. She put in brief polite queries, she smiled now and again; she even quoted two lines of a French poem. In this way she succeeded for minutes together in forgetting the pangs of jealousy and the ache of her longing for Frank. She knew men too well to overlook the state this little Japanese was in, his wrought-up and fevered excitement, his supplications and courtship, his discouragement and gratitude, and she thought half in pity and half in amusement: How much in love he is with me!

" . . . you ask how I live, Jelena; can it really interest you to know how a paltry and modest and untalented journalist lives in Tokyo? I am married, and when I say that my wife is stupid I do not mean it in the conventional manner as polite modesty. No, Jelena, forgive me if I am outspoken: he who has known you, who has had the good fortune to know you as I have, is stricken—or blessed—with restlessness and discontent for the rest of his life. You do not know, Jelena, you cannot know, what it means to me to have you give me your company tonight. I will confess the truth to you, Jelena. If Yo had not met you tonight he would have gone home and destroyed himself."

Yoshio was shocked into silence. But that is the truth I am saying, he thought; I am doing it all wrong again, I am telling the truth instead of lying; I must tell her things to rouse her curiosity, anything, but only not the truth.

"And as I have had an important mission laid upon me, my suicide would have been more than desertion," he added feebly. Helen had not been listening, but she noticed the silence that fell when he had ended. She caught at the echo of his last words and succeeded in recovering them.

"You Japanese with your suicide," she said, with a smile. "Have you all got the hara-kiri complex? I was taken to see a mountain in Japan and was told that young people threw themselves down by hundreds, just as the finale of a happy Sunday's outing. Is that really true? Is it as catching as measles with us?"

"Miharayama in Oshima. Yes, it is true, many people commit suicide there for almost no reason and many merely in imitation of others. It is a fascination hard to explain," Yoshio said reflectively. "You know, Jelena, my younger brother committed hara-kiri, and it has made my own life completely ridiculous. Worthless. Useless and undignified. It is much more honorable to be a name on an ancestors' tablet than fourth reporter on a second-rate newspaper, and much easier too, I can assure you."

Helen had become more attentive. "Another complex?" she asked with a smile. "Cain and Abel? Are you jealous of your brother and envious of his death? Has the idea never occurred to you that a living man too can do something heroic and worthy? You Japanese prize your dead too highly, it seems to me."

Yoshio made a rapid effort of concentration. "You are right, Jelena," he said quickly and rather too loudly. "That is why I am trying at this very moment to carry out a mission of importance for Dai Nippon."

"Dai Nippon—is that your newspaper?" Helen asked, letting her attention wander again. Yoshio was unhappy over this for a moment, then he remembered that her indifference was only assumed. He was always forgetting that Jelena was a spy and more practised than he.

"You surely know what Dai Nippon is? Japan, the Great Nippon, Jelena, my country. In former days I could only tell you about it, but now you have seen it and know for yourself how beautiful Japan is. Dai Nippon. Are you still surprised that every Japanese is ready to die for his country?"

"Dying, always dying! The *idée fixe*——"

"Or live—you are right. To live for Dai Nippon."

The man's drunk, Helen thought as she observed his heated face and listened to his tirades. There were red patches on his high cheekbones. She remembered that with these yellow little people of Dai Nippon, red cheeks were the shameful sign of drunkenness. Dai Nippon, indeed!

"You were saying something about a mission you have, Yo? What have you got on? Are you going to assassinate Chiang Kai-shek? Or are you going to tie a bomb round your waist and blow up the arsenal in person? Honestly, I cannot imagine you in the part of one of these living bombs, these celebrated living bombs," she said rather more gaily. A cheering thought had found its way into her dazed head. Perhaps Frank will be sitting in the lounge talking with Madame Tissaud when I get back. Perhaps it is all quite simple. Good evening, Frank, I shall say, let us have one more cup of coffee together before I go. . . .

"Here is the Sakuran," Yoshio said, and the taxi stopped.

From the street the three-storied house looked like any other. It had a little Russian delicatessen shop at one side of its entrance and a French dressmaker's on the other. But the courtyard to which the entrance led was planted in the style of a Japanese garden, and beyond stood a second house, dimly illuminated behind its paper windows, and in general a fairly good imitation of a Japanese inn.

"Charming," Helen said, standing still to look at it. The evening breeze rustled in the bamboos, and water fell with a cool, trickling noise into a stone trough.

"Here one can forget Shanghai," Yoshio said at her elbow.

"Let's try, anyway," Helen replied with a sigh and walked on.

They were received with all ceremony; kneeling maidservants took their shoes off for them on the first wooden step, a polite hostess in a dark kimono led them up the narrow stairs into a room whose floor was covered with mats. More maidservants, kneeling beside the sliding door, brought them light, thin kimonos, fans, silk cushions and the slender little jug of warm sake. Helen, who for hours past had been inwardly trembling with cold and apprehension, drank it thankfully and quickly. Her headache lifted; it was no less but it went into a distance, as if it were no longer in her head but in that of another person.

"Have you forgotten it all?" Yoshio asked as Helen looked at her cushion and remained standing. She at once knelt down obediently and replied: "Almost, but I learned it over again when we were in Japan."

"How long were you in Japan?"

"I don't know exactly. Six weeks perhaps."

"And did it please you?"

"Yes, you patriot," Helen said with a smile, "it did please me." She drank up her little cup and said consolingly in answer to his hungering eyes: "I was very pleased indeed with your Dai Nippon. I have already quarreled with the whole English colony in Shanghai because I am too friendly to Japan."

"We are so little loved," Yoshio Murata said sadly. "And we do not deserve it. Can you tell me why nobody likes us?"

"Complex number three," Helen said and took a drink.

"Our land is beautiful, our people are industrious and honest. We have no debts, we beg of nobody, either for help or money, we buy more from foreign countries than we sell to them, we respect the laws of our own country and those of all foreign countries, of which we are guests, we are tolerant to all religions, we produce beautiful things for little money, we are frugal and unpretending, we are orderly and progressive—what has the world against us?" asked Yoshio from whose mouth poured a torrent of ever more complacent oratory as he drank the warm sake. He suddenly stopped, shocked by the immodesty with which he had expressed himself. "Certainly, our country is small and not to be compared with others," he quickly added for the sake of politeness and decency.

"Small and modest," Helen said in great amusement. "And crammed with soldiers who are burning to die for it, and ruled by a military clique which breaks all treaties, and dominated by five mighty families who keep the Mikado prisoner. And harried into wars of conquest by clans who carry on their primeval feuds as commanders of the army and the fleet, playing one off against the other and using Korea, Manchuria and China as the arenas for their rivalries. Small and modest, frugal and unpretending, industrious and honest. Possibly, yes, very possibly. But are those the qualities that make people like you? Have you ever known the model school-boy, whose exercises are faultless and who puts on airs for that reason, being liked by the other boys in his class? You are the little store at the corner that sells everything five cents cheaper, and you are the youth who has got a new shotgun and fires it off bang-bang day and night so that no one can sleep, and you are the neighbor who dumps his rubbish over our hedge. That's what you are, and yet you ask why the world doesn't like you."

Yoshio opened his mouth several times to interrupt her. When she had done he went back to the only remark he had quite understood and which he was imperatively compelled to challenge.

"I would never permit myself, Jelena," he said, "to express myself so disrespectfully about any foreign statesman as you have just chosen to speak about the ruler of Dai Nippon. I fear you will never under-stand us as long as you do not bear in mind that our ruler is a divinity and descended in the direct line to the hundred and twenty-fourth generation from the sun goddess, Amaterasu. This fact natu-rally lays on us, his children, higher responsibilities and deeper rever-ence than is the case with other nations."

Helen looked at the little Japanese in utter astonishment. "Yo!" she said again and again several times. "Yo! But Yo!" Just as though he had to be roused out of a deep sleep. "A fact? Good God, Yo, do you call that a fact? You are surely not speaking seriously, Yo? You, a modern and enlightened person. Don't you remember the *rive gauche*, Yo, and all the Communists and Surrealists and I don't know what other 'ists' you used to be friends with? And then you go back to Japan, and the Middle Ages swallow you up and your blessed Mikado is a divinity! You surely don't believe that!"

Yoshio looked with an intent and obstinate expression into his sake cup. The delicate little vessel was decorated with the wavelike crest of the shoguns, which had no business in the sukiyaki restaurant in Shanghai and was only there for its beauty. The various layers of his education and mental make-up were so ingrown with one another that it was as painful and risky as a surgical operation to separate them.

"Japan," he began, " is a peaceful and divine country. We learned that at school, and something of what one learns as a child always remains behind, do you not think so, Jelena-san? Japan has never been conquered. That is a fact. But it has never sought for wars, it has never gone out to make conquests, it lived in peaceful isolation until the black ships of Commodore Perry forced it to open its ports and to enter into relations with foreign countries. We did not wish it, we are not responsible, it was forced upon us."

Helen began to find this discourse boring. The Japanese were hopelessly boring and thorough and tedious. Yoshio, on the other hand, gained fresh impetus for the execution of his task from this political discussion into which he had unexpectedly, and with the support of rice wine, become involved.

"It's a pity you're such hypocrites," she said amiably. "You're worse and even more hypocritical than the English."

"I thank you for your candor," Yoshio replied with a bow. She hates us, he thought, almost with satisfaction; she is a British secret agent and she means us nothing but harm. Good, she shall have what she is out for.

"Forgive me, Yo," Helen said, in response. "Sake on an empty stomach makes me quarrelsome. It is a matter of complete indifference to me on what terms Japan stands to the rest of the world. What does interest me is the sukiyaki."

The little waitress in the plum-blossom kimono who had been pouring out the sake for them now got up to help them into the light kimonos the restaurant supplied for its patrons. Helen wrapped herself closely in a soft blue one with a light red pattern of fluttering butterflies, and although Yoshio did not want to see how beautiful she was he couldn't help it. He himself at first declined to put on a kimono; but after a moment's reflection it dawned upon him that he could further his ends by doing so.

"I would prefer not to. I have important documents in the breast pocket of my coat," he said to Helen, and he said it in French as a secret he did not want the waitresses to hear.

"A kimono is more comfortable—and suits you better," Helen observed. "I promise to look after your coat with the important documents."

Yoshio floated on the crest of a wave of satisfaction. He took the documents out of his pocket and put them back again to make sure Helen knew where they were. Then he consented to be helped into the kimono. "Ever so much nicer, Yo," Helen remarked, approvingly. He knelt down on his cushion while two servants set out low tables and got the cooking apparatus ready and began cooking the finely cut slices of meat, vegetables and bean curd. The appetizing smell pervaded the room. Helen was right, for the rather plain and somewhat ridiculous little Japanese in his ostentatious and ill-fitting white ducks had changed into a creature of dignity and charm as soon as he put on the kimono and knelt down on his cushion. His smoothly gleaming hair, the shape of his mouth, his polite smile and the composure with which he put the first morsels on her plate, all combined to make a pleasing and harmonious picture. For a fleeting moment Helen could understand how his company—and that of others like him—had not been unpleasant to her. Next moment she had completely forgotten him and was back with Frank once more. She wondered whether this Yo could contrive any means of preventing the marriage. It was clear he would do anything she asked of him. Orientals were cunning, and possibly he might think of a plan. Chinese women poisoned their rivals; they were wise—there you had an old and highly cultivated civilization. "What is the time, Yo?" After ten. The boat sailed at one on the following afternoon: there were still fifteen hours—an eternity. "It's charming here, Yo. It was nice of you to take me here." If I could only have a few hours alone

with Frank, all would be well. Why am I not here with Frank—
alone? Are you afraid of me, Frank? Afraid, that means you love me.
I must not, must not think. Why are we not talking? Talking and
drinking—I must not think. I must forget. "What is that on the
kakemono in the niche there, Yo?"

"Can you not read Japanese letters any longer, Jelena? You have
such talent for languages."

"I've forgotten it all, Yo. It's a pity. Wait a moment—that is the
sign for 'great' and that for 'water.' That's all I know. What does
it all mean?"

"When the moon is at the full it begins to wane," Yoshio read out.
"When the ebb is lowest, the tide begins to flow."

The wisdom and the quiet consolation of the ancient proverb
affected him deeply in the state of relaxation he was in. The words
seemed to him profound and pregnant, they instilled steadfastness
and sounded a warning on the eve of war. Beneath the kakemono
stood a flat dish in which were three water lilies and a single brown-
flowering rush. Helen looked at Yoshio in surprise as he took off
his spectacles and shamefacedly dried his eyes.

"What's the matter, Yo?" she asked gently.

"Nothing," Yoshio replied quickly and with embarrassment. She
looked at him again and for a moment felt the relief of forgetting
to think about herself.

"Has it something to do with your secret mission?"

"No, I assure you."

"Or with your hara-kiri brother?" she went on cross-examining
him.

"No," Yoshio said. Once more he felt that strange sense of release
deep within him; listening as though to some distant sound, he said:
"I have always pretended to myself that I loved my brother. It is
not true. I hated him. He took from me all that was mine. My own
mother preferred him to me, although he was not her child. Since
he died I have no defense against him—he has grown too strong. I
may not even say to anyone what I think. I say it now for the first
time, Jelena-san: he was uneducated and without intelligence, and
he behaved in a criminal manner and did only harm to his country.

Seppuku and a white robe and the short sword—that is all very fine and affecting on the stage of a theater; that is the place for them, do you not agree, Jelena? They are all—what do you call it?—props. What did his death prove? Nothing. And what harm did it do? Much, oh, so much. No, I do not weep for Kitaro, Jelena, I weep perhaps for Yoshio, for Yoshio's unlived life."

Helen looked away in embarrassment when he had to wipe his spectacles once more, and now two tears rolled without restraint over his high cheekbones. "You are being tactless now, Yo," she said. "We don't need to take our skeletons out of their cupboards and show them to each other."

"Forgive me," Yoshio begged hurriedly. He was ashamed. "We Japanese weep too easily. It is a national weakness." He took his handkerchief from his sleeve and applied it to his nose.

"Really?" Helen asked with surprise. "That is new to me. How does that tally with your celebrated self-control and impassivity?"

"We have too much feeling," Yoshio explained, putting on his spectacles with every intention of keeping them dry this time. "We need control the more because we are so emotional. We are as easy to see through as water. Just consider that we never lie, unless, it may be, out of politeness. But we cannot express ourselves well—it is partly due to our language. We cannot explain or analyze ourselves. We prefer to be silent rather than to say what is untrue, and we prefer to smile rather than to give pain. We are—what do you say?—people of the soul. We read masses and pray for all the fish we have eaten, for our cats, for our broken dolls, even for the needles, the good, loyal needles, that have sewn for us all the year through. We are grateful and devoted, Jelena, even though it may seem otherwise at times. We are sentimentalists encased in concrete."

Yoshio had begun in earnest to explain the soul of Japan, but he ended with a smile. Helen had long since ceased to listen. When he stopped she pulled herself together. "Needles," she said in a state of complete abstraction.

Although she had complained of hunger and had eaten nothing for twenty-four hours, she left her food almost untouched. Her throat contracted as soon as she tried to swallow a mouthful: it was a ridiculous and childish protest of her exhausted nerves. I'm like a dog who can't find his master, she thought in a fury; if I don't look out I shall die of a broken heart, as anemic damsels do in old novels.

The three servant girls had taken the greatest pains over her, kneeling and smiling, daintily officious; their noiseless functioning was almost inhuman. Helen collected herself.

"People of the soul," she said. "Yes, I noticed that, too. We paid a visit to the Yoshiwara. In each house there's a government official seated beside the cash desk to receive the tax for every visit on the spot. In all the prostitutes' rooms there is a notice on the wall, letting them know how much they have to give the government out of every yen they earn. It's the most soulful regulation I've ever seen."

"How do you know what the notice says, Jelena-san?" Yoshio asked quickly. So she can read Japanese, the spy, he thought in sudden joy. Helen looked at him distractedly.

"It's printed in three languages, no doubt for the benefit of international visitors," she said. Yoshio was silenced.

"But," he said feebly, "you may perhaps have observed that in every one of those houses there is a little altar; the girls even have a god of their own." It was unpleasant to speak of Yoshiwara to a lady. He reflected that Helen was not a lady.

"Yes, whores are good-natured and pious all the world over," she said casually, as she poked about among the strawberries that had been put in front of her; she took one by the stalk with the intention of putting it to her mouth.

She stopped halfway: a panic, white hot, ice cold, seized her. She heard the telephone ringing in her bedroom, clearly, insistently, ceaselessly, beseechingly. Helen darling, Frank was saying, I must speak to you, I must see you once more tonight, now, this moment, I love you, I love you, I love you . . .

She put the strawberry back carefully in the little bowl and got up. Her legs were stiff with kneeling; she stretched them and beat on her thighs—it was a habit she had acquired in the days when she worked as a model. "I must go home—it's late," she said breathlessly.

Yoshio gazed at her in dismay. The game had only just begun.

He had made the first move, and now it was her turn to play. Instead, she impetuously stripped off her kimono, tore it off and threw it down and seized her hat. He could not understand it. "Don't let me disturb you, Yo," she said hurriedly. "I can find my way back to the hotel. I'm used to it."

"Why—so suddenly?" he asked, standing unsteadily on his numbed legs. He had lost the Japanese habit of kneeling, and his soles, calves and knees tingled with pins and needles.

"My husband," Helen said. "He'll be worrying about me."

She had no sooner said it than it seemed so idiotic she had to laugh. Yoshio was in despair. "Only one moment," he besought her. "You cannot go alone—I cannot allow it—the town is full of soldiers——"

He picked up his coat and then, changing his mind, put it down again. It was at this moment that a stroke of genius flashed so vividly upon him that he shut his bespectacled eyes as though dazzled. "One second, Jelena," he implored her. "It will only take half one second. The bill—you understand—it is the Japanese custom—I must see our hostess personally—impossible in presence of honored guest."

He caught his kimono round him and tiptoed in stockinged feet to the door. Two waitresses knelt and slid the two halves of the door apart.

"Please take care of my coat," Yoshio said, just to make sure, and then the door closed behind him.

Jelena took up the coat impatiently in the tips of her fingers and put it down again; it smelt of Yoshio's hair oil. You need to be very intimate with a man not to be repulsed by his clothes, she thought vaguely. This thought, as all others did, recalled Frank to her mind. The warmth of Frank's shoulders in his white duck coat, the scent of his cigarettes, the line of his brown neck emerging above his collar, even the creases in his collar after a night of dancing—every line of his clothing was familiar and exciting. Every inch of Yoshio's pretentious little coat nauseated her.

She was standing by the open window when he returned, looking down at the rustling bamboos and illumined by the soft light. His coat was still on the table, but not in the same place as before. "Have

I been long?" he asked, clearing his throat to strike the right pitch.

"Long enough," Helen said. He did not know what she meant. He did not know whether she had looked at the documents, substituted others for them and stolen them. He took off his kimono and put on his coat. It seemed to him that they were still in his pocket as before. For a moment he was overwhelmed with despair. I am not clever enough for this business, he thought. Helen watched him as he took out the long narrow envelopes adorned with a red-and-white emblem without which the tip for the waitresses would have been an insult, not a present.

"Charming," she said absently.

Yoshio Murata with a final effort succeeded in letting the documents fall from his pocket onto the mats that covered the floor. One of the little waitresses picked them up. He held his breath and from the corner of his spectacles he watched the expression in Helen's face. She gave the papers a passing glance.

"Japanese?" she asked.

"In cipher," he replied. "Secret documents." He thrust them back into his pocket, trying to look alarmed or embarrassed.

"What a pity I am not a spy," Helen remarked. He did not know whether she said it contemptuously or in deepest guile. *"Sayanaro,"* she said to the serving maids as she went out. *"Domo arigato gazai mashita,"* she said to the hostess and the girls who put on her shoes for her and remained kneeling with their hands on the ground.

"You know Japanese after all," Yoshio said as they crossed the courtyard. His heart was thumping so loudly that the noise it made verged on impoliteness.

"It has been a delightful evening," Helen said, becoming once more the conventional English lady in good society. A young boy had summoned a taxi, and it was waiting in the street outside the entrance. Yoshio opened the door for her.

"My dear Yo," she said amiably, "don't be cross with me—but I don't want you to come with me. Please don't misunderstand—it's my husband, he is very jealous. Ridiculous, I know. But I don't want him to make a scene if he saw me in your—in the company of another man."

Yoshio took a step back: the insult froze him. An Englishman! he thought. I have kept his wife, Japanese have picked up his wife from the street and kept her. Now she may not so much as be seen with a Japanese. All through the evening he had tossed on a sea of agitation, now high on the crest of a wave, now deep down in its trough and drowning. Fear and rage, triumph and insult ran together in a violent and almost uncontrollable desire to board the taxi and take Helen by assault. He took a step forward; she held out her hand. He blanched with the effort of self-control.

"Good night, Jelena-san, and thank you for your esteemed company. I hope I shall see you again." He took off his spectacles and bent down to kiss her hand as he had learned to do in Paris.

"We are sure to meet again somewhere," Helen. said above his bent head. "We sail tomorrow at midday on the *Soerabaya*. Perhaps we may meet in Hong Kong—or Singapore—or London. It has been a charming evening. And good luck to your secret mission."

He let her hand go and stared at her. The taxi drove off. She waved once with an odd distraught gesture and leaned back in her seat— she was gone. Yoshio stood there, staring at the empty street. He had been pale before; now he felt his blood ebb in slow pulsations with a dragging pain in his breast, his kidneys and the joints of his knees. The boy who had got the taxi gazed at him in amazement.

He had gone as gray as the pavement at his feet.

XVI

DR YUTSING CHANG sat in a taxi on his way to the Shanghai Hotel. It was getting close to midnight, and the streets were full of people. The paper boys shouted out that Japanese troops had landed and been fired on in Hongkew. But Yutsing heard nothing as he sat hunched in the taxi, tugging at his handkerchief, rolling it into a ball, twisting it into a cord, while tears of rage ran down his cheeks. He was in the state of fury and despair that occasionally breaks the surface of Chinese calm and brings with it rebellions, lootings, massacres and the cruel torturing of enemies. Yutsing Chang had heard news that sounded so improbable, so impossible, so utterly criminal that it reduced him to tears even before he had been able to convince himself of its truth.

"Mr Bogum Chang is with his guests in the Silver Chamber," the boy at the elevator in the rear of the hotel said. Yutsing Chang had paid off his taxi and hurried through the colonnades and the domed hall in order to avoid the lounge and the people there.

"To the Silver Chamber, then," he said with clenched teeth. The boy shut the door of the elevator, and it ascended. It was all Chang could do to force back his tears, and his eyes smarted and his breath came in gasps. He had thrown the golden mean to the winds and was left now to his uncontrollable fury and fear.

The "Silver Chamber" was the name given by the Chinese staff to one of the smaller banqueting rooms which were at the service of wealthy clients on the third floor. As many foreigners had fallen into the Asiatic habit of entertaining and amusing their friends, particularly important business friends, away from their homes, the capable management of the hotel had equipped and furnished four of these rooms with the luxury that was to be expected of it. The walls of the Silver Chamber were occupied almost entirely by mirrors in dull silver frames. The architect had selected bright red silk curtains to go with the mirrors in their silver frames, and the floor shone with the smooth black lacquer of Ningpo which reflected the figures of the guests almost as clearly as the mirrors themselves. As Yutsing went along the corridor to the Silver Chamber he could hear music and the voices of men and women. Afraid lest his inward commotion might be seen in his face, he went back again to the mirror which was let into the wall between two porcelain flower pots near the elevator. He straightened his tie, tried to smooth his hair, which in spite of his efforts rose up again with a rebellious crackle, and took a few deep breaths to calm the beating of his heart. He put on his spectacles to hide his burning eyes and went straight to the outer door of the Silver Chamber.

"Yutsing? What wind brings you here?" asked Mr Chai, his father's young secretary, who was standing in the vestibule, superintending a row of waiters in white jackets before they carried in the covered dishes. Yutsing pushed his way past the young man, who was clearly taken aback, and opened the tall massive door. There he came to a standstill, for what he saw was still worse than what he had expected.

His father's guests were seated at a long table, and beside each one was a girl in a bright-colored silk dress. The guests were Japanese. Three Japanese girls in shimmering kimonos were dancing on a small dais which had been provided for the purpose of such displays. The other girls, partly Chinese, partly Koreans, were showing as much solicitude for their neighbors as though they were infants at the breast who had to be induced to drink. In the center of one side of the table sat Chang, his father, in a European white dinner jacket. There were small silver Chinese wine cups in front of him and also larger Japanese porcelain cups for sake and an array of glasses for the drinks of the West. The guest of honor was at his side—a Japanese admiral in uniform, with gray hair and finely cut features which at that moment seemed to Chang no better than those of a monkey.

This Japanese, one of the admirals of the fleet which had landed its bluejackets the day before, was watching the dancing girls with a smile on his face and one arm round the Korean girl at his side, though he paid her no further attention. From time to time he exchanged a few words with Chang Bogum, and each time he accompanied them with a rapid, cursory bow.

The sight of this Japanese whom his father was feasting, while outside Chinese troops were desperately digging trenches, took Yutsing's breath away. He had hurried there to ward off a nightmare of shame and humiliation. Now the reality confronted him, and he stood transfixed in the doorway of the Silver Chamber and did not know what to say. Yet his giant of a father soon seemed to feel his son's eyes upon him, though possibly he looked towards the door only because, as host, he was waiting impatiently for the next course to be brought in. Whatever it may have been that took his eyes to the door, Yutsing observed that an almost inperceptible shadow clouded his father's face and that he instantly began to laugh and raised his wine cup to him from the other side of the room. "An unexpected guest is here, my son Chang Yutsing!" he cried out in

a voice that rose above the phonograph and the Japanese lutes and
the drunken clamor round the table. At this several faces were turned
to Yutsing: Japanese faces, the grinning and detested faces of the
mortal foe. It was odd that Yutsing noticed just at this very moment
a. pallor on his father's face; the copper color of his northern complexion was flecked with white as though he were sick or frightened.
As Yutsing could not stand forever in the doorway, rooted to the
ground, and as something had to happen, he tore himself with an
effort from the theshold and entered the room. He was not aware
that the train of waiters trooped in at his heels, giving him the air
of a ridiculous master of ceremonies in white linen suit, ushering in
the dishes.

He walked straight up to his father and said in a loud voice, "What
is the meaning of this feast at a moment like this?"

Chang was not in the least disconcerted.

"I have invited my friends to a little meal in honor of their arrival,"
he said smoothly. "Admiral Sagami, may I introduce my son? I have
told you about him. Mr Nakano, this is my son, Dr Chang Yutsing.
You will have much to talk about together, for he too has studied in
America." He clapped his hands, and two girls came running. "A
chair and a cover for my son," he cried out.

B. G. Chang spoke English with his guests, the hard but fluent
English of a man in big business, and the polite Japanese smiled and
bowed to Yutsing. He moistened his parched lips three times before
feeling able to speak; even so his voice was hoarse. "I must talk to
you at once, Father," he said.

Chang briefly scrutinized his son's disheveled appearance. "Later,
my son, later," he said in a low voice in Chinese.

"Now. This moment," Chang replied.

His father looked at him in silence for several seconds, and at the
same time the talk died away all along the table. The girls held their
fans still in their arrested hands and looked on. Chang saw that his
son swayed as a tree in a storm or a boat in a tempest. He got up
and bowed to his guests.

"I beg your forgiveness—urgent news, a domestic circumstance,"
he said. He put his arm round the shoulder of his son, who was

much shorter than himself, to give the guests the impression that they were on the best of terms, and guided him by the pressure of his massive arm to a door concealed by the bright red curtains. They were now in the white-tiled anteroom of the gentlemen's cloakroom in which the management, thoughtful as ever, had placed two sofas for the benefit of drunken or drowsy banqueters. Chang Bogum sank down on one of them as if he found standing difficult. Yet, as Yutsing well knew, his father was not drunk, for he had never been drunk in his life.

"Now—what is it?" Chang asked, still for some odd reason speaking in English. Probably he had had to talk so much in that language during the evening that his brain could not change over again. "Why do you turn up like a ghost and cause me to be rude to my guests?"

Yutsing remained on his feet in front of the sofa, looking down at his father, who even when seated was nearly as tall as he.

"How can you possibly give a dinner to our enemies? A dinner on the very night when we are erecting barricades in Chapei and Hongkew and the first dead are lying in the streets?" he asked in a voice that became hoarser the longer he spoke. "I did not believe it, I did not think it possible, but I have had to see it with my own eyes. My father feasting the Japanese, the Japanese who want to make China a Japanese colony! I have been told that you have given the Japanese money. Is that true also?"

Chang smiled; his face was still flecked with white. "The gentlemen I have invited are old friends," he said with exaggerated complacency. "Admiral Sagami, Mr Nakano, director of the Osaka Bank, Tsuneo Fujita, who owns the *Daily Advertiser* at Kobe, Toro Sato, my partner in the Tsingtao mills—why should I not entertain them? I have known all of them for over twenty years. They are honorable and well-behaved, polite men."

"Have you given them money? Money to buy guns, to blow us to pieces?" Yutsing shouted in a voice that broke in his agitation.

B.G. merely smiled. "My experience with the Japanese has taught me that they are almost unbribable," he said. "For that reason subtler means of influence have to be used."

He got up and went to the marble washbasin, filled his cupped hands with water as he had done in his early days as a coolie and washed his face. Then he returned to his son.

"It gives me small pleasure to entertain these men today," he resumed in Chinese, "for I have pains in my side and I would prefer to rest myself. But it is my opinion that it is of great use to have friends among the enemy."

"Father," Chang Yutsing said, trying to be calm, "you gave the government six airplanes as a present. What sense is there in it if you give the enemy also six airplanes with which to fight against ours?"

"I gave Nanking the six airplanes to please you," Chang said, "and not because I expect great benefit from them. You do not know perhaps that though the government has good airplanes and good pilots, they forgot to store an adequate supply of gasoline," he said, falling back into English, a language more suitable to this topic. "We Chinese make ourselves ridiculous when we come on the scene as soldiers. It is easy to send soldiers to the war who don't know what all this is about. It is easy to slaughter hogs that cannot defend themselves. But the people who know better are irresponsible. They give the soldiers English rifles with French ammunition and American planes with Italian spare parts. One does not fit the other, and the army is miserably equipped. You can't kill anyone with slogans. In war it depends on who can kill the better, not who has more soldiers to be killed."

Yutsing's mouth filled with a bitter taste at these words of his father. "It is bad enough that we live in a time and in a world that can be convinced only by guns and warships and bombs," he cried in exasperation. "But we have prepared for this war, and we shall carry it through even if it lasts a hundred years or two hundred years, if it lasts until not a single soldier is left alive. And if necessary we shall destroy people like you who sow unbelief and make terms with the Japanese."

While his son was speaking, Chang Bogum had pressed his hand to his side, where for some days he had felt a pain that he had tried in vain to forget. "You need not try your propaganda talk on me," he said. "Keep your big words for those who believe in them. What do you really require of me?"

Yutsing thought this question over. It was not an easy one to answer.

"I require you to go back at once to those Japanese and show them the door. I require you to withdraw every cent you have put into Japanese enterprises. I require you to love China and to believe in China and to help China, our country, our poor unhappy country. *Your* country. Don't you understand that?"

The elder Chang now began by degrees to lose his temper. "And what if I told you that I believe China would be happier under Japanese rule than it is now?" he asked angrily.

His son stared at him for a long time in silence as though words failed him. Chang had not quite turned off the tap, and the faint regular drip was mingled with the shouts and laughter, the rattle of plates and singing in high-pitched women's voices from the banqueting room.

As Yutsing did not reply, his father went on speaking: "The Japanese have a talent for ruling, and we have not, it seems to me. Uncorruptible officials, peace and order in the country, no famines, no plagues, rice for all. You promise it: the Japanese give it. Do you think it makes any difference to the common people who is at the top as long as there is enough to eat at the bottom and the taxes are not too high? What does the peasant care about the catchwords you have been taught at school? Liberty or slavery—unity or division—the common man does not even understand what they mean. A full belly is more to him than his liberty. Of liberty he has plenty, but too little food. And the more soldiers there are in the country the hungrier the people will be. But you and your like, you go around and make the people discontented, who would have been as contented as their forefathers were but for the schoolboy clamor of you hotheads without human understanding."

Yutsing listened in dismay, and then he remembered where he had heard the same thing. Sun Yat-sen, the Great Master, the revolutionary, the father of the New China, had said it too. Do not offer the people liberty, for China has had liberty for two thousand years, too much liberty. But offer it money and it will rise up, for the nation is poor, and every nation desires what it does not possess. It was a shock to him that his father, opportunist, capitalist, unscrupulous profiteer, should reach the same conclusion as the Great Master and revolutionary.

"The Japanese have got one thing—they are patriots, they have national pride. They will spit on you if you have no feeling for your country. They drink with you, but they despise you just as I am forced to despise you," he shouted in his effort to ward off his father's imperturbable common sense. The blood rose into Chang Bogum's face and made the white patches on his skin glow like copper.

"The son despises the father. That is the morality of the New Life," he said quietly. Chang had been afraid for a moment that his father would knock him down as he had done once, ten years ago. The quiet and carefully controlled reply put him to shame, for it put him in the wrong.

"What are you buying from the Japanese with this shameless feast you are giving them?" he asked, whipping up again the anger he had felt at his first entry. His father had gone pale again, paler than before.

"What business is it of yours?" he asked scornfully. "Perhaps it is safety of the house in which your mother lives. Perhaps the future of the business I have built up. Perhaps, since you ask, perhaps your own life."

"I forbid you," Yutsing said, trembling with rage. "I forbid you to bargain with the Japanese for my life. My life belongs to me, and I will not have it bought off at the price of humiliation and infamy."

Chang Bogum broke into a laugh again. He leaned his head on the back of the sofa and laughed aloud.

"Is that in your schoolbooks?" he asked. "Have you not kept a spark of humor? Or of tolerance? I let you play your political games because youth must have its follies and age of itself teaches reason. I have even taken the pains to be kind to my foreign, barren daughter-in-law whom you brought into my family without asking my permission. But I demand tolerance from you also for my own insignificant life and my doubtless stupid and worthless opinions. Tolerance, you understand, son, and not inveterate and unfeeling arrogance. I began life as a coolie, and you have filled your belly with complicated and costly education, but I appear to know one thing you have never learned: It is a sickness of humanity to neglect one's own fields, to look for weeds in the neighbor's fields."

"Opium and Confucius—with those you have kept the people in subjection like a beast that cannot think," Yutsing said grimly.

"Allow me to tell you that you do not know the people. I know it because I grew up in it: the people does not want war, no people in the world wants war. I can tell you that without having to read books. The Japanese too do not want war, and the Europeans and the Americans and whatever else the peoples of the world choose to call themselves—none of them wants war. The people wants its share of happiness and peace. And all men who drive the plow and all men who carry burdens and all men who work hard are brothers and want the same thing. They want to eat their plate of rice or noodles, they want to sleep with their wives and beget sons, they want to labor and to rest from labor, they want to laugh sometimes or to sing a song or to play cards, and if they can now and then afford themselves a little dissipation with wine, opium or dice, then life is good and dying easy. And all that you and your like preach to them and all that you goad them into is strange to them and makes them sick inside and discontented with the world and bitter." Chang Bogum drew a deep breath after he had said this and once more pressed the pain in his side back into his body with his gigantic hands, for a comic thought had struck him and it hurt him to laugh.

"I can still remember the day when I put on foreign leather boots, for the first time. They were hard and hurt my feet. I thought to myself: that is why all foreigners are bad-tempered and unfriendly and without goodness. They wear tight, hard boots, and their feet hurt them, so how can they be happy and good? When you give the people your education and your hygiene and your New Life and your 'Three Principles' and your feud with our Japanese neighbors, you are giving them foreign, tight, hard boots which pinch them and do not fit. And now, my son, you will have to excuse me," he said. "I must go back to my guests."

Yutsing stepped quickly forward and barred his father's way. "Father," he said resolutely, "if you do that, if you go back, if you take the side of the Japanese—then you will never see me again. I shall disown you. I shall disown you," he shouted. "I shall no more be your son and you shall no more be my father. Decide! Choose!"

Chang went past his son with no more than a push of his elbow. But at the door he stopped again and turned round and faced him. He made an ironical gesture towards the white-tiled and sumptuous gentlemen's cloakroom, its dripping tap, the row of washbasins along the wall, the clean, round bottles of liquid soap, the automatic machines for paper towels and the two white-covered sofas for the benefit of drunken guests.

"This is neither the time nor the place for such decisions," he said, almost amused. Chang felt void for a moment while the white, shining, sparkling tiled walls revolved before his eyes.

"It is on your head," Yutsing said, gripping the gun in his coat pocket. He charged his father with his head down as he had seen footballers do. Chang had been too often in dangerous situations not to realize the menace of the gun barrel in Yutsing's pocket. His son had already opened the door and only the red silk curtain concealed him from the guests within.

"What are you doing, crazy child?" Chang Bogum muttered. And as he leaped on his son he felt a sharp stab in his aching side. Yutsing bared his teeth in a grin, but made no answer. He opened a small chink in the curtain.

B. G. Chang had three times in his life been present when political or military opponents had been invited to a friendly meal and then been killed there. But as on each occasion he had been on the side of the killers, it had been quite amusing. It was quite another matter if his own son was going to murder his guests, Japanese guests, when a Japanese fleet lay in the river and a Japanese army had landed. Such was Chang Bogum's character, that he did not have to think in moments of danger but did the right thing, like an animal.

In the next moment Yutsing's arm hung limp, and he crashed to the floor, because his father had at the same time given him a crippling blow on the arm and thrown him over by a push in the back. Next he took the gun out of Yutsing's pocket, slipped down the safety catch and put it out of harm's way. Then he dragged his son, who was somewhat dazed by the fall, back into the white-tiled lavatory and shut the door behind him with his foot. Altogether it did not take him more than three seconds. Then he felt the pain in his side again and quickly sat down.

The moment Yutsing came to himself he jumped to his feet and threw himself on his father. He was senseless with rage and shame and possessed by a purely physical lust for revenge. Curses came from his mouth which he must have heard when he worked as a coolie among coolies; they broke out from a hidden corner of his brain in an obscene torrent: "Coolie, beast, fatherless son of a bitch in heat, grandson of a whore," he shouted hoarsely as he gripped the old man's throat and tried to strangle him.

Mr Chai, the young secretary, must have been eavesdropping behind a narrow door that led from the cloakroom to the service quarters of the hotel; otherwise he would not have been on the spot at the right moment and able to separate the two before they destroyed each other. It cost him severe, silent and panting exertion, for father and son were at each other's throat like fighting dogs. By the time Mr Chai had separated them neither could do anything but pant. There was blood on Chang Bogum's smart white dinner jacket from a scratch on Yutsing's forehead. Yutsing was crouching on the floor in exhaustion, with his collar wrenched from his torn shirt. He fumbled at his green tie in an effort to put it straight again. The secretary looked from one to the other and finally took out his pocket handkerchief and, after steeping it in water at a washbasin, began to wipe the faces of the two men, first the old Chang and then the young one.

It was such an unexampled situation that the young man did not know where to look. For there was always loss of face when anybody allowed himself to be carried away by rage and violence; when scuffles occurred, the one who began it was always in the wrong; but a fight between a father and a son, even in these modern times of

relaxed family ties, was a thing of unimaginable scandal. As Mr Chai
had the good or bad luck to have been an eyewitness of this horrible
scene, there were only two things that could happen to him: either
B. G. Chang would have him kidnaped and put out of the way, or
else he would give him the coveted position of bank manager in
order to buy his silence.

"Go to my guests and make my excuses for another moment or
two," Chang Bogum whispered when he had gained control over
himself. "Say that my nose bled, say anything. Go and give them
more to drink and see to the girls, I will be back in a moment."

Mr Chai crept reluctantly away. As he opened the door to the
Silver Chamber a loud burst of merriment came through and the
phonograph had passed from Japanese songs to the latest American
hits.

Dr Yutsing Chang was still crouching on the floor. He looked in
his father's face. He ought to have brought himself to ask his forgiveness. But he could not. He clenched his teeth and waited for his
father to speak. Chang Bogum twice opened his mouth, but not a
word came. He pulled an extraordinary sort of face. His eyebrows
met over the bridge of his nose, his chin quivered, his mouth shut
over his strong jaws; but it was not until he put his hands in front
of his eyes and a cry, as grotesque and comic as the high-pitched cry
of an infant, emerged from behind those enormous hands, that Yutsing realized that his father was weeping.

As Chang, the giant, had no experience of or practice in weeping,
it came on him as a cramp rather than as a release. Yutsing got up
and pretended to be looking for his gun. He did so partly from
shame and partly from defiance and with the air of not understanding what was the matter with his father. He found the gun and put
it back in his coat pocket, which was torn at the corner and hanging
down.

"I am the richest man in Shanghai. I am the richest man in Shanghai," Chang moaned behind his hands. "The richest man in Shanghai.
I have everything but what the poorest coolie has—his son's affection."

Yutsing marched erectly and stiffly from the room. He went out by the small door the secretary had come in by and made his way blindly down the back stairs of the hotel. When he reached the back entrance he took out his pocket handkerchief and held it against the scratch on his forehead.

The night had suddenly become cool. The air smelt strange and acrid. He stood in a daze at the end of the colonnade waiting for an empty taxi. At last one of those gilded vehicles drew up.

"Celestial Mansions, Bubbling Well Road," Yutsing told the driver. It was the address of Meilan, the young concubine.

XVII

PEARL CHANG GOT BACK at about ten o'clock at night from a mothers' meeting, which she had been addressing on the care of infants. She gave these lectures every Friday evening at one of the branches of the "Daughters of the New Life," the aim of which was the enlightenment and education of the wives of the laborers and coolies. She had been that evening to Nantao; the meeting was sparsely attended, and there had been more coughing than usual. After trying hard to hold the attention of her listeners, who were chewing melon seeds and had brought their children and babies with them as though it were a theater, Pearl was tired and rather discouraged when she got home. It was clear that the war would lay waste much of the little that had been built up in recent years.

Yutsing had not come home, and Pearl tried not to feel uneasy. His absence left her the free run of the bathroom, and she dawdled for a long time over her bath until she felt less wrought up and could hope to fall asleep quickly. But as soon as she had lain down in bed and turned out the light she became more wakeful every minute. This had been her fate for a week, this week during which danger tightened its hold round the city, while at the same time her husband seemed to get further and further away from her. The empty bed beside her with its hard little head prop prevented her from sleeping. Yutsing had spent three of the seven nights away from home. He is worried about China, she thought sympathetically. All he has built up is tumbling down.

He tortures himself over all these children, she thought. It was a heavy responsibility, she knew that. The Boy Scouts were still in Shanghai; they could not be got away, for the trains were reserved for the transportation of the troops and there were not enough motor coaches to take the three thousand boys back to their villages; the roads were blocked, the Kiangwan barracks were overcrowded. The Scouts had become a burden, an insoluble problem for all who were responsible for the Jamboree. It was growing more difficult every day to provide them with food and shelter, no one knew what was to be done about them if the war actually descended on Shanghai. Yutsing has stayed at Civic Center, Pearl thought; he forgets food and sleep in his anxiety over the Scouts. But a dark and vague presentiment told her that something else was taking her husband from her, something she had feared ever since she came to live in China. . . .

When the war is over we will take a holiday and go home for a few months, she thought, while she tossed restlessly from side to side, throwing back the bedclothes and then pulling them up again. Home—to her that was America, not China, as Pearl noticed with a slight shock. America. It seemed to her that she needed the air of America to recover the old impetus and her early confidence. Shanghai had taken much of it from her. When midnight struck from the Catholic church she turned on the light, got up and looked for a sleeping powder in the little medicine cabinet in the bathroom. She dissolved it and drank it, standing absent-mindedly in front of the mirror with the tumbler in her hand, and then lay down again. Her thoughts were a wheel that turned more and more slowly, and at last she fell asleep.

She was awakened by the telephone by her bed; it was nearly four in the morning. It was already gray outside. Her head was dull, her ears sang as she listened into the receiver. I haven't slept off the veronal, she thought with annoyance. It took a minute or two before she realized it was Dr Hain who was speaking to her.

"Pearl," he said, "can I speak with your husband? . . . No? Where is he? . . . You do not know? But we must find him and as quickly as possible. What has happened? . . . Listen, Pearl, your father-in-law is ill. Acute appendicitis. . . . Yes, the abdomen is distended. He ought to be taken to hospital at once. . . . Yes, there is the risk of a perforation, he must be operated, but he refuses. You know him better than I. He is very obstinate, very obstinate indeed. . . . Yes, I have called in two Chinese doctors whom his secretary recommended to me. We hoped he would have more confidence in them. But no, he fights like a buffalo—excuse me, Pearl! We need your husband in order to decide what is to be done—and, Pearl, you understand—it is urgent. He asks without ceasing for Dr Chang. His secretary tells me that something happened between them last night. Mr Chang Bogum seems to imagine he has fallen sick because he was angry with your husband. . . . No, that is nonsense, of course. . . . Yes, appendicitis, undoubtedly. Please send your husband here at once. I am sorry to alarm you, Pearl. He is very strong, it may all still go well if he is operated soon. . . . Then—auf Wiedersehen."

Pearl put down the receiver in dismay. She had put in a few brief questions and knew quite enough. She frowned and passed her hand over her drowsy forehead. Then she went into the sitting room where her surgical bag was and rummaged about in it. She turned on every light in the flat, and it mingled sadly with the hint of dawn from outside. She took out her hypodermic syringe and gave herself a caffein injection to get rid first of the effect of the sleeping powder, for she needed a clear head now. She had no idea where Yutsing might be at this first gray hour of dawn. I must drive to Liu. He may perhaps know something, Pearl thought, almost falling asleep again. She stood under the pitiless cold shower to wake herself up. Her Number One boy made his appearance with the passive clairvoyance of the race. She sent him for a taxi, for there was reason to despair of the telephone. Number One came back with a taxi even before she had finished dressing. It was a long drive to Hongkew, where Liu lived; even if the telephone were to be relied upon it would have been of no use, for Liu, the aesthete, had no telephone in his Chinese house, as a demonstration against American ways and because he wanted to have peace.

It had rained during the night, the streets were wet and cool. Pearl, with the caffein at work in her veins, became wakeful and over-excited as the taxi took her on her way. Twice she met soldiers, once a squad of small, dusky French colonial troops and once a detachment of the international guard. She had to show her pass before she could cross Soochow Creek, and she was glad she had had the forethought to provide herself with it, for it enabled her as a doctor to go where she pleased. The streets near the creek had a strange look about them, and the day dawned unwillingly and slowly, for the sky was overcast, and in the gray light she thought she saw barbed wire and barricades. But perhaps it was only the caffein which made everything look distorted and peculiar.

When she had crossed the creek and turned into the Chinese side of North Szechuan Road, a long brown column of Chinese soldiers came marching along. They were mostly very young fellows, whose faces looked out impassively and without expression from under their steel helmets. They were not marching in step; rather they were strolling along more like people returning from an outing.

"The warehouses along the river are full of them," the driver said, turning round to Pearl when she looked after the soldiers.

Liu's house stood in a maze of narrow alleys where many Chinese houses were built along a little stream. The house had a doorway and two windows on each side of it, and when Pearl pulled the bell a drowsy and ruffled doorkeeper made his appearance after some delay. Although it was Liu's pleasure to affect poverty and a simple manner of life, his doorkeeper was fat and indolent, and the house was always crowded with servants and parasites, as befitted the household of a man of a great family. Pearl impatiently gave the reason for her untimely visit. The doorkeeper left her waiting in the street while he retreated into the dark interior of the house to inform the master. It seemed to Pearl that days had gone by since Dr Hain's urgent call, and she began to feel angry with her husband, who had vanished without letting her knew where he had gone and forced her to hunt the town for him in the gray of dawn.

Liu made his appearance with surprising speed, buttoning up his long brown robe down the side. There was laughter on the surface of his face, but there was worry underneath.

"Liu, I am sorry to burst in on you like this," Pearl said as they walked to the taxi which was waiting at the corner of the impassably narrow lane. "My father-in-law is very ill and wants to see Yutsing. It's idiotic, but I don't know where his son has got to."

She laughed irritably and added:

"Perhaps it's a mad idea, but I thought that you as his friend might perhaps know where he was."

"I—think I can find him," Liu said, getting into the taxi without more ado. "I suggest that you drive straight to the Shanghai Hotel to take care of old Chang. I will go on in the taxi and look for Yutsing. Shanghai Hotel!" he shouted to the driver, and they set off in the direction from which Pearl had come.

"Do you know where he is?" Pearl asked again. She looked at him; Liu smiled awkwardly and made no reply.

"I cannot go to my father-in-law without Yutsing, it would only agitate him," Pearl said. "I shall stick with you till we've found him."

Liu considered her reply for a little while. Finally he said, "Good—as you like, Pearl. Perhaps it is just as well."

Pearl urged the driver to drive as fast as he could, and so they soon overtook the soldiers she had met shortly before. Liu looked out of the window while they drove slowly along the narrow strip of road the troops left them. When finally they had passed them he said, "So it's going to be serious. What a pity!"

"You don't believe in fighting, and yet you hate the Japanese. That's not logical."

"Logic, Pearl, is a thin-blooded affair that doesn't suit us. But if you want logic—we have never won a war, and we shall lose this one also. What we need is not ammunition but patience—and that we have got. Let us wait—five hundred years, a thousand years. Time's no object. We lose wars, but we are unconquerable. Let the Japanese come——"

"It doesn't seem that we can do anything else but let them come," Pearl exclaimed bitterly. "We don't want to fight. It is forced upon us."

"Quite right," Liu said. "But the mistake lies in allowing ourselves to be forced to fight. We are not strong as the tiger is strong. Our strength is the strength of ants, of amoeba, of the coral insect, of innumerable seething particles of life that beget and bring forth and split up and increase, unalterably and insuperably without end. We shall always be there. But Japan—where will Japan be in ten thousand years?"

Pearl let her eyes fall on his hand, which with a casual gesture swept Japan away. Liu's hand, finest ivory whose haughtiness, delicacy and pride had been turned on the lathe of a thousand years.

"That is too biological for me," she said. "I am a woman. What is going to happen ten thousand years from now does not interest me. Today, Liu, today we have to defend ourselves."

"Put a piece of ice into a tub of boiling water. Must the water defend itself? Can the ice survive?" Liu asked, smiling at her vehemence. His metaphors made Pearl furious.

"I suppose you'll bring out the old, well-worn platitude next and tell me that China will turn the Japanese into Chinese," she said, and her voice went deeper, as it always did when she got excited.

"It may seem strange, Pearl, but platitudes arise where a truth is repeated too often," Liu said, feeling sorry for her. "It is indisputable that China has absorbed its conquerors every time. And not only that: it has had a new birth every time new blood has poured into it from the north. Believe me, Pearl, it is not worth while to fight Japan. China is always strongest when she does nothing and just exists."

Pearl had ceased to listen. She was worrying about Yutsing's father, she was anxious about her husband. "Faster, faster," she called out to the driver.

"You American!" Liu said, teasing her good-naturedly.

"I am a doctor," Pearl answered. "I happen to know what minutes may mean."

They drove on for a time in silence. Where is Yutsing? Pearl thought without ceasing. What has happened to him? Where shall I find him? What has taken him from me and made a stranger of him day by day? How is it that Liu knows more about him than I do?

We used to be friends, she thought sadly. Were we not friends, Yutsing? And yet what do I know about you? What do you know about me? Our joys are shallow, our sorrows deep, she thought. Her father had written out the old proverb when her little brother died and hung it on the wall. She saw the large, rather stiff characters in her father's brush strokes. Hurrying along beneath the cool, gray morning sky, she was aware of the peculiar pride that is known only to those who dwell in loneliness. . . .

When they got near the bridge, they were held up by a small detachment of Chinese soldiers. A young officer, cigarette in his mouth, came up to the taxi and spoke to Liu. The woman he ignored. Liu endeavored to explain the haste they were in and the motive of their journey at that early hour, but it was not until Pearl showed her pass that the officer saluted and let the taxi go on. Meanwhile it had got much lighter, the sun would soon be shining behind the houses and clouds. Liu leaned back and considered how he could best tell Pearl what he had to tell her. On they went and reached the International Settlement without being held up by the English soldiers patrolling the creek; they drove along Nanking Road, which was still vacant and silent, and past the Shanghai Hotel with a sleepy doorman lounging at the door.

"Where are we going?" Pearl asked. Liu made the plunge.

"If Yutsing is where I think he is, we shall find him in Celestial Mansions," he said with hesitation. He glanced quickly at Pearl, and as she had her expression under control and showed neither surprise nor curiosity, he went on with relief: "You will have to know it, after all, sooner or later, Pearl, and it is perhaps as well you should know it now. Yutsing would gladly have confided in you, but he was afraid you might misunderstand him. I am not speaking now as a Chinese, Pearl, but straight to the point, for I know you are much too intelligent and high-minded to attribute too much importance to unavoidable—and unimportant—matters. Yutsing has . . . he has done as his father asked and taken a concubine. It has nothing to do with feelings or love or anything that concerns Yutsing Chang as an individual. Please, please understand that, Pearl. It is purely a matter of having issue. It's part of what I was saying about China. There

must be future generations, there must be the certainty that China
will live on century after century. Old B.G. is a bandit and a pirate
and an old sinner—but he has the right to grandchildren, and Yutsing has no right to refuse the old man grandchildren. You see that,
Pearl? You must see it. You must not take it hard and let your
wretched little modernized heart and your Christian notions of
monogamy get the better of you. Will you promise me that, Pearl?
Promise me to smile like a good, dutiful matriarch when we pick
up Yutsing at Celestial Mansions."

Liu looked at Pearl, and she smiled obediently. Whatever might
have been going on inside her, she smiled. Liu heaved a sigh of relief. Yutsing can thank me for taking that off his shoulders, he
thought with satisfaction.

"You are a good wife, Pearl. You are almost perfection," he said
gaily in order to make her smile even more. "I shall take the liberty
of composing a poem to you, an ode in the classical style. Have you
no sister? I would travel all the way to America to ask your sister to
be my wife, if she was like you."

"You have a wife, or wives, already," Pearl said, smiling still.

The taxi stopped. "Here we are," Liu said.

Celestial Mansions was an enormous building of innumerable
floors, inhabited by modern smartness and elegance. We are modern,
its façade shouted to the world at large, we are the newest thing, the
last word. We are the streamlined, chromium-plated, sophisticated,
costly and cosmopolitan Shanghai of tomorrow. The entrance
sparkled with metal and glass. A flower shop on the ground floor had
cascades of water pouring day and night down its plate-glass windows in order to keep the many orchids fresh.

"Might you want to be so kind as to fetch Yutsing? I wait here,"
Pearl said. Sometimes these Chinese phrases cropped up in her English. She folded her hands in her lap and dropped her eyes. Liu gave
her a last searching and grateful look and vanished in the chromium
splendors of Celestial Mansions. Pearl went on smiling, although no
one saw her. Her smile weighed five hundred pounds, and she trembled with the effort of holding it up as the strong man at the fair
trembles as he lifts his heaviest dumbbell. Her world had crashed

down on her in the last ten minutes. She was surprised she did not have to cry. It must be the caffein, she thought. But it was not that. From some hidden depth in her Chinese blood there came composure and submission to man and his laws.

Pearl had put on a modern tailor-made suit, as she did not like going to the Shanghai Hotel in Chinese dress. She put her hands in the pockets of her jacket as Yutsing appeared with Liu in the doorway of Celestial Mansions. He looked like a whipped dog.

"Pearl!" he said as he sat down beside her.

"We have lost a lot of time," she said, continuing to smile. "I hope you will be able to persuade your father to have the operation. I am sorry to be the bearer of such bad news."

Yutsing looked at the palms of his hands as though there were something to be read there. "Pearl!" he said again and felt for her hand on the seat. But her arms were unbending like steel, and she kept her hands to herself in the pockets of her modern suit. She felt she would break at his first touch.

"Shall I send a telegram to your mother?" Liu asked, trying to make a practical diversion.

"No, I think not," Yutsing said. "She can't get here now. All the railways are blocked, so why agitate her?"

"Dr Hain is a very good doctor," Pearl said. "He was a celebrated surgeon in his own country. I am glad he was at hand at the time."

The vacuum cleaners were at work in the lounge of the Shanghai Hotel. They had to wake up the elevator boy, for it was his last hour of duty and he had fallen asleep.

"Shall I come, too?" Liu asked. "Perhaps I might be of some use." Pearl held her hand out to him. "We need you, Liu," she said imploringly. He gazed at the object as though not knowing what he was supposed to do with it. Then he remembered his English education and cautiously shook it. They went up in silence to the roof garden.

In Bogum Chang's large reception room the three girls whom Yutsing had once before seen in his father's company were huddled together like little monkeys. He knew by now that the eldest of them was Meilan's sister. Servants, hangers-on, employees and distant relations sat, squatted or stood about. Some of them were smoking, and there was a game of mahjong in progress on a window seat. They interrupted their doleful whisperings when Pearl entered. Dr Hain advanced to meet her. "I have sent Mr Chai for the ambulance, the telephone is out of order again," he said in a low voice. "Let us hope your husband will have enough influence with his father."

Pearl followed Yutsing into the bedroom. She exchanged a few polite words with the Chinese doctors who were moving to and fro on the tips of their toes. Their shoes squeaked, they were intent on giving their wealthy patient an impression of ceaseless activity. For the moment their pains were wasted, for Chang lay in his large bed and appeared to be asleep. His eyelids were half shut, leaving only a tiny black slit visible, and he appeared to be naked.

"The temperature has gone up—102 degrees," Dr Hain said over Pearl's shoulder as she bent down to the sick man. Her husband was at her side and looked questioningly at her. "Speak to him," she said. Yutsing sat on the edge of the bed and cleared his throat.

"Father!" he said.

Chang Bogum's naked shoulders rose in such a mighty structure under the bedclothing that his son could not believe it a dangerous sickness. His face too, which the night before had been flecked with pallor, was again copper-colored, and the blood surged under his skin. "Father!" Yutsing said again. The three girls had followed in his wake to the door, now they stood there leaning together, a touching picture of sorrow and anxiety. The bed was high and broad, a genuine Chinese bed with silk curtains and no mosquito net and a hard, red-covered box of a pillow. The lights were still on, although it was by now broad daylight. Apparently in the general agitation no one had thought of turning them out. Mr Chai, the secretary, went to and fro offering the doctors tea. Then the rasping sound of the telephone was heard in the room without. Pearl went out quickly. The ambulance of the Hopkins Hospital had arrived. She told the stretcher bearers to come up and wait in the anteroom.

Chang opened his eyes and became alert at once. In whatever realms his soul might have been wandering, he now came to himself and smiled at his son. He lifted his great hand from under the bed-covering and stroked Yutsing's forehead with a strange and gentle movement. Yutsing understood that he was thinking of the wound he had given him the night before. Tears came to his eyes, and he grasped his father's hand and put it back on the quilt.

"I have come to implore on my knees the exalted person's forgiveness," he said with all the reverence due to a father.

"Where is Meilan?" Chang asked, moistening his lips. "Have you brought her with you?"

Yutsing shook his head in astonishment. His father sat up in sudden annoyance. "I insist that you bring her here at once. You must bring your two wives here and keep them under this roof," he ordered.

"I will send for Meilan, Father," Yutsing said obediently. He looked round for the two officious doctors. "Is he delirious?" he asked in a whisper when Chang Bogum's eyes closed again.

One of the doctors felt his father's pulse, the other laid his hand on his forehead. "A broken thread," said the one who was feeling his pulse.

Pearl came back from the telephone and announced softly: "The ambulance is here. Can we have him carried down?"

Chang was already on the alert again, more alert than before. He sat up and, ignoring his pain, gave his daughter-in-law an unfriendly glance. "I will not leave this building in any circumstances," he said loudly. "And I refuse to have myself cut up. I ate rather too much yesterday, and I got slightly agitated on a full stomach. And that wasn't good for me." As he said this he shot an almost mischievous and meaning glance at his son. "As soon as my rebellious belly is reduced to order, I shall be well again. But if it is my destiny to go to my fathers today I insist on being buried whole and unmutilated. Moreover, I prefer," he added, and once more the mischievous expression passed over his face, "to die of a well-filled belly rather than of the bombs of the Japanese. I am safer here than in a hospital."

When he had said this he drew a deep breath, pressed his hand to his side, muttered a coarse coolie oath in the Shantung dialect and looked from face to face to see whether his orders had been understood. Pearl was the only one who ventured on a counterattack. "It is better for the high person of the honored father to be taken to the sickhouse," she said. "There are means there of taking away the pains. We, his children, have the right to ask that the father shall try to protect his health by every means."

Chang surveyed his American daughter-in-law for a time in silence, as though the sight of her amused him. Then he beckoned to her to sit down on the bed. "Wife of my son," he said confidentially, "the father is no such fool as you seem to believe. And in order that you may understand what is in my thoughts, I will tell you the following: The town will be bombed today. I know that from a sure source. This roof and building are safe. The Japanese have promised me that they will not drop bombs on it. And the Japanese—say what you like against them—are people who keep their word. For this reason I am going to stay here, and I desire that all who belong to me shall also come under this roof."

After making this astonishing announcement he sank back; a dark and fevered flush spread over his face, he clenched his teeth, shut his eyes. Immediately afterwards there was no more than a low regular groaning which showed that he had relapsed into semiconsciousness again. Time went by, the mahjong pieces rattled outside, an electric clock ticked in a corner, time went by. Once the windows rattled faintly as though from a distant explosion, but no one paid any attention. Pearl went into the next room to smoke a cigarette and came back again. Her husband was still sitting on the bed, listening to his father's subdued groans. He raised his head, looked at her as she stood in the doorway. For a fleeting moment all was well between them, and Pearl wished she could return to that yesterday of friendly confidence, of happy and now irrecoverable ignorance.

"Yutsing," she said softly, "you are the only son, you have the entire responsibility. If you give the order he can be taken to hospital. To wait is murder."

Dr Chang got up from the bed and signaled to Pearl and the three doctors to follow him into the large room. "Is it certain that an operation will save his life? Or is that too a risk?" he asked.

Pearl looked at him in surprise. "But Yutsing, you are a doctor yourself," she said. "You can see that the distention of the abdomen is increasing. Pressure on the McBurney, two vomitings. The danger of a perforation is obvious."

Dr Chang wondered at himself. He had almost forgotten that he had begun as a doctor. He spent his life in bureaus and offices, in consultations and on committees, attending meetings and giving lectures, drawing up documents and waging the bureaucratic war for money, which the campaign for hygiene swallowed up. "Dr Hain, you are the eldest, what is your opinion?" he asked. Ever since his early association with Dr Lee his confidence in elderly and foreign doctors had been firmly rooted. Dr Hain adjusted his eyeglasses and stood up.

"I am convinced that every moment of delay is at the risk of his life, whereas the operation is without any risk whatever," he said quickly. It was long since he had had his say in an important consultation. "I could not prevent my Chinese colleagues giving the patient an injection which has somewhat blurred the picture, but the diagnosis stands fast."

"If that is so, we must take my father to the hospital—if necessary by force," Yutsing decided. He went to the telephone to order the ambulance stretcher bearers to come up. While he was speaking, the door opened and Liu came in behind the secretary, followed by a demure little figure in a tight green dress.

It was Meilan, whom Yutsing had sent the secretary to fetch, since his father was so anxious to have her under the protected roof of the Shanghai Hotel. She crossed the threshold with downcast eyes, and her sister, Chingliu, went quickly up to her and took her by the shoulders. Yutsing put the receiver down. Even in this dread and agitated hour when his father's life was at stake, he saw with an inward elation and delight how beautiful Meilan was and how desirable in her artful helplessness. Pearl stood beside Dr Hain with her hands dug into the pockets of her jacket. She looked as if she felt cold.

"Pearl," Yutsing said to his wife, "this is—Meilan. Will you be so good as to bid her welcome? She is afraid of you," he added in English.

"Have you eaten, Meilan?" Pearl said mechanically. It was the greeting of the simple folk.

"Thank you, I have eaten," Meilan answered.

I shall be divorced, Pearl thought. The experiment has failed. I am not suited to China. The endless chain of desperate efforts and almost imperceptible successes which had made up her life in that country passed before her eyes. And now the war on top of it all. It was to please Yutsing that she had labored; it was for him she had come here. She looked at the concubine under her eyelids. She was very young and very beautiful, but it was not the beauty of a human being who thinks and knows and fights; it was the beauty of a flower, vegetative and without life of its own. I shall get a divorce and go back to America, Pearl thought once more, smarting with a fiercer pain than before. But when she thought of Chinatown, of the narrow life in its few lanes, its ostracism and limitations, she knew that she did not belong there, either. She went to the window, which reached to the floor, and opened it and looked out. But she saw nothing.

Dr Hain glanced at the electric clock ticking in the corner. Five minutes past nine. "We are losing hours and hours," he said nervously, for he was used to the anxious haste with which in Europe cases of life and death were handled. Never had the Chinese seemed to him so foreign as that morning. "I will try to persuade him," Yutsing said, and he returned to the bedroom. The telephone rasped again, the secretary, Mr Chai went to it.

"It is for you, Dr Hain," he said. "A Mrs Russell wants to speak to you."

"Me?" the doctor said, going to the small table on which the telephone stood. "What does she want from me?"

As he took up the receiver, a roar as of a great refractory animal came from the bedroom. It was the emphatic tones with which old Chang refused to be taken to hospital. His voice was so loud and so amazingly vehement that Dr Hain could not understand a word he heard on the telephone and had to ask twice. "Forgive me, it is so loud here, I do not understand. What were you saying? Would you repeat it once more, Mrs Russell?"

He listened with open mouth. He adjusted his eyeglasses straight. "I'm coming," he said as he hung up the receiver.

XVIII

FRANK TAYLOR HAD SET his alarm clock for seven from a vague feeling that it was fitting to get up earlier than usual on his wedding morning. But when the ringing and buzzing started, he seized the unpleasant apparatus without opening his eyes and throttled it under his pillow; but as he had told Ah Sinfu to bring his morning tea at seven, it was of no avail. Ah Sinfu appeared, drew the curtains, made a rattling with cups and saucers, put down shining white, freshly cleaned shoes and turned on the shower bath.

"Master velly much happy, Ah Sinfu velly much happy. Missie velly much happy," he said, giving his good wishes with an expectant smile.

Frank got up, drank his first cup of tea with his eyes still shut and woke up at the second one. He went across into Morris' room, but the reporter had not come home that night, either. He plunged under the shower and emerged from it singing a few minutes later. Ah Sinfu stood ready with the towel to rub him down. While this was proceeding, Frank gave him his final orders. Trunks had to be packed, the flat handed over in good order and two suits sent to the laundry. Also Frank had promised that Ah Sinfu should help to serve the wedding breakfast which Mrs B.S. was giving for them. What would not get into Ah Sinfu's head was the fact that his master was going to sleep the next night in the Shanghai Hotel, as the new flat would not be free until the morning of the fifteenth.

"Master no can catch house?" he asked again and again, and Frank repeated with growing impatience, "No can do, savvy, no can do. Tomorrow can do. Today no can do."

Just as Ah Sinfu, with an air of resignation, went to clear away the tea things, the telephone rang in the next room. Ruth, Frank thought instantly, and it was the first time he had thought of her since he woke up. Marrying was a thicket of formalities in which the people who were getting married completely vanished. He went half dressed to the telephone.

"Good morning, Midget," he called into the telephone. "How's Confucius? I've just sent you a telegram with the information that I've changed my mind." Nonsense of this kind was the easiest way of bridging the gap, as wide and deep as the Grand Canyon, which had opened between him and Ruth.

"I'm sorry," he heard in the telephone, "it's not Ruth, it's Helen."

"Oh!" Frank said and pulled himself together. "Helen—good morning, Helen. I thought you were leaving today——"

"My luggage is on board," she said. "The boat sails at one. I'm so sorry, Frank, to bother you, but I don't know what to do. You must come. You must help me."

Frank kept the receiver pressed to his ear without answering. "I —you know—I'm rather occupied today," he said when the silence had to be broken.

"I know, I know, Frank. I'm dreadfully sorry, but I have nobody but you. It's about Bobbie—he's disappeared. You must help me," her voice went on.

"What do you mean, disappeared?" Frank asked in bewilderment. "What do you mean by that, Helen?"

"Come, please, Frank, come to the hotel. I cannot explain to you on the telephone. I have been trying for half an hour—it's so difficult to get through, and I don't know how many people may be listening in," the voice went on. In fact there was a continual counterpoint of noises and ringings accompanying Helen's words. Frank thought it over for a moment longer.

"Right. I'll come. Don't get worried, darling," he said. He was filled to suffocation with good and noble instincts.

"Thank you. I knew it—Sir Galahad," the telephone said with an attempt at a little joke.

As Frank put down the receiver, he muttered a few curses. Nevertheless, an incongruous joy had crept into his heart at the prospect of seeing Helen once more. The parting at the elevator the night before had left a nasty taste behind it. Finished. Over. The damned

part of it was that it was not finished and over and did not stop the
moment one told it to. Finished? Nonsense. And yet—finished. I
can shave later, he thought, as he rapidly finished dressing.

As he was only three blocks from the hotel he did not take a
ricksha but went on foot, and as he went he drew in deep breaths
of the fresh air and from time to time whistled to himself. It was an
innocent way of trying to convince himself that Helen's call for help
did not excite him. It was early in the morning, most of the stores
were still shut. He hesitated when he came to the colonnade, then
walked quickly to the premises of the Eos Film and Foto Company.
Petrus, the office boy, whose duties began at half-past seven, was already visible in the gloom within, as he dreamily wiped the glass
cases, in which cameras were on display. Frank took a look at the
window, where already at this early hour transparent colored slides,
much enlarged, passed by in continuous procession. He had taken
some of them himself, and as always he felt even now a fleeting pride
in the new Eos color film "Colopan," which made such surprisingly
good pictures. He hesitated a moment longer, then entered the shop.
Petrus looked at him in astonishment and wiped much faster than
before. Frank went to the telephone and called up Ruth in her room.
"Well, well!" he said when he was connected on the instant.

"Tiny," he said, "don't forget it's your wedding day today. Wash
properly behind your ears and be a good girl. I've still one or two
odd jobs to do before we take our seats on the electric chair. Then
I'll come for you. You'll stay in your room? . . . Good, yes, please,
wait for me there. A kiss to Confucius. See you soon."

He rang off, stood for a moment at the telephone, began to whistle
again. "The forty packets of the Hundred and Sixteen must be
packed today for Soochow," he told Petrus. "Allight, Mister Tai-lo,"
the boy said with a grin. "Mr B.S. and I will not be here today, Mr
Wang will see to everything," Frank added. "I have written it all
down for him." He gave the boy a list and took another look in the
drawer where the developed films lay, tidily packed in wrappers on
which his photo of the Lunghua Pagoda with the airplane above it
was printed. "What are you making such a face for?" he asked the
boy. Petrus was in the pangs of congratulations which he was unable

to reduce to English; before he could get them out, Frank was already at the door. He sighed as he left the store to go to Helen. The store was no paradise, certainly, but it was a home. He entered the hotel from the back, crossed the domed hall and took the second elevator up to the sixteenth floor.

His chest was somewhat contracted as he knocked at No. 1678. As there was no answer, he pressed down the handle and entered the Russells' sitting room, where the lights were on and the heavy curtains drawn, so that he seemed to step out of daylight back into the night. Helen came at once out of her bedroom, the door of which she left open. She was not, as Frank had dimly feared or hoped, in negligee, but dressed for the voyage in a jacket and skirt of white Shantung silk.

"Thank you, Frank," she said, giving him her hand. "I knew you would not leave me in the lurch." She went to the window and drew the curtains aside. "What will you have for breakfast? Tea? Coffee? Eggs?"

"Coffee and two soft-boiled eggs," Frank muttered as she went to the telephone to call up the bedroom waiter. Frank felt extremely silly. He had expected something else, he did not exactly know what. Helen in tears, despairing, helpless, appealing for his advice and relying on his strength, sobbing on his shoulder. "And toast," he said.

"The thing is this," Helen said, sitting down opposite him in front of the fireplace. "The ship sails at one o'clock this afternoon. I sent Potter and Clarkson on board last night with the luggage so that they could make the cabins a bit comfortable. Boats are horrible, don't you think? But Bobbie has not come home. He disappeared the night before last, and I don't know where on earth to look for him. He has not been back for two nights, you see. I can't possibly leave the British colony a scandal to revel in after we've gone. What am I to do?"

"Have you no notion where he's gone?" Frank asked.

"Yes, if you like to call it a notion. He left the bar with that little pianist. I imagine they were both after opium. But I have no idea where they may have got to."

Frank laughed irritably. "There are four thousand opium dens in the city at the lowest guess," he said. "Tell me, has the pianist vanished, too?"

"Yes," Helen said. "I made inquiries. Do you think there's any danger in those places? Can anything have happened to Bobbie?"

It was meant to sound anxious, but it sounded hopeful. Frank was too busy with his thoughts to notice.

"You wouldn't like to inform the International Police? Best thing to do. I believe the fellows are discreet," he said tentatively. Although the whole thing was deeply repulsive to him and he was reluctant to be drawn into the unsavory and obscure affairs of the Russells, he was unable to resist the unfailing excitement and enchantment caused by the mere sight of Helen, Helen's presence, her voice, her movements, the way she pushed back her hair or crossed her feet.

"It must be a chemical reaction," he said aloud.

"What?" Helen asked in surprise.

"What's that? What did you say?" he asked back.

"What must be a chemical reaction?" she asked, smiling. Frank did not know that he had spoken aloud.

"You know that quite well," he said almost roughly.

"Psychology zero," she replied. There was a knock, and the waiter wheeled in the breakfast wagon and put it between them in front of the fireplace.

"Good morning, Gaston," Helen said. "Thanks, we'll help ourselves."

Gaston, with an injured air, resigned the silver pots and the rolls of butter, which nestled among crushed ice and shone like roses in dew.

"Thank you, Gaston. I will ring if I want you," Helen said when Gaston made no move to leave them alone. Jealous, she thought with amusement. Ever since she had succeeded in decoying Frank into that room, large triumphant bubbles of laughter rose irrepressibly in her throat. She looked at him, he was there, he was with her. He was holding onto his cigarette, and he looked gloomy, poor boy.

It was the waiter's expressive look that first opened Frank's eyes to the compromising nature of the situation: breakfast for two and the husband mislaid.

"I'm so sorry, Mrs Russell, that you can't come to my wedding," he said much too loudly and hurriedly, in the hope that the waiter might still hear it before he shut the door behind him.

"You little Babbitt," Helen said tenderly and mockingly and got up to pour out his coffee. She went round the table and stood behind Frank to do so. He quickly drank a glass of iced water. "This is not the way to find your husband," he said severely. "I must call Morris up, perhaps he's in the club. He may have some suggestion."

He walked across to the telephone and tried hard for several minutes to get through.

"Well?" Helen asked as he put down the receiver with a curse.

"The telephone boy at the club will call me up again if he can get through," he said, standing at the window.

"Your breakfast, Frank," Helen said gently.

"Thanks. I'm not hungry," he replied. He thought the matter over again. "Why don't you simply go on board and leave as arranged?" he asked. "That's the best thing you can do, in my opinion. If your husband doesn't turn up, that's his own affair. Perhaps he may go straight to the boat. What do you think?"

Helen stayed by the fireplace and looked at him.

"How impatient you are to be rid of me, Frank!" was all she said. He rubbed the palms of his hands together. They had got moist, and there was that nervous, dirty feeling again.

"Excuse me, can I wash my hands somewhere?" he asked. She pointed with her chin to the open door of her bedroom.

The air there was heavy with Helen's perfume, although the windows were wide open. The broad bed was tumbled about and in disorder. Frank walked quickly, as through a blazing fire, to the bathroom; he looked about for some soap and found a small piece of the hotel soap wrapped in paper; he turned on the tap, unwrapped the soap and began to wash his hands with a feeling of relief. As he dried his hands he looked without thinking at the wet marks of Helen's naked feet on the blue-tiled floor. The light imprints were so finely arched and curved, as if even the smallest trace of the woman bore the stamp of her beauty. Frank smiled at the sight of her footmarks and the vision of her nakedness that rose from them.

As he put down the towel and turned to leave the bathroom with clean, cool hands, he found that Helen was standing behind him.

Man had always been her enemy—to be conquered and taken by surprise. She had pitiless knowledge of the signs that betrayed a man's weakness. The play of the chin muscles and of the veins of the temples, the sudden pallor, cold lips, quivering nostrils, the deepening voice. Frank might wish her a happy voyage and say as many conventional things as he liked—she knew the state he was in.

He put the towel down, turned round, and there was Helen behind him. The next moment they were in a wild, furious and insensate embrace that filled the whole world and left no room for anything else. As they fell, locked together, on the bed, the windows once or twice faintly trembled, and a little later the yellow shafts of sun on the floor paled and storm clouds gathered and obscured the sky. Helen was the first to emerge from the rainbows in which they were lost. "Like in a jungle——" she said softly. Frank sat up. The windows rattled again.

"It's begun, I believe," Frank said.

"What has?" she asked.

"The bombardment," he said.

She looked at him searchingly and absent-mindedly and smiled passingly over the care he took to smooth his hair. There were moments which were inborn in the species man and came up again and again with all men in the same situations. She took his pocket handkerchief out of his breast pocket and pressed it to her lips. A few drops of blood stained the linen.

"What now?" Frank asked.

"Now we want a bomb to hit and take us away," Helen said, almost singing.

"Why now particularly?" Frank asked, although he knew the answer.

"We can never be happier than we are now," Helen said. They were still sitting on the wide and tumbled bed. They had only kissed each other and nothing more.

"It can be a lot more beautiful still," Frank said longingly. Helen let her fingertips slide over his mouth in a strange caress: "Frank," she said, "you know you can't marry. You know it."

Now it was Frank's turn to wish for a bomb. "What shall I do?" he asked himself and Helen and the walls of that alien room. "What shall I do?"

"If I give up everything, will you do the same?" Helen said breathlessly. She did not understand herself, but she had got to a state when she was ready to give up all for a thing whose existence she had always denied: love.

"And then?" Frank asked. "Do you want to trail an out-of-work chemist around the world with you? I daresay you spend more on perfume in a month than I earn in a year."

"Now don't be so practical," Helen said reproachfully. "If we stick together you will become rich and famous—anything you like. You will make a great discovery—plastic film, for example. You only need to be got out of yourself. You live in much too narrow a way, there is far more in you than people think, but I know you, I know you better than you do yourself. If we stick together——" She broke off and listened.

"It's not bombs," Frank said.

She put her hand over his mouth. The door opened in the next room and shambling steps shuffled in.

"Bobbie!" Helen's lips said without a sound. For the last twenty minutes Frank had utterly forgotten Bobbie Russell's existence.

Helen released herself and, darting to the looking glass, gave a glance at her white Shantung silk jacket and skirt. She quickly tore the jacket off and threw on a kimono; Frank saw the embroidered butterflies on a black background more distinctly than he had ever seen anything before in his life. Meanwhile her husband was mumbling and grumbling round the sitting room. "Helen!" he now shouted and knocked at the door. At the same moment Helen was there and turned the key in the lock.

"Yes, Bobbie?" she called out. "I'm just dressing. Go to your room, Bobbie."

Frank was still sitting dumfounded on the bed. Helen smiled at him reassuringly.

"Damn you, open the door!" Bobbie shouted outside. "Damn you, damn you!" He gave the door a kick that made the bottles on the dressing table ring. Helen gave Frank an imploring glance and pointed to the bathroom. It was like an evil dream but also slightly comic. He crept into the bathroom as quietly as he could. He kept the door open on a crack.

"Don't smash up this expensive hotel," he heard Helen telling her husband on the other side of the room; but she did not let Bobbie come in. She pushed him back into the sitting room.

"Where on earth have you been? I was just going to get the police to look for you," she said in a hostile tone. But Bobbie was not in the mood to be domineered over.

"In Elysium," he said. "In Elysium, my lady. Right down in the Elysium dirt, where you always say I belong."

"Don't be ridiculous, Bobbie," Helen said. "Get dressed. We must go on board."

From the bathroom Frank could hear all that was said. He discovered that there was another door out of it, probably into the passage. He tried the handle. The door was locked, and no key to be seen. He opened the door into Helen's bedroom a little wider and listened. It was the most damnably uncomfortable situation he had ever been in in his life. The night the detective had caught him with the little film whore came to his mind—the stuffy smell, the rain-swept street and his mortal dread. But this was far worse. My wedding day, he thought savagely; it actually made him laugh. But I can never get married now; it's all over, he thought as he sat down on the white-painted chair beside the bath.

By this time a quarrel was in progress in the sitting room beyond. Bobbie had discovered the breakfast table laid for two and, in the alert and aggressive condition his overdose of opium seemed to have induced, he was in no mind to let it pass.

"What's this?" Frank heard him roar. "What's the meaning of this? You've had a lover here. You poison me with booze and dope so that you can have time for your dirty affairs. But you make a mistake, you whore. I picked you up out of the dirt," he shouted, "and you behave like a—like a—— Who was it? Gaston? The bedroom waiter?

Is it him you've been making eyes at or some stinking Chinese? Speak or I'll——"

Helen's cool voice broke in with unruffled composure: "Go and shave."

Frank involuntarily felt his own chin. Immediately afterwards there was a tremendous crash of broken crockery. Bobbie had kicked over the table with its elegant breakfast service and had flung himself on his wife. Frank threw discretion to the winds and made for the door. There was now nothing but a panting noise to be heard on the other side.

"Let me go, you're mad!" Helen said breathlessly. Thuds, groans, a shriek from Helen. Frank seized the door handle. The groans had got weaker, there was a dull sound of repeated blows.

"Frank! Help!" Helen screamed. Frank rushed into the room. He saw it all in a flash, as if he were all eyes. Helen was lying on the floor, with Bobbie kneeling on her; his face was limp and idiotic, but all the same distorted with rage. A trickle of saliva fell onto Helen from his drooping underlip, and he was banging her head with both hands again and again on the floor. The floor all round them was strewn with broken crockery, there was a streak of yellow on the mantel where an egg had been smashed, and on the ledge above sat the little Buddha, looking on with stupid imperturbability.

"Bobbie!" Frank shouted. The man at once let go of his wife and, staggering to his feet, went for Frank with a shriek. Frank's fist got him straight in the face and Bobbie dropped. Frank rubbed his knuckles. Helen sat up and pulled her torn kimono straight. Her face and mouth were glowing—her eyes too. "Thank you, Sir Galahad," she said tonelessly but with a smile. "This time it was—dangerous."

Frank helped her from the floor and stroked her consolingly.

"It was all for me," he said and his voice, too, was hollow. She gave his bleeding knuckles a quick and fleeting kiss.

"Have you been a prize fighter?" she asked, laughing again already.

Frank then bent down over the prostrate Bobbie, who had the dazed smile of a man who has been knocked out.

"That's the second time you've had to let him have it," she said. Bobbie's face quivered, but he did not come to. "Now you must help me," Helen said.

She put her hands under Bobbie's shoulders to drag him from the room.

"Where are you going to put him?" Frank asked.

"In his bedroom. He can come round there," Helen said.

Frank took hold of him by the legs, with a glance at the dirt on his white dinner jacket, and they hauled him out. They put him on the low sofa in his bedroom. His bed was turned down and untouched. The thoughtful Potter had put out a fresh, white suit and all the accessories on the quilt. The curtains were drawn and the light was on, not only on the bedside table but in the middle of the ceiling. To all appearances everything was exactly as it had been left for Bobbie's arrival on the evening before. When they had deposited him as if he were a sack, he muttered incomprehensibly but did not come round. Frank could well understand the look of nausea with which Helen surveyed her husband before they left the room.

"Gaston will be surprised," Helen said as she looked at the shattered plates and glasses in the sitting room. "He took us for people of quality. Now he will begin to entertain doubts about the superiority of the English aristocracy."

Frank admired Helen's composure and poise. He himself still felt breathless and distraught. His only comfort was the physical pleasure that every man feels who has knocked out an opponent. She pushed up the loose sleeves of her kimono and examined the bronze skin of her arms.

"You see what it is," she said. "Since I married Bobbie there has never been a day when I haven't been black and blue."

Frank took hold of her arm and kissed it wherever the skin was beginning to grow discolored. Helen looked down with raised eyebrows at his handsome brown neck and the dark Hawaiian hair with which she had first fallen in love. "Do you see now that you must take me away out of this horrible life?" she asked softly. Frank only nodded as he bent over her arm. He had never known there was so much love in the world as he felt within him at that moment.

"Pity I let Potter go," she said, laughing quietly. 'He's had so much practice in clearing up these scrap heaps."

She gently released herself and rang for the Chinese bedroom boy. He came at once with a polite cough and knock at the door and shuffled into the room in his cotton shoes. Helen merely pointed to the catastrophe. The boy smiled and vanished and came back again with a cloth, in which he collected the fragments, and disappeared again, smiling still. While this went on, Frank stood at the window looking out at the clouds that seemed to forebode a storm.

"It's time I went," he said irresolutely as he turned back into the room.

"Now? You don't mean that seriously? You can't leave me alone with Bobbie now. If he comes to himself——" she said and left the sentence unfinished. "We've got to talk to him," she added. Frank sighed from the bottom of his heart. That he had to talk to Bobbie appeared indispensable, but what he was to say was more than he knew. Helen came up to him, and her torn kimono fell away from her breast. Frank noticed that she had tanned to bronze under her clothes too in provocative contrast to her red hair. But as soon as she put her arms round his neck, everything cooled and paled. He stayed helplessly where he was when, with her finger to her lips, she glided on tiptoe into Bobbie's bedroom.

She went right up to the sofa on which her husband lay. Bobbie's head had rolled to one side, and he was breathing regularly, with a little catch in every breath. He had come to after the blow Frank had given him and had simply fallen asleep. His mouth was open, his chin had dropped, and little bubbles of saliva appeared every time he exhaled. Helen switched on one more of those idiotic baby-ribbon-pink lamps in the curtained room and looked pitilessly and closely into his face in the strong light. It was pale and sunken and covered with freckles, which in some places ran together in large brown patches. His clothing was dirty, and he smelt of dirt—of the acrid, putrid dirt of the places where he had presumably spent his last two nights. He's worse than a corpse, Helen thought. She listened to his breathing. The loud and regular catch in his breath sounded as if he had difficulty in breathing at all. She put one hand on his chest to test the beating of his heart. It still beat on—that miserable heart. She removed her hand, for the mere feel of him overwhelmed her with nausea. She had knelt down beside the sofa to examine him. Now she stood up and looked aimlessly round the room. She walked softly to the bed and picked up the pillow which had had a fresh pillowcase put on it. The name "Shanghai Hotel" was woven into the linen. She never let her husband, her sleeping or unconscious husband, out of her eye as she came back to him with the pillow in her hands. She hesitated only one moment and then knelt down again beside the low sofa and pressed the pillow with all her strength over his face.

At first he made no resistance, then his hands groped about in the air. Helen leaned all her weight on the pillow. Bobbie's hands gripped her kimono, he drew up his knees and jerked them up and down spasmodically and grotesquely. She did not know how long it lasted before he ceased to move. His fingers went limp and relaxed their grip. Without releasing the pressure on the pillow she put one hand on his chest again.

His heart beat no longer.

I never thought it was so easy, Helen thought. But she found trouble in relaxing her own limbs, for they were quite cramped. Then, as soon as she was able to move and stand up, she began to tremble violently. The pillow was still on Bobbie's face, but she no longer held it down. For some moments she heard her own blood singing loudly in her ears; then this too ebbed away. The telephone rang in the next room; then she heard Frank's voice in answer. It brought her back, out of the ghostly and unreal world in which she had been, to the bedroom where she had just choked her husband. Slowly she withdrew the pillow from his face. She put her ear close to his open mouth. No, not a breath issued from it. Remembering what she had perhaps read, perhaps seen in a film, she got up and fetched Bobbie's shaving mirror from the dressing table and held it in front of his stiffened face. No, the glass was not misted. She put the mirror down again and the pillow back on the bed. Then she pondered for a second over its crumpled surface and took it back to the sofa. She lifted up his head, which was no limper but much heavier than it had been on the many other occasions when she had taken care of Bobbie in his frequent bouts of drunkenness and pushed the pillow under it.

As she turned out the lamp on the wall above him she was vexed to see that Bobbie's pale face had gone darker. The freckles seemed accentuated. She stretched her arms and her fingers. She went into the sitting room, the light there seemed dazzling, and she stood and waited until Frank had finished his conversation on the telephone.

"No," he was saying. "If that's so you're quite right. The wedding will have to be put off. How many bombs, d'you say? . . . Rotten luck, but what can you do? Will you be at the club? I want to see you. I want to have a long talk. . . . Well—so long. Don't be too crazy if you can help it. Aloha."

"That was Morris," he said as he put down the receiver. "He says there's fighting in Chapei but he can't get there. He says it's out of the question to have the wedding today. I must go straight to Ruth and tell her. That will give us time to think over what we are going to do about it all. In any case you must go on board. Perhaps I shall be able to come to Hong Kong in a few days' time. We have a branch there, too."

"Frank," Helen said, "Bobbie is dead."

"What?" Frank asked.

"Bobbie is dead," Helen repeated. Only now he saw her quivering lips and also that her face had altered and become almost strange. "Bobbie is dead," she said for the third time.

"But how—how is it possible?" Frank asked. The whole room lay between them, an abyss over which a rich green carpet was stretched. The Buddha on the mantelpiece did not care. . . .

"It must have happened when you knocked him down. Perhaps he broke his skull—or something," Helen whispered from the other side.

"Nonsense!" Frank said. He pulled himself together, braced his shoulders and went into the next room. He came back after a while and began walking mutely up and down the room. Helen's eyes never left him for a second.

"A nice mess we're in," he said finally. "He's boozed or smoked or whored himself to death for all I know. I'll have nothing to do with it."

"No," Helen said, almost smiling at this demonstration of masculine folly. "Of course not."

"What are we to do now?" Frank asked. "What are we to do now, I'd like to know? What are we to do now?"

"Stick together," Helen said. She looked down at herself and walked quickly across the room. "Excuse me, I must change my clothes," she muttered as she went through the door.

Stick together, Frank thought. It was worse than an earthquake, a hurricane, an explosion. It was the end. His head was utterly vacant. That blue face on the white pillow . . .

Helen returned in a fresh white dress. Frank recognized it with a ferocious sort of amusement as the dress in which he had seen her for the first time, out there at the Lunghua Pagoda. She had emerged then, without a crease and spotless, from the riot of leprous beggars, and she was just as uncreased and immaculate now when she supposed that he had killed her husband. He looked at his wrist watch with the aimless, flitting gesture of a man in desperation. After nine. In had been ten minutes to eight when he entered the hotel. Time had ceased to have its absolute significance and had become merely relative as in dreams. Helen took up the telephone.

"I want to speak to Dr Hain," she said. It occurred to Frank that she spoke with a slightly foreign accent; she was becoming another woman to his very eyes and his very ears. Helen did not know that she was too exhausted to keep up the discipline in which she lived her life of lies. Her lips trembled, her Russian origin broke through. She had lost control over the expression of her face too, and it looked wild and radiant with a joy which was ill suited to the occasion. It was remarkable also that the form she saw hovering before her eyes was not that of her murdered husband. It was—though dimly seen and made up of fragments that parted and came together again— the form of the beggar Grischa, the Russian beggar outside the Peony Club.

"Doctor!" Helen said into the telephone. "Please come at once.

My husband has had a frightful fit—I am afraid that it may be serious . . ."

Frank heard this with surprise. But he's dead already, he thought. He wanted to go. Ruth! he thought with longing. But he remained standing by the window as though paralyzed, and not another word passed between them until the doctor came. Only at the very last moment Helen said: "Leave it all to me. Don't say a word—I'll get us through." Then there was a knock and the old German doctor came in with his bag and spectacles.

XIX

DR HAIN WAS FEELING the effects of his sleepless night as he entered the Russells' suite, for his watch with the sick Chinese banker, the obstinacy of his patient, his consultations with his Chinese colleagues and the family, the ever-increasing number of relations, hangers-on and concubines assembled up there, had combined to fatigue him. At the same time he was wide awake and feeling more himself than for a long time, for this was a real case, and it was on the cards that he might still have to operate. It was the bugle call at which the old war horse pricks up his ears. Mrs Russell's urgent summons gave him a pleasant feeling of important and manifold activities.

"Where is our patient?" he asked with professional cheerfulness and followed Mrs Russell into the bedroom. "Again some excess or other?" he asked, putting down his bag. "Would you have the goodness to let in the daylight?"

And then it came out that Mr Russell was not suffering from a fit, as his wife had said, but was dead.

"A heart attack?" his wife asked. Dr Hain made no reply. He examined the eyes, the lids of which he raised and shut again, and the condition of the dead man's skin. He loosened the cramped fingers from the sofa and looked at them closely.

"Excuse me," Helen muttered: she had hoped to see it through, but she felt everything spinning round and a dead faint coming on as this examination proceeded before her very eyes. She fled to Frank in the next room, and he put a distracted and impassive arm round her shoulder.

After some time Dr Hain came back into the sitting room and with a casual good morning to Frank Taylor, whom he had not noticed on entering the suite, he sat down in front of the fireplace with his fingers interlaced in an arch. "I am very sorry, dear lady," he said. "It is a terrible shock for you."

"I am very grateful to you, Doctor, for your sympathy. It lessens the blow a little," Helen said. Frank was standing behind her chair, gripping the back of it.

"There are just a few formalities," the doctor said. "I should very much like to hear from you how it all happened before I make out the certificate of death. Forgive me, but it must be."

"Is my presence necessary?" Frank asked in an access of sheer cowardice. If only he could get away, hear no more and see no more. Ruth—he was longing for Ruth as a sleepless man longs for sleep.

"Yes, you must stay here, Frank. You cannot leave me alone now," Helen said in that new hard accent of hers. Frank bowed.

"May I use the telephone meanwhile?" he asked. He put a call through to Ruth's room. "Pips," he said (it was another of Ruth's nicknames). "Good morning, Pips. Bad news for us! Did you know that shells had been flying about? Haven't you heard the windows rattle? Listen to me, Tiny, it is possible we may have to put off the wedding. . . . Yes, Morris called me up. He says it's impossible to get across the town. . . . Where am I? In the office, I am making my will. Please stay in your room, Midget, promise me. Don't even put the tip of your nose out of the window or out of the door. Otherwise you'll have it shot away, and it's much too short in any case. I'll come soon, as soon as I am through here. Wait for me."

He put back the receiver, exhausted by his efforts at cheerfulness. Then he resumed his post behind Helen's chair. Helen had meanwhile given the doctor an account which corresponded to the truth at many points and departed from it in some others. It horrified Frank to see how coolly she handled the business. And he had gone to her that morning to help her. He had expected tears and helplessness. Idiot, fool, Sir Galahad . . .

Helen explained that Bobbie had not come home for two nights and that in her anxiety she had begged Frank Taylor to come to her aid: that Bobbie had then appeared in that kind of state she was accustomed to call fits and which took the form of raging, claustra-phobia, tears very often, but usually violence. With Frank Taylor's help she had succeeded in getting her husband to lie down on the sofa and in calming him a little. But then he had begun to groan and had fought for breath, he had struggled, gripped hold of her and shown all the symptoms of a man who was at the point of death. She had run in horror to the telephone and summoned the doctor. When she returned to her husband he was lying motionless. But she had no idea that it was all over with him. Now, she ended, she felt perfectly helpless, she did not know what to do, she didn't know what these formalities were he talked about, she knew nothing, nothing . . .

Dr Hain listened to all this attentively and often gave confirmatory nods of his head. When Helen had done, he said thoughtfully: "All that does not explain to me what has really happened. There is something, namely, that does not fit. There will have to be an autopsy, Mrs Russell. I am sorry, but the cause of death must be ascertained."

"But isn't it a heart attack?" Helen asked. "What else could cause death so suddenly?"

Dr Hain looked at the palms of his hands and said: "Heart attack is only the popular name for a process which can have many causes. Drowning, for example, suffocation, certain poisonings. I cannot conceal from you that your husband makes not the impression of a man who has died peacefully and easily. He must also have been much longer dead than you say, at least twenty minutes. I must call up Dr Bradley."

"Who is Dr Bradley?" Helen asked in a weak voice.

"Dr Bradley will make the autopsy, he is the coroner," Dr Hain said. "I advise, meanwhile, informing the British consul. All kinds of formalities will be necessary. I am sorry, Mrs Russell, but it must be found out what happened with your husband before he died."

"But I can tell you that, Doctor. He has been with a countryman of yours—that pianist in the bar. Opium—I presume. It would be a pity if the young man got mixed up in an opium scandal, don't you think?" Helen said tentatively. She could see from the doctor's expression that this had gone home, and she gave careful thought to what she went on to say.

"I'm sorry if I was not quite accurate about the exact time of Bobbie's death. It was a terrible shock to find him in those spasms," she added. "In such moments, as you can imagine, Doctor, one loses all sense of time. Perhaps he was dead already and I simply did not know it."

Dr Hain thoughtfully shook his head. Something does not fit, he thought, something does not fit. He had nothing to go by, only a vague feeling, unscientific to the last degree. His nerves were on edge after his sleepless night. They received a kind of warning from the inexplicably cramped and rigid attitude of the still warm body in the next room.

"In any case I must call up Dr Bradley and the consulate," he said obstinately. "It is the regulation——"

"But listen to me, Doctor," Helen said quickly. "My husband is dead, and it won't bring him to life again to establish what particular form of excess brought him to his end. Dying is after all a private matter, isn't it? Why raise a lot of dust and bring other people into it? It cannot do poor Bobbie any good, and it will perhaps do other people harm. His heart was weak and, as we know, he overtaxed it with poisons of all kinds." She tried to smile as she went on more slowly: "It may be childish of me, but this—this autopsy makes things so horrible for me. I do not want my poor Bobbie to be dissected, it makes his death so ghastly. Please, please, Doctor, help me to prevent it."

"That is the standpoint of the laity," the doctor said. "An autopsy is nothing ghastly, it is purely and simply science, Mrs Russell. The scalpel is as fine an instrument as the violin. I play the violin myself, I know what I talk of . . ."

Frank felt worse and worse while all these words buzzed in his ears. And all this time Bobbie Russell was lying next door with a fractured skull, of which this chattering old German appeared to be completely unaware. All the time he was conscious of Ruth waiting for him, while an irresistible tide swept him further from her. All the time his knees were trembling, and for minutes together he forgot what had happened in the effort to control those unmanly and terror-stricken knees of his.

"Interesting," he heard himself saying when the doctor had stopped and a silence fell. It sounded completely idiotic. He was aware of Helen leaning hard against his hands, which were clasping the back of her chair. The doctor sat with his back to the light, and half the room was reflected in his spectacles. His eyebrows were drawn up by the furrows in his forehead, his large nose was pitted with large, open pores. Frank saw all this vaguely, and it displeased him, and he thought: The Jew . . .

"You may be right," Helen said, "but I think all the same——"

A report like thunder seemed to split the world. A window, which was shut, broke in splinters, the wall seemed to quiver, the air was driven so violently against their eardrums that it hurt.

"Bombs!" Dr Hain said with blanched lips. He was not afraid, but his nerves were reminded of the Great War, and his heart missed a beat. "One soon gets used to them. After a time one hears them no more—as with the trams," he said reassuringly.

"They won't bomb the Settlement," Frank said. Oddly, the explosion had strengthened his knees again. Ruth will be frightened, he thought. "I'd like to go to Ruth for a moment," he said beseechingly to Helen. "Just to reassure her——"

"You must wait till these formalities are finished with," Helen said inexorably.

Frank realized with horror that he was in her hands. She can do what she likes with me, he thought, and again gripped the back of her chair with his hands. They were moist and dirty, no washing was of any use now.

"It's raining bombs outside and we are quarreling over formalities," Helen began subtly. "I want to ask you, Doctor, to have a little regard for English psychology. We are hypocrites, as all the world knows, and think of the scandal in Shanghai, where the prestige of the English counts for so much. Perhaps you don't know that poor Bobbie's brother is an M.P., and what may not this autopsy reveal? That poor Bobbie has been to places where he ought not to have gone and drunk things and smoked things that are prohibited. Why not let him be taken quietly to the crematorium without blackening his name? I am his widow, and I alone am responsible to his family. I must protect the family name, Doctor."

She felt that she was now in good form. Unconsciously she wrung her hands, though she still had in them the feeling of the struggling body—a feeling of which she could not get rid. She was still not absolutely sure that Bobbie was dead once and for all. At the bottom of her mind was the cold and horrid dread that he might suddenly come through the door of his bedroom as a living man.

The longer this woman talked, the less could Dr Hain believe what she said. Something here does not fit, he thought again, something does not fit. Helen puzzled over the expression of his face and then said: "I daresay you think me heartless because I do not weep. But you know something of the circumstances. I have wept so much during my married life that I have no tears left. All I can do now is to avoid a scandal."

"I am convinced that the British authorities will do their utmost to help you in that," Dr Hain said. "It will be as much the interest of the British colony here as it is yours."

Dr Hain got up and put his instruments back in his bag. He was impatient to be gone. Russell was dead. Chang still lived and had to be operated on. The doctor wanted to get back to his more urgent case. Helen was in his way.

"Wait one moment, Doctor," she said hurriedly. "Let us look at this matter from another angle. It is a matter of complete indifference to you, I presume, what it may have been that brought my husband's ailing heart to a standstill. In all probability it was opium. But to me—and to his family—it is of the utmost importance to give him a reputable death, even if his life was disreputable. Do us the service of signing the death certificate, attributing his death to heart disease, let us say, and spare me all these complications that

can lead to nothing. If I have understood you rightly, you mean
that there must be an autopsy in the case of a sudden heart attack,
but not in the case of chronic heart disease that finally proves mortal. Well then, you told me yourself a few days ago that Bobbie's
heart was far from sound. I am not asking you for anything out of
the way, only for a little consideration. I don't know whether money
means anything to you, but as, unfortunately, I have no other means
of showing my gratitude for your kindness—I mean that I would
very gladly leave it to you to name your price if you would make
the necessary formalities as simple as possible."

She looked at the doctor and observed that his hands trembled
as he put the stethoscope back and shut his bag. She quickly took
a checkbook of the Hong Kong-Shanghai bank from the table
drawer and wrote her long fine signature in the bottom right-hand
corner. "Please, Doctor, make it out for what you like," she said as
she put the piece of paper down on the table and held out the pen.
He shook his head. "I cannot do that," he said. Helen smiled encouragingly.

"What shall we make it out for?" she asked, now feeling much
more sure of her ground, for she thought he was giving way. "Five
hundred pounds?"

She waited, and still he shook his head. Madame Tissaud had told
her all about the wretched poverty in which Dr Hain lived, and she
supposed that everyone in Shanghai had his price.

"A thousand," she said, beginning to enter the amount. "A thousand pounds for an unblemished name. Poor Bobbie!" she said as
she handed him the check. He did not take it, but he did not
refuse it, either.

"I must in any case come again," he said irresolutely. "It does not
depend upon me alone. I shall speak with Dr Bradley. If he agrees
with my finding of heart disease and dispenses with the autopsy
——"

Without ending the sentence he picked up his bag and fled from
the room. The check was left lying on the table. Helen smiled at
his retreating figure.

"So that's settled," she said, heaving a sigh as his footsteps died away along the passage. She raised her face to Frank, who was still standing behind her chair. He had been standing there the whole time—hypnotized, paralyzed. It was worse than the worst of bad dreams. And, on top of it all, the sky was overcast with even blacker clouds, the air was oppressive and surcharged. The light was tinged with a lurid yellow, in which Helen's face shone strange and hard and bright. She came up to him and he stood rigidly, lest he should retreat to the wall as his instinct bade him. "Frank," Helen said softly. "Frank, now you belong to me. I have rescued you from hell, and now there is nothing but us, together, forever."

Another bomb exploded, this time further away. Two planes with black wings droned along just under the dark clouds. Helen threw a quick glance at the door behind which Bobbie lay. But the dead man was deaf, and no bombs could rouse him any more.

There was a bench in the passage near the elevator. Dr Hain sat down on it to think. He put his black bag beside him, sunk his chin on his chest and put his hand over his eyes, as his habit was when he had a problem to solve.

A thousand pounds, a thousand pounds. Enough to take him and Irene to America, out of this place of damnation, back to the living. A thousand pounds. A year of work and preparation with Irene at his side. A thousand pounds. The future, work, justification, the one hope he lived for. A thousand pounds.

Against it was to be set the death of a drunken decadent, a worthless person whose dishonored corpse lay there in that room. What business is it of mine? Dr Hain thought, fighting grimly against his better self. He has drugged himself to death, he has died by his own folly. Perhaps his wife poisoned him, but what does it matter to me? What do these people matter to me, what have I to do with them? A thousand pounds—and a dead man will be buried and the survivors will be happy and relieved of care. He thought with joy of San Francisco. He had dim recollections of pictures in illustrated magazines: hills and skyscrapers, bays and bridges. He could almost scent the smell of the operating theater in his nostrils. He could see the white and brilliant light on the area to be operated, feel the tense and silent activity, the unerring precision of the knife in his hand.

A man is worth what his work is worth and not a jot more, he thought. He himself without his work was nothing but a wastrel, a bum, a man who had run to seed. But with his work—oh, Irene, Irene, Irene . . . He got up and pressed the bell for the elevator. His smile was a contortion, for he had for a long time given up the habit of smiling. I could not have stood it for another month, he thought as he descended to the ground floor.

He went to the reception desk and asked for the telephone directory. "I want Dr Bradley's number," he said, turning the pages.

"How is the Great Old Man?" the reception clerk asked, trying to imitate the intonation of a Chinese. Hain looked at him in surprise. "Who?" he asked absent-mindedly. Then at last he remembered old Chang's condition. "It is still uncertain," he replied as he went on turning the pages. Probably, he thought, Bradley would not come as long as the bombardment went on. The cause of death would be left to him, and he would make out the death certificate.

The junior clerk was looking through a ledger.

"There's a registered letter come for you, Doctor," he said. "Will you sign this, please?"

Hain took the letter and signed. It was from Irene. He left the directory open at the B's and opened the letter and read it where he stood. He read it once, he read it twice. He put it in his pocket, consulted the directory again, but instead of letters he saw ants. He took his spectacles off and put them on again—vacantly, in desperation. It was not until he had read the letter for the third time that he was able to grasp its contents:

DEAR EMANUEL:

I have hesitated for a long time to write this letter to you, but it must be done. I think you must already have a suspicion of its contents. You must have felt as I have that we have got further and further apart during the last three years and have now reached a point where we have nothing left in common. You have gone to foreign countries and adapted yourself to life there. I have stayed here and come to see that Germany is the only country I belong to and where I can live. I have come to see that our Führer is right, and I have learned to believe in him and the Third Reich. I need say no more.

It was a grievous error that we ever married, and for this error we have both paid with our hearts' blood. I know that you will not grudge me the effort to build up on the ruins a life that corresponds to my nature and my origin. I wish you happiness in your future, and I am sure that the ambition, the intelligence and the adaptability of your race will take you far in whatever country you may be. I have applied for a divorce which in our case goes through of itself.

Forget me as I try to forget you——

IRENE

That was the letter, and that was the end.

Perhaps she is right, Dr Hain thought. I was going to sell myself for a thousand pounds. Intelligent and adaptable. But not so adaptable as to make common cause with the murderers of my son, he thought with an access of hot, despairing and utterly uncontrollable rage.

"Shall I put you through to Dr Bradley, Doctor?" the assistant asked. Dr Hain took off his spectacles which were misted.

"No," he said. "I have changed my mind. Call up Sir Henry Kingsdale-Smith at the British consulate. Something has happened."

XX

B. G. CHANG HAD BEEN brandishing his great fists and refusing with astonishing violence to be transported to the hospital. As the Chinese doctors were afraid that the excitement and the vehement movements would have fatal results, they had advised against contradicting him for the time being. In any case he could not be operated on without his consent. After winning the round, the obstreperous patient had again fallen into a drowse or a state of semiconsciousness, from which nobody dared to rouse him. But soon he woke up of his own accord and reached out for his son's hands with great tenderness. Yutsing was deeply moved and gave them to him gladly.

"I remember," the sick man said after a moment, "I remember the day quite clearly when Elder Sister put an oar into my hands for the first time. I was very proud. I was not four years old, for I had no pigtail, but only four little tiny braids in which Elder Sister had woven red wool. It was at the beginning of winter. Four-coat weather, and I hadn't even one. Elder Sister put her own jacket round me and rolled herself in the mat. When I die you must be good to Elder Sister."

"You are not going to die," Yutsing said, although he knew that it was a portent of death when the spirit of the sick man took flight into the past.

"I can see it all as clearly as if it were in this room," his father said. "The river and the rapids. There were goats on the bank, there was an old gray goat with her two black kids. It seems to me that I have lived five lives, not one—as if I had not been one man but five different men. That is because the times have altered so quickly during my span of life. Go, my son, and call your two wives."

Yutsing hesitated.

"Go," his father said impatiently. He went.

Pearl and Meilan had put the whole length of the big room between them. Pearl, with her hands in her jacket pockets and a cigarette in her mouth, was talking earnestly with the Chinese doctors. The lurid light of the overcast sky fell on her through the tall windows. At the other end of the room, near the door, Meilan was kneeling beside her sister, looking like a broken reed or a shot bird. Yutsing went from one to the other and asked them to go to his father's bedside. Pearl led the way, Meilan crept behind her. He did not look round at her, although he was conscious of her presence with every drop of blood in his body.

"Come to me, my daughters, sit by my bed," Chang said more gently than his son had ever heard him speak, and the women sat down obediently on two chairs which the secretary officiously pushed forward. Chang, the son, realized with a flash of intuition that his giant of a father must have won women as well as bought them; it was a new thought to him that Chang Bogum understood tenderness as well as force.

As soon as the two women, who were as different from one another as any two beings of the same sex and race could be, were seated by his bedside, he looked from one to the other, not as one who was on the brink of death but as a man who was enjoying himself.

"It is a good word that says: The ugly wife serves well in the house, but at the feast the beautiful one is preferred," he said finally. "I beg your forgiveness, wife of my son, if I have not received you with the love and understanding that you perhaps deserve. I am a stupid, uneducated and old-fashioned man, who has only a poor appreciation of your undoubtedly high qualities. But as you seem to possess common sense and the strength to preside over a great house, I speak to you rather than to her whom I have had brought up only for my son's pleasure." At these words Meilan crumpled up a little more, and Pearl suppressed a smile, for her father-in-law apparently meant well, although his approval sounded like an insult.

"Daughter," he said sternly, "you are unfortunately incapable of giving the house and the family of the Changs a child. This girl here, the concubine Meilan, has conceived and will, we may hope, bear a son—many sons, for she comes from a garden where the trees bear plentifully. I put her in your charge and desire that you take care of her as an elder sister. You will protect her in the war and nurse her in childbirth and in sickness, and you will not embitter and poison her life with ridiculous jealousy. For you are the wife and companion and Number One. As your womb is barren, you must love your husband's children by another woman as your own. You must promise me that, so that I may die in peace. And you—" he told Meilan, who trembled lightly as a leaf at evening, "you will bear sons to reverence the ancestors and to offer up offerings and to light incense after the old manner. Otherwise," he said, pointing a menacing forefinger at her, "I shall come back as a discontented spirit, and I shall be an angry and a strong spirit to persecute you if you do not do what I expect of you. Go into the temple, ask the priests for the right prayers and the right god to whom you shall light incense and burn spirit money so that you shall have sons, and if you have sons," he said, waxing ever more angry, "if you have sons, then see to it that you are not proud towards the wife of your master and a cause of trouble, and mark this: not even the five fingers of a hand can be of the same length, and so do not forget your place. She is over you, and I bought you as a slave for eight dollars."

He lay back in contentment and motioned the two women to go. "You stay," he told Yutsing. His son knelt down beside the bed.

"I made my will long since, and you will find everything in order," Chang said. "It depends on you whether you keep the automobile or not. I have given the chauffeur a small pension in case you dismiss him. I have made a trust fund for you and for your mother, which will later descend to your children. Last night I had thoughts of casting you off, but death extinguishes all anger, and who among us is without fault? What horse never stumbles?"

"Does not talking tire you, Father?" Yutsing asked anxiously, for old Chang's voice got louder and louder, and his great hands gesticulated more and more vigorously.

"No," he said. "It is well with me, and I scarcely feel the pain any more. I am unwilling to die, my son, extremely unwilling," he said emphatically. "Even though it is said that the affairs of this world pass like a day in spring and that we should think of death as a homecoming. The affairs of this world are not so simple, my son. They are not simple but more interesting than the wildest gamble. It is just as hard to tear oneself from them as it is to get up from the gambling table or to leave the bottle half empty or to rise from a woman's bed in the middle of the night. I am not old," he said, "and there is enough strength in me for three men. Why should I die? A living beggar is better than a dead king, they say. What then is a dead banker? I should like much to have waited for my first grandson. You were born with a tooth in your mouth—what will my grandson look like? You must see to it that I am brought plenty of food offerings, for I have always been a hungry man, and my spirit too will be hungry I fear——"

There was a loud droning close overhead, and the air burst in with a sudden tempestuous inrush. Furniture fell over, and glass was shattered. The women screamed in the large room. Yutsing had involuntarily seized his father's hand, perhaps to protect him, perhaps to be protected by him. The doctors came to the door with white faces to see what effect the shock had had on their patient. Yutsing was annoyed to find that he was trembling. The last ten years had made a weakling of him. He had almost forgotten what it was to be under fire, to sleep on shells and to carry bombs on him, to throw at the enemy in the nick of time.

Chang Bogum had pushed back the clothes and was sitting up. "What is that?" he shouted. "Bombs? Bombs in Nanking Road? It must have been quite close. What is the meaning of it? They promised me to leave this quarter in peace. The swine, the dogs, the turtles, the sons and grandsons of devils, the Japanese dwarfs, the liars, the traitors, thieves and bandits, they're dropping bombs, they're breaking their word, they take my money and then they murder my family into the bargain . . ."

Chang Bogum in a rage was a spectacle worth seeing. All those who were awaiting his death in the next room came in one after another and stood looking at the naked man in the huge bed. He made more noise and was more terrifying than the bombs. The outbreak was all the more astonishing, as he had been on the point of calming himself down to that gentle and submissive composure which became a dying man and would leave him a good name behind him. Pearl was the first to see the humor of the situation and to have the courage to interrupt the infuriated banker.

"They are not Japanese bombs, Father," she said, stepping forward from the rest. "They are our own airmen—Chinese airmen and Chinese bombs."

"Chinese? Why Chinese? Are you going to tell me that our planes are chucking bombs on Nanking Road?" Chang asked, growing suddenly calm from sheer astonishment. As though in answer came the roaring of several airplanes close at hand, diving steeply down over the houses and climbing up to the clouds again on their flight from the spot they had just destroyed. Mr Chai, the secretary, looked out of the window. There they were, black-winged and in a triangle like wild ducks at evening over the lake. They all involuntarily held their breath in dread of the next bomb, but the roar of the engines died away and was soon inaudible.

"Where is the sense of that? What have the Chinese to gain by bombing the Concessions?" Chang asked as coolly as though he were presiding over a stockholders' meeting. "What would be the benefit?" he asked. "What would be the profit of such an undertaking?"

As no one could answer him, and as his son could only shrug his shoulders, Chang, the banker, looked from one to another. "Why do you stand there? What are you doing here at all when a bomb may hit us at any moment?" he suddenly shouted. "If it is not the Japanese but the Chinese, then this building is the most dangerous place in the whole town. Can't you understand that! The Chinese! Chinese airmen! A fine joke it would be if they murdered us with the very bombs I presented to those worms in Nanking. Get out, bestir yourselves, what are you standing there for, run for safety," he cried, wrenching himself to an upright position and putting his feet to the floor. "Chingliu, you turtle," he roared at Meilan's sister who was standing open-mouthed at the back. "Quick, bring me my clothes! Chai, the automobile, at once. We're leaving this moment."

Yutsing stood amazed and bewildered in the midst of this scene of flurry and confusion.

"Where is there safety, Father?" he asked. "Where is the place that this war will not reach?"

"Any place is better than under this roof, you fool," Chang roared. "Has no one enough sense in his guts to get me out of here?" At that moment he caught sight at the back of the two white-clothed stretcher bearers, who emitted a strong hospital smell.

"Who are those two?" he asked and repeated with growing annoyance: "Who are those two fellows?" Thrusting everyone who barred his way aside, he confronted the two dazed men in all his massive nakedness. Slowly a grin spread over their faces.

"We are the stretcher bearers, Excellency," one of them said. "We are waiting to carry Your Excellency to the ambulance."

"Ambulance!" Chang exclaimed, more amused than annoyed. "And you are going to carry me? Have you ever tried to carry a man of my weight? Six men like you could not carry me on that matchstick stretcher of yours. Get out of it, my good friends, you and your ridiculous apparatus. I know something about porterage.

I was a coolie porter, and you cannot teach me anything about that job. You have the legs of flies. I should be afraid of breaking all your bones, sick man as I am. Give them some money to buy tea and send them away," he told his secretary, relenting abruptly, and the two astonished men were hurried out and dismissed.

It was Pearl again who had been the first to offer her shoulder to her father-in-law when he left his bed. He leaned heavily but with caution on it, for he was accustomed to dealing gently with women in case he crushed them to bits. He stood there, gigantic, naked and without shame, and there was no question any longer of dying.

"Will he get through it?" Yutsing whispered to his wife. He was astounded by his father's unexpected energy.

She bit her lip to prevent herself from laughing. "It almost looks like it," she whispered back. She led Chang Bogum to a large chair and looked up at him. He looked down on her from his towering height. He patted her cropped hair.

"The ugly ones have sense, the stupid ones beauty," he said, teasing her mischievously, and Pearl knew that her father-in-law's heart turned to her for the first time.

Chingliu and Meilan came in with their master's vast apparel, vest and stockings, shoes and silk robe, and began dressing him with the quick and careful fingers of nursemaids. The large reception room was a turmoil of people—servants, women and hangers-on. The mahjong pieces had been upset on the floor and a teapot broken when the bomb landed, and a precious glazed camel of the Tang dynasty lay in fragments, although the old massive horses' heads of the Han period had kept their position on the shelves along the walls. After the shock and terror and amazement, all talked at once, and the hangers-on bowed to each other and shook their own hands as they congratulated themselves on their escape and the improvement in the health of Chang, the banker, their lord and father. Liu sat in a corner smoking minute pellets of tobacco in his long thin pipe.

"Well?" he asked as Pearl sat down beside him and produced a fresh cigarette.

"We must wait until the High Person expresses his further wishes," she said, smiling. Liu considered this, then he smiled too.

"Doesn't the High Person remind you of the straggler out of the Shiking?" he asked gaily.

> "There is no rest for me
> Nor for my tired feet.
> Give me to drink and eat,
> Do what is best for me.
> Order an ambulance car
> And carry me, carry me on."

Even before he had concluded his quotation, a commanding roar came from the sickroom.

"The ambulance did not go down very well with the High Person," Pearl remarked with amusement. She folded her hands in her lap and contentedly waited for further events.

XXI

THE MECHANISM OF THE HUMAN SOUL is finely constructed and offers many merciful ways of escape. No one is allotted a greater pain or a heavier weight than he can bear. Nature provides faintings and comas as merciful narcotics.

When Dr Hain had read his wife's letter, and when every last living hope and every last aim in life had slipped away from under his feet, as the ground might in a landslide, he became completely numb and insensitive. As a surgeon he had made condemned limbs numb and insensitive in this way by freezing. But although after the final blow nothing was left of him, of the man and doctor Emanuel Hain, he still found himself perfectly capable of functioning in a rational and normal manner. He succeeded in getting a call through on the refractory telephone in a city where panic was taking possession of the streets and all communications were giving out; in breaking through a wall of obstructive, agitated and arrogant consulate officials and in forcing himself upon the much preoccupied Crown Advocate, Sir Henry Kingsdale-Smith. He reported tersely and tactfully that Mr Robert George Russell had died in so questionable a manner that he, as a doctor, could not do otherwise than advise an inquest. He observed further that he had not applied to the International Police, whose business it was, but to him, Sir Henry, a friend of the family and British representative, since he wished to do what he could to avoid publicity and scandal. He also politely if with a bad accent begged Sir Henry to excuse him for bothering him at an awkward moment, when he was so busily occupied, and requested this high official to deal with the matter before it became public property. Sir Henry thanked him, coughed once or twice into the telephone, and then hurriedly said that he would come at once in person to the Shanghai Hotel to offer Mrs Russell his help.

Dazed as he was, Dr Hain succeeded in confining Madame Tissaud's curiosity, which rose snapping at him as he crossed the lounge, to the weather and the bombs. And now what? he thought with an effort, for his thoughts had developed an extraordinary tendency to desert his brain. This vacancy and silence at the back of his head, where as a rule a restless, never-ending hum of activity went on, was a very odd feeling. The factory of thought is closed down, he told himself, and it seemed to him very witty. He stood in front of the elevator staring at the elevator boy, who stared back at him with a wondering smile. Chang! the doctor remembered.

"To the roof," he said. On the way he changed his mind. "Tenth floor," he said. He got out and made his tortuous way to Kurt Planke's room or closet. There was no answer to his knock, and he cautiously turned the handle.

In there the light was burning and fell on the sleeping young man. Dr Hain sat down on the edge of the bed and looked at Kurt reflectively for a while. It seemed that he had thrown himself on his bed just as he had come in, in his one, dirty, crumpled suit. He lay on his side with his cheek pillowed in his bent arm, and in the relaxation of sleep he looked much younger than he was—almost a child. In spite of his dazed condition the doctor felt sorry to wake him, but as it could not be helped he shook Kurt carefully by the shoulder. Kurt opened his eyes and smiled at the doctor in a friendly way, without showing the least surprise.

"What day is it?" he asked in the voice of a child who wants to be pampered. Dr Hain did not enter into the spirit of this question. Instead he asked: "Have you been on the spree with Russell?"

"Yes," Kurt said, rather more wakefully. "I pretty well succeeded in breaking the Honourable's English arrogance."

"He is dead," Hain said.

"You don't say," Kurt remarked without surprise. "Well, he's to be congratulated."

"Do you know anything about how it can have happened?" the doctor asked.

"Perhaps the Honourable was allergic to opium refuse, although I must say it seemed to have the best possible effect on his disposition. You'd have been surprised, Doctor. Quite tame—almost decent. Not to say intelligent at isolated moments."

"Did you return in his company?" the doctor asked, feeling somewhat impatient with Kurt's fanciful and dreamy irony. "Were you with him up to the last? Your evidence will be taken. Get up, take a cold shower, pull yourself together."

"Get up, take a cold shower, pull yourself together," Kurt repeated. "Cruel, very cruel. But a matter of indifference all the same; everything is a matter of indifference. Everything is merely illusion." He described a narrow circle with his hand to include his room, himself and the doctor. "Illusion," he repeated, "all nonexistent and therefore quite unimportant. You and I, life and death. Particularly death: illusion. You ought to become a morphine addict, Doctor, most doctors do, don't they? Get up, take a cold shower, pull yourself together." He sat up, holding with both hands to the edge of his mattress as though he felt dizzy. "You want to help me, Doctor, I know. I want to help you, too. But you see it's like this—nobody can help anybody. Thanks. Thanks all the same." He started laughing. "I don't believe in chamber music," he said. Dr Hain was in no mood for a philosophical discussion. People under the influence of drugs had a way of bringing forth the most frightful commonplaces as deep inspirations—it made him impatient. He left the room, faintly hoping that Kurt in his uplifted condition would be equal to the cross-examination that lay ahead of him. He came to a stop outside the door and thought hard. Something of importance occurred to him. First Chang must be operated on; there will still be time afterwards, he thought.

But what there would be time for afterwards, he did not know.

He made his way back to the elevator and was taken up to the eighteenth floor. Even from the anteroom he could hear the raging and storming of the sick banker, but the Chinese collected there were too excited to bother about him, and the two stretcher bearers were squatting impassively beside their stretcher and eating rice. Dr Hain pushed his way into the large room. In there it looked as though a party were in full progress. Tea was being drunk, a whisky bottle circulated, people had divided up into small groups and talked and argued and laughed among themselves. Dr Hain thought for a moment that he must have come to the wrong place, then he discovered Pearl in a corner and beckoned her aside. He had come to a stop near the door, and while she was crossing the room the cloud upon his consciousness lifted for a moment and then descended again. During this brief moment he realized what had happened to him in the short time since leaving the room and returning to it again. A cold fear crept to the roots of his hair, and he thought: How many deaths can a man die and yet live on? A scrap of banal music came to his ears from the phonograph, and at the same time a voice from the radio, explaining or reassuring; he understood the tone but not the words. Then once more he became an automaton which functioned mechanically. "Have you been able to persuade him into an operation?" he asked Pearl.

"No, Doctor," Pearl Chang said. "It does not look like it. Apparently the bomb has done my father-in-law good. It is certainly a medicine that corresponds to his usual vein."

"The bomb?" the doctor asked.

Pearl gave a sharp look at him. "Yes, the bomb, haven't you noticed that they're bombarding the Settlement?"

"Oh, of course," Dr Hain said. "But that was early today." He's had a shock, Pearl thought after examining the distraught face of her old colleague.

"Did it give you a horrible fright?" she asked kindly. "We two are not so hardened as these Shanghai people, are we?"

"Yes, yes," Dr Hain said, "I am hardened." The World War came into his mind. "I was in the war," he went on. "So no operation?"

"No, I think not. It looks as if he were going to get through without an operation," Pearl said. Dr Hain's face fell.

"Then my presence here has become quite superfluous," was all he said.

Pearl felt sorry for him. "No, no, stay here, please," she said quickly. "There is still the question of removing him. Who knows what may happen yet? In this country you never know."

Liu came up looking slender and quite at his ease in his casual brown garment. "Our lord and master's órders," he said in English. "I have got to take you and the precious concubine at once in a taxi to the bank and deposit you among the vaults in the basement. It's safe there, as everyone knows. Are you ready?"

"And what about my father-in-law?" Pearl asked.

"The High Person has decided to wait here for his own car. The High Person is more obstinate than ever. Besides that, good old Chang is in pain again, and it is taking some time to get him dressed and bundled up. But he's a glorious fellow all the same. You know the Chinese proverb, Doctor: Have the coffin ready and you won't die."

Dr Hain stood there irresolutely a few moments longer, then he slipped out. He had remembered something, where he might be of use. Sir Henry Kingsdale-Smith and Dr Bradley will need me, he thought· it was his last crutch, and on it he limped to the elevator. Pearl did not even notice that he left. "Is Yutsing coming, too?" she asked Liu.

"The son remains with the father," Liu answered.

She nodded. She had grasped in the last hour that she existed for the family and not for her isolated companionship with Yutsing. The new responsibility his father had laid upon her softened her grief and dulled her jealousy.

She gave herself a prod, lit a cigarette to keep countenance and, taking her hands out of her pockets, she went across to Meilan.

"If it would please you, Meilan," she said kindly, "it is the father's wish that we shall stay together until he has come to a further decision. If you like we can go now; and do not be afraid—Meilan."

"Great honor for my low person," Meilan whispered and made a little bow. She put her hand, as delicate as a piece of carved ivory, in Pearl's large work-roughened paw and thought: No wonder Yutsing is not very pleased with its caresses.

The elevator boy was a little bewildered. He kept on talking about the bombs. "Did the ladies hear the bombs? They say that three hundred people were blown to pieces not half a li from here. Bombs, bombs!" Meilan felt the silk of Pearl's coat and skirt between her fingers. "Beautiful silk," she said confidingly. "I could embroider you a jacket of silk like this if you would like it. I can embroider. I love embroidering. I know the Peking stitch, too."

Little silkworm, Pearl thought with a touch of condescending warmth. Thin, anemic blood, reared in the shade. She recollected a phrase she had heard or read. "Why do they say 'eyebrows like a silkworm'?" she asked Liu in English. Liu understood her at once and looked at Meilan. "You have never looked at a silkworm, Pearl. You are too intellectual altogether, that is the trouble with you." He said it as parents in China do who scold their children, call them "bad boy" and "stupid daughter," instead of petting them. For that might make the spirits envious.

The elevator stopped at the tenth floor, and more passengers got in: Kurt Planke between two plain-clothes men whose profession could be recognized a mile off. Only detectives have those shoulders, those necks and that benevolently menacing expression. Meilan shrank together at this unexpected encounter and tried to make herself invisible. Kurt did not see her at first, and when he did, he opened his mouth to greet her with the last little gleam of lightheartedness left him from his opium trance. Do you recognize my tie, Gretchen? I wear it as a talisman, today as in the hour of our parting, amen. But Meilan shrank behind Pearl and put a finger beseechingly and imploringly to her lips, while at the same time her eyes sparkled with the joy of intrigue. Kurt said nothing. Pearl noticed nothing. Liu, the poet, noticed everything. He had even made the first two lines of a poem by the time the elevator stopped at the third floor and Kurt and his escort got out.

"Right turn, my lad," one of the two said. Kurt looked back as long as the door of the elevator was open. During those few moments he had managed to stand close to Meilan and to seize her hand and hold it fast. Playful hand, tiny foreign Chinese hand. The hint of warmth, the hint of scent from her hair, the last hint of beauty that left him forever as it vanished down the narrow shaft of the elevator and on to the ground floor.

Madame Tissaud was sitting in the crowded lounge. Excited people were all shouting at once, and the chirping of the string quartet came from the large dining room.

"Madame Chang, Madame Chang!" she cried out. "How is your father-in-law? Is he dead? And who is that you have there? One of his orphan children?"

"My father-in-law is not one of those people who just die," Pearl replied almost gaily. She took Meilan's hand and led her through the revolving door and out to a gilded taxi that was waiting for them.

XXII

YOSHIO MURATA HAD BEEN LEFT in front of the Sakuran Restaurant, gray in the face and utterly wretched, after Jelena had made her escape in the taxi. It began to rain. The wet streets became dim mirrors in which the lamplight swam. He put his hand to the documents in his pocket and had no idea what to do next. He hated himself, he hated the forged documents and the mission that had been forced upon him, and worst of all he hated Jelena, who was sailing off on a boat instead of stealing those cursed sheets of paper.

Perhaps she isn't a spy after all, he thought in a lucid interval, but he rejected the notion again instantly. The monomania of all Japanese, the fear of espionage, was in the marrow of his bones. His respect for the government of his country was too deeply rooted for him to imagine that Mr Endo could have made a mistake. I have failed, he thought abjectly. It is all my stupidity and my clumsiness. While he was still standing at the edge of the road, brooding on all this, a fresh torrent of rain descended. The large drops pelted down on his shoulders, the air pressed against his face like a moist warm cloth. Although the interval between him and his suicide had worn now to paper thinness, Yoshio was glad all the same that he had brought his umbrella. He opened it and felt a little better. I shall have to see Mr Endo, he thought in a panic. It was some comfort to remember that the telephone was only operating spasmodically and also that Mr Endo would only make chrysanthemic allusions on the telephone. Once Yoshio had convinced himself that there was no question of using the telephone, he walked on in a rather more hopeful mood beneath his black umbrella.

In the Rue Thibet he found a taxi; he had made up his mind to be driven to Mr Endo's and to make his report before he went home to his razor blade and the oath he had sworn in the secrecy of his own heart. It stopped raining as suddenly as it had begun. Small patrols were everywhere in the streets: French, English, American and International guards. He had twice to show the pass Mr Endo had sent him. It was a long way, and when Yoshio reached Mr Endo's house in Yangtze Po it was past midnight. He looked up at the four-storied front of the house and saw narrow streaks of light gleaming through the bamboo shutters. The street door was open, there was a light on the stairs. It seemed that Mr Endo was expecting late visitors.

Yoshio rang the bell. There was a long interval, then Mr Endo himself came to the door. He was in shirt sleeves and his blue braces looked sweat-stained and disreputable.

"I regret profoundly that I have to disturb your honorable night rest," Yoshio said. "I have a pressing report to make."

Mr Endo gave him a fleeting glance and an even more fleeting bow. "No success?" he said shortly and almost impolitely.

"Unfortunately, no—a promising opening but a disappointing close," Yoshio murmured quietly. It was only now that Mr Endo asked him to come in.

"Be so kind as to follow me," he said, leading the way through the empty office, then down the narrow back stairs to the floor below. As they descended the creaking wooden stairs Yoshio had a new inspiration.

"Possibly these plans are clumsily forged?" he remarked loudly to Mr Endo's back. "Jelena is a clever woman, a very clever woman. Perhaps she looked at the papers and rejected them."

Mr Endo stopped and turned round. "Then she looked at the plans?" he asked.

"I—I imagine so," Yoshio stammered. Mr Endo went on again. It seemed to Yoshio that they had been descending these stairs forever and getting nowhere.

"I recommend abandoning that hypothesis," Mr Endo said. "The documents are an unusually skillful piece of work."

He opened a door and ushered Yoshio in. "My modest quarters," he said. It was a graceless and sparsely furnished room, and the only object in it that caught Yoshio's eye was a scroll of exquisite calligraphy. This specimen of calligraphy was the cause of his bowing three times with his hands on his knees. It was Japan. All the rest was Shanghai. Four young Japanese were seated at the table with whisky, ice and soda water before them. The night was loud with the hooting of sirens, either from the ships or from factories working on night shift. Yoshio noticed that Mr Endo did not make him acquainted with the other Japanese; he poured him out a whisky and soda without introducing him. He drank, full of gratitude and thirst.

"Is it raining again?" one of the men asked with a glance at Yoshio's wet suit.

"It has been raining but now it is over," he said.

"It has cooled off," another of them said.

"It was 104 degrees at midday," Mr Endo said.

"The barometer has fallen," the first one said, and they talked on for a time about the weather, then Mr Endo begged the four Japanese to excuse him and took Yoshio into the next room.

"Now tell me," he said.

Yoshio began to tell his story. As he spoke he felt better. He made a great deal out of his tête-à-tête dinner with Jelena and of the renewal of their intimacy. He felt that, on the whole, he had made a very good job of it. Mr Endo smiled a gold-plugged, appraising smile at more than one passage in his report. Even when Yoshio with diminishing confidence came to Jelena's abrupt departure, Mr Endo still went on smiling. Yoshio then drew to a close, bowed thrice and waited for his death sentence.

"On the *Soerabaya*—to Hong Kong—tomorrow at midday," Mr Endo said reflectively. He took a notebook from a drawer and jotted down a few notes. The room they were sitting in was bare and lighted by a naked electric bulb. There were chairs in a row along the wall as in a dentist's waiting room. There were cupboards built into the walls and drawers of Japanese make. Yoshio involuntarily looked round for flowers, but there were none.

"I presume you are ready to carry your task to its conclusion now that you have got so far with it?" Mr Endo asked finally.

"Is not that the end of it then?" Yoshio asked, flustered. Mr Endo scrutinized him lingeringly. Yoshio did not know that his very harmless and obvious innocence had induced the authorities to appoint him for his task.

"The end of it? No, not by any means," Mr Endo said absently. "You have done good work, honored friend. We know now that the lady is after the plans. Otherwise why should she go and eat sukiyaki with you? We know also that she can speak and read Japanese, although she tries to hide it. She has to leave because her lunatic and drunken husband wishes it. Very probably she is furious about it. Well then, we will come to her help in her awkward situation and all will end happily."

At these words Yoshio's heart weakly fluttered its little stunted wings—hopefully, but also a little resentfully. Perhaps in his subconscious depths he had believed that Jelena had gone out with him for his own sake, not because of forged documents; perhaps the tumultuous and abnormal condition in which he had been plunged throughout the whole evening was due, not to the carrying out of a patriotic duty, but to the presence—to the close, exciting, challenging presence—of the woman who had once been his mistress. Perhaps his blood had congealed in cold little clots when Jelena abruptly took her departure—because he had failed, not as a secret agent, but as a man. But however these influences might cross and recross within him, they became none the clearer. Instead of that, a few lines of a German poem, which he had vainly tried to recover during the last day or two, came to his mind:

> *Über allen Gipfeln ist Ruh,*
> *In allen Wipfeln*
> *Spürest du*
> *Kaum einen Hauch——*

He pulled himself together. "What have I got to do?" he asked resolutely.

"I suggest you go to Hong Kong—I will try to get you a cabin on the *Soerabaya*. It will not be easy, but I hope I shall be able to fix it. A voyage would give you an excellent opportunity. The continuous propinquity, the lack of constraint—you understand. All the advantages are on your side. You must, of course, behave as though you had pursued the lady in excess of romantic passion. There is not a woman who is too clever to believe that. As soon as you get to Hong Kong, be so kind as to get in touch with Mr Yamado. He works in the Japanese Tourist Agency, right near the harbor. You must be tired now."

"Not in the least," Yoshio Murata said rather dizzily. "On the contrary, I am ready for anything. I should like to end up this business as quickly as possible, for I want to be here when the fighting starts. You see, I am a journalist, and wars are good copy."

Yoshio stood up. Mr Endo remained seated. "You will still find plenty of copy when you come back," he said dryly. He considered Yoshio for another moment in silence and not with strict politeness and then added: "I propose that you spend the night here. You cannot return to the Myako Hotel tonight. Tomorrow morning you will go straight on board from here."

Mr Endo did not wait for Yoshio's consent. Without another word he produced a Japanese bed out of one of the cupboards, consisting of a quilt, a light covering and a diminutive pillow, and spread it out on the floor.

"Unfortunately, we have mosquitoes," he said. He seemed to be concerned to keep Yoshio from his visitors in the next room whose

shouts of laughter could be heard through the door. When Yoshio
saw the bed he suddenly felt sleepy.

"But my luggage is at the hotel," he said.

"Your honorable luggage will, at worst, have to be sacrificed," Mr
Endo replied with a smile of regret.

The windows were open, but the bamboo blinds were let down.
As soon as Endo had made three bows and left him, Yoshio stood
in confusion for a few minutes in the empty room. Not even in Manchuria had so many things happened in so short a time. He undressed, folded his suit carefully, put out the light and lay down in
the strange bed.

Sirens, a streak of lamplight where the bamboo blinds did not fit
closely to the window frames. An automobile hoot, then another.
Next a sound that reminded him of home—the wooden clatter of
Japanese getas in the street. Yoshio smiled in the darkness; geishas,
invited to a party, he thought. Again a line or two from a poem:

> The geishas trip to a feast,
> You getas, why
> Do you tread on my heart?

He had written that himself when he was eighteen years old.
A shot. Or perhaps it was only the burst tire of a late auto. The
trill of a police whistle. Silence. Sirens again. A little later a gentle
rain rustled down, and this finally lulled him to sleep.

Mr Endo waked him himself and brought him his tea. "A happy
day to the honorable guest," he said gaily and with more ceremony
than usual. Yoshio did not know for a moment where he was.

"I recommend a speedy departure," Mr Endo said. "The launch
does not go today, and later on things might arise to delay the auto
and prevent your getting off."

"Am I really going? Have you got a berth for me?" Yoshio asked,
becoming wide awake. Mr Endo smiled amiably. "Indeed you are,"
he replied. "It is true that every steamer is full up, but a worthy fellow countryman of ours, Mr Watanabe, had engaged a cabin for his
wife and daughter, whom he wanted to send to relations in Singapore while there was fighting here. He is only too happy to put his

cabin at your disposal. I hope you have had a good rest. The bathroom, I am sorry to say, is as primitive as your night quarters."

"Was there shooting last night, or did I only dream it?" Yoshio
asked.

"Reports are contradictory," Mr Endo answered cautiously.

Yoshio went to the so-called bathroom to wash. He was in better
spirits than for a long time past. The night on an improvised bed had
jerked him out of the daily round, and he was in the midst of adventure. His task seemed pleasant and had an extremely hopeful
air in the morning light. He did not know it was the voyage with
Jelena that rejoiced him. Just as he was buttoning his suspenders,
doors, windows and furniture began to rattle and the tea things
clinked on the table. Guns, he thought, guns already. He remembered the dull, distant sound of shelling in the Manchurian campaign. Mr Endo came in, a smiling mask. "Here is your honorable
ticket," he said without mentioning the shooting. "Don't forget
when you reach Hong Kong to look for our travel agency. I have
written the name down for you here: Mr Yonosuke Yamado. He
will lend you a hand, if it should be necessary. The auto is waiting
below. It's a fairly long drive to the pier. And unforeseen hindrances
must be allowed for. A good voyage and—success! It was a great
honor to me to have you under my poor roof. If you must go already,
please come again. . . ."

His politeness was brought out so mechanically that Mr Endo
might just as well have said: Get out of here, there are more important things to be done now and more dangerous ones. Yoshio
bowed himself out of the house. He had ceased to do things: they
merely happened. A little Filipino in cap and white suit was waiting
outside the house with a large private automobile. Yoshio got in,
feeling dazed. He had nothing with him but his black umbrella, and
it annoyed him that his suit did not look fresh. He had shaved with
Mr Endo's razor, he smelt of Mr Endo's May-blossom soap. It was a
long way, as Mr Endo said, and it led through districts that Yoshio
did not know, through a maze of narrow lanes in which he lost all
sense of direction. The chauffeur, however, seemed to be following
definite instructions in avoiding the main streets. During the ride

Yoshio again felt the soundless explosions, a numbing pressure on his eardrum, which might, he thought, be caused by the firing of distant guns. The Filipino turned round and pointed earnestly to the sky. Yoshio now detected the roar of planes, but he could not see them in the scrap of sky which came down like a lid over the narrow lanes. After a long time, and yet unexpectedly, the river spread before him with its multitude of ships of every kind and size. Large gray warships lay motionless like resting buffaloes in muddy water, black cargo boats, red tugs, dapper white motorboats and fussy junks and sampans nosing everywhere among the other craft. Dark clouds were massed above, and their reflection turned the yellow of the river to a somber gray.

The *Soerabaya* was a little white steamer with a squat funnel. An old-fashioned gangway had been lowered from her side, and a procession of passengers was scrambling up the swaying steps. Coolies in blue squatted on the planks of the pier, waiting patiently and impassively to be taken on board and despatched to the East Indies. Every one of them had a new, gaudy-colored blanket, part of their wages. Some of them passed the time of waiting by gambling for pierced copper coins on the planks. Yoshio clambered up the gangway behind an old lady and was received by a gigantic Dutch steward. He handed him over to the small Javanese cabin boy, whose batiked headcloth gave him a serious and dignified air. Yoshio went straight on deck before being shown his cabin. Nothing was to be seen of Jelena. His cabin was tiny, and two bunks were placed or rather jammed at right angles to one another. But there was a surprise in store for Yoshio: his luggage was all there on the blue-patterned bedcover which positively crackled with cleanliness. Yoshio hastened to unpack, for he wanted to change before encountering Jelena. Phonograph music could be heard from a loudspeaker, and there was a burble of confused voices in the passage outside. As Yoshio opened his second trunk, the books that Miss Anderson had lent him on the voyage to Shanghai leaped to his eyes. He took them out, then stood dumfounded with the books in his hands. The blood shot into his face, he could feel himself blushing; in the stress of all his anxieties and defeats and agitations of the last days he had forgotten to return Miss Anderson her books.

What ever would Miss Anderson think of him? he reflected, stirred to his depths; for his Japanese sense of honor and responsibility was of so delicate a nature, and the unwritten laws of the Bushido were so deeply engraven in his Japanese breast beneath his white American linen suit, that he appeared to himself no better than a thief. This feeling was complicated by the innumerable slights and evidences of distrust to which his race as a whole and he as an individual were subjected by the white races, by his admiration of those arrogant and barbarous people of the Western world, and by the never-ending, insistent and miserable ambition to extort their respect and appreciation, even if not their understanding, which is the driving force of nearly everything the Japanese do. And so Yoshio Murata persuaded himself that he still had time to take the honorable books to the Shanghai Hotel and to get back again before the boat sailed. He caught sight of the little Filipino driver still on the quay; he had stopped in curiosity to watch the coolies at their gambling. Yoshio took this as a sign and an assurance that his enterprise was rational and practicable.

And thus a short while later he was once more being driven back the way he had come, faster and more impatiently this time, back into the town over which Chinese airplanes circled like black birds, back to Nanking Road, where the first bombs of the opening hostilities were falling, with no other object but to return to an American young lady, who had shown her kindness, four books which represented all told an outlay of two dollars and eighty cents. . . .

XXIII

"AND HOW DO YOU EXPLAIN that Mr Russell's pocketbook, money and rings were found on you?" Sir Henry Kingsdale-Smith asked, looking at the wall past Kurt Planke's head.

"The Honourable gave me all his possessions to take care of before he got fuddled," Kurt replied without concern.

The interview was taking place in a room on the third floor, which was sometimes used for meetings of big business people from Hong Kong, Singapore and Saïgon who were staying in the Shanghai Hotel. Sir Henry had hurried to the scene. He had viewed Bobbie's dead body, he had had a brief talk with Dr Hain and Dr Bradley and a longer one with the widow. He had endeavored to be tactful and helpful, and he wore a formal dark suit which was much too hot. The more he saw of the business the less he was able to conceal his distaste and ill-humor. He had ordered an immediate autopsy of the corpse, and the gruesome transportation of the dead man was actually taking place while the first Chinese bombs were falling on the town, while the A.A. guns of the Japanese warships thundered out and hundreds of people were being killed. Sir Henry was still anxious to keep the police out of the business, but the discussion took on more and more the character of a trial. The advocate had brought two of his officials with him in case they might be wanted. After the two hotel detectives, gigantic Russians, had fetched Kurt Planke along, Sir Henry sent down to the lounge for his own people, whom Madame Tissaud had by this time taken possession of. One of them was a watery-eyed, red-haired English secretary and the other a Eurasian interpreter for Chinese who looked like a very young and rather corrupt Buddha. They were all seated round the long table which served as a rule for business meetings, and at the further end sat Helen and Frank Taylor. The two Russians, after handing over Kurt Planke, had gone down to find the ricksha coolie who had brought Russell home that morning. The windows were open, but very little noise came up from the street, for ever since a bomb had hit Nanking Road lower down everyone who could permit himself to do so stayed at home.

Sir Henry took his eyes off the wall and focused them on Kurt Planke's flippant, handsome face.

"I want now an exact account of all that happened since Thursday night at twelve-twenty, when you left the hotel in Mr Russell's company, until this morning, when he came back—to die twenty minutes later. I advise you to stick closely to the truth. I recommend it in your own interest. I won't conceal from you that you have got yourself into a very awkward, not to say incriminating situation."

"Do you mind if I have a cigarette?" Kurt said, obviously not in the slightest degree impressed. Sir Henry was well enough acquainted with opium to know what was the cause of the witness's indifference and his flights of irony. The interpreter gave him an inquiring look and then offered Kurt his heavy vulgar case.

"Thanks," Kurt said, lighting his cigarette. "So you want to hear the truth about the deceased Russell? You can have it—only it won't be of any use for his gravestone, for he was a swine through and through. *De mortuis nil nisi bonum,* Amen."

Sir Henry was not annoyed; he found the nonchalance with which Planke dealt with the matter rather amusing. All the same he was convinced that the young German had drugged, robbed and plundered the dead man, even if he had not murdered him. He was proud of his ability to unravel complicated problems. He had instantly detected what even Russell's wife apparently had not noticed—that the dead man must have been robbed, since neither his pocketbook nor the two rings, which he was never known to take off, were to be found on his person. The doorman, when questioned about Russell's return that morning, declared that he and the pianist had arrived together in two rickshas and that the pianist had helped the gentleman through the revolving door and across the lounge, trying to be as unobtrusive as possible, as people usually did when escorting a drunkard. After hearing this, Sir Henry had sent the two detectives to Planke's room, where they had found him in a deep sleep; but under his pillow were all Russell's missing personal belongings. Sir Henry was on a straight course and kept to it. Kurt, on his side, took it all as a good joke and behaved accordingly.

"Well then, on Thursday night we were so slack in the bar that we closed at midnight," he began. "The Honourable had been pestering me the whole night to go on the razzle. As it happened, I was just in the mood for it. We took two rickshas and went to the Chrysanthemum Hotel. I don't know exactly how long we were there."

"What was the attraction in the Chrysanthemum Hotel?" Sir Henry asked.

"You know it as well as everybody else in Shanghai," Kurt said, getting cross. "Girls to prepare your pipe for you." The secretary wrote it all down, and the interpreter, whose services were not yet required, smiled. Sir Henry blinked his eyelids two or three times very fast. He hated those vulgar haunts where people smoked opium to dope themselves, to work themselves up and fancy themselves more important than they were. He himself smoked opium, and treasured it as the noblest means of clarifying the spirit, of freeing it from the limitations of physical life and releasing its sublime powers from the fears and sorrows that lay at the bottom of every soul. He had been an opium addict for twenty years, and he never smoked more than two pipes in the morning and two at night. He was proud of the victory he had won over himself, for he never gave way, he curbed his craving until the appointed time and stopped smoking before intoxication supervened and when only the first soaring lightness of spirit was attained. He had no sympathy whatever for people who went to the Chrysanthemum Hotel and prostituted the divine gift of opium.

Sir Henry had once been at the British legation at Peking. Europeans in Peking are very different from Europeans in Shanghai. Shanghai attracts all those who want to make money. In Peking are to be found those who have fallen in love with China and submit to the country's passive enchantment. Sir Henry read and wrote the classic Chinese of the mandarins and had even begun a translation of the works of the great Tu Fu, but he needed an interpreter when it came to talking to a coolie. As happened to many foreigners in Peking, he had become somewhat Chinese in appearance and even in character. His skin was stretched tightly over his cheekbones, his fingers were long and thin and clearly articulated at every joint. His eyes even became a little oblique when he fixed them on any object. Quotations from Lao-tse often slipped into his conversation. Like most people of his kind, he lost his identity as a European without becoming Chinese. After 1927, when his government had decided to support Chiang Kai-shek against the menace of the Japanese as well as against Russian influence and the spread of Communism in China, a new policy was entered on. Up to now China had been treated without compunction, like a colony. Now officials were required who had some slight understanding of the country and its tor-

tuous psychology and who were liked by the Chinese. So it came
about that Sir Henry Kingsdale-Smith, who had retired to a former
temple of the western hills, was appointed crown advocate in Shanghai. The appointment was a sympathetic gesture towards the Chinese, who respected him as much as they had hated his predecessor,
and he had little to do.

It was after ten o'clock, the hour at which Sir Henry was accustomed to smoke his two morning pipes, and he was becoming more
restlessly impatient and nervous the longer the inquiry went on. Kurt
Planke was suffering the same symptoms, for the soothing effect of
his last pipe was dying away.

"Why did you go to the Chrysanthemum Hotel of all places?"
Sir Henry asked reproachfully.

"I happened to have had an introduction there," Kurt said. "As
you know, one has to be taken there. For a short time I had an affair
with one of the little Japanese girls. I had already given Russell a letter to the girls, but they would not admit him without me. For that
reason he stuck to me like a leech. He wouldn't let me go to bed.
When I had done my job in the bar, he dragged me from place to
place and drank like a maniac—he was not a pleasant fellow when he
was drunk," Kurt said, looking to Helen for corroboration.

Helen did not even see the look, nor did she listen to what was
going on at the upper end of the table. Her eyes were fascinated by
Frank's hands: he had just lighted a cigarette and was now extinguish-
ing the match in the ash tray, which was already full of cigarette ends.
On one of his hands there was still the red imprint of lipstick from
her own mouth. Neither in spirit nor conscience was she aware of the
murder she had committed, but merely as an unpleasant physical
memory; it was not unlike the feeling that was left behind when she
had once run over a dog. Now and then the skin of her spine contracted in a little shudder at the recollection, that was all. But at the
same time it was all she could do to keep back the hysterical and
triumphant laughter which was always threatening to break out while
Sir Henry Kingsdale-Smith obstinately pursued his idiotic line of in-
vestigation. You belong to me, she thought, with her eyes on Frank's
brown hands. I have rescued you from the depths of hell, and I shall

never give you up. You belong to me now. Frank Taylor's thoughts were very different as he smoked faster and faster, stubbing out a half-smoked cigarette and the next moment lighting a fresh one.

The door opened and Dr Hain crept in. Sir Henry gave him an inquiring glance as he noiselessly sat down.

"I have just spoken to Dr Bradley on the phone," Dr Hain said.

"We are coming to that later," Sir Henry said, once more fixing his gaze on Kurt Planke. "Was Mr Russell an opium smoker?" he asked.

"No, not until he came here, but I must say opium suited him better than alcohol," Kurt remarked. "It brought to light what little sense he had."

"Do you mean that Thursday night was the first night he'd smoked opium?"

"No, that's not right, either. He'd already been taken by some swindlers who'd sold him a box of miserable refuse for ten dollars—a perfect farce. He came into the bar with it a few days ago. He had no lamp, pipe or needle, as far as I know, and he had no idea what to do with it. I was positively sorry for the man, and after the bar closed I took him to some girls in Chapei who had no opium of their own but knew how to prepare a pipe. That was—let me see—Monday."

"Did you smoke too on this occasion?"

"No, sir. Sorry. I had the pleasure of looking on."

"That doesn't sound very plausible, Mr—er—Planke."

"Perhaps you know the Chinese proverb, sir: To cure yourself of drunkenness, you must watch a drunkard while you're sober yoursef," Kurt replied. It was obviously irony.

"Do you mean to tell me that you tried to cure yourself of opium by those means?" Sir Henry asked, getting annoyed himself.

"Certainly. I have made one or two modest and not very successful efforts in that direction," Kurt observed with a smile.

Dr Hain shifted uneasily in his chair. If he was still alive it was on a purely provisional basis. I have still got to operate this banker Chang, he had told himself that morning. But Chang was not going to be operated. Then later he told himself that he still had to wait until the

autopsy was completed. Now he thought: I must stand by and help
Kurt through this business. Kurt smiled almost consolingly at him.

"We have got to Thursday night, when you took Mr Russell to
the Chrysanthemum Hotel. Did you know how much money he had
on him?" Sir Henry asked severely.

"I should like to take the opportunity of clearing up a psychological error. Money does not interest me. I don't care about it."

"No? I was under the impression that you took payment in one
way or another from women for—for services—which—how shall I
put it——"

"If you mean that I am a gigolo, sir, I must make a confession that
may sound very ludicrous. I have never been to bed with a woman
I didn't love. I would much rather have given diamonds to every one
of them than taken so much as a necktie," Kurt said, involuntarily
touching the tie which Meilan had given him.

"So you and Mr Russell smoked opium in the Chrysanthemum
Hotel," Sir Henry said, without taking up this elucidation. "How
many pipes? How long were you there? Did you sleep there?"

"I did not smoke. I only listened and looked on while the Honourable did. He was very openhearted when he was smoking. He complained bitterly. He was afraid of his wife."

"Afraid? Why afraid?"

Helen leaned forward to draw attention to herself.

"It is unfortunately no longer any secret that my husband had a
vicious and profligate character. He suffered from attacks of a kind
of claustrophobia. I have been told by doctors that they are the pre-
monitory symptoms of delirium tremens," she said, leaning back
again. She gave Frank a quick look, but she did not succeed in catching his eye.

Sir Henry gave a deep sigh. A forlorn and weeping widow would
have pleased him better. It won't be easy to whitewash this fellow
Russell, he thought. Not even death can clean him up.

"You had no designs on Mr Russell's pocketbook. You had no desire for opium, you did not even find the deceased sympathetic. Can
you tell me what induced you to spend every night of this week in his
company?" he asked with severity. Kurt looked at him reflectively;

he surveyed him as an amusing object. Sir Henry began to feel uncomfortable. His heart had suffered from his long stay in China; if he did not have his two pipes punctually, his heart began to beat in an uneasy, feeble and irregular manner.

"Let me think," Kurt said casually. "You touch on a matter there, —wait a bit," he said. "I think I know. Russell belonged to a class I've always hated and—yes, hated and despised and considered ridiculous. He belonged to society. He belonged to society, and nevertheless he went to the dogs. That delighted me. Yes, I have gone to the dogs too, you said as much a moment ago when you made your kind allusion to my relations with women. I went to the dogs, Sir Henry, because I got into circumstances that were too much for me. I'll put it this way: I got involved in circumstances that only a Jew can survive. Jews flourish in exile and persecution. A man like me goes to the dogs. Thomas Mann says somewhere that difficult circumstances are the most favorable circumstances, or something of the sort, but he also says that there is nothing more unhygienic than life. For that reason——"

"Who is Thomas Mann?" Sir Henry asked.

"You would not have heard of him, sir," Kurt said airily. "A writer. Nobel Prize. The greatest living German. It doesn't matter, anyway. What I wanted to say was this: Russell was born to the most fortunate circumstances: money, family, in a country of wealth, security and liberty. He had everything. Nevertheless he went to the dogs. That delights a fellow like me, sir. It does me all the good in the world. I was only too pleased to look on while this Honourable made a swine of himself without the excuse I had of being up to my neck in it. I don't know whether you can understand that, sir. There was something in common between Russell and me, and you must excuse me if I employ a big word for it: self-annihilation. That was it—self-annihilation. It gave me pleasure to watch the fellow at it. Self-annihilation."

Sir Henry pulled a face as though he had a bad taste in his mouth.

"Let's get back to the facts and leave psychology alone," he said. "You went to the Chrysanthemum Hotel and you stayed there——"

"Not very long—in any case not long enough for the Honourable.

He had only had about five pipes. I say 'only,' because it took a long time for the opium to have any effect on him. He had a certain immunity, you see. I believe drunkards are very difficult to anesthetize," he said with a questioning look at Dr Hain. The doctor gave a hurried nod in confirmation. "Five pipes were nothing at all for a fellow like that. Just enough to wake him up. Then there was an interruption—police or something of the kind. Possibly the police wanted to shake up the Japanese who own the hotel. In any case, the girls pushed us out by a back door, and there we were in the street at two in the morning, I dead sober and the Honourable shouting for more. Not a hope of getting him home and tucking him up in his four-poster. After the fifth pipe he was more afraid of his wife than after his second. So there."

"Yes?" Sir Henry asked, positively curious to hear the further adventures of the night, but before Kurt could go on, the door opened and the two Russians led in a ricksha coolie by the elbows.

It was Yen. He was in fairly clean clothes, an open blue jacket and crumpled trousers, with his European hat on his head, for he could not part with it even after the glorious hours in his son's company were over and he had sold the silk robe again.

"Wait," Sir Henry said, pointing his thin forefinger. Yen stood against the wall near the door, gasping, as though waiting for his execution.

"As you know, sir, the Chrysanthemum Hotel is close to Nanking Road. Yes, close to Nanking Road. As there was nothing more to be done there, we tried North Szechuan Road and Foochow Road and every other damn dirty corner of the town. But the devil was in it. Every place I knew was shut, shutters up or else boards nailed across and no light inside. Everyone afraid of the Japanese, you see. At last I told the coolie to take us to Kwe Kuei's." Kurt pointed to Yen with his chin. "Kuei's, you must know, is the lowest, dirtiest, filthiest place in the whole of Greater Shanghai. You have to lie on the same mat with coolies, and the only difference is the price the white men have to pay. I told the Honourable that. I didn't disguise from him what sort of hop joint it was. But he was crazy for opium. He had to have more, at once, that very night, he couldn't wait. Of course, I was only too delighted to drag him through the mud in his smart dinner jacket. It was just what I wanted. If he was set on sinking lower and lower, I was not the man to hold him back. And so we were taken to Kwe Kuei's. There too it was bolted and barred, but the coolie seemed to be a *persona grata,* and for his sake they let us in. There he Honourable got all the opium he wanted. Before he fell asleep he gave his money and his rings and everything else he had on him into my charge. No doubt the company did not seem to him implicitly to be trusted. But that of course was nonsense. The coolies there are as good as gold."

"Have you any other witnesses to prove that Mr Russell gave these things into your charge?" Sir Henry asked aggressively. Kurt shrugged his shoulders. "I don't know whether the coolie was clear enough in the head at the time to take notice of it," he said.

Nevertheless it appeared that Yen knew all about it, when the interpreter questioned him.

"The coolie corroborates the statement," the interpreter announced. "He says: the tall gentleman handed the little good Mr Ku his money case and his rings. The little good Mr Ku laughed and put them in his pocket without giving them a look, just as if they were pebbles."

Sir Henry Kingsdale-Smith reflected with a shudder on the depths to which the craving for opium had brought Russell: smoking in the company of his ricksha coolie, who was smoking, too. Sir Henry was aware of elegant séances where the pipe went from mouth to mouth, and even these lax coteries sickened him. His imagination quailed before those bunks in Kwe Kuei's den. "Go on," he said, involuntarily putting his hand to his heart, which was troubling him.

"Later on I fell asleep too, for I had not smoked for a long time and soon became drowsy. When I woke up, or rather when the coolie and Kuei waked me, the Honourable was still sleeping like a log. The Chinese were gabbling nineteen to the dozen, and I did not understand a word of it. I said to the coolie: 'Franz, what's all this about?'—I call them all Franz, just a habit of mine, sir—but in his excitement the fellow had forgotten whatever little pidgin he ever knew. Fact was that though Kuei had let us into his stinkhole it was quite impossible for him to let us out. Everything was barricaded and boarded up, and Chinese troops had been fortifying the street with sandbags and barbed wire and other such warlike preparations I could see through a chink in the shutters. Kuei and the coolie tore down all the bunks from the walls, simply throwing the people out of them and barricading the windows. The Honourable alone noticed nothing at all of these excitements and slept blissfully on. We were in a thoroughly awkward situation—prisoners in an opium den. The window looked over low roofs, for we were at the back of the house. Outside we heard the banging of tin plates or something or other the soldiers were carting around, and one of them never stopped singing through his nose—the stuff they sing here that makes one so melancholy one could howl like a dog when it hears the violin. At last the Honourable woke, and I told him what was up. He was surprisingly gentle and well behaved. He thought it funny. He was so bungfull of opium that he thought it fun. He asked for something to eat. Kuei gave him some cooked rice that tasted of rat dung—or at least, as I imagine rat dung would taste——"

"Could this rice have been poisoned?" Sir Henry asked quickly

"How do you mean, poisoned?" Kurt asked. His examination had been becoming more and more of a monologue. "Oh, you mean because the Honourable—— No, I don't think so. I consider Kwe Kuei an honest fellow in his way, and after all I ate the same food a the Honourable without turning blue in the face. You think Kue meant to poison us and rob us and then throw us on the rubbish heap? Funny, I should never have thought of that. No, I feel quite sure the rice wasn't poisoned. It only tasted like that."

Sir Henry Kingsdale-Smith shook his head. If Kurt Planke wa guilty of the death of this wretched Russell, he was certainly doing very little to prove his innocence.

"Well, go on," he said and tapped the table with his long thin Chinese forefinger.

"Towards evening the Honourable grew obstreperous," Kurt wen on. "He kicked up such a row that Kuei brought out the pipes again He smoked like a lunatic, I must say. I smoked again, too. It wa sheer madness, I grant you. But after all, the pipe was the only pleasure left us. We hadn't had a very pleasant day of it. I don't know what sort of stuff it was Kuei gave us to smoke: it looked as black as bootblacking and had a hellish taste. Instead of making us drowsy and contented it roused us up. At any rate it roused the Honourable up to a quite extraordinary degree. He became very unpleasant, particularly when Kuei told him that he had no more of the stuff in the house. Very unpleasant, even more unpleasant than when he was under the influence of alcohol. I considered the situation, and I thought: we can't wait in this hole forever to see whether the war is going to spread to Shanghai or not. I took a hundred dollars out of the pocketbook the Honourable had entrusted to me and showed them to Kwe Kuei. He nearly had a stroke. I don't know how the hundred dollars were shared out, but anyway he let us out next morning. We encountered a few difficulties in getting out of the Chinese quarter of Chapei and through the guards into the International Settlement, but they were smoothed out somehow. Then I took the Honourable as far as his door, for he was not very strong on his legs. That was only this morning. Only this morning——" Kurt repeated in profound surprise.

"And then?" Sir Henry said impatiently.

"And then? I was dog tired. I threw myself down on my bed and went to sleep. If the two friendly ambassadors you sent hadn't waked me, I should probably be asleep at this moment."

"Then how did you know, when you woke up, that Mr Russell was dead?" Sir Henry asked, pouncing like a falcon on his prey.

"Yes—how did I?" Kurt asked back and stared at him in astonishment.

Dr Hain stood up at the end of the table and said: "I was in Kurt's room and told him of it. He must have fallen asleep again and have forgotten that I had spoken with him."

"Now I want to ask you a question," Sir Henry said. "Didn't you possibly just throttle Mr Russell a bit when you were alone with him in the hotel corridor, and did you not take away his pocketbook while he was unconscious in consequence?"

"No," Kurt said and merely laughed at the suggestion.

Once more Dr Hain had something to say.

"There was no kind of trace of strangling on the neck of the corpse," he announced. Frank Taylor started when he heard Russell described as a corpse. As if this expression made everything final.

"You know it's against the law to smoke opium and that you incur severe penalties by doing so," Sir Henry Kingsdale-Smith said. Kurt did not think such a remark worth the trouble of a reply. "So why did you smoke, and in such degrading circumstances into the bargain?" Sir Henry asked. He was not hypocritical; it was only that he could see no relation between opium as he smoked it and opium as others smoked it.

"I hardly need explain that to you, sir," Kurt parried. He let his chin fall on his chest to think it over. "You probably would not understand it," he went on. "It was really on account of the music."

"Music?" Sir Henry asked blankly. Dr Hain bent forward as if he had been called upon.

"Yes, on account of the music," Kurt said, nodding his head. "When you have had enough smoke—just before you fall asleep—there is music, music such as was never written down. So—so clear—such—music, in fact. It may sound ridiculous, but I always used to think: If I could remember this music and write it down, then——I am a musician, by the way," he put in hurriedly. "It would have been a justification, don't you see? If I had become a great composer," he added with a fleeting glance at the doctor. "Well, there you are," he ended, "that is probably the whole misfortune in getting drunk—that one believes in oneself."

Sir Henry Kingsdale-Smith had sunk into silent and abstracted pondering. "We'll take the coolie now," he said finally.

"Step forward, coolie," the interpreter said, and he said the word coolie as if it were an insult. Yen detached himself from the wall and took a step forward.

"May I have a cigarette?" Kurt asked again, and as soon as he got it he inhaled the smoke eagerly.

Yen stood there with his hands hanging down and his mouth open; his wasted chest showed through his open jacket, his teeth in his protruding Mongolian jaws looked naked, and he smelt like a frightened animal, since his skin was continually breaking out with the

old sweat of fear. Some of the hotel pages had called out to him
that his fare of that morning was dead. Although he could not see
how he could be implicated, one thing had profoundly startled him—
the presence, namely, of the old doctor who a few days before had
pricked him with the merciful needle. The skin of Yen's face was
stretched leanly over his cheekbones, and he took the greatest pains
neither to cough nor to spit and to understand the questions the interpreter put to him. The only thing that gave him a certain assurance was the consciousness of the expensive hat on his head. He accompanied each yes and no with a little bow and did not utter a
single other word.

His replies confirmed the account that Kurt Planke had just concluded. It was only when he was asked whether he too had smoked
opium that he became stubborn and began to lie.

Did he know the gentleman who had just been talking?

"Yes," Yen said.

Had he carried this man and another gentleman on Thursday
night? Yes, said Yen, he and one of his friends had taken them in
their rickshas. Had he taken the two gentlemen to the opium den of
a certain Kwe Kuei in Chapei and remained there with them until
that morning? Yes. Had the young gentlemen ridden with him to
Kuei's on a previous occasion? Yes. Had he, Yen, smoked opium
there too? No. Was he sure? Yes. Not on his oath? No. Yen's face
betrayed nothing, but from the way his Adam's apple bobbed up and
down in his wasted neck, Sir Henry Kingsdale-Smith could see that
he was lying.

"Tell him it is known to us that he has smoked opium because his
name is registered as an opium smoker with the anti-opium office,"
he told the interpreter. At these words Yen felt that something
within him was shattered and overturned, but his face remained impassive. He only glanced out of the corner of his eye at the foreign
doctor, for he was convinced that it was this man who had handed
him up to justice and to inevitable execution. It did not enter his
head that the white people were acquainted with mercy and prac-
ised it.

"Ask him why he took the foreigners to Kwe Kuei's," Sir Henry

said. A haze of opium had gathered over the whole affair. It veiled
every fact, and in Sir Henry himself the hunger for the peace of the
pipe grew ever more intense.

"On account of *komsha,*" the interpreter answered. "Twenty per
cent for each foreigner."

"Ask him whether he smoked the same pipe as Russell. And
whether he knows what the stuff was that this Kuei sold them. I
want to find out whether it was some sort of poison," Sir Henry
insisted impatiently. Kurt took the liberty of putting in a remark.

"A white man can very easily be finished off by something a Chinese would never notice," he said casually.

The interpreter announced: "Kuei collected the dregs of the pipes
of the day before and cooked them up with some fresh opium. It's
the most horrible stuff and much stronger than the ordinary opium,"
he added on his own account. Sir Henry turned to Dr Hain.

"Is it possible that this was the cause of Mr Russell's death?" he
asked.

Dr Hain reflected before replying.

"Theoretically it would be possible that he died of anything whatever, even of a glass of whisky," he declared in a low voice.

"Mrs Russell," Sir Henry said, trying to give his voice a note of
compunction, "did you get the impression that your husband was seriously ill—even dying, let us say—when he came back this morning?"

"I really can't say," Helen replied curtly. "He was very excited and
unsteady and reeling on his legs. I thought he was drunk, but perhaps he was ill."

Frank moved restlessly. He wanted to stand up and say something,
but Helen put her hand on his knee under the table and forced him
to keep his seat. The pressure of her hand was hard and heavy, and
she held him back as she might a runaway horse. It was hot in the
room, but the touch of Helen's hand struck a chill through Frank's
suit, and he felt a fleeting and quickly vanishing pity for her cold
and heavy hand. When he looked up he saw a surprised expression
on Sir Henry's face. After she had made her reply, Helen took a
cigarette from the box in front of them, and Frank mechanically
struck a match for her. She tried to smile at him while he held the

match to her cigarette. She had become incomprehensibly foreign. She talked like a Russian, with hard consonants and softly slurred vowels. She looked like a Russian with her red untidy hair and her large wild mouth. Jelena Trubova—she thought she had herself in control, she was proud of herself, and she did not know that she was already in a state of disintegration, with every eye upon her.

"Did you wish to say something, Mr Taylor?" Sir Henry asked after an interval of silence.

"I was present when Bobbie came in, and I am convinced he was quite well," Frank said quickly.

"You are an American, aren't you?" Sir Henry asked thoughtfully.

"I am," Frank said. "I believe I——"

Suddenly Yen began to speak—the coolie at the back of the room against the wall, whom everyone had forgotten.

For the last minute or two he had been looking from one to another, and he had become more and more convinced that what was at stake was his own head and nothing else. His heart went small and tried to find a way out of his chest; you could see it beating against his emaciated ribs. Since his life was at stake, he opened his mouth and began to talk.

"Who takes the slow coolie?" he said. "Who takes the weak, slow coolie? 'Quick!' cry the gentlemen. 'Quick, quick, coolie, run to the right, run to the left,' and they kick you in the behind if you stop to take breath. Who gives the poor coolie anything to eat if he is too slow to earn money? Who gives the coolie quick feet and a good wind? It is unjust to punish him who eats the Great Smoke, for the smoke is the only friend the coolie has. It makes the empty belly full and the tired feet agile, it stills the pains in the breast and gives dreams to him whose life is a weariness. The coolie dies without the Great Smoke, but if he eats of the Great Smoke his head is cut off. The coolie's lot is unjust. 'Come home, come back to your family,' the son says. 'Bitter are the tears of exile,' the storyteller says in the market. I want to go back with my son, but I have debts; they are never out of my head, I must earn much money, I must earn eight dollars to pay my debts. Then I can go back to my son and my home. For a week long I did not pull a ricksha and ate no smoke, sir. That makes the bones crumble and sucks the breath out of the chest. How am I to earn money when I am so wretched? How shall I ever see my son again? Is it a sin when the coolie smokes to get strength for his work and to pay his debts? Kwe Kuei gives me twenty cents for every foreign devil I bring him. 'Bring plenty of them and you pay your debts,' says Kuei. 'I give smoke for nothing,' says Kuei, 'to show you that I am your friend, for I can see that you perish for weakness.' Is it a sin to take medicine when the body is sick? The Great Smoke is the medicine of the poor. I was not born a coolie," Yen said, and he was so exhausted that tears came to his eyes and rolled down his cheeks. "I was not born a coolie. I belong to the honorable family of Lung, and my grandfather was a village elder and a worthy and respected man. So now I want to go back home and forget the foreigners as an evil dream. Since seeing my son, there is no other wish left within me but to go home. Soon, I keep on thinking, soon the debts will be paid and freedom earned and I will go back to my village. There I shall not need the smoke, there everything is good and nobody shouts: 'Quick, coolie, quick!' But I shall not go home. Now my head will be cut off. What does the foreign Old Doctor want with my head? Why does he deliver up my head? Is he paid for it? Is he paid for my head? How much?" Yen shouted, and stepping up to Dr Hain he raised his two fists. "The foreigners too have heads that can be cut off," he shouted in the bitterness of his heart. "The time will come when their heads shall be cut off so that they do not see their sons any more. That is what we are told and promised: that the foreigner shall be driven out of the country and killed, and then we shall have the riches that now they keep fast hold of. But I," he said, weeping, "but I shall not be there. I shall be executed and my head cut off. I shall never see my son again, and there is none of my family near to bury my body——"

When Yen got thus far he put his hands before his face and wept in great heaving sobs, for it dawned on him that even his corpse would be without honor and mutilated. There would be nobody there to sew his head on again, and so he would be fated to be a restless and ignoble spirit forever instead of an ancestor who would be honored with incense and rice. And in his despair he imagined hell as the life of a coolie but without the consolation of opium.

Dr Hain had quailed a little when the coolie shook his fists in his face, and he heard and understood only one word of all he said, the word *tsu,* which means "son." He had just a glimmer of Yen's fate, and he felt great pity for him. Sir Henry Kingsdale-Smith asked the interpreter: "What's all that he says?"

The interpreter, who had had some trouble himself in following the incoherent torrent of words that had poured from Yen's lips, shrugged his shoulders. "Communist talk," he said. Kurt Planke put out his hand for an ash tray and stubbed out his cigarette on it.

"If it will help to prove the coolie's innocence, I am very ready to confess that I strangled Mr Russell, poisoned him and stabbed him from behind," he said casually, although every nerve in his body quivered in sympathy with the Chinaman's inarticulate grief.

"I must establish whether Mr Russell was in good health when he got out of the ricksha," Sir Henry said obstinately. "That is the point. Was the cause of death contracted in Chapei, or did something happen in the brief interval between his reaching the hotel and entering his bedroom? This was the only time when you, Mr Planke, were with the deceased without a witness. There has been no explanation of the highly incriminating circumstance that his pocketbook and rings were found in your possession."

Sir Henry, as he made these remarks, looked past Kurt to the bottom of the table where Helen sat with lowered eyes as though to avoid seeing the pitiful scene. Her knee was pressed against Frank's under the table, but the contact did nothing to still the trembling of her limbs. Suddenly Frank stood up, threw his cigarette on the floor, rested both hands on the table and said:

"Excuse my interrupting, sir. I should have talked long ago. There was nothing wrong with Russell when he got home. He was so well, he almost killed his wife. As I unfortunately was a witness of this domestic scene, I knocked him down. He fell with his head on the edge of the table. I suppose I am responsible for his death. Smashed his skull on something. There is no object in letting you follow a false scent any longer, sir. I did it, and the responsibility is mine."

Helen uttered a strange little cry of grief as he said this. Frank paid no attention. During the last hour he had interposed whole oceans and continents between this woman and himself. When he had finished, he stood where he was with his hands on the table, waiting to see what would happen next. Sir Henry, addressed so abruptly, looked like a man near whose ear an alarm clock has just gone off. But before he could speak, Dr Hain jumped up and called:

"I have spoken with Dr Bradley. A broken skull or any other outward injury is quite out of the question. The post-mortem has put that beyond a doubt. Mr Taylor has, as far as that goes, nothing to do with Russell's death—not directly at least." He sat down again, astonished at himself. He was deeply surprised that he still took any part in human problems and still tried to serve the ends of justice. His sleepless night and the disaster he carried in his coat pocket in the shape of a crumpled letter had put him into a strange condition of thin-skinnedness and made him oversensitive. He was convinced that neither Kurt nor the coolie had anything to do with Russell's death. Yet only at the very moment when Frank began to speak it became clear to him that it was the wife who had murdered her husband. Sir Henry had not got as far as this; his brain, on the contrary, grew more and more dazed the further the hour for his two pipes was left behind. He leaned far over the table and said kindly: "You see, Mr—er—Taylor, you caused no fatal injury, that is certain. If Mr Russell really attacked his wife and you knocked him down, as I have no reason to doubt, it was an entirely natural and even praiseworthy act. Not one of us would look on while a woman was being maltreated without defending her."

"Thank you, sir," Frank said and sat down again. Suddenly the tension in him gave way, everything went limp. He took hold of the cigarette box. It was empty. I need a whisky, he thought. Now his limbs began to grow strong again. He had been dead. Now he was alive once more.

"By the way, how did it happen that you were there when Mr Russell came home?" he heard Sir Henry asking. The table was long, and Sir Henry sat far away, on the opposite shore of a broad stream. He was still hesitating when Helen said, without taking her eyes from her clasped hands:

"Mr Taylor came to say good-by to us before we went on board. He wanted to thank us for the wedding present we sent him. It's his wedding day today."

Frank did not grasp the bitter and immeasurable triumph in these words. Sir Henry murmured politely:

"Sorry to upset your wedding day; you didn't hit on a very good date," he added, for the air was rent at ever shorter intervals by dull explosions. It might be thunder. There were flashes sometimes, and they all tried to believe it was only thunder. Frank stood up again and said: "I was just going to ask permission to go and look after my fiancée. She is sure to be worried about me. She's staying in the hotel, so I shall be here in case I'm wanted. I am entirely at your disposal. But if you could just spare me for the next few minutes——" Frank breathed deeply, he swallowed great breaths of the thunderous air that broke in from outside. He greedily devoured the air in the room, the stale oppressive air, laden with the Chinese coolie's cold sweat of fear and with the vapors of distant explosions. He dug his way on like a buried miner, when he grasped that he had nothing to do with Russell's death. It was only now he noticed that his hands and feet had gone dead. His blood now began to pulse in them, it tingled and pricked as if he had been frozen and restored to life again. The table still spread on and on, becoming thinner and longer, as though it were a railway track bearing Sir Henry away. It was a crazy sensation. Then everything became normal again and Sir Henry was near enough for Frank to see that he was smiling. "Yes, I think we could spare you for a time," he said. "But don't go too far away, Mr—er—Taylor. And may I suggest that you say nothing to your fiancée? We'll try and keep this matter to ourselves—if possible. You understand that this is not a trial, it is simply a little discussion. We are both friends of the Russells."

Decent fellow, this American, Sir Henry thought, as Frank Taylor got up to go. Tried to take it all on himself. Straight, very straight. "I shall ask you to stay here a moment longer, Dr Hain, and you too, Mr Planke." He pointed his thin forefinger at Yen. "The coolie can wait outside."

Yen was standing against the wall, feeling quite vacant and insensible with fear after his outbreak. He misunderstood the imperious gesture of this bony finger. He took it for his death sentence. At the moment when the two gigantic Russians laid hands on him to conduct him outside, he collapsed without a sound, like an empty sack. "Poor Franz," Kurt Planke said spontaneously. The two giants picked Yen up and carried him out.

Frank made two bows, one in the direction of Sir Henry and a second one, vague and badly aimed, to Helen. She sat very stiffly and did not look at him as he went to the door. She only turned white under her dark powder and grew many years older. Sir Henry put his Chinese fingers together and said: "And now for you, Mrs Russell . . ."

Frank shut the door behind him; he was outside, he was in the passage, he reached the elevator, he rang, he stood and waited and rang again. He discovered that he was whistling, as was his habit. I still have to shave, he thought. Ruth, he thought. Whisky, he thought also. He slowly came to himself as though out of a deep trance. Oh boy, oh boy, he thought to himself, *that* could have gone wrong. And so it was simply a heart attack . . .

The elevator came, he got in, he whistled louder, he went up the two floors, he got out, he walked along the passage again, he stood outside Ruth's door. He listened, but he heard nothing. He stood outside the door for several minutes before knocking, for he had first to regain his balance. When there was no answer to his knock, he cautiously turned the door handle and the door opened.

He hoped to find that Ruth had fallen asleep after waiting so long for him. But Ruth was not there. Confucius was not there. The room was silent and vacant. A silver salver, complete with cocktail shaker and twelve silver cups, was on the table. Frank went into the bathroom and washed his hands.

Already the first bomb has fallen on Nanking Road, the first, bitter blood has flowed, the first confused cry of agony has rung out, the first houses have had their walls shattered. The city will never again be as it was an hour before, for a fresh war is branding its battle-worn

face with fresh scars. And for the handful of people too whom we
have followed from their birth to this moment, the end has begun.
Life has swept them on to the mouth of the great sluggish river, it
has thrown them ashore at this gigantic crossroads of the world, in
order to annihilate them there. Some of them have already been
through frightful things; some are so innocent that they cannot
recognize death when they meet it in the open street. These people
are the product of the times in which they live, just as river pebbles,
round and angular and oddly shaped, are the product of the current
which has rolled them hither and thither and worn them to their
shape without their being able to do anything about it. These times,
however, the stretch covered by the last fifteen years—no one can
say yet whether the future will see them as a period of renewal or
as one of defeat and destruction. In any case, this period, in the
perspective of the whole destiny of the small, cool, dark planet which
is our dwelling place, will seem no more important than a passing
step that lays waste an ant heap; except that the tiny ants, busily
building up their home again, are sexless and concentrated only on
their duties to the commonwealth, while we atoms of humanity live
slavishly yet indomitably bound up with sex: immortal in the brief
songs it makes us sing, in the tears it extorts and in the grotesque
dances in which we are intertwined, crossing and recrossing, only
to part again. . . .

XXIV

RUTH ANDERSON WOKE EARLY that morning and thought of Frank. He
has changed, she thought; Shanghai has changed him. He will be as
he used to be as soon as we are together. She lay for a time in bed
with her arms behind her head, smiling reflectively, and then she fell
asleep again. She dreamt a short and joyful dream, which she was
unable to remember when she woke the second time. By this time
the air was full of noises, cups and plates clattered below, someone
was singing in a foreign Chinese voice, and Ruth wondered passingly
that Chinese kitchenmaids sang at their work just as kitchenmaids

did at home. She jumped out of bed with both feet at once, for that was very important on her wedding morning. It might have spoiled everything to get out of bed with the wrong foot first.

Confucius had got out of his basket; it was empty in its corner, not a trace of warmth left in it. Ruth began to search anxiously for the duckling, she called and enticed and wheedled, but Confucius would not reply. She found him at last under the bed, squeezed close to the wall with his head under his own inadequate wings. When she called out to him he gave a tiny plaintive quack. She lay flat on the floor and crept under the bed and cautiously pulled him out.

"Are you sick? What is the matter? Are you hungry—or cold?" she asked as she hollowed her hands and made a nest for him. She could feel the small downy body trembling weakly and unceasingly and felt very sorry for him. She put the little creature against her face and began to cajole it.

"Listen, Confucius," she said, "you must not be sick today, you can't do that to me, today is my wedding day." She rubbed her cheek against his down, and Confucius seemed to become more cheerful. He took his little head from under his wing and preened himself. "That's right," Ruth said. "There's a good boy." (Confucius' sex was not yet ascertained, but Ruth called him a boy.) "Make yourself nice for Mamma." He was just a tiny little duckling, a little ball, pale yellow with dark gray spots here and there. His beak was so soft she was afraid he would bend it. "Careful!" she said. "Don't overdo it." She put him back in his basket, but he worked his way out again after great exertions and a quack or two.

"What's the matter?" she asked, looking at him in anxiety. "Don't you like your home any more? Wait, we're going to move soon. You must have a little patience, don't you know that? I've had to wait too, Conny."

She sighed as she looked at the little duck for a moment or two longer, and then she turned on the radio to cheer them both up, and soon there was some jazz. She went into the bathroom, carefully leaving the door open so that Confucius could follow if he wanted to. After a while the little duck did in fact come waddling in after her. Ruth was enchanted. "You little darling," she cried in ecstasy, "you sweet little thing, that was really sweet of you. Do you like Mamma? Do you love Mamma a little?" she asked earnestly. Nevertheless, she could tell that all was not well with Confucius. If he had been one of her patients, she would have taken his temperature. Under the shower bath she hummed the jazz tune she had heard on the radio. She rubbed herself dry and went back into her bedroom with Confucius following behind her. She grew very serious as she sat down in front of the small dressing table to make up. It was of particular importance that morning, as everything else was. She studied her face and her hair and her skin narrowly and almost reproachfully, for she was not pleased with herself. She had already observed that there were very beautiful women in Shanghai. Every day crowds of smart, sophisticated and coquettish women, who were on world cruises, came into Frank's store. Ruth felt lamentably inexperienced and ordinary in comparison. Flathill, she thought. I am just a small-town product. She wrinkled her forehead in an effort to recall the words of an article she had read in a magazine on board ship: "No one can take my husband from me." The description the authoress gave of her husband seemed to Ruth an exact portrait of Frank. Tall, slender, good-looking, well educated, of a good family, good-tempered, a sportsman, popular with everybody. Just like Frank. "I am the slave of my husband, that is the secret," the authoress had written. Ruth gave a deep sigh. She was ready to be Frank's slave if that would help. Before she had got as far as putting her lipstick on, the telephone rang. Frank. Ruth automatically put on her dressing gown before she spoke to him; she did it from an impulse of modesty of which she was quite unconscious. So I've got to wait, she thought with disappointment when the brief talk was over and she sat down again. She was so restless she felt she might explode. She looked at the clock. It was not eight yet. The wedding was at one. A slave, she thought, and telephoned for her breakfast and a hard-boiled egg for Confucius. She looked in the mirror again, finished with her lipstick and finally put on the dress in which she was to be married, one of those nineteen-fifty dresses which marched in the van of her wardrobe. It was white and simple and it pleased her.

Ruth had a secret from Frank. She bought all her dresses from the children's departments of the stores, for any others were too large for her. As her breakfast appeared before her room had been done, she herself made her bed quickly, as she had thousands of sick-beds, put everything straight and then sat down at the window to feed the duckling and drink her coffee and orange juice. Confucius pecked fancifully at the hard-boiled egg and left it. Ruth looked at the time and found that only ten minutes had passed since Frank's call. It's going to be one of those turtle days, Ruth thought with a sigh. By degrees she grew annoyed. Ever since I've been in Shang-hai, my life, all told, has been nothing but waiting for Frank, she thought petulantly. She took Confucius on her lap, and he went to sleep there. I must learn to be lazy, she thought further, for she could not bear sitting still and got so weary of it that she opened her mouth and yawned. She went into the bathroom and washed three pairs of stockings, and then that too was done. There was a knock, and a Chinese boy dragged in an enormous heavy parcel. Ruth was always embarrassed when it came to giving tips. As soon as the boy had gone, she put Confucius into his basket and then unpacked the parcel. It was the ostentatious wedding present that Helen had chosen. Ruth was quite overcome. She picked up one cup after an-other and then the cocktail shaker and lastly the salver. She read the card enclosed: "Best wishes to you both." Real silver, she thought with veneration. She set the whole affair out on the little table in the middle of the room and sat down on the only armchair and gazed at it with folded hands. I must write to Mother about that, she thought in her gratitude.

Time simply refused to move. Just for the sake of doing some-thing, Ruth rubbed the pink varnish from her toenails and, with her tongue between her teeth, varnished them all over again. It was a ticklish business that took time and one's whole attention. Next she produced an old newspaper and tried an old crossword puzzle. She looked out of the window, from which there was nothing to see. She lay down on her bed to think, taking care not to crush her dress. Possibly she may have slept for a few moments. She tried to call

Frank up at the store, but she could not get through, she turned the radio off, then on again. At last Frank called her up again.

All she could understand from what he said was that the wedding would have to be put off and that she had to stay in her room because it looked dangerous somewhere. "Where are you?" she asked. "At the store," Frank said. His voice sounded strange and wrought-up, as though the danger he spoke of were behind him and looking over his shoulder while he telephoned. Ruth took her white dress off again when this conversation was over. There was no object in making it dirty, she thought sensibly. A few more days of waiting made little difference, she thought also. After all, she had waited for Frank for years. Being impatient was no help, she thought, impatient with her own impatience. She took out her coral-red dress, the one she was wearing when she arrived. Just as she was standing before the mirror in her salmon-pink slip, there came the first thunderous explosion. She stood there, completely dazed, with the dress in her hands, wondering what was happening. A thunderstorm, was her first thought, but her knees were trembling. Danger, she thought next. This was the danger Frank had spoken of. Ever since the day of her arrival there had been a continual talk of shooting and danger, and nothing happened. Ruth had put it down to nerves or to a way these jumpy Shanghi-ers had of speaking. But now the very air roared, the walls shook and danger was at her very elbow. Confucius made loud and bitter complaint and tried to scramble out of his basket, but he always fell back again, probably because he too had gone weak in the knees. He beat his ridiculous little wings and wanted to get away. Ruth had dressed and put on her hat and slipped her handbag under her arm before she knew what she was doing. She looked back at the despairing little duckling from the door and, turning back with a short and pitying laugh, she picked up the basket with Confucius in it and took him along with her. "Keep quiet, nothing will happen to us," she told him. The windows rattled again as she shut the door behind her. She was going to Frank, for if it was really getting dangerous she naturally wanted to be where he was.

Neither Frank nor B.S. were in the store, and Mr Wang was so hysterical that it was clearly beyond him to give any rational information.

"It's coming," he said over and over again. "It's begun, it's the end, this time they will shoot everything to pieces."

Ruth was surprised. She had always been told that the Chinese thought nothing whatever of dying, and she had supposed that death in Chinese was not at all the same thing as in American. And yet Mr Wang did not by any means give the impression of a man who faced death with composure: rather he ran to and fro like a hen about to have its head chopped off. Ruth left the store in disappointment. She stood under the colonnade and wondered where Frank could be, since he was not where he had said he was. Either he is at the club, Ruth thought, or else he's already had to turn out as a volunteer. She had a dim vision of tending Frank among other soldiers, with a steel helmet on his head—perhaps she had seen a picture of the sort somewhere. Those Japanese! she thought, hot with anger. Since her arrival in Shanghai the campaign of hatred against the Japanese had affected her, too. The propaganda had entered her through her eyes, her ears, and even through the pores of her skin. It was obvious to her that these Japanese would not hesitate to destroy Frank if he stood in the way of their lust for conquest.

Ruth marched off resolutely, out of the colonnade and along Nanking Road, which, though it could not be more crowded than usual, was certainly not emptier. She turned into a side street and arrived at the house in which Frank and Morris lived and climbed the dark narrow stairs and rang the bell. No one answered it. Ruth rang several times while she reluctantly breathed in the peppery smell on the stairs. When nobody came, she sighed and went out again. Confucius had fallen asleep.

She found Morris at the club, but no Frank. She had him called to the entrance, for she knew that women were not admitted there. He came out, a ghost, smelling of whisky, green-faced, red-haired and with red stubble on his chin. He tried to hide his face with his hand. "Not been to bed for three nights," he said in excuse. "Too busy with the news." The club resembled the entrance to a beehive.

"Where's Frank?" Ruth asked.

"Well, if *you* don't know——" Morris replied.

"I don't even know where to look for him," she said helplessly, for she had expected to find him at the club.

"Nonsense! You don't want to look for him. You must go straight back to the hotel, see? Holy Madonna, women are the most unreasonable creatures God ever made! You're safe in the hotel. It's too near the river here, where all those nice little Japanese warships are lying. Do you want to be hit? Do you want America to go to war with Japan on your account? If Frank knew you were gadding around here he'd spank you. I know Frank. And what are you hauling a farmyard about with you for, in the name of Heaven?"

Every man that passed in or out gave her a look. Girls were not looked at in this way in America. Ruth retreated as Morris, with a muttered excuse, dived back into the club, back to the telephone, the whisky and the news. This was really the first time Ruth had been alone in the streets of Shanghai. When she was with Frank she saw only Frank; now for the first time she realized something of the city's crowds and color and movement. Dark clouds obscured the sky; the thousands of banners and pennants and flags hung limply in front of the stores—only now and again they were stirred as suddenly as if an invisible hand had twitched them. The little Chinese newspaper boys shouted themselves hoarse at the street corners, the ricksha coolies ran, the motorcars crowded one upon another, the sidewalk was a seething mass of hurrying Europeans and Chinese. Ruth marveled, in passing, at three young Chinese women who went by, wearing their modern dresses and hats with all the chic of New York. She herself was hot, her coral-red dress was beginning to stick to her skin. She had lost her way in a maze of small streets running off behind the tall buildings on the Bund; she must have taken the wrong turn when she left the club. It was quite an adventure, and she almost enjoyed it—at least it passed the time. There's going to be a storm, she thought as she gasped for air. She stopped where two narrow streets crossed and looked up at the clouds. The sky was humming with planes.

When the next bomb fell, Ruth was standing in a narrow street

looking at the show window of a linen store. She was just wondering at the cheapness of the fine embroidered table linen. We'll have
to set the table for eight when we invite the B.S.'s, she was thinking
when the explosion came. It was so loud that she did not know
quite what had happened—there was a tremendous roar and a shock
that threw her to the ground. Darkness and wild terror, but no pain.
She would have lost consciousness if the cries from a thousand
throats had not kept her awake. People rushed past her as she lay
on the ground against the wall of a house, where she had been
flung, with the basket of the little duck still clasped to her. The show
window of the linen store lay in splinters on the sidewalk, she herself had been thrown some yards away. The outcry grew louder and
wilder while Ruth tried to collect her senses. That was a bomb, she
thought, looking first up at the sky and its low-hanging thunder-
clouds. She was now aware of a dull pain at the back of her head,
and when she felt with her hand she found a bruise where her head
had struck the ground as she fell. She laughed, for it seemed funny,
and she shook her head to get it clear. She saw a man running by,
a white man with a bleeding woman thrown over his shoulder like
a sack. She saw a Chinese woman in black trousers dragging two
children along with her. She saw a young Chinese who tripped over
his long robe and scrambled forward. She saw another woman with
children, one of whom was in her arms; its head hung limp and
was bleeding.

Ruth pulled herself together and stood up. She felt rather dizzy
and unsteady on her feet, but she was unhurt. She began at once
making her way against the stream of fleeing people, for it was her
nature not to run away from danger but to seek it and to go where
help was needed. She only stopped once to look at Confucius. He
looked smaller in his blanket. She touched him: he was warm and
limp. She took him out and held him up to her face: he was dead. She
laid him carefully back again and put the basket down. "I have no
time, little fellow. I am so sorry . . ." she murmured.

She pushed her way on and came to a corner, but she did not
realize that she was now in Nanking Road again, for the street was

unrecognizable. Half of the front of a building had been wrecked, thick clouds of dust were still rising from the rubble and rubbish of the ruins. The injured were writhing about in the dust clouds with strange wormlike contortions of pain. A strange and deadly smell hovered in the dense air. Ruth was now so close to the screaming people that her eardrums began to vibrate after the numbness caused by the explosion. By this time people were running into the street from a building and giving first aid to the wounded in a heap of rubbish in the middle of the street. Ruth climbed over the wreckage and got busy. The soles of her shoes were soon sticky and slippery with blood. The smell of blood soon drowned the stinging smell of mortar and dust and explosives.

Many were already dead, and that was just as well. Others lay mutilated, torn, as the house was whose walls had fallen on them. Bits of limbs, parts and fragments of what ten minutes before had been human beings, came to light as the men removed pieces of masonry and lifted up what was underneath. Ruth took hold of a woman's hand which projected from the rubble as though seeking help. The hand was followed by an arm and a scorched and bleeding piece of shoulder. The woman to whom the hand belonged had been flung somewhere else or blown to pieces. It did not make Ruth sick, for she had learned to control herself in the operating theater and in the dissecting room. She wiped the sweat from her face with her shoulder and continued to reach for bodies amidst the wreckage. White people and Chinese were inextricably mixed up in their gruesome death. "All men are brothers," somebody said close to Ruth. It had a ghostly sound, and when she looked she saw it was an old Chinese with an impassive face. He picked up a white child and carried it into the nearest building—a hotel with revolving doors in which no glass was left.

Not far from the devastated sidewalk Ruth found a woman who appeared to be uninjured but who was writhing in contortions; she was a Chinese of the lower classes, in black trousers and white linen jacket. As soon as Ruth bent down to help her she grasped what was wrong. The woman was pregnant, and the shock had brought on her labor. She poured out a torrent of muttered words, and her hair was moist with the sweat of her agony. Ruth thought it over for a second and then, exerting all her strength, she got the woman onto her back and carried her away from the scene of the disaster into a side street which was emptier and quieter. The woman stopped muttering at once, and something like a smile bared her large teeth. As soon as Ruth put her down on the ground and undid her trousers and pulled them down she began to groan again. It seemed a miracle to Ruth that a child was to be born amidst these scenes of death and destruction. She had often been present at childbirth, but she had never herself delivered a baby. The lack of any kind of antiseptic was grievous to her well-trained nurse's mind. But at the same time a fierce joy that she could be of help swept through her.

The woman lay on the ground with her thighs bared, and she arched her back and pulled her knees up to her chin. People were still running past, but the cries had died down. Nobody had time for the woman in childbirth over whom Ruth bent. The dark wet head of the child could already be seen, and Ruth grasped it with both hands and pulled it from the mother's body. It was a tiny, copper-colored baby boy. She gave it a smack on its little behind; it opened its mouth, showing bright red gums, and uttered a cry. It still lay between its mother's thighs, attached by the cord. The mother raised her head and tried to see her baby. Ruth understood, and lifted up the little piece of crumpled living flesh, so that its mother could see its head and body, arms and legs, delicate little hands and feet with perfect nails—a child complete with voice and sex. The woman let her head fall again.

Ruth knelt on the ground beside her, at a loss for a moment what to do next. She then tore her salmon-pink underslip from its shoulder straps. The silk tore and broke with a rending noise. She pulled it off under her dress and, bundling it up, put it under the little Chinese baby between its mother's knees. Then she thought again and felt for the broken shoulder straps under her dress and, when she found them, she knotted them together and tied the umbilical cord with them. She looked about her, and God knows from what primitive depths the little American girl discovered what she had to do next. She bent over the body of the mother and bit the cord through. There were a few drops of blood, and then no more. Ruth now felt her heart beating as it had never beaten before. Again she wiped the sweat from her face with her shoulder, in the primitive way of workers in the open field. Now the woman began to talk. "It's all right, it's all right," Ruth said consolingly, stroking the wet black streaks of hair from the woman's face. She wrapped the baby in her slip of rayon silk and put it in the woman's arms. After a few minutes the woman's face was contorted with a fresh onset of pain, and Ruth quickly took the child out of her arms; then she helped the woman to get rid of the afterbirth.

All this took place on the paved street, but it was no different from births in the heart of the jungle. Ruth had forgotten Frank as completely in the last quarter of an hour as if he had never existed. The baby—newborn, hungry little animal—now began to seek her breast. Ruth laughed loudly, and the mother laughed, too. Ruth put the child down again, reluctant to part from its living warmth. She dressed the mother again, and she, who was slowly regaining her strength, made an exclamation and pointed to Ruth's dress. It was only now, when she looked down, that Ruth saw that she was soaked with the blood of the wounded she had helped to carry. She shook her head and smiled at the Chinese woman.

There was a shrill whistle, and a white ambulance turned into the side street and stopped at the corner. Doctors and orderlies jumped out. Ruth ran up to them with the child in her arms.

"There's a woman here who has just given birth to a child," she told them. The doctor merely pushed her aside.

"There's no room," he muttered and hurried off with his men. Ruth went back to her patient. She was filled with a wild joy, something she had never known was in her. She tried to get the Chinese woman onto her feet; she wanted to help her to get away from the street. But the woman shut her eyes and shook her head. She seemed to be very tired and perfectly happy, and she wanted to stay where she was. Ruth got into a momentary panic over tetanus and Semmelweiss bacilli, but she got over it. She knelt on the ground and took the woman's head in her lap and clasped the child in her arms. Its little hands moved. It certainly was better than a million sick cats, and starlings with broken wings, and dead ducklings.

It was thus Pearl found them when she drove along the street in her gilded taxi, on her way to deposit the precious concubine in the vaults of the bank. She had long since made up her mind not to seek their protection for herself but to be driven straight on to Chapei and to open a first-aid station at the clinic.

"What's all this?" she said, stopping the taxi. "Stay where you are," she told Liu when he started to get out, too. Meilan covered her eyes with her hands when she caught sight of Ruth splashed with blood and of the woman lying dead or asleep in a pool of blood. Ruth looked up when Pearl bent down over her. "Do you speak English? Could you take the woman and the child in your taxi? It's only just born."

"Of course," Pearl answered, beginning to undress the woman again. "I am a doctor," she said in reply to Ruth's astonished gaze.

"It's all in order, placenta and everything," Ruth reported. "I happen to be a hospital nurse. If the woman could be taken to a hospital! What she really needs is a tetanus injection."

"I'll see to it all," Pearl said. "Wait a moment," she went on. "You are a nurse? Are you—are you not Mr Taylor's fiancée? He showed me your photo——"

"You know Frank?" Ruth asked, now at last remembering his existence.

"Yes, we used to be friends," Pearl said casually. "Come along and help us get the woman into the taxi," she called out to Liu. She had never seen Frank again since the abrupt and insulting termination of the dinner they had given for the Russells. Liu lifted the woman up; she muttered drowsily as Pearl settled her down in the taxi. Ruth followed with the child. The driver laughed. "We'll take her with us to the bank," Pearl said as she pushed Meilan aside to make room for the woman.

"Won't you come with us, too? There are bombproof vaults there," she said to Ruth, who was holding out the baby but not proposing to get in herself.

"How well you speak English!" Ruth said instead of answering.

"I am an American," Pearl replied. What a world it is, Ruth thought wonderingly. She put the child carefully down on the seat that Liu had pulled down.

"Good-by, little man," she said tenderly. It was her child. It was no easy matter to part from him. "I must go back to the Shanghai Hotel," she said hurriedly. "Frank may be looking for me. He'll be anxious——"

This had only just occurred to her. Pearl was still holding the door open.

"The hotel is not particularly safe," she said. "It would be better if you came with us. We could call Mr Taylor up from the bank. Jump in."

"No," Ruth said. "Thank you all the same. I must go and look for Frank. So pleased to have met you," she added very properly, for the conventions were slowly regaining their hold.

"Jump in all the same," Pearl said, "we can at least take you to the hotel. Anyone can see you've been working hard."

"I look like a pig," Ruth replied as she got in and quietly took the baby in her arms again. They sat closely squeezed together, and there was a smell of childbirth. Meilan bent shyly forward and looked at the newborn child over Ruth's shoulder. "A man," she said, smiling at Pearl and Liu. The taxi went by side streets, as the driver was afraid. The mother opened her eyes when the car started. She took the child away from Ruth and pressed it possessively to her breast. Liu made himself as small as possible. He smiled to himself. These four women, different as they were, strange, even hostile and antagonistic, formed a complete unity, while he, the man, sat hunched up in his corner, knowing nothing of this mystery of birth. Blood sisters, he thought, smiling indulgently.

"We'll meet again soon," Pearl said when the taxi stopped once more outside the Shanghai Hotel which it had left only a few minutes before. The Chinese woman was saying something.

"She wishes you a hundred sons and ten thousand years of life," Liu said with a little bow. Ruth laughed.

"Too much—too much of everything," she said as she got out. The doorman swung the revolving door open for her.

XXV

WHEN RUTH OPENED THE DOOR of her room she saw Frank, by the table on which she had set out the wedding present, staring at her like a ghost. Before she had time to shut the door he had taken her in his arms and was kissing her on her hair, her eyes, her face. He kissed her as a dog licks the master who has just come home. She gave herself up to this torrent of tenderness for some minutes and listened to his broken, stammering whisper. It did not sound like Frank, although it was a Frank she had often dreamed of.

"Where have you been? What has happened to you? Has someone hurt you? You must never leave me again; never, never, never, Ruth, my darling, my——"

Ruth got loose at last and put her hands against his chest. "I delivered a Chinese baby," she said, her eyes shining. "All by myself. A Chinese baby, so sweet——"

"What have you been doing?" Frank asked in astonishment. "Helping at a confinement? You look as if you had been wading up to your knees in blood."

Ruth now saw herself in the glass for the first time. She had lost her hat, her coral dress was covered in blood, she had no underslip, her hands were dirty, her stockings soaked and caked with the mud and blood she had knelt in.

"Excuse me," she said. "I'll get myself clean——"

But Frank followed her into the bathroom. "No——" Ruth said weakly as he picked her up in his arms. "This is our wedding day," Frank replied and began to undress her as if she were a child. He turned on the bath and poured in some lavender water out of a bottle he found. He put Ruth carefully in the warm bath and began washing her down with soap and a brush. In some places blood was so caked on her skin that it stuck fast, and he had to work with tender earnestness to get her clean. "Thank God you're here again, Ruth," he said over and over again.

"Were you afraid?" she asked. She sat with her knees to her chin and her arms folded over her breasts, so that there was little to be seen of her.

"Afraid?" Frank said. "Was I afraid? Ruth, you don't know what I have been through. Afraid!"

He lifted her out when he thought she was clean enough, wrapped her in a large bath towel and carried her to her bed.

"I feel tired all at once," she said plaintively and let her hand fall on his shoulder. And although she was so small and he so tall, he arranged matters so that his head rested on her breast, on the most peaceful, safest, cleanest place in the world. "Oh, Ruth," he said. "Oh —Ruth——"

He put his arm round her waist and lay quite still.

"Confucius is dead. The shock was too much for him," Ruth said. Frank's hair was close to her mouth, warm and comforting.

The childbirth had intervened between her and the frightful things she had seen, but now, as soon as she shut her eyes and relaxed in Frank's arms, it all came back.

"Bombs are horrible," she said, beginning to tremble. Frank stroked her. He took her hand and put it to his mouth and then looked at it.

"What's that?" he asked when he discovered a little wound on it.

"Nothing. It's where the woman bit me during her labor," Ruth said, forgetting the bombs again in a moment.

"Bit you!" Frank said indignantly.

"Yes, it was the pain, and she bit me. I'll bite, too," she added, nodding her head emphatically. Frank laughed softly. "My wife!" he said. "My boy!" Ruth replied.

"Never to be alone again," he said.

"Never again," Ruth said. You were never like this before, she thought wonderingly.

But Frank had no idea that the hours between morning and afternoon had so shaken him up and flung him into Ruth's arms that for the first time he gave up his banter and showed the naked feeling that overwhelmed him.

"Bombs—that's only the beginning," he said. "There's a lot worse to come. I've thought it all out, Ruth. We're not going to stay in Shanghai. We're going to go. It's a wretched sort of a place."

"As you like," Ruth said obediently. But she didn't really believe him. "Where shall we go? You have your job here," she said sensibly.

Frank waved all this away with his hand. "I've had enough of Shanghai. You go to the dogs here, Tiny. I tell you, three hundred dollars a month is no compensation. And now war and bombs on top of it. Besides, I can see already that you will always be where the bombs are falling thickest."

"And what about you?" Ruth asked.

"Yes, I too, I daresay," he said absently. "Listen, I'll tell you what I've decided. We'll clear out. We'll be cowards and run away. What do the Chinese and Japanese matter to us? What does Shanghai matter? There is nothing to be got here but dirty hands. We'll sail on the next American boat and go to Hawaii. What do you say to that?"

"Hawaii," was all Ruth said.

"Hawaii," Frank went on. "That's the place for us. We'll go to Hawaii," and as he said it, visions opened before his closed eyes: palm trees, flowers, endless stretches of sugar cane, the songs of the laborers, the golden rain, and last of all Mamo, young and on a little horse, Mamo on the sand at the seashore, Mamo who swam by his side when he was a little boy. . . .

"I did not really have a mother, you know; that was the trouble," he said. Ruth clasped him closer and began rocking him to and fro.

"Little mother!" he said almost inaudibly, for it was something inexpressible.

"We'll go to Hawaii," he said again. "My stepfather will find something for me to do. Besides we can live on stolen bananas and coconuts and fish. Fried *Humahuma nukanukaapuaa*," he said, smiling as the quaint and long-forgotten words came back to him. "We'll be shamelessly happy in Hawaii, shamelessly and boundlessly happy. What do you say?" he asked, leaning on his elbow and looking at Ruth intently and earnestly as though it were a very difficult question to answer.

Ruth had begun to feel anxious. "Have you been drinking?" she asked. He went on looking at her so intently that she moved her head to ward off his gaze.

"Perhaps I'll tell you someday," he said. "Later on."

"What?" Ruth asked uneasily. "What will you tell me?"

"Everything," Frank said. He lay down again beside her. Tense and relaxed at the same time. Now he could hear her heart beating against his temples. "Little bird!" he said. Then he pulled himself up until his lips were on her mouth. Ruth gave a deep sigh as though asleep. Slowly the years dissolved away, the years of separation, of estrangement, of distance, of loneliness and fear. They lay for a long time in silence, breathing in time with one another.

I never knew, thought Ruth, that there could be anything like this.

"I can see nothing but rainbows now," she said much later without opening her eyes.

"Don't speak," Frank murmured. "Don't speak, don't speak, just stay with me—always."

There was a knock at the door, gentle at first and then repeated, shyly certainly, but yet a little louder.

Frank sat up.

"Don't worry," he said. "Don't be afraid. It's nothing—no one can separate us. Nothing more can happen to us. Don't be afraid."

Ruth looked at him in astonishment. "Why should I be afraid?" was all she said.

Frank went to the door, but he hesitated to open it. There was a third knock. He smoothed back his hair, turned the key in the lock and opened the door. Outside, in the dusk of the corridor, stood a little Japanese. He had a parcel in his hand, and he bowed and smiled.

"I bring the books," he said.

Then the bomb fell that wrecked the building, burying people in the ruins and putting an end to fear and happiness and hate and life. And there is nothing left to report of those whom we have accompanied thus far but the moment in which they died.

Ruth, sitting on the edge of the bed, with her eyes fixed on Frank in a tender surprise, almost amused at the excess of bliss that this day had hammered into her good little everyday soul. It is well to die on the heights before the descent begins.

Frank, in the first flush of feeling that a woman can be the home for which he had longed all his life. Protection and warmth, the deep longings that had driven him hither and thither stilled: the return to the womb, to the warm maternal darkness before birth—so near to death that he did not know it when he died.

Yoshio Murata, the little Japanese, standing at the door with his borrowed books, touching and ridiculous, caught in the politeness of a bow. Thankful, perhaps, in the moment of his death, for the Chinese bomb which gave a warlike ending to his empty, aimless and absurd life.

The Changs, father and son, buried in the ruins of the shaft as they were rushing down in the elevator which was to be their escape to safety. Enemies in their points of view, chained to one another through the love that springs from the blood. Epicurean and ascetic, materialist and idealist, the exploiter and the flagbearer, the international capitalist and the defender of national rights and progress. Irreconcilable and yet indissolubly bound to one another. Chang, the father, to whom life had given everything and yet had denied him one thing: the respect of his son. And Chang, the son, distraught and distracted, weighed down by the responsibility for three thousand boys who were caught in a trap at Kiangwan by his fault, by his fault. One of those hundreds of thousands of young Chinese who preach courage and the fighting spirit and faith in their country and who yet know in the bottom of their hearts that China cannot be rescued thus.

Kurt Planke, a lost soul in relentless toils, whose future was nothing but the prison he had fled his country to escape. A tremendous chord crashed about his head, deep organ notes, the rush of wings. His spirit went to meet his death, for death is a stronger intoxication than opium and love.

Emanuel Hain, faint specter of a dim liberal epoch, a man who had outlived his death, a shell without content. The bomb that annihilated him spared him the exercise of courage required to swallow a dose of cyanide.

Jelena Trubova, the adventuress, shipwrecked on the first feeling she had ever allowed to enter her life. She had loved, murdered, lived in vain. Her reckoning all at fault. She stared at her palms, vacant, numbed, chilled hands which could take but could not hold. The doors were barred, the exits buried, her life played out. She did not die at once. She had still to be purified. She went through yellow, green and white hells of pain, and the half-second she lived was an eternity of suffering. Then she became clear and hard and transparent and without feeling; a piece of shattered crystal beneath the ruins—that was Jelena Trubova.

The coolie, Lung Yen, was unconscious when death found him, and he died unmutilated—his head, which already belonged to the executioner, unparted from his sick and tortured body. Lung Yen will never see his son again, nor his village, nor the earth his forefathers tilled, nor the graves wherein they rest—and that is sad. But he will never know that his son was to be killed out there in Kiangwan, after much hardship and desperate fighting—and that is good. Killed—one among hundreds of thousands, children, women, old men, the defenseless, the unresisting, the innocent. Killed as one of those whom Japan goes on killing in order—as its official reports say—to alter the hostile feeling against Dai Nippon.

Madame Tissaud, who was sitting close to a marble pillar when it collapsed, was not hurt. Only her white wig was slightly awry when all was over. She drank an absinthe and then found the whole affair rather amusing, for she had seen too many wars to take it seriously.

"There you have Shanghai," she told B.S., who came to see to the store of the Eos Film and Foto Company. "Chinese shoot at Chinese, and no one can say whether it is because they are so stupid or so clever. What I say is, better a dog in peace than a man in war. But what will you, Monsieur Scott? *Maskee* is what we all say here in such eventualities. What must happen, happens."

*Some other Oxford Paperbacks for readers
interested in Central Asia, China and
South-East Asia, past and present*

CAMBODIA

GEORGE COEDES
Angkor

CENTRAL ASIA

PETER FLEMING
Bayonets to Lhasa

LADY MACARTNEY
An English Lady in
Chinese Turkestan

ALBERT VON LE COQ
Buried Treasures of
Chinese Turkestan

AITCHEN K. WU
Turkistan Tumult

CHINA

All About Shanghai:
A Standard Guide

HAROLD ACTON
Peonies and Ponies

VICKI BAUM
Shanghai '37

ERNEST BRAMAH
Kai Lung's Golden
Hours*

ERNEST BRAMAH
The Wallet of Kai
Lung*

ANN BRIDGE
The Ginger Griffin

CHANG HSIN-HAI
The Fabulous
Concubine*

CARL CROW
Handbook for China

PETER FLEMING
The Siege at Peking

CORRINNE LAMB
The Chinese Festive
Board

W. SOMERSET
MAUGHAM
On a Chinese Screen*

G.E. MORRISON
An Australian in China

PETER QUENNELL
Superficial Journey
through Tokyo and
Peking

OSBERT SITWELL
Escape with Me! An
Oriental Sketch-book

J.A. TURNER
Kwang Tung or Five
Years in South China

HONG KONG

The Hong Kong Guide
1893

INDONESIA

S. TAKDIR
ALISJAHBANA
Indonesia: Social and
Cultural Revolution

DAVID
ATTENBOROUGH
Zoo Quest for a
Dragon*

VICKI BAUM
A Tale from Bali*

MIGUEL COVARRUBIAS
Island of Bali*

BERYL DE ZOETE AND
WALTER SPIES
Dance and Drama in
Bali

AUGUSTA DE WIT
Java: Facts and Fancies

JACQUES DUMARÇAY
Borobudur

JACQUES DUMARÇAY
The Temples of Java

GEOFFREY GORER
Bali and Angkor

JENNIFER LINDSAY
Javanese Gamelan

EDWIN M. LOEB
Sumatra: Its History and
People

MOCHTAR LUBIS
Twilight in Djakarta

MADELON H. LULOFS
Coolie*

COLIN McPHEE
A House in Bali*

HICKMAN POWELL
The Last Paradise

E.R. SCIDMORE
Java, Garden of the East

MICHAEL SMITHIES
Yogyakarta: Cultural
Heart of Indonesia

LADISLAO SZEKELY
Tropic Fever: The
Adventures of a
Planter in Sumatra

EDWARD C. VAN NESS
AND SHITA
PRAWIROHARDJO
Javanese Wayang Kulit

MALAYSIA

ABDULLAH ABDUL
KADIR
The Hikayat Abdullah

ISABELLA L. BIRD
The Golden Chersonese:
Travels in Malaya in
1879

PIERRE BOULLE
Sacrilege in Malaya

MARGARET BROOKE
RANEE OF SARAWAK
My Life in Sarawak

C.C. BROWN (Editor)
Sejarah Melayu or Malay
    Annals

K.M. ENDICOTT
An Analysis of Malay
    Magic

HENRI FAUCONNIER
The Soul of Malaya

W.R. GEDDES
Nine Dayak Nights

JOHN D. GIMLETTE
Malay Poisons and
    Charm Cures

JOHN D. GIMLETTE
AND H.W. THOMSON
A Dictionary of Malayan
    Medicine

A.G. GLENISTER
The Birds of the Malay
    Peninsula, Singapore
    and Penang

C.W. HARRISON
Illustrated Guide to the
    Federated Malay States
    (1923)

TOM HARRISSON
World Within: A
    Borneo Story

DENNIS HOLMAN
Noone of the Ulu

CHARLES HOSE
The Field-Book of a
    Jungle-Wallah

SYBIL KATHIGASU
No Dram of Mercy

MALCOLM MacDONALD
Borneo People

W. SOMERSET
MAUGHAM
Ah King and Other
    Stories*

W. SOMERSET
MAUGHAM
The Casuarina Tree*

MARY McMINNIES
The Flying Fox*

ROBERT PAYNE
The White Rajahs of
    Sarawak

OWEN RUTTER
The Pirate Wind

ROBERT W.C.
SHELFORD
A Naturalist in Borneo

J.T. THOMSON
Glimpses into Life in
    Malayan Lands

RICHARD WINSTEDT
The Malay Magician

PHILIPPINES

AUSTIN COATES
Rizal

SINGAPORE

PATRICK ANDERSON
Snake Wine: A
    Singapore Episode

ROLAND BRADDELL
The Lights of
    Singapore

R.W.E. HARPER AND
HARRY MILLER
Singapore Mutiny

JANET LIM
Sold for Silver

G.M. REITH
Handbook to Singapore
    (1907)

J.D. VAUGHAN
The Manners and
    Customs of the
    Chinese of the
    Straits
    Settlements

C.E. WURTZBURG
Raffles of the Eastern
    Isles

THAILAND

CARL BOCK
Temples and
    Elephants

REGINALD CAMPBELL
Teak-Wallah

MALCOLM SMITH
A Physician at the Court
    of Siam

ERNEST YOUNG
The Kingdom of the
    Yellow Robe

Titles marked with an asterisk have restricted rights